McGraw-Hill Education

Strategies for the GED® Test

in
Mathematical Reasoning

McGraw-Hill Education

Strategies for the GED® Test

in
Mathematical Reasoning

McGraw-Hill Education Editors

Contributor: Jouve North America

New York Chicago San Francisco Athens London Madrid
Mexico City Milan New Delhi Singapore Sydney Toronto

1 2 3 4 5 6 7 8 9 10 RHR/RHR 1 2 1 0 9 8 7 6 5 (book for set)

1 2 3 4 5 6 7 8 9 10 RHR/RHR 1 2 1 0 9 8 7 6 5 (book alone)

Book alone:
ISBN: 978-0-07-184038-5
MHID: 0-07-184038-9

Book/DVD set:
ISBN: P/N   978-0-07-184040-8 of set
             978-0-07-184042-2
MHID: 0-07-184040-0 of set
             0-07-184042-7

E-book:
Book alone:
ISBN: 978-0-07-184039-2
MHID: 0-07-184039-7

Library of Congress Control Number: 2014940571

GED® is a registered trademark of the American Council on Education (ACE) and administered exclusively by GED Testing Service LLC under license. This content is not endorsed or approved by ACE or GED Testing Service.

McGraw-Hill Education products are available at special quantity discounts to use as premiums and sales promotions or for use in corporate training programs. To contact a representative, please visit the Contact Us pages at www.mhprofessional.com.

Contents

CHAPTER 2 Exponents, Roots, and Radicals and Properties of Numbers 81

CHAPTER 3   Fractions   109

CHAPTER 5   Ratios and Proportions   177

CHAPTER 6   Percents   197

CHAPTER 7   Probability and Statistics   209

CHAPTER 8   Geometry   235

CHAPTER 9   Polynomials and Rational Expressions   305

CHAPTER 12   Functions   467

FORMULAS YOU NEED TO KNOW 533

MATHEMATICAL REASONING POSTTEST 535

CHAPTER EXERCISE ANSWER KEYS 549

Introducing the GED® Test

Welcome to *McGraw-Hill Education Strategies for the GED Test in Mathematical Reasoning*! Congratulations on choosing the preparation guide from America's leading educational publisher. You probably know us from many of the textbooks you used in school. Now we're ready to help you take the next step—and get the high school equivalency credential you want.

Before you start your study program, this chapter will give you a brief introduction to the exam. In the following pages, you'll learn:

- The history of the GED® test and how it took its current shape
- The structure of each part of the GED® test
- How the test is scored
- Some basic test-taking strategies
- Some dos and don'ts for test days

About the GED® Test

"GED®" stands for General Educational Development. The GED test is commonly referred to as a "high school equivalency" test because passing scores on all the test sections are usually accepted as equal to a high school diploma.

The GED program started in 1942 during World War II. Many young people had joined the armed services before completing high school. As a way to help returning veterans reenter civilian life with the equivalent of a high school diploma, which would help them get better jobs or go on to college, the U.S. military asked the American Council on Education (ACE) to develop the GED test.

The GED test was revised several times over the years, but many things remained constant. There were five separate test sections: Language Arts—Reading, Language Arts—Writing, Social Studies, Science, and Mathematics. These were standard "paper and pencil" tests that featured mostly multiple-choice questions. In 2002 a computerized version of the test was introduced. It did not differ much from the paper-and-pencil version.

ACE, a nonprofit organization, administered the GED program until 2011. In that year, ACE formed a new partnership with Pearson, a major educational publisher, to create the GED Testing Service. The first major goal of the new joint venture was to overhaul the old GED test series and create a new series of tests that use modern computer technology to measure career and college readiness.

The current version of the GED test is a major departure from the 2002 and earlier versions. Some key differences are:

- There is no paper-and-pencil version of the test. Only a computer version is available.
- There are four, not five, test sections: Reasoning through Language Arts, Social Studies, Science, and Mathematical Reasoning.

- The tests use some new question formats that may be unfamiliar to test takers.

- Multiple-choice questions have four, not five, answer options.

There are some other major differences that are more important to test designers and teachers than to test takers like you, but in case you are interested, here they are:

- Instead of using Benjamin Bloom's Taxonomy for measuring the difficulty of questions, the revised tests use Norman Webb's Depth of Knowledge measurements.

- Questions are aligned to the Common Core Standards rather than to standards generated by various boards or groups of educators as they were in the past.

Again, these are not changes you need to be concerned about. These changes tell the test designers what to test and how difficult to make each item.

How Do I Register?

The GED test is one of the most widely administered tests in the world. Luckily, that means you will probably have a lot of options about where to take the exam. The quickest way to register is to do so online at:

gedcomputer.com

Visit this website and follow the step-by-step instructions for registering and scheduling your test.

You can also register in person at an official GED testing location. You can find the location nearest you by visiting this site:

http://www.gedtestingservice.com/testers/locate-a-testing-center

You must register and schedule your test times in advance, and the times tests are offered vary from place to place. Each of the GED tests is scheduled separately.

Test-taking accommodations are available for those who need them, but test takers must get approval in advance for these accommodations. Accommodations include:

- An audio version of the test

- A private testing area

- Extended testing periods

- Additional break times

- Font size options

You must get the appropriate approval form filled out and approved. You can find the forms at this website:

http://www.gedtestingservice.com/testers /accommodations-for-disability#Accommodations4

In general, you will need documentation from your doctor or your school that proves testing accommodations are recommended and necessary.

What Are the Question Formats?

Do not worry too much about the question formats. The bulk of the current version of the GED tests is made up of multiple-choice questions, which almost everyone has experienced at one point or another. But you may need to get used to some new question types. Here is what to expect:

- **Drag-and-drop:** Drag-and-drop questions can look a variety of different ways, but what they ask you to do is use the computer mouse to select an object (it could be a word, a shape, a set of numbers, or another object) and "drag" it into a correct position in some kind of diagram. If you use a computer, you are probably familiar with the concept of "dragging" and "dropping." It is exactly what you do when you move the icon for a document from one folder to another. Look at the simple question below:

  Drag and drop the numbers below into the correct location on the chart.

Even Numbers	Odd Numbers

6

2

5

8

3

1

In this case, it is clear you should drag *6*, *2*, and *8* into the "**Even Numbers**" column and *5*, *3*, and *1* into the "**Odd Numbers**" column. Your correct answer would look like this:

Even Numbers	Odd Numbers
6	5
2	3
8	1

This is the basic idea of a drag-and-drop question. You will find many more examples in the practice tests and instructional chapters of this book.

- **Hot spot:** Hot spot items appear mostly in the Mathematical Reasoning test. They require you to plot points on a graph or alter a chart or complete a similar task. Here is an example:

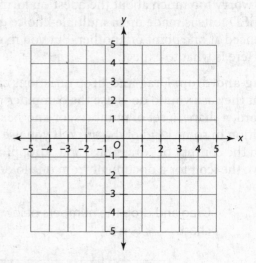

Click on the grid above to plot the point
indicated by the ordered pair (1, –3).

To answer this question, you have to "click" with your mouse on the correct point on the graph. In this case, you would move one place over along the *x* axis to 1 and then move down the *y* axis to –3. Your correct answer would look like this:

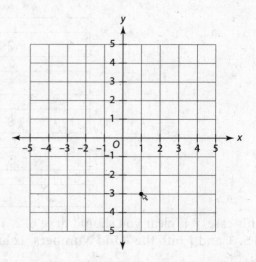

- **Fill in the blank:** This is a question type that is familiar to most people. On the GED tests, you will simply type in the correct answer. For example, look at this item:

    Forty percent of _____ is 8.

This question tests whether you know how to use percentages. So your correct answer would look like this:

    Forty percent of _____ 20 _____ is 8.

- **Drop-down:** In a drop-down item, you will see a blank space. At the start of the space, you will see the word "Select…" If you "click" on the space with your mouse, you will see a drop-down menu showing several answer options that could fill the blank space. This concept will be familiar to you if you often use the Internet. Many web pages have "menus," and if you use your mouse to click on them, multiple options appear. Here is a simple example:

The number six is a | Select... ▾ | number.

If you "click" on "Select" and the blank space, here is what you will see:

The number six is a | Select... ▾ | number.

| prime |
| even |
| decimal |
| negative |

In this case, you should select *even* as the best answer option.

The Mathematical Reasoning Test

The Mathematical Reasoning test is 115 minutes long and features 46 items in a variety of formats. The test starts with a short section consisting of five questions on which a calculator is not allowed, but for the bulk of the test, a calculator is allowed. The calculator is available on the computer screen.

About half of the test focuses on quantitative problem solving, and about half focuses on basic algebraic problem solving. There are some geometry questions as well. The test measures skills both with straightforward math problems and with hypothetical real-world situations that require you to decide how to use your problem-solving skills to arrive at the correct answer.

More About the Test Interface

Taking a test on a computer understandably makes many people nervous. Test-taking features you may be familiar with, such as the ability to mark skipped questions with a pencil so that you can return to them later, are not available. Scratch paper is not allowed. However, there are many features and functions of the new test that can improve the test-taking experience.

- **Built-in clock:** Keeping track of the time used to present a challenge, but the test now has a built-in clock that appears in the upper right-hand corner of the screen.

- **Erasable note boards:** You cannot use scratch paper, but the test offers erasable note boards that work just as well as regular scratch paper. You can request one at the time of your test, and you may exchange it for a new one if needed. You will be given an erasable marker to use, and you will deliver the note board to the test administrator after completing your test.

- **Marking skipped items:** In the past, when the GED test was a paper-and-pencil exam, test takers often marked skipped items on their answer sheets and returned to them as time allowed. Now the computerized GED test allows you to mark questions as "skipped" as you proceed from one to the next. When you reach the end of the test, you can see a list of skipped items and return to them if desired.

- **Zooming and color palette:** You have the option of zooming in on text to make it easier to view, or to change the color palette of the test to improve visibility.

- **No more separate answer sheets:** One of the problems with conventional bubble-in answer sheets is that one row accidentally skipped on the answer sheet can throw off a test taker's entire score. On the computerized GED test, you are presented with one question on the screen at a time, and you answer directly on that screen before moving on, so there is no chance of "bubbling in" on the wrong line of an answer sheet.

How the Tests Are Scored

As computerized tests have evolved, there have been two main types: adaptive and linear. Computerized adaptive tests are designed to zero in quickly on the test-taker's ability. Test takers get a "medium" level question first. If they answer correctly, they get a harder question. If they answer incorrectly, they get an easier question, and so on. Critics of this procedure point out that this format does not necessarily give a full picture of a test-taker's abilities because the test taker is not able to attempt all of the questions.

A linear test is just a test with a set number of questions, all of which are available to the test taker. The computerized GED tests are linear, so scores are determined based on the number of correctly answered questions. All questions, however, are not weighted equally. Because of the new question types, some questions are worth more than others. The tests are scored in their entirety by an automated scoring engine—even short-response and extended-response items will be scored by computer. Scores are reported within three hours of completion of the test.

Test-Taking Strategies

Clearly, the best preparation for the GED tests is a solid course of study using a book like the one you have in your hands. The best path to a good score is simply knowing the material. However, no matter how hard you study, there will probably be some questions on the GED tests that throw you for a loop. In those cases, you need to have some test-taking strategies ready.

There are a number of tried-and-true test-taking strategies that have been proven to help test takers, particularly in solving multiple-choice questions. The GED test still relies mainly on multiple-choice questions, so it is a good idea to keep the following strategies in mind:

- **The correct answer is staring you in the face.** Remember, the great thing about multiple-choice questions is that the correct answer is right in front of you. You just have to identify it. You do not have to retrieve it from your memory or come up with it on your own. Use this fact to your advantage.

- **Use the process of elimination:** On the GED test, there is no penalty for wrong answers, so if you don't know the answer to a question, you have nothing to lose by guessing. And if you must guess, you can improve your chances of guessing correctly by using the process of elimination, or POE.

  Think about it this way: on the GED test, multiple-choice items have four answer choices. If you just guess randomly, you still have a one-in-four chance of being correct. But what if you know that one of the answer choices is definitely wrong? Go ahead and eliminate that option. Now you have a one-in-three chance of guessing correctly. Your odds have just improved considerably. If you can eliminate two options, you are up to a 50 percent chance of selecting the correct answer. That's even better. Here is an example of how this works:

  > A pie is cut into 12 equal-sized slices. Eight slices remain. What fraction of the pie is left?
  >
  > A. $\dfrac{3}{4}$
  >
  > B. $\dfrac{2}{3}$
  >
  > C. $\dfrac{1}{2}$
  >
  > D. $\dfrac{1}{3}$

  Let's say you are not sure of the answer. It seems clear, though, that you can eliminate response D as a choice. Eight slices left from 12 is more than half of the pie, and $\dfrac{1}{3}$ is smaller than $\dfrac{1}{2}$. By the same reasoning, Choice C can be eliminated; if more than half the pie remains, then exactly half is not correct. But which of the remaining choices is correct? You have no idea? No matter. You are down to two options. Go ahead and guess. You have a 50 percent chance of being correct. (By the way, it is choice B: 8 slices out of 12 translates to the fraction $\dfrac{8}{12}$, which reduces to $\dfrac{2}{3}$.)

- **Keep an eye on the clock, and do not get hung up.** It may be tempting to keep wrestling with a difficult question until you have it mastered, but remember that you do not have all day. You have a set amount of time, and your goal should be to at least attempt every single question on the test. If you do some quick math based on the time limits and question totals, you will see that the longest you should spend on any given question is about two minutes. If you have been struggling and coming up empty for five minutes, mark the question as "skipped" and move on. You probably have many questions ahead of you that you can answer correctly, so go get those points!

- **Save the last five minutes for guessing—and always guess!** Suppose that you have gone through every item on the test. You have returned to skipped items and applied POE and come up with an acceptable answer. If there are still a few questions that leave you completely stumped, don't sweat it. Just guess. You still have a one-in-four chance of being right on multiple-choice items. The GED test does not penalize you for wrong answers. They simply count as zeroes. So why miss out on possible points? Pick something, even on one of the new question types. Put down some kind of answer. Never leave a question unanswered.

- **Use short, simple sentences.** On short-answer and extended-response questions, do not try to get too fancy. You can always make sure you are being grammatically correct if you keep your sentences simple and clear.

- **Use your erasable note board to outline your extended responses.** Before just starting to write an answer to an extended-response question, think for a minute or two about what you want to say, in what order, and how you intend to support your opinions or assertions. Make a quick outline. It does not have to follow a formal format. Just know where you are going with a response before you start typing.

- **Proofread your work.** Once you finish your short answer or extended responses, read through them carefully to make sure there are no obvious mistakes.

Test Day Tips

This will all sound like very commonsense advice, but you would be surprised at how often people do not prepare properly for test day. So here is your pretest and test-day checklist:

1. Congratulate yourself for having used *McGraw-Hill Education Strategies for the GED® Test in Mathematical Reasoning* to prepare yourself thoroughly for the mathematics portion of your test. You are ready.

2. At least a day or two before the test, make a dry run at getting yourself to the test-taking facility. Are you sure you know *exactly* where to show up—not just which building, but which room on which floor? If you are driving, is parking available? Where, and how far from the facility? How much does it cost? What is traffic like at the time your test is scheduled? Is there gas in the car? If you are taking public transportation, do you know the quickest, best route to your test-taking facility?

3. Plan to arrive 30 minutes early. Yes, that seems like it is very early. But the unexpected always happens, so be prepared. If you are early, so what? Sit down, relax, and visualize yourself acing the test. But if there is unexpected road construction or if the subway or bus is delayed, you will be glad you had a little time cushion. You do not want to arrive barely in the nick of time, and you definitely do not want to be late. At some facilities, you will not even be admitted if you are late.

4. Don't stay up all night studying the night before the test. Go ahead and review a little, but a good night's sleep is more beneficial than last-minute cramming.

5. Eat breakfast. Or lunch. Or whatever meal comes right before your test time. Just do not let yourself go into the test hungry and thirsty.

6. Dress in layers. Some testing facilities are as cold as freezers. Others are as hot as ovens. Be ready for anything so you can stay comfortable.

How to Use This Book to Set Up a Study Plan

This book features a Pretest and a Posttest. Before you begin your course of study, take the Pretest. Use the Answer Key to see how well you performed. Your performance on the Pretest will give you a good idea of which areas you need to work on and which areas you have already mastered.

How much time you decide to devote to each topic depends completely on your own schedule and your own level of mastery of each topic. There is no set prescription. This book is broken into short, manageable chunks of information, so you can take it one step at a time at your own pace.

If you have a packed daily schedule with very little time to devote to studying and you find that you need a lot of review in a given area, you will probably need to give yourself plenty of time. For example, if you are a parent with a full-time job, you may find that by the time you get the children to bed, you have only enough energy for 30 minutes of studying. That's fine. Just try to do one topic a night, and give yourself at least six weeks to finish your study.

On the other hand, if you want to take your GED test as quickly as possible in order to achieve some further goal (get a certain job or promotion, apply to college, or the like) and you have several hours or more of free time every day, you could conceivably prepare yourself for the test in two weeks.

Whatever you decide, write down your plan on a calendar (how many pages per night, for example) and stick to it. It may take a lot of determination, but you can do it.

Finally, turn to family and friends for support and encouragement. What you are doing is important, hard work. You deserve plenty of praise and pats on the back.

We wish you the best of luck on the test and beyond!

Using a Calculator

You can use a calculator on most of the GED test in mathematical reasoning. Part I consists of five questions designed to test your ability to do calculations by hand. A calculator is not available on this part of the exam. After completing Part I, you move on to Part II of the exam, where an on-screen calculator is available. You will not be able to return to Part I. There are no time limits for the individual parts of the exam, but the total time limit for both parts together is 115 minutes. The calculator you will use is an on-screen version of the Texas Instruments TI-30XS MultiView Scientific Calculator. You will not be allowed to bring your own calculator to the exam.

In the upper right of the keypad there are four direction keys used for moving the cursor around the display, and also a key labeled $\boxed{\text{clear}}$. You should press the $\boxed{\text{clear}}$ key before doing any calculation to prepare the calculator for a new calculation.

For basic arithmetic, the TI-30XS works like most ordinary calculators: for instance, to subtract 3 from 5, you press the following sequence of keys:

$$\boxed{5}\,\boxed{-}\,\boxed{3}\,\boxed{\text{enter}}$$

The display will show 2. Note that the TI-30XS uses an $\boxed{\text{enter}}$ key instead of an equal sign.

Adding, multiplying, and dividing two numbers at a time works in a similar fashion. More complicated expressions can be entered as printed on the page. For example the expression $4(7 + 8 \div 2) - 1$ can be computed with the sequence

$$\boxed{4}\,\boxed{\times}\,\boxed{(}\,\boxed{(}\,\boxed{7}\,\boxed{+}\,\boxed{8}\,\boxed{\div}\,\boxed{2}\,\boxed{)}\,\boxed{)}\,\boxed{-}\,\boxed{1}\,\boxed{\text{enter}}$$

The display should show 43.

Certain calculations with fractions may require operations in either or both of the numerator and denominator. As written, the fraction bar acts as both a grouping symbol and a division sign. You will need to insert the grouping symbols yourself. For instance, to calculate $\frac{6+3}{4-7}$, use the key sequence

$$\boxed{(}\,\boxed{6}\,\boxed{+}\,\boxed{3}\,\boxed{)}\,\boxed{\div}\,\boxed{(}\,\boxed{4}\,\boxed{-}\,\boxed{7}\,\boxed{)}\,\boxed{\text{enter}}$$

The display will show −3.

To use the calculator with negative numbers, use the $\boxed{(-)}$ key. This is a different key than the subtraction key, which is $\boxed{-}$. Be careful not to use one when you mean to use the other. When entering a negative number, you must press the $\boxed{(-)}$ before you enter the number. To calculate −5 + (3), use the following key sequence

$$\boxed{(-)}\,\boxed{5}\,\boxed{+}\,\boxed{(-)}\,\boxed{3}\,\boxed{\text{enter}}$$

The display should show −8.

To raise a number to a power, use the $\boxed{\wedge}$ key. Enter the base, press the $\boxed{\wedge}$ key, then enter the power and press $\boxed{\text{enter}}$. For example, to compute 2^9, use the sequence

$$\boxed{2}\,\boxed{\wedge}\,\boxed{9}\,\boxed{\text{enter}}$$

The display will show 512.

There is a shortcut for computing the square of a number. The $\boxed{x^2}$ key will square the number in the display without the need to enter the power separately. The same two keys, $\boxed{\wedge}$ and $\boxed{x^2}$, can be used with the key labeled $\boxed{\text{2nd}}$ to find decimal approximations of roots. The $\boxed{\text{2nd}}$ key accesses the function printed above another key, if any. Pressing $\boxed{\text{2nd}}$ again cancels the access to the alternate function. The sequence

$$\boxed{\text{2nd}}\,\boxed{\sqrt{}}\,\boxed{9}\,\boxed{\text{enter}}$$

will compute $\sqrt{9}$, displaying 3. To find $\sqrt[5]{32}$, use the sequence

$$\boxed{5}\,\boxed{\text{2nd}}\,\boxed{\sqrt[x]{}}\,\boxed{3}\,\boxed{2}\,\boxed{\text{enter}}$$

and the calculator will tell you that the fifth root of 32 is 2. With the power keys and the root keys, you can type an expression for the power. If you have more of an expression to enter that isn't part of a power, pressing the right-arrow key $\boxed{\triangleright}$ on the calculator will bring the cursor out of the exponent. The key sequence

$$\boxed{2}\,\boxed{\wedge}\,\boxed{(}\,\boxed{1}\,\boxed{+}\,\boxed{3}\,\boxed{)}\,\boxed{\triangleright}\,\boxed{+}\,\boxed{4}\,\boxed{\text{enter}}$$

will calculate $2^{1+3} + 4$, which is 20. Note that you must enclose the expression in the exponent within a pair of grouping symbols.

Certain calculations in geometry use the number π. There is a $\boxed{\pi}$ key on the TI-30XS, which displays π as accurately as it can be in the calculator. Unless a problem's instructions tell you to do otherwise, you should use this key. For example, the volume of a sphere with a radius of 6 inches is $\frac{4}{3}\pi(6)^3$. This can be found with the key sequence

$$\boxed{4}\,\boxed{\div}\,\boxed{3}\,\boxed{\times}\,\boxed{\pi}\,\boxed{\times}\,\boxed{6}\,\boxed{\wedge}\,\boxed{3}\,\boxed{\text{enter}}$$

after which, the calculator will display 904.7786842.

When you take the exam, a calculator reference sheet will be available onscreen. The reference sheet has a few basic examples of key sequences for certain types of problems as a reminder. The reference sheet is available for preview at the official GED test website; see

http://www.gedtestingservice.com/uploads/files
/e1b1e508627299978104548e9f2f6640.pdf

The official GED test website has more information about using the calculator; see

http://www.gedtestingservice.com/testers/calculator

There is a tutorial on using the calculator at

http://www.gedtestingservice.com/ged_calc_en_web/

The tutorial also has a link to the reference sheet.

The TI-30XS has far more functionality than can be explored here. Much of that functionality is not needed for the exam, though some of it could help you save time on the exam if you are proficient in its use. However, the time you spend preparing for the exam should include only a small amount of time trying to master the TI-30XS. The vast majority of your time should be spent on reviewing and learning the content of the test. A familiarity with the TI-30XS is good to have, but even if you only use the calculator for addition, subtraction, multiplication, division, and estimating roots, you will still be able to pass the exam because of the mathematics you know, not because of the capabilities of the calculator.

Mathematical Reasoning Pretest

This Mathematical Reasoning Pretest is designed to introduce you to this section of the GED® test and to give you an idea of your current skill level in this subject area.

This pretest has 30 items in various formats. The question formats mimic some of those on the actual GED® test. There are multiple-choice and free-response questions. On the real GED® test, you will indicate your answers by clicking on the computer screen. For this paper-and-pencil practice test, you can mark your answers directly on the page.

To get an idea of how you will do on the real exam, take this test under actual exam conditions. Complete the test in one session and with a time limit of 75 minutes. Refer to the second page of formulas as needed, found on page 534, but not the first page. If you do not complete the test in the time allowed, you will know that you need to work on improving your pacing. Try to answer as many questions as you can. There is no penalty for wrong answers, so guess if you have to. In multiple-choice questions, if you can eliminate one or more answer choices, you can increase your chances of guessing correctly.

After you have finished the test, check your answers in the Pretest Answer Key on page 19. Dividing the number of correct answers by 0.3 will give you the percentage of problems correct.

Mathematical Reasoning

30 questions | **75 minutes**

Directions: Write your answers in the blanks, or circle the correct answer when given answer choices.

1. What is the place value of 9 in 119,237,856?

   A. ten-thousands
   B. hundred-thousands
   C. millions
   D. ten-millions

2. What is the absolute value of |−20|? _____

3. Round 786 to the nearest ten. _____

4. Simplify $(-12)^2$. _____

5. What is 4^0?

   A. 4
   B. 0
   C. 1
   D. −4

6. Reduce $\dfrac{45}{180}$ to its lowest terms. _____

7. Arrange the following fractions in descending order: $\dfrac{12}{16}, \dfrac{5}{8}, \dfrac{21}{32}, \dfrac{1}{2}, \dfrac{15}{16}$. _____

8. Add: $61.88 + 38.85$ _____

9. Find the product: 13.95×64.76 _____

10. Which of the following is the decimal equivalent of $\dfrac{1,089}{10,000}$?

    A. 0.1089
    B. 0.001089
    C. 0.01089
    D. 0.010089

11. Express the ratio 50:100 in its simplest form.

    A. 1:2
    B. 2:3
    C. 3:4
    D. 1:4

12. The ratio of boys to girls in a class is 2:3. If there are 12 boys in the class, what is the total number of students in the class? _____

13. Convert 115% to a decimal. _____

14. Convert $\dfrac{25}{20}$ to a percent. _____

15. 78 is 24 percent of what number?

    A. 325
    B. 352
    C. 335
    D. 345

16. What is the mean of the following data? _____
    2, 7, 7, 9, 10, 15, 20, 23

17. Find the range of the dollars saved data. _____

Name	James	David	Thomas	Angel	Robin
Dollars Saved	7	4	2	5	10

18. A graph that uses vertical bars to represent data is called a _____.

    A. line graph
    B. pictograph
    C. bar graph
    D. pie graph

19. What is the supplement of an angle with a measure of 135°?

    A. 35°
    B. 45°
    C. 180°
    D. 90°

20. Find the area of a trapezoid having parallel sides measuring 5 meters and 7 meters and having a height of 2 meters. _____

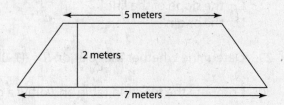

21. What is the volume of a sphere having a radius of 3 feet? _____

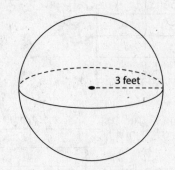

22. Add: $(7h^2 + 4) + (3h^2 + 6 + h^5)$ _____

23. Subtract: $(4p^2 - 8p^4) - (6p^4 + 7p^2)$ _____

24. Factor: $x^3 - 5x^2 + 3x - 15$

    A. $(x^3 + 3)(x - 5)$
    B. $(x + 3)(x^2 - 5)$
    C. $(x^2 + 2)(x - 4)$
    D. $(x^2 + 3)(x - 5)$

25. Solve: $3x + 15 = 6$.

    A. $x = 3$
    B. $x = 4$
    C. $x = -3$
    D. $x = -4$

26. Solve: $-5 \geq 15p - 10(p - 2)$. _____

27. What is the x-intercept of $10x - 6y = 30$? _____

28. What does the parameter *m* in the linear equation $y = mx + b$ denote?

    A. the *x*-intercept
    B. the *y*-intercept
    C. the slope of the line
    D. the origin

29. Determine whether the relation $R = \{(1, 0), (2, 2), (1, 2)\}$ is a function. _____

30. Compute the function table and draw a graph of the function $f(x) = x + 5$.

x	*f(x)*
−6	
−5	
−3	
1	
3	

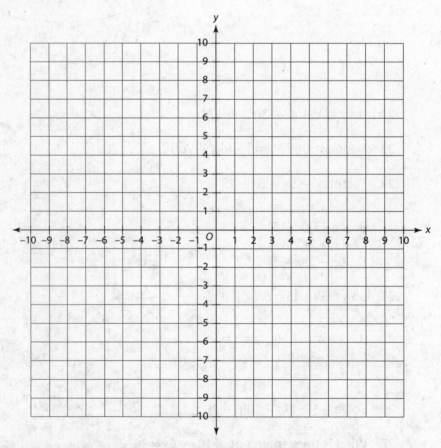

This is the end of the Mathematical Reasoning Pretest.

Answer Key

1. C

2. 20

3. 790

4. 144

5. C

6. $\frac{1}{4}$

7. $\frac{15}{16}, \frac{12}{16}, \frac{21}{32}, \frac{5}{8}, \frac{1}{2}$

8. 100.73

9. 903.402

10. A

11. A

12. 30

13. 1.15

14. 125%

15. A

16. 11.6

17. 8

18. C

19. B

20. 12 meters^2

21. 113.04 feet^3

22. $h^5 + 10h^2 + 10$

23. $-14p^4 - 3p^2$

24. D

25. C

26. $p \le -5$

27. (3, 0)

28. C

29. No

30.

x	$f(x)$
−6	−1
−5	0
−3	2
1	6
3	8

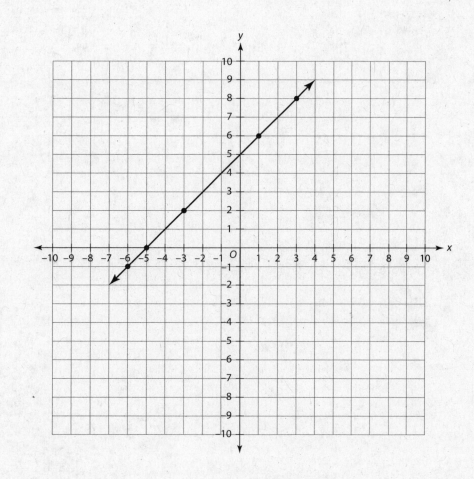

CHAPTER 1

Integers

The set of **natural numbers** is made up of the numbers 1, 2, 3, 4, … . The set of **whole numbers** is made up of the number 0 and the natural numbers. Whole numbers do not have a fractional part, a decimal part, or a negative sign.

For example, the number 37 is a whole number. The number $5\frac{1}{2}$ (read "five and one-half") is not a whole number because it has a fractional part. The number 16.0 (read as "sixteen point zero") is a whole number because it can be written as 16. The number −6, read as "negative 6," is not a whole number because of its negative sign.

Understanding Place Value

Place value means that the position of each digit of a whole number determines its value. The smallest place value for a whole number is the ones digit. Place value is generally read from right to left. The following diagram shows a place-value chart for a number with up to ten digits.

Place-value Chart

Millions			Thousands			Ones		
Hundred Millions	Ten Millions	Millions	Hundred Thousands	Ten Thousands	Thousands	Hundreds	Tens	Ones
100,000,000	10,000,000	1,000,000	100,000	10,000	1,000	100	10	1

EXAMPLE 1

Determine the place value of each digit of the number 408.

The number 408 is a three-digit number. The 8 is in the ones place, 0 is in the tens place, and 4 is in the hundreds place. You can show the value in the chart below.

Place-value Chart

Millions			Thousands			Ones		
Hundred Millions	Ten Millions	Millions	Hundred Thousands	Ten Thousands	Thousands	Hundreds	Tens	Ones
100,000,000	10,000,000	1,000,000	100,000	10,000	1,000	100	10	1
						4	0	8

EXAMPLE 2

Determine the place value of each digit of 4,800.

If you read the digits from right to left in 4,800, you find 4 is in the thousands place. Therefore, the value of 4 in 4,800 is 4 × 1,000 or 4,000. The value of 8 in 4,800 is

8 × 100 or 800, and so on. Its place value can be shown in the following place-value chart.

Place-value Chart

Millions			Thousands			Ones		
Hundred Millions	Ten Millions	Millions	Hundred Thousands	Ten Thousands	Thousands	Hundreds	Tens	Ones
100,000,000	10,000,000	1,000,000	100,000	10,000	1,000	100	10	1
						4	8	0	0

EXAMPLE 3

Determine the place value of each digit of 1,433,721.

If you read the digits from right to left in 1,433,721, you find 1 is in the millions place. Therefore, the value of 1 in 1,433,721 is 1 × 1,000,000 or 1,000,000. The value of 4 in 1,433,721 is 4 × 100,000 or 400,000, and so on. The place value of the digits in 1,433,721 can be shown in the following place-value chart.

Place-value Chart

Millions			Thousands			Ones		
Hundred Millions	Ten Millions	Millions	Hundred Thousands	Ten Thousands	Thousands	Hundreds	Tens	Ones
100,000,000	10,000,000	1,000,000	100,000	10,000	1,000	100	10	1
		1	4	3	3	7	2	1

EXAMPLE 4

Determine the place value of each digit of 31,421,782,012.

If you read the digits from right to left in 31,421,782,012, you find 3 is in the ten billions place. Therefore, the value of 3 in 31,421,782,012 is 3 × 10,000,000,000 or 30,000,000,000. The value of 1 in 31,421,782,012 is 1 × 1,000,000,000 or 1,000,000,000, and so on. The place value of the digits in 31,421,782,012 can be shown in the following place-value chart.

Place-value Chart

Trillions			Billions			Millions			Thousands			Ones		
Hundred Trillions	Ten Trillions	Trillions	Hundred Billions	Ten Billions	Billions	Hundred Millions	Ten Millions	Millions	Hundred Thousands	Ten Thousands	Thousands	Hundreds	Tens	Ones
100,000,000,000,000	10,000,000,000,000	1,000,000,000,000	100,000,000,000	10,000,000,000	1,000,000,000	100,000,000	10,000,000	1,000,000	100,000	10,000	1,000	100	10	1
				3	1	4	2	1	7	8	2	0	1	2

EXAMPLE 5

Determine the place value of each digit of 5,263,674,122,517.

If you read the digits from right to left in 5,263,674,122,517, you find 5 is in the trillions place. Therefore, the value of 5 in 5,263,674,122,517 is 5 × 1,000,000,000,000 or 5,000,000,000,000. The value of 2 in 5,263,674,122,517 is 2 × 100,000,000,000 or 200,000,000,000, and so on. The place value of the digits in 5,263,674,122,517 can be shown in the following place-value chart.

Place-value Chart

Trillions			Billions			Millions			Thousands			Ones		
Hundred Trillions	Ten Trillions	Trillions	Hundred Billions	Ten Billions	Billions	Hundred Millions	Ten Millions	Millions	Hundred Thousands	Ten Thousands	Thousands	Hundreds	Tens	Ones
100,000,000,000,000	10,000,000,000,000	1,000,000,000,000	100,000,000,000	10,000,000,000	1,000,000,000	100,000,000	10,000,000	1,000,000	100,000	10,000	1,000	100	10	1
	5		2	6	3	6	7	4	1	2	2	5	1	7

While moving from the right, notice that each place value is 10 times its preceding place value. The hundreds place is 10 times the tens place ($10 \times 10 = 100$). The thousands place is 10 times the hundreds place ($100 \times 10 = 1,000$). The ten thousands place is 10 times the thousands place ($1,000 \times 10$), and so on. Note that in each place, the number of zeros goes on increasing by 1, that is, ones place (1), tens place (10), hundreds place (100), thousands place (1,000), ten thousands place (10,000), and so on.

EXERCISE 1

Understanding Place Value

Directions: Answer the following questions about place value.

1. What is the place value of 3 in 7,430,521?

2. What is the place value of 8 in 108,926,441?

3. What is the digit in the ten millions place in 123,456,789?

Directions: Underline the digit in the tens place in each number.

4. 48

6. 75,325

8. 308

5. 218

7. 5,564

Directions: Underline the digit in the thousands place in each number.

9. 53,512   10. 178,321   11. 1,254,745   12. 28,580

13. In what place is the digit 3 in 436,781?

16. What is the value of the digit 8 in 2,826,567?

14. In what place is the digit 5 in 95,360,873?

17. What is the value of the digit 4 in 54,683,321?

15. What is the value of the digit 2 in 75,321?

18. What is the value of the digit 1 in 102,854,683,233?

Answers are on page 549.

Zero as Placeholder

The number zero, written as 0, is used as a placeholder in the place-value system.

EXAMPLE 1

Take a look at the number 607 in the place-value chart.

Hundreds	Tens	Ones
6	0	7

The number is read as "six hundred seven." A zero is used between 6 and 7 to keep the digits in their correct places. If the zero is missing, then you would have the number 67, which is completely different from 607.

Hundreds	Tens	Ones
	6	7

When determining place value, all digits of the number are written in the place-value chart, including 0.

EXAMPLE 2

The number 50 is written in the following place-value chart. Note that 0 is written in the ones place and is not omitted. The ones digit of 50 has a value of 0.

Hundreds	Tens	Ones
	5	0

Expanded Form of Whole Numbers

The number 47,635 is in standard form. Let's place the number in a place-value chart. This will help you write the **expanded form** of the number.

Place-value Chart

Millions			Thousands			Ones		
Hundred Millions	Ten Millions	Millions	Hundred Thousands	Ten Thousands	Thousands	Hundreds	Tens	Ones
100,000,000	10,000,000	1,000,000	100,000	10,000	1,000	100	10	1
				4	7	6	3	5

In this number, 5 is in the ones place, 3 is the in tens place, 6 is in the hundreds place, 7 is in the thousands place, and 4 is in the ten thousands place. Let's find out the place value of each digit. The place value of 5 is $5 \times 1 = 5$, the value of 3 is $3 \times 10 = 30$, and the value of 6 is $6 \times 100 = 600$. Continuing on, the value of 7 is $7 \times 1,000 = 7,000$, and the value of 4 is $4 \times 10,000 = 40,000$. The largest place value is 40,000.

When you add the values in descending order, you get the expanded form of 47,635:

$40,000 + 7,000 + 600 + 30 + 5.$

EXAMPLE

Write 4,285,403 in expanded form.

First, find the place of each digit in the number with a place-value chart:

Place-value Chart

Millions			Thousands			Ones		
Hundred Millions	Ten Millions	Millions	Hundred Thousands	Ten Thousands	Thousands	Hundreds	Tens	Ones
100,000,000	10,000,000	1,000,000	100,000	10,000	1,000	100	10	1
		4	2	8	5	4	0	3

Going from right to left, the value of 3 is 3, the value of 0 is 0, and the value of the first 4 from the right is 400. The value of 5 is 5,000, the value of 8 is 80,000, the value of 2 is 200,000, and the value of the leftmost 4 is 4,000,000. Thus, the expanded form of the number in descending place value order is:

4,000,000 + 200,000 + 80,000 + 5,000 + 400 + 0 + 3, or

4,000,000+ 200,000 + 80,000 + 5,000 + 400 + 3.

Generally, 0 is not included in the expanded form.

Rules for Reading and Writing a Whole Number

To read or write the word form of a whole number, use the following figure to help you.

Place-value Chart

Trillions			Billions			Millions			Thousands			Ones		
Hundred Trillions	Ten Trillions	Trillions	Hundred Billions	Ten Billions	Billions	Hundred Millions	Ten Millions	Millions	Hundred Thousands	Ten Thousands	Thousands	Hundreds	Tens	Ones
100,000,000,000,000	10,000,000,000,000	1,000,000,000,000	100,000,000,000	10,000,000,000	1,000,000,000	100,000,000	10,000,000	1,000,000	100,000	10,000	1,000	100	10	1

While writing whole numbers, use a comma to separate each group of three digits. In the figure, note that each successive three places are grouped into one **period**. The first period is ones, the second period is thousands, the third is millions, the fourth is billions, the fifth is trillions, and so on. A comma is used while writing a number to separate each of these periods. Each of these periods contains three places: ones, tens, and hundreds. The ones period contains ones, tens, and hundreds. The thousands period contains thousands, ten thousands, and hundred thousands. The millions period contains millions, ten millions, and hundred millions.

EXAMPLE 1

Write the number 10000 with commas.

For the number 10000, count three digits from the right and place a comma between the third and fourth zeros: 10,000. This is read as "ten thousand."

EXAMPLE 2

Write the number 10000000 with commas.

For the number 10000000, count three digits from the right and place a comma between the third and fourth zeros: 10000,000. Next, count three digits from the comma and place another comma between the sixth and seventh zeros: 10,000,000. This is read as "ten million."

EXAMPLE 3

Similarly, for writing the number 100000000000, count three digits from the right and place a comma between the third and fourth zeros: 100000000,000. Next, count three digits from the comma and place another comma between the sixth and seventh zeros: 100000,000,000. After that, count three digits from the second comma and place another comma between the ninth and tenth zeros: 100,000,000,000. This is read as "one hundred billion."

When reading a number with more than three digits, read the digits in each period followed by the period name.

EXAMPLE 4

To read 53128, place a comma after counting three digits from the right: 53,128. The 53 is in the thousands group. Therefore, it is read or written out as "fifty-three thousand, one hundred twenty-eight."

EXAMPLE 5

The number 78,436,571 is read or written out as "seventy-eight million, four hundred thirty-six thousand, five hundred seventy-one."

Note that the commas are also used between periods in the written forms.

EXERCISE 2

Expanded Form of Whole Numbers

Directions: Answer the following questions.

1. If a number is read as "thirty-two thousand, one hundred twenty-seven," what is the number?

2. If a number is read as "two hundred eighty-one thousand, three hundred twenty-one," what is the number?

3. The expanded form of a number is 50,000 + 1,000 + 70 + 8. What is the number?

4. The expanded form of a number is 600,000 + 40,000 + 3,000 + 200 + 60. What is the number?

Directions: Write the expanded form of the following numbers.

5. 1,039,670	**7.** 326,756	**9.** 311,234,077,090
6. 45,010	**8.** 123,577,899	**10.** 42,198,521

Directions: Write the word form of each number.

11. 46,142	**13.** 4,675,212	**15.** 91,532,277,563
12. 678,451	**14.** 44,411,763	**16.** 34,982

Answers are on page 549.

The Number Line

A **number line** is a convenient way to visualize whole numbers (and eventually, other types of numbers). A horizontal line with two arrows on the end is drawn with small straight lines, called tick marks. One tick mark is assigned the number 0, and consecutive whole numbers are used to label the other tick marks to the right of 0. The arrow at each end of the line signifies that the line and the numbers are understood to continue on, even though they are not drawn. The number line continues to the left of 0, which is the negative direction. This will be looked at later on in the chapter.

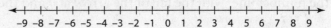

Numbers as Points

A specific number can be designated on a number line by placing a solid dot on the tick mark for that number.

EXAMPLE

Plot the number 6 on the number line.

A solid dot is drawn on the tick mark above 6 to indicate the number 6.

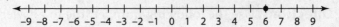

Scaling Considerations

Different scales are used for plotting numbers on the number line.

1. When larger numbers are plotted, a different scale may be needed.

EXAMPLE

Plot 40 on the number line.

A solid dot is drawn on the tick mark above 40 to indicate the number 40.

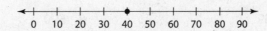

2. A different scale may call for using an estimation of the location of a point.

EXAMPLE

Plot 535 on the number line.

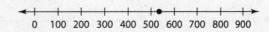

3. When there are several numbers to be plotted, the scale may be omitted if the numbers are labeled.

EXAMPLE

Plot 20, 239, 511, and 700 on the number line.

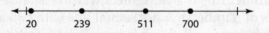

Numbers as Directed Line Segments

Another method for designating a number on the number line is by placing an arrow above the number line, with the tail of the arrow at 0 and the head of the arrow above the number.

EXAMPLE

Plot 6 on the number line.

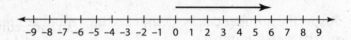

EXERCISE 3

The Number Line

Directions: Use the following number line to answer the questions.

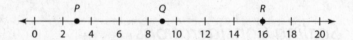

1. What number is represented by point *P*?
2. What number is represented by point *Q*?
3. What number is represented by point *R*?

Directions: Plot each number on a number line.

4. 35   7. 301   10. 996
5. 69   8. 500   11. 26
6. 187   9. 765

Answers are on page 549.

Integers

The set of the negatives of the natural numbers is a set of numbers less than 0 and is written as −1, −2, −3, … . The set of **integers** is made up of the whole numbers (0, 1, 2, 3, 4, …) and the negatives of the natural numbers (−1, −2, −3, −4, …). The natural numbers 1, 2, 3, 4, … are the **positive integers**. These are to the right of zero on the number line.

Negative integers refer to the negative numbers –1, –2, –3, –4, … , etc., and are to the left of zero on the number line.

The sign of an integer, except for 0, is either positive (+) or negative (–). The number zero can be written as + 0 or –0, but either number is still equal to 0. To represent integers on a number line, draw a number line, mark the middle of the line, and label it as zero. Draw tick marks on both sides of 0. Label the tick marks to the right of 0 with positive integers 1, 2, 3, 4, … , etc., and label the tick marks to the left of 0 with negative integers –1, –2, –3, –4, … , etc.

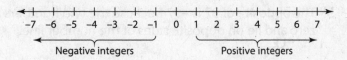

From the number line, you can observe that:

1. Every integer has a preceding value and a succeeding value. For example, 5 is the successor of 4 and –5 is the successor of –6. Also, 4 is the predecessor of 5 and –4 is the predecessor of –3.

2. Every integer on the number line is greater than those integers that are on its left. For example, 6 is greater than –4.

3. Alternatively, every integer on the number line is less than those integers that are on its right. For example –3 is less than –1.

4. All the positive integers are greater than the negative integers.

5. Zero is less than every positive integer and is greater than every negative integer.

Opposite Integers

Two integers are **opposites** if they are each the same distance away from zero but on opposite sides of the number line. One will have a positive sign while the other will have a negative sign. The opposites of positive integers are the negative integers, and the opposites of negative integers are the positive integers.

If a is a positive integer, then its opposite is $-a$. Similarly, the opposite of $-a$ is a.

Look at 2 and –2 on the number line.

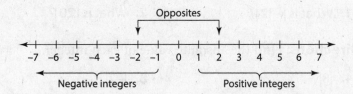

These two integers are the same distance away from zero but on the opposite sides of the number line. Therefore 2 and –2 are opposites, that is, 2 is the opposite of –2 and –2 is the opposite of 2.

EXAMPLES

1. The opposite of 4 is −4 because the two numbers are the same distance away from zero and lie on the opposite sides of the number line.

2. The opposite of −9 is 9 because the two numbers are the same distance away from zero and are on the opposite sides of the number line.

3. The opposite of −34 is 34 because the two numbers are the same distance from zero and are on the opposite sides of the number line.

4. The opposite of zero is zero itself.

5. The opposite of 97 is −97 because the two numbers are the same distance away from zero and lie on opposite sides of the number line.

Absolute Value

The **absolute value** of an integer is the distance of the integer from 0. For example:

The absolute value of −3 is 3 because its distance from 0 is 3 units.

The absolute value of 5 is 5 because its distance from 0 is 5 units.

The absolute value is always nonnegative (greater than or equal to 0). The absolute value of a number is shown with two straight lines with the number between the lines. For example, the absolute value of −4 is shown as $|-4|$ and is equal to 4. This means that −4 is 4 units away from 0.

If you consider 6 and −6 on a number line, both of the integers are situated at a distance of 6 units from 0, i.e.,

$$|-6| = |6| = 6$$

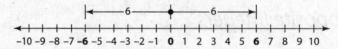

EXERCISE 4

Absolute Value

Directions: Find the absolute values.

1. What is $|-12|$?   2. What is $|20|$?   3. What is $|-1|$?

Directions: Find the absolute value of each integer.

4. $|8|$ 8. $|-7|$ 12. $|235|$

5. $|-8|$ 9. $|-881|$ 13. $|405|$

6. $|-22|$ 10. $|-1,058|$

7. $|14|$ 11. $|-144|$

Answers are on page 550.

Ordering of Integers

When you have two distinct numbers, one number is greater than the other. This can be represented using the inequality symbols < and >. Geometrically, the symbol < means "less than" or lies farther to the left on the number line and the symbol > means "greater than" or lies farther to the right on the number line. When two numbers are not distinct, meaning they are equivalent to the same number, then they are equal and the equal sign, =, is used to show that they are equal.

Take a look at the following number line.

215   784

In the number line, 215 is to the left of 784, which means that 215 is less than 784. Thus, you can write 215 < 784. In other words, 784 is to the right of 215, which means that 784 is greater than 215. Thus, you can also write 784 > 215. Notice that the order of the numbers matters depending on which symbol you use.

EXAMPLE

Compare 683 and 692 using <, >, or =.

683 and 692 have the same first digit, so compare the second digits. The 8 in 683 is less than the 9 in 692, so 683 is less than 692. Write 683 < 692.

Alternatively, you can think of 683 as to the left of 692 on the number line, and so 683 < 692.

When comparing two negative numbers, it might seem that the order is turned around. The statement −7 < −3 may not seem right until the position of the numbers on the number line is properly considered. The number −7 is to the left of −3, and so −7 < −3. Also, every negative number (those on the left side of the number line) is to the left of every positive number, so even a statement like −999,999 < 1 is a true statement.

There are two other inequality symbols that are common in mathematics. They are ≤, read as "less than or equal to," and ≥, read as "greater than or equal to." Each is a combination of < or > and part of an equal sign, =. These symbols are used extensively in algebra; they will be discussed further in other chapters.

EXERCISE 5

Ordering of Integers

Directions: Write each set of integers from least value to greatest value.

1. 65, 9, 0   **2.** 34, −11, 42   **3.** −87, −120, −18

Directions: Compare each pair of numbers by writing <, >, or = in the box.

4. 7,927 ☐ 8,904   **5.** 273 ☐ 279   **6.** 12,582 ☐ 12,562

Answers are on page 550.

Adding Whole Numbers

Addition is a mathematical operation that refers to the total amount of objects in a collection. It is represented by the plus sign, +. The total amount of objects is the **sum** of the objects.

> For example, if there are 3 apples and 3 oranges in a basket, then the sum of the fruits is 3 + 3, which is a total of 6 fruits. Therefore, you can write 3 + 3 = 6.

Generally, smaller numbers are added horizontally, i.e., the numbers and the sum are written from left to right, for example, 5 + 2 = 7. However, larger numbers can be written vertically, that is, the numbers and the sum are written above and below one another. When adding numbers vertically, it is important to use the correct setup of the numbers. The number digits should be placed vertically in such a manner that the ones are under the ones place, tens are under the tens place, hundreds are under the hundreds place, and so on.

Adding on the Number Line

Addition of whole numbers can be shown on a number line.

EXAMPLE

Add: 5 + 7.

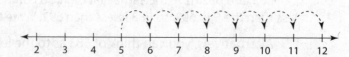

> As shown in the above number line, you start from 5 and make 7 jumps to the right. This is because you are required to add 7 to 5. The jumps are from 5 to 6, 6 to 7, 7 to 8, 8 to 9, 9 to 10, 10 to 11, and 11 to 12 as shown above. The jumps end at 12.

> Hence, 5 + 7 = 12. The sum of 5 and 7 is 12.

Adding Numbers with One Digit

Numbers with one digit can be easily added. Refer to the following addition table for adding one-digit numbers.

Addition Table of 1	Addition Table of 2	Addition Table of 3	Addition Table of 4	Addition Table of 5
1 + 1 = 2	2 + 1 = 3	3 + 1 = 4	4 + 1 = 5	5 + 1 = 6
1 + 2 = 3	2 + 2 = 4	3 + 2 = 5	4 + 2 = 6	5 + 2 = 7
1 + 3 = 4	2 + 3 = 5	3 + 3 = 6	4 + 3 = 7	5 + 3 = 8
1 + 4 = 5	2 + 4 = 6	3 + 4 = 7	4 + 4 = 8	5 + 4 = 9
1 + 5 = 6	2 + 5 = 7	3 + 5 = 8	4 + 5 = 9	5 + 5 = 10
1 + 6 = 7	2 + 6 = 8	3 + 6 = 9	4 + 6 = 10	5 + 6 = 11
1 + 7 = 8	2 + 7 = 9	3 + 7 = 10	4 + 7 = 11	5 + 7 = 12
1 + 8 = 9	2 + 8 = 10	3 + 8 = 11	4 + 8 = 12	5 + 8 = 13
1 + 9 = 10	2 + 9 = 11	3 + 9 = 12	4 + 9 = 14	5 + 9 = 14
1 + 10 = 11	2 + 10 = 12	3 + 10 = 13	4 + 10 = 14	5 + 10 = 15

Addition Table of 6	Addition Table of 7	Addition Table of 8	Addition Table of 9	Addition Table of 10
$6 + 1 = 7$	$7 + 1 = 8$	$8 + 1 = 9$	$9 + 1 = 10$	$10 + 1 = 11$
$6 + 2 = 8$	$7 + 2 = 9$	$8 + 2 = 10$	$9 + 2 = 11$	$10 + 2 = 12$
$6 + 3 = 9$	$7 + 3 = 10$	$8 + 3 = 11$	$9 + 3 = 12$	$10 + 3 = 13$
$6 + 4 = 10$	$7 + 4 = 11$	$8 + 4 = 12$	$9 + 4 = 13$	$10 + 4 = 14$
$6 + 5 = 11$	$7 + 5 = 12$	$8 + 5 = 13$	$9 + 5 = 14$	$10 + 5 = 15$
$6 + 6 = 12$	$7 + 6 = 13$	$8 + 6 = 14$	$9 + 6 = 15$	$10 + 6 = 16$
$6 + 7 = 13$	$7 + 7 = 14$	$8 + 7 = 15$	$9 + 7 = 16$	$10 + 7 = 17$
$6 + 8 = 14$	$7 + 8 = 15$	$8 + 8 = 16$	$9 + 8 = 17$	$10 + 8 = 18$
$6 + 9 = 15$	$7 + 9 = 16$	$8 + 9 = 17$	$9 + 9 = 18$	$10 + 9 = 19$
$6 + 10 = 16$	$7 + 10 = 17$	$8 + 10 = 18$	$9 + 10 = 19$	$10 + 10 = 20$

EXERCISE 6

Adding Numbers with One Digit

Directions: Add.

1. $2 + 5$

2. $6 + 1$

3. $4 + 3$

4. $9 + 9$

5. $7 + 4$

6. $8 + 3$

7. $8 + 9$

8. $1 + 6$

9. $7 + 7$

10. $9 + 3$

Answers are on page 550.

Properties of Addition

The properties of addition help you understand the numbers better and simplify the addition operation. These will make adding easier in some problems.

There are four properties of addition:

The Associative Property of Addition

If a, b, and c are three numbers, then $(a+b)+c = a+(b+c)$.

When three or more numbers are added, the sum of the numbers is the same regardless of the grouping of the numbers. For example:

$$(5+4)+2 = 5+(4+2) = 11.$$

The Commutative Property of Addition

If a and b are two numbers, then $a+b = b+a$.

When two or more numbers are added, the sum of the numbers remains the same regardless of the order of the numbers. This means that you can add two or more whole numbers in any order. For example:

$$3+7=7+3=10.$$

The Identity Property of Addition

If a is a number, then $a + 0 = 0 + a = a$.

The sum of any number and zero is the number itself. For example:

$$6+0=0+6=6.$$

The Inverse Property of Addition

If a is a number and $-a$ is the opposite of a, then $a + (-a) = 0$.

The sum of a number and its negative number is zero. For example:

$$8 + (-8) = -8 + 8 = 0.$$

EXERCISE 7

Properties of Addition

Directions: Use the properties to add.

1. $9 + 2$	**3.** $2 + 0$	**5.** $-4 + 4$	**7.** $-9 + 9$
2. $1 + 5$	**4.** $5 + (-5)$	**6.** $7 + 0$	**8.** $(4 + 9) + 1$

Answers are on page 550.

Adding Numbers with Two or More Digits Vertically

When adding numbers with two or more digits vertically, align the numbers starting with the ones digits. Write the numbers such that the ones digit of one number is under the ones digit of the numbers above it, the tens are under tens, hundreds are under hundreds, and so on. Then add the digits in each column from right to left.

EXAMPLE 1

$$34 + 23 = ?$$

First, place the numbers directly one below the other such that the ones digits are placed one below the other and the tens digits are placed together under tens.

```
  34
+ 23
```

Then add the ones first, followed by the addition of the tens digits.

$$
\begin{array}{r}
34 \\
+\ 23 \\
\hline
57
\end{array}
$$

Thus, $34 + 23 = 57$.

EXAMPLE 2

$25 + 36 = ?$

Place the numbers directly one below the other such that the ones digits are placed together one below the other and the tens digits are placed together under tens.

$$
\begin{array}{r}
25 \\
+\ 36 \\
\hline
\end{array}
$$

Add the ones first. If you get a double-digit number on adding the ones, then carry the digit on the left of each sum to the next column. Add the digits at the tens place including the carryover to get the final sum.

$$
\begin{array}{r}
{}^{1}\ \ \\
25 \\
+\ 36 \\
\hline
61
\end{array}
$$

Thus, $25 + 36 = 61$.

EXAMPLE 3

$125 + 86 = ?$

Place the numbers directly one below the other such that the ones digits are placed together one below the other and the tens digits are placed together under tens.

$$
\begin{array}{r}
125 \\
+\ 86 \\
\hline
\end{array}
$$

Then add the ones first. In case of double-digit sum for any column, carry the digit on the left of each sum to the next column, and so on. Add the digits at the tens place including the carryover. Then add the digits at the hundreds place including the carryover to get the final sum.

$$
\begin{array}{r}
{}^{1\,1}\ \ \\
125 \\
+\ 86 \\
\hline
211
\end{array}
$$

Thus, $125 + 86 = 211$.

EXAMPLE 4

2,675 + 45 = ?

First, place the numbers directly one below the other such that the ones digits are placed together one below the other, the tens are under tens, and so on.

```
  2,675
+   45
  ─────
```

Then add the ones first and carry the digit on the left of each sum to the next column.

```
   1 1
  2,675
+   45
  ─────
  2720
```

Thus, 2,675 + 45 = 2,720.

EXAMPLE 5

5,670 + 675 + 453 + 9,876 = ?

First, arrange the numbers vertically,

```
  5,670
    675
    453
+ 9,876
  ─────
```

Then add the numbers one digit at time, from right to left. Add the ones first and carry the digit on the left of each sum to the next column.

```
  2 2 1
  5,670

    675

    453

+ 9,876
  ─────
 16,674
```

Therefore, 5,670 + 675 + 453 + 9,876 = 16,674.

EXERCISE 8

Adding Numbers with Two or More Digits Vertically

Directions: Add.

1. 85
   +13

2. 92
   +68
    61

3. 36
   +73

4. 451
    678
  + 564

5. 176
    230
   +15

6. 1,035
    + 42

7. 8,062
    + 675

8. 9,061
     36
   + 679

9. 5,099
    6,786
  + 5,643

10.   76
    3,000
     458
    + 45

Answers are on page 550.

Adding Two Integers

Adding whole numbers involves only adding 0 and positive numbers. However, you can also perform addition for the set of both positive and negative integers.

Addition of Two Positive Integers

The sum of two positive integers is positive. To add two positive integers, add the two integers. Placing a positive (+) sign in front of the sum is optional because a number is assumed to be positive if there is no sign in front of it.

EXAMPLE

Find $(+56) + (+42)$.

First, add the absolute values of the numbers: $|+56| = 56$ and $|+42| = 42$.

     56
   + 42
   ————
     98

Now, place a + sign on the sum. Thus, the answer is +98, or just 98.

Addition of Two Negative Integers

The sum of two negative integers is negative. To add two negative integers, add the absolute values of the two integers and then place a negative sign (–) before the sum.

EXAMPLE

Find $(-35) + (-87)$.

First, find the absolute value of the negative integers: $|-35| = 35$ and $|-87| = 87$.

Now add the absolute values:

$$\begin{array}{r} \overset{1}{3}5 \\ +87 \\ \hline 122 \end{array}$$

Place a negative sign in front because both numbers that were added were negative numbers. Thus, the sum is –122.

Addition of a Positive Integer and a Negative Integer

To add positive and negative integers, find the absolute values of the integers. Then, subtract the smaller number from the larger number. Assign the sign of the integer that has the larger absolute value to the difference obtained.

EXAMPLE

Find $(+55) + (-31)$.

First, find the absolute values of the integers: $|+55| = 55$ and $|-31| = 31$.

Now subtract the smaller value from the larger one:

$$\begin{array}{r} 55 \\ -31 \\ \hline 24 \end{array}$$

The larger absolute value is 55 and the integer had a "+" sign. Hence, the answer is +24. But positive integers are usually written without the "+" sign. Therefore, $(+55) + (-31) = 24$.

EXERCISE 9

Adding Two Integers

Directions: Add.

1. $85 + 45$
2. $(-62) + 75$
3. $36 + (-79)$
4. $(-99) + (-67)$
5. $(-76) + (-30)$
6. $(-40) + 40$
7. $92 + 56$
8. $(-68) + (-34)$

Answers are on page 550.

Adding Several Integers

The rules for adding pairs of integers will help you add several integers easily. When all the integers have the same sign, add the absolute values of the integers and then write the sign of the integers on the sum.

When adding both positive and negative integers, follow these steps:

Step 1: Add the positive integers separately. You may have to change the order of the integers. The commutative property of addition allows you to change the order.

Step 2: Add the negative integers separately.

Step 3: Find the difference of the absolute value of the two sums obtained in the previous steps. Give this difference the sign of the sum from the previous steps with the larger absolute value.

EXAMPLE

Add: $56 + (-21) + 9 + 30 + (-62)$.

Step 1: Change the order of the integers to two groups. Add the positive integers.

$56 + (-21) + 9 + 30 + (-62)$
$= (56 + 9 + 30) + [(-21) + (-62)]$
$= 95 + [(-21) + (-62)]$

Now, assign the sign of the sum having the larger absolute value, i.e., the "+" sign.

Step 2: Add the negative integers.

$95 + [(-21) + (-62)]$
$= 95 + (-83)$

Step 3: Find the difference of the absolute values of the two integers.

$|95| - |83| = |12| = 12$

Now determine the sign of this difference. The difference takes on the sign of the sum of 95 because it has a larger absolute value than −83. So the sign is positive.

Thus, $56 + (-21) + 9 + 30 + (-62) = +12 = 12$.

EXERCISE 10

Adding Several Integers

Directions: Add.

1. $55 + 5 + (-30)$

2. $(-42) + (-62) + 33$

3. $9 + (-79) + (-98) + (-44)$

4. $(-59) + (-27) + 46 + (-54)$

5. $(-84) + (-90) + 42 + 45 + (-32)$

6. $42 + 12 + (-10) + (-40) + 10$

7. $65 + (-21) + 16 + (-10) + 30 + (-12)$

Answers are on page 550.

Subtracting Whole Numbers

Subtraction is a mathematical operation that refers to the removal of objects from a collection. It is represented by the minus sign, –. The answer of a subtraction problem is called the **difference**.

For example, if you take out 6 apples from a basket containing 10 apples, then the number of remaining apples in the basket is 10 – 6, which is 4 apples. Therefore, 10 – 6 = 4.

Subtraction is not commutative; i.e., if you change the order of numbers in a subtraction problem, the result also changes. For example, 20 – 5 = 15, but 5 – 20 = –15. So do not change the order of the numbers in subtraction problems.

Generally, subtraction problems of smaller numbers are done horizontally, for example, 8 – 3 = 5. However, subtraction problems of larger numbers can be done vertically. When subtracting numbers vertically, it is important to use the correct setup of the numbers. The number digits should be placed vertically in such a manner that the ones are under the ones place, tens are under the tens place, hundreds are under the hundreds place, and so on.

Relation to Addition

Subtraction is the opposite of addition. If a and b are two integers, then subtraction of b from a means to add the opposite of b to a, that is,

$$a - b = a + (-b) \qquad \text{[opposite of } b \text{ is } (-b)]$$
$$a - (-b) = a + b \qquad \text{[opposite of } (-b) \text{ is } b]$$

EXAMPLE 1

Subtract: 7 – 3.

Here, you have to find the value of 7 – 3.

$7 - 3$

$= 7 + (-3)$

$= 4$

EXAMPLE 2

Subtract: –10 – (–4).

Here, you have to find the value of –10 – (–4).

$-10 - (-4)$

$= -10 + 4$

$= -6$

EXAMPLE 3

Subtract: −12 − 5.

Here, you have to find the value of −12 − 5.

$-12 - 5$

$= -12 + (-5)$

$= -17$

EXAMPLE 4

Subtract: −18 − (−4).

Here, you have to find the value of −18 − (−4).

$-18 - (-4)$

$= -18 + 4$

$= -14$

Subtracting on the Number Line

The subtraction of two whole numbers can also be shown on a number line.

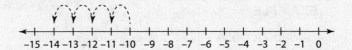

Let's find −10 − 4. As shown in the number line, you start from −10. Since 4 is to be subtracted, move toward the left of −10 making jumps of 1 unit each. Make 4 such jumps, that is, from −10 to −11, −11 to −12, −12 to −13, and −13 to −14. Thus, you reached the point −14.

Therefore, −10 − 4 is −14.

EXERCISE 11

Subtracting on the Number Line

Directions: Subtract.

1. 10 − 4	**5.** 7 − 3	**9.** −2 − 6
2. 15 − 10	**6.** 12 − 7	**10.** 9 − 3
3. −9 − 2	**7.** 5 − 1	
4. −3 − 4	**8.** −10 − 1	

Answers are on page 550.

Subtracting Multi-Digit Numbers Vertically

As seen in addition, alignment of place value is necessary in the subtraction of numbers.

EXAMPLE

Subtract: 56 − 32.

Step 1: Place the larger number on top and arrange the numbers with the ones digits of both numbers lined up vertically. Then line up all other digits accordingly.

```
  56
 −32
```

Step 2: Now, subtract column-wise as in addition, starting with the column of ones.

```
  56
 −32
  24
```

Thus, 56 − 32 = 24.

Sometimes you have to "borrow" when one digit in the top number is less than its corresponding digit in the second number.

EXAMPLE

Subtract: 654 − 175.

Step 1: Write 654 and then align 175 underneath it.

```
  654
 −175
```

Step 2: Look at the ones column: the number 4 is less than 5. Therefore, you need to borrow 1 from the next column. When you borrow from the column to the left, you are borrowing 1 ten, or 10, and adding it to the 4 to get 14. Write a 1 above and to the left of 4 so it looks like 14. Subtract the borrowed 1 from 5 in the tens place by crossing it out, so it becomes 4. The problem now looks like this:

```
   4 1
  6 5̸ 4
 −17 5
```

Now subtract 5 from 14 in the ones column: 14 − 5 = 9. Write 9 underneath the ones column:

```
   4 1
  6 5̸ 4
 −17 5
      9
```

Step 3: Now subtract the tens columns. The number 4 is smaller than 7 in the tens column, so you borrow 1 from 6 in the next column, which means you add another 10 to 4 (since the hundreds column is 10 times the tens column). Write a 1 next to the 4 in the second column and cross out the 6 in the third column. Write a 5 above the 6.

$$
\begin{array}{r}
\overset{\overset{1}{5}\;\overset{4}{\cancel{6}}\;1}{\cancel{6}\,\cancel{5}\,4} \\
-175 \\
\hline
9
\end{array}
$$

Then subtract the second column: $14 - 7 = 7$. The number 7 is the second digit in the answer.

$$
\begin{array}{r}
\overset{\overset{1}{5}\;\overset{4}{\cancel{6}}\;1}{\cancel{6}\,\cancel{5}\,4} \\
-175 \\
\hline
79
\end{array}
$$

Step 4: Now subtract $5 - 1$ in the hundreds column. The number 4 is the third digit.

$$
\begin{array}{r}
\overset{\overset{1}{5}\;\overset{4}{\cancel{6}}\;1}{\cancel{6}\,\cancel{5}\,4} \\
-175 \\
\hline
479
\end{array}
$$

Thus, $654 - 175 = 479$.

EXERCISE 12

Subtracting Multi-Digit Numbers Vertically

Directions: Subtract.

1.
$$
\begin{array}{r}
95 \\
-15 \\
\hline
\end{array}
$$

2.
$$
\begin{array}{r}
72 \\
-34 \\
\hline
\end{array}
$$

3.
$$
\begin{array}{r}
102 \\
-\ 87 \\
\hline
\end{array}
$$

4.
$$
\begin{array}{r}
1,172 \\
-\ 532 \\
\hline
\end{array}
$$

5.
$$
\begin{array}{r}
667 \\
-\ 99 \\
\hline
\end{array}
$$

6.
$$
\begin{array}{r}
1,972 \\
-\ 893 \\
\hline
\end{array}
$$

7.
$$
\begin{array}{r}
895 \\
-588 \\
\hline
\end{array}
$$

8.
$$
\begin{array}{r}
593 \\
-275 \\
\hline
\end{array}
$$

9.
$$
\begin{array}{r}
716 \\
-484 \\
\hline
\end{array}
$$

10.
$$
\begin{array}{r}
971 \\
-439 \\
\hline
\end{array}
$$

Answers are on page 551.

Zero Digits in the Minuend

When the top number has zeros, you may need to do double borrowing in the same step. Take a look at the example below.

EXAMPLE

Find the difference: 5,004 − 236.

Step 1: Write the numbers vertically. The first number is on top.

$$
\begin{array}{r}
5{,}004 \\
-236 \\
\hline
\end{array}
$$

Step 2: Now subtract using borrowing. Notice that you need to move two places over to 5 to borrow because the two places are zeros from which you cannot subtract or even borrow. You need to borrow 1 from the 5 first. This makes the hundreds place into a 10 and the 5 as a 4.

$$
\begin{array}{r}
\overset{4}{\cancel{5}},\overset{1}{}004 \\
-\ 236 \\
\hline
\end{array}
$$

Step 3: Now you can borrow 1 from the 10, thus making the 0 in the tens place as 10 and the 10 from which you borrowed as 9.

$$
\begin{array}{r}
\overset{4}{\cancel{5}},\overset{9}{\cancel{0}}\overset{1}{}04 \\
-\ 236 \\
\hline
\end{array}
$$

Step 4: Finally, you borrow 1 from 10 in the tens place for the ones column, making the 4 as 14 and the 10 as 9.

$$
\begin{array}{r}
\overset{4}{\cancel{5}},\overset{9}{\cancel{0}}\overset{9}{\cancel{0}}\overset{1}{}4 \\
-\ 236 \\
\hline
\end{array}
$$

Step 5: Subtract.

$$
\begin{array}{r}
\overset{4}{\cancel{5}},\overset{9}{\cancel{0}}\overset{9}{\cancel{0}}\overset{1}{}4 \\
-\ 236 \\
\hline
4{,}768 \\
\end{array}
$$

The difference is 5,004 − 236 = 4,768.

EXERCISE 13

Zero Digits in the Minuend

Directions: Subtract.

1.	$20 - 5$	**6.**	$\begin{array}{r} 6{,}900 \\ -\ 934 \\ \hline \end{array}$	**9.**	$\begin{array}{r} 7{,}060 \\ -\ 439 \\ \hline \end{array}$
2.	$60 - 28$				
3.	$304 - 165$	**7.**	$\begin{array}{r} 1{,}000 \\ -\ 487 \\ \hline \end{array}$	**10.**	$\begin{array}{r} 9{,}009 \\ -\ 675 \\ \hline \end{array}$
4.	$560 - 124$				
5.	$900 - 340$	**8.**	$\begin{array}{r} 7{,}002 \\ -1{,}086 \\ \hline \end{array}$		

Answers are on page 551.

Checking Answers by Adding

The answer of a subtraction problem can be checked by adding the answer with the second number in the subtraction (the number following the minus sign). If the result is equal to the top number, then your answer is correct.

EXAMPLE 1

Verify the answer of $56 - 32 = 24$.

To check subtraction, add the answer to the number following the minus sign in the problem. The sum should be equal to the larger, or top, number.

$$\begin{array}{r} 24 \\ +32 \\ \hline 56 \end{array}$$

The sum obtained is equal to the top number of the subtraction problem. So, the answer of the subtraction problem is correct.

EXAMPLE 2

Verify the answer of $654 - 175 = 479$.

To check subtraction, add the answer to the number following the minus sign in the problem. The sum should be equal to the larger, or top, number.

$$\begin{array}{r} 479 \\ +175 \\ \hline 654 \end{array}$$

The sum obtained is equal to the top number of the subtraction problem. So, the answer of the subtraction problem is correct.

EXAMPLE 3

Verify the answer of $5,004 - 236 = 4,768$.

To check subtraction, add the answer to the number following the minus sign in the problem. The sum should be equal to the larger, or top, number.

$$
\begin{array}{r}
\overset{1\ \ 1\ 1}{4,768} \\
+\ 236 \\
\hline
5,004
\end{array}
$$

The sum obtained is equal to the top number of the subtraction problem. So, the answer of the subtraction problem is correct.

Definition of Integer Subtraction

Subtraction of integers can be simplified by using the addition of opposites; if a and b are two integers, then $a - b = a + (-b)$, where $-b$ is the opposite of b.

Recall:

$a - b = a + (-b)$

$a - (-b) = a + b$

Subtracting Two Integers

As mentioned earlier, the subtraction of two integers is the opposite of addition. Here, the subtraction of one integer from another integer means to add the opposite of the former integer to the latter integer.

EXAMPLE 1

Subtract: $8 - 4$.

Subtraction is the opposite of addition of integers, that is, if a and b are two integers, then $a - b = a + (-b)$, where $-b$ is the opposite of b.

Therefore, $8 - 4 = 8 + (-4) = 4$.

EXAMPLE 2

Subtract: $8 - (-4)$.

Subtraction is the opposite of addition of integers, that is, if a and b are two integers, then $a - (-b) = a + b$, where $-b$ is the opposite of b.

Therefore, $8 - (-4) = 8 + 4 = 12$.

EXAMPLE 3

Subtract: $-8 - 4$.

Subtraction is the opposite of addition of integers, that is, if a and b are two integers, then $a - b = a + (-b)$, where $-b$ is the opposite of b.

Therefore, $-8 - 4 = -8 + (-4) = -12$.

EXAMPLE 4

Subtract: $-8 - (-4)$.

Subtraction is the opposite of addition of integers, that is, if a and b are two integers, then $a - (-b) = a + b$, where $-b$ is the opposite of b.

Therefore, $-8 - (-4) = -8 + 4 = -4$.

EXERCISE 14

Subtracting Two Integers

Directions: Subtract.

1. $69 - (-34)$	**4.** $-706 - (-39)$	**7.** $219 - 44$
2. $-100 - (-87)$	**5.** $-909 - (-65)$	**8.** $-221 - 123$
3. $72 - 16$	**6.** $-120 - 18$	

Answers are on page 551.

Multiplying Whole Numbers

Multiplication is the mathematical operation that refers to the addition of a number to itself for a certain number of times. It can be represented by the $\times$ symbol, by the $\cdot$ symbol, or by using parentheses around each number. The answer of a multiplication problem is known as the **product**.

Relation to Addition

Multiplication is a shorthand way to represent repeated addition. For example, 5×7 means 5 groups of 7, which means to add $7 + 7 + 7 + 7 + 7$. The result is 35. Now, 5×7 could also be written as 7×5 and represent 7 groups of 5. This means to add $5 + 5 + 5 + 5 + 5 + 5 + 5$. Instead of writing out this addition with repeated numbers, use multiplication.

EXAMPLE

Multiply 6×3 using repeated addition.

Since you have to multiply 6 and 3, add 6 three times repeatedly:

$6 + 6 + 6 = 18$

Therefore, $6 \times 3 = 18$.

Multiplying on the Number Line

Multiplication of whole numbers can also be shown on the number line.

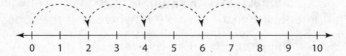

Consider 2 × 4. As shown in the number line, start from 0 and move 2 units at a time toward the right. Make 4 jumps of 2 each (0 to 2, 2 to 4, 4 to 6, and 6 to 8) and reach the point 8. Thus, 2 × 4 is 8.

Multiplying Single Digits

You should try to memorize the multiplication facts for multiplying by 1 to 9. Here is the multiplication table of 1 to 10 for you to review.

Multiplication Table of 1	Multiplication Table of 2	Multiplication Table of 3	Multiplication Table of 4	Multiplication Table of 5
1 × 1 = 1	2 × 1 = 2	3 × 1 = 3	4 × 1 = 4	5 × 1 = 5
1 × 2 = 2	2 × 2 = 4	3 × 2 = 6	4 × 2 = 8	5 × 2 = 10
1 × 3 = 3	2 × 3 = 6	3 × 3 = 9	4 × 3 = 12	5 × 3 = 15
1 × 4 = 4	2 × 4 = 8	3 × 4 = 12	4 × 4 = 16	5 × 4 = 20
1 × 5 = 5	2 × 5 = 10	3 × 5 = 15	4 × 5 = 20	5 × 5 = 25
1 × 6 = 6	2 × 6 = 12	3 × 6 = 18	4 × 6 = 24	5 × 6 = 30
1 × 7 = 7	2 × 7 = 14	3 × 7 = 21	4 × 7 = 28	5 × 7 = 35
1 × 8 = 8	2 × 8 = 16	3 × 8 = 24	4 × 8 = 32	5 × 8 = 40
1 × 9 = 9	2 × 9 = 18	3 × 9 = 27	4 × 9 = 36	5 × 9 = 45
1 × 10 = 10	2 × 10 = 20	3 × 10 = 30	4 × 10 = 40	5 × 10 = 50
Multiplication Table of 6	Multiplication Table of 7	Multiplication Table of 8	Multiplication Table of 9	Multiplication Table of 10
6 × 1 = 6	7 × 1 = 7	8 × 1 = 8	9 × 1 = 9	10 × 1 = 10
6 × 2 = 12	7 × 2 = 14	8 × 2 = 16	9 × 2 = 18	10 × 2 = 20
6 × 3 = 18	7 × 3 = 21	8 × 3 = 24	9 × 3 = 27	10 × 3 = 30
6 × 4 = 24	7 × 4 = 28	8 × 4 = 32	9 × 4 = 36	10 × 4 = 40
6 × 5 = 30	7 × 5 = 35	8 × 5 = 40	9 × 5 = 45	10 × 5 = 50
6 × 6 = 36	7 × 6 = 42	8 × 6 = 48	9 × 6 = 54	10 × 6 = 60
6 × 7 = 42	7 × 7 = 49	8 × 7 = 56	9 × 7 = 63	10 × 7 = 70
6 × 8 = 48	7 × 8 = 56	8 × 8 = 64	9 × 8 = 72	10 × 8 = 80
6 × 9 = 54	7 × 9 = 63	8 × 9 = 72	9 × 9 = 81	10 × 9 = 90
6 × 10 = 60	7 × 10 = 70	8 × 10 = 80	9 × 10 = 90	10 × 10 = 100

EXAMPLE 1

Multiply: 9×3.

On referring to the multiplication table of 9, you would find that $9 \times 3 = 27$.

EXAMPLE 2

Multiply: 6×5.

On referring to the multiplication table of 6, you would find that $6 \times 5 = 30$.

EXERCISE 15

Multiplying Single Digits

Directions: Multiply.

1. 9×2	**5.** 7×9	**9.** 8×8
2. 3×3	**6.** 3×7	**10.** 9×6
3. 4×8	**7.** 5×6	
4. 9×2	**8.** 2×4	

Answers are on page 551.

Properties of Multiplication

As with addition, there are properties of multiplication that hold for all numbers. These properties will make it easier to simplify expressions with multiplication. There are five properties of multiplication: the associative, commutative, identity, zero, and distributive properties.

Associative Property of Multiplication

If a, b, and c are three numbers, then $(a \times b) \times c = a \times (b \times c)$.

When three or more numbers are multiplied, the product of the numbers is the same regardless of the grouping of the numbers.

EXAMPLE

$$(5 \times 4) \times 2 = 20 \times 2$$

$$= 40$$

Also, $5 \times (4 \times 2) = 5 \times 8$

$$= 40$$

Thus, $(5 \times 4) \times 2 = 5 \times (4 \times 2)$.

Commutative Property of Multiplication

If a and b are two numbers, then $a \times b = b \times a$.

When two or more numbers are multiplied, the product of the numbers remains the same regardless of the order of the numbers. This means that you can multiply two or more whole numbers in any order and you would still get the same product.

EXAMPLE

$3 \times 7 = 21$ and $7 \times 3 = 21$.

Identity Property of Multiplication

If a is a number, then $a \times 1 = 1 \times a = a$.

The product of any number and one is the number itself.

EXAMPLE

$4 \times 1 = 4$ and $1 \times 4 = 4$.

Zero Property of Multiplication

If a is a number, then $a \times 0 = 0 \times a = 0$.

The product of any number and zero is zero.

EXAMPLE

$(-6) \times 0 = 0$ and $0 \times (-6) = 0$.

Multiplicative Inverse

The **multiplicative inverse** is the reciprocal of the number. Any nonzero number multiplied by its reciprocal equals 1.

EXAMPLE

The multiplicative inverse of 5 because $5 \times \dfrac{1}{5} = \dfrac{5}{5} = 1$.

Distributive Property of Multiplication

If a, b, and c are three numbers, then $a \times (b + c) = (a \times b) + (a \times c)$.

The product of a number and the sum of numbers equals the sum of the products of the first number with each of the other numbers. In other words, you can distribute the outer factor a over the sum of $b + c$. Multiplying a sum by a number is the same as multiplying each of the numbers in the sum by the outer number and then adding. This property also works with subtraction in the parentheses: $a \times (b - c) = (a \times b) - (a \times c)$.

EXAMPLE

$$2 \times (3 + 4) = 2 \times 7 = 14$$

$$\text{Also, } 2 \times (3 + 4) = (2 \times 3) + (2 \times 4)$$
$$= 6 + 8$$
$$= 14$$

EXERCISE 16

Properties of Multiplication

Directions: Multiply.

1. 7×1

2. 3×0

3. 1×0

4. 9×1

5. $2 \times (2 \times 3)$

6. $7(4 + 5)$

7. $3 \times (8 - 3)$

8. $(2 + 11) \times 3$

9. $7(5 - 2)$

Answers are on page 551.

Multiplying Multi-Digit Numbers by One-Digit Numbers

Using your knowledge of the multiplication facts, you can multiply multi-digit numbers by one-digit numbers.

EXAMPLE 1

Multiply: 34×2.

Step 1: Generally, it is easier to multiply when the number with the most digits is on top. Arrange the digits vertically such that the ones digit of the top number is above the ones place of the second number.

$$\begin{array}{r} 34 \\ \times 2 \\ \hline \end{array}$$

Step 2: Multiply the digits in the ones place, that is, $4 \times 2 = 8$. You get the ones digit of the answer. Write the answer in the columns with the ones digits.

$$\begin{array}{r} 34 \\ \times 2 \\ \hline 8 \end{array}$$

Step 3: Multiply the digit in the tens place with the single digit 2, that is, $3 \times 2 = 6$, which is the second digit in the answer.

$$\begin{array}{r} 34 \\ \times 2 \\ \hline 68 \end{array}$$

Therefore, $34 \times 2 = 68$.

This example illustrates a simple multiplication problem with no carryover. In the next example, there is a carryover to the next digit.

EXAMPLE 2

Multiply: 53 × 6.

Step 1: Align the numbers vertically.

$$
\begin{array}{r}
53 \\
\times\,6 \\
\hline
\end{array}
$$

Step 2: Multiply the digits in the ones place, that is, 3 × 6 = 18. Since the product obtained is a double-digit number, write 8 below in the answer and carry over 1 to the tens place.

$$
\begin{array}{r}
\overset{1}{5}3 \\
\times\ \ 6 \\
\hline
8 \\
\end{array}
$$

Step 3: Multiply the digit in the tens place with the single digit 6, that is, 5 × 6 = 30. Add the carryover to this product: 30 + 1 = 31. Place this value, 31, in the answer.

$$
\begin{array}{r}
\overset{1}{5}3 \\
\times\ \ 6 \\
\hline
318 \\
\end{array}
$$

Therefore, 53 × 6 = 318.

EXERCISE 17

Multiplying Multi-Digit Numbers by One-Digit Numbers

Directions: Multiply.

1. 69 × 5
2. 1,005 × 7
3. 702 × 6

4. 576 × 9
5. 909 × 2
6. 1,320 × 8

7. 1,123 × 3
8. 672 × 8

Answers are on page 551.

Multiplying Multi-Digit Numbers by Multi-Digit Numbers

Multiplication of multi-digit numbers involves several steps similar to multiplying a two-digit number by one digit.

EXAMPLE 1

Multiply: 25 × 12.

Here, both the numbers contain multiple digits. Hence, 25 × 12 can be multiplied in the following way:

Step 1: Align the numbers vertically by place value.

$$
\begin{array}{r}
25 \\
\times 12 \\
\hline
\end{array}
$$

Step 2: Multiply the first number with the ones digit of the second number. Follow the process of multiplication of multi-digit numbers by single-digit numbers.

$$
\begin{array}{r}
25 \\
\times 12 \\
\hline
50 \\
\end{array}
$$

Step 3: Place a zero in the ones column underneath the product you found. This is a placeholder because you are multiplying the top number with the tens digit of the second number. Then multiply the second digit with the tens digit of the second number. Follow the same multiplication process. Then arrange the two obtained products vertically such that the second product ends below the tens place of the first number.

$$
\begin{array}{r}
25 \\
\times 12 \\
\hline
50 \\
250 \\
\end{array}
$$

Step 4: Add the products to get the final answer.

$$
\begin{array}{r}
25 \\
\times 12 \\
\hline
50 \\
250 \\
\hline
300 \\
\end{array}
$$

Therefore, 25 × 12 = 300.

EXAMPLE 2

Multiply: 57 × 27.

Step 1: Align the numbers vertically.

$$
\begin{array}{r}
57 \\
\times 27 \\
\hline
\end{array}
$$

Step 2: Multiply the first number with the ones digit of the second number. Follow the process of multiplication of multi-digit numbers by single-digit numbers.

$$
\begin{array}{r}
57 \\
\times\, 27 \\
\hline
399
\end{array}
$$

Step 3: Write the 0 as a placeholder in the ones column of the second row. Multiply the second digit with the tens digit of the second number. Follow the same multiplication process. Then arrange the two obtained products vertically such that the second product ends below the tens place of the first number.

$$
\begin{array}{r}
57 \\
\times\, 27 \\
\hline
399 \\
1{,}140
\end{array}
$$

Step 4: Add the products to get the final answer.

$$
\begin{array}{r}
57 \\
\times\, 27 \\
\hline
399 \\
1{,}140 \\
\hline
1{,}539
\end{array}
$$

Therefore, $57 \times 27 = 1{,}539$.

EXERCISE 18

Multiplying Multi-Digit Numbers

Directions: Multiply.

1. 28×12
2. 32×15
3. 112×10

4. 99×52
5. 875×74
6. 32×16

7. 56×97
8. 299×25

Answers are on page 551.

Multiplying Two Integers

You can also multiply numbers with different signs. The multiplication process is the same as you have seen for two positive numbers. The only difference is that the sign of the product must be considered when numbers have different signs or two negative signs.

If you consider two integers that are both positive or both negative, then their product is positive and its value is equal to the product of their absolute values.

EXAMPLE 1

Multiply: $(+3) \times (+8)$.

Here, first find their absolute values: $|+3| = 3$, $|+8| = 8$.

Product of their absolute values: $3 \times 8 = 24$.

Therefore, $(+3) \times (+8) = +24 = 24$.

EXAMPLE 2

Multiply: $(-3) \times (-8)$.

Here, first find their absolute values: $|-3| = 3$, $|-8| = 8$.

Product of their absolute values: $3 \times 8 = 24$.

Therefore, $(-3) \times (-8) = 24$.

If you consider two integers of different signs, then their product is negative and its value is equal to the product of their absolute values.

EXAMPLE 3

Multiply: $(+3) \times (-8)$.

Here, first find their absolute values: $|+3| = 3$, $|-8| = 8$.

Product of their absolute values: $3 \times 8 = 24$.

Therefore, $(+3) \times (-8) = -24$.

EXAMPLE 4

Multiply: $(-3) \times (+8)$.

Here, first find their absolute values: $|-3| = 3$, $|+8| = 8$.

Product of their absolute values: $3 \times 8 = 24$.

Therefore, $(-3) \times (+8) = -24$.

EXERCISE 19

Multiplying Two Integers

Directions: Multiply.

1. -9×21

2. $(-75) \times (-74)$

3. $\begin{array}{r} 72 \\ \times 16 \\ \hline \end{array}$

4. $69 \times (-75)$

5. $\begin{array}{r} -39 \\ \times -25 \\ \hline \end{array}$

6. -49×51

7. $\begin{array}{r} 62 \\ \times -24 \\ \hline \end{array}$

8. $\begin{array}{r} -175 \\ \times -4 \\ \hline \end{array}$

Answers are on page 551.

Multiplying Several Integers

For multiplying more than two integers, it is important to remember the following points:

1. The product of positive integers is always positive.

2. If an even number of negative integers are multiplied, the product is positive.

3. If an odd number of negative integers are multiplied, the product is negative.

4. It is easiest to multiply pairs of integers from left to right.

EXAMPLE 1

Multiply: $2 \times 3 \times 4$.

Step 1: Multiply the first two integers: $2 \times 3 = 6$.

Step 2: Multiply the product of 6 with the third integer: $6 \times 4 = 24$.

Therefore, $2 \times 3 \times 4 = 24$.

EXAMPLE 2

Multiply: $(-2) \times (-3) \times 4$.

Step 1: Multiply the first two integers: $(-2) \times (-3) = 6$.

Step 2: Multiply the product of 6 with the third integer: $6 \times 4 = 24$.

Therefore, $(-2) \times (-3) \times 4 = 24$.

EXAMPLE 3

Multiply: $(-2) \times (-3) \times (-4)$.

Step 1: Multiply the first two integers: $(-2) \times (-3) = 6$.

Step 2: Multiply the product of 6 with the third integer: $6 \times -4 = -24$.

Therefore, $(-2) \times (-3) \times (-4) = -24$.

EXAMPLE 4

Multiply: $(-3) \times (-4) \times (-5) \times (-6)$.

Step 1: Multiply the first two integers: $(-3) \times (-4) = 12$.

Step 2: Multiply the product of 12 with the third integer: $12 \times -5 = -60$.

Step 3: Multiply the product of −60 with the fourth integer: $-60 \times -6 = 360$.

Thus, $(-3) \times (-4) \times (-5) \times (-6) = 360$.

Multiplying Several Integers

Directions: Multiply.

1. $(-3) \times 4 \times (-5)$

2. $4 \times (-2) \times 5$

3. $(-3) \times (-6) \times (-7)$

4. $(-9) \times 21 \times 12$

5. $(-5) \times (-7) \times (-4)$

6. $2 \times 6 \times 7$

7. $(-9) \times (-7) \times (-5) \times (-3)$

8. $(-9) \times (-2) \times (-5)$

Answers are on page 551.

Dividing Whole Numbers

When a number is divided by another number, you get a **quotient**, which is the answer to the division problem.

Consider 35 divided by 5 equals 7. Here, 35 is called the **dividend**, which is the number to be divided, and 5 is called the **divisor**, which is the number that divides. The quotient is 7.

This problem can be represented in the following ways:

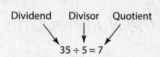

Dividend   Divisor   Quotient

$$35 \div 5 = 7$$

Quotient → 7
Divisor → $5 \overline{)35}$ ← Dividend

Dividend → $\dfrac{35}{5} = 7$ ← Quotient
Divisor →

Dividend   Divisor   Quotient

$$35/5 = 7$$

Relation to Subtraction

If you clearly observe a division problem, you will find that division is repeated subtraction. If you repeatedly subtract 7 from 35, you get 0. The number of times you subtract 7 is 5:

$$35 - 7 = 28$$
$$28 - 7 = 21$$
$$21 - 7 = 14$$
$$14 - 7 = 7$$
$$7 - 7 = 0$$

Thus, 35 divided by 7 is 5.

EXAMPLE

Divide 12 ÷ 3 using repeated subtractions.

Since you have to divide 12 ÷ 3, you can subtract 3 repeatedly from 12 till you get zero.

$$12 - 3 = 9$$
$$9 - 3 = 6$$
$$6 - 3 = 3$$
$$3 - 3 = 0$$

You had to subtract 3 four times from 12 to get zero. Therefore, 12 ÷ 3 = 4.

Relation to Multiplication

The inverse operation of division is multiplication. You can solve division problems that involve the multiplication facts by using the multiplication table.

EXAMPLE

Divide: 45 ÷ 9.

Ask: what number times 9 gives a product of 45? You know that 9 times 5 gives a product of 45. Thus, 45 ÷ 9 = 5 because 9 × 5 = 45.

Dividing on the Number Line

Division of whole numbers can also be shown on the number line.

EXAMPLE 1

Divide: 6 ÷ 3.

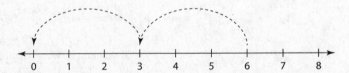

As shown on the number line, you start from 6 and move groups of 3 units left until you reach 0. You make 2 such jumps (6 to 3 and 3 to 0). Hence, 6 ÷ 3 = 2.

EXAMPLE 2

Divide 10 ÷ 2 using the number line.

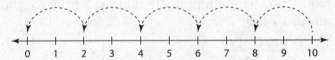

As shown, you start from 10 and move 2 units at a time to 0. You make 5 such jumps (10 to 8, 8 to 6, 6 to 4, 4 to 2, and 2 to 0). Thus, 10 ÷ 2 = 5.

Dividing on the Number Line

Directions: Divide.

1. $50 \div 5$
2. $16 \div 2$
3. $49 \div 7$
4. $27 \div 3$

5. $24 \div 6$
6. $72 \div 8$
7. $18 \div 3$
8. $72 \div 9$

9. $90 \div 10$
10. $32 \div 4$

Answers are on page 551.

Long Division Algorithm

The **long division process** is a division process in which each step of the division is written down. This process is used to divide a large divisor. The following examples show exact division using the long division process.

EXAMPLE 1

Divide: $654 \div 3$.

Step 1: Divide the first digit of the dividend by the divisor: $6 \div 3 = 2$.

$$\begin{array}{r} 2 \\ 3\overline{)654} \\ \underline{3} \\ 0 \end{array}$$

Step 2: Carry down the second digit, 5, of the dividend and divide it by the divisor: $5 \div 3$. Since 3 does not exactly divide 5, you get a remainder, 2.

$$\begin{array}{r} 2\,1 \\ 3\overline{)6\,54} \\ \underline{6}\!\!\downarrow \\ 5 \\ \underline{3} \\ 2 \end{array}$$

Step 3: Carry down the next digit, 4, of the dividend. Since you have a carryover, 2, from the previous division, use both digits to form a new number, 24. Now divide 24 by 3.

```
       2 18
   3)6 54
     6↓↓
     ‾‾‾‾
       5↓
       3↓
     ‾‾‾‾
       2 4
       2 4
     ‾‾‾‾
         0
```

Thus, 654 ÷ 3 = 218.

EXAMPLE 2

Divide: 1,234 ÷ 2.

Here, the dividend is a large number of four digits whereas the divisor is a single-digit number.

Step 1: Divide the first digit of the dividend by the divisor: 1 ÷ 2. Since 1 is less than 2, you cannot divide 2 into 1. Hence, consider the next digit with 1 and see if 12 can be divided by 2. Now divide 12 by 2; you get a quotient of 6 and no remainder.

```
        6
   2)1234
     12
     ‾‾‾
      0
```

Step 2: Carry down the next digit 3 and divide by 2. You get a quotient of 1 and a remainder of 1.

```
       61
   2)1234
     12↓
     ‾‾‾
       3
       2
     ‾‾‾
       1
```

Step 3: Carry down the next digit 4. Since you have a remainder, 1, from the previous division, use both digits to form a new number, 14. Divide 14 by 2. You get a quotient of 7 and no remainder.

$$
\begin{array}{r}
617 \\
2\overline{)1234} \\
\downarrow\downarrow \\
\overline{12\downarrow\downarrow} \\
12\downarrow\downarrow \\
\overline{3\downarrow} \\
2\downarrow \\
\overline{14} \\
14 \\
\overline{0}
\end{array}
$$

Thus, $1,234 \div 2 = 617$.

EXERCISE 22

Long Division Algorithm

Directions: Divide.

1. $500 \div 5$
2. $390 \div 2$
3. $900 \div 2$

4. $921 \div 3$
5. $786 \div 2$
6. $5\overline{)1,900}$

7. $4\overline{)28,204}$
8. $9\overline{)1,026}$
9. $3\overline{)2,352}$

Answers are on page 552.

Answers with Remainders

Sometimes, when the divisor does not divide the dividend exactly, you will get a **remainder** at the end of the division process. For example, consider $25 \div 4$; 25 is not divisible by 4. The nearest number to 25 that is divisible by 4 is 24. So, subtract 24 from 25. You get 1, which is the remainder of the division problem.

$$
\begin{array}{r}
6 \\
4\overline{)25} \\
24 \\
\overline{1}
\end{array}
$$

The division process is continued till all the digits of the dividend are divided by the divisor, that is, no digits of the dividend are left to divide.

EXAMPLE 1

Divide: 110 ÷ 8.

Here, you can divide 110 by 8 in the following way, using the long division process:

```
        1 3
     8)110
        8↓
        ──
        30
        24
        ──
         6
```

Notice that you divide until you divided with the 0 digit. Therefore, the quotient is 13 and the remainder is 6. Remember that the remainder should always be less than the divisor. Otherwise, you have to redivide to find the right quotient.

EXAMPLE 2

Divide: 659 ÷ 3.

Here, you divide 659 by 3 using the long division process:

```
        2 19
     3)659
        6↓↓
        ──
        5↓
        3↓
        ──
        29
        27
        ──
         2
```

Therefore, the quotient is 219 and the remainder is 2.

EXAMPLE 3

Divide: 4,144 ÷ 12.

Here, you can divide 4,144 ÷ 12 using the long division process:

```
          345
     12)4144
         36↓↓
         ──
         54↓
         48↓
         ──
         64
         60
         ──
          4
```

Therefore, the quotient is 345 and the remainder is 4.

EXAMPLE 4

Divide: 5,557 ÷ 10.

Here, you can divide 5,557 ÷ 10 using the long division process:

```
        5 55
  10)5557
      50↓↓
      55↓
      50↓
      57
      50
       7
```

Therefore, the quotient is 555 and the remainder is 7.

EXERCISE 23

Answers with Remainders

Directions: Divide. Write the quotient and remainder.

1. 788 ÷ 3	**3.** 5,660 ÷ 11	**5.** 12,345 ÷ 13	**7.** 6,786 ÷ 11
2. 1,227 ÷ 5	**4.** 19,098 ÷ 12	**6.** 9,811 ÷ 15	**8.** 5,681 ÷ 12

Answers are on page 552.

Checking Answers with Multiplication

Once you have obtained an answer to a division problem, you can check the answer by multiplying the divisor and the quotient and then adding any remainder. The result should be equal to the original dividend.

EXAMPLE 1

Divide: 108 ÷ 9 = 12. Check your answer.

```
      12
   9)108
      9↓
      18
      18
       0
```

Here, 12 is the quotient. To check the answer, first find the value of 9 × 12, which is 108. Since the remainder is zero, you do not have to add anything to the product. The product is equal to the original dividend (108). Therefore, 108 ÷ 9 = 12 is correct.

EXAMPLE 2

Divide: 110 ÷ 8. Check your answer.

$$
\begin{array}{r}
13 \\
8\overline{)110} \\
\underline{8\downarrow} \\
30 \\
\underline{24} \\
6
\end{array}
$$

Here, the quotient is 13 and the remainder is 6. To check the answer, first find the value of 8 × 13, which is 104. Since the remainder is 6, add it to the product, that is, 104 + 6 = 110. The sum is equal to the original dividend, 110. Therefore, the answer of 110 ÷ 8 is correct.

EXAMPLE 3

Divide: 1,445 ÷ 12. Check your answer.

$$
\begin{array}{r}
120 \\
12\overline{)14\ 45} \\
\underline{12\downarrow\downarrow} \\
24\downarrow \\
\underline{24\downarrow} \\
5 \\
\underline{0} \\
5
\end{array}
$$

Here, the quotient is 120 and the remainder is 5. To check the answer, first find the value of 120 × 12, which is 1,440. Since the remainder is 5, add it to the product, that is, 1,440 + 5 = 1,445. The sum is equal to the original dividend, 1,445. Therefore, the answer of 1,445 ÷ 12 is correct.

Fractions Representing Division

As mentioned earlier, a division problem can also be represented as a fraction. If a and b are two integers, then $a \div b$ can also be written as $\frac{a}{b}$. Divide the top number by the bottom number to simplify a fraction.

EXAMPLE

Simplify: $\frac{8}{2}$.

$$\frac{8}{2} = 8 \div 2 = 4$$

Therefore, $\frac{8}{2} = 4$.

EXERCISE 24

Fractions Representing Division

Directions: Simplify.

1. $\dfrac{12}{3}$ **5.** $\dfrac{81}{3}$ **9.** $\dfrac{625}{5}$

2. $\dfrac{42}{2}$ **6.** $\dfrac{132}{11}$ **10.** $\dfrac{882}{18}$

3. $\dfrac{72}{8}$ **7.** $\dfrac{306}{34}$ **11.** $\dfrac{665}{5}$

4. $\dfrac{60}{5}$ **8.** $\dfrac{84}{14}$ **12.** $\dfrac{822}{3}$

Answers are on page 552.

Dividing Two Integers

1. If both the dividend and divisor are positive or negative integers, then the quotient is positive. For example, $16 \div 4 = 4$ and $(-16) \div (-4) = 4$.

2. However, if the dividend and the divisor have opposite signs, then the quotient is negative. For example, $(-16) \div 4 = -4$ and $16 \div (-4) = -4$.

The following diagram shows all possible combinations of signs for the dividend and divisor and the resulting sign of the quotient. This will help you remember when the quotient is negative.

$$
\begin{array}{c c c c c}
\textit{Dividend} & \textit{Divisor} & & \textit{Quotient} & \\
(+) & \div & (+) & = & (+) \\
(+) & \div & (-) & = & (-) \\
(-) & \div & (+) & = & (-) \\
(-) & \div & (-) & = & (+) \\
\end{array}
$$

Division by 0

If you divide 1 by 0, it will be expressed as $\dfrac{1}{0}$. Assume $\dfrac{1}{0} = x$. When simplified, $1 = x \times 0$ by cross multiplying. Any number multiplied by 0 will be 0, so $x \times 0 = 0$. Thus $1 = 0$, which is a contradiction. Therefore, division by 0 is undefined.

Dividing Two Integers

Directions: Divide.

1. $(-21) \div 3$ **4.** $(-204) \div 4$ **7.** $561 \div (-3)$

2. $86 \div (-2)$ **5.** $999 \div (-9)$ **8.** $(-721) \div (-7)$

3. $(-900) \div (-5)$ **6.** $(-235) \div (-5)$

Answers are on page 552.

Rounding Whole Numbers

In certain situations, you may have to estimate numbers. **Estimation** is using approximations of numbers in calculations instead of using exact numbers.

For example, suppose that you want to buy 6 notebooks that cost $1.99 each. When you go to buy them, the shopkeeper tells you that the cost of 6 notebooks is $14. Is the cost correct?

The cost of one notebook is $1.99. Consider its rounded value, 2; 6 times 2 is 12. So, the cost of 6 notebooks should be approximately $12. But, the cost asked by the shopkeeper is $14, which is over your estimate. You may ask the shopkeeper to check the cost of notebooks again.

Rules for Rounding Whole Numbers

When estimating, a number is **rounded** to a given place value. To round, follow these steps:

Step 1: Find the given place value. Circle or box that digit.

Step 2: Look at the next place value to the right. Underline that digit. One of the following two possible ways will apply for rounding that digit:

1. If that digit has a value of 5 or more, change the given place value that you are rounding to be 1 greater. Change all other place values to the right to 0. This is the rounded number.

2. If that digit to the right is less than 5, meaning it has a value of 0, 1, 2, 3, or 4, keep the given place value that you are rounding. Change all other place values to the right to 0. This is the rounded number.

Take a look at examples of rounding to specific place values.

Estimating to the Nearest Tens

Rounding to the nearest tens means that you use the ones digit in the number to round.

EXAMPLE 1

Round 527 to the nearest tens.

Step 1: Find the value of the tens place.

5[2]7

Step 2: Underline the digit to the right. This is the digit that will help you round.

5[2]7

Now, compare the underlined digit to 5. The digit 7 is greater than 5. Thus, the boxed place value of 2 is changed to 3. To make the rounded number, you then drop 7 and change it to 0. You keep all digits to the left of the tens digit.

5[2]7 → 530

Thus, when you round 527 to the nearest tens, you get 530. This is one way to estimate 527.

EXAMPLE 2

Round 873 to the nearest tens.

Step 1: Find the value of the tens place.

8[7]3

Step 2: Underline the digit to the right. This is the digit that will help you round.

8[7]3

Now, compare the underlined digit to 5. The digit 3 is less than 5. Thus, the boxed place value of 7 will remain unchanged. To make the rounded number, you then drop 3 and change it to 0. You keep all digits to the left of the tens digit.

8[7]3 → 870

Thus, when you round 873 to the nearest tens, you get 870. This is one way to estimate 873.

Estimating to the Nearest Hundreds

Rounding to the nearest hundreds means that you use the tens digit in the number to round.

EXAMPLE 1

Round 789 to the nearest hundreds.

Step 1: Find the value of the hundreds place.

[7]89

Step 2: Underline the digit to the right. This is the digit that will help you round.

7̲89

Now, compare the underlined digit to 5. The digit 8 is greater than 5. Thus, the boxed place value of 7 is changed to 8. To make the rounded number, you then drop 8 and 9 and change them to 0.

7̲89 → 800

Thus, when you round 789 to the nearest hundreds, you get 800.

EXAMPLE 2

Round 3,422 to the nearest hundreds.

Step 1: Find the value of the hundreds place.

3 4̲ 22

Step 2: Underline the digit to the right. This is the digit that will help you round.

3 4̲ 2̲2

Now, compare the underlined digit to 5. The digit 2 is less than 5. Thus, the boxed place value of 4 will remain unchanged. To make the rounded number, you then drop both the 2s and change them to 0. You keep all digits to the left of the hundreds digit.

3 4̲ 2̲2 → 3,400

Thus, when you round 3,422 to the nearest hundreds, you get 3,400.

Estimating to the Nearest Thousands

Rounding to the nearest thousands means that you use the hundreds digit in the number to round.

EXAMPLE 1

Round 56,789 to the nearest thousands.

Step 1: Find the value of the thousands place.

5 6̲ 789

Step 2: Underline the digit to the right. This is the digit that will help you round.

5 6̲ 7̲89

Now, compare the underlined digit to 5. The digit 7 is greater than 5. Thus, the boxed place value of 6 is changed to 7. To make the rounded number, you then drop 7, 8, and 9 and change them to 0.

5 6̲ 7̲89 → 57,000

Thus, when you round 56,789 to the nearest thousands, you get 57,000.

EXAMPLE 2

Round 238,454 to the nearest thousands.

Step 1: Find the value of the thousands place.

23$\boxed{8}$454

Step 2: Underline the digit to the right. This is the digit that will help you round.

23$\boxed{8}$454

Now, compare the underlined digit to 5. The digit 4 is less than 5. Thus, the boxed place value of 8 will remain unchanged. To make the rounded number, you then drop 4, 5, and 4 and change them to 0. You keep all digits to the left of the hundreds digit.

23$\boxed{8}$454 → 238,000

Thus, when you round 238,454 to the nearest thousands, you get 238,000.

EXERCISE 26

Rules for Rounding Whole Numbers

Directions: Round to the nearest tens.

1. 14	**3.** 145	**5.** 1,282
2. 264	**4.** 987	

Directions: Round to the nearest hundreds.

6. 765	**8.** 2,311	**10.** 13,210
7. 999	**9.** 1,142	

Directions: Round to the nearest thousands.

11. 1,765	**13.** 2,311	**15.** 13,166
12. 9,599	**14.** 77,891	

Answers are on page 552.

Rounding to Estimate Sums, Differences, Products, or Quotients

You can use rounding to estimate a sum or difference. A common method of estimating sums or differences is to round each individual number to the greatest place value common to both numbers and then perform the given operation. For example, the greatest place value common to 56 and 120 is the tens place. Thus, you would round 56 and 120 to the nearest tens.

Rounding to Estimate Sums

Take a look at this example.

EXAMPLE

Estimate: 6,180 + 18,657.

Step 1: Find the greatest place value common to both numbers. The greatest place value common to both 6,180 and 18,657 is the thousands place. Note that if you round 18,657 to the nearest ten thousands then the estimate of 20,000 could be considered unreasonable because it is too large when compared to 6,180.

Round: 6,180 to 6,000

18,657 to 19,000

Step 2: Find the sum of the rounded numbers: 6,000 + 19,000 = 25,000.

The actual sum is 24,837. Therefore, an estimated sum by using the largest common place value is quite reasonable.

Rounding to Estimate Differences

Take a look at this example.

EXAMPLE

Estimate: 4,676 − 516.

Step 1: Find the greatest place value common to both numbers. The greatest place value common to both 4,676 and 516 is the hundreds place. Note that if you round 4,676 to the nearest thousands then the estimate, 5,000, could be considered unreasonable because it is too large.

Round: 4,676 to 4,700

516 to 500

Step 2: Find the difference of the rounded numbers: 4,700 − 500 = 4,200.

The actual difference is 4,160. Therefore, the estimated difference is quite reasonable.

Rounding to Estimate Products

Take a look at this example.

EXAMPLE

Estimate: 24 × 75.

Step 1: Find the greatest place value common to both numbers. The greatest place value common to both 24 and 75 is the tens place.

Round: 24 to 20

75 to 80

Step 2: Find the product of the rounded numbers: $20 \times 80 = 1,600$.

The actual product is 1,800. Therefore, the estimated product is reasonable.

Rounding to Estimate Quotients

Take a look at this example.

EXAMPLE

Estimate: $761 \div 34$.

Step 1: Find the greatest place value common to both numbers. The greatest place value common to both 761 and 34 is the tens place.

Round: 761 to 760

34 to 30

Step 2: Find the quotient of the rounded numbers:

$$
\begin{array}{r}
25 \\
30\overline{)760} \\
\underline{60} \\
160 \\
\underline{150} \\
10
\end{array}
$$

The quotient is 25 with a remainder of 10. When estimating, ignore the remainder and use the quotient of 25 as the estimate. The actual quotient is approximately 22.38. Therefore, the estimated quotient is reasonable.

EXERCISE 27

Rounding to Estimate

Directions: Estimate the sum.

1. $561 + 32$

2. $669 + 432$

3. $6,745 + 1,897$

4. $2,234 + 213$

Directions: Estimate the difference.

5. $674 - 24$

6. $588 - 113$

7. $1,271 - 876$

8. $6,762 - 1,261$

Directions: Estimate the product.

9. 34×78

10. 657×108

11. $1,021 \times 31$

12. $2,123 \times 689$

Directions: Estimate the quotient.

13. $378 \div 27$

14. $4,512 \div 142$

15. $766 \div 12$

16. $8,912 \div 312$

Answers are on page 552.

Powers

If a is a number and n is a natural number, then you can write $a^n = \underbrace{a \times a \times a \times ... \times a}_{n \text{ factors of } a}$. The number a is the **base** and n is the **power** or **exponent**.

a^n is read as one of the following:

a to the power n

a raised to the power n

a raised to the nth power

Note that $a^1 = a$, because the exponent 1 just means to write one factor of a. For example, $3^1 = 3$. Also, 1 raised to any power of n is 1. For example, $1^5 = 1$.

While working with n as a natural number, the zeroth power of a number can be defined. A number raised to 0 is 1. For example, $67^0 = 1$.

Powers of Ten

Powers of ten refers to raising 10 to the values 0, 1, 2, etc.

The first few powers of ten are as follows:

$$10^0 = 1$$

$$10^1 = 10$$

$$10^2 = 100$$

$$10^3 = 1,000$$

$$10^4 = 10,000$$

The powers of ten follow a pattern. The exponent on 10 indicates the number of zeros in the number that represents that power of ten. You do not have to multiply out the various tens to find its value. For example, 10^4 has 4 zeros. Thus, when you write the value of 10^4, write down a 1 and 4 zeros.

EXERCISE 28

Powers of Ten

Directions: Find each power of ten.

1. 10^3 3. 10^6 5. 10^4

2. 10^7 4. 10^9

Answers are on page 552.

Multiplication by Powers of Ten

When you multiply a number with powers of ten, the product can be found by these steps without having to carry out the multiplication in the usual way.

Step 1: Count the number of zeros in the power of ten.

Step 2: Write the other number down. Then write down that many zeros to the right of the number. Place commas as needed. This is the product.

EXAMPLE 1

Find the product: 54×10.

Step 1: There is 1 zero in 10.

Step 2: Write down 54. Then write down 1 zero to the right of 54: 540.

Thus, $54 \times 10 = 540$.

EXAMPLE 2

Find the product: 321×10^3.

Step 1: There are 3 zeros in 10^3.

Step 2: Write down 321. Then write down 3 zeros to the right of 321: 321,000.

Thus, $321 \times 10^3 = 321,000$.

EXAMPLE 3

Find the product: $7,681 \times 10^7$.

Step 1: There are 7 zeros in 10^7.

Step 2: Write down 7,681. Then write down 7 zeros to the right of 7,681: 76,810,000,000.

Thus, $7,681 \times 10^7 = 76,810,000,000$.

Multiplication by Powers of Ten

Directions: Multiply.

1. 534×10^4

2. $1{,}234 \times 10^5$

3. $6{,}726 \times 10^3$

4. 652×10^8

5. $8{,}713 \times 10^5$

6. $9{,}851 \times 10^6$

7. 654×10^7

8. $4{,}311 \times 10^2$

Answers are on page 552.

Multiplying Numbers Ending in Strings of Zeros

Multiplying numbers with zeros is similar to multiplying by powers of 10. These are the steps for multiplying such numbers:

Step 1: Ignoring the zeros for now, multiply the nonzero parts of the numbers together.

Step 2: Count the number of zero digits in both numbers. Write that many zeros next to the product found in Step 1. Write commas as needed. This is the product of the two numbers.

EXAMPLE 1

Multiply: $3{,}600 \times 40{,}000$.

Step 1: Multiply the nonzero portion of the numbers: 36×4.

$$
\begin{array}{r}
\overset{2}{3}6 \\
\times 4 \\
\hline
144
\end{array}
$$

Step 2: Count the total number of zeros present in the given numbers. The number 3,600 has 2 zeros and 40,000 has 4 zeros. Thus, the total number of zeros is $2 + 4 = 6$.

Add 6 zeros and commas to the product you obtained earlier: 144,000,000.

Therefore, $3{,}600 \times 40{,}000 = 144{,}000{,}000$.

EXAMPLE 2

Multiply: $5{,}412{,}000 \times 760{,}000$.

Step 1: Multiply the nonzero portion of the numbers: $5{,}412 \times 76$.

$$
\begin{array}{r}
\overset{2}{} \overset{1}{} \\
5412 \\
\times 76 \\
\hline
32472 \\
37884 \\
\hline
411312
\end{array}
$$

Step 2: Count the total number of zeros present in the given numbers. The number 5,412,000 has 3 zeros and 760,000 has 4 zeros. Thus, the total number of zeros is $3 + 4 = 7$.

Add 7 zeros and commas to the product you obtained earlier: 4,113,120,000,000.

Therefore, $5,412,000 \times 760,000 = 4,113,120,000,000$.

EXERCISE 30

Multiplying Numbers Ending in Strings of Zeros

Directions: Multiply.

1. $400 \times 39,000$
2. $120 \times 9,000$
3. $11,400 \times 8,000$
4. $1,000 \times 70$
5. $17,400 \times 20,000$
6. $80 \times 3,200$
7. $720,000 \times 7,100$
8. $35,000 \times 15,000$

Answers are on page 552.

Integers to Powers—Even and Odd Powers

When a positive integer is raised to either an even or odd power, the result is positive. In other words, a positive integer remains a positive integer irrespective of the even or odd powers. However, the result of a negative integer raised to an even power is positive. When a negative integer is raised to an odd number, the result is negative.

To summarize:

If a is greater than 0 and n is an even number, then $(-a)^n = a^n$.

If a is greater than 0 and n is an odd number, then $(-a)^n = -a^n$.

EXAMPLE 1

Find $(-4)^4$.

$$(-4)^4 = (-4) \times (-4) \times (-4) \times (-4)$$
$$= (4 \times 4 \times 4 \times 4)$$
$$= 256$$

The result is positive.

EXAMPLE 2

Find $-(-2)^3$.

$$-(-2)^3 = -(-2 \times -2 \times -2)$$
$$= -(-8)$$
$$= 8$$

Find the negative of the term $(-2)^3$ last.

EXERCISE 31

Integers to Powers—Even and Odd Powers

Directions: Evaluate.

1. $(-2)^5$ 5. $(-8)^3$ 9. $(-2)^{10}$

2. $-(-3)^5$ 6. $(-6)^4$ 10. $-(41)^2$

3. $(-8)^4$ 7. 11^3

4. 4^5 8. $(-4)^2$

Answers are on page 553.

Order of Operations

Accurate calculations involve the correct usage of mathematical operations, such as addition, subtraction, multiplication, and division. When two or more of these operations are present in a single problem, the operations must be performed in a certain order. The rules that describe the order in which the operations are to be performed are known as the **Order of Operations**. All operations have to be performed as you move from left to right in the problem.

Need for Agreement

The presence of multiple operators in a single problem complicates the entire problem-solving process. Various approaches could be used to solve such problems, which might result in different solutions. Hence, to standardize the method of solving such problems, mathematicians have agreed upon a specific order of operations to follow.

The order of operations is given in the steps below. Follow each step one after another without skipping steps. However, skip a step if no such operation is present.

1. First, perform operations within the parentheses.

2. Evaluate the exponents. This includes powers and square roots.

3. Multiply and divide as they come up in the problem. In other words, perform each operation as you move from left to right.

4. Add and subtract as you move from left to right.

EXAMPLE 1

Evaluate: $(35 + 74) - (36 - 12)$.

Step 1: First, solve the operations within the parentheses:

$$(35 + 74) - (36 - 12) = 109 - 24$$

Step 2: Now, subtract the answers obtained in the previous step:

$$109 - 24 = 85$$

EXAMPLE 2

Evaluate: $(15 + 40) \times 10 - (36 - 12) \div 2^2$.

Step 1: Evaluate operations in parentheses.

$$(15 + 40) \times 10 - (36 - 12) \div 2^2$$

$$= (55) \times 10 - (24) \div 2^2$$

Step 2: Evaluate any powers or square roots.

$$= (55) \times 10 - (24) \div 2^2$$

$$= 55 \times 10 - 24 \div 4$$

Step 3: Multiply or divide from left to right.

$$= 55 \times 10 - 24 \div 4$$

$$= 550 - 24 \div 4$$

$$= 550 - 6$$

Step 4: Add or subtract from left to right.

$$550 - 6 = 544$$

EXERCISE 32

Order of Operations

Directions: Evaluate.

1. $5 \times (5 \times 3 - 9^2) + 3$

2. $(14 + 22 - 4) - 8 - 4^2$

3. $(10 - 3)^2 + (6 + 12 + 2)$

4. $(12 + 20 - 2) - 15 - 7^2$

5. $(10 + 6) \times (10 + 4) - 6^2$

6. $8 \times (4 \times 2 - 7^2) + 6$

7. $(17 - 8) \times (13 + 6) - 2^2$

8. $(12 + 37 - 5^2) + (8 + 4)$

9. $(8 - 5)^2 + (8 + 15 + 3)$

Answers are on page 553.

Grouping Symbols

Grouping symbols are used to group numbers or variables so as to simplify the problem solving process. Three types of grouping symbols are used in mathematical problems: parentheses ( ), brackets [ ], and braces { }.

Sometimes these pairs of grouping symbols are used within each other. When working the order of operations, work from the innermost set of grouping symbols, usually parentheses, and work outward.

EXAMPLE 1

Simplify: $6(2 + 3)$.

Carry out the addition in parentheses first.

$$6(2 + 3) = 6(5)$$
$$= 6 \times 5$$
$$= 30$$

EXAMPLE 2

Simplify: $3\{1 + [5(3 - 1) + 6]\}$

Step 1: Carry out the operation in the innermost pair of parentheses.

$$3\{1 + [5(3 - 1) + 6]\}$$
$$= 3\{1 + [5(2) + 6]\}$$

Step 2: Simplify the operations in the brackets [ ]. Remember the order of operations applies within the brackets.

$$= 3\{1 + [5(2) + 6]\}$$
$$= 3\{1 + [5 \times 2 + 6]\}$$
$$= 3\{1 + [10 + 6]\}$$
$$= 3\{1 + [16]\}$$

Step 3: Simplify the operations in the outermost braces { }.

$$= 3\{1 + [16]\}$$
$$= 3\{1 + 16\}$$
$$= 3\{17\}$$

Step 4: Simplify all other operations in the expression.

$$= 3\{17\}$$
$$= 51$$

EXAMPLE 3

Simplify: $((1 + 2) \times 4) + 5$.

$$((1+2)\times 4)+5$$
$$=((3)\times 4)+5$$
$$=(3\times 4)+5$$
$$=(12)+5$$
$$=12+5$$
$$=17$$

EXERCISE 33

Grouping Symbols

Directions: Simplify.

1. $\{[(5+6)-8]\times 6\}-2$

2. $[(5-2)^3+7]-5$

3. $(9\times 2)+[1+6(8+5)]$

4. $1+[(5-4)+(3-2)]+7+5-(6-3)$

5. $\{6+[(5+2)+5]\}-4$

6. $[11+(10+5-8)]+9$

7. $[9+(14+2+6)]+9$

8. $(10-5)+[(12+2)\times 4]$

9. $[(11-7)+(18-6)]\times 6$

10. $17+[9+(15-8)]-7$

Answers are on page 553.

Memory Device for Order of Operations (PEMDAS)

Sometimes, it is confusing to remember which operators need to be performed first. In such a case, you can use **PEMDAS**, or "**P**lease **E**xcuse **M**y **D**ear **A**unt **S**ally." This memory device will help you to remember the order of operations for solving complicated problems.

Memorize PEMDAS or "Please Excuse My Dear Aunt Sally":

1st	P stands for Parentheses
2nd	E stands for Exponents
3rd	M stands for Multiplication
	D stands for Division
4th	A stands for Addition
	S stands for Subtraction

Now, you can solve any complicated problem that includes addition, subtraction, multiplication, and division operations.

EXAMPLE

Evaluate: $\{[(5 \times 4) - 5] + 14 + [(20 - 12) \div 2^3]\} + 5$.

Here, the problem includes multiple operations and you use PEMDAS to simplify.

$\{[(5 \times 4) - 5] + 14 + [(20 - 12) \div 2^3]\} + 5$

$= \{[(20) - 5] + 14 + [(8) \div 2^3]\} + 5$

$= \{[20 - 5] + 14 + [8 \div 8]\} + 5$

$= \{[15] + 14 + [1]\} + 5$

$= \{15 + 14 + 1\} + 5$

$= 30 + 5$

$= 35$

Therefore, the answer is 35.

EXERCISE 34

Memory Device for Order of Operations (PEMDAS)

Directions: Evaluate.

1. $4^2 + (6 + 7) - (5 + 6) \times 2$

2. $(9 - 8) + 18 \div 6 + (6 + 2)$

3. $(9 - 2) \times (5 - 2)$

4. $(1 + 7)^2 + 6 \div 3 + (3 \times 2 \times 5)$

5. $(9 - 4) + (8 - 4) + (5 \times 3) + (8 \div 2)$

6. $[7^2 + (8 - 4 + 4^2)] + 4^2$

7. $18 + [5 \times (4 + 6)^2] + 2$

8. $[(3 + 4)^2 + 4] - 7 - 2^2$

9. $[(16 - 2) + (10 - 5)^2] + 7^2$

10. $[(9 - 7) + (12 - 6)^2] \times 4^2$

Answers are on page 553.

Exponents, Roots, and Radicals and Properties of Numbers

Before studying exponents and radicals, you need to understand the concept of prime numbers, the prime factorization process, and the Fundamental Theorem of Arithmetic.

Fundamental Theorem of Arithmetic

The Fundamental Theorem of Arithmetic describes an important aspect of the relationship between natural numbers and numbers. It states that prime numbers are the building blocks of natural numbers. To understand this theorem, it is important to understand the concept of prime numbers.

Prime Numbers

A **prime number** is a **natural number** that is greater than 1 and is divisible only by 1 and itself. Remember, a natural number includes all the counting numbers such as 1, 2, 3, 4, … onward. The least prime number is 2, which is greater than 1 and is divisible by 1 and itself. Other prime numbers are 3, 5, 7, 11, 13, 17, etc. All of these numbers are greater than 1 and are divisible only by 1 and themselves. You can check whether the above numbers are divisible by any other number other than 1 and themselves.

For example, $7 \rightarrow 1, \cancel{2}, \cancel{3}, \cancel{4}, \cancel{5}, \cancel{6}, 7$. If you check the divisibility of 7 from each number 1 to 7, you will find that 7 is divisible only by 1 and 7.

Similarly, $11 \rightarrow 1, \cancel{2}, \cancel{3}, \cancel{4}, \cancel{5}, \cancel{6}, \cancel{7}, \cancel{8}, \cancel{9}, \cancel{10}, 11$. If you check the divisibility of 11 from each number 1 to 11, you will find that 11 is divisible by 1 and 11 only.

EXERCISE 1

Prime Numbers

Directions: Check whether the following numbers are prime or non-prime numbers.

1. 11
2. 15
3. 51
4. 63

5. 29
6. 65
7. 43
8. 79

9. Find the set of prime numbers between 30 and 50.

Answers are on page 553.

Prime Factorization of a Whole Number

Whole numbers include 0 and all the other natural numbers, that is, whole numbers are 0, 1, 2, 3, 4, 5, etc. Sometimes, you need to find out the factors of a given whole number. To find out the factors, it is important to understand what a factor means.

A **factor** is a number that can divide another number exactly. In other words, a factor of a number is an exact divisor of that number.

EXAMPLE 1

6 is divisible by 1, 2, 3, and 6. So, the factors of 6 are 1, 2, 3, and 6.

EXAMPLE 2

8 is divisible by 1, 2, 4, and 8. So, the factors of 8 are 1, 2, 4, and 8.

EXAMPLE 3

Similarly, 12 is divisible by 1, 2, 3, 4, 6, and 12. So, the factors of 12 are 1, 2, 3, 4, 6, and 12.

Prime factorization is the process by which a number is expressed as the **product of prime factors**. It means all the factors of a given number are expressed in terms of prime numbers, such that some prime numbers may be repeated more than once.

Prime factorization is calculated by using the repeated division method, which is suitable for large numbers. In the repeated division method, the number is divided by a prime number that divides it exactly. Then the quotient is divided by a prime number till the resultant quotient is a prime number itself. The prime factors are the list of prime numbers used in the division process.

EXAMPLE 4

Find the prime factors of 12 using the repeated division method. 12 is divisible by 2.

$$2\underline{|12}$$
$$2\underline{|06}$$
$$3$$

The quotient 6 is then again divided by 2. The final quotient is 3, which is a prime number. Thus, the prime factors of 12 are 2, 2, and 3.

EXERCISE 2

Prime Factorization of a Whole Number

Directions: Find the prime factors of each number using the repeated division method.

1. 540	**5.** 140	**9.** 565
2. 630	**6.** 220	**10.** 777
3. 1,650	**7.** 155	
4. 210	**8.** 192	

Answers are on page 553.

Fundamental Theorem of Arithmetic

The **Fundamental Theorem of Arithmetic** states that every natural number (numbers that you can count) greater than 1 is either a prime number itself or is the product of prime numbers. It further states that even if the order of the prime numbers is arbitrary, the prime factors themselves are unique. This theorem is also known as the Unique Factorization Theorem or Unique-Prime Factorization Theorem.

EXAMPLE 1

$$1,000 = 2 \times 2 \times 2 \times 5 \times 5 \times 5 = 2 \times 5 \times 2 \times 5 \times 2 \times 5$$

EXAMPLE 2

$$1,500 = 2 \times 2 \times 3 \times 5 \times 5 \times 5 = 5 \times 2 \times 3 \times 5 \times 2 \times 5$$

Finding All the Factors/Divisors of a Number

Finding all the **factors of a number** will help find **common factors** and **common multiples**. The examples show how to find all the factors of a number.

EXAMPLE 1

Write all the factors of 66.

Divide 66 by each and every natural number.

$$66 = 1 \times 66$$
$$66 = 2 \times 33$$
$$66 = 3 \times 22$$
$$66 = 6 \times 11$$
$$66 = 11 \times 6$$

Since 6 and 11 have occurred earlier, stop here. If you continue, you will get the same numbers in reverse order; the product of which will always be the same.

Therefore, all the factors of 66 are 1, 2, 3, 6, 11, 22, 33, and 66.

EXAMPLE 2

Find the factors of 45.

Divide 45 by each and every natural number.

$$45 = 1 \times 45$$
$$45 = 3 \times 15$$
$$45 = 5 \times 9$$
$$45 = 9 \times 5$$

Stop here as 5 and 9 have occurred earlier. Therefore, the factors of 45 are 1, 3, 5, 9, 15, and 45.

EXERCISE 3

Finding All the Factors/Divisors of a Number

Directions: Find all the factors of each number.

1. 68   **5.** 312   **9.** 352

2. 180   **6.** 325   **10.** 200

3. 680   **7.** 195

4. 145   **8.** 274

Answers are on page 553.

Finding All the Common Factors of Two Numbers

Since you know how to find all the factors of a number, it will be easy to find the factors that are shared by two or more numbers. These factors are known as **common factors**.

EXAMPLE 1

Find the common factors between 30 and 40.

The factors of 30 are <u>1</u>, <u>2</u>, 3, <u>5</u>, 6, <u>10</u>, 15, and 30.

The factors of 40 are <u>1</u>, <u>2</u>, 4, <u>5</u>, 8, <u>10</u>, 20, and 40.

Therefore, the common factors of 30 and 40 are 1, 2, 5, and 10.

EXAMPLE 2

What are the common factors of 25 and 625?

The factors of 25 are <u>1</u>, <u>5</u>, and <u>25</u>.

The factors of 625 are <u>1</u>, <u>5</u>, <u>25</u>, 125, and 625.

The common factors of 25 and 625 are 1, 5, and 25.

EXERCISE 4

Finding All the Common Factors of Two Numbers

Directions: Find the common factors of each pair of numbers.

1. 36 and 45   **5.** 15 and 125   **9.** 150 and 175

2. 98 and 132   **6.** 108 and 144   **10.** 182 and 198

3. 100 and 125   **7.** 136 and 172

4. 55 and 99   **8.** 115 and 100

Answers are on page 554.

Finding All the Common Factors of More Than Two Numbers

For finding the common factors of two or more numbers, you can simply find all the factors of the numbers and then compare them. Any number that is on the list of factors for all of the numbers is a common factor. The examples show the process.

EXAMPLE 1

Find the common factors of 15, 30, and 60.

The factors of 15 are 1, 3, 5, and 15.

The factors of 30 are 1, 2, 3, 5, 6, 10, 15, and 30.

The factors of 60 are 1, 2, 3, 4, 5, 6, 10, 12, 15, 20, 30, and 60.

Therefore, the common factors of 15, 30, and 60 are 1, 3, 5, and 15.

EXAMPLE 2

What are the common factors of 10, 25, and 125?

The factors of 10 are 1, 2, 5, and 10.

The factors of 25 are 1, 5, and 25.

The factors of 125 are 1, 5, 25, and 125.

The common factors of 10, 25, and 125 are 1 and 5.

EXERCISE 5

Finding All the Common Factors of More Than Two Numbers

Directions: Find the common factors of each set of numbers.

1. 90, 120, and 135
2. 36, 48, and 60
3. 10, 50, and 100
4. 5, 50, and 150
5. 56, 78, and 108
6. 120, 128, and 144
7. 100, 125, and 150
8. 72, 112, and 142
9. 120, 140, and 160
10. 48, 152, and 168

Answers are on page 554.

Finding the Greatest Common Factor of Two or More Numbers

The **greatest common factor** (**GCF**) of two or more numbers is the largest factor common for all the given numbers.

EXAMPLE 1

Find the GCF of 30 and 40.

The factors of 30 are 1, 2, 3, 5, 6, 10, 15, and 30.

The factors of 40 are <u>1</u>, <u>2</u>, 4, <u>5</u>, 8, <u>10</u>, 20, and 40.

The common factors of 30 and 40 are 1, 2, 5, and 10.

Of the common factors, the greatest factor is 10.

So, the GCF of 30 and 40 is 10.

EXAMPLE 2

What is the GCF of 10, 25, and 125?

The factors of 10 are <u>1</u>, 2, <u>5</u>, and 10.

The factors of 25 are <u>1</u>, <u>5</u>, and 25.

The factors of 125 are <u>1</u>, <u>5</u>, 25, and 125.

The common factors of 10, 25, and 125 are 1 and 5.

Of these factors, the greatest factor is 5. Therefore, the GCF of 10, 25, and 125 is 5.

Sometimes, it is difficult to list all the factors of the given numbers. To find out the GCF of two or more numbers, use the prime factorization method.

EXAMPLE 1

Find the GCF of 30 and 40 using the prime factorization method.

First, find the prime factors of 30 and 40 using the prime factorization method.

$$
\begin{array}{cc}
 & 2\underline{|40} \\
2\underline{|30} & 2\underline{|20} \\
3\underline{|15} & 2\underline{|10} \\
5 & 5
\end{array}
$$

The prime factors of 30 are <u>2</u>, 3, and <u>5</u>.

The prime factors of 40 are <u>2</u>, 2, 2, and <u>5</u>.

The common factors of 30 and 40 are 2 and 5. The GCF of 30 and 40 is $2 \times 5 = 10$.

EXAMPLE 2

What is the GCF of 10, 25, and 125?

Find the prime factors of 10, 25, and 125 using the prime factorization method.

$$
\begin{array}{ccc}
 & & 5\underline{|125} \\
2\underline{|10} & 5\underline{|25} & 5\underline{|25} \\
5 & 5 & 5
\end{array}
$$

The prime factors of 10 are 2 and <u>5</u>.

The prime factors of 25 are 5 and <u>5</u>.

The prime factors of 125 are 5, 5, and <u>5</u>.

The common factor of 10, 25, and 125 is 5. Therefore, the GCF of 10, 25, and 125 is 5.

EXERCISE 6

Finding the Greatest Common Factor of Two or More Numbers

Directions: Find the GCF of each set of numbers.

1. 21 and 35

2. 36 and 48

3. 90, 120, and 150

4. 70, 100, and 150

Directions: Find the GCF of each set of numbers by using the prime factorization method.

5. 18 and 45

6. 100, 110, and 120

7. 12, 84, and 144

8. 250, 365, and 660

9. 148, 152, and 168

10. 120, 140, and 180

Answers are on page 554.

Finding All the Multiples of a Number

A **multiple** of a number is formed when you multiply a number with a natural number (1, 2, 3, …). To find all the multiples of a number, simply multiply the number with each and every natural number starting from 1.

EXAMPLES

1. The multiples of 2 are $2 \times 1 = 2$, $2 \times 2 = 4$, $2 \times 3 = 6$, $2 \times 4 = 8$, $2 \times 5 = 10$, …

2. The multiples of 3 are $3 \times 1 = 3$, $3 \times 2 = 6$, $3 \times 3 = 9$, $3 \times 4 = 12$, $3 \times 5 = 15$, $3 \times 6 = 18$, …

3. The multiples of 11 are 11, 22, 33, 44, 55, 66, …

EXERCISE 7

Finding All the Multiples of a Number

Directions: Find the first six multiples of each number.

1. 18

2. 25

3. 50

4. 61

5. 76

6. 21

7. 45

8. 55

9. 34

10. 15

11. 62

12. 100

Answers are on page 554.

Finding All the Common Multiples of Two Numbers

The **common multiples** of two numbers are the multiples of the two numbers that are the same. To find the common multiples, first find the multiples of each number given. Then underline or circle the multiples that are common for both the numbers. This gives you the list of common multiples.

EXAMPLE 1

Find the first three common multiples of 25 and 50.

To find the common multiples, first list the multiples of 25 and 50.

25: 25, 50, 75, 100, 125, 150, 175, 200, 225, 250, 275, 300, …

50: 50, 100, 150, 200, 250, 300, …

Common multiples of 25 and 50 are the multiples that are common between the numbers. So the first three common multiples are 50, 100, and 150.

EXAMPLE 2

Find the first two common multiples of 12 and 60.

12: 12, 24, 36, 48, 60, 72, 84, 96, 108, 120, …

60: 60, 120, 180, 240, 300, …

The first two common multiples of 12 and 60 are 60 and 120.

EXERCISE 8

Finding All the Common Multiples of Two Numbers

Directions: Find the first common multiple of each set of numbers.

1. 36 and 45	**5.** 6 and 8	**9.** 30 and 40
2. 98 and 196	**6.** 36 and 54	**10.** 60 and 72
3. 18 and 23	**7.** 19 and 20	
4. 30 and 45	**8.** 25 and 30	

Answers are on page 554.

Finding All the Common Multiples of More Than Two Numbers

To find the common multiples of more than two numbers, first write down the multiples of each number and then find the multiples that are common for the given numbers.

EXAMPLE

Find the first two common multiples of 8, 16, and 32.

The multiples of 8, 16, and 32 are:

8: 8, 16, 24, 32, 40, 48, 56, 64, …

16: 16, 32, 48, 64, …

32: 32, 64, 96, …

The first two common multiples of 8, 16, and 32 are 32 and 64.

EXERCISE 9

Finding All the Common Multiples of More Than Two Numbers

Directions: Find the first three common multiples of each set of numbers.

1. 36, 40, and 45

2. 5, 18, and 36

3. 15, 30, and 45

4. 6, 8, 10, and 12

5. 14, 28, and 54

6. 60, 72, and 120

7. 3, 8, and 12

8. 18, 36, and 72

9. 24, 84, and 96

Answers are on page 554.

Finding the Least Common Multiple of Two or More Numbers

The **least common multiple** (**LCM**) of two or more numbers is the smallest number that is a multiple of each of the given numbers.

EXAMPLE 1

Find the LCM of 2 and 5.

First, write the multiples of both 2 and 5.

2: 2, 4, 6, 8, 10, 12, 14, 16, 18, 20, …

5: 5, 10, 15, 20, 25, 30, …

Common multiples of 2 and 5 are 10, 20, … Therefore, the LCM of 2 and 5 is the smallest common multiple, that is, 10.

EXAMPLE 2

Find the LCM of 20 and 25.

First, write the multiples of both 20 and 25.

20: 20, 40, 60, 80, 100, 120, 140, 160, 180, 200, …

25: 25, 50, 75, 100, 125, 150, 175, 200, …

Common multiples of 20 and 25 are 100, 200, …

Therefore, the LCM of 20 and 25 is 100.

From the examples, notice that it is difficult to write down all the multiples of the given numbers. For this, calculate the LCM of two or more numbers by using the prime factorization method.

To find the LCM of numbers using the prime factorization method, follow these steps:

1. Find the prime factors of each number.

2. The LCM is the product of all the different prime numbers using the highest number of times they appear.

3. Find the LCM of 16, 18, and 20 using the prime factorization method.

First, write down the prime factors for each number.

$16 = 2 \times 2 \times 2 \times 2$

$18 = 2 \times 3 \times 3$

$20 = 2 \times 2 \times 5$

As shown, the highest number of times 2 occurs as a prime factor is four times, 3 occurs two times, and 5 occurs one time.

Therefore, the LCM of 16, 18, and 20 is $2 \times 2 \times 2 \times 2 \times 3 \times 3 \times 5 = 720$.

EXERCISE 10

Finding the Least Common Multiple of Two or More Numbers

Directions: Find the LCM of each set of numbers.

1. 24, 36, and 60

2. 42, 48, and 50

3. 34, 46, and 90

4. 4, 8, 12, and 14

Directions: Find the LCM of each set of numbers using the prime factorization method.

5. 15, 30, 60, 90, and 120

6. 5, 50, 168, and 200

7. 32, 36, 40, and 44

8. 5, 16, and 54

9. 12, 14, and 16

10. 20, 24, and 32

11. 18, 20, 24, and 32

12. 5, 15, 18, and 24

Answers are on page 554.

Roots and Radicals

In this section and subsequent sections, you will learn the definitions, properties, and rules of exponents and radicals and how to simplify expressions with exponents or radicals.

Perfect Squares and Perfect Cubes

Perfect Squares

A number is squared when it is multiplied by itself. The product of this multiplication is called the **square** of the number.

EXAMPLES

1. The square of the number 1 is $1 \times 1 = 1$.

2. The square of 3 is $3 \times 3 = 9$.

3. The square of 6 is $6 \times 6 = 36$.

If the squared number is a whole number, then the resulting product is called a **perfect square**.

EXAMPLES

1. 9 is a perfect square because $3 \times 3 = 9$.
2. 25 is a perfect square because $5 \times 5 = 25$.

Only certain numbers are perfect squares. For example, 32 is not a perfect square. The number 32 occurs between the square numbers 25 and 36, which are products of 5^2 and 6^2, respectively. If 32 is a square number, it must be the square of a whole number between 5 and 6. However, there is no whole number between 5 and 6. Therefore, 32 is not a perfect square. Perfect squares are whole numbers. The first 10 perfect squares are listed in the table below.

Perfect Squares

$1 = 1 \times 1$	$36 = 6 \times 6$
$4 = 2 \times 2$	$49 = 7 \times 7$
$9 = 3 \times 3$	$64 = 8 \times 8$
$16 = 4 \times 4$	$81 = 9 \times 9$
$25 = 5 \times 5$	$100 = 10 \times 10$

Perfect Squares

Directions: Find the square of each number.

1. 3		**5.** 13		**9.** 60	
2. 5		**6.** 15		**10.** 100	
3. 7		**7.** 25			
4. 10		**8.** 30			

Answers are on page 554.

Perfect Cubes

A **perfect cube** or **cubed** number is obtained by multiplying a number to itself three times.

EXAMPLES

1. The cube of 1 is $1 \times 1 \times 1 = 1$.

2. The cube of 4 is $4 \times 4 \times 4 = 64$.

The table shows the first few perfect cubes.

Perfect Cubes

$1 = 1 \times 1 \times 1$	$216 = 6 \times 6 \times 6$
$8 = 2 \times 2 \times 2$	$343 = 7 \times 7 \times 7$
$27 = 3 \times 3 \times 3$	$512 = 8 \times 8 \times 8$
$64 = 4 \times 4 \times 4$	$729 = 9 \times 9 \times 9$
$125 = 5 \times 5 \times 5$	$1,000 = 10 \times 10 \times 10$

EXAMPLE

Determine if 9 is a perfect cube.

There is no natural number that can be multiplied by itself three times to give a product of 9. The number 9 is not a perfect cube.

EXERCISE 12

Perfect Cubes

Directions: Find the cube of each number.

1. 2	**5.** 8	**9.** 12
2. 3	**6.** 9	**10.** 13
3. 5	**7.** 10	
4. 7	**8.** 11	

Answers are on page 555.

Square Roots

Finding the **square root** of a number is the inverse operation of squaring the number. The radical symbol, $\sqrt{}$, is used for square root. There is usually a number under the radical symbol. For example, $\sqrt{9}$ is read as "the square root of 9" and $\sqrt{9} = 3$ because $3 \times 3 = 9$.

EXAMPLES

1. $\sqrt{1} = 1$ because $1 \times 1 = 1$.

2. $\sqrt{25} = 5$ because $5 \times 5 = 25$.

Square Roots of Perfect Squares

Square roots are only taken of nonnegative numbers (numbers greater than or equal to 0). Knowing the **perfect squares** helps you easily recall many square roots. If you see a perfect square under a square root symbol, you have to just remove the radical sign ($\sqrt{}$) and write down the square root of that perfect square. For example, $\sqrt{25}$ is equal to 5 because 25 is a perfect square.

Square Root Property

$\sqrt{ab} = \sqrt{a}\sqrt{b}$ for $a, b > 0$: If a and b are positive real numbers, then $\sqrt{ab} = \sqrt{a}\sqrt{b}$. This property helps to simplify the square root of any number, not just perfect square roots.

$$\sqrt{ab} = \sqrt{a}\sqrt{b}$$

EXAMPLES

1. $\sqrt{4 \times 9} = \sqrt{4} \times \sqrt{9} = 2 \times 3 = 6$.

2. $\sqrt{81 \times 16} = \sqrt{81} \times \sqrt{16} = 9 \times 4 = 36$.

Simplifying Square Roots of Non-Perfect Squares

If the number is very large and you are not sure if it is a perfect square, try taking the square root of it on the calculator. If the answer is a whole number, then the original number is a perfect square.

Become familiar with the following keys on your calculator and how to use them.

$\boxed{x^2}$ squares a number.

$\boxed{\text{SHIFT}}$ accesses key operations indicated above the key.

$\boxed{\sqrt{}}$ finds the square root of a number.

If you need to find the square root of a number that is not a perfect square, you have to explore all of the numbers that can multiply to make that number, which helps you simplify the square root of the number. If the number is even, divide it by 2. If the number is not divisible by 2, try 3, 4, 5, and so on.

The divisors 2, 3, 5, and so on are called prime numbers. A **prime number** is a whole number greater than 1 and can be divided evenly only by 1 or itself. The first few prime numbers are 2, 3, 5, 7, 11, 13, and 17.

The process of getting the square root is called the **prime factorization method**, which was discussed in the section on the Fundamental Theorem of Arithmetic. Prime factorization is finding which prime numbers multiply together to make the original number. Using the process, you find prime factors and group together identical pairs of the prime factors. If no factor is left out after grouping, then the number is a perfect square. However, if one of the prime factors is a single factor, then the number is not a perfect square.

EXAMPLE 1

Simplify: $\sqrt{98}$.

The number 98 is even. You divide 98 by 2 as shown below. The quotient is 49, which is a perfect square.

$$2 \underline{| 98}$$
$$7 \underline{| 49}$$
$$7$$

Here, 7×7 is a group and 2 is a single factor.

So you can write $\sqrt{98} = \sqrt{7 \times 7 \times 2} = \sqrt{7 \times 7} \times \sqrt{2} = 7\sqrt{2}$.

EXAMPLE 2

Find the value of $\sqrt{50}$.

By using the prime factorization method, divide 50 by 2. The quotient is 25, which is a perfect square. You get $\sqrt{50} = \sqrt{5 \times 5 \times 2} = \sqrt{5 \times 5} \times \sqrt{2} = 5\sqrt{2}$.

EXERCISE 13

Square Roots

Directions: Find the square root of each number.

1. 9	**5.** 121	**9.** 44
2. 25	**6.** 196	**10.** 99
3. 81	**7.** 625	
4. 100	**8.** 900	

Answers are on page 555.

Cube Roots

The **cube root** of a number is a number that is multiplied three times to give the original number. The symbol $\sqrt[3]{}$ denotes "cube root." For example, $\sqrt[3]{125} = 5$. The cube root of 125 is 5 because 5 multiplied three times gives 125. On a calculator, use the $\boxed{x^y}$ key.

EXAMPLES

1. $\sqrt[3]{8} = 2$ since $2 \times 2 \times 2 = 8$.

2. $\sqrt[3]{729} = 9$ since $9 \times 9 \times 9 = 729$.

3. $\sqrt[3]{1,000} = 10$ since $10 \times 10 \times 10 = 1,000$.

Cube Roots of Perfect Cubes

The **cube root of a perfect cube** can be found using the prime factorization method. If the number is even, divide it by 2. If the number is not divisible by 2, try 3, 4, 5, and so on.

EXAMPLE 1

Find the cube root of 216.

Using the prime factorization method, you get $\sqrt[3]{216} = \sqrt[3]{6 \times 6 \times 6} = 6$.

EXAMPLE 2

Find the cube root of 343.

Using the prime factorization method, you get $\sqrt[3]{343} = \sqrt[3]{7 \times 7 \times 7} = 7$.

EXAMPLE 3

Find the cube root of 1,331.

Using the prime factorization method, you get $\sqrt[3]{1331} = \sqrt[3]{11 \times 11 \times 11} = 11$.

Cube Roots of Perfect Cubes

Directions: Find the cube root of each number.

1. 8	**5.** 512	**9.** 3,375
2. 27	**6.** 1,728	**10.** 8,000
3. 64	**7.** 2,197	
4. 343	**8.** 2,744	

Answers are on page 555.

Cube Root Property

Cube roots can be distributed over multiplications: $\sqrt[3]{ab} = \sqrt[3]{a}\sqrt[3]{b}$ for all a and b.

EXAMPLE

$$\sqrt[3]{8 \times 27} = \sqrt[3]{8} \times \sqrt[3]{27} = 2 \times 3 = 6.$$

Simplifying Cube Roots of Non-Perfect Cubes

If the number is very large and you are not sure if it is a perfect cube, find its prime factors and group together three of the same factor. If no factor is left out, then the number is a perfect cube. However, if one of the prime factors is a single factor or a double factor, then the number is not a perfect cube.

EXAMPLE

Find the cube root of 243.

Using the prime factorization method,

$$\sqrt[3]{243} = \sqrt[3]{3 \times 3 \times 3 \times 3 \times 3} = \sqrt[3]{3 \times 3 \times 3} \times \sqrt[3]{3 \times 3} = 3\sqrt[3]{9}.$$

Simplifying Cube Roots of Non-Perfect Cubes

Directions: Simplify.

1. $\sqrt[3]{24}$	**5.** $\sqrt[3]{54}$	**9.** $\sqrt[3]{135}$
2. $\sqrt[3]{32}$	**6.** $\sqrt[3]{56}$	**10.** $\sqrt[3]{392}$
3. $\sqrt[3]{40}$	**7.** $\sqrt[3]{72}$	
4. $\sqrt[3]{48}$	**8.** $\sqrt[3]{80}$	

Answers are on page 555.

nth Roots

Like the "2nd," "3rd," or "16th" root, you can find the **nth root**. The "nth root" is multiplied by itself n times to find the original number.

nth Roots of Perfect nth Powers

When a value has an exponent of n and you take the nth root, you will get the value back again. If a is positive or zero, then $\sqrt[n]{a^n} = a$.

EXAMPLE

$\sqrt[3]{2^3} = 2$.

nth Root Properties

1. $\sqrt[n]{ab} = \sqrt[n]{a}\sqrt[n]{b}$ for all a, b when n is odd.

EXAMPLE

$\sqrt[3]{128} = \sqrt[3]{64 \times 2} = \sqrt[3]{64} \times \sqrt[3]{2} = 4\sqrt[3]{2}$.

2. $\sqrt[n]{ab} = \sqrt[n]{a}\sqrt[n]{b}$ for all a, $b > 0$ when n is even.

EXAMPLE

$\sqrt{64} = \sqrt{16 \times 4} = \sqrt{16} \times \sqrt{4} = 4 \times 2 = 8$.

EXERCISE 16

*n*th Roots

Directions: Simplify.

1. $\sqrt[3]{3^3}$
2. $\sqrt[4]{5^4}$
3. $\sqrt[10]{7^{10}}$
4. $\sqrt[11]{11^{11}}$

5. $\sqrt[10]{10^{10}}$
6. $\sqrt[3]{256}$
7. $\sqrt[3]{625}$
8. $\sqrt[3]{1,296}$

9. $\sqrt[3]{6,561}$
10. $\sqrt[3]{10,000}$

Answers are on page 555.

Relations

A relation is a set of ordered pairs. The elements a and b written in the form (a, b) is known as an ordered pair. The first component is a and b is the second component of (a, b). For example, the whole numbers and their squares can be set as ordered pairs: $(1, 1)$, $(2, 4)$, $(3, 9)$.

Note that the elements of a set can be written in any order, but the elements of an ordered pair have to be written in proper order, that is, (3, 2) ≠ (2, 3).

Relations between two objects are called binary relations in mathematics. As with the equal sign and inequality signs, you use a binary relation to make a statement about two objects.

Properties of Relations

The symbols =, >, and < are used to relate numbers. The symbols > and < are called inequality signs. Their meanings are in the table.

Relation Symbols

Symbol	Meaning	Example
=	equal sign	6 = 6 means 6 is equal to 6.
>	greater than	8 > 2 means 8 is greater than 2.
<	less than	0 < 3 means 0 is less than 3.

Using these relation symbols you can make statements about two numbers.

The reflexive, symmetric, and transitive properties of equality are satisfied by the equal sign.

Reflexive Property of Equality

The **reflexive property of equality** says that for any real number a, $a = a$.

EXAMPLE

$2 = 2$.

Symmetric Property of Equality

The **symmetric property of equality** says that if $a = b$, then $b = a$.

EXAMPLE

If orange = fruit, then fruit = orange.

Transitive Property of Equality

The **transitive property of equality** says that if $a = b$ and $b = c$, then $a = c$.

EXAMPLE

If John's height = Mary's height and Mary's height = Peter's height, then John's height = Peter's height.

(Note: You must be cautious when attempting to develop arguments using the transitive property in other settings.)

Transitive Property of Inequalities

The following statements are part of the **transitive property of inequalities**:

If $a < b$ and $b < c$, then $a < c$.　　　If $a \le b$ and $b \le c$, then $a \le c$.

If $a > b$ and $b > c$, then $a > c$.　　　If $a \ge b$ and $b \ge c$, then $a \ge c$.

(Note: You must be cautious when attempting to develop arguments using the transitive property in other settings.)

EXERCISE 17

Properties of Relations

Directions: What property is reflected in each statement?

1. If $x < y$ and $y < z$, then $x < z$.

2. If $2 = 3$, then $3 = 2$.

3. If $x = y$ and $y = z$, then $x = z$.

4. If $11 > 9$ and $9 > 5$, then $11 > 5$.

5. If $x \le y$ and $y \le z$, then $x \le z$.

6. If $x \ge y$ and $y \ge z$, then $x \ge z$.

Answers are on page 555.

Properties of Exponents

Exponential expressions are useful when writing very small or very large numbers. To perform operations on these numbers, **properties of exponents** can be used. You can also use these properties to simplify answers.

Definition of Exponents

An **exponent**, written as a **superscript number** and placed to the upper right of the base number, tells how many times the base number is to be multiplied to itself. For now, you assume the base to be greater than 0.

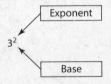

For the exponential expression 3^2, 3 is the base number and 2 is the exponent. The exponent 2 tells you to multiply 3 to itself two times: $3 \times 3 = 9$. The expression 3^2 is read as "three to the second power" or as "3 squared." The "squared" term is used for powers of two.

The exponent or power can be considered to be an instruction because it tells you what to do with the base number. When the exponent is 3 and the base number is 2, the expression will be 2^3. The exponent 3 tells you to multiply the base number 2 to itself three times: $2 \times 2 \times 2 = 8$.

In the expression 5^1, the exponent is 1 and the base number is 5. So 1 times 5 is 5, that is, $5^1 = 5$.

EXAMPLES

1. $2^5 = 2 \times 2 \times 2 \times 2 \times 2 = 32$.

2. $3^5 = 3 \times 3 \times 3 \times 3 \times 3 = 243$.

3. $2^6 = 2 \times 2 \times 2 \times 2 \times 2 \times 2 = 64$.

4. $5^4 = 5 \times 5 \times 5 \times 5 = 625$.

Product Rule

The **product rule** tells you that when multiplying two powers that have the same base, you can add the exponents to find the product: $(a^m)(a^n) = a^{(m+n)}$.

EXAMPLE

$10^2 \times 10^3 = 10^{2+3} = 10^5$, or

$10^2 \times 10^3 = (10 \times 10) \times (10 \times 10 \times 10) = 10 \times 10 \times 10 \times 10 \times 10 = 10^5$.

Extended Product Rule

The **product rule** can be **extended** to more than two terms with the same base:

$(a^1)(a^2)(a^3) \ldots (a^n) = a^{(1+2+3+\cdots+n)}$.

EXAMPLE 1

$3^2 \times 3^3 \times 3^4 = 3^{2+3+4} = 3^9$, or

$3^2 \times 3^3 \times 3^4 = (3 \times 3) \times (3 \times 3 \times 3) \times (3 \times 3 \times 3 \times 3)$

$= 3 \times 3 \times 3 \times 3 \times 3 \times 3 \times 3 \times 3 \times 3 = 3^9$.

EXAMPLE 2

$2^2 \times 2^2 \times 2^3 \times 2^4 \times 2^5 = 2^{2+2+3+4+5} = 2^{16}$, or

$2^2 \times 2^2 \times 2^3 \times 2^4 \times 2^5 = (2 \times 2) \times (2 \times 2) \times (2 \times 2 \times 2) \times (2 \times 2 \times 2 \times 2) \times (2 \times 2 \times 2 \times 2 \times 2)$

$= 2 \times 2 \times 2 \times 2 \times 2 \times 2 \times 2 \times 2 \times 2 \times 2 \times 2 \times 2 \times 2 \times 2 \times 2 \times 2 = 2^{16}$.

Quotient Rule

The **quotient rule** tells you to divide two powers with the same base by subtracting the exponents.

1. For $m > n$, $\dfrac{a^m}{a^n} = a^{(m-n)}$.

EXAMPLE

$\dfrac{2^4}{2^2} = 2^{(4-2)} = 2^2$ or $\dfrac{2^4}{2^2} = \dfrac{2 \times 2 \times \cancel{2} \times \cancel{2}}{\cancel{2} \times \cancel{2}} = 2 \times 2 = 2^2$.

2. If $m < n$, $\dfrac{a^m}{a^n} = \dfrac{1}{a^{(n-m)}}$.

EXAMPLE

$$\frac{2^2}{2^3} = \frac{1}{2^{(3-2)}} = \frac{1}{2^1} = \frac{1}{2} \text{ or } \frac{2^2}{2^3} = \frac{\cancel{2} \times \cancel{2}}{2 \times \cancel{2} \times \cancel{2}} = \frac{1}{2}.$$

Factor Rule

The **factor rule** says that when a product is raised to a power, you can raise each factor in the product to the power: $(ab)^n = (a^n)(b^n)$.

EXAMPLE

$(3 \times 5)^2 = 3^2 \times 5^2 = 9 \times 25 = 225$ or $(3 \times 5)^2 = 15^2 = 225$.

Extended Factor Rule

The **factor rule** can be **extended** to more than two terms in parentheses:

$(abc \ldots z)^n = (a^n)(b^n)(c^n) \ldots (z^n)$.

EXAMPLE

$(2 \times 3 \times 4 \times 5)^2 = 2^2 \times 3^2 \times 4^2 \times 5^2 = 4 \times 9 \times 16 \times 25 = 14{,}400$ or

$(2 \times 3 \times 4 \times 5)^2 = 120^2 = 14{,}400$.

Fraction Rule

The fraction rule says that when raising a fraction to a power, you can raise the numerator to the power and the denominator to the power: $\left(\dfrac{a}{b}\right)^n = \dfrac{a^n}{b^n}$.

EXAMPLE

$$\left(\frac{2}{3}\right)^2 = \frac{2^2}{3^2} = \frac{4}{9} \text{ or } \left(\frac{2}{3}\right)^2 = \left(\frac{2}{3} \times \frac{2}{3}\right) = \frac{4}{9}.$$

Power Rule

The **power rule** tells you to multiply the exponents when a power is raised a power to a power: $(a^m)^n = a^{(mn)}$.

Note that there is only one base.

EXAMPLE

$(3^2)^2 = 3^{(2 \times 2)} = 3^4 = 81$ or $(3^2)^2 = (3 \times 3)^2 = 9^2 = 81$.

EXERCISE 18

Exponents

Directions: Find the value of each expression.

1. $1{,}000^1$

2. 9^3

3. 10^4

4. 11^5

5. 8^4

6. $4^2 \times 4^3$

7. $3^2 \times 3^2 \times 3$

8. $\dfrac{5^3}{5^2}$

9. $\left(\dfrac{3}{8}\right)^2$

10. $(6^2)^2$

Directions: Which rule of exponents is used in each expression?

11. $(2^2)(2^3) = 2^{2+3} = 2^5 = 32$

12. $5^2 \times 5^3 \times 5^4 \times 5^5 = 5^{14} = 6{,}103{,}515{,}625$

13. $\dfrac{3^4}{3^2} = 3^{(4-2)} = 3^2 = 9$

14. $\dfrac{3^2}{3^5} = \dfrac{1}{3^{5-2}} = \dfrac{1}{3^3} = \dfrac{1}{27}$

15. $(7 \times 6)^2 = 7^2 \times 6^2 = 49 \times 36 = 1{,}764$

16. $(3 \times 2 \times 4 \times 6)^2 = 3^2 \times 2^2 \times 4^2 \times 6^2 = 144^2 = 20{,}736$

17. $\left(\dfrac{3}{4}\right)^2 = \dfrac{3^2}{4^2} = \dfrac{9}{16}$

18. $(5^2)^2 = 5^{(2 \times 2)} = 5^4 = 625$

Answers are on page 555.

Special Cases of b^n

$1^n = 1$

The integer powers of one are all one: $1^n = 1$.

EXAMPLES

1. $1^2 = 1 \times 1 = 1$.

2. $1^5 = 1 \times 1 \times 1 \times 1 \times 1 = 1$.

$0^n = 0 \ (n > 0)$

If the exponent n is positive, then zero raised to any power is zero: $0^n = 0$.

EXAMPLE

$0^2 = 0 \times 0 = 0$.

$b^1 = b$

A number raised to the power of one equals itself: $b^1 = b$.

EXAMPLE

$3^1 = 3$.

$b^0 = 1 \ (b \neq 0)$

Any nonzero number raised to the power of zero equals 1: $b^0 = 1$.

b^0 could also be written as $\dfrac{b^3}{b^3} = b^{3-3} = b^0$. In other words, $b^0 = \dfrac{b^3}{b^3} = \dfrac{\cancel{b} \times \cancel{b} \times \cancel{b}}{\cancel{b} \times \cancel{b} \times \cancel{b}} = 1$. Similarly,

5^0 could be written as $\dfrac{5^2}{5^2} = 5^{2-2} = 5^0$. In other words, $5^0 = \dfrac{5^2}{5^2} = \dfrac{\cancel{5} \times \cancel{5}}{\cancel{5} \times \cancel{5}} = 1$.

0^0 Is Undefined

Zero raised to the zero power is undefined.

EXERCISE 19

Special Cases of b^n

Directions: Simplify.

1. 1^{11}	5. 331^0	9. 0^{100}
2. 0^5	6. 0^0	10. 81^1
3. 32^1	7. 1^{25}	
4. 100^0	8. 75^1	

Answers are on page 555.

Negative Bases and Powers

Negative Bases

Sometimes the base in an **exponential expression** could be **negative**, such as with $(-5)^2$. To show that -5 is squared with its negative sign, parentheses are written around -5. Also, to evaluate expressions involving negative bases, you will use the fact that a negative number times a negative number is a positive number.

Let's look at the difference between -5^2 and $(-5)^2$. The missing parentheses mean that you find 5 squared and then take its negative: $-5^2 = -(5)(5) = -25$. On the other hand, $(-5)^2$ means to multiply -5 by -5: $(-5)^2 = (-5)(-5) = 25$. Here, the negative sign is part of the base, and a negative number times a negative number is a positive product. So be careful with simplifying negative bases and exponents.

Assume b as the base and n as the exponent:

If n is even, $(-b)^n = b^n$.

If n is odd, $(-b)^n = -b^n$.

EXAMPLE

Find the values of $(-5)^3$, $(-6)^4$, and $(-9)^3$.

$$(-5)^3 = (-5) \times (-5) \times (-5) = -125$$

$$(-6)^4 = (-6) \times (-6) \times (-6) \times (-6) = 1{,}296$$

$$(-9)^3 = (-9) \times (-9) \times (-9) = -719$$

EXERCISE 20

Negative Bases

Directions: Simplify.

1. $(-1)^3$

2. $(-1)^4$

3. $(-2)^3$

4. $(-3)^3$

5. $(-5)^4$

6. $-(10)^2$

7. $(-10)^2$

8. $(-11)^3$

Answers are on page 555.

Negative Powers

Any nonzero number raised to a **negative power** equals its reciprocal raised to the opposite power. To simplify an expression with a negative exponent, you need to "flip" the base, remove the minus sign from the exponent, and put the expression underneath 1.

EXAMPLE

$$4^{-2} = \frac{1}{4^2} = \frac{1}{16}.$$

Definition of Negative Exponent

An expression with a **negative exponent** is defined as: $a^{-n} = \frac{1}{a^n}$. This definition will work with all the rules you have learned so far about exponents.

EXAMPLE

Simplify 8^{-2}.

Remove the negative sign from the exponent and put the expression underneath 1.

Thus $8^{-2} = \frac{1}{8^2} = \frac{1}{64}$.

Quotient Rule Revisited

The **quotient rule** tells you that you can divide two powers with the same base by subtracting the exponents. With the definition of a negative exponent, you don't have to worry about the exponent on the bottom being larger than the exponent on top. The quotient rule can be restated without regard to the relative sizes of the exponents:

$$\frac{a^m}{a^n} = a^{(m-n)}.$$

EXAMPLE 1

$$\frac{2^{-4}}{2^{-2}} = 2^{(-4-(-2))} = 2^{-2} = \frac{1}{2^2} = \frac{1}{4}.$$

EXAMPLE 2

$$\frac{2^{-2}}{2^{-4}} = 2^{(-2-(-4))} = 2^2 = 4.$$

EXERCISE 21

Negative Powers

Directions: Simplify each expression.

1. 2^{-3} 5. 10^{-3} 9. 20^{-3}

2. 5^{-3} 6. 10^{-4} 10. 25^{-2}

3. 6^{-3} 7. 11^{-3}

4. 9^{-3} 8. 15^{-2}

Answers are on page 556.

Fractional Exponents

Fractional exponents can be rewritten as radicals. This will allow you to simplify expressions more easily.

1. $b^{\frac{1}{n}} = \sqrt[n]{b}$

EXAMPLE

$$4^{\frac{1}{2}} = \sqrt{4} = 2.$$

$4^{\frac{1}{2}}$ times itself is 4: $4^{\frac{1}{2}} \times 4^{\frac{1}{2}} = 4^{\left(\frac{1}{2}+\frac{1}{2}\right)} = 4^{\left(\frac{1+1}{2}\right)} = 4^{\left(\frac{2}{2}\right)} = 4^1 = 4.$

$4^{\frac{1}{2}}$ multiplied by itself gives 4, and $\sqrt{4}$ multiplied by itself also gives 4. Thus $4^{\frac{1}{2}} = 4$.

You can say that 2 is the **square root** of 4 because $2 \times 2 = 4$. Write $\sqrt{4} = 2$.

2. $b^{\frac{m}{n}} = b^{\left(m \times \frac{1}{n}\right)} = (b^m)^{\frac{1}{n}} = \sqrt[n]{b^m}$

A fractional exponent such as $\dfrac{m}{n}$ can be evaluated in two ways.

1. Find the mth power of the base and then take the nth root.

2. Find the nth root and then find the mth power.

EXAMPLE

$$4^{\frac{3}{2}} = 4^{\left(3 \times \frac{1}{2}\right)} = (4^3)^{\frac{1}{2}} = \sqrt{4^3} = \sqrt{64} = 8.$$

3. $\left(\sqrt[n]{b}\right)^m = \sqrt[n]{b^m}$, when $\dfrac{m}{n}$ is in lowest terms.

EXAMPLE

$$\left(\sqrt[2]{5}\right)^3 = \sqrt[2]{5^3} = \left(5^{\frac{1}{2}}\right)^3 = (5^3)^{\frac{1}{2}} = 5^{\frac{1}{2} \times 3} = 5^{\frac{3}{2}}.$$

EXERCISE 22

Fractional Exponents

Directions: Simplify.

1. $9^{\frac{1}{2}}$

2. $4^{\frac{1}{3}}$

3. $4^{\frac{1}{4}}$

4. $27^{\frac{1}{3}}$

5. $(27)^{\frac{4}{3}}$

6. $(25)^{\frac{1}{2}}$

7. $(81)^{\frac{1}{2}}$

8. $(81)^{\frac{1}{4}}$

9. $8^{\frac{1}{3}}$

10. $(1,000)^{\frac{1}{3}}$

Answers are on page 556.

Simplifying Expressions with More Than One Factor

Fractional exponents may have more than one term. Here is how to simplify these expressions.

EXAMPLE

Simplify $\left(\dfrac{3^2}{27^{-1}}\right)^2$.

Rewrite $\left(\dfrac{3^2}{27^{-1}}\right)^2$ as $\left(\dfrac{3 \times 3}{\frac{1}{27}}\right)^2$.

As discussed earlier in this chapter, an expression with a **negative exponent** can be written in the form $a^{-n} = \dfrac{1}{a^n}$. Remove the negative sign from the denominator and put it underneath 1, and then simplify.

$$\left(\frac{3 \times 3}{\frac{1}{27}}\right)^2 = \left(\frac{3 \times 3 \times 27}{1}\right)^2 = \left(\frac{243}{1}\right)^2 = (243)^2 = 59{,}049$$

EXERCISE 23

Simplifying Expressions with More Than One Factor

Directions: Simplify each expression.

1. $\left(\dfrac{2^2}{3^{-3}}\right)^2$

2. $\left(\dfrac{2^2}{4^{-2}}\right)^2$

3. $\left(\dfrac{3^2}{5^{-1}}\right)^{-1}$

4. $\left(\dfrac{3^2}{7^{-1}}\right)^{-2}$

Answers are on page 556.

Simplifying Radicals

A radical expression consists of three parts: a **radical** symbol, a **radicand**, and an **index**.

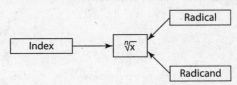

As shown here, $\sqrt{}$ is the radical symbol, n is the index, and x is the radicand. The index n gives the degree of the root. The value inside the radical symbol is the radicand. Take the root of the radicand after determining the index of the radical.

A radical is the reciprocal of the exponent. To understand radicals, have a look at some exponents.

$2^2 = 4$, which means 2 is the square root of 4 or $2 = \sqrt{4}$.

$2^3 = 8$, which means 2 is the cube root of 8 or $2 = \sqrt[3]{8}$.

$2^4 = 16$, which means 2 is the fourth root of 16 or $2 = \sqrt[4]{16}$.

$2^5 = 32$, which means 2 is the fifth root of 32 or $2 = \sqrt[5]{32}$.

If $n = 2$, then it is a square root. If $n = 3$, then the root is a cube root. If $n = 4$, then it is the fourth root, and so on.

To **simplify radicals**, find the prime factorization of the number inside the radical. The process is similar to simplifying square roots. Start by dividing the number by 2 and continue dividing by 2 until you get a remainder. Then divide by 3, 5, 7, and so on.

Then determine the index of the radical. The index tells you how many of the same factor is needed in order to simplify the radical. For example, if the index is 2 (a square root), then you need two of the same factor for a square root to be evaluated. If the index is 3 (a cube root), then you need three of a kind to take a cube root.

If there are not enough numbers or variables to make a group of two, three, or whatever is needed, then leave those numbers inside the radical.

Simplify the terms outside the radical by multiplication. Multiply all numbers inside the radical together. Multiply all numbers and variables outside the radical together.

EXAMPLE

Simplify $\sqrt{252}$.

Using the prime factorization method:

$$\sqrt{252} = \sqrt{2 \times 2 \times 3 \times 3 \times 7}$$

Since you have two factors of 2 and 3 each, group pairs of 2 and 3 and take the square root. Leave the single factor 7 inside the radical.

$$\sqrt{252} = \sqrt{\underline{2 \times 2} \times \underline{3 \times 3} \times 7} = 2 \times 3\sqrt{7} = 6\sqrt{7}$$

EXERCISE 24

Simplifying Radicals

Directions: Simplify each expression.

1. $\sqrt[4]{81}$
2. $\sqrt[3]{216}$
3. $\sqrt[3]{729}$
4. $\sqrt[3]{1,000}$

5. $\sqrt[4]{10,000}$
6. $\sqrt{48}$
7. $\sqrt{92}$
8. $\sqrt{90}$

Answers are on page 556.

Fractions

Fractions are parts of whole numbers such as halves, thirds, or quarters. In this chapter you will learn about the meaning and use of fractions, and how to combine them using the operations of arithmetic.

Understanding Fractions

A **fraction** is a number that represents a part of a whole. For example, divide a circle into eight equal parts. This circle represents the whole and can be represented by the number 1. Shade one part of the eight parts of the circle. One shaded part of the 8 equal parts can be represented by the number $\frac{1}{8}$ (one-eighth). Notice that the top number, 1, represents a part of the whole and the bottom number, 8, represents the number of parts of the whole. Two shaded parts of the 8 equal parts can be represented by the number $\frac{2}{8}$ (two-eighths). Similarly, three shaded parts of the 8 equal parts can be represented by the number $\frac{3}{8}$ (three-eighths), and so on.

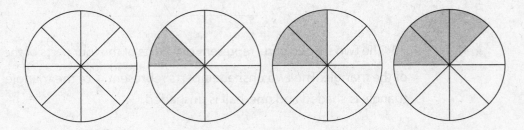

In the fraction $\frac{3}{8}$, the top number, 3, is called the **numerator**, which refers to the number of parts of the whole you have. The bottom number, 8, is called the **denominator**, which refers to the number of equal parts of the whole. If you consider the fractions obtained in the example of the circle, $\frac{1}{8}$, $\frac{2}{8}$, and $\frac{3}{8}$, the numerators are 1, 2, and 3 and the denominator is 8 in all three fractions.

Fractions as Parts of a Whole

To understand how a fraction represents a part of a whole, consider some more examples.

EXAMPLE 1

The following rectangle is divided into six equal parts.

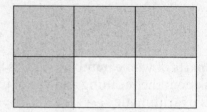

The four shaded parts represent four parts of the six parts of the rectangle. In other words, the shaded area represents $\frac{4}{6}$ of the rectangle. Likewise, the two unshaded parts represent $\frac{2}{6}$ of the rectangle.

EXAMPLE 2

The following triangle is divided into four equal parts.

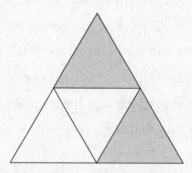

The two shaded parts represent two parts of the four parts of the triangle, that is, $\frac{2}{4}$ of the triangle. The two unshaded parts represent $\frac{2}{4}$ of the triangle. One-half of the triangle is shaded and one-half is unshaded.

Fractions as Parts of a Set

A fraction can be represented as parts of a set. Consider the following figure. There are 12 circles in the figure, and 7 of them are shaded. The shaded parts can be represented as a fraction: $\frac{7}{12}$. The fraction means 7 parts of the set of 12 circles.

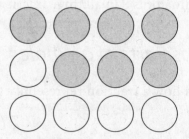

Consider these examples.

EXAMPLE 1

A basket has 10 apples.

If 4 apples are taken out of the basket, then it can be said that $\frac{4}{10}$ of the apples have been taken out of the basket. Here, 10 represents the number in the whole set and 4 represents the number of the part of the set.

EXAMPLE 2

In a family, there are six members. Of them, five members are females. Thus, the female members can be represented as $\frac{5}{6}$. Here, 6 is the number of family members and 5 represents the number of the part of the set that is female.

Fractions as Division Problems

A fraction can also represent a division problem, that is, the numerator is divided by the denominator. The fraction $\frac{3}{8}$ means 3 *divided by* 8. Similarly, a fraction $\frac{11}{10}$ means 11 *divided by* 10.

Some problems require you to determine the value of a fraction, which can be calculated by dividing the numerator of the fraction by the denominator.

Fractions on the Number Line

As with other numbers, fractions can also be presented on the number line. Consider marking $\frac{1}{2}$ on a number line. The fraction $\frac{1}{2}$ is greater than 0 and less than 1. It divides the interval between 0 and 1 exactly in half. To show this fraction in the number line, divide the gap between 0 and 1 into two equal parts and show one part as $\frac{1}{2}$.

If you want to show $\frac{1}{3}$ (one part of three equal parts of the whole) on the number line, divide the interval between 0 and 1 into three equal parts. The first equal part is labeled as $\frac{1}{3}$.

Similarly, you can show $\frac{2}{3}$ (two parts of three equal parts of the whole) on the same number line.

Types of Fractions

When solving fraction problems, you will come across many types of fractions. The most commonly used fractions are proper fractions, improper fractions, and mixed numbers.

Proper Fractions

In a **proper fraction**, the numerator is smaller than its denominator and the value is always less than one, for example, $\frac{2}{5}, \frac{19}{43}, \frac{66}{99}$, and $\frac{10}{11}$. Note that in all of these fractions, the numerators are less than their respective denominators. When you divide the numerator by its respective denominator, you will get a value less than 1.

Improper Fractions

In an **improper fraction,** the numerator is equal to or larger than its denominator, for example, $\frac{29}{15}, \frac{31}{31}, \frac{58}{9}$, and $\frac{110}{11}$. In all of these fractions, the numerator is either larger than the denominator or is equal to the denominator. Any whole number can be written as an improper fraction. The whole number forms the numerator and the denominator is 1, because any number divided by 1 will always result in the same number. Therefore, 5 can be written as $\frac{5}{1}$, 10 can be written as $\frac{10}{1}$, and 1 can be written as $\frac{1}{1}$.

Mixed Numbers

A **mixed number** is a combination of a whole number and a proper fraction. Examples of mixed numbers are $5\frac{1}{2}$ (five and one-half) and $7\frac{7}{8}$ (seven and seven-eighths). For these two examples, 5 and 7 are the whole number parts and $\frac{1}{2}$ and $\frac{7}{8}$ are the fractional parts.

While solving fraction problems, you may often come across problems that require you to convert mixed numbers to improper fractions and improper fractions to mixed numbers. Each conversion process is shown next.

Converting Improper Fractions to Mixed Numbers

An **improper fraction** can be converted to a mixed number by using these steps:

Step 1: Divide the numerator by the denominator of the fraction.

Step 2: The obtained quotient of the division presents the whole number part of the mixed number. A quotient is the answer obtained on dividing two numbers.

Step 3: Write the remainder as a fraction. The remainder is considered as the numerator and is placed over the original denominator to get the fractional part of the mixed number.

Step 4: Write the mixed number. Reduce the fraction if necessary.

EXAMPLE 1

Change $\frac{18}{7}$ to a mixed number.

Step 1: Divide 18 by 7.

$$\begin{array}{r} 2 \\ 7\overline{)18} \\ \underline{14} \\ 4 \end{array}$$

Step 2: Because the quotient is 2, the whole number part is 2.

Step 3: The remainder is 4. The fractional part of the mixed number is $\frac{4}{7}$.

Step 4: The mixed number is $2\frac{4}{7}$.

EXAMPLE 2

Change $\frac{10}{4}$ to a mixed number.

Step 1: Divide 10 by 4.

$$\begin{array}{r} 2 \\ 4\overline{)10} \\ \underline{8} \\ 2 \end{array}$$

Step 2: The quotient is 2; hence, the whole number part is 2.

Step 3: The remainder is 2. The fractional part of the mixed number is $\frac{2}{4}$.

Step 4: Thus, the mixed number is $2\frac{2}{4}$. After reducing to its lowest terms, the mixed number becomes $2\frac{1}{2}$.

Converting Mixed Numbers to Improper Fractions

A mixed number can be converted to an improper fraction by using these steps:

Step 1: Multiply the whole number of the mixed number by the denominator of the fraction.

Step 2: Add the numerator of the fraction to the product found in Step 1.

Step 3: Write the sum over the denominator to form an improper fraction.

EXAMPLE

Change $5\frac{5}{8}$ to an improper fraction.

Step 1: Multiply the whole number by the denominator, that is, $5 \times 8 = 40$.

Step 2: Add this value to the numerator: $40 + 5 = 45$.

Step 3: Write the sum over the original denominator: $\frac{45}{8}$.

Therefore, $5\frac{5}{8}$ can be written as $\frac{45}{8}$.

EXERCISE 1

Converting Mixed Numbers to Improper Fractions

Directions: Work the following problems to become familiar with fractions.

1. Identify the proper fractions: $\frac{3}{8}, \frac{5}{5}, \frac{1}{4}, \frac{7}{2}, \frac{21}{13}$.

2. Identify the improper fractions: $\frac{3}{8}, \frac{7}{3}, \frac{9}{9}, \frac{5}{1}, \frac{11}{19}$.

3. Write $\frac{7}{3}$ as a mixed number.

4. Write $1\frac{9}{10}$ as an improper fraction.

Directions: Convert each improper fraction into a mixed number.

5. $\frac{6}{4}$

6. $\frac{19}{15}$

7. $\frac{9}{5}$

8. $\frac{8}{3}$

Directions: Convert each mixed fraction into an improper fraction.

9. $5\frac{2}{3}$

10. $7\frac{4}{5}$

11. $2\frac{5}{6}$

12. $13\frac{14}{15}$

Answers are on page 556.

Equivalent Fractions

If more than two fractions have the same value, they are known as **equivalent fractions**. These fractions represent the same part of a whole or the same part of a set. Such fractions are used for comparing, ordering, adding, and subtracting fractions with different denominators.

Consider the following figures.

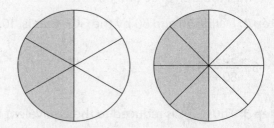

The shaded area in the first figure represents $\frac{3}{6}$ and the shaded area in the second figure represents $\frac{4}{8}$. Both represent half parts of the whole. Thus, the fractions $\frac{3}{6}$ and $\frac{4}{8}$ are equivalent fractions.

Reducing Fractions to Lowest Terms

Reducing a fraction means to find an equivalent fraction in lowest terms. A **fraction in lowest terms** means that the only common factor shared by the numerator and denominator is 1.

To reduce a fraction to lowest terms:

Step 1: Find the greatest common factor (GCF) of both the numerator and denominator.

Step 2: Divide both the numerator and the denominator by the GCF.

Step 3: The result is a fraction that is equivalent to the original fraction. When the fraction is reduced using the GCF, the fraction will be reduced to lowest terms.

EXAMPLE 1

Reduce $\frac{8}{10}$ to its lowest terms.

Step 1: Find the GCF of the numerator and the denominator. For 8 and 10, the GCF is 2.

Step 2: Divide 8 and 10 by the GCF, that is, 2.

$$\frac{8 \div 2}{10 \div 2} = \frac{4}{5}$$

Step 3:: Thus, $\frac{8}{10}$ is reduced to the equivalent fraction of $\frac{4}{5}$. You can say $\frac{8}{10} = \frac{4}{5}$.

EXAMPLE 2

Reduce $\frac{50}{80}$ to lowest terms.

Step 1: Find the GCF of 50 and 80.

The factors of 50 are 1, 2, 5, 10, 25, and 50.

The factors of 80 are 1, 2, 4, 10, 20, 40, and 80.

Thus, the GCF of 50 and 80 is 10.

Step 2: Divide 50 and 80 by the GCF, that is, 10.

So $\dfrac{50 \div 10}{80 \div 10} = \dfrac{5}{8}$.

Step 3: Thus, $\dfrac{50}{80}$ is reduced to the equivalent fraction of $\dfrac{5}{8}$.

EXAMPLE 3

Reduce $\dfrac{35}{45}$ to lowest terms.

Step 1: Find the GCF of 35 and 45.

The factors of 35 are 1, 5, 7, and 35.

The factors of 45 are 1, 5, 9, and 45.

Thus, the GCF is 5.

Step 2: Divide both 35 and 45 by the GCF, that is, 5.

$\dfrac{35 \div 5}{45 \div 5} = \dfrac{7}{9}$

Step 3: Thus, $\dfrac{35}{45}$ reduces to $\dfrac{7}{9}$.

EXERCISE 2

Reducing Fractions to Lowest Terms

Directions: Work the following problems to become familiar with rewriting fractions.

1. What is the GCF of 12 and 24?

2. Reduce $\dfrac{24}{48}$ to an equivalent fraction with a denominator of 2.

3. Explain why $\dfrac{100}{10}$ is in lowest terms.

Directions: Reduce each fraction to lowest terms.

4. $\dfrac{100}{10}$ 7. $\dfrac{51}{289}$ 10. $\dfrac{50}{55}$ 13. $\dfrac{16}{64}$

5. $\dfrac{45}{63}$ 8. $\dfrac{99}{99}$ 11. $\dfrac{33}{77}$

6. $\dfrac{75}{300}$ 9. $\dfrac{19}{38}$ 12. $\dfrac{33}{90}$

Answers are on page 556.

Building Up Single Fractions

Another way to make an equivalent fraction is to build up fractions. **Building up** means to raise fractions to higher terms. This is the opposite of reducing a fraction to lowest terms.

To raise a fraction to any higher term:

Step 1: Find the number that should be multiplied to the fraction to get the higher term.

Step 2: Multiply both the numerator and the denominator by the same number.

Step 3: You will get an equivalent fraction to the original fraction. For example, $\frac{5 \times 3}{8 \times 3} = \frac{15}{24}$.

EXAMPLE 1

Raise $\frac{3}{8}$ to its next higher term.

Step 1: On multiplying the fraction with 1, you would get the same fraction. The next higher term means both the numerator and the denominator should be multiplied by 2.

Step 2: Multiply both the numerator and denominator by 2.

$$\frac{3 \times 2}{8 \times 2} = \frac{6}{16}$$

Step 3: Thus, the equivalent fraction is $\frac{6}{16}$.

EXAMPLE 2

Convert $\frac{2}{5}$ to a fraction with a denominator of 10.

This means $\frac{2}{5} = \frac{?}{10}$.

Step 1: First, divide the new denominator by the original denominator.

$$10 \div 5 = 2$$

This means that the denominator was multiplied by 2 to get the denominator of 10.

Step 2: To get an equivalent fraction, multiply the numerator 2 by 2:

$$\frac{2 \times 2}{5 \times 2} = \frac{4}{10}$$

Step 3: Thus, the equivalent fraction is $\frac{4}{10}$.

EXERCISE 3

Building Up Single Fractions

Directions: Work the following problems to become familiar with building up a fraction.

1. Convert $\frac{3}{4}$ to an equivalent fraction with a denominator of 8.

2. Find the next higher term of $\frac{6}{14}$.

3. What is $\frac{1}{2}$ raised to the denominator of 12?

Directions: Raise each fraction to its next higher term.

4. $\frac{4}{10}$

6. $\frac{14}{6}$

5. $\frac{8}{5}$

7. $\frac{7}{8}$

Directions: Raise each fraction to a denominator of 36.

8. $\frac{17}{6}$

10. $\frac{19}{12}$

12. $\frac{24}{9}$

9. $\frac{11}{3}$

11. $\frac{54}{4}$

Answers are on page 556.

Building Up Two or More Than Two Fractions

If there are more than two fractions, then the fractions can be raised by using the **lowest common denominator** (LCD). The smallest number that can be divided evenly by all the denominators is known as the lowest common denominator, or the LCD.

The LCD for two or more fractions can be found by using one of the following:

1. Consider the largest denominator and check whether the other denominators divide it exactly.

2. Alternatively, find the smallest multiple of the largest denominator that can be divided exactly by the other denominators.

EXAMPLE 1

Find the LCD of $\frac{3}{4}$ and $\frac{5}{12}$.

The largest denominator is 12. The other denominator, 4, divides evenly into 12. Thus, the LCD is 12.

EXAMPLE 2

Find the LCD of $\frac{5}{4}$, $\frac{1}{12}$, and $\frac{5}{8}$.

The largest denominator of the three fractions is 12. The denominator 4 divides into 12, but 8 does not divide into 12. You have to find the smallest multiple of 12 into which both 4 and 8 will divide evenly:

$1 \times 12 = 12$, which is not divisible by 8.

$2 \times 12 = 24$, which is evenly divisible by both 4 and 8.

Therefore, the LCD for the three fractions is 24.

Once the LCD is calculated, you can raise two or more fractions by raising each fraction to that of the LCD.

EXAMPLE 3

Build up $\frac{5}{4}, \frac{1}{12}$, and $\frac{5}{8}$ by using the LCD.

Step 1: Calculate the LCD for 4, 12, and 8.

This has been calculated in the previous example. The LCD of 4, 12, and 8 is 24.

Step 2: Change $\frac{2}{4}, \frac{4}{8}$, and $\frac{8}{12}$ so that they each have a denominator of 24.

$$\frac{2}{4} = \frac{2 \times 6}{4 \times 6} = \frac{12}{24}$$

$$\frac{4}{8} = \frac{4 \times 3}{8 \times 3} = \frac{12}{24}$$

$$\frac{8}{12} = \frac{8 \times 2}{12 \times 2} = \frac{16}{24}$$

Step 3: The raised fractions are $\frac{12}{24}, \frac{12}{24}$ and $\frac{16}{24}$. Note that these fractions are respectively equivalent to $\frac{2}{4}, \frac{4}{8}$ and $\frac{8}{12}$.

EXERCISE 4

Building Up Two or More Than Two Fractions

Directions: Work the following problems to become familiar with building up fractions.

1. What is the LCD of $\frac{3}{5}$ and $\frac{7}{15}$?

2. What is the LCD of $\frac{3}{4}, \frac{5}{6}$, and $\frac{7}{8}$?

3. If $\frac{3}{4}$ is raised to the denominator of 12, what is the equivalent fraction?

Directions: Write each set of fractions as fractions with the LCD.

4. $\frac{1}{2}, \frac{3}{5}$

5. $\frac{2}{6}, \frac{7}{8}$

6. $\frac{1}{2}, \frac{3}{5}, \frac{5}{7}$

7. $\frac{4}{6}, \frac{3}{5}, \frac{1}{3}$

8. $\frac{5}{2}, \frac{2}{5}, \frac{5}{7}$

9. $\frac{1}{3}, \frac{5}{9}, \frac{7}{12}$

10. $\frac{1}{7}, \frac{3}{5}, \frac{5}{9}$

11. $\frac{4}{3}, \frac{5}{8}, \frac{5}{6}$

Answers are on page 557.

Comparing and Ordering Fractions

Some mathematical problems may require you to compare two or more fractions. **Comparing** two fractions means to determine whether one fraction is equal to (=), greater than (>), or less than (<) the other fraction. A fraction is said to be not equal to (≠)

another fraction if the two values are not equal. It is best to compare fractions when they have a common or same denominator. If the denominators are not the same, then find the LCD and write the fractions with this new denominator.

Fractions can be compared using the following steps:

Step 1: Check whether the denominators of the fractions are equal. If the denominators are not the same, find the LCD.

Step 2: Raise the fractions to the denominator of LCD.

Step 3: Compare the fractions.

Step 4: Write the original fractions in place of the raised fractions.

EXAMPLE 1

Compare $\dfrac{9}{15}$ and $\dfrac{17}{30}$.

Step 1: The LCD of 15 and 30 is 30.

Step 2: Raise the denominator of the first fraction to the LCD.

$$\frac{9}{15} = \frac{9 \times 2}{15 \times 2} = \frac{18}{30}$$

Step 3: On comparing $\dfrac{18}{30}$ and $\dfrac{17}{30}$, notice that the first numerator, 18, is greater than the second numerator, 17, that is, 18 > 17. Thus, $\dfrac{18}{30} > \dfrac{17}{30}$.

Step 4: Write the original fractions in place of the raised fractions: $\dfrac{9}{15} > \dfrac{17}{30}$.

EXAMPLE 2

Compare $\dfrac{5}{8}$ and $\dfrac{4}{5}$.

Step 1: The LCD of 8 and 5 is $8 \times 5 = 40$.

Step 2: Raise the denominators of both the fractions to the LCD.

$$\frac{5}{8} = \frac{5 \times 5}{8 \times 5} = \frac{25}{40}$$

$$\frac{4}{5} = \frac{4 \times 8}{5 \times 8} = \frac{32}{40}$$

Step 3: On comparing $\dfrac{25}{40}$ and $\dfrac{32}{40}$, notice that the first numerator, 25, is less than the second numerator, 32, that is, 25 < 32. Thus, $\dfrac{25}{40} < \dfrac{32}{40}$.

Step 4: Write the original fractions in place of the raised fractions: $\dfrac{5}{8} < \dfrac{4}{5}$.

Thus, $\dfrac{5}{8} < \dfrac{4}{5}$.

EXAMPLE 3

Compare $\dfrac{3}{4}$ and $\dfrac{15}{20}$.

Step 1: The LCD of 4 and 20 is 20.

Step 2: Raise the denominator of the first fraction to the LCD.

$$\frac{3}{4} = \frac{3 \times 5}{4 \times 5} = \frac{15}{20}$$

Step 3: On comparing the two fractions, notice that the first and second numerators are equal, that is, $\dfrac{15}{20} = \dfrac{15}{20}$.

Step 4: Write the original fractions in place of the raised fractions: $\dfrac{3}{4} = \dfrac{15}{20}$.

Ordering two or more fractions means to arrange the fractions according to a particular order, that is, in ascending or descending order. **Ascending order** means the fractions are arranged from the smallest to the largest value, and **descending order** means the fractions are arranged from the largest to the smallest value. It is easier to order fractions if they have the same denominator.

Here are the steps for ordering fractions:

Step 1: Check whether the denominators of the fractions are equal. If the denominators are not the same, find the LCD.

Step 2: Raise the fractions to the denominator of the LCD.

Step 3: Compare the fractions and arrange them in the required ascending or descending order.

Step 4: Write the original fractions in place of the raised fractions.

EXAMPLE 1

Arrange the following fractions in ascending order: $\dfrac{5}{6}, \dfrac{3}{8}, \dfrac{11}{12}, \dfrac{7}{4}$.

Step 1: The LCD of 6, 8, 12, and 4 is 24.

Step 2: Raise the denominators of the fractions to 24:

$$\frac{5}{6} = \frac{5 \times 4}{6 \times 4} = \frac{20}{24}$$

$$\frac{3}{8} = \frac{3 \times 3}{8 \times 3} = \frac{9}{24}$$

$$\frac{11}{12} = \frac{11 \times 2}{12 \times 2} = \frac{22}{24}$$

$$\frac{7}{4} = \frac{7 \times 6}{4 \times 6} = \frac{42}{24}$$

Step 3: On comparing the numerators of the equivalent fractions, notice that $9 < 20 < 22 < 42$.

You can arrange the fractions in the ascending order, that is, smallest to largest value: $\dfrac{9}{24}, \dfrac{20}{24}, \dfrac{22}{24}, \dfrac{42}{24}$.

Step 4: Thus, the ascending order of the fractions is $\dfrac{3}{8}, \dfrac{5}{6}, \dfrac{11}{12}, \dfrac{7}{4}$.

EXAMPLE 2

Arrange the following fractions in descending order: $\dfrac{3}{2}, \dfrac{6}{7}, \dfrac{10}{8}, \dfrac{9}{4}$.

Step 1: The LCD of 2, 7, 8, and 4 is 56.

Step 2: Raise the fractions to LCD, that is, 56:

$$\frac{3}{2} = \frac{3 \times 28}{2 \times 28} = \frac{84}{56}$$

$$\frac{6}{7} = \frac{6 \times 8}{7 \times 8} = \frac{48}{56}$$

$$\frac{10}{8} = \frac{10 \times 7}{8 \times 7} = \frac{70}{56}$$

$$\frac{9}{4} = \frac{9 \times 14}{4 \times 14} = \frac{126}{56}$$

Step 3: On comparing the numerators of the equivalent fractions, notice that 126 > 84 > 70 > 48.

You can arrange the fractions in descending order, that is, largest to smallest value: $\dfrac{126}{56}, \dfrac{84}{56}, \dfrac{70}{56}, \dfrac{48}{56}$.

Step 4: Thus, the descending order of the fractions is $\dfrac{9}{4}, \dfrac{3}{2}, \dfrac{10}{8}, \dfrac{6}{7}$.

EXERCISE 5

Comparing and Ordering Fractions

Directions: Work the following problems to become familiar with comparing fractions.

1. Which fraction is greater than $\dfrac{15}{16}$?

    A. $\dfrac{5}{6}$ **B.** $\dfrac{7}{8}$ **C.** $\dfrac{5}{4}$ **D.** $\dfrac{1}{30}$

2. Which fraction is less than $\dfrac{18}{30}$?

    A. $\dfrac{5}{6}$ **B.** $\dfrac{7}{8}$ **C.** $\dfrac{5}{4}$ **D.** $\dfrac{6}{15}$

3. Which fraction is equivalent to $\frac{72}{45}$?

A. $\frac{24}{15}$ **B.** $\frac{7}{8}$ **C.** $\frac{36}{30}$ **D.** $\frac{24}{20}$

Directions: Write <, >, or = in the box to compare.

4. $\frac{7}{12} \square \frac{5}{21}$ **6.** $\frac{15}{7} \square \frac{20}{56}$ **8.** $\frac{10}{5} \square \frac{12}{6}$

5. $\frac{19}{18} \square \frac{15}{9}$ **7.** $\frac{7}{20} \square \frac{5}{21}$ **9.** $\frac{7}{9} \square \frac{11}{13}$

Directions: Arrange the following fractions in ascending order.

10. $\frac{9}{16}, \frac{3}{8}, \frac{11}{12}, \frac{7}{4}$ **11.** $\frac{1}{2}, \frac{2}{3}, \frac{3}{5}, \frac{5}{7}$ **12.** $\frac{5}{12}, \frac{13}{8}, \frac{10}{12}, \frac{7}{20}$

Directions: Arrange the following fractions in descending order.

13. $\frac{6}{7}, \frac{3}{21}, \frac{2}{35}, \frac{17}{14}$ **14.** $\frac{6}{5}, \frac{5}{9}, \frac{3}{7}, \frac{7}{11}$ **15.** $\frac{10}{18}, \frac{3}{6}, \frac{5}{12}, \frac{7}{9}, \frac{5}{18}$

Answers are on page 557.

Adding and Subtracting Fractions

Addition and subtraction are basic mathematical operations that can be performed with fractions. When adding or subtracting fractions, the same denominator is needed for all of the fractions. In the case of fractions having different denominators, you need to convert all denominators to the same denominator before adding or subtracting.

Adding or Subtracting Proper Fractions with the Same Denominator

To add or subtract fractions with the same denominator:

Step 1: Add or subtract all the numerators as indicated.

Step 2: Write the result over the denominator.

Step 3: Reduce the resultant fraction to its lowest terms.

EXAMPLE 1

Add: $\frac{3}{5} + \frac{1}{5}$.

Step 1: Here, the denominators are the same. Thus, simply add the numerators.

$3 + 1 = 4$

Step 2: Now, write the sum over the denominator, that is, $\frac{4}{5}$.

Step 3: The sum is in lowest terms and cannot be reduced further. Thus, the final answer is $\frac{4}{5}$.

EXAMPLE 2

Add: $\frac{1}{9} + \frac{4}{9} + \frac{7}{9}$. Write the answer in lowest terms.

Step 1: Here, the denominators are the same. Hence, add the numerators of each fraction.

$1 + 4 + 7 = 12$

Step 2: Place the sum over the denominator, that is, $\frac{12}{9}$.

Step 3: The resultant sum can be reduced further. Both the numerator and the denominator are divisible by 3: $\frac{12 \div 3}{9 \div 3} = \frac{4}{3}$. The sum is $\frac{4}{3}$, or $1\frac{1}{3}$.

EXAMPLE 3

Subtract: $\frac{3}{5} - \frac{1}{5}$.

Step 1: When the denominators are the same, subtract the numerators.

$3 - 1 = 2$

Step 2: Place the result over the denominator, that is, $\frac{2}{5}$.

Step 3: The fraction $\frac{2}{5}$ cannot be reduced further. Hence, the difference is $\frac{2}{5}$.

EXERCISE 6

Adding or Subtracting Proper Fractions with the Same Denominator

Directions: Add the fractions.

1. What is $\frac{5}{6} + \frac{3}{6}$ in lowest terms?

2. What is $\frac{7}{9} - \frac{2}{9}$ in lowest terms?

Directions: Add. If necessary, reduce the answer to lowest terms. Keep your answer as a fraction.

3. $\frac{22}{25} + \frac{12}{25}$ **5.** $\frac{2}{5} + \frac{10}{5} + \frac{32}{5}$ **7.** $\frac{25}{100} + \frac{75}{100}$

4. $\frac{64}{12} + \frac{18}{12}$ **6.** $\frac{50}{67} + \frac{12}{67}$ **8.** $\frac{3}{20} + \frac{5}{20} + \frac{1}{20}$

Directions: Subtract. If necessary, reduce the answer to lowest terms.

9. $\dfrac{20}{24}-\dfrac{11}{24}$

10. $\dfrac{22}{25}-\dfrac{12}{25}$

11. $\dfrac{45}{8}-\dfrac{12}{8}$

12. $\dfrac{65}{54}-\dfrac{30}{54}$

13. $\dfrac{99}{90}-\dfrac{43}{90}$

14 $\dfrac{9}{15}-\dfrac{1}{15}-\dfrac{3}{15}$

Answers are on page 557.

Adding or Subtracting Proper Fractions with Different Denominators

To add or subtract fractions with different denominators:

Step 1: Find the LCD of the fractions and build all fractions to the new LCD.

Step 2: Add or subtract the numerators.

Step 3: Write the sum or difference over the common denominator.

Step 4: If necessary, reduce the sum or difference to lowest terms.

EXAMPLE 1

Add: $\dfrac{17}{12}+\dfrac{40}{48}$.

Step 1: Here, the denominators are different. So, first find the LCD for the fractions. 48 is the largest common denominator, and 12 divides 48 exactly. Hence, the LCD is 48.

The first fraction has to be raised to a denominator of 48.

$$\frac{17}{12}=\frac{17\times4}{12\times4}=\frac{68}{48}$$

Step 2: Add the numerators: $68+40=108$.

Step 3: Write the sum over the denominator, that is, $\dfrac{108}{48}$.

Step 4: The resultant fraction can be reduced further: $\dfrac{108}{48}=\dfrac{9}{4}$. Thus, the answer is $\dfrac{9}{4}$, or $2\dfrac{1}{4}$.

EXAMPLE 2

Add: $\dfrac{2}{4}+\dfrac{4}{8}+\dfrac{8}{12}$.

Step 1: Find the LCD of the fractions. 12 is the largest denominator, and 4 divides into 12 but 8 does not divide into 12. You have to go through the multiplication table of 12 until you find the smallest multiple that both 4 and 8 will divide into evenly.

$1 \times 12 = 12$, which is not divisible by 8.

$2 \times 12 = 24$, which is evenly divisible by both 4 and 8.

Therefore, the LCD for the three fractions is 24.

Now, raise $\frac{2}{4}, \frac{4}{8}$, and $\frac{8}{12}$ to the denominator of 24.

$$\frac{2}{4} = \frac{2 \times 6}{4 \times 6} = \frac{12}{24}$$

$$\frac{4}{8} = \frac{4 \times 3}{8 \times 3} = \frac{12}{24}$$

$$\frac{8}{12} = \frac{8 \times 2}{12 \times 2} = \frac{16}{24}$$

Step 2: Add the numerators: $12 + 12 + 16 = 40$.

Step 3: Place the sum over the denominator, that is, $\frac{40}{24}$.

Step 4: The fraction can be further reduced: $\frac{40}{24} = \frac{5}{3}$. Therefore, the answer is $\frac{5}{3}$, or $1\frac{2}{3}$.

EXAMPLE 3

Subtract: $\frac{10}{12} - \frac{1}{9}$.

Step 1: Find the LCD of the fractions. 12 is the largest denominator, and 9 does not divide 12. List multiples of 12 until you find the smallest multiple that 9 will divide into evenly:

$1 \times 12 = 12$, which is not divisible by 9.

$2 \times 12 = 24$, which is not divisible by 9.

$3 \times 12 = 36$, which is evenly divisible by 9.

Thus, the LCD is 36.

Raise the fractions to the denominator of the LCD.

$$\frac{10}{12} = \frac{10 \times 3}{12 \times 3} = \frac{30}{36}$$

$$\frac{1}{9} = \frac{1 \times 4}{9 \times 4} = \frac{4}{36}$$

Step 2: Subtract the numerators: $30 - 4 = 26$.

Step 3: Place the result over the denominator: $\frac{26}{36}$.

Step 4: This can be further reduced: $\frac{26}{36} = \frac{13}{18}$. The final answer is $\frac{13}{18}$.

EXERCISE 7

Adding or Subtracting Proper Fractions with Different Denominators

Directions: Add the fractions.

1. What is $\frac{2}{5} + \frac{3}{7}$ in lowest terms?

2. What is $\frac{5}{3} - \frac{7}{9}$ in lowest terms?

Directions: Add. Write your answer in lowest terms.

3. $\frac{23}{22} + \frac{12}{25}$

4. $\frac{64}{10} + \frac{18}{15}$

5. $\frac{2}{3} + \frac{10}{7} + \frac{32}{9}$

6. $\frac{50}{67} + \frac{12}{65}$

7. $\frac{25}{30} + \frac{75}{10} + \frac{32}{20}$

8. $\frac{3}{20} + \frac{5}{14} + \frac{1}{2}$

Directions: Subtract. Write your answer in lowest terms.

9. $\frac{29}{36} - \frac{4}{9}$

10. $\frac{7}{8} - \frac{1}{2}$

11. $\frac{45}{23} - \frac{12}{24}$

12. $\frac{65}{5} - \frac{27}{4}$

13. $\frac{99}{90} - \frac{13}{30}$

14. $\frac{17}{20} - \frac{1}{5} - \frac{3}{10}$

Answers are on page 558.

Adding Mixed Numbers

Mixed numbers with the same denominator can be added without simplification.

Step 1: Add the fractional parts of the whole numbers. If necessary, reduce to lowest terms. In case you get an improper fraction, write it as a mixed number or whole number.

Step 2: Then add only the whole number parts (including any whole number obtained in the sum of Step 1).

Step 3: Write the sum of the fractional parts and the whole number sum as a new mixed number.

EXAMPLE 1

Add: $8\frac{1}{12} + 6\frac{5}{12}$.

Step 1: Add only the fractional part of the whole numbers:. $\frac{1}{12} + \frac{5}{12} = \frac{6}{12}$.

This can be reduced to $\frac{1}{2}$.

Step 2: Add only the whole number parts separately: $8 + 6 = 14$.

Step 3: Now, write the sum of the fractional parts and the sum of the whole numbers as a new mixed number: $14\frac{1}{2}$. Therefore, the answer is $14\frac{1}{2}$.

EXAMPLE 2

Add: $7\frac{2}{7} + 5\frac{3}{7}$.

Step 1: Add only the fraction part of the whole numbers: $\frac{2}{7} + \frac{3}{7} = \frac{5}{7}$.

Step 2: Add only the whole number parts separately: $7 + 5 = 12$.

Step 3: Now, write the sum of the fractional parts and the sum of the whole numbers as a new mixed number: $12\frac{5}{7}$. Therefore, the answer is $12\frac{5}{7}$.

EXAMPLE 3

Add: $8\frac{5}{6} + 3\frac{5}{6}$.

Step 1: Add only the fractional part of the whole numbers: $\frac{5}{6} + \frac{5}{6} = \frac{10}{6}$.

The fraction can be reduced to $\frac{5}{3}$. Note that the fraction formed is an improper fraction and should be written as a mixed number: $1\frac{2}{3}$.

Step 2: Add only the whole number parts separately. Include the whole number obtained from the sum in the previous step: $8 + 3 + 1 = 12$.

Step 3: Now, write the sum of the fractional parts and the sum of the whole numbers as a new mixed number $12\frac{2}{3}$. Therefore, the answer is $12\frac{2}{3}$.

EXAMPLE 4

Add: $3\frac{5}{8} + 7\frac{7}{8}$.

Step 1: Add only the fractional part of the whole numbers: $\frac{5}{8} + \frac{7}{8} = \frac{12}{8}$. The fraction can be reduced: $\frac{12}{8} = \frac{3}{2}$. Note that the fraction formed is an improper fraction and can be written as a mixed number: $1\frac{1}{2}$.

Step 2: Add only the whole number parts separately. Include the whole number obtained from the sum in Step 1: $3 + 7 + 1 = 11$.

Step 3: Now, write the sum of the fractional parts and the sum of the whole numbers as a new mixed number: $11\frac{1}{2}$. Therefore, the answer is $11\frac{1}{2}$.

EXERCISE 8

Adding Mixed Numbers

Directions: Add the mixed numbers.

1. What is the sum of $2\frac{1}{3}+1\frac{1}{3}$?

2. What is the sum of $1\frac{2}{3}+1\frac{1}{3}$?

Directions: Add. Reduce to lowest terms.

3. $7\frac{1}{12}+5\frac{5}{12}$

4. $10\frac{11}{12}+5\frac{3}{12}$

5. $9\frac{10}{17}+2\frac{1}{17}$

6. $5\frac{2}{23}+3\frac{1}{23}$

7. $19\frac{9}{19}+13\frac{5}{19}$

8. $2\frac{8}{11}+4\frac{3}{11}$

9. $10\frac{1}{4}+5\frac{3}{4}$

10. $11\frac{3}{15}+4\frac{7}{15}$

Answers are on page 558.

Adding Mixed Numbers and Simplifying

For adding mixed fractions with different denominators, follow these steps.

Step 1: Find the LCD of the denominators. Raise the fractional parts to the LCD.

Step 2: Add the fractional parts of the mixed numbers. If necessary, reduce to lowest terms. In case you get an improper fraction, write it as a mixed fraction.

Step 3: Then add the whole number parts (including any whole number in a mixed fraction obtained in the previous step).

Step 4: Write the mixed number with the sum of the whole number parts and the sum of the fractional parts.

EXAMPLE 1

Add $2\frac{1}{3}$ and $6\frac{5}{9}$.

Step 1: Find the LCD of the denominators, that is, 3 and 9. The LCD of 3 and 9 is 9.

Raise $\frac{1}{3}$ to the LCD (i.e., to a denominator of 9): $\frac{1\times3}{3\times3}=\frac{3}{9}$.

Step 2: Add the fractional parts of the whole numbers: $\frac{3}{9}+\frac{5}{9}=\frac{8}{9}$.

Step 3: Add the whole numbers: $2+6=8$.

Step 4: Write the sum of the fractional parts and the sum of the whole numbers as a new whole number: $8\frac{8}{9}$. Therefore, the sum is $8\frac{8}{9}$.

EXAMPLE 2

Add: $7\frac{1}{4}+5\frac{1}{2}$.

Step 1: Find the LCD of the denominators, that is, 4 and 2. The LCD of 4 and 2 is 4.

Raise $\frac{1}{2}$ to the LCD (i.e., to a denominator of 4): $\frac{1\times2}{2\times2}=\frac{2}{4}$.

Step 2: Add the fractional parts of the whole numbers: $\frac{1}{4}+\frac{2}{4}=\frac{3}{4}$.

Step 3: Add the whole numbers: $7+5=12$.

Step 4: Write the sum of the fractional parts and the sum of the whole number parts as a new whole number: $12\frac{3}{4}$. The sum is $12\frac{3}{4}$.

EXAMPLE 3

Add: $8\frac{4}{5}+3\frac{5}{6}$.

Step 1: Find the LCD of the denominators, that is, 5 and 6.

The LCD of 5 and 6 is $5\times6=30$.

Raise $\frac{4}{5}$ and $\frac{5}{6}$ to the LCD (i.e., to a denominator of 30):

$$\frac{4\times6}{5\times6}=\frac{24}{30}$$

$$\frac{5\times5}{6\times5}=\frac{25}{30}$$

Step 2: Add the fractional parts of the whole numbers: $\frac{24}{30}+\frac{25}{30}=\frac{49}{30}$. The fraction is an improper fraction and can be written as a mixed number: $1\frac{19}{30}$.

Step 3: Add the whole number parts (including the whole number obtained in the sum of the previous step): $8+3+1=12$.

Step 4: Write the fractions sum and the whole numbers sum as a new mixed number: $12\frac{19}{30}$.

Therefore, the sum is $12\frac{19}{30}$.

EXERCISE 9

Adding Mixed Numbers and Simplifying

Directions: Add the mixed numbers and simplify.

1. What is $10\frac{1}{4}+3\frac{2}{5}$?

2. What is $1\frac{2}{3}+2\frac{3}{4}$?

Directions: Add. Reduce your answer to lowest terms, if necessary.

3. $10\frac{1}{4} + 3\frac{2}{12}$

4. $13\frac{10}{14} + 7\frac{3}{7}$

5. $9\frac{6}{10} + 2\frac{1}{5}$

6. $9\frac{7}{22} + 3\frac{2}{11}$

7. $6\frac{9}{15} + 1\frac{5}{10}$

8. $3\frac{10}{15} + 2\frac{5}{10}$

9. $5\frac{7}{8} + 1\frac{5}{9}$

10. $8\frac{8}{28} + 5\frac{6}{14}$

11. $3\frac{5}{8} + 4\frac{1}{2}$

Answers are on page 558.

Subtracting Mixed Numbers

Subtracting mixed numbers with the same denominator is similar to adding mixed numbers with the same denominator.

Here are the general steps for subtracting mixed numbers:

Step 1: Subtract the fractional parts of the whole numbers. Reduce the fraction to its lowest terms, if necessary.

Step 2: Subtract the whole number parts of the mixed numbers.

Step 3: Write the difference of the fractional parts and the difference of the whole numbers as a new mixed number.

EXAMPLE

Subtract: $7\frac{5}{6} - 2\frac{1}{6}$.

Step 1: Subtract the fractional parts of the mixed numbers: $\frac{5}{6} - \frac{1}{6} = \frac{4}{6}$. This can be reduced to $\frac{2}{3}$.

Step 2: Subtract the whole numbers: $7 - 2 = 5$.

Step 3: Write the difference of the fractional parts and the difference of the whole number parts as a new whole number: $5\frac{2}{3}$. Thus, the answer is $5\frac{2}{3}$.

Sometimes you have to subtract mixed numbers that have different denominators, as these steps will show how.

Step 1: Find the LCD of the denominators of the fractional parts. Raise the fractions to the LCD.

Step 2: Subtract the fractional parts of the whole numbers. If necessary, reduce to lowest terms.

Step 3: Subtract the whole number parts of the mixed numbers.

Step 4: Write the difference of the fractional parts and the difference of the whole numbers as a new mixed number.

EXAMPLE 1

Subtract: $6\frac{5}{9} - 2\frac{1}{3}$.

Step 1: Calculate the LCD of the two denominators, that is, 3 and 9. The LCD of 3 and 9 is 9. Raise $\frac{1}{3}$ to the denominator of 9: $\frac{1 \times 3}{3 \times 3} = \frac{3}{9}$.

Step 2: Now subtract the fractional parts: $\frac{5}{9} - \frac{3}{9} = \frac{2}{9}$.

Step 3: Subtract the whole numbers: $6 - 2 = 4$.

Step 4: Write the difference of the fractional parts and the difference of the whole number parts as a new whole number: $4\frac{2}{9}$. Thus, the difference is $4\frac{2}{9}$.

EXAMPLE 2

Subtract: $8\frac{4}{5} - 3\frac{1}{3}$.

Step 1: Calculate the LCD of the two denominators, that is, 5 and 3. The LCD of 5 and 3 is $5 \times 3 = 15$.

Raise $\frac{4}{5}$ and $\frac{1}{3}$ to the denominator of LCD:

$$\frac{4 \times 3}{5 \times 3} = \frac{12}{15}$$

$$\frac{1 \times 5}{3 \times 5} = \frac{5}{15}$$

Step 2: Now subtract the fractional parts: $\frac{12}{15} - \frac{5}{15} = \frac{7}{15}$.

Step 3: Subtract the whole numbers: $8 - 3 = 5$.

Step 4: Write the difference of the fractional parts and the difference of the whole number parts as a new mixed number: $5\frac{7}{15}$. Thus, the answer is $5\frac{7}{15}$.

EXERCISE 10

Subtracting Mixed Numbers

Directions: Subtract. Reduce your answer to lowest terms, if necessary.

1. $8\frac{5}{7} - 3\frac{1}{7}$

2. $10\frac{11}{12} - 5\frac{5}{12}$

3. $9\frac{10}{17} - 2\frac{1}{17}$

4. $5\frac{2}{23} - 3\frac{1}{23}$

5. $19\dfrac{9}{19} - 13\dfrac{5}{19}$

6. $8\dfrac{4}{5} - 3\dfrac{1}{5}$

7. $24\dfrac{9}{10} - 3\dfrac{3}{5}$

8. $20\dfrac{8}{15} - 13\dfrac{2}{5}$

9. $19\dfrac{8}{21} - 10\dfrac{1}{3}$

10. $5\dfrac{5}{8} - 1\dfrac{1}{2}$

11. $7\dfrac{2}{3} - 3\dfrac{4}{9}$

12. $11\dfrac{3}{8} - 4\dfrac{1}{6}$

Answers are on page 558.

Subtracting Mixed Numbers with Borrowing

Sometimes, when subtracting fractions, the first fraction is smaller than the second fraction. You have to borrow the equivalent of the number 1 and add it to the first fraction. This will allow the subtraction to be carried out.

EXAMPLE

Subtract: $9\dfrac{2}{3} - 5\dfrac{3}{4}$.

Step 1: The LCD of 3 and 4 is 12. Raise $\dfrac{2}{3}$ and $\dfrac{3}{4}$ to their LCD, that is, 12.

$$\dfrac{2}{3} = \dfrac{2 \times 4}{3 \times 4} = \dfrac{8}{12}$$

$$\dfrac{3}{4} = \dfrac{3 \times 3}{4 \times 3} = \dfrac{9}{12}$$

Step 2: Subtract: $\dfrac{8}{12} - \dfrac{9}{12}$. The first number is smaller than the second number. Thus, borrow 1 from the whole number 9. So, $9\dfrac{8}{12} = 8\dfrac{8}{12} + \dfrac{12}{12}$. The borrowed 1 can be written as $\dfrac{12}{12}$ because the LCD is 12.

Step 3: Add the fractions: $\dfrac{8}{12} + \dfrac{12}{12} = \dfrac{20}{24}$. The new whole number is $8\dfrac{20}{12}$.

Step 4: Now, find $8\dfrac{20}{12} - 5\dfrac{9}{12}$. First, subtract the fractional parts: $\dfrac{20}{12} - \dfrac{9}{12} = \dfrac{11}{12}$.

Then subtract the whole numbers: $8 - 5 = 3$.

Step 5: Write the difference of the fractional parts and the difference of the whole number parts as a mixed number: $3\dfrac{11}{12}$.

Thus, the difference is $3\dfrac{11}{12}$.

Subtracting Mixed Numbers with Borrowing

Directions: Subtract. Reduce your answer to lowest terms, if necessary.

1. $5\frac{1}{4} - 1\frac{3}{4}$

2. $7\frac{1}{3} - 2\frac{2}{5}$

3. $4\frac{5}{8} - 1\frac{7}{8}$

4. $7\frac{2}{5} - 2\frac{4}{5}$

5. $13\frac{5}{8} - 10\frac{3}{4}$

6. $9\frac{1}{2} - 2\frac{4}{5}$

7. $25\frac{5}{9} - 15\frac{7}{9}$

8. $16\frac{1}{2} - 5\frac{6}{7}$

9. $19\frac{1}{4} - 11\frac{2}{5}$

10. $7\frac{1}{4} - 2\frac{1}{3}$

11. $8\frac{1}{3} - 3\frac{11}{18}$

12. $9\frac{2}{3} - 6\frac{3}{4}$

Answers are on page 558.

Multiplying and Dividing Fractions

Multiplication and division of fractions do not require finding a common denominator. You will use your multiplication and division facts and knowledge of reducing to lowest terms for these two processes.

Multiplying Fractions

To multiply two or more fractions, you simply need to multiply all the numerators and multiply all the denominators to get the resultant fraction. Then, reduce the fraction to lowest terms, whenever necessary.

EXAMPLE 1

Multiply: $\frac{3}{8} \times \frac{5}{7}$.

Step 1: Multiply the numerators together: $3 \times 5 = 15$.

Step 2: Multiply the denominators together: $8 \times 7 = 56$.

Step 3: The product of the fractions is $\frac{3}{8} \times \frac{5}{7} = \frac{15}{56}$, which is in lowest terms.

EXAMPLE 2

Multiply: $\frac{1}{9} \times \frac{2}{5} \times \frac{4}{7}$.

Step 1: Multiply the numerators together: $1 \times 2 \times 4 = 8$.

Step 2: Multiply the denominators together: $9 \times 5 \times 7 = 315$.

Step 3: The product of the fractions is $\frac{1}{9} \times \frac{2}{5} \times \frac{4}{7} = \frac{8}{315}$. The product $\frac{8}{315}$ cannot be reduced further.

EXAMPLE 3

Multiply: $\frac{7}{6} \times \frac{2}{5}$.

Step 1: Multiply the numerators together: $7 \times 2 = 14$.

Step 2: Multiply the denominators together: $6 \times 5 = 30$.

Step 3: The product of the fractions is $\frac{7}{6} \times \frac{2}{5} = \frac{14}{30}$. The product $\frac{14}{30}$ can be reduced further: $\frac{14}{30} = \frac{7}{15}$.

Reducing Before Multiplying

To make the process of multiplying fractions easier, you can first reduce the fractions and then multiply to obtain the result. The fractions can be reduced by **canceling**, which reduces the sizes of the numbers in the numerators and denominators. In order to cancel, you must find a number that divides evenly into one numerator and one denominator. The numerator and denominator may belong to different fractions, or they could be part of the same fraction.

EXAMPLE 1

Multiply: $\frac{6}{20} \times \frac{5}{18}$.

Step 1: Note that 6 and 18 share a GCF of 6. Divide both 6 and 18 by 6.

$$\frac{\overset{1}{\cancel{6}}}{20} \times \frac{5}{\underset{3}{\cancel{18}}}$$

Step 2: Check all pairs of numerators and denominators. Notice that 5 and 20 share a GCF of 5. Divide 5 and 20 by 5.

$$\frac{\overset{1}{\cancel{6}}}{\underset{4}{20}} \times \frac{\overset{1}{\cancel{5}}}{\underset{3}{\cancel{18}}}$$

Step 3: Multiply the new numerators and denominators to get the result: $\frac{1}{4} \times \frac{1}{3} = \frac{1}{12}$.

The answer is reduced to its lowest terms. Therefore, the product is $\frac{1}{12}$.

EXAMPLE 2

$$\frac{5}{16}\times\frac{8}{12}\times\frac{6}{15}\times\frac{9}{7}=?$$

Step 1: Divide both 5 and 15 by 5.

$$\frac{\overset{1}{\cancel{5}}}{16}\times\frac{8}{12}\times\frac{6}{\underset{3}{\cancel{15}}}\times\frac{9}{7}$$

Step 2: Then divide 8 and 16 by 8.

$$\frac{\overset{1}{\cancel{5}}}{\underset{2}{\cancel{16}}}\times\frac{\overset{1}{\cancel{8}}}{12}\times\frac{6}{\underset{3}{\cancel{15}}}\times\frac{9}{7}$$

Step 3: Divide 6 and 12 by 6.

$$\frac{\overset{1}{\cancel{5}}}{\underset{2}{\cancel{16}}}\times\frac{\overset{1}{\cancel{8}}}{\underset{2}{\cancel{12}}}\times\frac{\overset{1}{\cancel{6}}}{\underset{3}{\cancel{15}}}\times\frac{9}{7}$$

Step 4: Multiply the new numerators and denominators to get the result.

$$\frac{1}{2}\times\frac{1}{2}\times\frac{1}{3}\times\frac{9}{7}=\frac{9}{84}$$

Step 5: Check if the product can be reduced further. Both 9 and 84 can be divided evenly by 3.

$$\frac{9}{84}=\frac{3}{28}.$$

The product, in lowest terms, is $\frac{3}{28}$.

EXERCISE 12

Multiplying Fractions

Directions: Multiply. If necessary, reduce the answer to lowest terms.

1. $\frac{4}{5}\times\frac{7}{10}$

2. $\frac{6}{10}\times\frac{3}{5}$

3. $\frac{5}{9}\times\frac{10}{6}$

4. $\frac{1}{7}\times\frac{4}{9}$

5. $\dfrac{2}{9} \times \dfrac{5}{9}$

6. $\dfrac{4}{7} \times \dfrac{8}{9} \times \dfrac{5}{11}$

7. $\dfrac{1}{12} \times \dfrac{5}{6} \times \dfrac{10}{3}$

8. $\dfrac{7}{6} \times \dfrac{1}{5} \times \dfrac{4}{11}$

9. $\dfrac{2}{6} \times \dfrac{12}{10}$

10. $\dfrac{7}{6} \times \dfrac{6}{7}$

11. $\dfrac{14}{15} \times \dfrac{3}{7}$

12. $\dfrac{5}{9} \times \dfrac{18}{20}$

13. $\dfrac{5}{6} \times \dfrac{7}{8} \times \dfrac{9}{10}$

14. $\dfrac{4}{8} \times \dfrac{3}{9} \times \dfrac{2}{4}$

15 $\dfrac{26}{5} \times \dfrac{20}{13} \times \dfrac{1}{5}$

16. $\dfrac{2}{3} \times \dfrac{6}{12} \times \dfrac{4}{5}$

Answers are on page 558.

Multiplying Mixed Numbers

For multiplying mixed numbers, first convert the mixed numbers to improper fractions and then multiply as fractions.

EXAMPLE 1

Multiply: $4\dfrac{2}{3} \times 1\dfrac{1}{2}$.

Step 1: Change the mixed numbers to improper fractions: $4\dfrac{2}{3} = \dfrac{14}{3}$ and $1\dfrac{1}{2} = \dfrac{3}{2}$.

Step 2: Multiply by canceling. Cancel both 3s.

$$\dfrac{14}{\cancel{3}} \times \dfrac{\cancel{3}^{\,1}}{2}$$

Step 3: Then divide 2 and 14 by 2.

$$\dfrac{\cancel{14}^{\,7}}{\cancel{3}_{\,1}} \times \dfrac{\cancel{3}^{\,1}}{\cancel{2}_{\,1}}$$

Step 4: Multiply the new numerators and denominators to get the result:

$$\dfrac{7}{1} \times \dfrac{1}{1} = \dfrac{7}{1} = 7.$$

The answer is reduced to its lowest terms. Therefore, the product is 7.

EXAMPLE 2

Multiply: $7\frac{1}{3} \times 3\frac{3}{4}$.

Step 1: Change the mixed numbers to improper fractions: $7\frac{1}{3} = \frac{22}{3}$ and $3\frac{3}{4} = \frac{15}{4}$. Rewrite the multiplication problem: $\frac{22}{3} \times \frac{15}{4}$.

Step 2: See if you can cancel. Divide 3 and 15 by 3.

$$\frac{22}{\cancel{3}_1} \times \frac{\cancel{15}^5}{4}$$

Step 3: Then divide 4 and 22 by 2.

$$\frac{\cancel{22}^{11}}{\cancel{3}_1} \times \frac{\cancel{15}^5}{\cancel{4}_2}$$

Step 4: Multiply the new numerators and denominators to get the result:

$$\frac{11}{1} \times \frac{5}{2} = \frac{55}{2} = 27\frac{1}{2}.$$

Therefore, the product is $27\frac{1}{2}$.

EXERCISE 13

Multiplying Mixed Numbers

Directions: Multiply. Write your answer as a mixed number. If necessary, reduce the answer to lowest terms.

1. $3\frac{1}{5} \times 5\frac{1}{2}$

2. $6\frac{2}{3} \times 5\frac{5}{6}$

3. $1\frac{1}{2} \times 5\frac{1}{7}$

4. $9\frac{1}{2} \times 7\frac{4}{9}$

5. $3\frac{1}{4} \times 5\frac{4}{5} \times 4\frac{1}{2}$

6. $3\frac{3}{4} \times 5\frac{1}{3}$

7. $8\frac{1}{4} \times 2\frac{1}{2}$

8. $3 \times 6\frac{1}{7}$

9. $2\frac{1}{6} \times 5\frac{2}{3}$

10. $9\frac{1}{2} \times 2\frac{4}{5} \times 11$

Answers are on page 559.

Dividing Fractions

A division problem has three different parts. The number that is being divided is the dividend. The number that divides the dividend is the divisor. The answer of the division problem is the quotient.

To divide two fractions or two mixed numbers, follow these steps:

Step 1: If the numbers are not fractions, write each number as a fraction.

Step 2: Invert the numerator and denominator of the divisor and change the ÷ sign to a × sign.

Step 3: Follow the steps of multiplying fractions.

EXAMPLE

Divide: $\frac{7}{8} \div \frac{1}{4}$.

Step 1: Both numbers are fractions: $\frac{7}{8} \div \frac{1}{4}$.

Step 2: Invert the numerator and denominator of the divisor and change the ÷ sign to a × sign.

$$\frac{7}{8} \times \frac{4}{1}$$

Step 3: Multiply the fractions.

$$\frac{7}{8} \div \frac{1}{4} = \frac{7}{\overset{}{\underset{2}{8}}} \times \frac{\overset{1}{4}}{1} \text{ (cross-cancel and multiply)}.$$

$$= \frac{7}{2}$$

Therefore, the answer is $\frac{7}{2}$.

EXERCISE 14

Dividing Fractions

Directions: Divide. Write your answer as a mixed number. If necessary, reduce the answer to lowest terms.

1. What is $\frac{3}{8} \div \frac{15}{16}$?

2. What is $\frac{4}{10} \div \frac{20}{100}$?

Directions: Divide. If necessary, reduce the answer to lowest terms.

3. $\dfrac{2}{4} \div \dfrac{5}{8}$

4. $\dfrac{6}{5} \div \dfrac{18}{10}$

5. $\dfrac{3}{4} \div \dfrac{9}{12}$

6. $\dfrac{5}{11} \div \dfrac{15}{11}$

7. $\dfrac{13}{26} \div \dfrac{13}{26}$

8. $\dfrac{7}{10} \div \dfrac{14}{15}$

9. $\dfrac{1}{9} \div \dfrac{2}{3}$

10. $\dfrac{10}{100} \div \dfrac{50}{20}$

Answers are on page 559.

Dividing Mixed Numbers

To divide mixed numbers, follow these steps:

Step 1: Convert the mixed numbers to improper fractions.

Step 2: Then divide as if dividing fractions.

EXAMPLE

Divide: $3\dfrac{1}{2} \div 5\dfrac{1}{2}$.

Step 1: Convert the fractions into improper fractions:

$$3\dfrac{1}{2} = \dfrac{7}{2}$$
$$5\dfrac{1}{2} = \dfrac{11}{2}$$

Step 2: The reciprocal of the divisor $\dfrac{11}{2}$ is $\dfrac{2}{11}$.

Thus, $\dfrac{7}{2} \div \dfrac{11}{2} = \dfrac{7}{2} \times \dfrac{2}{11} = \dfrac{7}{\overset{1}{\cancel{2}}} \times \dfrac{\overset{1}{\cancel{2}}}{11} = \dfrac{7}{11}$. The quotient is $\dfrac{7}{11}$.

EXERCISE 15

Dividing Mixed Numbers

Directions: Divide. If necessary, reduce the answer to lowest terms. If the answer is an improper fraction, write your answer as a mixed number.

1. $3\frac{1}{2} \div 5\frac{1}{3}$

2. $6\frac{2}{3} \div 5\frac{5}{6}$

3. $1\frac{1}{2} \div 5\frac{1}{7}$

4. $9\frac{1}{2} \div 7\frac{4}{9}$

5. $3\frac{1}{4} \div 5\frac{4}{5}$

6. $7\frac{1}{3} \div 3\frac{1}{2}$

7. $8\frac{1}{2} \div 7\frac{2}{3}$

8. $4\frac{3}{4} \div 3\frac{1}{2}$

9. $4\frac{2}{3} \div 8\frac{2}{5}$

10. $8\frac{3}{4} \div 4\frac{1}{3}$

Answers are on page 559.

Raising Fractions to Powers

As with whole numbers, fractions can be written with exponents to indicate repeated multiplication. Consider the base is $\frac{2}{3}$ and is raised to the 4th power and represents the expression $\frac{3}{4} \times \frac{2}{3} \times \frac{2}{3} \times \frac{2}{3}$. Reduce the product if necessary.

EXAMPLE 1

Evaluate $\left(\frac{5}{6}\right)^2$.

Step 1: To evaluate the fraction, write the fraction twice with a × sign: $\frac{5}{6} \times \frac{5}{6}$.

Step 2: Then multiply the fractions.

$$\frac{5}{6} \times \frac{5}{6} = \frac{25}{36}$$

Thus, the answer is $\frac{25}{36}$.

EXAMPLE 2

Evaluate $\left(\frac{3}{5}\right)^3$.

Step 1: Write the fraction three times along with the × sign: $\frac{3}{5} \times \frac{3}{5} \times \frac{3}{5}$.

Step 2: Then multiply the fractions.

$$\left(\frac{3}{5}\right)^3 = \frac{3}{5} \times \frac{3}{5} \times \frac{3}{5} = \frac{27}{125}$$

The answer is $\frac{27}{125}$.

EXERCISE 16

Raising Fractions to Powers

Directions: Raise the fractions to the indicated power.

1. What is the square of $\frac{1}{10}$?

   A. $\frac{1}{10}$ B. $\frac{1}{20}$ C. $\frac{1}{50}$ D. $\frac{1}{100}$

2. What is the cube of $\frac{2}{3}$?

   A. $\frac{8}{27}$ B. $\frac{4}{9}$ C. $\frac{6}{27}$ D. $\frac{8}{3}$

Directions: Find the square and cube of each fraction.

3. $\frac{1}{8}$ 5. $\frac{6}{12}$ 7. $\frac{7}{3}$ 9. $\frac{3}{8}$

4. $\frac{3}{4}$ 6. $\frac{5}{6}$ 8. $\frac{2}{9}$ 10. $\frac{2}{7}$

Answers are on page 559.

Square Roots and Cube Roots of Fractions

Finding the square root and cube root of fractions is the opposite of finding squares and cubes of fractions. The process of evaluating such roots is similar to the process with whole numbers.

Step 1: Write the roots of the entire fraction as individual roots of the numerator and denominator.

Step 2: Find the root of the numerator and the denominator separately.

Step 3: Write the roots in the form of a fraction.

EXAMPLE 1

Find $\sqrt{\dfrac{4}{9}}$.

Step 1: Write $\sqrt{\dfrac{4}{9}}$ as $\dfrac{\sqrt{4}}{\sqrt{9}}$.

Step 2: Find the square root of the numerator and the denominator separately.

Find the square root of 4: $\sqrt{4}=2$.

Find the square root of 9: $\sqrt{9}=3$.

Step 3: Therefore, $\sqrt{\dfrac{4}{9}}=\dfrac{2}{3}$.

EXAMPLE 2

Find $\sqrt[3]{\dfrac{8}{27}}$.

Step 1: Write $\sqrt[3]{\dfrac{8}{27}}$ as $\dfrac{\sqrt[3]{8}}{\sqrt[3]{27}}$.

Step 2: Find the cube root of the numerator and the denominator separately.

Find the cube root of 8: $\sqrt[3]{8}=2$.

Find the cube root of 27: $\sqrt[3]{27}=3$.

Step 3: Therefore, $\sqrt[3]{\dfrac{8}{27}}=\dfrac{2}{3}$.

EXAMPLE 3

Find $\sqrt{\dfrac{18}{25}}$.

Step 1: Write $\sqrt{\dfrac{18}{25}}$ as $\dfrac{\sqrt{18}}{\sqrt{25}}$.

Step 2: Find the square root of the numerator and the denominator separately.

Find the square root of 18: $\sqrt{18}=\sqrt{2\times9}=3\sqrt{2}$.

Find the square root of 25: $\sqrt{25}=5$.

Step 3: Therefore, $\sqrt{\dfrac{18}{25}}=\dfrac{3\sqrt{2}}{5}$.

EXAMPLE 4

Find $\sqrt[3]{\dfrac{27}{40}}$.

Step 1: Write $\sqrt[3]{\dfrac{27}{40}}$ as $\dfrac{\sqrt[3]{27}}{\sqrt[3]{40}}$.

Step 2: Find the cube root of the numerator and the denominator separately.

Find the cube root of 27: $\sqrt[3]{27} = 3$.

Find the cube root of 40: $\sqrt[3]{40} = \sqrt[3]{8 \times 5} = 2\sqrt[3]{5}$.

Step 3: Therefore, $\sqrt[3]{\dfrac{27}{40}} = \dfrac{3}{2\sqrt[3]{5}}$.

When a radical is left in the denominator, it needs to be rationalized. Multiply a number to both the numerator and the denominator such that the denominator contains no radical.

$$\frac{3}{2\sqrt[3]{5}} = \frac{3\sqrt[3]{25}}{2\sqrt[3]{5} \times \sqrt[3]{25}}$$

$$= \frac{3\sqrt[3]{25}}{2\sqrt[3]{25}}$$

$$= \frac{3\sqrt[3]{25}}{2 \times 5} = \frac{3\sqrt[3]{25}}{10}$$

Thus, $\sqrt[3]{\dfrac{27}{40}} = \dfrac{3\sqrt[3]{25}}{10}$.

EXERCISE 17

Square Roots and Cube Roots of Fractions

Directions: Find the square root.

1. $\sqrt{\dfrac{49}{144}}$

2. $\sqrt{\dfrac{169}{121}}$

3. $\sqrt{\dfrac{16}{50}}$

4. $\sqrt{\dfrac{32}{81}}$

5. $\sqrt{\dfrac{225}{625}}$

Directions: Find the cube root.

6. $\sqrt[3]{\dfrac{125}{343}}$

7. $\sqrt[3]{\dfrac{648}{125}}$

8. $\sqrt[3]{\dfrac{125}{512}}$

9. $\sqrt[3]{\dfrac{64}{343}}$

10. $\sqrt[3]{\dfrac{27}{250}}$

Answers are on page 559.

Fractions and the Order of Operations

When two or more mathematical operations are present in a single problem, the operations must be performed in a certain order. The rules that describe the correct order are known as the **order of operations**.

Here is the order of operations to follow when evaluating an expression. A step may be skipped if there is no operation to be performed at that step.

Step 1: Perform all operations within each set of parentheses.

Step 2: Evaluate the exponents: powers and roots.

Step 3: Multiply and divide numbers as you move from left to right.

Step 4: Add and subtract numbers as you move from left to right.

The order of operations can be thought of as "Parentheses, Exponents, Multiply and Divide, Add and Subtract." Remember to use the acronym PEMDAS or "Please Excuse My Dear Aunt Sally" to help you remember the order of the steps for evaluating or simplifying expressions.

EXAMPLE 1

Evaluate: $\dfrac{(7+3)^2}{5}+45$.

Step 1: Simplify the parentheses: $7 + 3 = 10$.

Step 2: Evaluate the exponent on the parentheses: $10^2 = 10 \times 10 = 100$.

Step 3: Divide 100 by 5: $\dfrac{100}{5} = 20$.

Step 4: Add $20 + 45 = 65$.

Step 5: $\dfrac{(7+3)^2}{5}+45 = 65$.

EXAMPLE 2

Evaluate $4 \times \dfrac{1}{2}\left\{\dfrac{(3+1)^2}{8}\right\} \div 4$.

Step 1: Simplify the inner set of parentheses: $3 + 1 = 4$.

Then simplify the outer set of parentheses: $\dfrac{4^2}{8} = \dfrac{16}{8} = 2$.

Step 2: Multiply: $4 \times \dfrac{1}{2} \times 2 = 4$.

Step 3: Divide 4 by 4: $\dfrac{4}{4} = 1$.

Step 4: $4 \times \dfrac{1}{2}\left\{\dfrac{(3+1)^2}{8}\right\} \div 4 = 1$.

EXAMPLE 3

Evaluate $9 \div \left(1 + \dfrac{1}{2}\right) - 3 \times \dfrac{4}{8} \times \dfrac{6}{9} + \sqrt{4}$.

Step 1: Simplify the parentheses: $1 + \dfrac{1}{2} = \dfrac{2+1}{2} = \dfrac{3}{2}$.

Step 2: Find the square root of 4: $\sqrt{4} = 2$.

Step 3: Divide 9 by $\dfrac{3}{2}$: $9 \div \dfrac{3}{2} = 9 \times \dfrac{2}{3} = 6$.

Step 4: Multiply: $3 \times \dfrac{4}{8} \times \dfrac{6}{9} = 1$.

Step 5: Subtract: $6 - 1 = 5$.

Step 6: Add: $5 + 2 = 7$.

Step 7: $9 \div \left(1 + \dfrac{1}{2}\right) - 3 \times \dfrac{4}{8} \times \dfrac{6}{9} + \sqrt{4} = 7$.

EXAMPLE 4

Evaluate $\sqrt{8} + 6 + 2^3 - 10 \times \dfrac{1}{2}$.

Step 1: Evaluate the square roots: $\sqrt{8} = 2\sqrt{2}$.

Find the cube of 2: $2^3 = 8$.

Step 2: Multiply: $10 \times \dfrac{1}{2} = 5$.

Step 3: Add: $2\sqrt{2} + 6 + 8 = 2\sqrt{2} + 14$.

Step 4: Subtract: $2\sqrt{2} + 14 - 5 = 2\sqrt{2} + 9$.

Step 5: $\sqrt{8} + 6 + 2^3 - 10 \times \dfrac{1}{2} = 2\sqrt{2} + 9$.

EXAMPLE 5

Evaluate $15 + 16 - 10 \times 2 - 2 + 3 \div \dfrac{3}{9}$.

Step 1: Multiply: $10 \times 2 = 20$.

Step 2: Divide: 3 by $\dfrac{3}{9}$: $3 \div \dfrac{3}{9} = 3 \times \dfrac{9}{3} = 9$.

Step 3: Add: $15 + 16 = 31$.

Step 4: Subtract: $31 - 20 = 11$.

Step 5: Subtract: $11 - 2 = 9$.

Step 6: Add: $9 + 9 = 18$.

Step 7: $15 + 16 - 10 \times 2 - 2 + 3 \div \dfrac{3}{9} = 18$.

EXERCISE 18

Fractions and the Order of Operations

Directions: Evaluate using the order of operations.

1. $(32 + 54) - (43 - 32)$

2. $\dfrac{(8-2)}{4} + 42 - 10$

3. $\dfrac{3}{4} + (5 + 18) - (3 + 7)$

4. $\dfrac{(3+5+7)}{((3+2)-4)}$

5. $(4 \times 5) + \dfrac{7}{9}$

6. $\{2^2 + (32 \times 2 + 4)\} \div 8 \times 2$

7. $\dfrac{\left(\sqrt{4}\right)^2}{8} + (5^2 - 5 \div 5) + 10 \div 2$

8. $\dfrac{3}{4} \times (5 + 18 \div 9) + 3^2$

9. $\dfrac{(3 \times 5 - 7) \times 2}{8 \div 2 - 2 + 4 \times 2}$

10. $\sqrt{(4 \times 5)} + \dfrac{3^2 + 7}{4}$

Answers are on page 559.

CHAPTER 4

Decimals

Decimal numbers are used daily. You buy a packet of snacks for $3.98. The stock market gains 120.55 points. A neighbor travels 36.2 miles to reach his workplace. In this chapter, you will learn about the place-value system with decimals, using decimals, comparing decimals, performing decimal operations, and converting decimals to fractions and fractions to decimals.

Understanding Decimals

Fractions whose denominators are 10 or a higher power of ten are called **decimal fractions**.

For example, $\frac{2}{10}$, $\frac{31}{100}$, and $\frac{45}{1,000}$ are decimal fractions. These fractions can be converted into decimal numbers by division. A **decimal number** is a number with a period called a decimal point with numbers to the right of the decimal point. These numbers are not whole numbers (although whole numbers can be written with a decimal point). A decimal number has two parts: a whole number part and a decimal part. The whole number is to the left of the decimal point and the number to the right is the decimal part.

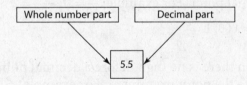

The value of a decimal number does not change if you add one or more zeros to the right of it. For example, $73.31 = 73.310 = 73.3100$.

Extending the Place-Value System

The **place values** of the digits in the whole number part from right to left are 1, 10, 100, 1,000, ... and in the decimal part from left to right is $\frac{1}{10}$, $\frac{1}{100}$, $\frac{1}{1,000}$, ... (one-tenth, one-hundredth, one-thousandth, ...). Each decimal part represents part of a whole because it is a fraction less than 1.

The following place-value chart can be used to read whole numbers and decimal numbers. The whole numbers are to the left of the decimal point. The decimals, which are parts of a whole, are to the right of the decimal point. The decimal places are to the right of the decimal point.

1,000	100	10	1	•	$\frac{1}{10}$	$\frac{1}{100}$	$\frac{1}{1,000}$	$\frac{1}{10,000}$
Thousands	Hundreds	Tens	Ones	AND	Tenths	Hundredths	Thousandths	Ten-thousandths
	1	2	5		8	5		

Note that the names of the decimal places end in *th*. The decimal point, read as "and," separates the whole number part from the decimal part.

In the chart, the number 125.85 has two decimal places (tenths and hundredths), but only the last decimal place is named when the number is read. The number is read as "125 and 85 hundredths." Thus, 125.85 can be thought of as 125 and $\frac{85}{100}$.

Padding the Decimal Part of a Number on the Right with Zeros

To convert a **decimal fraction** to a decimal number, put the **decimal point** in the numerator before as many digits in the number as there are zeros in the denominator. If the number of places in the numerator is less than the number of zeros in the denominator, put as many zeros as needed to the left of the numerator before placing the decimal point. For example, $\frac{7}{10} = .7$, $\frac{213}{100} = 2.13$, $\frac{988}{1,000} = 0.988$, $\frac{555}{10,000} = .0555$, and $\frac{71}{100,000} = .00071$.

When there is no digit before a decimal point, then a zero is generally written before it to make the point prominent. For example, .51 is written as 0.51 and .015 as 0.015.

Decimals on the Number Line

Like fractions, decimals can also be represented on a **number line**. Take representing 0.6 on a number line as an example. Since 0.6 is more than zero but less than one, there are 6 tenths in it. Divide the number line between 0 and 1 into equal parts and count six parts from 0.

Similarly, you can show, for example, 1.5 and 2.3 on the number line.

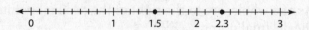

EXAMPLES

1. What is the place value of the underlined digit: 538.60<u>5</u>?

   The underlined digit, 5, is in the thousandths place and stands for 5 thousandths.

2. What is the place value of the underlined digit: 2.<u>8</u>02?

   In this number, the underlined 8 is in the tenths place and represents 8 tenths.

3. What is the place value of the underlined digit: 527.1<u>0</u>7?

   In this number, the underlined digit, 0, is in the hundredths place. It is a placeholder.

EXERCISE 1

Understanding Decimals

Directions: Write each fraction as a decimal.

1. $\dfrac{1}{10}$ 2. $\dfrac{2}{100}$ 3. $\dfrac{10}{100}$ 4. $\dfrac{8}{1,000}$ 5. $\dfrac{11}{10,000}$

6. Show 63 on the number line.

7. Show 75.5 on the number line.

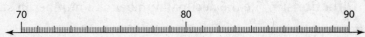

8. Show 101.2 on the number line.

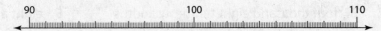

Directions: Write the place value of the underlined digit.

9. 5.<u>5</u>49   **10.** 22.35<u>7</u>   **11.** 263.4<u>5</u>32   **12.** 478.219<u>7</u>

Answers are on page 560.

Reading and Writing Decimals

Rules for Reading Decimals

Decimals are read in the following way:

Step 1: Read the whole number part first.

Step 2: Say "and" for the decimal point.

Step 3: Read the decimal number part.

Step 4: Say the place value of the last decimal digit. Use the place-value chart if needed to find the name of the last decimal digit.

EXAMPLES

1. The number 825.35 is read as "eight hundred twenty-five and thirty-five hundredths."
2. If there is no whole number, start at Step 3 above. The decimal 0.009 is read as "nine thousandths," and 0.0009 is read as "nine ten-thousandths."

Rules for Writing Decimals

The use of zero is very important in writing and reading decimal numbers. For example, before writing nine thousandths as a decimal, first notice that there are no whole number, tenths, or hundredths parts in the word form. To indicate this, in the number form, write 0 for the whole number part, tenths place, and hundredths place: 0.009.

EXERCISE 2

Reading and Writing Decimals

Directions: Write the decimal number as a number in standard form.

1. six tenths
2. fifteen hundredths
3. four thousand eight ten-thousandths
4. six hundred nine thousandths
5. one hundred-thousandth

6. sixteen and five tenths
7. one and eight thousandths
8. eight and four thousand four millionths
9. thirty and thirty-two hundredths
10. forty-two and five hundredths

Answers are on page 560.

Comparing Decimals

As with whole numbers and integers, you can compare decimal numbers. A decimal number has two parts: the whole number part and the decimal part. The whole number is to the left of the decimal point, and the number to the right is the decimal part. When comparing two or more decimal numbers, look first at the whole number parts. If the whole number parts are the same, then look at the decimal parts of the numbers to do the comparison.

When comparing decimal numbers, you can use inequality signs < and > to show which number is smaller than or larger than the other. The notation $a < b$ means that a is less than b. The notation $a > b$ means that a is greater than b.

Comparing Decimals Based on Digits and Place Value

When comparing the decimal parts, make sure that each number has the same number of digits to the right of the decimal point to help in the comparison. If the decimal numbers do not have the same number of digits to the right of the decimal point, the decimal numbers can be rewritten by attaching zeros because it is easier to compare numbers that have the same number of decimal places. Attaching zeros to the right of the last decimal digit does not change the value of the number. For example, $11 can also be written as $11.00. Similarly, 15.5, 15.50, and 15.500 all have the same value.

Next are some examples to understand the process of decimals comparison.

EXAMPLE 1

Compare 5.294 and 6.12.

If you look at the whole number parts of 5.294 and 6.12, you find 5 is smaller than 6. Therefore, 5.294 < 6.12. No comparison of the decimal parts is required.

EXAMPLE 2

Compare 19.22 and 15.25.

If you look at the whole number parts of 19.22 and 15.25, you find 19 is greater than 15. Therefore, 19.22 > 15.25. No comparison of the decimal parts is required.

EXAMPLE 3

Compare 0.12 and 0.125.

Since the whole number parts are the same (both are 0), compare the decimal parts. Attach a zero to 0.12 to make it 0.120 so that both the numbers have the same number of digits (three) to the right of the decimal point. Now both 0.125 and 0.120 are expressed in thousandths and have the same number of decimal places.

0.125 = 0.125

0.12 = 0.120

You can see that 120 thousandths is smaller than 125 thousandths because 120 is less than 125.

Therefore, 0.12 < 0.125.

EXAMPLE 4

Compare 3.72 and 3.78.

Since the whole number parts are the same (both are 3), compare the decimal parts. The decimal parts of both the decimal numbers have the same number of digits (two). The decimal number 3.72 has 72 hundredths, while the decimal number 3.78 has 78 hundredths.

As 3.72 has fewer hundredths than 3.78, 3.72 < 3.78.

EXAMPLE 5

Compare 7.15 and 7.148.

Since the whole number parts are the same (both are 7), compare the decimal parts. Attach a zero to 7.15 to make it 7.150 so that both the numbers have the same number of digits (three) to the right of the decimal point.

The decimal number 7.150 has 150 thousandths, while the decimal number 7.148 has 148 thousandths. As 7.150 has more thousandths than 7.148, 7.15 > 7.148.

EXAMPLE 6

Arrange 32.2, 32.02, 32.19, and 32.098 in order from the smallest to the largest.

Since the whole number parts are the same (32), compare the decimal parts to know the order from the smallest to the largest. First attach zeros so that each number has the same number of decimal places.

32.2 = 32.200

32.02 = 32.020

32.19 = 32.190

32.098 = 32.098

Then rank the mixed decimals in order from the smallest to the largest after comparing the decimal parts.

32.2 = 32.200 = 4th

The decimal number 32.200 has 200 thousandths.

32.02 = 32.020 = 1st

The decimal number 32.020 has 20 thousandths.

32.19 = 32.190 = 3rd

The decimal number 32.190 has 190 thousandths.

32.098 = 32.098 = 2nd

The decimal number 32.098 has 98 thousandths.

Now you can put the original numbers in order from the smallest to largest: 32.02, 32.098, 32.19, 32.2. This order can also be written in the form 32.02 < 32.098 < 32.19 < 32.2.

EXAMPLE 7

For the set of numbers below, find the smallest number and the largest number.

0.34, 0.306, 0.2986

Compare the decimal digits as all three numbers have a whole number part of 0. The third number 0.2986 has only 2 tenths, while the others have 3 tenths. Two tenths is less than three tenths (and adding hundredths to it will not make it more). Therefore, 0.2986 is the smallest number.

One of the remaining two numbers is the largest of the set. When comparing 0.34 and 0.306, the first decimal digits in the tenths place are equal. So compare the second digits: 0.34 has 4 hundredths and 0.306 has 0 hundredths. Since 4 hundredths are more than 0 hundredths, 0.34 is the largest number.

Comparing Decimals Using the Number Line

Decimal numbers can be compared using **number lines**.

EXAMPLE

Represent the numbers 0.3 and 0.8 on a number line and find which one is larger.

Since 0.3 and 0.8 are more than zero but less than one, you can divide the interval between 0 and 1 into 10 equal parts and count 3 tenths and 8 tenths as shown above. Notice that 0.8 is to the right of 0.3. Thus, 0.8 > 0.3.

EXERCISE 3

Comparing Decimals

Directions: Choose the largest or smallest as indicated.

1. Which amount is the greatest?

   A. $115.53
   B. $115.55
   C. $115.15
   D. $114.15

2. Which number is the smallest?

   A. 129.786
   B. 129.886
   C. 129.986
   D. 129.486

3. Which number is the largest?

   A. 146.56

   B. 145.52

   C. 146.55

   D. 146.50

4. Which number is the smallest?

   A. 515.88

   B. 516.89

   C. 516.91

   D. 514.99

Directions: Choose the smallest number in each set.

5. 0.012, 0.12, 0.021

6. 0.3113, 0.3133, 0.3131

7. 72.0456, 72.4056, 72.4506, 72.4566

8. 9.1565, 9.01565, 9.15065, 9.9565

Directions: Choose the largest number in each set.

9. 105.001, 105.011, 105.1

10. 0.6151, 0.6515, 0.6415

11. 0.8901, 0.89001, 0.8801, 0.88001

12. 90.0105, 90.1005, 90.1004, 90.0104

Answers are on page 560.

Rounding Decimals

When you are asked to round a number to a given number of decimal places, first identify the place of the last digit to be reported. If you need to round to two decimal places, count right from the decimal point to the second digit. Underline the second digit so you do not lose your place. Now look at the next digit to the right. If this digit is 5 or greater, round up by adding 1 to the underlined second digit. If the digit is 4 or less, round down by leaving the underlined digit alone. Ignore all digits that are to the right of the specified place.

EXAMPLE 1

Round 51.5356 to two decimal places.

    Underline the second decimal place: 51.5356. Now see the digit to the right of 3 is 5. So you add 1 to the 3 and round 51.5356 as 51.54.

EXAMPLE 2

Round 323.45331 to three decimal places.

    Underline the third decimal place: 323.45331. The digit to the right is less than 5, so ignore all numbers to the right of that place and round 323.45331 as 323.453.

Estimation with Decimals

Estimation is a tool for making a **rough calculation** of amounts of money, lengths of time, distances, and many other physical quantities. Here you will read about two estimation strategies that could be used to estimate the sum of decimals.

The first strategy is to add the whole number part and the decimal part separately. Then adjust the estimate.

EXAMPLE 1

Jim and Charlene went to a restaurant for lunch. The waiter handed them the bill with the price of each lunch but forgot to add up the total. Estimate the total bill if Jim's lunch was $4.75 and Charlene's lunch was $4.29.

$$\begin{array}{cc} 4 & 0.75 \\ \underline{+4} & \underline{+0.29} \\ 8 & 1.04 \end{array}$$

$$\$4.75 + \$4.29 = \$8 + (0.75 + 0.29)$$

First add the whole number part: $4 + 4 = 8$. Then add the decimal part: $0.75 + 0.29 = 1.04$, or 1 when rounded down. Thus, an estimate of the total bill is $8 + $1 = $9.

Another strategy is to first round up each decimal to a designated place value, and then add both to estimate the sum.

EXAMPLE 2

You bought a wallet for $3.05 and an umbrella for $4.51. Estimate the total cost of your purchase.

Rounding each decimal to the nearest dollar amount you get $3 and $5. So an estimate of the total cost of your purchase is $3 + $5 = $8.

EXERCISE 4

Rounding Decimals

Directions: Round the numbers to the specified number of places.

1. 157.825 to two decimal places
2. 0.1034 to three decimal places
3. 5.78925 to four decimal places
4. $125.456 to the nearest hundredths

Directions: Estimate each sum by first rounding up each decimal to the nearest tenths.

5. 0.4925 + 0.85
6. 0.466 + 0.342
7. 0.914 + 0.138
8. 0.5309 + 0.3
9. 0.53 + 0.1435
10. 3.52 + 6.79

Answers are on page 560.

Basic Operations with Decimals

The four arithmetic operations of addition, subtraction, multiplication, and division are performed with decimal numbers in much the same way as they are with whole numbers. The difference is the way that you need to keep track of the decimal point.

Addition of Decimals

When **adding decimal numbers**, line up the decimal points and add. Put in zeros as placeholders so that the numbers have the same length. This will make it easier to add. Add the numbers as you would with whole numbers, starting with the right column. Then place the decimal point below the column of decimal points.

EXAMPLE 1

Add: 1.452 + 1.3.

```
  1.452
 +1.300  ← zeros are added so the numbers have the same length.
  2.752
```

EXAMPLE 2

Find 3.25 + 0.075 + 5.

Write 5 with a decimal point and 3 zeros. Then add.

```
  3.250
  0.075   Zeros are added so the numbers have the same length.
 +5.000
  8.325
```

EXERCISE 5

Addition of Decimals

Directions: Add.

1. 93.59 + 4.7

2. 136.04 + 102.27

3. 5.84 + 8 + 12.79

4. 5.649 + 39.27

5. 2.372 + 14.04

6. 3.93 + 0.04 + 0.9

7. 20.15
    0.083
   +6.9
   _____

8.   3.032
     7.89
   +103.2
   _____

9. 902.03
    78.3054
    40.039
   +1.1326
   _____

10. 72.13
     0.259
     839.702
    +91.4332
    _____

Answers are on page 560.

Subtraction of Decimals

Subtraction of decimals is similar to addition. Line up numbers vertically and place zeros in missing places. Subtract as with whole numbers, including borrowing.

EXAMPLE 1

Subtract: 1.1 − 0.03.

$$
\begin{array}{r}
1.10 \\
-0.03 \quad \leftarrow \boxed{\text{zero added}} \\
\hline
1.07
\end{array}
$$

To do subtraction in the decimal system, use the borrow method as you did with whole numbers. Here, borrow a 10 from the tenths column as 0 is smaller than 3 in the hundredths column. Move 10 to the hundredths column and subtract 3. Once you move 10 from the tenths column to the hundredths column, the tenths column becomes empty and is left with 0. After subtracting, you get 7 in the hundredths place and 0 in the tenths place, and 1 as the whole number part. Therefore, 1.1 − 0.03 = 1.07.

EXAMPLE 2

Subtract: 7.005 − 0.55.

$$
\begin{array}{r}
7.005 \\
-0.550 \quad \leftarrow \boxed{\text{zero added}} \\
\hline
6.455
\end{array}
$$

First, subtract the numbers in the thousandths column, that is, 5 − 0 = 5. In the hundredths column and the tenths column, you see the 0s are smaller than the 5s in the second row. So borrow a 1 from 7 in the ones column. When you move 1 to the tenths column, the 0 in the tenths column becomes 10 and 6 is left in the ones column.

Next, borrow a 1 from the 10 in the tenths column to make the 0 in the hundredths column 10. After 1 is lent to the hundredths column, 9 is left in the tenths column. Now subtract 5 from 10 in the hundredths column and 5 from 9 in the tenths column. Therefore, 7.005 − 0.55 = 6.455.

EXERCISE 6

Subtraction of Decimals

Directions: Subtract.

1. 2.9
 −1.07

2. 90.9009
 −9.09

3. 34.91
 −14.214

4. 12.00942
 −12.0087

5. 198.9
 −198.132

6. 159.02
 −87.835

7. 1,001.1001
 −110.01

8. 21.45
 −7.32

Answers are on page 560.

Multiplication of Decimals

Decimal numbers are multiplied the same way as with whole numbers, except for keeping track of the decimal points. Follow these steps to multiply two decimal numbers.

Step 1: Remove the decimal points from the numbers temporarily.

Step 2: Multiply as with whole numbers.

Step 3: Count the total number of places to the right of the decimal points in both of the original numbers. These are called the decimal digits of the numbers.

Step 4: Starting from the right, count that many places to the left in the product you found in Step 2. If you don't have enough digits, add zeros in as placeholders as you count. Write a decimal point at the place you stopped.

EXAMPLE 1

Multiply: 0.25×0.2.

Step 1: Change 0.25×0.2 to 25×2.

Step 2: Multiply: $25 \times 2 = 50$.

Step 3: Count the number of decimal places in the original problem: 0.25×0.2. The number 0.25 has 2 decimal places, and the number 0.2 has 1 decimal place. There are 3 decimal places in the final product.

Step 4: Count three digits from the right side of 50. Since 50 has only 2 digits, place a 0 to the left of 5 as a placeholder.

<u>0 5 0</u>
3 digits

Write the decimal digit down. Since there is no whole number part after you write the decimal digit, write a 0 for the whole number part. It is standard to write 0 when the whole number part is 0: 0 . <u>0 5 0</u>. Thus, $0.25 \times 0.2 = 0.050$.

EXAMPLE 2

Multiply: 102×0.22.

Step 1: Change 102×0.22 to 102×22.

Step 2: Multiply: $102 \times 22 = 2244$.

Step 3: Count the number of decimal places in the original problem: 102×0.22. The number 102 does not have any decimal places, and the number 0.22 has 2 decimal places. There are 2 decimal places in the final product.

Step 4: Count two digits from the right side of 2244.

22<u>44</u>
2 digits

Insert the decimal point to the left of the two decimal digits 44: 22.<u>44</u>. Thus, $102 \times 0.22 = 22.44$.

EXERCISE 7

Multiplication of Decimals

Directions: Multiply.

1. 0.0005×8

2. 47.4×45

3. 7.382×5

4. 0.004×0.73

5. $\begin{array}{r} 17.88 \\ \times 25.96 \\ \hline \end{array}$

6. $\begin{array}{r} 12.64 \\ \times 34.77 \\ \hline \end{array}$

7. $\begin{array}{r} 55.38 \\ \times 14.11 \\ \hline \end{array}$

8. $\begin{array}{r} 20.69 \\ \times 41.36 \\ \hline \end{array}$

Answers are on page 560.

Division of Decimals

Division with decimal numbers is similar to **whole number division**. The division process continues until the desired number of digits is reached and the number is rounded, or there is no remainder.

Before you start dividing decimal numbers, move the decimal point in both the divisor and dividend so that the divisor becomes a whole number. Then carry out the long division as you would when you divide whole numbers. Follow the steps in the examples.

EXAMPLE 1

Divide: $142.45 \div 0.05$.

Step 1: Write: $0.05\overline{)142.45}$. Move the decimal in the divisor two places to the right to make the divisor, 0.05, into a whole number, 5. Move the decimal the same number of places to the right in the dividend: 142.45 becomes 14,245. The long division problem $0.05\overline{)142.45}$ becomes $5\overline{)14245}$.

Step 2: Divide as with whole numbers.

$$
\begin{array}{r}
2849 \\
5\overline{)14245} \\
\underline{-10} \\
42 \\
\underline{-40} \\
24 \\
\underline{-20} \\
45 \\
\underline{-45} \\
0
\end{array}
$$

The remainder is 0, and so the division process stops.

Step 3: The quotient is 2,849.

Once the last digit in the dividend is brought down in the division process, the process does not stop with a remainder until there is no remainder. If needed, the process is continued by adding zeros to the dividend and then bringing them down to subtract. It works because every whole number can be treated as a decimal number whose decimal part consists of as many zeros as is needed: 5 = 5.0000.

EXAMPLE 2

Divide: 47.1 ÷ 3.2.

Step 1: Write: 3.2)47.1. Move the decimal in the divisor one place to the right to make the divisor, 3.2, into a whole number, 32. Move the decimal the same number of places to the right in the dividend: 47.1 becomes 471. The long division problem 3.2)47.1 becomes 32)471.

Step 2: Divide.

$$
\begin{array}{r}
14 \\
32 \overline{)471} \\
-32 \\
\hline
151 \\
-128 \\
\hline
23
\end{array}
$$

After going through the steps of carrying the remainders forward, bringing down the digits from the dividend, and subtracting, you get a remainder of 23. Since you have reached the end of the whole numbers, add a decimal point both in the quotient and the dividend. Then add zeros to the dividend since adding zeros after the decimal point does not change the value of the number, and continue the long division process.

$$
\begin{array}{r}
14.71875 \\
32 \overline{)471.00000} \\
-32 \\
\hline
151 \\
-128 \\
\hline
230 \\
-224 \\
\hline
60 \\
-32 \\
\hline
280 \\
-256 \\
\hline
240 \\
-224 \\
\hline
160 \\
-160 \\
\hline
0
\end{array}
$$

The last remainder you get is 0, so stop dividing. As long as the subtraction gives a number above zero, the long division process can go on. Sometimes you will be asked to carry out division to a certain decimal place.

Step 3: So 14.71875 is the quotient.

Division When Rounding to a Specific Place

On many occasions, when the division does not terminate/stop by itself, you need to stop the process and round off the answer. This is used a lot when dividing amounts that represent money. When estimating dollar values, rounding is usually done in the hundredths place, or to the nearest cent.

EXAMPLE

Find the quotient of 0.001451 ÷ 0.0004 to the nearest hundredths.

Step 1: Write: $0.0004\overline{)0.001451}$. Move the decimal in the divisor four places to the right to make the divisor, 0.0004, into a whole number, 4. Move the decimal the same number of places to the right in the dividend: 0.001451 becomes 14.51. The long division problem $0.0004\overline{)0.001451}$ becomes $4\overline{)14.51}$.

Step 2: Divide up until the thousandth place. Add zeros in the dividend as needed.

$$
\begin{array}{r}
3.627 \\
4\overline{)14.510} \\
\underline{-12} \\
25 \\
\underline{-24} \\
11 \\
\underline{-8} \\
30 \\
\underline{-28} \\
2
\end{array}
$$

Step 3: Since you have been asked to round the quotient to the hundredths place, you need to look at the digit, 7, in the thousandths place of the quotient. The 7 tells you to round the hundredths digit up to the next number, so the properly rounded quotient is 3.63.

Division When Not Told to Round to a Specific Place

When you are not asked to round off the product of the division, go on dividing the dividend by adding zeros as placeholders to the dividend until you get zero as remainder.

EXAMPLE

Divide: 12.111916 ÷ 0.4.

Step 1: Write: $0.4\overline{)12.111916}$. Move the decimal in the divisor one place to the right to make the divisor, 0.4, into a whole number, 4. Move the decimal the same number of places to the right in the dividend: 12.111916 becomes 121.11916. The long division problem $0.4\overline{)12.111916}$ becomes $4\overline{)121.11916}$.

Step 2: Divide.

```
        30.27979
    4)  121.11916
       -12
         0
        -0
         11
         -8
         31
        -28
         39
        -36
         31
        -28
         36
        -36
          0
```

Here, the division continued until the remainder became zero.

Step 3: So 30.27979 is the quotient.

EXERCISE 8

Division of Decimals

Directions: Divide and round as indicated.

1. Find the quotient of 3.64 divided by 0.77 to the nearest hundredths.

2. Find the quotient of 52.37 divided by 11 to the nearest thousandths.

Directions: Divide. Round the quotient to the nearest hundredths, if necessary.

3. $86.8 \div 2.7$ 5. $463.4 \div 3.2$ 7. $1,504.8 \div 6$ 9. $0.275 \div 0.25$

4. $86.4 \div 3.1$ 6. $487.2 \div 5.6$ 8. $0.0325 \div 0.013$ 10. $4.214 \div 0.5$

Answers are on page 560.

Multiplication and Division by Powers of Ten

When **multiplying** or **dividing** by **powers of ten** (e.g., 10, 100, 1,000), you can just move the decimal point based on the number of zeros in the powers of ten. In multiplication, move the decimal point to the right by the same number of digits in the divisor that is the power of ten. Add zeros as needed for placeholders to get the correct number of places.

EXAMPLE 1

Multiply: 30.24×10.

There is one zero in 10. Move the decimal point one place to the right in 30.24.

$30.24 \times 10 = 302.4$

EXAMPLE 2

Multiply: $71.58 \times 1,000$.

There are 3 zeros in 1,000. Move the decimal point 3 places to the right in 71.58. Since there are two digits after the decimal point, add a zero after the 8 as a placeholder.

$71.58 \times 1,000 = 71,580$

In division, the decimal point is moved to the left the number of places equal to the number of zeros in the divisor that is the power of ten. Add zeros as needed for placeholders to get the correct number of places in the product.

EXAMPLE 1

Divide: $3.15 \div 100$.

There are 2 zeros in 100. Move the decimal place 2 places to the left in 3.15. Insert a 0 before the 3 as a placeholder.

$3.15 \div 100 = 0.0315$

EXAMPLE 2

Divide: $295 \div 10,000$.

Since there are 4 zeros in 10,000, move the decimal point 4 places to the left in 295. Insert one zero as a placeholder.

$295 \div 10,000 = 0.0295$

EXERCISE 9

Multiplication and Division by Powers of Ten

Directions: Find the products or quotients with powers of 10.

Directions: Multiply.

1. 20.77×10 **3.** $95.22 \times 1,000$ **5.** $0.005 \times 10,000$

2. 21.59×100 **4.** $252.627 \times 1,000$

Directions: Divide.

6. $63.4 \div 10$ **8.** $68.4 \div 1,000$ **10.** $0.05 \div 10,000$

7. $456.89 \div 100$ **9.** $1.45 \div 1,000$

Answers are on page 561.

Conversion of Decimals to Fractions

To convert a decimal number to a fraction, determine the last place value of the decimal number. To write the fraction, write the decimal part of the number (without the decimal point) as the numerator, and the number representing the last place value as the denominator.

EXAMPLE 1

Convert 0.225 to a fraction. Reduce to lowest terms, if necessary.

The decimal part of the number is 225. The last place value of 0.225 is the thousandths, so the denominator of the fraction is 1,000. Thus, $0.225 = \frac{225}{1,000}$. The fraction does reduce further, so $0.225 = \frac{9}{40}$.

EXAMPLE 2

Convert 0.0435 to a fraction. Reduce to lowest terms, if necessary.

The decimal part is 435. The last place value of 0.0435 is the ten-thousandths. Thus, $0.0435 = \frac{435}{10,000}$. The fraction reduces, so $0.0435 = \frac{87}{2,000}$.

EXAMPLE 3

Convert 1.22 to a fraction. Reduce to lowest terms, if necessary.

The number 1.22 has 2 decimal places. The decimal part is 0.22 and the last place value is the hundredths. You can write 1.22 as $1\frac{22}{100} = 1\frac{11}{50}$. The result is a mixed number.

Another way to write a decimal number with a whole number part is to just put the entire number over 100: $\frac{122}{100} = \frac{61}{50}$. The result is an improper fraction and is equivalent to $1\frac{22}{100} = 1\frac{11}{50}$.

EXERCISE 10

Conversion of Decimals to Fractions

Directions: Convert to a fraction. Reduce to lowest terms, if necessary.

1. 0.625	**3.** 0.85	**5.** 0.375	**7.** 0.425	**9.** 0.475
2. 0.333	**4.** 0.64	**6.** 0.825	**8.** 0.15	**10.** 0.9875

Answers are on page 561.

Converting Fractions to Non-Repeating Decimals

A **non-repeating decimal** is a **rational number** whose decimal representation eventually ends. For example, 0.34, 0.125, and 0.838383 are non-repeating decimals.

Some fractions are non-repeating decimals. To find out if a fraction is a non-repeating decimal, divide the numerator by the denominator.

EXAMPLE 1

Convert $\frac{3}{8}$ to a decimal.

Use the long division method to do the conversion. Keep dividing until the remainder is 0.

$$
\begin{array}{r}
0.375 \\
8\overline{)\,3.000} \\
\underline{-0} \\
3\,0 \\
\underline{-2\,4} \\
6\,0 \\
\underline{-5\,6} \\
4\,0 \\
\underline{-4\,0} \\
0
\end{array}
$$

Thus, $\frac{3}{8} = 0.375$.

EXAMPLE 2

Convert $\frac{1}{4}$ to a decimal.

Use the long division method to do the conversion. Keep dividing until the remainder is 0.

$$
\begin{array}{r}
0.25 \\
4\overline{)\,1.00} \\
\underline{-0} \\
1\,0 \\
\underline{-8} \\
2\,0 \\
\underline{-2\,0} \\
0
\end{array}
$$

Thus, $\frac{1}{4} = 0.25$.

EXERCISE 11

Converting Fractions to Non-Repeating Decimals

Directions: Convert to a decimal.

1. $\dfrac{4}{5}$ 3. $\dfrac{3}{4}$ 5. $\dfrac{8}{25}$ 7. $\dfrac{7}{8}$ 9. $\dfrac{19}{125}$

2. $\dfrac{2}{5}$ 4. $\dfrac{5}{8}$ 6. $\dfrac{17}{20}$ 8. $\dfrac{1}{4}$ 10. $\dfrac{11}{16}$

Answers are on page 561.

Converting Fractions to Repeating Decimals with a Single Repeating Digit

A **repeating decimal** is a decimal that has a digit or a block of digits that repeats over and over again without ever ending. For example, 22.67777… and 1.3333… have repeating decimal parts. The part that repeats is usually shown by writing three dots after showing the repeating part or by writing a bar over the repeating part. For example, 22.6777… can be written as $22.6\overline{7}$ because the digit 7 repeats continually. The examples show how to convert a fraction to a repeating decimal.

EXAMPLE

Convert $\dfrac{4}{9}$ to a decimal.

Use the long division method to do the conversion.

```
      0.444...
  9)  4.000
     -3 6
     ─────
       40
      -36
      ─────
       40
      -36
      ─────
        4
```

Stop dividing when you notice that the quotient has a single digit 4 that keeps repeating. The remainder never changes at each step. Thus, $\dfrac{4}{9} = 0.\overline{4}$ or $\dfrac{4}{9} = 0.444\ldots$.

EXERCISE 12

Converting Fractions to Repeating Decimals with a Single Repeating Digit

Directions: Convert to a decimal.

1. $\frac{5}{9}$　**2.** $\frac{4}{9}$　**3.** $\frac{1}{3}$　**4.** $\frac{7}{9}$　**5.** $\frac{11}{9}$　**6.** $\frac{2}{3}$　**7.** $\frac{1}{9}$　**8.** $\frac{8}{9}$

Answers are on page 561.

Converting Fractions to Repeating Decimals with Several Repeating Digits

Sometimes when you convert a fraction to a decimal, the quotient has more than one digit in a repeating pattern.

EXAMPLE

Convert $\frac{1}{7}$ to a repeating decimal.

Use the long division method to do the conversion.

```
        0.142857 ...
     7)  1.000000
        −0
         10
         −7
         30
        −28
         20
        −14
         60
        −56
         40
        −35
         50
        −49
          1
```

Notice that you can stop the division when the remainder becomes 1, which is the beginning of the divisor at the beginning of the process. This indicates that the quotient's pattern will start again. Thus, $\frac{1}{7} = 0.142857\ldots = 0.\overline{142857}$ with a bar on top of the entire part that repeats.

Converting Fractions to Repeating Decimals with a Single Repeating Digit Following Non-Repeating Digits

In some fraction-decimal conversions, you find **single repeating digits** following **non-repeating digits**.

EXAMPLE

Convert $\dfrac{77}{600}$ to decimal.

Use the long division method to do the conversion.

```
        0.128333
600)77.000000
     −0
     770
    −600
    1700
   −1200
    5000
   −4800
    2000
   −1800
    2000
   −1800
    2000
   −1800
     200
```

Thus, $\dfrac{77}{600} = 0.128333\ldots = 0.128\overline{3}$. Here the single digit "3" repeats. Note that you have to carry out many steps to find the part of the quotient that repeats.

EXERCISE 13

Converting Fractions to Repeating Decimals with Several Repeating Digits or to Decimals with a Single Repeating Digit Following Non-Repeating Digits

Directions: Convert to a decimal.

1. $\dfrac{9}{11}$ 3. $\dfrac{22}{7}$ 5. $\dfrac{1}{7}$ 7. $\dfrac{2}{7}$ 9. $\dfrac{1}{13}$

2. $\dfrac{7}{12}$ 4. $\dfrac{5}{74}$ 6. $\dfrac{3}{7}$ 8. $\dfrac{4}{7}$ 10. $\dfrac{5}{7}$

Answers are on page 561.

Converting Non-Repeating Decimals to Fractions

To convert a **non-repeating decimal** to a fraction, find the last place value of the decimal part. Write the decimal part over the power of ten representing the last place value. Reduce to lowest terms, if needed. This is the same process as converting a decimal to a fraction, which you saw earlier.

EXAMPLE

Express 0.425 as a fraction in lowest terms.

Since the number is 425 thousandths, write $\dfrac{425}{1,000}$. Now you have to reduce the fraction to lowest terms: $\dfrac{425}{1,000} \div \dfrac{25}{25} = \dfrac{17}{40}$.

Converting Decimals with a Single Repeating Digit to Fractions

To convert a decimal with a **single repeating digit** to a fraction, follow the steps given in the example below.

EXAMPLE

Express 0.555… as a fraction.

Step 1: Let x be the number 0.555…. Here the repeating part is 5.

$x = 0.555…$

Step 2: Place the repeating digit "5" to the left of the decimal point. For this, you need to move the decimal point one place to the right. Moving a decimal point one place to the right is done by multiplying the decimal number by 10.

Step 3: When you multiply one side by a number, you have to multiply the other side by the same number to keep the equation balanced. So

$10x = 5.555….$

$x = 0.555….$

Step 4: Subtract the second equation from the first equation:

$10x - x = (5.555…) - (0.555…)$

The repeated part is subtracted out and you are left with a whole number on the right side.

$9x = 5$

Step 5: Then divide both sides of the equation by 9.

$x = \dfrac{5}{9}$

Thus, $0.555… = 0.\overline{5} = \dfrac{5}{9}$.

EXERCISE 14

Converting Non-Repeating Decimals or Decimals with a Single Repeating Digit to Fractions

Directions: Convert to a fraction. Reduce to lowest terms, if necessary.

1. 0.09	**3.** $0.\overline{7}$	**5.** $0.\overline{6}$	**7.** $0.\overline{1}$	**9.** $0.\overline{4}$
2. 0.125	**4.** $0.\overline{3}$	**6.** $0.\overline{5}$	**8.** $1.\overline{2}$	**10.** $0.\overline{8}$

Answers are on page 561.

Converting Decimals with Multiple Repeating Digits to Fractions

You can convert a decimal with **multiple repeating digits** to a fraction by following similar steps given in the previous section.

EXAMPLE

Convert $1.0\overline{42}$ to a fraction.

Step 1: You can write $1.0\overline{42}$ as 1.04242424242… . Let $x = 1.0424242…$. The repeating part is 42.

Step 2: Place the repeating digit "42" to the left of the decimal point. For this, you need to move the decimal point three places to the right. Moving a decimal point three places to the right is done by multiplying the decimal number by 1,000.

Step 3: Remember that when you multiply one side of an equation by a number, you have to multiply the other side by the same number to keep the equation balanced. So, multiply x by 1,000. Thus, $1,000x = 1,042.42424242…$.

Now you have to place the repeating digits "42" in 1.04242424242… to the right of the decimal point. Here the repeating digit is not immediately to the right of the decimal point. There is a zero between the repeating digit and the decimal point.

So you have to move the decimal point one place to the right by multiplying both sides by 10.

$x = 1.04242424242…$

$10x = 10.4242424242…$

Step 4: Use these two modified equations in this step:

$1,000x = 1,042.42424242…$.

$10x = 10.4242424242…$

Subtract the second equation from the first equation.

$1{,}000x - 10x = (1{,}042.42424242\ldots) - (10.4242424242\ldots)$

$990x = 1{,}032$

$$x = \frac{1{,}032}{990}$$

Thus, $1.04242424242\ldots = \dfrac{1{,}032}{990} = \dfrac{516}{495}$. Alternatively, you could have written just the decimal part as the fractional part: $1.04242424242\ldots = 1\dfrac{21}{495}$. The whole number part of the decimal form is the same as the whole number part of the fraction form, so it would have sufficed to convert only the decimal part, $0.04242\ldots$.

EXERCISE 15

Converting Decimals with Multiple Repeating Digits to Fractions

Directions: Convert to a fraction. Reduce to lowest terms, if necessary.

1. $0.\overline{81}$ **2.** $0.\overline{63}$ **3.** $0.0\overline{9}$ **4.** $0.\overline{567}$ **5.** $0.\overline{285714}$

Answers are on page 561.

Converting Decimals with Non-Repeating Digits Followed by Repeating Digits to Fractions

You can convert a decimal with **non-repeating digits followed by repeating digits** to a fraction by following these steps.

Step 1: Let x be the decimal number.

Step 2: Find the number of non-repeating digits after the decimal point.

Step 3: Suppose there are n non-repeating digits. Multiply both sides by 10^n so that only the repeating decimal digit is on the right side of the decimal point. This is the first equation that you will need in the process of conversion.

Step 4: Write the repeating digits at least twice.

Step 5: Find the number of repeating digits after the decimal point.

Step 6: For n repeating digits, multiply both sides by 10^n. You get a second equation in this step.

Step 7: Subtract the equation of Step 3 from the equation of Step 6.

Step 8: Divide both sides of the equation by the coefficient of *x*.

Step 9: Reduce the fraction to lowest terms.

EXAMPLE

Express 0.43213213213… as a fraction.

Step 1: Let $x = 0.43213213213…$.

Step 2: The number of non-repeating digits is 2.

Step 3: Multiply both sides by 100.

$$100x = 43.213213213…$$

Step 4: There are already at least two sets of repeating digits after the decimal point.

$$100x = 43.213213213…$$

Step 5: The number of repeating digits after the decimal point is three. Multiply by 1,000.

Step 6: $100x \times 1,000 = 43.213213213… \times 1,000$

$$100,000x = 43,213.213…$$

Step 7: Now subtract the two equations found.

$$100,000x - 100x = 43,213.213 - 43.213213$$

$$99,900x = 43,170$$

Step 8: Divide by 99,900. Reduce, if necessary.

$$x = \frac{43,170}{99,900} = \frac{43,17\cancel{0}}{99,90\cancel{0}} = \frac{4,317}{9,990}$$

Step 9: Therefore, $0.43213213213… = \dfrac{4,317}{9,990}$.

EXERCISE 16

Converting Decimals with Non-Repeating Digits Followed by Repeating Digits to Fractions

Directions: Convert to a fraction. Reduce to lowest terms, if necessary.

1. $0.08\overline{3}$ **2.** $0.7\overline{162}$ **3.** $0.5\overline{428571}$ **4.** $0.1\overline{283}$ **5.** $0.3\overline{81}$

Answers are on page 562.

Estimating Roots

To find the square root of a decimal number that is a perfect square, you can follow these steps:

Step 1: Remove the decimal point.

Step 2: Estimate the square root of the resulting number using the prime factorization method.

Step 3: After you find the root, place (from the right) as many decimal numbers as there are number of *pairs* of decimal places under the radicand of the original number.

EXAMPLE

Simplify $\sqrt{0.36}$.

Step 1: If you remove the decimal point, $\sqrt{0.36}$ will become $\sqrt{36}$.

Step 2: Using the prime factorization method, you get the following:

$$
\begin{array}{r|l}
2 & 36 \\
2 & 18 \\
3 & 9 \\
  & 3
\end{array}
$$

Thus, $36 = 2 \times 2 \times 3 \times 3$.

So, $\sqrt{36} = \sqrt{2 \times 2 \times 3 \times 3} = 2 \times 3 = 6$.

Step 3: Since there is one pair of decimal places under the radicand of the original number, put the decimal point after one number. So $\sqrt{0.36} = 0.6$.

Estimating Square Roots of Non-Perfect Squares

You can estimate the square root of a **non-perfect square** by using a calculator.

EXAMPLE

Simplify $\sqrt{9.8}$.

Enter 9.8 in the calculator and press the $\sqrt{}$ key to get the result. So you get $\sqrt{9.8} = 3.130495168499706$, which can be rounded to 3.13.

An alternate way to find the square root on a calculator is to use the power key x^y or $\wedge$, depending on your calculator. So, to find $\sqrt{9.8}$, you could follow this sequence: 9.8, x^y, 0.5, =. If you have a $\wedge$ key, enter this sequence: 9.8, $\wedge$, 0.5, =.

Estimating Cube Roots of Non-Perfect Cubes

You can also estimate the cube root of a **non-perfect cube** by using a calculator.

EXAMPLE

Simplify $\sqrt[3]{24.3}$.

Enter 24.3 in the calculator and press the " $\sqrt[3]{}$ " key to get the result. So you get $\sqrt[3]{24.3} = 2.896468$, which can be rounded to 2.9.

An alternate way to find the square root on a calculator is to use the power key x^y or ^, depending on your calculator. So, to find $\sqrt[3]{24.3}$, you could follow this sequence: 24.3, x^y, (, 1, ÷, 3,), =. If you have a ^ key, enter this sequence: 24.3, ^, (, 1, ÷, 3,), =. Be sure to use parentheses around the 1, ÷, 3 sequence.

EXERCISE 17

Estimating Roots

Directions: Find the indicated root using a calculator.

1. $\sqrt{0.0169}$ **3.** $\sqrt{0.00021025}$ **5.** $\sqrt[3]{23.435}$ **7.** $\sqrt{17.64}$ **9.** $\sqrt[3]{85.5}$

2. $\sqrt{0.4225}$ **4.** $\sqrt[3]{5.832}$ **6.** $\sqrt{761.76}$ **8.** $\sqrt{16.81}$ **10.** $\sqrt[3]{96.49}$

Answers are on page 562.

Ratios and Proportions

As long as numbers have existed, people have been comparing them. Ratios and proportions are all about comparing numbers. In this chapter you will learn about the rules for using these comparisons, and what they are used for, and how.

Understanding Ratios

Ratios, rates, and proportions can be used in the real world when dealing with several quantities that come in relative sizes.

Concept of Ratio

A **ratio** is the quotient of two quantities. A ratio can be written in three different ways, using the word *to*, using a colon (:), or as a fraction. For example, the quantities 9 hours and 5 hours can be compared as a ratio and can be written as $\dfrac{9 \text{ hours}}{5 \text{ hours}} = \dfrac{9}{5}$, 9:5, or 9 to 5. They are all read the same way, "nine to five." A ratio of a to b can be written as $\dfrac{a}{b} = a \div b = a : b$. The ratio needs to be stated in the order given.

EXAMPLE 1

Find the ratio of 45 miles to 7 miles.

$$\frac{45 \text{ miles}}{7 \text{ miles}} = \frac{45}{7} \text{ or } 45{:}7$$

EXAMPLE 2

Express as a ratio: $56 to $73.

$$\$56{:}\$73 = \frac{\$56}{\$73} = \frac{56}{73} \text{ or } 56{:}73$$

EXERCISE 1

Concept of Ratio

Directions: Find fraction notation for each ratio. You do not need to simplify.

1. $7 to $10

2. 15 miles to 35 miles

3. 50 km to 40 km

4. 45 hours to 60 hours

5. 7 days to 15 days

6. 1.2 minutes to 3.6 minutes

7. 8 boys to 12 girls

8. 19 fishes to 76 fishes

9. 6 pounds to 48 pounds

Answers are on page 562.

Using Ratio Language to Describe Ratio Relationships

The order of the items in a ratio is important.

EXAMPLE 1

Refer to the triangle.

a. What is the ratio of the length of the longest side to the length of the shortest side?

$$\frac{\text{longest side}}{\text{shortest side}} = \frac{5}{3}$$

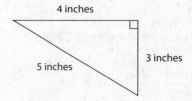

4 inches

3 inches

5 inches

b. What is the ratio of the length of the shortest side to the length of the longest side?

$$\frac{\text{shortest side}}{\text{longest side}} = \frac{3}{5}$$

EXAMPLE 2

There are 18 students in Art class and the school has 427 students. Find the ratio of students in Art class to all the students.

The ratio can be written as $18{:}427 = \dfrac{18}{427}$.

EXERCISE 2

Using Ratio Language to Describe Ratio Relationships

Directions: Answer the following questions. Do not write the units.

1. In the figure, find the ratio of the longest side to the shortest side.

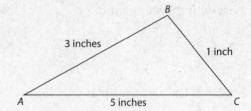

2. In the figure, find the ratio of the two equal sides.

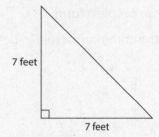

3. In the figure, find the ratio of bananas to apples.

4. In the figure, find the ratio of triangles to circles.

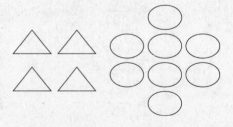

5. Find the ratio of 15 out of 20 students who participated in the essay competition.

6. The zoo has two tigers and an elephant. What is the ratio of elephants to tigers?

Answers are on page 562.

Ratios in Simplest Form

Sometimes a ratio can be simplified. Simplifying provides a means of finding other numbers with the same ratio.

EXAMPLE 1

Find the ratio of 6 honeydews to 15 honeydews. Then simplify to find two other numbers with the same ratio.

$$\frac{6}{15} = \frac{2 \cdot 3}{3 \cdot 5} = \frac{2 \cdot \cancel{3}}{\cancel{3} \cdot 5} = \frac{2}{5}$$

2 to 5 has the same ratio as 6 to 15.

EXAMPLE 2

Express $\frac{16}{48}$ in simplest form.

Cancel the common factors in both the numerator and the denominator.

$$\frac{\cancel{16}^{1}}{\cancel{48}_{3}} = \frac{1}{3}$$

The simplest form of $\frac{16}{48}$ is $\frac{1}{3}$.

EXERCISE 3

Ratios in Simplest Form

Directions: Express the ratios in simplest form.

1. $\frac{8}{20}$ 4. $\frac{55}{100}$ 7. $\frac{3}{30}$ 10. $\frac{0.28}{0.54}$

2. $\frac{35}{45}$ 5. $\frac{4}{16} : \frac{6}{20}$ 8. $\frac{17}{102}$

3. $\frac{3.2}{4.8}$ 6. $\frac{52}{104}$ 9. $\frac{3.4}{1.7}$

Answers are on page 562.

Equivalent Ratios and Comparing Ratios

A ratio remains unchanged if both the numerator and denominator are multiplied or divided by the same nonzero number. When you multiply or divide the ratio by the same number, you are creating an **equivalent ratio**.

EXAMPLE 1

Write two equivalent ratios for $\frac{8}{10}$.

$$\frac{8}{10} = \frac{8 \times 2}{10 \times 2} = \frac{16}{20}$$

$$\frac{8}{10} = \frac{8 \div 2}{10 \div 2} = \frac{4}{5}$$

EXAMPLE 2

Ben can eat 4 apples in 7 minutes, and Bess can eat 3 apples in 5 minutes. Who eats apples at a faster rate?

The ratios in the given context are $\frac{4}{7}$ and $\frac{3}{5}$. In the first ratio, the denominator is 7, and in the second ratio, the denominator is 5. The lowest common denominator (LCD) of 7 and 5 is 35. Write both fractions with the common denominator.

$$4:7 = \frac{4}{7} = \frac{4 \times 5}{7 \times 5} = \frac{20}{35}$$

$$3:5 = \frac{3}{5} = \frac{3 \times 7}{5 \times 7} = \frac{21}{35}$$

Now, $20 < 21$, that is, $\frac{20}{35} < \frac{21}{35}$. Therefore, $\frac{4}{7} < \frac{3}{5}$.

This means that Bess eats apples at a faster rate than Ben does.

EXAMPLE 3

Shop A sells 3 oranges for $1.50 and shop B sells 9 oranges for $2.30. Which one sells oranges at a cheaper price?

Shop A sells 3 oranges for $1.50. So the price of 1 orange is $\frac{1.50}{3}$. Shop B sells 9 oranges for $2.30. So the price of 1 orange is $\frac{2.30}{9}$. The ratios can be written as

$$1.5:3 = \frac{1.5}{3} = \frac{15}{30}$$

$$2.3:9 = \frac{2.3}{9} = \frac{23}{90}$$

Since 90 is a multiple of 30, the LCD of 30 and 90 is 90. Write each fraction with the common denominator.

$$\frac{15}{30} = \frac{15 \times 3}{30 \times 3} = \frac{45}{90}$$

$$\frac{23}{90} = \frac{23}{90}$$

Now 45 > 23. Thus shop B sells oranges at a cheaper price.

EXERCISE 4

Equivalent Ratios and Comparing Ratios

Directions: Find two equivalent ratios for each of the following ratios.

1. $\frac{5}{10}$ 3. $\frac{2}{3}$ 5. $\frac{11}{12}$

2. $\frac{7}{28}$ 4. $\frac{6}{10}$

Directions: Compare the following ratios.

6. At the Village Market, 5 cans of green beans cost $4. In Bess's Club, 10 cans of the same beans can be bought for $4.90. Which store has the best buy?

7. The bakers at Bagel Barn can make 260 bagels in 5 hours, whereas the bakers at the Bagel Factory can make 700 bagels in 14 hours. Which bakery can make bagels at a faster rate?

8. An experimental jet M travels 520 miles in 5 hours. Another experimental jet N travels 1,200 miles in 14 hours. Which jet can travel faster?

9. The test results of car A show that the car can travel 320 miles on 10 gallons of gas. The test results of another car B show that the car can travel 2,300 miles on 65 gallons of gas. Which car can travel farther on a single gallon of gas?

10. Ben's ice cream factory can make 170 quarts of ice cream in 5 hours. Sarah's ice cream factory can make 450 quarts in 12 hours. Which ice cream factory can make more ice cream in less time?

Answers are on page 562.

Ratios Comparing More Than Two Quantities

More than two quantities can be compared by using a common second term (i.e., denominator) for all the ratios.

EXAMPLE 1

Three cars A, B, and C, can travel 300 miles on 10 gallons of gas, 600 miles on 15 gallons of gas, and 900 miles on 25 gallons of gas, respectively. Find the car that can travel farthest per gallon of gas.

Car A can travel 300 miles on 10 gallons of gas. So, it can travel $\frac{300}{10}$ miles on a gallon of gas.

Car B can travel 600 miles on 15 gallons of gas. So it can travel $\frac{600}{15}$ miles on a gallon of gas.

Car C can travel 900 miles on 25 gallons of gas. So it can travel $\frac{900}{25}$ miles on a gallon of gas.

You need to compare the three ratios: $\frac{300}{10}$, $\frac{600}{15}$, and $\frac{900}{25}$.

The second terms in the three ratios are 10, 15, and 25, respectively.

The LCD of 10, 15, and 25 is 150. Rewrite each fraction with the LCD.

$$\frac{300}{10} = \frac{300 \times 15}{10 \times 15} = \frac{4,500}{150}$$

$$\frac{600}{15} = \frac{600 \times 10}{15 \times 10} = \frac{6,000}{150}$$

$$\frac{900}{25} = \frac{900 \times 6}{25 \times 6} = \frac{5,400}{150}$$

Thus, car B can travel farther on a single gallon of gas.

EXAMPLE 2

Compare: $\frac{1.5}{3}$, $\frac{1.3}{3.5}$, and $\frac{2.3}{6}$.

The ratios can be rewritten as follows.

$$\frac{1.5}{3.0} = \frac{15}{30}$$

$$\frac{1.3}{3.5} = \frac{13}{35}$$

$$\frac{2.3}{6} = \frac{23}{60}$$

The LCD of 30, 35, and 60 is 420. Now, raise the denominators of the fractions to 420 ($420 \div 30 = 14$, $420 \div 35 = 12$, $420 \div 60 = 7$).

$$\frac{15}{30} = \frac{15 \times 14}{30 \times 14} = \frac{210}{420}$$

$$\frac{13}{35} = \frac{13 \times 12}{35 \times 12} = \frac{156}{420}$$

$$\frac{23}{60} = \frac{23 \times 7}{60 \times 7} = \frac{161}{420}$$

Now, $210 > 161 > 156$, that is, $\frac{210}{420} > \frac{161}{420} > \frac{156}{420}$. Therefore, $\frac{15}{30} > \frac{23}{35} > \frac{13}{35}$.

EXERCISE 5

Ratios Comparing More Than Two Quantities

Directions: Compare the following ratios.

1. $\frac{16}{20}$, $\frac{2}{5}$, and $\frac{3}{5}$

2. $\frac{4}{5}$, $\frac{21}{35}$, and $\frac{8}{21}$

3. $\frac{2}{7}$, $\frac{5}{6}$, and $\frac{18}{36}$

4. $\frac{20}{24}$, $\frac{12}{16}$, and $\frac{12}{20}$

5. $2:2\frac{1}{2}$, $\frac{32}{40}$, and $1:1\frac{1}{3}$

6. $\frac{0.4}{0.2}$, $\frac{0.6}{0.8}$, and $\frac{1.2}{0.4}$

7. $\frac{1}{2}$, $\frac{7}{54}$, and $\frac{6}{48}$

8. $\frac{7.2}{1.2}$, $\frac{0.7}{4.2}$, and $\frac{8}{16}$

9. $\frac{1}{2}:\frac{1}{3}$, $\frac{5}{7}:\frac{9}{2}$, and $\frac{1}{2}:\frac{7}{2}$

Answers are on page 563.

Understanding Rates and Unit Rates

The Concept of Rates

When a ratio is used to compare two different kinds of measure, it is called a **rate**. For example, 45 miles per hour is a rate. When rates are written as fractions, the units cannot be canceled because they are not common, but common numerical factors can be canceled to reduce to the lowest term.

EXAMPLE

Compare 98 miles and 4 hours using a fraction and a colon.

$$\frac{98 \text{ miles}}{4 \text{ hours}} = \frac{49 \text{ miles}}{2 \text{ hours}}; 49 \text{ miles}:2 \text{ hours}$$

EXERCISE 6

The Concept of Rates

Directions: Write each rate using a fraction and a colon. Do not simplify the rates.

1. 450 cashews and 32 people

2. $145 and 20 minutes

3. 54 miles and 2 hours

4. $150 and 4 people

5. 45 flowers and 2 children

6. $790 and 4 books

Answers are on page 563.

Use of Rate Language in the Context of Rate Relationships

It was mentioned earlier in this chapter that ratio relationships are of three types: part to part, part to whole, and relationship between different units or terms. The third type represents rate relationships, that is, relationships between different units or terms. Rate relationships can be phrased in different ways, as in the following examples:

- The car traveled at a speed of 150 miles per hour.
- In the school, there are 2 teachers to every 15 students.
- There were 10 chocolates per student.

EXAMPLE

Andrew covers a distance of 150 miles in 4 hours. What is the rate relationship?

According to the sentence, the rate relationship is 150 miles:4 hours.

It can be written as $\dfrac{150 \text{ miles}}{4 \text{ hours}} = \dfrac{\overset{75}{\cancel{150}} \text{ miles}}{\underset{2}{\cancel{4}} \text{ hours}} = 75{:}2 = 75 \text{ miles:2 hours.}$

Thus the rate relationship is 75 miles:2 hours.

EXERCISE 7

Use of Rate Language in the Context of Rate Relationships

Directions: Find the rate in the following sentences.

1. In a fish farm, there are 5 fishes per aquarium.
2. A new park has 1 bench for every 5 children.
3. A garden has 5 trees to 14 flowers.
4. There are 10 cashews per student.
5. The school has assigned 3 teachers per classroom.
6. The zoo has an elephant to two tigers.

Answers are on page 563.

Rates in Simplest Form

Rates can be simplified to lowest form by canceling all the common factors in the given quantities.

EXAMPLE

102 miles and 4 hours. Find the rate and reduce to simplest form.

This can be written as $\dfrac{102 \text{ miles}}{4 \text{ hours}} = \dfrac{\overset{51}{\cancel{102}} \text{ miles}}{\underset{2}{\cancel{4}} \text{ hours}} = \dfrac{51 \text{ miles}}{2 \text{ hours}} = 51 \text{ miles:2 hours.}$

EXERCISE 8

Rates in Simplest Form

Directions: Write each rate in simplest form.

1. 450 cashews for 32 people

2. $145 earnings in 20 minutes

3. 54 miles in 2 hours

4. $150 for 4 people

5. 45 flowers for 3 children

6. total cost of $790 for 4 books

Answers are on page 563.

Meaning and Computation of a Unit Rate

A **unit rate** has a denominator of 1. Any ratio can be converted into a unit ratio by dividing the numerator by the denominator. Depending on how the unit rate is used, either mixed numbers or decimal numbers are appropriate for the numerical part of the unit rate.

EXAMPLE 1

Write 600 miles in 10 hours as a unit rate.

600 miles in 10 hours can be written as a unit rate.

$$\frac{600 \text{ miles}}{10 \text{ hours}} = \frac{60 \text{ miles}}{1 \text{ hour}} = 60 \frac{\text{miles}}{\text{hour}} = 60 \text{ miles per hour.}$$

EXAMPLE 2

Write $150 for 3 books as a unit rate.

$150 for 3 books can be written as a unit rate.

$$\frac{\$150}{3 \text{ books}} = \frac{\$50}{\text{book}} = \$50 \text{ per book.}$$

EXAMPLE 3

Write 200 miles to 10 hours as a unit rate.

200 miles to 10 hours can be written as a unit rate.

$$\frac{200 \text{ miles}}{10 \text{ hours}} = \frac{20 \text{ miles}}{1 \text{ hour}} = 20 \text{ miles per hour.}$$

EXAMPLE 4

Write 66 feet to 15 seconds as a unit rate with a mixed number.

$$\frac{66 \text{ feet}}{15 \text{ seconds}} = \frac{22 \text{ feet}}{5 \text{ seconds}} = 4\frac{2}{5} \text{ feet per second.}$$

EXAMPLE 5

Write 25 pounds to 4 boxes as a unit rate with a decimal number.

$$\frac{25 \text{ pounds}}{4 \text{ boxes}} = 6.25\frac{\text{pounds}}{\text{box}}$$

EXERCISE 9

Computation of Unit Rates

Directions: Determine the unit rate.

1. 574 houses and 14 blocks

2. 318 miles to 3 hours

3. 105 flowers to 4 children using a mixed number.

4. 110 mice and 26 cages rounded to the nearest one

5. 215 rooms and 6 floors with a decimal number

6. $117 and 2 books with a decimal number

Answers are on page 563.

Using the Equation Unit Rate × Quantity = Total

Unit rates can be used to find total quantities by using different versions of the following equation:

Total quantity = unit rate × number of items

Here are some examples with different names for the parts of the equation:

Distance = rate of speed × time

Earnings = hourly wage × hours worked

Total cost = unit cost × number of items bought

EXAMPLE 1

A train is traveling at 45 miles per hour for 6 hours. What is the distance traveled?

The rate is 45 miles per hour. The time is 6 hours.
Distance = rate of speed × time = $45 × 6 = 270$ miles.

EXAMPLE 2

A worker earns $12.58 per hour and works a 40-hour week. What is his pay for the week?

Earnings = hourly wage × hours worked = $12.58 × 40 = $503.20.

Therefore, the worker earns $503.20 in a 40-hour workweek.

EXAMPLE 3

A pound of organic tomatoes is $2.00 per pound. How much does $3\frac{3}{4}$ pounds cost?

Total cost = cost per pound × quantity in pounds = $2 × 3\frac{3}{4} = \cancel{2} × \frac{15}{\cancel{4}_2} = \frac{15}{2} = $7.50.

The total cost of the tomatoes is $7.50.

EXAMPLE 4

Fiona has 5 bags of apples with 25 apples in each bag. What is the total number of apples?

Total quantity = unit rate × number of items = $25 × 5 = 125$.

Therefore, Fiona has 125 apples in total.

EXERCISE 10

Using the Equation Unit Rate × Quantity = Total

Directions: Use unit rates to find the total quantities.

1. There are 25 students per classroom in a school that has 32 classrooms. What is the total number of students in the school?

2. The cost of strawberries is $3.99 per bucket. What is the cost of 5 buckets of strawberries?

3. Each dump truck contains 5.5 tons of sand. If there are 12 trucks, what is the total amount of sand contained in those trucks?

4. Find the distance traveled if a car is driven at 70 miles per hour for 4 hours.

5. A box contains 80 nails. Jeremy has 12 boxes of nails. How many nails does he have in all?

6. Jenna earns $10 per hour and works 25 hours per week. What is her total pay for the week?

7. Ryan has a can of paint that says it will cover 100 square feet. How many square feet can he cover with $7\frac{1}{2}$ cans of paint?

8. If Michael works for 12 hours per day for 7 days, how many hours did he work in all?

Answers are on page 563.

Understanding Proportions

When two pairs of numbers, such as 6, 4 and 3, 2, have the same ratio, they are said to be **proportional** or **in proportion**. A **proportion** is a statement that two ratios are equal. A proportion may be written in the form of fractions or with colons or may be written in words.

Means and Extremes

In the expression $\frac{a}{b} = \frac{c}{d}$, a and d are called **extremes** and b and c are called **means of the proportion**. If $\frac{a}{b} = \frac{c}{d}$, then $ad = bc$. Thus, in a proportion, product of means = product of extremes. For example, if $\frac{3}{4} = \frac{18}{24}$, $3(24) = 4(18)$, the means equal the extremes.

EXERCISE 11

Means and Extremes

Directions: Find the means and extremes of each proportion.

1. $\frac{1}{2} = \frac{4}{8}$

2. $\frac{7}{2} = \frac{14}{4}$

3. $\frac{9}{7} = \frac{36}{28}$

4. $\frac{5}{6} = \frac{40}{48}$

5. $\frac{5}{10} = \frac{2}{4}$

6. $\frac{9}{3} = \frac{18}{6}$

Answers are on page 563.

Determining Whether Two Quantities Are Proportional

Two quantities are proportional if and only if the product of extremes and the product of means are equal. Therefore, $\frac{a}{b} = \frac{c}{d}$ if and only if $ad = bc$. This is where the phrase "cross multiply" comes from: you are multiplying the terms that are across the equal sign.

EXAMPLE 1

Determine whether the number pairs 6, 15 and 3, 45 are proportional.

$a = 6$, $b = 15$, $c = 3$, and $d = 45$. Find the cross products.

$$\frac{6}{15} = \frac{3}{45}$$
$$6(45) = 3(15)$$
$$270 = 45$$

Since the cross products are not the same, the numbers are not proportional.

EXAMPLE 2

Determine whether the number pairs 9, 10 and 18, 20 are proportional.

$a = 9$, $b = 10$, $c = 18$, and $d = 20$. Find the cross products.

$$\frac{9}{10} = \frac{18}{20}$$
$$10(18) = 9(20)$$
$$180 = 180$$

Since the cross products are the same, the numbers are proportional.

EXERCISE 12

Deciding Whether Two Quantities Are in Proportional Relationships

Directions: Determine whether the two number pairs are proportional.

1. 2, 3 and 4, 6

2. 3, 15 and 30, 45

3. 1, 7 and 9, 63

4. 4.5, 0.3 and 1.5, 1

5. 5, 2 and 6, 3

6. 0.3, 0.5 and 1, 1.2

7. 3, 9 and 2, 6

8. 1, 2 and 7, 14

Answers are on page 563.

Solving Proportions with a Single Missing Value

You can use *cross multiplication* to solve proportions with a missing value.

EXAMPLE 1

Solve the proportion $\frac{x}{5} = \frac{14}{35}$.

$$\frac{x}{5} = \frac{14}{35}$$

$$x \cdot 35 = 5 \cdot 14$$

$$35x = 70$$

$$\frac{35x}{35} = \frac{70}{35}$$

$$x = 2$$

Thus, $x = 2$.

EXAMPLE 2

The ratio of girls to boys in a club is 5:6. If there are 20 girls, what is the total number of people in the club?

Let x = the number of boys. Set up the proportion:

$$\frac{\text{girls}}{\text{boys}} = \frac{\text{girls}}{\text{boys}}$$

$$\frac{5}{6} = \frac{20}{x}$$

$$5x = 6(20)$$

$$5x = 120$$

$$\frac{5x}{5} = \frac{120}{5}$$

$$x = 24$$

The number of boys is 24. So, the total number of people in the club is $20 + 24 = 44$.

EXAMPLE 3

A football team's win-loss ratio was 2:3. If the team lost 15 matches, how many did it win?

Let the number of wins be x.

$$\frac{2}{3} = \frac{x}{15}$$

$$2 \times 15 = x \times 3$$

$$30 = 3x$$

$$3x = 30$$

$$x = \frac{30}{3} = 10$$

Thus, the number of wins is 10.

Solving Proportions with a Single Missing Value

Directions: Find the missing numbers in the following proportions.

1. $\dfrac{2}{5} = \dfrac{7}{x}$

2. $\dfrac{3}{7} = \dfrac{x}{21}$

3. $\dfrac{4}{x} = \dfrac{36}{81}$

4. $\dfrac{0.3}{1.5} = \dfrac{1.2}{x}$

5. $\dfrac{8}{16} = \dfrac{x}{8}$

6. $\dfrac{x}{5} = \dfrac{20}{25}$

Directions: Answer the following questions.

7. An orchard has apricot trees and peach trees in the ratio 4:5. If there are 3,000 apricot trees, what is the number of peach trees?

8. A store ordered soaps and shampoos in the ratio 3:7. If the total number of soaps purchased is 4,500, what is the number of shampoos purchased?

9. The sports club has a girls-to-boys ratio of 5:6. If the team has 18 boys, what is the number of girls on the team?

10. A family bought vegetables and meat in the ratio 1:9. If they bought 81 pounds of meat, how many pounds of vegetables were bought?

Answers are on page 564.

Solving Proportions with More Than One Missing Value

To solve proportion problems with more than one missing value, you can use multiple proportions for finding each missing value and then use cross multiplication on each.

EXAMPLE 1

A store sells T-shirts in three colors: red, green, and yellow. The colors are in the ratio of 2:3:5. If the store has 30 red shirts, how many shirts does it have altogether?

Here, you have to find the number of green and yellow shirts.

Let the number of green shirts be *x* and the number of yellow shirts be *y*.

For the given question, you can find two proportions for each of the variables.

First proportion for variable *x*: $\dfrac{\text{red}}{\text{green}} = \dfrac{2}{3} = \dfrac{30}{x}$.

Second proportion for variable *y*: $\dfrac{\text{red}}{\text{yellow}} = \dfrac{2}{5} = \dfrac{30}{y}$.

Solve the first and second proportions using cross multiplication.

$$\frac{2}{3} = \frac{30}{x}$$

$$2 \cdot x = 3 \times 30$$

$$2x = 90$$

$$x = \frac{90}{2} = 45$$

$$\frac{2}{5} = \frac{30}{y}$$

$$2 \cdot y = 5 \times 30$$

$$2y = 150$$

$$y = \frac{150}{2} = 75$$

Thus, the total number of shirts = $30 + 45 + 75 = 150$.

EXAMPLE 2

A cereal mixture contains rice, wheat, and corn in the ratio 3:4:5. If one bag of the cereal contains 4 ounces of rice, what is the number of ounces of wheat and corn in the bag?

Here, you have to find the amount of wheat and corn in the bag.

Let the amount of wheat be x and the amount of corn be y.

For the given question, you can find two proportions for each of the variables.

First proportion for variable x: $\dfrac{\text{rice}}{\text{wheat}} = \dfrac{3}{4} = \dfrac{4}{x}$.

Second proportion for variable y: $\dfrac{\text{rice}}{\text{corn}} = \dfrac{3}{5} = \dfrac{4}{y}$.

Solve the first and second proportions using cross multiplication.

$$\frac{3}{4} = \frac{4}{x}$$

$$3 \cdot x = 4 \cdot 4$$

$$3x = 16$$

$$x = \frac{16}{3} = 5\frac{1}{3}$$

$$\frac{3}{5} = \frac{4}{y}$$

$$3 \cdot y = 5 \cdot 4$$

$$3y = 20$$

$$y = \frac{20}{3} = 6\frac{2}{3}$$

The total amount is $4 + 5\frac{1}{3} + 6\frac{2}{3} = 16$ ounces.

Solving Proportions with More Than One Missing Term

Directions: Find the missing terms.

1. If three numbers A:B:C are in the ratio 1:2:3 and A is given to be 45, find the other two numbers.

2. Kate has collected three types of flowers x, y, and z, in the ratio 5:6:7. If she has 21 flowers of z type, what are the numbers of flowers of the other two types?

3. The library has books of three different types in the ratio 4:5:6. If the number of books of the second type is 60, what are the numbers of the other two book types?

4. A store sold apples, oranges, and pineapples in the ratio 10:15:3. If the number of pineapples sold is 9, find the numbers of apples and oranges sold.

5. Amy scored marks in three subjects in the ratio 3:5:7. If her score in the first subject is 18, find the scores of the other two subjects.

Answers are on page 564.

Analyzing and Solving Real-World Problems

Ratios and proportions can be used to analyze and solve real-world problems.

EXAMPLE 1

Betty is planning a trip from San Marcos, Texas, to Zapata, Texas. On a map, she found the distance between the two cities to be 10 inches. If the scale on the map is 1 inch = 28 miles, what is the actual distance in miles between the two cities?

The scale given is 1 inch:28 miles. Set up a proportion:

$$\frac{1 \text{ inches}}{28 \text{ miles}} = \frac{10 \text{ inches}}{x \text{ miles}}$$
$$1 \cdot x = 10 \times 28$$
$$x = 280$$

The actual distance between the two cities is 280 miles.

EXAMPLE 2

The scale on a map is $\frac{1}{4}$ inch = 15 miles. If the distance between two cities on the map is 8 inches, what is the actual distance between the two cities?

The scale given is $\frac{1}{4}$ inch:15 miles. Set up a proportion.

$$\frac{\frac{1}{4} \text{ inches}}{15 \text{ miles}} = \frac{8 \text{ inches}}{x \text{ miles}}$$

$$\frac{1}{4} \cdot x = 8 \times 15$$

$$x = 120 \times 4$$

$$x = 480$$

The actual distance between the two cities is 480 miles.

EXAMPLE 3

The blueprint of a house has a scale of 2 inches = 5 feet. Find the actual height of the house if the height of the house given on the blueprint is 10 inches.

The ratio of inches to feet given in the blueprint is 2:5. Call the actual height of the house x feet.

$$\frac{2 \text{ inches}}{5 \text{ feet}} = \frac{10 \text{ inches}}{x \text{ feet}}$$

$$2 \cdot x = 10 \cdot 5$$

$$2x = 50$$

$$x = \frac{50}{2} = 25$$

The actual height of the house is 25 feet.

EXAMPLE 4

Harry went hiking for 2 days. For how many hours did he go hiking?

You know that 1 day = 24 hours. Call the number of hours Harry went hiking x.

$$\frac{1 \text{ day}}{24 \text{ hours}} = \frac{2 \text{ days}}{x \text{ hours}}$$

$$1x = 2(24)$$

$$x = 48$$

Harry went hiking for 48 hours.

EXAMPLE 5

Mr. Ivan used 60 cups of water to feed his chickens. How many gallons of water did he use?

1 gallon = 16 cups. Call the number of gallons used x.

$$\frac{1 \text{ gallon}}{16 \text{ cups}} = \frac{x \text{ gallon}}{60 \text{ cups}}$$

$$1 \cdot 60 = x \cdot 16$$

$$60 = 16x$$

$$\frac{16x}{16} = \frac{60}{16}$$

$$x = \frac{\overset{15}{\cancel{60}}}{\underset{4}{\cancel{16}}} = \frac{15}{4} = 3\frac{3}{4}$$

Mr. Ivan used $3\frac{3}{4}$ gallons of water to feed his chickens.

EXERCISE 15

Analyzing and Solving Real-World Problems

Directions: Solve the following problems.

1. A concrete mix is made up of 3 parts cement, 3 parts sand, and 6 parts gravel. If 12 kilograms of cement is used, how much sand and gravel are needed?

2. Tom is 70 inches tall. Find his height in feet. (Hint: 1 foot = 12 inches.)

3. If your cousins are going to take a 4-week vacation, how many days will they be gone? (Hint: 1 week = 7 days.)

4. A cake recipe calls for $\frac{1}{3}$ cup of sugar. How much sugar is needed for 5 cakes?

5. A recipe for a gallon of punch requires $\frac{2}{3}$ cup of lime juice. How much lime juice is needed for $\frac{1}{2}$ gallon of punch?

6. A concrete mix has 1 part cement and 2 parts sand. If 5 kilograms of cement is used, how much sand is needed?

7. If the scale on a map is 1 inch = 150 miles, what is the actual distance between two locations that are 4 inches apart on the map?

8. The height of a window on a scale drawing is 2 inches. If the scale is 1 inch = 3 feet, what is the actual height of the window?

9. If the length of a boat on a scale drawing is 4 centimeters, what is the actual length of the boat? (Scale: 1 centimeter = 2 meters.)

10. On a map, 1 inch represents 200 miles. If the distance between two cities is 5,000 miles, what is the distance between the two cities on the map?

Answers are on page 564.

CHAPTER 6

Percents

Percents are everywhere. Changes in population and other quantities are given as percents. Tax rates are expressed as percents. Businesses offer discounts in terms of percents. In this chapter you will learn about conversions, uses, and applications of percents.

Understanding Percents

Like a decimal or a fraction, a percent (%) represents some part of a whole. *Percent* means "per 100," and 100% represents whole or all. Percent is used to express rates of interest, proportions, etc. If a student scores 100 out of a total of 100 marks, his score is 100%. If he scores 50 out of 100, then his score is 50%. Similarly, 20% means 20 out of 100, so when 20% of students have computers, that means that 20 out of 100 students have computers.

Converting Percents

To solve problems, you may need to convert percents to fractions or decimals and vice versa. Since *percent* means "per 100," a percent should be divided by 100 to get a purely numerical equivalent. So 30% means $\frac{30}{100}$, or $\frac{3}{10}$ or 0.3, and 100% means $\frac{100}{100}$ or 1 (100% of any number is the number itself). Two hundred percent means $\frac{200}{100}$ or 2 (200% of any number is twice the number) and similarly 300% is $\frac{300}{100}$ or 3 (300% of any number is three times the number). Dividing by 100 is the same as multiplying by $\frac{1}{100}$ or multiplying by 0.01. For example, $13\% = 13 \times \frac{1}{100} = \frac{13}{100}$ or $13\% = 13 \times 0.01 = 0.13$. The following methods can be used for conversion:

Percent to Fraction

To change a percent to a fraction, remove the percent sign and write the percent over 100. This has the effect of multiplying by $\frac{1}{100}$. Reduce if possible.

EXAMPLES

1. $41\% = \frac{41}{100}$

2. $20.5\% = \frac{20.5}{100} = \frac{20.5}{100} \times \frac{10}{10} = \frac{205}{1,000} = \frac{41}{200}$

3. $10\% = \dfrac{10}{100} = \dfrac{1}{10}$

4. $83\dfrac{1}{3}\% = \dfrac{83\frac{1}{3}}{100} = \dfrac{\frac{250}{3}}{\frac{100}{1}} = \dfrac{250}{3} \times \dfrac{1}{100} = \dfrac{5}{3} \times \dfrac{1}{2} = \dfrac{5}{6}$

Percent to Decimal

To change a percent to a decimal, remove the percent sign and multiply by 0.01 (as given above, percent means multiplying by 0.01). Multiplying by 0.01 moves the decimal point two places to the left.

EXAMPLES

1. $19.7\% = 19.7 \times 0.01 = 0.197$

2. $3\% = 3 \times 0.01 = 0.03$

3. $0.05\% = 0.05 \times 0.01 = 0.0005$

4. $213\% = 213 \times 0.01 = 2.13$

Fraction to Percent

To change a fraction to a percent, multiply the fraction by $\dfrac{100}{1}$ and attach the percent sign.

EXAMPLES

1. $\dfrac{1}{5} = \left(\dfrac{1}{5} \times \dfrac{100}{1}\right)\% = 20\%$

2. $\dfrac{2}{3} = \left(\dfrac{2}{3} \times \dfrac{100}{1}\right)\% = 66\dfrac{2}{3}\%$

3. $1 = \left(1 \times \dfrac{100}{1}\right)\% = 100\%$

4. $1\dfrac{3}{4} = \left(\dfrac{7}{4} \times \dfrac{100}{1}\right)\% = 175\%$

Decimal to Percent

To change a decimal to a percent, multiply the decimal by 100 and attach the percent sign. Multiplying the decimal by 100 moves the decimal point two places to the right.

EXAMPLES

1. $0.29 = (0.29 \times 100)\% = 29\%$

2. $0.015 = (0.015 \times 100)\% = 1.5\%$

3. $4.1 = (4.1 \times 100)\% = 410\%$

4. $12 = (12 \times 100)\% = 1,200\%$

EXERCISE 1

Converting Percents

Directions: Carry out the indicated conversions.

Convert to a fraction. Reduce to lowest terms.

1. 80%

2. 125%

3. $12\frac{1}{2}$%

4. $16\frac{2}{3}$%

Convert to a decimal.

5. 39.2%

6. 1.38%

7. 150%

8. 0.002%

Convert to a percent.

9. $\frac{2}{5}$

10. 65.25

11. 0.32

12. $\frac{3}{8}$

13. $\frac{5}{6}$

14. $6\frac{5}{12}$

15. 400

16. 0.0075

Answers are on page 564.

Solving Percent Problems

Solving Percent Problems Using a Proportion

A percent problem can be solved by creating a proportion describing how the relationship between the part and the whole is the same as the relationship of the percent to 100. In the language of proportions, the part is to the whole as the percent is to 100. The proportion below shows how to set up a problem:

$$\frac{\text{Part}}{\text{Whole}} = \frac{\text{Percent}}{100}$$

A key to solving any percent problem is identifying the part, the whole, and the percent. The *percent* is the quantity that comes right before the word "percent" or the percent symbol, the *whole* is the quantity that comes immediately after the phrase "percent of," and the *part* is the quantity that comes on the opposite side of the word "was" or "is." For example, think about the statement "25% of 80 is 20." The number

20 is the part, 80 is the whole, and 25 is the percent. The numbers can be set up in a proportion format:

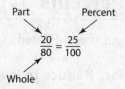

Part   Percent

$$\frac{20}{80} = \frac{25}{100}$$

Whole

Use the following steps to solve percent problems:

1. Determine which of the part, the whole, and the percent are known values and which is the missing value. Label the missing value with N.

2. Depending on the problem, you may need to do the following:

   2a. If the whole and the percent are known and the part is missing, then set up the proportion $\frac{N}{\text{Whole}} = \frac{\text{Percent}}{100}$, and solve for N.

   2b. If the part and the percent are known and the whole is missing, then set up the proportion $\frac{\text{Part}}{N} = \frac{\text{Percent}}{100}$, and solve for N.

   2c. If the part and the whole are given and the percent is missing, then set up the proportion $\frac{\text{Part}}{\text{Whole}} = \frac{N}{100}$, and solve for N.

3. To solve for N, cross multiply and divide both sides of the equation by the number multiplying N.

EXAMPLE 1

What is 30% of 150?

Here you are looking for the part, given a whole of 150 and a percent of 30. Set up the proportion:

$$\frac{N}{150} = \frac{30}{100}$$

$N \times 100 = 30 \times 150$ (cross multiply)

$$N = \frac{30 \times 150}{100} = 45$$

Therefore, 30% of 150 is 45.

EXAMPLE 2

15 is what percent of 75?

You are looking for the percent, given a whole of 75 and a part of 15. Set up the proportion:

$$\frac{15}{75} = \frac{N}{100}$$

$N \times 75 = 15 \times 100$ (cross multiply)

$$N = \frac{15 \times 100}{75} = 20$$

Therefore, 15 is 20% of 75.

EXAMPLE 3

49 is 140% of what number?

You are looking for the whole, given a part of 49 and a percent of 140. Set up the proportion:

$$\frac{49}{N} = \frac{140}{100}$$

$N \times 140 = 49 \times 100$ (cross multiply)

$$N = \frac{49 \times 100}{140} = 35$$

Therefore, 49 is 140% of 35. Notice here that the part (49) is larger than the whole (35). This is because the percent is 140%, which is more than 100%.

EXAMPLE 4

A clothing store owner buys jackets for $80 each from the factory. He puts a 30% markup on each jacket for his customers. Find the amount of the markup.

Here, $80 is the whole, 30% is the percent, and you are looking for the part. Set up the proportion:

$$\frac{N}{80} = \frac{30}{100}$$

$N \times 100 = 80 \times 30$ (cross multiply)

$$N = \frac{80 \times 30}{100} = 24$$

The markup amount is $24.

EXAMPLE 5

Amy makes $500 a week. She pays $80 a week for food. The food budget is what percent of Amy's income?

$80 is the part and $500 is the whole. You are looking for the percent. Set up the proportion:

$$\frac{80}{500} = \frac{N}{100}$$

$N \times 500 = 80 \times 100$ (cross multiply)

$$N = \frac{80 \times 100}{500} = 16$$

Amy spends 16% of her income on food.

EXAMPLE 6

Jack got a 5% commission for selling a product. His commission was $120. Find the selling price of the product.

Here, 5% is the percent, $120 is the part, and you are looking for the whole. Set up the proportion:

$$\frac{120}{N} = \frac{5}{100}$$

$N \times 5 = 120 \times 100$ (cross multiply)

$$N = \frac{120 \times 100}{5} = 2{,}400$$

The selling price of the product is $2,400.

EXERCISE 2

Solving Percent Problems Using a Proportion

Directions: Answer the following questions.

1. Find 5% of 35.

2. Find 150% of 50.

3. 6 is 1.5% of what number?

4. 245 is what percent of 700?

5. 15% of what number is 18?

6. What percent of 350 is 122.5?

Answers are on page 564.

Solving Percent Problems Using Percent × Whole = Part

Percent problems can be solved using the equation Percent × Whole = Part. This formula can be used in three different ways: to find the part when the percent and the whole are known; to find the whole when the percent and the part are known; or to find the percent when the whole and the part are known. In the first two cases the percent is known, and must be converted to a decimal or fraction to be used in the equation. In the last case the percent is unknown and must be converted to a percent after using the equation.

Missing Part

If the percent and the whole are known and the part is missing, then solving the equation is a matter of carrying out a calculation.

EXAMPLE 1

Find 20% of 140.

Here, 20% is the percent, 140 is the whole, and you are looking for the part. Convert 20% to 0.20 and write the equation $0.20 \times 140 =$ Part. This equation simplifies to $28 =$ Part. Therefore, 20% of 140 is 28.

EXAMPLE 2

Tom wants to buy a house for $12,900. He plans to make a down payment of 8%. How much is the down payment?

The down payment is 8% of the price of the house, so the price of the house is the whole and you are looking for the part. Convert 8% to 0.08 and write the equation 0.08 × 12,900 = Part. Simplifying gives 1,032 = Part. Therefore, the down payment is $1,032.

Missing Whole

If the percent and the part are known and the whole is missing, then using the equation Percent × Whole = Part will include solving the equation for Whole by dividing both sides of the equal sign by Percent.

EXAMPLE 1

100 is 40% of what number?

Here, 100 is the part, 40% is the percent, and you are looking for the whole. Convert 40% to 0.40 and write the equation 0.40 × Whole = 100. To find the whole, divide both sides of the equal sign by 0.40:

$$0.40 \times \text{Whole} = 100$$

$$\frac{0.40 \times \text{Whole}}{0.40} = \frac{100}{0.40}$$

$$\frac{0.40 \times \text{Whole}}{0.40} = \frac{1,000}{4}$$

$$\text{Whole} = 250$$

(Note: To eliminate the decimal from the denominator, multiply both the numerator and the denominator by 10.) Whole is 250. Therefore, 100 is 40% of 250.

EXAMPLE 2

Eighteen students came to Ms. Paul's math class. This was 75% of the students registered for the class. How many students were registered for the class?

Here, the part is 18, the percent is 75%, and you are looking for the whole. Convert 75% to 0.75 and write the equation 0.75 × Whole = 18. To find the whole, divide both sides of the equal sign by 0.75:

$$0.75 \times \text{Whole} = 18$$

$$\frac{0.75 \times \text{Whole}}{0.75} = \frac{18}{0.75}$$

$$\frac{0.75 \times \text{Whole}}{0.75} = \frac{1,800}{75}$$

$$\text{Whole} = 24$$

Whole is 24. Therefore, 18 is 75% of 24, and there were 24 students registered for the class.

Missing Percent

If the part and the whole are known and the percent is missing, then using the equation Percent × Whole = Part will include solving for percent by dividing both sides of the equal sign by Whole. After solving the equation, the result will need to be converted into a percent.

EXAMPLE 1

175 is what percent of 700?

Here, 175 is the part, 700 is the whole, and you are looking for the percent. Write the equation Percent × 700 = 175. To find the percent, divide both sides of the equal sign by the whole:

$$\text{Percent} \times 700 = 175$$

$$\frac{\text{Percent} \times 700}{700} = \frac{175}{700}$$

$$\frac{\text{Percent} \times \cancel{700}}{\cancel{700}} = \frac{175}{700}$$

$$\text{Percent} = 0.25$$

The result, 0.25, needs to be converted to a percent. Move the decimal point two places to the right to get 25%. Percent is 0.25. Therefore, 175 is 25% of 700.

EXAMPLE 2

There were 70 trees in a garden. Due to a storm, 14 trees fell. What percent of trees are still standing?

Here, the whole is 70, the part is 14, and you are looking for the percent. Write the equation Percent × 70 = 14. To find the percent, divide both sides of the equal sign by the whole:

$$\text{Percent} \times 70 = 14$$

$$\frac{\text{Percent} \times 70}{70} = \frac{14}{700}$$

$$\frac{\text{Percent} \times \cancel{70}}{\cancel{70}} = \frac{14}{70}$$

$$\text{Percent} = 0.20$$

The result, 0.20, needs to be converted to a percent. Move the decimal point two places to the right to get 20%. Percent is 0.20. Therefore, 14 is 20% of 70, and the number of trees that fell was 14. Subtract 14 from 70 to get the number of trees still standing: 70 − 14 = 56. There are 56 trees still standing.

EXERCISE 3

Solving Percent Problems Using Percent × Whole = Part

Directions: Answer the following questions.

1. Find 25% of 96.

2. 15 is 20% of what number?

3. What percent of 68 is 34?

4. Find 12.5% of 40 kilograms.

5. 60 is what percent of 75?

6. A survey of 500 children showed that 25% liked playing baseball. How many children liked playing baseball?

7. A local soccer club played 20 matches in one season. It won 25% of them. How many matches did it win?

8. Harry took his family out to a restaurant. The bill was $40. He left the waiter a tip of $6. The tip was what percent of the bill?

Answers are on page 564.

Percent Increase or Decrease

The previous example, where 14 out of 70 trees were lost in a storm, is a problem of *percent decrease*. Had the problem been stated in terms of 14 additional trees being planted, the problem would have been one of *percent increase*. There are two main things to keep in mind when working problems of percent increase or decrease:

1. The whole is the original value before the increase or decrease.

2. The part is the actual increase or decrease.

EXAMPLE 1

In a few months the price of heating oil increased from $1.20 a gallon to $1.80 a gallon. By what percent did the price increase?

Original price = $1.20, new price = $1.80. Therefore, the increase in price = $1.80 − $1.20 = $0.60. Use Whole = 1.20 and Part = 0.60 and find Percent.

$$\text{Percent} \times 1.20 = 0.60$$

$$\frac{\text{Percent} \times 1.20}{1.20} = \frac{0.60}{1.20}$$

$$\frac{\text{Percent} \times \cancel{1.20}}{\cancel{1.20}} = \frac{6}{12}$$

$$\text{Percent} = \frac{1}{2} = 0.50$$

Percent = 0.50, so the price increased 50%.

EXAMPLE 2

The population of a small town last year was 2,500. Due to an oil boom, the population this year is greater by 20%. Find the population this year.

Original population = 2,500, percent increase = 20%. Use Whole = 2,500 and Percent = 0.20. The part will be the actual increase in population, which will be added to the original population of the town to get the new population.

$$0.20 \times 2,500 = \text{Part}$$

$$0.20 \times 2,500 = \text{Part}$$

$$500 = \text{Part}$$

Part = population increase = 500. Adding the increase to the town's original population gives the new population: 500 + 2,500 = 3,000. The new population is 3,000. Percent increase and decrease problems often include a step with addition or subtraction. The next example shows that there may need to be an addition or subtraction of percents.

EXAMPLE 3

Johnny went on a diet last year. He lost 6% of his weight, and this year he weighs 188 pounds. How much did Johnny originally weigh?

Here, the equation Percent × Whole = Part has to be used with care. Since the original weight, the whole, is not available, the actual decrease in weight, the part, cannot be computed. On the other hand, if Johnny lost 6% of his weight, then he still has 100% − 6% = 94% of his weight, which is 188 pounds. Use Percent = 0.94 and Part = 188 to find Whole, Johnny's original weight:

$$0.94 \times \text{Whole} = 188$$

$$\frac{0.94 \times \text{Whole}}{0.94} = \frac{188}{0.94}$$

$$\frac{\cancel{0.94} \times \text{Whole}}{\cancel{0.94}} = \frac{18,800}{94}$$

$$\text{Whole} = 200$$

Johnny originally weighed 200 pounds.

EXERCISE 4

Percent Increase or Decrease

Directions: Answer the following questions.

1. The enrollment in a school increased by 12% from the year 2010 to 2011. If 1,500 enrolled in 2010, what was the enrolment in 2011?

2. This year the profit of a company was 15% higher than last year. This year the profit was $17,480. What was it last year?

3. Michael bought an old car and spent an additional 20% of the cost on repairs. If the total cost including repairs was $12,000, at what price did he buy the car?

4. Christopher's income is 20% more than Joseph's income. Joseph's income is what percent less than Christopher's income? (*Hint:* Make up a convenient value for someone's income.)

5. Carol bought stock for $28 per share. In three months, it rose to $49 per share. Find the percent of increase of the stock.

6. A college's enrollment dropped from 9,152 to 3,520 over the course of 10 years. What is the percent of decrease in enrollment? Round to the nearest whole percent.

7. At 8 years of age, George was 4'2" tall. At 14, he is 5'5". Find the percent of increase in George's height.

8. Alex bought a used car for $8,200. He drove it for six years, then sold it for $1,400. By what percent did the value of the car decrease? Round to the nearest whole percent.

Answers are on page 565.

Serial Increase or Decrease

The term *serial* means "following one after the other." In serial percent problems you find a percent of a number, calculate a new amount, and then find a percent of the new amount.

For example, suppose you are buying an item on sale. To know the sale price of the item, you calculate the discount and subtract the discount from the original price. Then, to know the final price, you calculate any sales tax based on the sale price and add the sales tax to the sale price.

EXAMPLE 1

A silk tie originally costs $50. It is on sale for 10% off. What is the sale price of the silk tie in a state where the sales tax is 5%?

First find the discount. Discount = 10% of $50 = 0.10 × $50 = $5.

Then find the sale price. Sale price = $50 − $5 = $45.

Find the sales tax by calculating 5% of $45 = 0.05 × $45 = $2.25.

Add the sales tax to the sale price: $45 + $2.25 = $47.25.

The sale price including tax is $47.25.

(Note: In this example, the sales tax is calculated on the sale price $45, not the original price.)

EXAMPLE 2

A laptop was originally listed at $280. For a Christmas sale, a store offered a 10% discount on all electronics. The store offered an additional 5% discount on all items for paying in cash. How much did a buyer pay if he purchased the laptop on sale and paid in cash?

The 10% sale discount and additional 5% cash discount are not both based on the list price, so you cannot add the percents. Find the sale discount first: 10% of $280 = 0.10 × $280 = $28, so the sale price is $280 − $28 = $252. The 5% cash discount is based on $252. Find the cash discount next: 5% of $252 = 0.05 × $252 = $12.60, so after the cash discount, the buyer paid $252 − $12.60 = $239.40.

EXERCISE 5

Serial Increase or Decrease

Directions: Answer the following questions.

1. A total of 30% of 2,000 employees of a company belong to a union. Of these union members, 25% voted in favor of a strike. How many union members at the company did not vote to strike?

2. Nancy's gross salary is $2,500 a month. Her employer withholds 10% for federal tax, 5% for social security, and 5% for state tax. Find her net salary for the month.

3. A farm with a market value of $150,000 was assessed for 65% of its market value. The farm is taxed at 3% of the assessed value. Find the tax on the farm.

4. Peter buys a bicycle at a cost of $600 and sells it at a 6% discount to Mike. Mike sells it at a 3% markup to Sarah. Find the price that Sarah paid Mike.

5. The value of a machine decreases by 13% every year. Brian bought the machine yesterday for $20,000. What will be its value after two years?

6. A gym reduces its regular fee by 10% for senior citizens. It also takes 5% off of a member's fee for members who pay before the 15th of the month. If the regular fee is $15, what is the reduced fee for a senior citizen who pays before the 15th?

Answers are on page 565.

Probability and Statistics

Probability is the extent to which an event is likely to occur. Statistics is about collecting and analyzing numerical data in large quantities. Together, they bring to mathematics techniques that are used to deal with uncertainty.

Basics of Statistics

Data are facts or information from which conclusions may be drawn. Data can be values, measurements, observations, or even just descriptions of things. Data can be collected from sources or by conducting observations, surveys, or experiments. Data can be categorized as shown in the following figure.

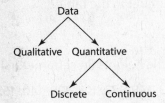

Qualitative data are the descriptive information collected.

Quantitative data are concerned with the numerical information.

Discrete data contain only certain values such as whole numbers.

Continuous data can take any value within a certain range.

Depending on the **source**, data can be divided into *primary data* and *secondary data*. Some typical data sources are as follows:

1. Information about the age groups of the people living in a country at a particular time.

2. Information about the age of the workers in a factory as well as their monthly wages.

3. Information about the maximum and minimum temperatures of a city during a certain period of time.

Data Representation and Creation

After being collected, data need to be displayed. One way to display data is in a table. A **table** uses rows and columns to present the data.

EXAMPLE 1

Use the table to answer the following questions.

Section	Students
A	39
B	25
C	15
D	33
E	19
F	21

Which section has the least number of students?

The answer is Section C; the total number of students in the section is 15, which is the lowest number in the table.

Which section has the greatest number of students?

The answer is Section A; the total number of students in the section is 39, which is the greatest number in the table.

EXAMPLE 2

Below are the heights (in centimeters) of 11 boys of a class:

146, 143, 148, 132, 128, 139, 140, 152, 154, 142, 149

Arrange the above data in an order and find the following: (a) the height of the tallest boy, and (b) the height of the shortest boy.

Arranging the data in ascending order, you get: 128, 132, 139, 140, 142, 143, 146, 148, 149, 152, 154.

(a) The height of the tallest boy = 154 centimeters, and (b) the height of the shortest boy = 128 centimeters.

A **bar chart** or graph is a good way for showing comparisons. A bar graph is a pictorial representation of numerical data. Bar graphs may be drawn horizontally or vertically.

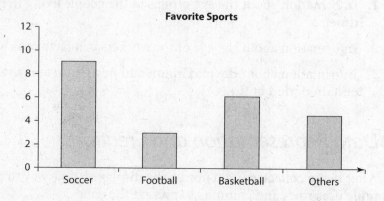

A **histogram** is similar to a bar graph, but there is no space between the bars and it is used for continuous class intervals.

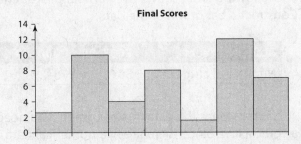

A **line graph** is often used to show a change over time as well as to indicate a pattern or trend.

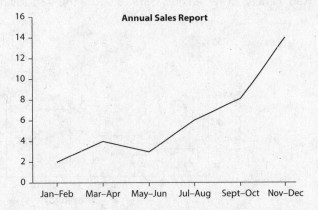

A **pie chart**, also called a circle graph, is used to show the percent of a quantity in each of several different categories.

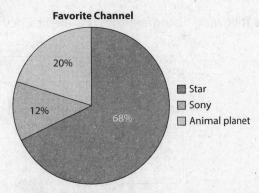

A **pictograph** is a type of graph that uses pictorial symbols.

EXAMPLE 3

The following table shows the number of students in a particular class by year. Construct a bar graph of the data.

Academic Years	2007–08	2008–09	2009–10	2010–11	2011–12
Number of students	50	75	125	150	200

To represent the data in a bar graph, you need to first draw a horizontal line and a vertical line. Since there are five numerical data, mark five points on the horizontal line at equal distances. Next, you scale the vertical axis. Look over the data and note that the numbers range from 50 to 200. Start the vertical scale at 0, labeling marks by 50. Finally, draw vertical bars to show the various numbers of students, as shown.

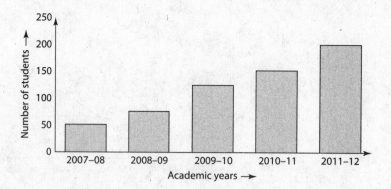

EXAMPLE 4

The following histogram shows the efficiency level (in miles per gallons) of 110 cars.

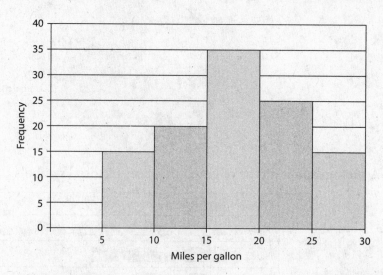

a. How many cars have efficiency between 20 and 25 miles per gallon?

In the histogram, the height of the rectangle between 20 and 25 is 25.

b. How many cars have efficiency greater than 15 miles per gallon?

In the histogram, cars with efficiency above 15 miles per gallon are ranging from 15 to 30.

15 to 20 range has 35 cars.

20 to 25 range has 25 cars.

25 to 30 range has 15 cars.

The total number of cars above 15 miles per gallon is $35 + 25 + 15 = 75$ cars.

c. What percent of cars has efficiency less than 25 miles per gallon?

You know the total number of cars is 110. The total number of cars with efficiency less than 25 miles per gallon is $15 + 20 + 35 + 25 = 95$. The percent of the cars below the efficiency of 25 miles per gallon is $\dfrac{95}{110} = 0.864 = 86.4\%$.

EXAMPLE 5

The following table shows declining membership totals at a local gym. Create a line graph of the data.

Month	Membership
January	68
March	63
May	60
July	58
September	55
November	50

EXAMPLE 6

The following table shows the goals made by five countries in a soccer competition. Create a pie chart of the data.

Country	Goals Made
Brazil	16
Portugal	8
Germany	12
Argentina	18
Spain	11

Goals

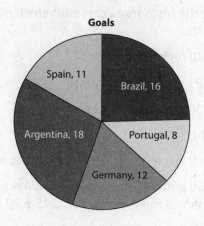

EXAMPLE 7

The following table shows the number of ice cream bars sold by five students in a class. Create a pictograph from the data.

Name	Ice Cream Bars Sold
Peter	8
Stuart	5
Ryan	2
David	4
Thomas	7

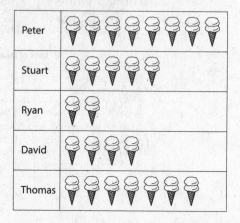

EXERCISE 1

Basics of Statistics

Directions: Answer the following questions.

1. The final grades of a group of 20 students are: 23, 75, 56, 42, 70, 84, 12, 61, 40, 63, 87, 58, 35, 80, 14, 63, 49, 72, 66, 61. What are the lowest and highest grades?

2. Create a bar graph with the data in the table. Then answer the questions based on the graph.

Student's Test Scores

Subject	Score
English	80
Debate	55
Math	73
Social Science	46
Science	68

    a) In which subjects did the student score higher than 70?
    b) In which subjects did the student score lower than 65?

3. The following chart shows the results of a survey of the favorite food items of 100 students. Create a pie chart of the data.

Favorite Food Items

Food Item	Votes
Cake	32
Bread	5
Burger	15
Hot dog	22
Cookies	26

4. Students' scores on a 25-point quiz are 12, 16, 18, 17, 24, 19, 22, 13, 21, 16, 21, 9, 23, 16, 23, 22, 7, and 24. Create a histogram for the class using the intervals 0–5, 5–10, 10–15, 15–20, and 20–25; then answer the following questions.
    a) What is the highest score on the quiz?
    b) How many scores are in the 10–15 range?

5. Create a line graph using the data in the table. Then answer the following questions based on the graph created.

Number of Employees

Year	Employees
1994	30
1995	50
1996	60
1997	50
1998	80
1999	80
2000	60

    a) In which consecutive pair of years was the number of employees the same?
    b) Between which two years was the difference between the numbers of employees the greatest?

6. Look at the picture depicting the balls sold by a seller in a day. Answer the following questions after studying the picture.

Type of Ball	Number of Balls
Football	⚽ ⚽ ⚽ ⚽ ⚽
Basketball	🏀 🏀 🏀
Tennis ball	🎾 🎾 🎾 🎾
Volleyball	🏐
Baseball	

a) How many balls were sold by the seller in total?
b) How many footballs were sold by the seller?
c) How many baseballs were sold by the seller?

Answers are on page 565.

Measures of Central Tendency for Data Sets

A **statistic** is a number describing a set of data. One such statistic is the **measure of central tendency**. The most common kind of center point is the **mean**.

Mean

The mean (or average) is the sum of all the data points divided by the number of items of data.

$$\text{Mean} = \frac{\text{Sum of all the observations}}{\text{Total number of observations}}$$

EXAMPLE 1

Joseph earned 10, 36, 95, 40, and 92 on quizzes. What was his average?

$$\text{Mean} = \frac{10+36+95+40+92}{5} = \frac{273}{5} = 54.6$$

In a **weighted mean**, more importance or weight is assigned to some values than other values

EXAMPLE 2

The grades in a science class are computed as shown below.

	Weight for Grade
Quizzes	20%
Homework	10%
Tests	50%
Exam	20%

Nicola has scored 70% on quizzes, 100% on homework, 87% on tests, and 92% on the exam. What is her average?

Because each category is weighted differently you must multiply each percentage by its weight, add the results, and divide by the total of the weights.

$$\frac{70(20)+100(10)+87(50)+92(20)}{100} = \frac{8,590}{100} = 85.9 = 86\%$$

Median

The **median** is useful when you want to de-emphasize unusually extreme numbers in a data set. Once a data set is listed in order, from smallest to largest, the **median** is the middle number if there is an odd number of data items. If there is an even number of data items, the median is the number that is the average of the two middle numbers.

EXAMPLE 1

Find the median of 9, 3, 44, 17, and 15.

List the numbers least to greatest: 3, 9, 15, 17, 44.

There is an odd number of data items. The median is the number exactly in the middle. The median is 15.

EXAMPLE 2

Calculate the median of 8, 3, 44, 17, 12, and 6.

List the numbers least to greatest: 3, 6, 8, 12, 17, 44.

There is an even number of data items. The median is the average of the middle two data points.

$$\frac{8+12}{2} = \frac{20}{2} = 10$$

The median is 10.

Mode

The **mode** is the value of the observation that occurs most frequently.

EXAMPLE

What is the mode of 9, 3, 3, 44, 17, 17, 44, 15, 15, 15, 27, 40, and 8?

Arrange the numbers in order: 3, 3, 8, 9, 15, 15, 15, 17, 17, 27, 40, 44, 44.

The mode is 15 because it occurs the most times.

If there is no value that occurs most frequently, or if there is more than one value that occurs most frequently, then the mode does not exist.

EXERCISE 2

Measures of Central Tendency for Data Sets

Directions: Calculate the measures of central tendency.

1. Find the mean of the following data.
   a) 19, 5, 9, 12, 10, 5
   b) 22, 2, 5, 12, 9
   c) 3, 12, 18, 7, 6, 12, 12
   d) 2, 3, 5, 9, 6
   e) 4, 7, 5, 3, 6
   f) 6, 2, 8, 3, 1
   g) 8, 6, 4, 7, 5
   h) 2, 9, 4, 1, 6, 8, 5
   i) 14, 15, 16, 14, 29, 8, 16
   j) 3, 2, 10, 19, 3, 2, 3

2. Find the median of the following data.
   a) 1, 14, 18
   b) 18, 8, 28, 9, 6, 9, 27
   c) 29, 19, 1, 26, 11, 29, 25
   d) 24, 6, 7, 2, 11
   e) 14, 27, 28, 2, 9
   f) 11, 20, 16, 23, 1, 23, 11
   g) 1, 10, 1, 12, 1
   h) 21, 18, 30, 16, 30
   i) 25, 10, 25, −1, 5, 25, 2
   j) 2, 0, 13, 3, 13, 11, 7

3. Find the mode of the following data.
   a) 4, 22, 4, 28, 17, 28, 23
   b) 27, 14, 23, 8, 4, 30, 20
   c) 20, 16, 7, 21, 6, 20, 1
   d) 11, 26, 10, 12, 11
   e) 13, 4, 28, 6, 16, 29, 23
   f) 15, 1, 8, 3, 3, 14, 26
   g) 24, 29, 22, 22, 18, 28, 25
   h) 18, 14, 16
   i) 20, 2, 21, 7, 20, 7, 14
   j) 30, 21, 25, 19, 25

4. Find the mean, median, and mode of the following data.
   a) 1, 39, 48, 52, 46, 62, 54, 40, 96, 52, 98, 40, 42, 52, 60
   b) 2, 8, 2, 1, 2
   c) 7, 2, 9, 5, 2
   d) 9, 7, 5, 6, 7, 5, 3, 5, 7
   e) 3, 7, 5, 1, 3, 6, 1, 7, 3
   f) 8, 3, 7, 5, 3, 4

5. The following table shows the numbers of students who earned various scores on a recent test. Calculate the weighted mean average test score.

Test Score	Number of Students Earning the Score
90	4
89	6
79	4
60	3
55	2
49	1

Answers are on page 566.

Probability

In day-to-day life, when something is likely to happen, people say that there is a *probability* that it will happen. "There is a probability that it will rain today." "There is a probability that he may be right."

The **probability of an event** is a measure of the likelihood that the event will occur. It is a number between 0 and 1, inclusive. When you perform a probability experiment, the different possible results are called **outcomes**. An **event** consists of a collection of outcomes. For example, in the roll of a six-sided number cube, an "even roll" consists of the outcomes 2, 4, and 6.

Counting

If there are three roads from Albany to Swanton and two roads from Swanton to Wauseon, in how many ways can you travel from Albany to Wauseon by way of Swanton? You can determine this answer by using the fundamental principle of counting. The **fundamental principle of counting** says that if one event can occur in m ways and a second event can occur in n ways, then both events can occur in mn ways, provided the outcome of the first event does not influence the outcome of the second event.

EXAMPLE 1

How many ways can you travel from Albany to Wauseon by way of Swanton?

There are three ways to get from Albany to Swanton. There are two ways to get from Swanton to Wauseon. 3(2) = 6; there are six ways.

EXAMPLE 2

A license plate has two letters followed by three digits. How many different license plates can be made using this scheme?

The number of decisions = 5 (2 letters and 3 digits).

The number of options for each decision = 26 for letters and 10 for digits.

Therefore, the number of possible license plates is $26 \times 26 \times 10 \times 10 \times 10 = 676{,}000$.

EXERCISE 3

Counting

Directions: Count the number of possibilities in the following scenarios.

1. Ben can take any one of the three routes from school to the town center and can then take five possible routes from the town center to his home. He does not retrace his steps. How many different possible ways can Ben walk home from school?

2. Sarah goes to her local pizza parlor and orders a pizza. She has two choices for the size. She has seven different choices for toppings and three different choices for crust. How many different single-topping pizzas could Sarah order?

3. Suppose there are four girls and three boys in the school science club. You must select one girl and one boy to represent the club on the school council. How many ways are there to do this?

4. Kendra has four skirts and five tops. How many different outfits could she wear?

5. For the literature course, Rachel has to choose one novel to study from a list of four, one poem from a list of six, and one short story from a list of five. How many different choices does Rachel have?

Answers are on page 566.

Factorials

When using the fundamental counting principle, you often have products such as $5 \cdot 4 \cdot 3 \cdot 2 \cdot 1$. For convenience you can write these products using the symbol $n!$ (read as "*n factorial*").

$n! = n \cdot (n-1) \cdot (n-2) \cdot \cdots \cdot 3 \cdot 2 \cdot 1$, with $0! = 1$ for convenience.

For example:

$$0! = 1$$
$$1! = 1$$
$$2! = 2 \times 1 = 2$$
$$3! = 3 \times 2 \times 1 = 6$$
$$4! = 4 \times 3 \times 2 \times 1 = 24$$
$$5! = 5 \times 4 \times 3 \times 2 \times 1 = 120$$

EXAMPLE 1

Evaluate 6!

$$6! = 6 \times 5 \times 4 \times 3 \times 2 \times 1 = 720$$

EXAMPLE 2

Evaluate $\dfrac{5!}{3!}$

$$\frac{5!}{3!} = \frac{5 \cdot 4 \cdot 3 \cdot 2 \cdot 1}{3 \cdot 2 \cdot 1} = \frac{5 \cdot 4 \cdot \cancel{3 \cdot 2 \cdot 1}}{\cancel{3 \cdot 2 \cdot 1}} = 20$$

EXAMPLE 3

In how many ways can 12 students sit in a row?

There are 12 ways to fill the first spot, 11 ways to fill the second spot, and so on.

Evaluate 12! = 479,001,600.

EXERCISE 4

Factorials

Directions: Calculate the expressions involving factorials.

1. Evaluate the following.

a) $\dfrac{8!}{5!}$ d) $\dfrac{10!}{5!}$ g) $\dfrac{7!}{3!\,2!}$ j) $\dfrac{4!}{(4-1)!\,1!}$

b) $\dfrac{2!}{17!\,4!}$ e) $\dfrac{7!}{2!\,5!} + \dfrac{7!}{4!\,3!}$ h) $\dfrac{6!}{(5-3)!\,3!}$

c) $\dfrac{155!}{152!}$ f) $2 \times \dfrac{5!}{2!\,3!}$ i) $\dfrac{7!}{(7-4)!\,4!}$

2. Sam's mother has framed his photos from first grade to seventh grade. She is now thinking of hanging them in the hall in a long row. In how many ways can she display them?

3. In how many ways is it possible for 15 students to arrange themselves among 15 seats in the front row of an auditorium?

4. There are four candidates for a job. The members of the search committee will rank the four candidates from the strongest to weakest. How many different outcomes are possible?

5. There are eight cars in a race. In how many different orders could they finish this race?

Answers are on page 566.

Permutations

A **permutation** is one of many possible ordered arrangements of the terms of a set. The arrangement may include all the terms in the set, or only some specified number of terms at a time. For example, there are six permutations of the terms of the set {*a*, *b*, *c*} using all of the terms: *abc*, *acb*, *bac*, *bca*, *cab*, and *cba*.

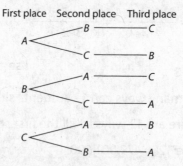

To find the number of possible permutations without listing them, the fundamental counting principle can be used. There are three ways to fill the first position; two ways to fill the second position, and one way to fill the last position.

The total number of permutations of *n* objects taken *r* at a time is denoted by *P*(*n*, *r*), given by

$$P(n,r) = \frac{n!}{(n-r)!}$$

Note that when $n = r$, $P(n,n) = n!$.

$$P(n,n) = \frac{n!}{(n-n)!} = \frac{n!}{0!} = \frac{n!}{1} = n!$$

EXAMPLE 1

How many possible permutations of the letters *a*, *b*, *c*, *d*, *e*, *f*, and *g* are there?

$$P(7,7) = 7! = 7 \cdot 6 \cdot 5 \cdot 4 \cdot 3 \cdot 2 \cdot 1 = 5,040$$

EXAMPLE 2

A museum has eight paintings to hang and four vacant locations. In how many different ways can these four locations be filled with paintings?

$$P(8,4) = \frac{8!}{(8-4)!} = \frac{8 \cdot 7 \cdot 6 \cdot 5 \cdot 4 \cdot 3 \cdot 2 \cdot 1}{4 \cdot 3 \cdot 2 \cdot 1} = 1{,}680$$

EXERCISE 5

Permutations

Directions: Work the following problems to become familiar with permutations.

1. Solve the following problems.

   a) $P(5, 3)$

   b) $P(6, 6)$

   c) $P(7, 4)$

   d) $P(10, 2)$

   e) $P(12, 4)$

   f) $P(9, 4)$

   g) $P(8, 7)$

   h) $P(5, 3)$

2. Five people walk into a hotel at the same time. In how many ways can they form a line?

3. How many four-letter sequences can be made from the letters in the word IMPEACH?

4. How many seven-digit numbers can be created from the digits 5, 1, 7, 6, 9, 3, and 8 without repeating any?

5. In an eight-person race, how many different ways can three runners arrive at the finish line?

6. How many ways can you arrange four letters from the word COMPUTER if repetitions are not allowed, and different orders of the same letter count as different arrangements?

7. How many different four-digit numbers are possible if you can choose any digits from 0 to 9?

8. In how many ways, can three books be arranged on a shelf out of seven books in a box?

9. In a class of 24 students, a first prize and a second prize are to be awarded. In how many ways can this be done?

10. A club has 28 members. In how many ways can the President, Treasurer, and Secretary be chosen?

Answers are on page 566.

Combinations

A **combination** is one of many possible selections of terms from a set in which the order of the terms does not matter. The number of ways of choosing r terms from a set of n terms without regard to the order of the terms, $C(n,r)$, is given by

$$C(n,r) = \frac{P(n,r)}{r!} = \frac{n!}{(n-r)!\,r!}$$

EXAMPLE 1

Find the number of possible ways in which three people can be selected from a set of seven people.

$$C(7,3) = \frac{7!}{(7-3)!\,3!} = \frac{7!}{4!\,3!} = \frac{7 \times 6 \times 5 \times 4 \times 3 \times 2 \times 1}{(4 \times 3 \times 2 \times 1)(3 \times 2 \times 1)} = \frac{7 \times 6 \times 5}{3 \times 2 \times 1} = 35$$

EXAMPLE 2

In how many ways can a committee consisting of 5 men and 6 women be formed from 8 men and 10 women?

5 men are to be chosen from 8 men.

6 women are to be chosen from 10 women.

So, the required number of ways is:

$$
\begin{aligned}
C(8,5) \times C(10,6) &= \frac{8!}{(8-5)!\,5!} \cdot \frac{10!}{(10-6)!\,6!} \\
&= \frac{8!}{3!\,5!} \cdot \frac{10!}{4!\,6!} \\
&= \frac{8 \times 7 \times 6 \times \overline{5 \times 4 \times 3 \times 2 \times 1}}{(3 \times 2 \times 1)\overline{(5 \times 4 \times 3 \times 2 \times 1)}} \cdot \frac{10 \times 9 \times 8 \times 7 \times \overline{6 \times 5 \times 4 \times 3 \times 2 \times 1}}{(4 \times 3 \times 2 \times 1)\overline{(6 \times 5 \times 4 \times 3 \times 2 \times 1)}} \\
&= \frac{336}{6} \cdot \frac{5,040}{24} = 56 \times 210 = 11,760
\end{aligned}
$$

EXERCISE 6

Combinations

Directions: Work the following problems to become familiar with combinations.

1. Solve the following problems.
   a) $C(6, 3)$
   b) $C(9, 4)$
   c) $C(9, 2)$
   d) $C(11, 9)$
   e) $C(16, 9)$
   f) $C(3, 3)$
   g) $C(15, 5)$
   h) $C(20, 3)$

2. In a class of 10 students, in how many ways can a club of 4 students be selected?

3. On an English exam, students are required to answer four essay questions from a list of nine questions. How many possible combinations of four questions can there be?

4. Eleven students put their names on slips of paper inside a box. Three names are going to be taken out. In how many different ways can the three names be chosen?

5. In how many ways can a group of 5 players on the varsity boys' sports team be chosen from a team of 14 players?

6. You want to paint three rooms of a house, each with a different color of paint. How many color combinations are possible for the three rooms if you have seven to choose from?

7. There are 18 astronauts who volunteer for a mission to Mars. However, there are only four seats on the rocket. How many different groups of four can go on the rocket?

8. Larry has 12 shirts. If he needs to pick three of them for a camping trip, how many different combinations are there?

Answers are on page 566.

Finding Probabilities Mathematically

If you toss a coin once, the outcome will be either heads (H) or tails (T). So for that coin toss, the total number of *possible* outcomes is 2. The total number of possible outcomes for an event like a coin toss is called the **sample space**. If you roll a number cube, there are six possible outcomes (1, 2, 3, 4, 5, and 6), so the size of the sample space is 6. Study the following examples.

EXAMPLE 1

A coin is flipped and a number cube is rolled at the same time. Identify the sample space (total number of possible outcomes) of the experiment. Let H = heads and T = Tails.

The possible outcomes are:

{(H, 1), (H, 2), (H, 3), (H, 4), (H, 5), (H, 6), (T, 1), (T, 2), (T, 3), (T, 4), (T, 5), (T, 6)}.

The size of the sample space is 12.

EXAMPLE 2

What is the size of the sample space when a pair of number cubes is thrown?

Each number cube has a possibility of six outcomes.

Two number cubes have 6×6 outcomes = 36 possible outcomes.

To calculate the probability of whichever event you choose (called the *favorable outcome*), you need to know the size of the sample space and the number of times that you could possibly get that favorable outcome. The probability is the ratio of the number of favorable outcomes to the total number of possible outcomes.

$$\text{Probability of an event} = \frac{\text{Number of favorable outcomes}}{\text{Number of possible outcomes}}$$

EXAMPLE 3

There are 3 black puppies and 5 yellow puppies in a litter of Labs. Picking at random, what is the probability of selecting a black Lab?

A favorable outcome is picking a black Lab. There are 3 black puppies out of 8, so there are 3 possible favorable outcomes out of a total of 8 possible outcomes. The probability is $\frac{3}{8}$ or 37.5%.

Probability of a Complementary Event

For every event E, there is another event E' that complements event E. For example, if you roll a number cube and get a 1, the complementary event would be to get a 2, 3, 4, 5, or 6. The probability of a complementary event is calculated as follows:

$$P(E') = 1 - P(E)$$

EXAMPLE 1

What is the probability of NOT rolling doubles when a pair of number cubes is rolled?

There are six ways to roll doubles.

$$P(\text{doubles}) = \frac{6}{36} = \frac{1}{6}. \quad P(\text{not doubles}) = 1 - \frac{1}{6} = \frac{5}{6}$$

EXAMPLE 2

What is the probability of rolling 10 or less when a pair of number cubes is rolled?

The complement of rolling "10 or less" is rolling 11 or 12.

$$\begin{aligned} P(10 \text{ or less}) &= 1 - P(11 \text{ or } 12) \\ &= 1 - [P(11) + P(12)] \\ &= 1 - \left(\frac{2}{36} + \frac{1}{36}\right) \\ &= \frac{33}{36} = \frac{11}{12} \end{aligned}$$

EXERCISE 7

Finding Probabilities Mathematically

Directions: Compute the probabilities in each scenario.

1. A number cube is rolled once. What are the probabilities of the following events?
   a) Rolling a 3 or 5
   b) Rolling a number greater than 10
   c) Rolling an even number
   d) Rolling a 3 or more

2. A number cube is rolled twice. What are the probabilities of the following events?
   a) Rolling a sum of 3 or more
   b) Rolling either a 1 or a 3 each time
   c) Rolling a sum greater than 10
   d) Rolling a 5 both times

3. A number is chosen at random from 1 to 25. Find the probability of NOT selecting a prime number.

4. Find the probability of rolling a number cube and getting a number smaller than 4.

5. Find the probability of rolling doubles when rolling two number cubes.

6. Find the probability of drawing a black face card from a deck of 52 cards.

7. Find the probability of drawing a black 3 through 7 card from a deck of 52 cards on the first draw, replacing it, and drawing a 10 card on the second draw.

8. Three unbiased coins are tossed. What is the probability of getting at most two heads?

Answers are on page 567.

Combining Probabilities

Independent Events

Two events are **independent events** if the outcome of one has no effect on the outcome of the other. For instance, if a coin is tossed twice, the outcome of the first toss (heads or tails) has no effect on the outcome of the second toss. If A and B are independent events, then the probability that both A and B occur is:

$$P(A \text{ and } B) = P(A) \cdot P(B)$$

EXAMPLE

A box contains three red paper clips, four green paper clips, and five blue paper clips. One paper clip is taken from the box and then replaced. Another paper clip is taken from the box.

What is the probability that the first paper clip is red and the second paper clip is blue?

The first paper clip taken from the box is replaced, so the sample space remains the same.

$$S = 3 + 4 + 5 = 12$$

$$P(R \text{ and } B) = P(R) \cdot P(B) = \frac{3}{12} \times \frac{5}{12} = \frac{15}{144} = \frac{5}{48}$$

Dependent Events

Two events are **dependent events** if the occurrence of one affects the occurrence of the other. The probability that B will occur given that A has occurred is written as $P(B|A)$. If A and B are dependent events, then the probability that both A and B occur is:

$$P(A \text{ and } B) = P(A) \cdot P(B|A)$$

EXAMPLE

A card is chosen at random from a standard deck of 52 playing cards. Without replacing it, a second card is chosen. What is the probability that the first card chosen is a queen and the second card chosen is a jack?

$P(\text{Queen on first pick}) = \dfrac{4}{52}$

$P(\text{Jack on second pick excluding the queen from the first pick}) = \dfrac{4}{51}$

$P(\text{Queen and Jack}) = \dfrac{4}{52} \times \dfrac{4}{51} = \dfrac{16}{2,652} = \dfrac{4}{663}$

EXERCISE 8

Independent Events

Directions: Compute the probabilities in each scenario.

1. A fair number cube is tossed twice. Find the probability of a 4 or 5 on the first toss and a 1, 2, and 4 on the second toss.

2. Two balls are drawn successively without replacement from a box that contains four white balls and three red balls. Find the probability that the first ball drawn is white and the second is red.

3. If the probability that person A will be alive in 20 years is 0.7 and the probability that person B will be alive in 20 years is 0.5, what is the probability that they will both be alive in 20 years?

4. If a pair of number cubes is rolled two times in a row, what is the probability that the sum of the numbers thrown is 4 both times?

5. If there is a 10% chance that Jupiter will align with Mars and a 50% chance that a coin's flip will be heads, then what is the possibility that Jupiter will align with Mars and that the coin flip will be heads?

6. There are six red, four green, five blue, and five yellow marbles in a jar. What is the probability of picking a green marble and then a blue marble, if you do NOT replace the first marble?

7. Three cards are chosen at random from a deck of 52 cards without being replaced. What is the probability of choosing three aces?

8. In a math test, 5 out of 20 students received an A. If three students are chosen at random without replacement, what is the probability that all three of them received an A on the test?

9. Two cards are chosen at random from a deck of 52 cards with being replaced. What is the probability that the first card is a jack and the second card is a 10?

10. In a shipment of 20 computers, 3 are defective. Three computers are randomly selected and tested. What is the probability that all three are defective if the first and second ones are not replaced after being tested?

Answers are on page 567.

Mutually Exclusive Events and Non–Mutually Exclusive Events

Two or more events are mutually exclusive if they cannot occur at the same time. In other words, events that have no outcomes in common are said to be mutually exclusive events or disjoint events. If two events A and B are mutually exclusive, then the probability of the occurrence of A or B is the sum of their individual probabilities. That is:

$$P(A \text{ or } B) = P(A) + P(B)$$

EXAMPLE

What is the probability of a number cube showing a 2 or a 5?

The size of sample space $= 6$, so $P(2) = \dfrac{1}{6}$ and $P(5) = \dfrac{1}{6}$.

$$P(2 \text{ or } 5) = P(2) + P(5) = \dfrac{1}{6} + \dfrac{1}{6} = \dfrac{2}{6} = \dfrac{1}{3}$$

Thus, the probability of a die showing 2 or 5 is $\dfrac{1}{3}$.

When two events, A and B, are non–mutually exclusive, the probability that A or B will occur is:

$$P(A \text{ or } B) = P(A) + P(B) - P(A \text{ and } B)$$

EXAMPLE 1

An urn contains six red marbles and four black marbles. Two marbles are drawn without replacement from the urn. What is the probability that both of the marbles are black?

Let $A =$ the event that the first marble is black; and let $B =$ the event that the second marble is black. There are 10 marbles in the urn, 4 of which are black. Therefore, $P(A) = \dfrac{4}{10}$. After the first selection, there are nine marbles in the urn, three of which are black. Therefore, $P(B|A) = \dfrac{3}{9}$.

$$P(A \text{ and } B) = P(A)P(B|A) = \dfrac{4}{10} \times \dfrac{3}{9} = \dfrac{12}{90} = \dfrac{2}{15}$$

EXAMPLE 2

A card is drawn randomly from a deck of ordinary playing cards. You win \$10 if the card is a spade or an ace. What is the probability that you will win the game?

Let $S =$ the event that the card is a spade; and let $A =$ the event that the card is an ace.

There are 52 cards in the deck. There are 13 spades, so $P(S) = \dfrac{13}{52}$. There are four aces, so $P(A) = \dfrac{4}{52}$. There is one ace that is also a spade, so $P(S \text{ and } A) = \dfrac{1}{52}$. Therefore, based on the rule of addition:

$$P(S \text{ or } A) = P(S) + P(A) - P(S \text{ and } A) = \dfrac{13}{52} + \dfrac{4}{52} - \dfrac{1}{52} = \dfrac{16}{52} = \dfrac{4}{13}$$

EXERCISE 9

Mutually Exclusive Events

Directions: Compute the probabilities in each scenario.

1. A pair of number cubes is rolled. What is the probability that the sum of the numbers rolled is either 8 or 12?

2. Tony had five red socks, three blue socks, and two white socks in a drawer. He pulled out two socks at random from the drawer. What is the probability that one sock is blue and the other is red?

3. Carol has five cookies, eight chocolates, and two cakes in her refrigerator. Find the probability of Carol choosing a chocolate and her sister choosing a cake.

4. A number cube is rolled. What is the probability of rolling a number less than 7?

5. A box contains cards labeled from A to Z. Sam drew a card and replaced it and drew another card. What is the probability that the first card was an E and the second was a B?

6. In a group of 101 students, 30 are freshmen and 41 are sophomores. Find the probability that a student picked from this group at random is either a freshman or sophomore.

7. In a group of 101 students 40 are juniors, 50 are female, and 22 are female juniors. Find the probability that a student picked from this group at random is either a junior or female.

8. Select two cards from the standard deck of 52 cards with replacement. Find the probability of selecting two kings.

9. Suppose you toss a coin and then roll a dice. What is the probability of obtaining a tail and then rolling a 5?

10. A committee consists of four women and three men. The committee will randomly select two people to attend a conference in Hawaii. Find the probability that both are women.

Answers are on page 567.

Conditional Probability

The probability of an event occurring given that another event has already occurred is called a **conditional probability**. The probability that event *B* occurs, given that event *A* has already occurred, is:

$$P(B|A) = \frac{P(A \text{ and } B)}{P(A)}$$

EXAMPLE

What is the probability that the total of two dice will be greater than 8, given that the first die is 6?

Let A = First die is 6.

Let B = Total of two dice is greater than 8.

Then, A and B will be {(6, 3), (6, 4), (6, 5) and (6, 6)}.

In total, there are 36 possible outcomes, when you throw two dice.

Thus, $P(B \text{ and } A) = \dfrac{4}{36} = \dfrac{1}{9}$.

Thus, $P(B|A) = \dfrac{P(B \text{ and } A)}{P(A)} = \dfrac{\frac{1}{9}}{\frac{1}{6}} = \dfrac{6}{9} = \dfrac{2}{3}$.

EXERCISE 10

Conditional Probability

Directions: Compute the probabilities in each scenario.

1. A bag contains 12 red pens, 12 blue pens, and 12 green pens. What is the probability of drawing two pens of the same color in a row?

2. In a school of 1,200 students, 250 are seniors, 150 students take math, and 40 students are seniors also taking math. What is the probability that a randomly chosen student is a senior who is taking math?

3. A company has three plants at which it produces a certain item. 30% are produced at Plant A, 50% at Plant B, and 20% at Plant C. Suppose that 1%, 4%, and 3% of the items produced at Plants A, B, and C, respectively, are defective. If an item is selected at random from all those produced, what is the probability that the item was produced at Plant B and is defective?

4. Jack and James are playing a game in which one number cube is rolled and whoever rolls the larger number wins. If the numbers are the same, they have to roll again. If Jack won, what is the probability that he rolled a 5?

5. If a couple wants to have three or four children, including exactly two girls, what is the probability that their wish will come true?

Answers are on page 567.

Probability Tree

A tree diagram is simply a way of representing a sequence of events. Tree diagrams are particularly useful in probability since they record all possible outcomes in a clear and uncomplicated manner. It shows all the possible events. The first event is represented by a dot. From the dot, branches are drawn to represent all possible outcomes of the event. The probability of each outcome is written on its branch.

Construction of Tree

Consider tossing a coin.

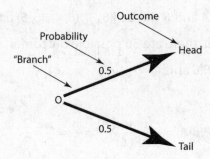

There are two "branches" (Heads and Tails).

The probability of each branch is written on the branch.

The outcome is written at the end of the branch.

Deriving Probabilities from a Probability Tree

You can extend the above tree diagram to show two tosses of a coin.

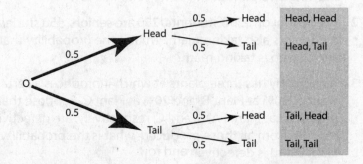

Multiply probabilities along the branches and add the probabilities down columns.

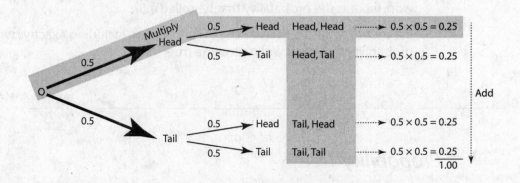

All probabilities add to 1.

The probability of "Head, Head" is $0.5 \times 0.5 = 0.25$.

The probability of "Tail, Tail" is $0.5 \times 0.5 = 0.25$.

The probability of "Head, Tail" is $0.5 \times 0.5 = 0.25$.

The probability of "Tail, Head" is $0.5 \times 0.5 = 0.25$.

The probability of getting at least one "Head" from two tosses is $0.25 + 0.25 + 0.25 = 0.75$.

The probability of getting at least one "Tail" from two tosses is $0.25 + 0.25 + 0.25 = 0.75$.

EXERCISE 11

Probability

Directions: Answer the following questions.

1. Find the probability that an even number is obtained when a die is rolled.

2. When three unbiased coins are tossed, what is the probability of getting at most two heads?

3. If you throw a number cube twice, what is the probability of getting a sum of 9?

4. A card is drawn at random from a deck of cards. Find the probability of selecting the three of diamonds.

5. A number cube is rolled. Find the probability that the number rolled is greater than 4.

6. Evaluate 13!

7. How many ways can four letters of the word NUMBER be arranged?

8. How many five-digit numbers can be written using all of the following digits? 3, 3, 8, 8, 9

9. How many combinations of 5 students can be selected from a class of 25?

10. From a group of six men and four women, how many committees of two men and three women can be formed?

11. If a person selects one ball at random from a bag with 15 balls numbered from 1 to 15, what is the probability that the number printed on the ball is a prime number greater than 5?

12. How many elements in the sample space consist of an even number and a tail when a number cube, with faces numbered 1 to 6, is rolled, and a penny are tossed at the same time?

13. What is the probability of getting a 7 after rolling a single number cube numbered 1 to 6?

14. What is the probability of choosing a green marble from a jar containing five red, six green, and four blue marbles?

15. If the probability of an event is $\frac{5}{9}$, what is the probability of its complementary event?

16. If 2 chocolates are drawn at random from 8 dark chocolates and 12 milk chocolates, what is the probability that both are milk chocolate? What is the probability that neither is milk chocolate?

17. Danica has four dimes, three quarters, and seven nickels in her purse. She reaches in and pulls out a coin, only to have it slip from her fingers and fall back into the purse. She then picks out another coin. What is the probability that she picked a nickel on both tries?

18. A bag of candy contains four lemon-flavored sour balls and five lime-flavored sour balls. If Jim reaches in, takes one out, and eats it, and then 15 minutes later selects another and eats that one as well, what is the probability that they were both lemon-flavored candies?

19. On a test, 6 out of 30 students earned an A. If three students are chosen at random without replacement, what is the probability that all three selected earned an A on the test?

20. A drawer contains pairs of socks folded together and matched up. The socks are the following colors: blue, brown, red, white, black. You reach into the sock drawer and choose a pair of socks without looking. You replace this pair and then choose another pair of socks. What is the probability that you will choose the red pair of socks both times?

21. A card is drawn from a deck of playing cards. What is the probability of drawing a heart or the king of spades?

22. Consider a pack of 52 playing cards. A card is selected at random. What is the probability that the card is either a diamond or ten?

23. In a group of 101 students, 40 are juniors, 50 are females, and 22 are female juniors. Find the probability that a student picked from this group at random is either a junior or female.

24. There are two identical baskets. One basket contains two green balls and one red ball. The other basket contains two red balls. A basket is selected at random and a single ball is drawn. What is the probability that the ball is red?

Answers are on page 567.

CHAPTER 8

Geometry

Geometry is the study of points, lines, angles, surfaces, and solids. The study of geometry is important because the world in which you live is made up of points, lines, angles, surfaces, and solids, and many other geometric shapes as well. In this chapter you will learn about basic object and the relations between them, and study formulas used to measure them.

Points, Lines, Planes, and Space

Point

A **point** is a location in space. It is shown as a dot denoted with a capital letter such as *A*, *B*, and *C*. A point has no length, width, or thickness.

Line

A **line** is a straight path of infinite points that continues in two directions. A line has only length and no width. It has no terminal point. In the following illustration, the arrows are drawn to indicate that the line continues.

In geometry, the word *line* generally means a straight line. A curved line is called a *curve* or *arc*.

Straight line   Curved line

A line can be horizontal (left to right), vertical (up or down), or diagonal (slanted).

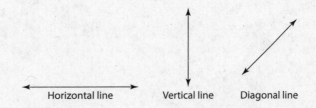

Horizontal line   Vertical line   Diagonal line

235

Uniquely Defined by Two Points

A line is uniquely defined by two points. If A and B are any two points on a line, then the line may be denoted by $\overleftrightarrow{AB}$ or $\overleftrightarrow{BA}$. The two arrows on the line above the name of the line indicate that the line continues indefinitely in both directions.

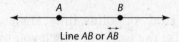

Line AB or $\overleftrightarrow{AB}$

Intersecting Lines

Two or more lines or line segments are said to be **intersecting lines** if they meet at a point of intersection.

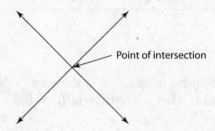

Point of intersection

Parallel Lines

Two or more lines or line segments are said to be **parallel** when they run in the same direction and are always at an equal distance apart. Parallel lines never cross, no matter how far they are extended.

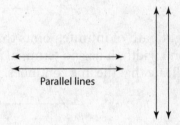

Parallel lines

Perpendicular Lines

Two lines or line segments are said to be **perpendicular** when the lines meet or intersect to make right angles.

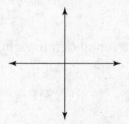

Skew Lines

Two or more lines in three-dimensional space are said to be **skew lines** if they do not intersect and are not parallel.

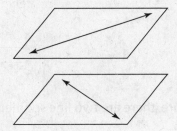

EXAMPLE

Use the figure below to answer the questions.

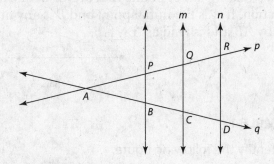

1. Name all pairs of parallel lines.

   The pairs of parallel lines are _l_ and _m_, _m_ and _n_, _l_ and _n_.

2. Name all pairs of intersecting lines.

   The pairs of intersecting lines are _l_, _p_; _m_, _p_; _n_, _p_; _l_, _q_; _m_, _q_; _n_, _q_; and _p_, _q_.

3. Name the lines intersecting at point _P_.

   Lines _l_ and _p_ intersect at point _P_.

4. Name the lines intersecting at point _C_.

   Lines _m_ and _q_ intersect at point _C_.

5. Name the lines intersecting at point _R_.

   Lines _n_ and _p_ intersect at point _R_.

Segment

A **line segment** is a portion of a line and has a definite length. Every line segment has two endpoints. If _A_ and _B_ are two points on a line, then the line segment can be denoted by $\overline{AB}$ or $\overline{BA}$.

_A_ ————————————————— _B_

Line segment _AB_

EXAMPLE

How many line segments are there in the following figure?

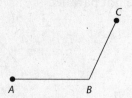

In the figure, there are two line segments: $\overline{AB}$ and $\overline{BC}$.

Ray

A **ray** is a straight path of points that begins at one point and continues indefinitely in one direction. If A is the initial point and B is any other point on the ray, then the ray is denoted by $\overrightarrow{AB}$ and is read as "ray AB."

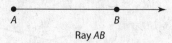

Ray AB

EXAMPLE 1

Identify the following figure.

The figure represents a line as it extends in both directions.

EXAMPLE 2

Identify the following figure.

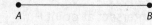

The figure represents line segment $\overline{AB}$.

Plane

A **plane** is a flat surface with no thickness that extends indefinitely in all directions. Two planes either intersect in a line or are parallel.

Planes Defined by Two Non-Skew Lines

A plane can be defined in terms of non-skew lines. For any two lines that intersect, the set of all points that lie on the line defined by two points (one from each line) specifies a **plane defined by these two lines**.

In the following figure, lines *m* and *l* are two lines that intersect, and points *P* and *Q* are two points on *m* and *l*, respectively.

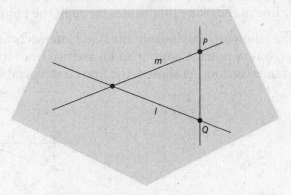

Intersecting Planes

Two planes are known as **intersecting planes** if they intersect. Two planes always intersect at a line.

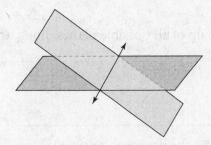

Parallel Planes

Two planes are said to be **parallel planes** if they do not intersect and are the same distance apart everywhere.

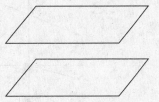

Perpendicular Planes

Two planes are said to be **perpendicular planes** if one plane contains a line perpendicular to the other plane, that is, one plane is perpendicular to the other plane.

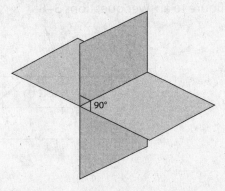

Line Perpendicular to Plane

A **line is said to be perpendicular to a plane** if it intersects the plane and is perpendicular to every line in the plane that passes through the point of intersection.

In the following illustration, the line l intersects and is perpendicular to the plane p at the intersection point A, and m and n are two lines in the plane p that pass through the point of intersection. As shown, the line l is perpendicular to the plane.

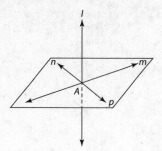

Space

Space is made up of all possible planes, lines, and points.

EXERCISE 1

Lines

Directions: Use the figures to answer the questions in each group.

Use the figure to answer questions 1 and 2.

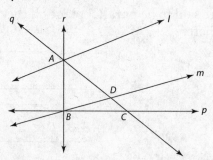

1. Name the lines intersecting at A.

2. Name the lines intersecting at B.

Use the figure to answer questions 3–8.

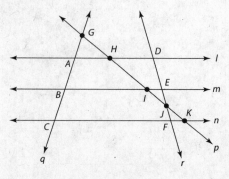

3. Name all pairs of parallel lines.

4. Name all pairs of intersecting lines.

5. Name the lines intersecting at point *I*.

6. Name the lines intersecting at point *D*.

7. Name the lines intersecting at point *E*.

8. Name the lines intersecting at point *A*.

9. Identify the following figure.

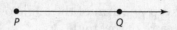

10. Identify the following figure.

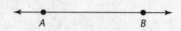

11. How many line segments are there in the following figure? Name all of them.

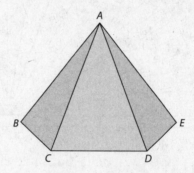

12. How many line segments are there in the following figure? Name all of them.

Answers are on page 568.

Angles

An **angle** is defined as the figure formed by two rays or lines extending from one point. The two rays or lines are known as the angle's **arms** or **sides**. The point from which the rays extend is the **vertex**. The symbol $\angle$ stands for the word *angle*. The angle shown in the following illustration is represented by $\angle ABC$ or $\angle CBA$ or $\angle B$. When using three points to write the name, the vertex point is always written in the middle.

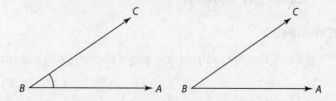

Units for Measuring Angles

Angles can be denoted using the symbol $\angle$ or $m\angle$. Here, m refers to the measure of an angle. The size of an angle depends on the amount of rotation of its sides, or the openness of the angle. One unit of angle measure is **degrees**, denoted with the symbol ° after the number measure. Special angles with certain degree measures have special names, as you will see in the next section.

Angles can be measured using a **protractor**. The curved edge of the instrument is divided into 180 equal parts. Each part is equal to a degree. The markings begin from 0 on the right side and end at 180° on the left side, and vice versa. While measuring angles on a protractor, keep one arm of the angle on the 0 marking of the protractor. The arm indicates the measure of the angle.

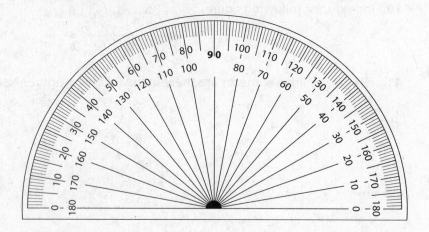

EXAMPLE 1

What is the measure of the angle shown with the protractor?

In the image, one arm of the angle is on 0 and the other arm is on 60°. Thus, the measure of the angle is 60°.

EXAMPLE 2

What is the measure of the angle shown with the protractor?

In the image, one arm of the angle is on 0 and the other arm is on 150°. Thus, the measure of the angle is 150°. Even though there are two numbers corresponding to the left arm, 150° is the correct measure because the angle opens wider than a right angle (90°). Thus, 30° would not be the measure.

EXAMPLE 3

Use a protractor to find the measure of the angle shown in the following figure.

The measure of the angle is 90°.

Angle Names Based on Size

Acute Angle

An **acute angle** has a degree measure of more than 0° but less than 90°.

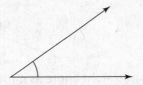

Right Angle

A **right angle** has a degree measure equal to 90°.

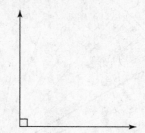

Obtuse Angle

An **obtuse angle** has a degree measure of greater than 90° but less than 180°.

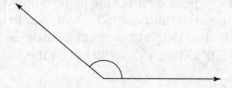

Straight Angle

A **straight angle** has a degree measure equal to 180°.

Reflex Angle

A **reflex angle** has a degree measure of more than 180° but less than 360°.

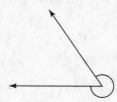

EXAMPLES

Identify the type of each angle.

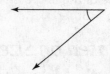

1. This angle is an acute angle as it measures more than 0° but less than 90°.

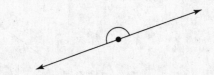

2. This angle is a straight angle as it measures 180°.

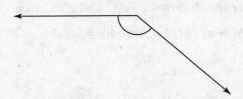

3. This angle is an obtuse angle as it measures more than 90° but less than 180°.

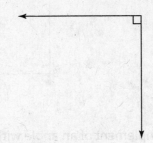

4. This angle is a right angle as it has a measure of 90°.

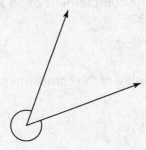

5. This angle is a reflex angle as it measures more than 180° but less than 360°.

Relationships Between Angles

Complementary Angles

Two angles are said to be **complementary angles** if the sum of their measures is 90°. Each of these angles is called the **complement** of the other.

In the following figure, $\angle ABC$ and $\angle CBD$ are complementary angles.

$m\angle ABC + m\angle CBD = 30° + 60° = 90°.$

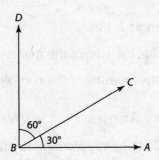

In the figure that follows, $\angle BAC$ and $\angle BCA$ are complementary angles.

$$m\angle BAC + m\angle BCA = 50° + 40° = 90°.$$

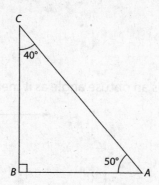

EXAMPLE 1

Find the complement of an angle with measure of 58°.

You know that the sum of the measures of complementary angles is 90°.

Therefore, the complement of an angle with measure of 58° has a measure of $90° - 58° = 32°$.

EXAMPLE 2

Find the measure of the complement of the following angle.

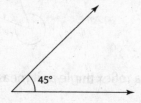

The given angle is 45°.

You know that the sum of the measures of complementary angles is 90°.

Therefore, the measure of the complement of $45° = 90° - 45° = 45°$.

EXAMPLE 3

Find the measure of the complement of the following angle.

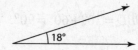

The given angle is 18°.

You know that the sum of the measures of complementary angles is 90°.

Therefore, the measure of the complement of $18° = 90° - 18° = 72°$.

Supplementary Angles

Two angles are said to be **supplementary** if the sum of their measures is 180°. Each of the angles is called the **supplement** of the other.

In the figure that follows, $\angle AOD$ and $\angle BOD$ are supplementary angles.

$m\angle AOD + m\angle BOD = 180°$.

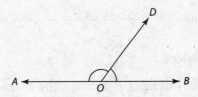

In the figure that follows, $\angle ABC$ and $\angle PQR$ are supplementary angles.

$m\angle ABC + m\angle PQR = 130° + 50° = 180°$.

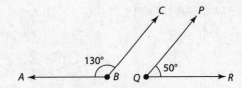

EXAMPLE 1

Find the supplement of an angle with measure of 143°.

You know that the sum of the measures of supplementary angles is 180°.

Therefore, the measure of the supplement of 143° = 180° − 143° = 37°.

EXAMPLE 2

Find the measure of the supplement of the following angle.

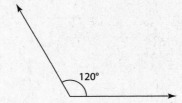

The given angle is 120°.

You know that the sum of the measures of supplementary angles is 180°.

Therefore, the measure of the supplement of 120° = 180° − 120° = 60°.

EXAMPLE 3

Find the measure of the supplement of the following angles.

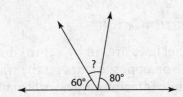

The given angles are 60° and 80°. The sum of the measures of these angles is 60° + 80° = 140°.

You know that the sum of the measures of supplementary angles is 180°.

Therefore, the measure of the supplement of 140° = 180° − 140° = 40°.

Vertical Angles

When two lines intersect at a point, the two sets of angles formed at the point of intersection that are opposite to each other are known as **vertical angles**. Vertical angles have measures that are equal.

In the following figure, $\angle a$, $\angle c$ are one pair of vertical angles, and $\angle b$, $\angle d$ are another pair of vertical angles.

Thus, $m\angle a = m\angle c$ and $m\angle b = m\angle d$.

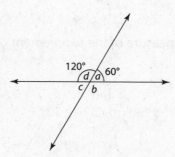

EXAMPLE

In the following figure, $m\angle a = 60°$ and $m\angle d = 120°$.

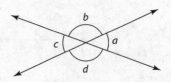

Find the vertical angles of $\angle a$ and $\angle d$ and their corresponding measures.

Vertical angles are opposite and have equal measures. The opposite angle of $\angle a$ is $\angle c$ and the opposite angle of $\angle d$ is $\angle b$. Thus, the vertical angle of $\angle a$ is $\angle c$ and of $\angle d$ is $\angle b$.

You know that vertical angles are equal. Therefore, if $m\angle a = 60°$, $\angle c = 60°$ and if $\angle d = 120°$, $\angle b = 120°$.

Alternate Interior Angles

When two parallel lines are cut by a third line, which is known as a **transversal**, the pair of angles that are on opposite sides on the transversal but inside the two parallel lines are known as **alternate interior angles**. Alternate interior angles have equal measures.

In the following figure, $\angle a$, $\angle d$ form one pair of alternate interior angles. The angles $\angle b$, $\angle c$ form another pair of alternate interior angles.

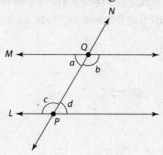

So, $m\angle a = m\angle d$ and $m\angle b = m\angle c$.

EXAMPLE

In the following diagram, $m\angle a = 30°$. Find the measures of $\angle b$, $\angle c$, and $\angle d$.

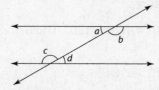

The pairs of alternate interior angles are $\angle a$, $\angle d$ and $\angle b$, $\angle c$.

Given, $m\angle a = 30°$. Thus, $m\angle d = 30°$ as alternate interior angles are equal.

The angles $\angle a$ and $\angle b$ are lying on a straight line and are supplementary angles.

Therefore,

$m\angle b = 180° - m\angle a$

$\qquad = 180° - 30°$

$\qquad = 150°$

The angles $\angle b$ and $\angle c$ are alternate interior angles and their measures are equal. Therefore, $m\angle c = m\angle b = 150°$.

Alternate Exterior Angles

The pair of angles that are on opposite sides on the transversal but outside the two parallel lines are known as **alternate exterior angles**. Alternate exterior angles have equal measures.

In the following figure, $\angle a$ and $\angle d$ form one pair of alternate exterior angles. The angles $\angle b$ and $\angle c$ form another pair of alternate exterior angles.

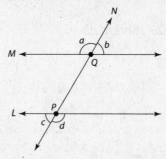

So, $m\angle a = m\angle d$ and $m\angle b = m\angle c$.

EXAMPLE

List the alternate exterior angles in the following figure. If $m\angle b = 50°$, find the measures of the other alternate exterior angles.

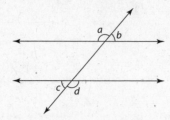

The alternate exterior angles in the given figure are these pairs: $\angle a$, $\angle d$ and $\angle b$, $\angle c$.

Since $m\angle b = 50°$, then $m\angle c = 50°$ because alternate exterior angles are equal. The angles $\angle a$ and $\angle b$ are on a straight line and are supplementary angles. This means that $m\angle a = 180° - 50° = 130°$. Also, $\angle a$ and $\angle d$ are alternate exterior angles and have equal measures.

So, $m\angle d = m\angle a = 130°$. Thus, $m\angle a = 130°$, $m\angle b = 50°$, $m\angle c = 50°$, and $m\angle d = 130°$.

Corresponding Angles

Two angles are said to be **corresponding angles** if both the angles lie on the same side of the transversal and are situated in the same way on two different parallel lines. Corresponding angles have equal measures.

In the following figure, the pairs of corresponding angles are:

$\angle a$ and $\angle g$

$\angle d$ and $\angle f$

$\angle b$ and $\angle h$

$\angle c$ and $\angle e$

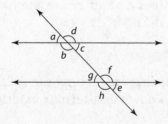

Therefore, $m\angle a = m\angle g$, $m\angle d = m\angle f$, $m\angle b = m\angle h$, and $m\angle c = m\angle e$.

EXAMPLE 1

If $m\angle a = 120°$, find $m\angle b$.

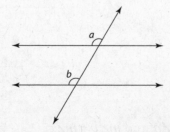

In the given figure, $\angle a$ and $\angle b$ are corresponding angles.

The measures of corresponding angles are equal.

Hence, $m\angle b = m\angle a = 120°$.

EXAMPLE 2

Find the corresponding angle of $\angle q$ and if $m\angle q = 70°$, find the measures of other angles.

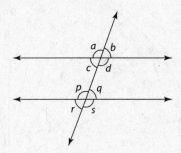

The corresponding angles in the given figure are $\angle a$ and $\angle p$, $\angle c$ and $\angle r$, $\angle b$ and $\angle q$, and $\angle d$ and $\angle s$.

Given, $m\angle q = 70°$. Thus, $m\angle b = 70°$ as the measures of corresponding angles are equal.

$\angle b$ and $\angle d$ are lying on a straight line and are hence supplementary angles.

Therefore,

$$m\angle d = 180° - m\angle b$$
$$= 180° - 70°$$
$$= 110°$$

1. $\angle d$ and $\angle s$ are corresponding angles and have equal measures. Therefore, $m\angle s = m\angle d = 110°$.

2. $\angle s$ and $\angle p$ are vertical angles. Therefore, $m\angle s = m\angle p = 110°$.

3. $\angle q$ and $\angle r$ are vertical angles. Therefore, $m\angle q = m\angle r = 70°$.

4. $\angle p$ and $\angle a$ are corresponding angles. Therefore, $m\angle p = m\angle a = 110°$.

5. $\angle r$ and $\angle b$ are corresponding angles. Therefore, $m\angle r = m\angle b = 70°$.

6. Thus, $m\angle a = 110°$, $m\angle b = 70°$, $m\angle c = 70°$, $m\angle d = 110°$, $m\angle p = 110°$, $m\angle q = 70°$, $m\angle r = 70°$, and $m\angle s = 110°$.

EXERCISE 2

Angles

Directions: Answer each question.

1. What is the measure of the angle shown in the diagram?

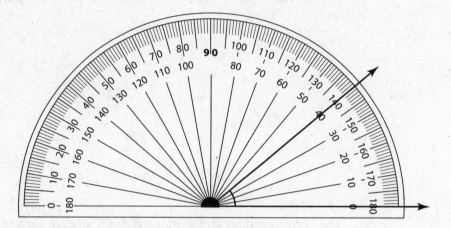

2. What is the measure of the angle shown in the diagram?

3. Use a protractor to find the measure of the angle shown in the diagram.

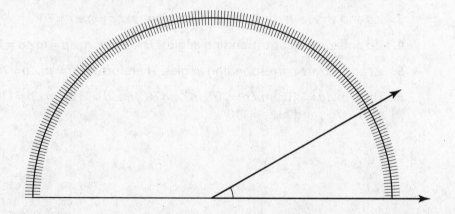

4. Use a protractor to find the measure of the angle shown in the diagram.

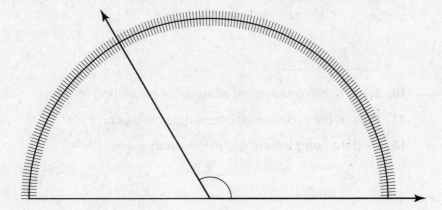

Identify the type of each angle.

5.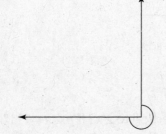

6.

7.

8.

9.

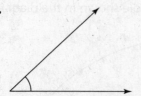

10. What is the complement of an angle measuring 56°?

11. What is the supplement of an angle measuring 138°?

12. Find the complement of the following angle.

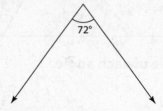

13. Find the supplement of the following angles.

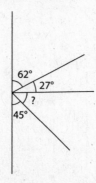

14. Using the diagram shown, which angle is vertical to ∠x? If $m∠x = 111°$, what is the measure of its vertical angle?

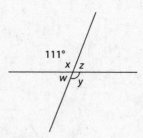

15. Using the diagram shown, list the alternate interior angles. If $m∠p = 73°$, find the measures of other alternate interior angles.

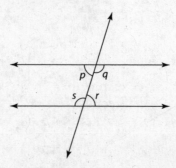

16. Find the alternate exterior angles, and if $m\angle x = 133°$, find the measures of the other angles.

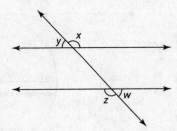

17. If $m\angle x = 64°$, find $m\angle y$.

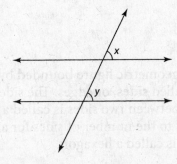

18. Find the corresponding angle of $\angle a$, and if $m\angle a = 70°$, find the measures of the other angles.

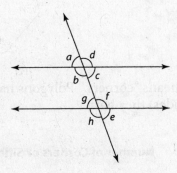

Answers are on page 568.

Two-Dimensional Figures

Circle

A **circle** is a closed curve in which the center point is at the same distance from the boundary from every direction. The center point is the **center** of the circle. A line segment connecting the center to a point on the boundary is the **radius** of the circle.

The **diameter** is any straight line segment passing through the center that joins any two points on the circle boundary. Its length is twice the length of the radius.

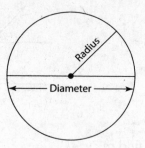

Polygon

A **polygon** is a geometric figure bounded by three or more line segments. These line segments are called **sides**, or edges. The sides do not have to be of equal length. The point of intersection between two sides is called a **vertex** (plural: **vertices**). The number of corners is equal to the number of sides for any polygon. The diagram shows an example of a polygon. It is called a hexagon.

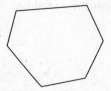

In Greek, *gon* means "corners." Polygons have different names according to the number of corners (or sides) they have.

Number of Corners or Sides	Polygon
3	Triangle
4	Quadrilateral
5	Pentagon
6	Hexagon
7	Heptagon
8	Octagon
9	Nonagon
10	Decagon

Regular Polygon

A regular polygon is a polygon with all sides of equal length. An example of a regular polygon is shown in the diagram. It is called a pentagon.

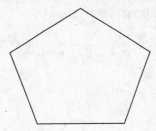

Triangle

A **triangle** is a closed plane figure with three sides and three angles. The sum of its angles is 180°.

- **Right Triangle:** A **right triangle** is a triangle that has a right angle. In the following figure, ∠B is a right angle; that is, it has a measure of 90°.

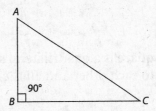

- **Equilateral Triangle:** An **equilateral triangle** is a triangle whose sides are all equal. All the angles have equal measures as well; that is, each one has a measure of 60°.

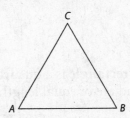

- **Acute Triangle:** An **acute triangle** is a triangle whose angles are all acute, that is, all measures are less than 90°.

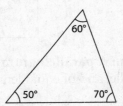

- **Obtuse Triangle:** An **obtuse triangle** is a triangle in which any one angle is an obtuse angle. In the following figure, ∠B is an obtuse angle; that is, its measure is greater than 90°.

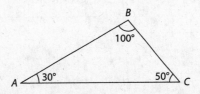

- **Isosceles Triangle:** An **isosceles triangle** is a triangle with two equal sides. The angles opposite the equal sides are also equal. In the following figure, $\overline{PQ}$ and $\overline{PR}$ are of equal lengths. The two marks on each side indicate that the sides are of equal length. Also, $\angle PQR = \angle PRQ$. $\angle Q$ and $\angle R$ are **base angles**, and $\angle P$ is the **apex angle** of the isosceles triangle.

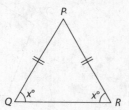

Quadrilateral

A **quadrilateral** is a polygon with four sides and four angles.

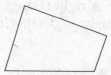

- **Square:** A **square** is a quadrilateral shape with four equal sides. The opposite sides are parallel to each other and all the angles are right angles.

- **Rectangle:** A **rectangle** is a quadrilateral shape with four sides. The opposite sides are parallel and are of equal length. All four angles are right angles.

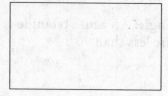

- **Parallelogram:** A **parallelogram** is a quadrilateral in which the pairs of opposite sides are parallel and of equal length.

- **Rhombus:** A **rhombus** is a parallelogram with four equal sides.

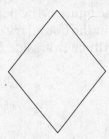

- **Trapezoid:** A **trapezoid** is a quadrilateral in which only one pair of opposite sides are parallel and the other pair of sides are not parallel.

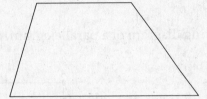

Composite Figures

Composite figures are made up of two or more geometric figures.

- **Square with Hole:** As the name suggests, this figure contains a square with a circular hole. In the following figure, the shaded portion represents the remaining portion of the square.

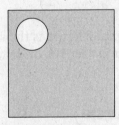

- **Rectangle with Semicircular Attachment:** This figure includes a rectangle having a semicircular attachment on one of its sides.

- **Triangle with Square Missing from Side:** This figure includes a triangle having a square portion missing from one of its sides. In the following figure, the shaded portion denotes the remaining portion of the triangle.

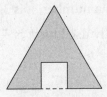

Altitude of Plane Figure

The altitude of a plane figure is the perpendicular distance from one side of the figure to the farthest point in the boundary of the figure. In the following diagram of an acute triangle, AD is the altitude from side BC to point A.

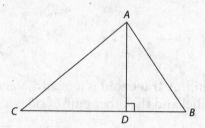

In the following diagram of a parallelogram, AE is the altitude from side CD to point A.

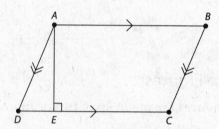

Perimeter

The **perimeter** of a plane figure is the measure of the distance of its boundary around the figure. Perimeter is a length or distance. Examples of perimeter measure are inches, meters, or feet.

Perimeter of a Circle

For a circle, the perimeter is called the **circumference**. It can be calculated using the length of the radius, r, or diameter, d. Note that the diameter is twice as long as the radius and can be calculated as $d = 2 \times r$, where d is the diameter and r is the radius.

The formula for finding the circumference C of a circle is:

$C = 2\pi r$, where r stands for radius;

Or

$C = \pi d$, where d stands for diameter.

The number π (**pi**) is the ratio of the circumference of any circle to the diameter of that circle: $\pi = \dfrac{C}{d}$. As a number, π is 3.14159… or, approximately, 3.14. The fractional approximation usually used for π is $\dfrac{22}{7}$, for the purpose of computation.

EXAMPLE

Find the circumference of a circle with radius measuring 2 feet. Use $\pi = 3.14$.

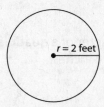

Circumference $= 2\pi r = 2 \times 3.14 \times 2 = 12.56$ feet.

Therefore, the circumference of the given circle is 12.56 feet.

Perimeter of a Polygon

- **Regular Polygon:** The perimeter of a regular polygon is n times the length of any side, where n is the number of sides.

EXAMPLE

Find the perimeter P of a regular pentagon having a side length of 2 feet.

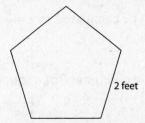

2 feet

A regular pentagon has 5 equal sides. The perimeter is 5 times the side length of 2 feet: $P = 5 \times 2 = 10$. Thus, the perimeter is 10 feet.

- **Triangle:** The perimeter P of a triangle is the sum of all three of its sides: $P = a + b + c$, where a, b, and c are the lengths of the sides of the triangle.

EXAMPLE

Find the perimeter of a triangle having sides with lengths of 4 inches, 3 inches, and 5 inches.

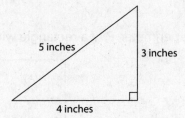

5 inches   3 inches

4 inches

$P = a + b + c$
$\quad = 4 + 3 + 5$
$\quad = 12$

The perimeter is 12 inches.

- **Quadrilateral:** The perimeter of any quadrilateral is the sum of its four sides: $P = a + b + c + d$, where a, b, c, and d are the sides of the quadrilateral.

EXAMPLE

Find the perimeter of a quadrilateral having sides with lengths of 5 inches, 6 inches, 4 inches, and 10 inches.

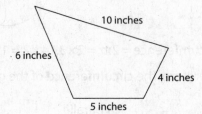

$$P = a + b + c + d$$
$$= 5 + 6 + 4 + 10$$
$$= 25$$

Thus, the perimeter of the quadrilateral is 25 inches.

- **Square:** Suppose s represents the length of one side of a square. The perimeter P of a square can be measured as $P = 4 \times s$. When the perimeter is known, the length of each side can be calculated by $s = \dfrac{P}{4}$.

EXAMPLE

Calculate the perimeter P of a square with each side measuring 6 feet.

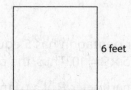

Here, the length of each side of the square s is 6 feet. The perimeter of a square is $4 \times s$. So, the perimeter is 4×6 feet $= 24$ feet.

- **Rectangle:** When the length, l, and width, w, of a rectangle are given, then the perimeter of the rectangle can be found by: $P = 2l + 2w = 2(l + w)$.

EXAMPLE

Find the perimeter, P, of a rectangle with a length of 6 inches and a width of 7 inches.

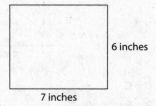

Here, length, l, is 6 inches and the width, w, is 7 inches.

So, the perimeter is $P = 2(l + w) = 2(6 + 7) = 2 \times 13 = 26$ inches.

- **Parallelogram:** The perimeter of a parallelogram is the sum of its sides. It is given by the formula $P = 2(a+b)$, where P is the perimeter and a, b are adjacent sides of the parallelogram.

EXAMPLE

Find the perimeter of the parallelogram with side lengths of 5 inches and 7 inches.

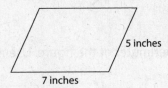

The perimeter of a parallelogram is $P = 2(a+b)$.

Thus, $P = 2(5+7) = 2 \times 12 = 24$ inches.

- **Rhombus:** The perimeter of a rhombus is $4 \times$ length of one side of the rhombus.

EXAMPLE

Calculate the perimeter of the rhombus with each side measuring 8 inches.

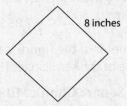

The perimeter of a rhombus is $4 \times$ length of the sides. So, P is 4×8 inches $= 32$ inches.

- **Trapezoid:** The perimeter of a trapezoid is the sum of all four sides. Here, $P = a+b+c+d$, where a, b, c, and d are the lengths of the sides of the trapezoid.

EXAMPLE

Find the perimeter of a trapezoid having sides with lengths of 7 inches, 6 inches, 5 inches, and 9 inches.

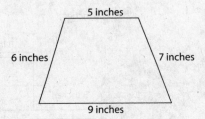

$$P = a+b+c+d$$
$$= 7+6+5+9$$
$$= 27$$

Thus, the perimeter of the trapezoid is 27 inches.

Perimeter of Composite Figures

The perimeter of a composite figure is the sum of its boundary. Sometimes, it is helpful to first calculate the perimeter of the simple figures in the composite figure and accordingly add or subtract the perimeters to get the perimeter of the composite figure.

- **Rectangle with Semicircular Attachment:** The perimeter of this figure includes the sum of the free sides of the rectangle and the circumference of the semicircle.

EXAMPLE

Find the perimeter of the figure. Use $\pi = 3.14$.

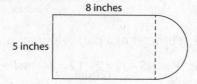

Look first at the half-circle or semicircle. The circumference of a circle in terms of diameter (d) is $C = \pi d$. So, the circumference of a semicircle will be $C = \dfrac{\pi d}{2}$.

The side of the rectangle on which the semicircle is attached is the diameter and has a length of 5 inches. Thus, the diameter is 5 inches.

Thus, $C = \dfrac{\pi d}{2} = \dfrac{3.14 \times 5}{2} = 7.85$ inches.

The perimeter of the figure is the sum of the three sides of the rectangle and the circumference of the semicircle. Thus, $P = 8 + 5 + 8 + 7.85 = 28.85$ inches.

- **Triangle with Square Chunk Missing from Side:** The perimeter of this figure includes part of the perimeter of the triangle plus part of the perimeter of the square.

EXAMPLE

Find the perimeter of the shaded portion of the following figure.

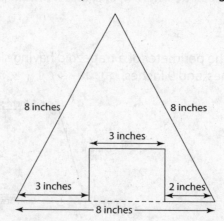

The perimeter of the figure is the sum of the sides of the shaded portion of figure.

The triangle has a side length of 8 inches and the square has a side length of 3 inches. Thus the perimeter of the figure is two sides of the triangle and three sides of the square, plus the third side of the triangle minus one side of the square (8 inches − 3 inches = 5 inches, broken into a 3-inch piece and a 2-inch piece):
$8 + 8 + 3 + 3 + 3 + 3 + 2 = 30$ inches.

EXERCISE 3

Perimeter

Directions: Find the distance around each figure.

1. Find the circumference of the circle. Use π = 3.14.

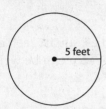

5 feet

2. Find the perimeter of the regular hexagon.

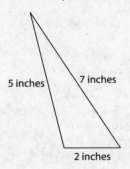

3 feet

3. Find the perimeter of the triangle.

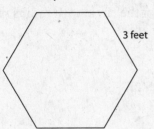

5 inches 7 inches

2 inches

4. Find the perimeter of the quadrilateral.

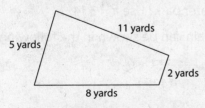

11 yards

5 yards

2 yards

8 yards

5. Calculate the perimeter of the square.

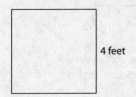

4 feet

6. Find the perimeter of the rectangle.

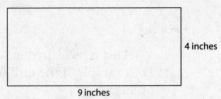

4 inches

9 inches

7. Find the perimeter of the parallelogram.

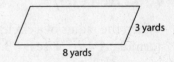

3 yards

8 yards

8. Calculate the perimeter of the rhombus.

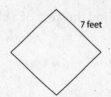

7 feet

9. Find the perimeter of the trapezoid.

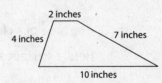

2 inches

4 inches 7 inches

10 inches

10. Find the perimeter of the following figure.

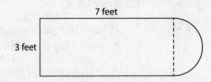

7 feet

3 feet

11. Find the perimeter of the shaded portion of the following figure.

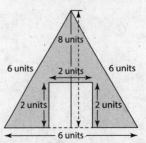

8 units

6 units 2 units 6 units

2 units 2 units

6 units

Answers are on page 568.

Area

The **area** of a plane figure is a measure of the amount of surface or space within the figure. The shaded portions of the following figures represent the areas of the figures.

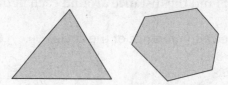

Area is measured in square units, such as square inches, square feet, and square meters. For example, if the unit of length is feet, then the unit of area can be written as square feet or feet².

Area of a Circle

When the radius of a circle is given, the area, A, of the circle with radius r is given by the formula $A = \pi r^2$. Use $\pi = 3.14$ for computing the area.

EXAMPLE 1

Find the area of a circle with a radius of 6 feet.

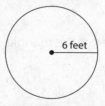

6 feet

The area of a circle can be calculated by $A = \pi r^2$.

Here, $r = 6$ feet and $\pi = 3.14$.

So, $A = 3.14 \times 6^2 = 3.14 \times 36 = 113.04$ square inches.

EXAMPLE 2

A fountain at a water park has a circular base of 10 feet radius. What is the area covered by the fountain in the water park? Use $\pi = 3.14$.

The circular base of the fountain can be shown in the following figure.

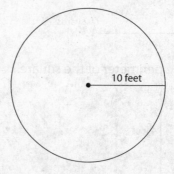

10 feet

$A = \pi r^2$

Here, $r = 10$ feet and $\pi = 3.14$.

So, $A = 3.14 \times 10^2 = 3.14 \times 100 = 314$ feet^2.

Therefore, the area of the fountain in the park is 314 square feet (sq ft or ft^2).

Area of a Polygon

- **Triangle:** The area of a triangle is $A = \frac{1}{2}bh$, where b is the length of the base and h is the height of the triangle. This works for all triangles regardless of shape.

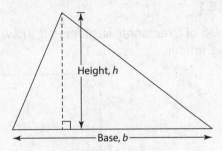

EXAMPLE

Find the area of the triangle with a base of 8 inches and height of 5 inches.

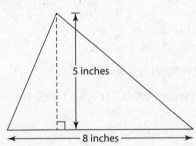

$$A = \frac{1}{2}bh = \frac{1}{\cancel{2}} \times \overset{4}{\cancel{8}} \times 5 = 20 \ \text{in}^2.$$

- **Square:** The area of a square with side s is $A = s^2 = s \times s$. When the area of the square is known, the length of the side can be measured by taking the square root of the area: $\sqrt{A}$.

EXAMPLE 1

Calculate the area of a square with each side measuring 7.5 feet.

Here, the length of each side of the square is 7.5 feet.

The area of a square is $A = s^2 = (7.5 \ \text{feet})^2 = 56.25 \ \text{feet}^2$.

EXAMPLE 2

The perimeter of a square is 69 inches. Find the area of the square.

Here, the perimeter of the square is 69 inches and it is known that $P = 4 \times$ length of the side.

Find the length of the side of the square from the perimeter:

$$\text{length of the side} = \frac{P}{4} = \frac{69}{4} = 17.25 \text{ inches.}$$

Thus, the area of the square is $A = (17.25 \text{ inches})^2 = 17.25 \times 17.25 = 297.56$ square inches or inches^2.

- **Rectangle:** When the length (l) and the width (w) are given, then the area, A, of the rectangle can be found by the formula $A = l \times w$. When the perimeter or the area of the rectangle is given and either the length or width is given, then the missing side of the rectangle can also be calculated.

EXAMPLE 1

The area of a rectangle is 36 feet^2. If the width of the rectangle is 4 feet, find its length and perimeter.

4 feet

You know: area = 36 feet^2, width = 4 feet.

$A = l \times w$

$l = \dfrac{A}{w} = \dfrac{36}{4} = 9$

The length is 9 feet.

The perimeter is $2\,(l + w) = 2\,(9 + 4) = 2 \times 13 = 26$ feet.

EXAMPLE 2

The perimeter of a rectangle is 42 units. If the length of the rectangle is 14 units, find its width and area.

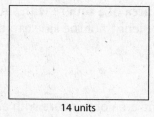

14 units

The perimeter P is 42 units and the length l is 14 units. The formula for the perimeter of a rectangle is $2(l + w)$.

Thus, substituting the value for P and l, find the width w.

$P = 2\,(l + w)$

$42 = 2\,(14 + w)$

$42 = 28 + 2w$

$$14 = 2w$$

$$w = 7$$

The width is 7 inches. Now find the area of the given rectangle.

$A = l \times w = 14 \times 7 = 98$ square units.

- **Parallelogram:** The area of a parallelogram is the product of its base and height, that is, $A = b \times h$.

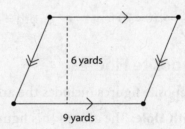

EXAMPLE

Find the area of the parallelogram with a base that is 9 yards long and a height of 6 yards.

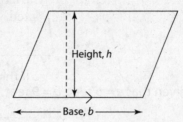

You are given that $b = 9$ and $h = 6$.

$$A = b \times h$$

$$= 9 \times 6 = 54 \text{ yards}^2$$

- **Trapezoid:** The area of a trapezoid is given by $A = \dfrac{a+b}{2} \times h$.

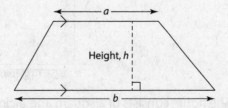

Here, a and b are the lengths of the two parallel sides and h is the height of the trapezoid.

EXAMPLE

Find the area of the trapezoid with parallel sides of lengths 5 feet and 9 feet and a height of 10 feet.

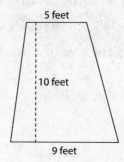

5 feet

10 feet

9 feet

You are given that $a = 5$ feet, $b = 9$ feet, and $h = 10$ feet.

$$A = \frac{a+b}{2} \times h$$

$$= \frac{5+9}{2} \times 10$$

$$= \frac{\overset{7}{\cancel{14}}}{\cancel{2}} \times 10 = 70 \text{ feet}^2$$

Area of Composite Figures

The area of composite figures includes the areas of individual figures.

- **Square with Hole:** The area of this figure is calculated by subtracting the area of the circle from the area of the square.

EXAMPLE

Find the area of the shaded portion.

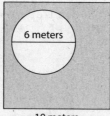

6 meters

10 meters

The figure consists of a square and a circle. The side of the square is given, $s = 10$ meters.

So, the area of the square is $s^2 = 10^2 = 100$ meters^2.

The radius of the circle is $r = \frac{d}{2} = \frac{6}{2} = 3$ meters.

So, the area of the circle $= \pi r^2 = 3.14 \times 3^2 = 3.14 \times 9 = 28.26$ meters^2.

The circle is within the square and is excluded from the square portion. Thus, the area of the shaded portion is the area of the square minus the area of the circle.

Area of the shaded portion = $100 - 28.26$ meters^2 = 71.74 meters^2.

- **Rectangle with Semicircular Attachment:** The area of this figure includes the sum of the area of the rectangle and the area of the semicircle.

EXAMPLE

Find the area of the following figure. Use $\pi = 3.14$.

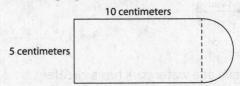

The area of the rectangle = $l \times w = 10 \times 5 = 50$ centimeters^2.

The area of the semicircle is $\dfrac{\pi r^2}{2}$.

The diameter of the circle is the length of the side of the rectangle to which the circle is attached. It is 5 centimeters long. So the radius r is 2.5 centimeters.

The area of the semicircle is $\dfrac{\pi r^2}{2} = \dfrac{3.14 \times 2.5^2}{2} = \dfrac{3.14 \times 6.25}{2} = \dfrac{19.625}{2} = 9.81$ centimeters^2.

Thus, the total area of the composite figure = area of the rectangle + area of the semicircle.

$A = 50 + 9.81 = 59.81$ centimeters^2.

- **Triangle with Square Chunk Missing from Side:** The area of this figure includes the area of the triangle minus the area of the square.

EXAMPLE

Find the area of the shaded figure.

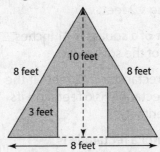

The area of the figure is the area of the triangle minus the area of the square.

The base of the triangle is 8 feet and the height is 10 feet.

So, the area of the triangle is $A = \dfrac{1}{2}bh = \dfrac{1}{2} \times \overset{4}{\cancel{8}} \times 10 = 40$ feet^2.

The length of one side of the square is 3 feet. Thus, the area of the square is $3 \times 3 = 9$ feet^2.

Total area of the composite figure = area of the triangle − area of the square.

$= 40 - 9 = 31$ feet^2

Therefore, the area of the shaded portion is 31 feet^2.

EXERCISE 4

Area

Directions: Find the area of the figures.

1. Find the area of the given circle.

2. A fountain at a water park has a circular base of 9 feet radius. What is the area covered by the circular base?

3. Find the area of the triangle.

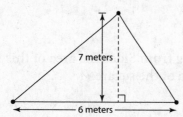

4. Calculate the area of a square with each side measuring 9.2 feet.

5. The perimeter of a square is 41 inches. Find the area of the square.

6. The area of a rectangle is 42 feet². If the width of the rectangle is 6 feet, find its length and perimeter.

7. The perimeter of a rectangle is 28 centimeters. If the length of the rectangle is 5 centimeters, find its width and area.

8. Find the area of the parallelogram of base 7 meters and height 5 meters.

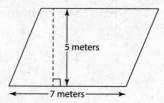

9. Find the area of the trapezoid.

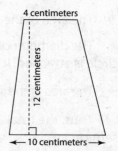

10. Find the area of the shaded portion.

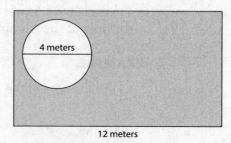

11. Find the area of the figure.

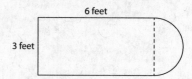

12. Find the area of the shaded figure.

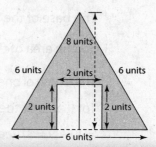

Sums of Interior Angles for Plane Figures

The angles within a plane figure are known as its **interior angles**. The **sum of interior angles** is the total of all the interior angles within the plane figure.

EXAMPLE 1

Find the sum of the interior angles of the triangle.

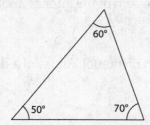

The interior angles of the given triangle are 50°, 60°, and 70°.

Thus, the sum of interior angles = 50° + 60° + 70° = 180°.

EXAMPLE 2

Find the sum of the interior angles of the hexagon.

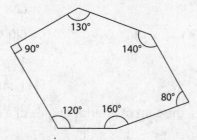

The interior angles of the given hexagon are 90°, 130°, 140°, 80°, 160°, and 120°.

Thus, the sum of interior angles = 90° + 130° + 140° + 80° + 160° + 120° = 720°.

General Plane Figure

If a plane figure has n sides, then the sum of its interior angles can be calculated by the formula $(2n-4) \times 90°$.

EXAMPLE 1

What is the sum of interior angles of a pentagon?

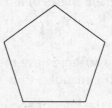

The pentagon has five sides, $n = 5$.

$$\text{The sum of the interior angles} = (2n - 4) \times 90°$$
$$= (2 \times 5 - 4) \times 90°$$
$$= (10 - 4) \times 90°$$
$$= 6 \times 90°$$
$$= 540°$$

Thus, the sum of the interior angles of a pentagon is 540°.

EXAMPLE 2

Find the sum of interior angles of a decagon.

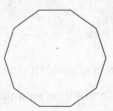

A decagon has 10 sides, $n = 10$.

$$\text{The sum of the interior angles} = (2n - 4) \times 90°$$
$$= (2 \times 10 - 4) \times 90°$$
$$= (20 - 4) \times 90°$$
$$= 16 \times 90°$$
$$= 1,440°$$

Thus, the sum of interior angles of a decagon is 1,440°.

Triangle

A triangle has three sides, that is, $n = 3$. Therefore, the sum of interior angles of a triangle can be calculated as:

$$(2n - 4) \times 90°$$
$$= (2 \times 3 - 4) \times 90°$$
$$= (6 - 4) \times 90°$$
$$= 2 \times 90°$$
$$= 180°$$

Thus, the sum of interior angles of a triangle is 180°.

EXAMPLE 1

Two angles of a triangle have measures of 30° and 60°. Find the measure of the third angle of the triangle.

The sum of the interior angles of a triangle is 180°. Thus, the sum of the measures of the two given angles is 30° + 60° = 90°. The third angle is the difference between the sum of the interior angles and the sum of the two given angles: 180° − 90° = 90°. Thus, the third angle of the triangle has a measure of 90°.

EXAMPLE 2

The measures of the angles of a triangle have the ratio 1:1:4. Find the angles.

The sum of interior angles of a triangle is 180°. The measures of the angles can be written as x, x, and $4x$.

$$x + x + 4x = 6x$$
$$6x = 180°$$
$$x = \frac{180°}{6} = 30°$$
$$4x = 30° \times 4 = 120°$$

Thus, the measures of the angles of the triangle are 30°, 30°, and 120°.

Quadrilateral

A quadrilateral has four sides, that is, $n = 4$. Therefore, the sum of interior angles can be calculated as:

$$(2n - 4) \times 90°$$
$$= (2 \times 4 - 4) \times 90°$$
$$= (8 - 4) \times 90°$$
$$= 4 \times 90°$$
$$= 360°$$

Thus, the sum of interior angles of a quadrilateral is 360°.

EXAMPLE 1

The measures of three angles of a quadrilateral are 30°, 50°, and 130°. Find the fourth angle of the quadrilateral.

The sum of the three angles is 30° + 50° + 130° = 210°. So, the measure of the fourth angle is the difference between the sum of the interior angles and the sum of the three given angles:

360° − 210° = 150°.

Thus, the fourth angle of the quadrilateral is 150°.

EXAMPLE 2

The angles of a quadrilateral are in the ratio 1:2:4:5. Find the angles.

The sum of interior angles of a quadrilateral is 360°.

The angles are in the ratio 1:2:4:5.

Let the angles be x, $2x$, $4x$, and $5x$. The sum of angles is $x + 2x + 4x + 5x = 12x$.

$$12x = 360°$$
$$x = \frac{360°}{12} = 30°$$
$$2x = 30° \times 2 = 60°$$
$$4x = 30° \times 4 = 120°$$
$$5x = 30° \times 5 = 150°$$

Thus, the angles of the quadrilateral are 30°, 60°, 120°, and 150°.

EXERCISE 5

Sums of Interior Angles for Plane Figures

Directions: Answer the following questions.

1. Find the sum of the interior angles of a heptagon.

2. Find the sum of the interior angles of a 14-sided plane figure.

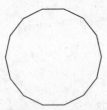

3. The measures of two angles of a triangle are 45° and 80°. Find the third angle of the triangle.

4. The measures of the angles of a triangle have the ratio 2:1:6. Find the measures of the angles.

5. Three angles of a quadrilateral have measures of 45°, 30°, and 160°. Find the measure of the fourth angle of the quadrilateral.

6. The measures of the angles of a quadrilateral have the ratio 2:1:3:4. Find the measures of the angles.

7. Find the sum of the interior angles of an octagon.

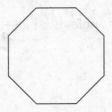

8. The measures of five interior angles of a hexagon are 100°, 140°, 110°, 115°, and 135°. Find the sixth angle.

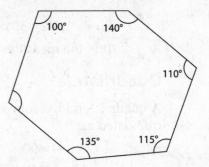

9. The measures of four angles of a pentagon are 68°, 121°, 103°, and 85°. Find the measure of the fifth angle.

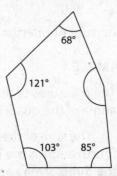

10. If the measures of three interior angles of a quadrilateral are 68°, 126°, and 106°, find the measure of the fourth angle.

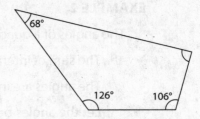

Answers are on page 569.

Three-Dimensional Figures

Types of Figures

Sphere

A **sphere** is a set of points all at the same distance from the central point in three-dimensional spaces. It is a geometric figure shaped like a ball and is described by the radius of the circle that passes through its center. The distance around this circle is the **circumference of the sphere**.

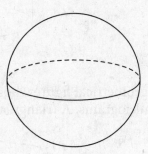

Cube

A **cube** is a three-dimensional solid object with six square faces, that is, the lengths of all edges are equal. All the corners of each face of a cube are right angles.

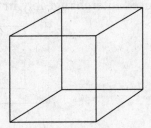

Rectangular Solid

A **rectangular solid** is a three-dimensional figure with rectangular sides and is described by its length, width, and height. The faces of a rectangular solid include the four sides, the bottom, and the top of the box. All corners of each face of a rectangular solid are right angles.

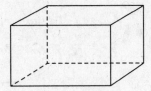

Cylinder

A **cylinder** is a solid figure whose top and bottom faces are circles and the sides are perpendicular to the bases. It is described by its radius and height. The **height of the cylinder** is the perpendicular distance between the top and bottom bases.

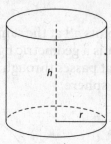

Prism

A **prism** is a solid geometrical figure whose two ends are equal, parallel figures. The sides of a prism are parallelograms. A triangular prism is shown below.

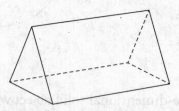

The following diagram shows a rectangular prism. It is also called a rectangular solid. The terms will be used interchangeably in this chapter.

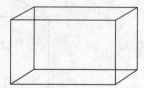

Cone

A **cone** is a three-dimensional solid figure with a circular base and a triangular cross-section with a vertex. The perpendicular distance from the vertex to the center of the circular base is the **height** of the cone.

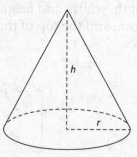

Pyramid

A **pyramid** is a solid figure made up of a base and triangular faces that meet at a common point called the **vertex/apex**. The number of triangular faces depends on the number of sides of the base. For example, a pyramid with a rectangular base has four triangular faces, while a pyramid with a hexagonal face is made up of six triangular faces. The **height** of a regular square pyramid is a vertical line from the vertex to the center of the square base. The triangular faces of the pyramid are called **lateral faces**.

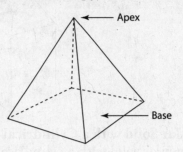

Polyhedron

A **polyhedron** is a three-dimensional solid object with flat faces, straight edges, and sharp corners (vertices). The following figure is a polyhedron.

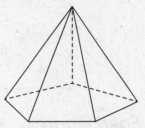

A **regular polyhedron** is polyhedron whose faces are identical regular polygons.

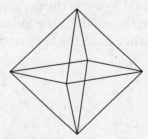

Composite Figures

Just as circles, squares, triangles, and rectangles may be combined, composite figures may be formed from various solids. Some of these are as follow.

- **Cylinder with One or Two Hemispherical Ends:** As the name suggests, this composite figure includes a cylinder with one or two hemispherical ends. The following diagrams show two such composite figures: one cylinder with a single hemispherical end and another cylinder with two hemispherical ends.

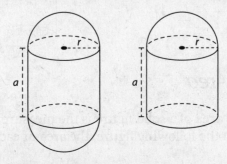

- **Prism with a Pyramidal End:** This figure consists of a prism with a pyramid attached to one end or one side.

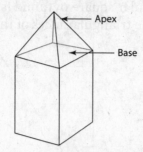

- **Rectangular Solid with a Cylindrical Hole Drilled Through It:** This figure consists of a rectangular solid with a cylindrical hole going through it.

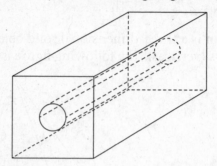

Altitude of a Solid Figure

The **altitude** of a solid figure is the perpendicular distance from the base of the figure to the highest point in the solid. In the following figure, the altitude of the pyramid is the perpendicular distance from the base of the pyramid to the vertex of the pyramid.

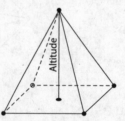

In the following figure, the altitude of a cylinder is the perpendicular distance from the base to the top of the cylinder.

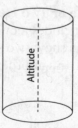

Surface Area

The **surface area** of a solid figure is the measure of the total area occupied by the surface. As shown in the following figure, the area of each of the shaded surfaces of a cube can be determined individually by using the formula for the area of a square. The total surface area of the cube is the sum of the areas of each of the six surfaces.

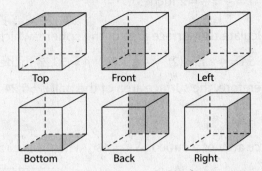

Surface area, *SA*, measures area, and thus its units are the same as those of any other area, that is, square units. These include square inches, square feet, etc.

Sphere

The surface area of a sphere is given by the formula $SA = 4\pi r^2$, where *r* is the radius of the sphere.

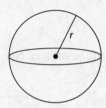

From the surface area, *SA*, of a sphere, its radius can be calculated with the formula $r = \sqrt{\dfrac{SA}{4\pi}}$, where *r* is the radius and $\pi = 3.14$.

EXAMPLE 1

If the radius is 7 feet for a given sphere, then what is the surface area of the sphere?

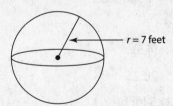

Surface area $= 4\pi r^2 = 4 \times \pi \times (7)^2 = 4 \times 3.14 \times 49 = 615.44$ feet^2

EXAMPLE 2

A ball has a diameter of 4 inches. What is its surface area?

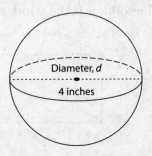

$$d = 2 \times r$$

$$r = \frac{d}{2} = \frac{4}{2} = 2 \text{ inches}$$

Calculate the surface area of the sphere, which is $4\pi r^2$.

$$SA = 4 \times \pi \times (2)^2 = 4 \times 3.14 \times 4 = 50.24 \text{ inches}^2$$

Therefore, the surface area of the ball is 50.24 inches².

Cube

The surface area of a cube is $SA = 6s^2$, where s is each edge of the cube.

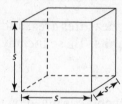

From the surface area of a cube, you can find the length of each edge by $s = \sqrt{\dfrac{SA}{6}}$.

EXAMPLE

Calculate the surface area of the cube with each edge measuring 4.5 inches.

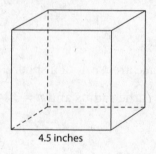

4.5 inches

Here, $s = 4.5$ inches.

$$SA = 6s^2$$

$$= 6 \times (4.5)^2$$

$$= 6 \times 20.25$$

$$= 121.5 \text{ inches}^2$$

Therefore, the surface area of the cube is 121.5 inches².

Rectangular Solid

The surface area of a rectangular solid is given by the formula $SA = 2(lw + wh + lh)$, where l is the length of the solid, w is the width of the solid, and h is the height of the solid.

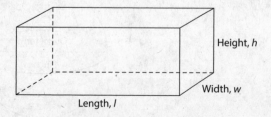

Height, h

Width, w

Length, l

EXAMPLE

Find the surface area of a rectangular solid with a length of 10 centimeters, a width of 3 centimeters, and a height of 5 centimeters.

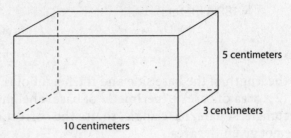

$l = 10$ centimeters, $w = 3$ centimeters, $h = 5$ centimeters

$SA = 2(lw + wh + lh)$

$\quad = 2\,[(10 \times 3) + (3 \times 5) + (10 \times 5)]$

$\quad = 2\,(30 + 15 + 50)$

$\quad = 2 \times 95 = 190$ centimeters^2

Cylinder

The surface area of a cylinder is $SA = 2\pi r^2 + 2\pi rh = 2\pi r(r + h)$, where r is the radius and h is the perpendicular height between the two bases.

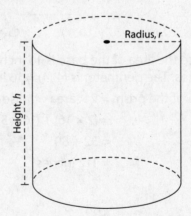

EXAMPLE

Find the surface area of a cylinder with radius 3 meters and height 7 meters.

$r = 3$ meters, $h = 7$ meters

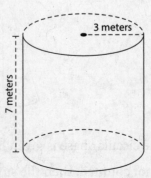

$$SA = 2\pi r(r + h)$$
$$= 2 \times 3.14 \times 3 \, (3 + 7)$$
$$= 18.84 \times 10$$
$$= 188.4 \text{ meters}^2$$

Prism

When the length of the base side and the height of the prism are given, then the surface area is (2 × area of base) + (perimeter of base × height of prism). The base of a prism may be a rectangle, square, or triangle, so use the correct formula for the area of the base if you are not given the area.

EXAMPLE

The area of the square base of a rectangular prism is 16 inches². The height of the rectangular prism is 5 inches. Find the surface area of the prism.

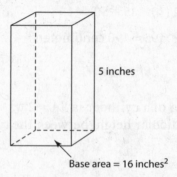

5 inches

Base area = 16 inches²

Since the area of the base is 16 inches², the length of one side of the square base is 4 inches. The perimeter is (4)(4) = 16 inches.

Area of the prism = 2 × area of base + (perimeter of base × height of prism)
$$= (2 \times 16) + (16 \times 5)$$
$$= 32 + 80$$
$$= 112 \text{ inches}^2$$

Cone

The surface area of a cone is $SA = \pi rh + \pi r^2$, where h is the slant height of the cone and r is the radius of the base. The **slant height** of a cone is the distance from any point on the outside edge of the base of the cone to the top, measured along the surface of the cone.

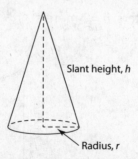

Slant height, h

Radius, r

The area of the circular base is given by $B = \pi r^2$.

If the base is not counted, then the surface area is $SA = \pi rh$.

EXAMPLE

Find the surface area of a cone if the slant height is 7 inches and radius is 2 inches.

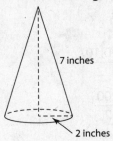

7 inches

2 inches

$h = 7$ inches, $r = 2$ inches

$SA = \pi rh + \pi r^2$

$\quad = (3.14 \times 2 \times 7) + (3.14 \times 2^2)$

$\quad = 43.96 + 12.56$

$\quad = 56.52$ inches^2

Pyramid

The total **surface area of a pyramid** is the sum of the areas of all its faces including its base. Use the formula $SA = B + \dfrac{PL}{2}$, where B is the area of the base, P is the perimeter of the base, and L is the slant height. Generally, you will work with pyramids with square, rectangular, or triangular bases.

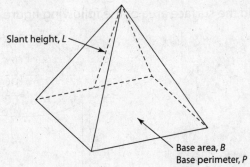

Slant height, L

Base area, B
Base perimeter, P

The **slant height** of a pyramid is the distance from the outside edge of the base of the pyramid to the apex, measured along the center of one lateral face. In other words, it is the altitude of the triangle that makes up that lateral face.

EXAMPLE

Find the surface area of a square pyramid (square base) if the base area is 25 feet^2 and the slant height is 10 feet.

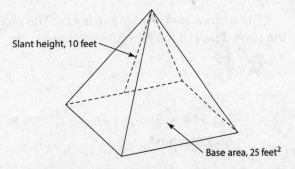

Slant height, 10 feet

Base area, 25 feet^2

The area of the square base is $B = 25$ feet². The length of each side of the base is 5 feet. So, the perimeter P is $4(5) = 20$ feet.

$$SA = B + \frac{PL}{2}$$

$$= 25 + \frac{20(10)}{2}$$

$$= 25 + \frac{200}{2}$$

$$= 125$$

Thus, the surface area of the pyramid is 125 feet².

Composite Solids

The surface area of a composite solid can be thought of as the sum of the surface areas of the separate solids. However, keep in mind that a base or face may not be counted because the solid figures will overlap. So the formulas that you use for surface area may have to be modified.

- **Cylinder with One or Two Hemispherical Ends:** For this figure, you need to find the surface area of the hemisphere and the surface area of the cylinder and then add the two surface areas.

EXAMPLE

Find the surface area of the following figure.

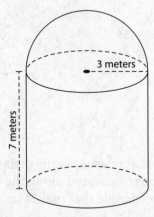

First, find the surface area of the hemisphere. The hemisphere consists of half a sphere. Notice that the circular base of the hemisphere overlaps with the base of the cylinder and is inside the solid. Thus, the area of the base is not considered for the surface area of the whole figure.

The surface area of a sphere is $4\pi r^2$. The radius is 3 meters. So, the surface area of the curved part of the hemisphere is given by:

$$SA = \frac{4\pi r^2}{2}$$

$$= 2\pi r^2$$

$$= 2 \times 3.14 \times 9$$

$$= 56.52 \text{ meters}^2$$

Next, find the surface area of the cylinder with $h = 7$. Notice that only the bottom end of the cylinder is counted as part of the surface area of the cylinder. So only find the area of one circle for the surface area of the cylinder. The formula for the surface area is modified.

$$SA = \pi r^2 + 2\pi rh$$
$$= 28.26 + 131.88$$
$$= 160.14 \text{ meters}^2$$

Thus, the surface area of the cylinder and hemisphere is $56.52 + 160.14 = 216.66 \text{ meters}^2$.

- **Prism with Pyramidal End:** Find the surface area of the prism and the surface area of the pyramidal end and then add the two surface areas to find the surface area of the entire figure. The base that the two figures share is not counted as part of the surface area, so the formulas for the surface area of both figures have to be adjusted.

EXAMPLE

In the following figure, the area of the base is 16 inches^2. The height of the prism is 8 inches and the slant height of the pyramid is 10 inches. Find the surface area of the figure.

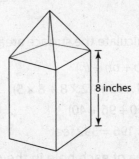

8 inches

The base of the pyramid and the prism are inside the solid figure because the solids overlap and meet at a base. So the base of the pyramid is not counted and one of the bases of the prism is not counted.

First, find the surface area of the prism. Since the area of the base is 16 square inches, one side has a length of 4 inches. The perimeter of the base is $(4)(4) = 16$ inches.

The surface area of the prism is the area of one square base + (perimeter of base × height of prism).

$$SA = 16 + (16 \times 8)$$
$$= 16 + 128$$
$$= 144 \text{ inches}^2$$

Now, the surface area of the pyramid is just $\frac{PL}{2}$, where P is the base perimeter and L is the slant height. So, $P = 16$ inches and $L = 10$ inches.

$$SA = \frac{16 \times 10}{2}$$
$$= \frac{160}{2}$$
$$= 80 \text{ inches}^2$$

Thus, the surface area of the prism with a pyramidal end is $144 + 80 = 224$ inches^2.

• **Rectangular Solid with a Cylindrical Hole Drilled Through It:** The surface area of this figure is calculated by subtracting the areas of the cylindrical holes from the areas of the ends and then adding the surface area of the cylinder, without its bases, inside the solid.

EXAMPLE

Find the surface area of the following figure if the radius of the cylindrical hole is 2 feet.

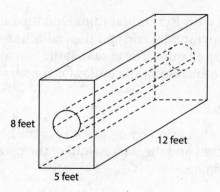

First, calculate the surface area of the rectangular solid.

$SA = 2(lb + bh + lh)$

$= 2(5 \times 12 + 12 \times 8 + 8 \times 5)$

$= 2(60 + 96 + 40)$

$= 2 \times 196 = 392$ feet²

The area of each hole in the ends of the rectangular solid is $\pi(2)^2 = (3.14)(4) = 12.56$ feet². Then the area of the two holes is $12.56 \times 2 = 25.12$ feet². This number will be subtracted from the surface area of the rectangular prism because the holes are cut out from the figure. With the hole drilled out, the surface of a cylinder without bases is present inside the solid. This surface area has to be found. The bases of the cylinder are not counted. Use the formula $SA = 2\pi rh$. The height of the cylinder is 12 feet.

$SA = 2(3.14)(2)(12)$

$= 150.72$ feet²

Thus, the surface area of this rectangular solid with the cylindrical hole drilled out is given by

$SA = 392 - 25.12 + 150.72 = 517.6$ feet².

The surface area for this figure is more than the surface area of the rectangular solid because the cylinder is cut out of the solid, exposing more surface area.

EXERCISE 6

Surface Area

Directions: Round your answer to the nearest hundredth. Use π = 3.14.

1. What is the surface area of the sphere?

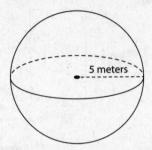

5 meters

2. What is the surface area of the ball?

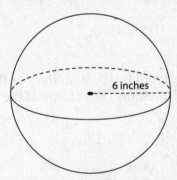

6 inches

3. Calculate the surface area of the cube.

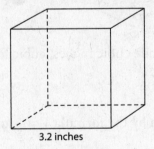

3.2 inches

4. Find the surface area of the rectangular solid.

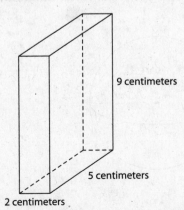

9 centimeters

5 centimeters

2 centimeters

5. Find the surface area of the cylinder.

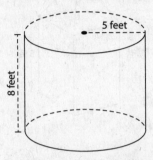

5 feet

8 feet

6. The base area and slant height of a square pyramid are 64 inches² and 20 inches, respectively. Find the surface area of the prism.

7. Find the surface area of the cone.

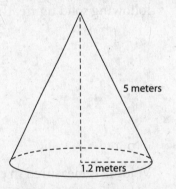

5 meters

1.2 meters

8. Find the surface area of a square pyramid if the base area is 36 centimeters² and the slant height is 9 centimeters.

9. Find the surface area of the solid.

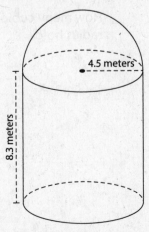

4.5 meters

8.3 meters

10. In the following composite solid, the area of the square base is 49 feet². The height of the rectangular prism is 5 feet, and the slant height of the pyramid is 3 feet. Find the surface area of the figure.

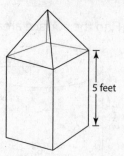

5 feet

11. Find the surface area of the solid if the radius of the cylindrical hole is 1.5 inches.

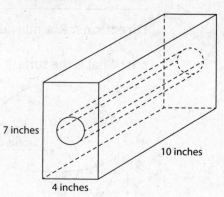

7 inches

10 inches

4 inches

Answers are on page 569.

Volume

The **volume** of a solid figure is the space enclosed by the boundary of the figure. In the following solid figure, the shaded portion represents the volume of the figure.

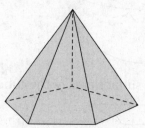

Volume is measured in cubic units. These include cubic inches, cubic feet, etc.

Sphere

The volume V of a sphere with radius r is given by the formula $V = \frac{4}{3}\pi r^3$.

EXAMPLE

How many cubic inches of water can a spherical water balloon with an 8-inch radius hold?

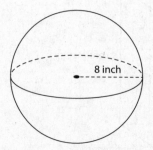

8 inch

To calculate the water content capacity of the balloon, find the volume.

$$V = \frac{4}{3}\pi r^3$$
$$= \frac{4}{3}\pi \times (8)^3$$
$$= \frac{4}{3} \times \pi \times 512$$
$$= 1.33 \times 3.14 \times 512$$
$$= 2{,}138.21 \text{ inches}^3$$

Therefore, the given balloon can hold 2,138.21 inches³ of water.

Cube

The volume V of a cube is $V = s^3$ cubic units, where s is the length of one edge of the cube and V is the volume. From the volume of a cube, you can find the length of one edge by $s = \sqrt[3]{V}$.

EXAMPLE

An underground water tank is in the shape of a cube of side 9 feet. What is its volume?

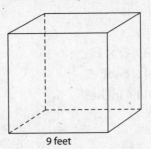

9 feet

The length of one side, *s*, of the tank is 9 feet.

$$V = s^3 = 9^3 = 729 \text{ feet}^3$$

Rectangular Solid

The volume V of a rectangular solid is given by $V = l \times w \times h$, where l, w, and h represent the length, width, and height, respectively, of the rectangular solid.

EXAMPLE

Find the volume of the rectangular solid whose length is 8 centimeters, width is 5 centimeters, and height is 7 centimeters.

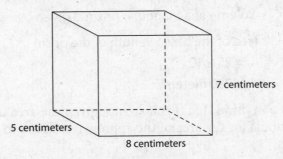

7 centimeters

5 centimeters

8 centimeters

$$V = l \times w \times h$$
$$= 8 \times 5 \times 7$$
$$= 280 \text{ centimeters}^3$$

Cylinder

The volume V of the cylinder is calculated by $V = \pi r^2 h$, where r is the radius of the cylinder and h is the height of the cylinder.

EXAMPLE

Find the volume of a cylinder whose radius is 8 inches and height is 15 inches.

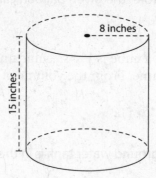

$$V = \pi r^2 h$$
$$= 3.14 \times 8^2 \times 15$$
$$= 3.14 \times 64 \times 15$$
$$= 3{,}014.4 \text{ inches}^2$$

Prism

The volume V of a triangular prism is given by the formula $V = A \times l$, where A is the area of the base and l is the length of the prism.

EXAMPLE

Find the volume of a triangular prism whose base has an area of 25 meters² and whose length is 10 meters.

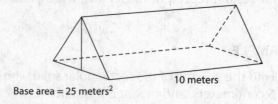

Base area = 25 meters²

Volume of a triangular prism is given by:

area of the base × length of the prism

$$= 25 \times 10$$
$$= 250 \text{ meters}^3$$

Keep in mind that if you are not given the area of the base of a prism, you need to use the formula for the area of the appropriate figure to find the area of that base.

Cone

The volume V of a cone is $V = \frac{1}{3}\pi r^2 h$, where r is the radius of the circular base and h is the height of the cone.

EXAMPLE

Find the volume of a cone if the radius is 5 feet and the height of the cone is 9 feet.

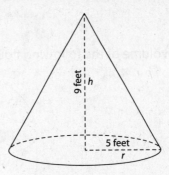

$$V = \frac{1}{3}\pi r^2 h$$

$$= \frac{1}{\cancel{3}} \times 3.14 \times 5^2 \times \cancel{9}^3$$

$$= 3.14 \times 25 \times 3$$

$$= 235.5$$

Thus, the volume of a cone is 235.5 feet^3.

Pyramid

The volume V of a pyramid is given by $V = \frac{1}{3}BH$, where B is the area of the base and H is the height of the pyramid (not the slant height).

EXAMPLE

The area of the base of a pyramid is 30 meters^2 and the height is 10 meters. Find the volume of the pyramid.

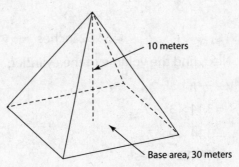

10 meters

Base area, 30 meters

$$V = \frac{1}{3}BH$$

$$= \frac{1}{\cancel{3}} \times \cancel{30}^{10} \times 10$$

$$= 100$$

Thus, the volume of the pyramid is 100 meters^3.

Composite Solids

The volumes of composites solids may be found in a fashion similar to finding areas of composite plane figures. Use volume formulas to find the volumes of the individual parts, and add them together, or subtract if there is volume missing.

- **Cylinders with One or Two Hemispherical Ends:** For this figure, the volume is calculated by adding the volumes of the cylinder and the hemisphere.

EXAMPLE

Find the volume of the following figure.

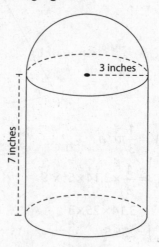

First, find the volume of the hemisphere.

The volume of a hemisphere is given by:

$$\frac{\text{volume of sphere}}{2} = \frac{4\pi r^3}{3 \times 2}$$

$$= \frac{2\pi r^3}{3}$$

$$= \frac{2}{3} \times 3.14 \times 3^2$$

$$= 2 \times 3.14 \times 9$$

$$= 56.52 \text{ inches}^3$$

Next, find the volume of the cylinder.

$$V = \pi r^2 h$$

$$= 3.14 \times 3^2 \times 7$$

$$= 3.14 \times 9 \times 7$$

$$= 197.82 \text{ inches}^3$$

Thus, the volume of the cylinder with a single hemispherical end is the sum of the volumes of the hemisphere and the cylinder and is given by 56.52 + 197.82 = 254.34 inches³.

- **Prism with Pyramidal End:** For this figure, find the volume of the prism and the volume of the pyramidal end and then add the two volumes.

EXAMPLE

In the following figure, the area of the base is 16 feet². The length of the rectangular prism is 8 feet, and the height of the pyramid is 10 feet. Find the volume of the figure.

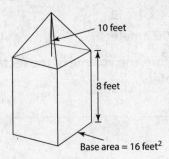

10 feet

8 feet

Base area = 16 feet²

First, find the volume of the prism.

$V = B \times l$

$= 16 \times 8$

$= 128 \text{ feet}^3$

Find the volume of the pyramid.

$V = \frac{1}{3}BH$

$= \frac{1}{3} \times 16 \times 10$

$= \frac{160}{3}$

$= 53.33$

Thus, the volume of the prism with the pyramidal end is $128 + 53.33 = 181.33 \text{ feet}^3$.

- **Rectangular Solid with a Cylindrical Hole Drilled Through It:** The volume of this figure is calculated by subtracting the volume of the cylindrical hole from the volume of the rectangular solid.

EXAMPLE

Find the volume of the figure if the radius of the cylindrical hole is 2 meters.

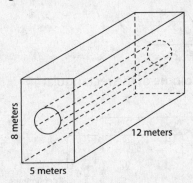

8 meters

12 meters

5 meters

First, calculate the volume of the rectangular solid.

$V = l \times w \times h$

$= 12 \times 5 \times 8$

$= 480 \text{ meters}^3$

Next, find the volume of the cylindrical hole.

$V = \pi r^2 h$

$= 3.14 \times 2^2 \times 12$

$= 3.14 \times 4 \times 12$

$= 150.72 \text{ meters}^3$

Therefore, the volume of the rectangular solid with the hole is $480 - 150.72 = 329.28 \text{ meters}^3$.

EXERCISE 7

Volume

Directions: Round your answers to the nearest hundredth. Use $\pi = 3.14$.

1. How many cubic inches of water can the spherical water balloon hold?

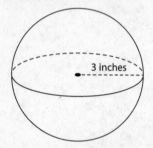

3 inches

2. An underground water tank is in the shape of cube as shown. What is its volume?

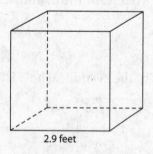

2.9 feet

3. Find the volume of the rectangular solid.

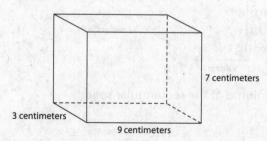

7 centimeters

3 centimeters

9 centimeters

4. Find the volume of the cylinder.

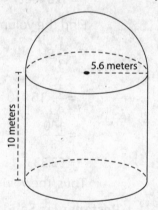

5.6 meters

10 meters

5. Find the volume of the triangular prism.

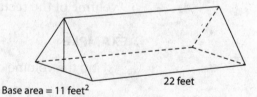

Base area = 11 feet²

22 feet

6. Find the volume of the cone.

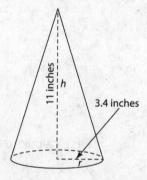

11 inches

h

3.4 inches

r

7. Find the volume of the pyramid.

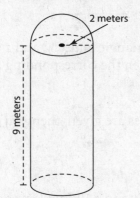

11.5 inches

Base area, 23 inches²

8. Find the volume of the composite solid.

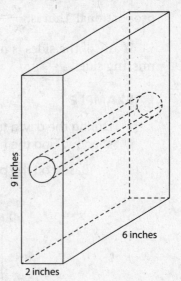

2 meters

9 meters

9. In the following figure, the base area of the rectangular prism is 11 feet². The length of the rectangular prism is 4 feet and the height of the pyramid is 8.7 feet. Find the volume of the figure.

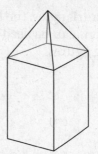

10. Find the volume of the solid if the radius of the cylindrical hole is 1.4 inches.

9 inches

6 inches

2 inches

Answers are on page 569.

Other Topics

Similar Triangles

Two triangles are said to be **similar triangles** if the measures of the corresponding angles of the triangles are equal and the lengths of the corresponding sides are in proportion. For example, refer to the following figures.

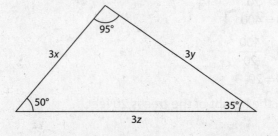

95°

$3x$ $3y$

50°   35°

$3z$

x 95° y

50°   35°

z

The triangles shown have equal corresponding angles and the corresponding sides are proportional, that is, $\dfrac{3x}{x}=\dfrac{3y}{y}=\dfrac{3z}{z}=\dfrac{3}{1}$. They are similar triangles.

Using Proportions to Find Missing Lengths

In similar triangles, the lengths of the corresponding sides are proportional. Thus, proportions can be used to find the length of any missing side of the triangle. Look at the following figures.

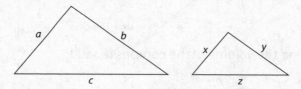

Consider that a, b, and c are the sides of one triangle and x, y, and z are the sides of another triangle. If the triangles are similar, then the corresponding sides will be proportional, that is, $\dfrac{a}{x}=\dfrac{b}{y}=\dfrac{c}{z}$.

If any of the sides is missing and the other sides are given, then you can find the missing side.

EXAMPLE

During the day, a tree casts a 40-foot shadow and a 10-foot lamppost casts a 20-foot shadow. Find the height of the tree.

Based on the problem, draw two similar triangles.

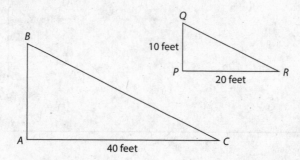

The corresponding sides are proportional. Thus, $\dfrac{AB}{PQ}=\dfrac{BC}{QR}=\dfrac{AC}{PR}$.

PQ, PR, and AC are given, and you have to find AB (height of the tree).

Therefore, write proportions using the lengths given and then solve.

$$\frac{AB}{PQ}=\frac{AC}{PR}$$

$$\frac{AB}{10}=\frac{40}{20}$$

$$20\,AB = 400$$

$$AB=\frac{400}{20}$$

$$AB=20$$

Thus, the height of the tree is 20 feet.

Pythagorean Theorem

The **Pythagorean theorem** states that the square of the length of the hypotenuse of a right triangle is equal to the sum of the squares of the lengths of the other two sides. This rule is applicable only to right triangles; that is, the triangle has to include a 90° angle. In a right triangle, the side opposite to the right angle is known as the **hypotenuse** and the other two sides are known as **legs of the triangle**.

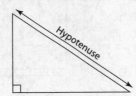

The theorem can be presented in a formula. If a and b are the lengths of the legs of a right triangle, and c is the length of the hypotenuse, then $a^2 + b^2 = c^2$.

Missing Hypotenuse

Given the Pythagorean theorem, the length of the hypotenuse of a right triangle can be found by the formula $c = \sqrt{a^2 + b^2}$.

EXAMPLE

Find the length of the hypotenuse of a right triangle with legs 3 meters and 4 meters.

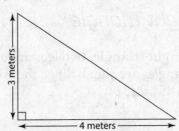

The lengths of the legs are given: $a = 3$ meters and $b = 4$ meters.

So, $c = \sqrt{a^2 + b^2}$

$= \sqrt{3^2 + 4^2}$

$= \sqrt{9 + 16}$

$= \sqrt{25} = 5$

Thus, the length of the hypotenuse c is 5 meters.

Missing Leg

Given the Pythagorean theorem, the length of the missing leg of a right triangle can be found by using the following formula:

$a^2 + b^2 = c^2$

$a^2 = c^2 - b^2$ or $b^2 = c^2 - a^2$

$a = \sqrt{c^2 - b^2}$ or $b = \sqrt{c^2 - a^2}$

Thus, to find the length of a leg of a triangle, you need to find the square root of the difference of the square of the hypotenuse and the square of the other leg.

EXAMPLE

A right triangle has a hypotenuse of 15 feet and a leg of 12 feet. Find the length of the other leg.

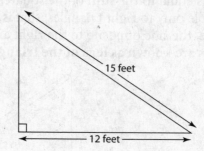

You are given that $c = 15$ feet and $b = 12$ feet. You need to find a.

$$a = \sqrt{c^2 - b^2}$$
$$= \sqrt{15^2 - 12^2}$$
$$= \sqrt{225 - 144}$$
$$= \sqrt{81} = 9$$

Thus, the length of the other leg is 9 feet.

Isosceles Right Triangle

In an **isosceles right triangle**, two legs are of equal lengths and the measures of the corresponding angles are equal. Since the triangle is a right triangle, the angles of the triangle are 45°, 45°, and 90°.

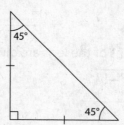

The Pythagorean theorem can be applied to this triangle. As the lengths of the two legs are equal (i.e., $a = b$), the hypotenuse can be calculated as follows:

$$c^2 = a^2 + b^2$$
$$= 2a^2$$

So, the length of the hypotenuse is $\sqrt{2a^2} = a\sqrt{2}$.

30°-60°-90° Right Triangle

A **30°-60°-90° right triangle** is a right triangle having angles 30°, 60°, and 90°.

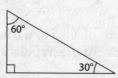

EXERCISE 8

Pythagorean Theorem

Directions: Find the length of the missing side.

1. Find the length of the hypotenuse of the following triangle.

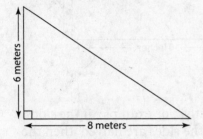

2. Find the length of the hypotenuse of the following triangle.

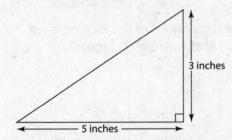

3. Find the length of the other leg in the following triangle.

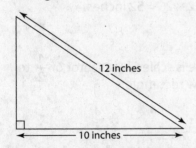

4. Find the length of the hypotenuse in the following triangle.

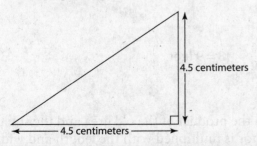

5. Find the length of the other leg in the following triangle.

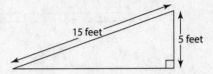

6. Find the length of the other leg in the following triangle.

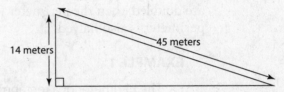

7. Find the length of the other leg in the following triangle.

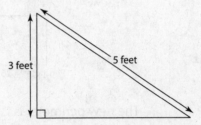

8. Find the length of the hypotenuse in the following triangle.

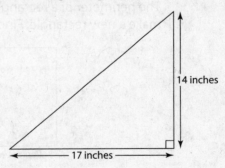

Effects of a Scale Factor

A **scale factor** is a ratio of the lengths of the corresponding sides of similar figures. The word *factor* implies that figures are scaled by multiplication or division. The scale factor affects the perimeter, area, and volume of the figures.

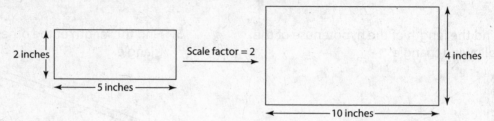

On Perimeter

The scale factor affects the perimeter of the figure directly. For example, if the sides are doubled, then the perimeter is also doubled, and if the sides are halved, then the perimeter is also halved.

EXAMPLE 1

The perimeter of a rectangle is 26 inches. If the dimensions of the rectangle are increased by a scale factor of 2, find the perimeter of the new rectangle.

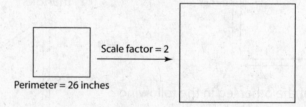

The new perimeter is 2 times the old perimeter: $2 \times 26 = 52$ inches.

EXAMPLE 2

The perimeter of a rectangle is 18 feet. The rectangle is scaled by a factor of $\frac{1}{2}$ to make a new rectangle. Find the perimeter of the new rectangle.

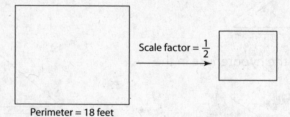

The perimeter is $\frac{1}{2} \times$ old perimeter: $\frac{1}{2} \times 18 = 9$ feet.

On Area

If the scale factor is given, then the new area is the product of the old area and the square of the scale factor. This is because the scale factor is multiplied with the length and width separately, giving two factors, or a square, of the scale factor.

EXAMPLE 1

The area of a square is 16 inches². The square is scaled by a factor of 3 to make a new square. Find the area of the new square.

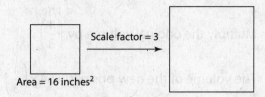

Area = 16 inches² Scale factor = 3

Multiply the original area of the square by 3^2.

The area of the new square is $16 \times 3^2 = 16 \times 9 = 144$ inches².

EXAMPLE 2

The area of a triangle is 24 meters². The triangle is scaled by a factor of $\frac{1}{2}$ to make a new triangle. Find the area of the new triangle.

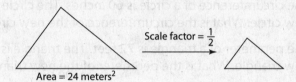

Area = 24 meters² Scale factor = $\frac{1}{2}$

Multiply the original area of the triangle by $\left(\frac{1}{2}\right)^2$.

The area of the new triangle is $\left(\frac{1}{2}\right)^2 (24) = \frac{24}{4} = 6$ meters².

On Volume

If the scale factor is given, then the new volume is the product of the old volume and the cube of the scale factor (raised to the third power).

EXAMPLE 1

The volume of a cylinder is 60 inches³. The cylinder is scaled by a factor of 2 to make a new cylinder. What is the volume of the new cylinder?

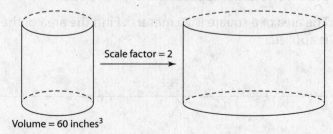

Volume = 60 inches³ Scale factor = 2

Multiply the original volume by 2^3.

The new volume is $60 \times 8 = 480$ inches³.

EXAMPLE 2

The volume of a rectangular prism is 54 centimeters³. The dimensions of the prism are scaled by a factor of $\frac{1}{3}$. Find the volume of the new prism.

Multiply the original volume by $\left(\frac{1}{3}\right)^3$.

The volume of the new prism is $= 54 \times \left(\frac{1}{3}\right)^3 = 54 \times \frac{1}{27} = 2$ centimeters³.

EXERCISE 9

Effects of a Scale Factor

Directions: Determine the effects of the scale factors on the given figures.

1. The circumference of a circle is 60 inches. The circle is scaled by a factor of 4 to make a new circle. What is the circumference of the new circle?

2. The perimeter of a triangle is 72 feet. The triangle is scaled by a factor of $\frac{1}{4}$ to make a new triangle. What is the perimeter of the new triangle?

3. The area of a cylinder is 144 meters². If a scale factor of 3 is applied, what is the new area?

4. The area of a triangle is 60 meters². The triangle is scaled by a factor of $\frac{1}{2}$ to make a new triangle. Find the area of the new triangle.

5. The volume of a pyramid is 81 feet³. The pyramid is scaled by a factor of 3. Find the volume of the new pyramid.

6. The volume of a cube is 125 inches³. The cube is scaled by a factor of $\frac{1}{5}$. Find the new volume.

7. The volume of a sphere is 15 feet². Find the new volume if a scale factor of 3 is applied.

8. The volume of a cylinder is 75 centimeters³. If a scale factor of 2 is applied, find the volume of the new cylinder.

9. The circumference of a circle is 10 inches. Find the new circumference of the circle if a scale factor of 5 is applied to the given circle.

10. The area of a square is 20 meters². Find the area of the new square if a scale factor of 7 is applied.

Answers are on page 569.

Polynomials and Rational Expressions

Polynomials play a very important role in algebra, much like the role whole numbers play in arithmetic. Fractions and decimals, ratios, and proportions are made up of whole numbers, so once you learn about whole numbers, you are ready to learn about other types of numbers. Likewise, polynomials are used to build rational expressions, radical expressions, exponential expressions, and other algebraic entities. Once you learn about polynomials, you will be ready to tackle more advanced algebraic constructs. This chapter will introduce you to polynomials and to rational expressions, which are built from polynomials.

Understanding Polynomials

In this chapter, you will study a particular type of algebraic expression, called a polynomial, and factorization of polynomials. In addition, you will learn to evaluate expressions.

Terms and Polynomials

The different parts of a polynomial are known as **terms**, which are separated by + or – signs. A **term** is a single algebraic expression that does not connect expressions with + or – signs. For example, 7, $-3cd$, $4x$, $\dfrac{3}{x^5}$, and $12t^5$ are all terms. The terms of a polynomial are of a special form, as you will see later. Any term with a **variable**, or letter, is called a **variable term**.

Polynomials

A **polynomial** is a special algebraic expression made up of added or subtracted terms of the form ax^n, where a is a real number and is multiplied by a variable x raised to a nonnegative power n ($n \geq 0$). The variable can be any letter, not just x, and there can be more than one variable multiplied together in the same term. The chart shows examples of polynomials and their terms. A minus sign is considered to be a negative sign on the term that follows it and is treated as part of that term when the polynomial is separated out into terms.

Polynomials	Terms
$a + 7$	a, 7
$2xy - 3y + 2$	$2xy$, $-3y$, 2
5	5
$4x^2 + 3x - 7$	$4x^2$, $3x$, -7
$3x^5 - 2x^3 - 4x + 7$	$3x^5$, $-2x^3$, $-4x$, 7

Note that multiplication and division signs do not separate the terms of an expression. Also, polynomial terms do not have square or cube roots of variables, fractional powers, or variables in the denominator of any fractions.

EXAMPLES

1. $5x^{-2}$: This is not a polynomial term because the variable has a negative exponent.

2. $\dfrac{1}{x^2}$: This is not a polynomial term because the variable is in the denominator.

3. $\sqrt[3]{x}$: This is not a polynomial term because the variable is inside a radical.

4. $9x^2$: This is a polynomial term because it has a whole number exponent in the variable term.

Monomials

A polynomial with one term, such as $2x$ or $4x^2$, may also be called a **monomial** (*mono* means "one"). A monomial can be a number, a variable, or the product of a number and variables with an exponent. You can think of a polynomial with several terms as being the sum or difference of monomials.

Constants

A term that is just a number is called a **constant**. Constants can be terms of polynomials because a constant term a can be written as ax^0. (Remember that x^0 is equal to 1.) For example, $3 = 3x^0$ is a constant term.

Factors

When two or more constants and/or variables are multiplied together, the result is called the **product** and each constant or variable is called a **factor**. For example, $3 \times a \times b \times b = 3ab^2$.

EXERCISE 1

Terms and Polynomials

Directions: List the terms of each polynomial.

1. $3x^2$
2. 3
3. $-2x^2$
4. $x + 1$
5. $3x - 2$
6. $-x^2 - 3$
7. $x^2 + x - 1$
8. $-2x^2 - 5x - 3$
9. $14x^4 - 2x^3y^4 + 15y^4$
10. $\dfrac{2}{3}x^2 - 4xy - 7$

Answers are on page 569.

Coefficients

The numerical factor of a term is called the **coefficient**.

EXAMPLES

1. In the terms $5xy$ and $4x^2$, 5 is the coefficient of xy and 4 is the coefficient of x^2.

2. In the term x, the coefficient of x is 1 (because $1 \times x = x$). It is understood that a variable term without a coefficient in front of it has a coefficient of 1.

3. In the term $-x$, the coefficient of x is -1 (because $-1 \times x = -x$). It is understood that a variable term with just a negative sign in front of it has a coefficient of -1.

Leading Term

Terms of polynomials are usually written in **decreasing order**; that is, the term with the largest exponent first, the next highest next, and so forth, and the plain number is written last.

EXAMPLE 1

If you look at the exponents on the terms in $4x^2 + 3x - 7$, you will see the first term has an exponent of 2; the second term has an understood exponent of 1; and the last term does not have any variable at all.

When terms of polynomials are written in **increasing order**, the plain number comes first, the term with the smallest exponent next, the next smallest next, and so forth.

EXAMPLE 2

The exponents on the terms in $-2 + 8x^4 + 3x^7$ increase from left to right.

When a polynomial is written in decreasing order, the first term with the largest exponent is called the **leading term**.

EXAMPLE 3

In $7x^4 + 6x^2 + x$, the term $7x^4$ is the leading term.

Leading Coefficient

The coefficient of the leading term is called the **leading coefficient**.

Constant Term

Any constant in a polynomial is called a **constant term**.

EXAMPLE

In the polynomial below, the coefficient of the leading term is 2; the coefficient of the second term is 3; and the term 7 is the constant term.

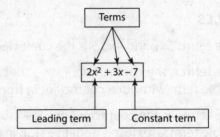

EXERCISE 2

Coefficients

Directions: Write the coefficient in each of the algebraic expressions.

1. $\frac{2}{3}x$ **2.** $-y$ **3.** $\frac{2}{3}xy$ **4.** $2x^2 + 3y$ **5.** $3x^2 + 2y + 7xy + 5$

Directions: Identify the leading term, leading coefficient, and constant term.

6. $4x^2 - 5x - 9$ **8.** $7x2 + 3xy + 8$ **10.** $x5 - 4x3 - x + 7$

7. $3x^3 - 2x^2 + 3$ **9.** $8x4 - 2 + 3x7$

Answers are on page 569.

Degree of a Term

The exponent on a term tells you the **degree of the term**. The term with the largest degree is the **leading term**.

EXAMPLE

The leading term in $2x^2 + 6x - 5$ is $2x^2$, which is also a second-degree term or a term of degree 2. The second term, $6x$, is a first-degree term. The last term, -5, is degree 0.

Degree of a Polynomial

The degree of the leading term tells the **degree of the polynomial**.

EXAMPLES

1. $3 - 5x$ is a polynomial of degree 1.

2. $2 + 3x - x^2$ is a polynomial of degree 2.

3. $1 - 3x + 4x^3$ is a polynomial of degree 3.

EXERCISE 3

Degree of a Polynomial

Directions: Give the degree of the polynomials.

1. $x^2 - y^4$

2. $5x + 2$

3. $x^2 + 2x^5 - x$

4. $4 + x + x^7$

5. $7x^4 + 6x^2 + x$

6. $2x^5 - 5x^3 - 10x + 9$

7. 3

8. $x^2 - 2x + 3$

9. $2y^6 + 1y^5 - 3y^4 + 7y^3 + 9y^2 + y + 6$

10. $-x^4 + x^2 + x$

Answers are on page 569.

Polynomials of One Variable

Polynomials of one variable are polynomials with only one letter used as the base in the terms. The degree of this kind of polynomial is the largest, or greatest, exponent in the polynomial. Here are some examples of polynomials and their degrees.

EXAMPLES

1. $3x^4 - 2x^3 + 5$ degree: 4

2. $5x - 7$ degree: 1

3. -8 degree: 0

But $2x - 3x^{\frac{1}{2}} - \dfrac{1}{x^2}$ is not a polynomial as the last term has a variable term in the denominator.

Polynomials of Several Variables

A polynomial can have two or more variables in one expression. To find the degree of this polynomial, find the sum of the powers of the variables in each term. The highest sum is the degree of the polynomial.

EXAMPLE

The polynomial $2x - 3xy + 4xy^2 - y^3$ has two variables, x and y. The degree of the polynomial is 3 because the term with the exponents that have the greatest sum is $4xy^2$.

Combining Like Terms

The terms that have the same variable factors are known as **like** or **similar terms**.

EXAMPLES

1. $7x, x, -2x$

2. $3ab, 7ab, \dfrac{4}{5}ab$

3. $\left(\dfrac{1}{3}\right)xy^2, -2xy^2, 6xy^2$

4. $-8x^2y, 3x^2y, -\dfrac{1}{3}x^2y$

Combining like terms means adding or subtracting terms having the same variables to the same power. Like terms are added or subtracted by adding or subtracting the coefficients. You can add like terms because of the distributive property of multiplication.

EXAMPLE 1

Add: $-3m + 9m - 4m$.

Using the distributive property, you can rewrite the expression and then add the coefficients. The variable term stays the same.

$$-3m + 9m - 4m = (-3 + 9 - 4)m$$
$$= 2m$$

EXAMPLE 2

Add: $(3x - y + z) + (2y - 5z) + (3z - 4x)$.

When adding several terms with different variable parts, you can write them in columns with like terms in the same column.

$$
\begin{array}{rrr}
3x & -y & +z \\
& +2y & -5z \\
-4x & & +3z \\
\hline
-x & +y & -z
\end{array}
$$

EXAMPLE 3

Add: $(2x^2y - 3xy + x) + (4xy - x^2y) + (2x - 3x^2y + xy)$.

$$
\begin{array}{rrr}
2x^2y & -3xy & +x \\
-x^2y & +4xy & \\
-3x^2y & +xy & +2x \\
\hline
-2x^2y & +2xy & +3x
\end{array}
$$

EXERCISE 4

Combining Like Terms

Directions: Add.

1. $-3x - 4 + 2x + 6$

2. $2x + 3y + 4x - 5y$

3. $(4x - 3y) + (3y - 5x) + (5z - 4x)$

4. $3xy - 4xyz + 3x - 8xy + 5xyz - 9x$

5. $8x - 5xy - 4x + 4xy$

6. $(2a - 3b + c) + (5a - 6b + c)$

7.
$$
\begin{array}{llll}
7xy & +5yz & -3xz & \\
& 4yz & +9xz & -4y \\
-2xy & & -3xz & +5x \\
\hline
\end{array}
$$

8.
$$
\begin{array}{lll}
3x & -y & +5z \\
-2x & +y & \\
-2x & +7y & +3z \\
\hline
\end{array}
$$

9.
$$
\begin{array}{lll}
3ab & -ab^2 & +7a^2b \\
-5ab & & +4a^2b \\
4ab & -2ab^2 & +a^2b \\
\hline
\end{array}
$$

10. $x^2 - 5xy^2 + 2x^2y + 3xy + 4x^2y + 7xy^2 - xy - y^2$

Answers are on page 570.

Descending or Ascending Order

Polynomials can be written in **ascending** or **descending order**. But most of the time polynomials are written in descending order, which may be called standard form. In the **descending order**, the term with the greatest exponent is written first, and the rest follow in order of decreasing exponents. In the **ascending order**, the terms are arranged from lowest exponent to highest exponent.

EXAMPLE 1

Arrange the terms in ascending and descending orders: $x^4 - x^2 + 5x^3$.

Ascending order: $-x^2 + 5x^3 + x^4$

Descending order: $x^4 + 5x^3 - x^2$

EXAMPLE 2

Arrange the terms in descending order: $8x^3y - y^2 + 6x^2y + xy^2$.

Descending order: $8x^3y + 6x^2y + xy^2 - y^2$

EXERCISE 5

Descending or Ascending Order

Directions: Arrange the terms in descending order.

1. $4x^2 - 5x^3 + 3$
2. $6x^3 + x - 4x^2 + 1$

Directions: Arrange the terms in ascending order.

3. $12x^4 - 5 + 6x^3$
4. $8x^2 + 3 - \dfrac{1}{2}x^3$

Answers are on page 570.

Opposite of a Polynomial

Two polynomials are **opposites** of each other if they are additive inverses. When they are combined together, the sum becomes zero. For example, the opposite of the term $4a^2$ is $-4a^2$ and $2xy$ is $-2xy$. Note that $-4a^2$ means $-1 \times 4a^2$, and $-2xy$ means $-1 \times 2xy$. To find the opposite, multiply the polynomial by -1.

EXAMPLE

Find the opposite of $4a^2 - 12a + 8$.

The opposite of $4a^2 - 12a + 8$ is $-(4a^2 - 12a + 8)$:

$$-(4a^2 - 12a + 8) = (-1)(4a^2 - 12a + 8)$$

Distribute -1 on each term.

$$= (-1)(4a^2) + (-1)(-12a) + (-1)(8)$$
$$= -4a^2 + 12a - 8$$

The opposite is $-4a^2 + 12a - 8$.

EXERCISE 6

Opposite of a Polynomial

Directions: Find the additive inverse or opposite of each polynomial. Write your answer in standard form.

1. $8y^2 + 5y$

2. $3x^2 + 2x + 2$

3. $-4x + 7 - 4x^2$

4. $9x^3 - 7x + 3$

5. $3x^2 + 7x + 2$

6. $9x^2 - 3x - 9$

7. $-3x^2 - 7x + 2$

8. $6x^2 - 3x + 3$

9. $7x^3 - 9x + 3$

10. $7x^2 + 3x + 3$

Answers are on page 570.

Operations on Polynomials

Evaluating Polynomials

Polynomials include variables, so it is important to be able to **evaluate polynomials** when values for the variables are known. To do this, replace each variable with the known value and then evaluate the polynomial using the order of operations.

EXAMPLE 1

Find the value of x^2y^3 if $x = 2$ and $y = 4$.

Replace the values of $x = 2$ and $y = 4$ in x^2y^3 and then simplify.

$x^2y^3 = (2)^2 \cdot (4)^3 = 4 \times 64 = 256$

EXAMPLE 2

Evaluate $bc^3 - ad$ if $a = -2$, $b = 3$, $c = -4$, and $d = 4$.

Replace the values of $a = -2$, $b = 3$, $c = -4$, and $d = 4$ in $bc^3 - ad$ and then simplify.

$bc^3 - ad = (3)(-4)^3 - (-2)(4)$

$= (3)(-64) - (-8)$

$= -192 + 8 = -184$

EXAMPLE 3

Evaluate $x^4 + 3x^3 - x^2 + 6$ if $x = -3$.

Replace the value of $x = -3$ in $x^4 + 3x^3 - x^2 + 6$ and then simplify.

$$x^4 + 3x^3 - x^2 + 6 = (-3)^4 + 3(-3)^3 - (-3)^2 + 6$$
$$= 81 + 3(-27) - (9) + 6$$
$$= 81 - 81 - 9 + 6$$
$$= -3$$

EXERCISE 7

Evaluating Polynomials

Directions: Evaluate the polynomials for the given values of the variables.

1. Evaluate a^2b if $a = -2$ and $b = 3$.

2. Evaluate $a - cd$ if $a = -2$, $c = -4$, and $d = 4$.

3. Evaluate $(b + d)^2$ if $b = 3$ and $d = 4$.

4. Evaluate $x^2 + y^2$ if $x = 3$ and $y = 4$.

5. Evaluate $3x^2 - 12x + 4$ if $x = -2$.

6. Evaluate $7x^2 - 3x + 2$ if $x = -2$.

7. Evaluate $x^2 + 3y^3$ if $x = 7$ and $y = -2$.

8. Evaluate $4x^2y - 2xy^2 + x - 7$ if $x = 3$ and $y = -1$.

9. Evaluate $4x^2 - 2x + 7$ if $x = 3$.

10. Evaluate $2x^3 - xy^2 + 6$ if $x = -2$ and $y = 5$.

Answers are on page 570.

Adding Polynomials

When **adding polynomials**, combine like terms. Recall that like terms have the same variables to the same power. All x^2, y^2, and xy terms are like terms, regardless of coefficient. For example, $2x^2$, $-x^2$, and $5\frac{1}{5}x^2$ are like terms. Also, $3x^2y$, $-x^2y$, and $\frac{1}{2}x^2y$ are like terms. All constants are like terms. Like terms are combined by adding their coefficients, as you saw earlier.

To add polynomials, arrange each polynomial in descending order. Write out the first polynomial, and next arrange the second polynomial below, aligning like terms vertically. Then add columns.

EXAMPLE

Add: $(3ab + bc - ac) + (4ab - 5bc) + (3ac - 2ab)$.

$$
\begin{array}{rrr}
3ab & +bc & -ac \\
4ab & -5bc & \\
-2ab & & +3ac \\
\hline
+5ab & -4bc & +2ac
\end{array}
$$

Subtracting Polynomials

When **subtracting polynomials**, arrange the two polynomials in descending order with all signs as given. Then change the sign of each term of the expression that is to be subtracted (the second polynomial). Now combine like terms.

EXAMPLE

Subtract: $(4x^3 + y^2) - (2x^3 - 3y^2)$.

$(4x^3 + y^2) - (2x^3 - 3y^2) = 4x^3 + y^2 - 2x^3 + 3y^2$

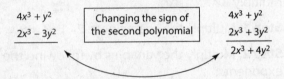

$$
\begin{array}{l}
4x^3 + y^2 \\
2x^3 - 3y^2 \\
\hline
\end{array}
\qquad
\boxed{\begin{array}{c} \text{Changing the sign of} \\ \text{the second polynomial} \end{array}}
\qquad
\begin{array}{l}
4x^3 + y^2 \\
2x^3 + 3y^2 \\
\hline
2x^3 + 4y^2
\end{array}
$$

EXERCISE 8

Adding and Subtracting Polynomials

Directions: Add or subtract.

1. $(3x^3 - 2x^2 + 1) + (2x^2 - 5x + 2) + (4x^3 - 3x + 7)$

2. $(4pq - 2qr + rp) + (3qr - 2rp + pq) + (pq - 3qr)$

3. $(5a - b + 3c) - (7a + 8b - c)$

4. $(4pq^2 + pq - p) - (3pq^2 - 2pq + p)$

5.
$$
\begin{array}{llll}
 & 3x^2 & -6x & +xy \\
2x^3 & -5x^2 & & \\
 & & 7x & +8y \\
 & & & -3y \\
\end{array}
$$

6. $(2x^2 - 4y + 7xy - 6y^2) - (-3x^2 + 5y - 4xy + y^2)$

7. $(3x^2 - 5x + 8y + 7xy + 2y^2) - (4x^2 + 2x - 3y + 7xy - 3y^2)$

8.
$$
\begin{array}{lll}
-4x^3 & +x^2y & -xy^2 \\
3x^3 & +5x^2y & -xy^2 \\
 & & 7xy^2 & +3y^3 \\
\end{array}
$$

9.

$$
\begin{array}{llllll}
5x^2y & -xy^2 & & & +5x & -3 \\
& 4xy^2 & -3y & +7xy & & -5 \\
2x^2y & & & -3xy & &
\end{array}
$$

10. If $A = 3x^2 + xy - 5y^2$, $B = 2x^2 - xy + 3y^2$, and $C = -6x^2 + 4xy - 7y^2$, what is $A + B - C$?

Answers are on page 570.

Multiplying Monomials

A monomial is a polynomial with one term. Polynomials with more than one term can be thought of as having several monomials as each term is a monomial. Looking at how to **multiply monomials** can help you understand some more complex multiplications. To multiply monomials, first multiply the coefficients and then multiply the variable parts, following the rules of exponents.

EXAMPLE

Multiply $2x^2 \cdot x^3 \cdot 3x^2$.

Step 1: Multiply the coefficients: $2 \cdot 1 \cdot 3 = 6$.

Step 2: Multiply the variables by following the product rule from the laws of exponents:

$$x^2 \cdot x^3 \cdot x^2 = x^{2+3+2} = x^7.$$

Step 3: Find the final product: $2x^2 \cdot x^3 \cdot 3x^2 = 6x^7$.

EXERCISE 9

Multiplying Monomials

Directions: Multiply.

1. $-5x^3 \cdot 6x^6$

2. $7y^7 \cdot 5y^6$

3. $y \cdot y^7 \cdot y^{10}$

4. $11b^5 \cdot 10b^7$

5. $16a^6 \cdot 12a^{10}$

6. $(19m^2n^4)(-m^4n^{10})$

7. $(6x^2)(-3y^3)(2z^5)$

8. $(8x^3y^4)(4x^2y^5)$

9. $(3a^3)(-5a^4)(2a^2)$

10. $(5xy)(-3y)(6xy^2)$

Answers are on page 570.

Multiplying a Monomial and a Polynomial

You can use the distributive property to multiply a monomial and a polynomial.

EXAMPLE

Multiply $5x(4x + 5)$.

Step 1: Distribute the monomial according to the distributive property:

$5x(4x + 5) = 5x(4x) + 5x(5)$.

Step 2: Multiply each term as a monomial times a monomial: $20x^2 + 25x$.

Thus, $5x(4x + 5) = 20x^2 + 25x$.

EXERCISE 10

Multiplying a Monomial and a Polynomial

Directions: Multiply.

1. $2(4 + x)$

2. $-2(9 - x)$

3. $x(3 + x)$

4. $x(7 - x + y)$

5. $(5x)(2x^{11} - 9x^{10} + 4x^3)$

6. $(-2x)(3x^7 - 9x^5 + 4)$

7. $(5x)(3x^6 + 2x + 5)$

8. $(7x)(3x^3 + 4x^2 - 5)$

9. $(9x)(5x^4 - 4x^{12} + 12)$

10. $(5x)(2x^{11} - 9x^{10} + 4x^3)$

Answers are on page 570.

Multiplying Polynomials

Using the distributive property and the process of multiplying monomials, you can multiply two polynomials.

EXAMPLE

Multiply $(2x + 5)(x^2 - 2x - 8)$.

Step 1: Distribute each of the two terms in the first parentheses:
$2x(x^2 - 2x - 8) + 5(x^2 - 2x - 8)$

Step 2: Distribute each term: $2x(x^2) - 2x(2x) - 2x(8) + 5x^2 - 5(2x) - 5(8)$.

Step 3: Multiply each pair of terms: $2x^3 - 4x^2 - 16x + 5x^2 - 10x - 40$.

Step 4: Combine like terms. The product is $2x^3 + x^2 - 26x - 40$.

Multiplying Polynomials

Directions: Multiply.

1. $(2n - 4)(n^2 + 6n - 4)$

2. $(4a + 2)(6a^2 - a + 2)$

3. $(7k - 3)(k^2 - 2k + 7)$

4. $(7r^2 - 6r - 6)(2r - 4)$

5. $(5x + 2)(3x^6 + 2x^5 + 5)$

6. $(3x + 4)(5x^4 + 7x^3 + 5x)$

7. $(6n^2 - 6n - 5)(7n^2 + 6n - 5)$

8. $(m^2 - 7m - 6)(7m^2 - 3m - 7)$

9. $(3x^6 + 2x^5 + 5)(4x^2 + x + 5)$

10. $(2x^7 + 4x^2 + 3x)(3x^8 + 2x^3 + 15x)$

Answers are on page 570.

Multiplying Binomials

A two-term polynomial, such as $(2x + y)$ or $(x^2 - 4)$, is called a **binomial**. Two binomials can be multiplied using a mnemonic called **FOIL**. Each letter of FOIL stands for a separate multiplication. The letters stand for First, Outside, Inside, Last. This refers to pairs of terms in the two binomials.

In order, multiply the **first** terms of the binomials. Next, multiply the terms on the **outside** of the binomials. Then, multiply the terms **inside** the problem. Finally, multiply the **last** terms in each binomial.

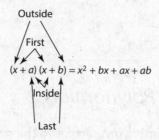

EXAMPLE 1

Multiply $(x + 4)(x - 5)$.

Using FOIL, multiply the **first** terms: $(\mathbf{x} + 4)(\mathbf{x} - 5)$ $\mathbf{x^2}$.

Next, multiply the **outside** terms: $(\mathbf{x} + 4)(x - \mathbf{5})$ $x^2 - \mathbf{5x}$.

Now multiply the **inside** terms: $(x + \mathbf{4})(\mathbf{x} - 5)$ $x^2 - 5x + \mathbf{4x}$.

Then, multiply the **last** terms: $(x + \mathbf{4})(x - \mathbf{5})$ $x^2 - 5x + 4x - \mathbf{20}$.

Combine like terms: $(x + 4)(x - 5) = x^2 - x - 20$.

The product is $x^2 - x - 20$.

EXAMPLE 2

Multiply $(2x + 3)(x + 5)$.

Using FOIL, multiply the **first** terms: $(\mathbf{2x} + 3)(\mathbf{x} + 5)$ $\mathbf{2x^2}$.

Next, multiply the **outside** terms: $(\mathbf{2x} + 3)(x + \mathbf{5})$ $2x^2 + \mathbf{10x}$.

Now multiply the **inside** terms: $(2x + \mathbf{3})(\mathbf{x} + 5)$ $2x^2 + 10x + \mathbf{3x}$.

Then, multiply the **last** terms: $(2x + \mathbf{3})(x + \mathbf{5})$ $2x^2 + 10x + 3x + \mathbf{15}$.

Combine like terms: $(2x + 3)(x + 5) = 2x^2 + 13x + 15$.

The answer is $2x^2 + 13x + 15$.

EXAMPLE 3

Multiply $(10x + 3y)(x - 6y)$.

Using FOIL, multiply the **first** terms: $(\mathbf{10x} + 3y)(\mathbf{x} - 6y)$ $\mathbf{10x^2}$.

Next, multiply the **outside** terms: $(\mathbf{10x} + 3y)(x - \mathbf{6y})$ $10x^2 - \mathbf{60xy}$.

Now multiply the **inside** terms: $(10x + \mathbf{3y})(\mathbf{x} - 6y)$ $10x^2 - 60xy + \mathbf{3xy}$.

Then, multiply the **last** terms: $(10x + \mathbf{3y})(x - \mathbf{6y})$ $10x^2 - 60xy + 3xy - \mathbf{18y^2}$.

Combine like terms: $(10x + 3y)(x - 6y) = 10x^2 - 57xy - 18y^2$.

The answer is $10x^2 - 57xy - 18y^2$.

EXERCISE 12

Multiplying Binomials

Directions: Multiply.

1. $(2n + 2)(6n + 1)$ **4.** $(x - 1)(3x + 8)$ **7.** $(x - 3)(6x - 2)$

2. $(3x + 2)(2x + 1)$ **5.** $(4x - 3)(5x - 2)$ **8.** $(8p - 2)(6p + 2)$

3. $(3x - 2)(2x + 1)$ **6.** $(4n + 1)(2n + 6)$ **9.** $(6p + 8)(5p - 8)$

Answers are on page 571.

Square of a Binomial

The **square of a binomial** is the product of a binomial times itself.

EXAMPLE

Find $(a + b)^2$.

$$(a + b)^2 = (a + b)(a + b) = a^2 + ab + ab + b^2 = a^2 + 2ab + b^2$$

The square of a binomial has this form: $a^2 + 2ab + b^2$. The first term of the product is the square of the first term of the binomial, the second term is twice the product of the terms of the binomial, and the last term is the square of the second term of the binomial. Use the formula $a^2 + 2ab + b^2$ to square a binomial.

EXAMPLE 1

Find $(x + 6)^2$.

$$(x + 6)^2 = x^2 + 2(6x) + 6^2 = x^2 + 12x + 36$$

EXAMPLE 2

Find $(3x - 4)^2$.

$$(3x - 4)^2 = 9x^2 + 2(-12x) + (-4)^2 = 9x^2 - 24x + 16$$

EXERCISE 13

Square of a Binomial

Directions: Simplify.

1. $(x + 4)^2$ **3.** $(2x + 1)^2$ **5.** $(3x - 2)^2$ **7.** $(2y - 3)^2$

2. $(x + 6)^2$ **4.** $(x - y)^2$ **6.** $(4p - 1)^2$ **8.** $(x + 7)^2$

Answers are on page 571.

Product of the Sum and Difference of Two Terms

The product of the sum of two terms multiplied by the difference of the same two terms is the difference of the squares of the two terms: $(a + b)(a - b) = a^2 - b^2$. When carrying out the FOIL method, the two middle terms cancel each other out because they are opposites.

EXAMPLE 1

Find $(x - 4)(x + 4)$.

$$(x - 4)(x + 4) = x^2 - 4^2 = x^2 - 16$$

EXAMPLE 2

Find $(ab - 5)(ab + 5)$.

$$(ab - 5)(ab + 5) = (ab)^2 - 5^2 = a^2b^2 - 25$$

EXERCISE 14

Product of the Sum and Difference of Two Terms

Directions: Find the product of the following.

1. $(4x - 2)(4x + 2)$
2. $(7y + 5)(7y - 5)$
3. $(2x + 3)(2x - 3)$
4. $(3y + 7)(3y - 7)$
5. $(a + 3b)(a - 3b)$

6. $(2x - 5y)(2x + 5y)$
7. $(12xy - 11)(12xy + 11)$
8. $(8 - 5t)(8 + 5t)$
9. $(3x + 2)(3x - 2)$
10. $(5c - 3d)(5c + 3d)$

Answers are on page 571.

Dividing Polynomials

There are two techniques for **dividing polynomials**: the division can be simplified by just reducing a fraction or by using long polynomial division.

EXAMPLE

Simplify $\dfrac{2x + 4}{2}$.

You can reduce this fraction because there is only one term in the polynomial that you are dividing by. There are two ways of doing this. The division can be written as a sum of two fractions and then reduced:

$$\frac{2x + 4}{2} = \frac{2x}{2} + \frac{4}{2} = \frac{\cancel{2}x}{\cancel{2}_1} + \frac{\cancel{4}^2}{\cancel{2}_1} = x + 2$$

You can also factor out the common factor from the numerator and the denominator, and then cancel.

$$\frac{2x + 4}{2} = \frac{2(x + 2)}{2} = \frac{\cancel{2}(x + 2)}{\cancel{2}_1} = x + 2$$

Monomial Divisor

Division, like multiplication, is distributive. For example, the problem $(8x + 6x - 2x) \div 2x$ may be solved by adding the numbers within the parentheses and then dividing the total by 2.

Thus, $\dfrac{8x + 6x - 2x}{2x} = \dfrac{12x}{2x} = 6.$

The problem can also be solved by dividing each term by $2x$.

$$\frac{8x + 6x - 2x}{2x} = \frac{8x}{2x} + \frac{6x}{2x} - \frac{2x}{2x} = 4 + 3 - 1 = 6$$

The distributive method can be applied to those polynomials with unlike terms divided by the same denominator. The distributive method can be used as in the following two problems:

EXAMPLE 1

Divide $\dfrac{2ax + aby + a}{a}$.

$$\frac{2ax + aby + a}{a} = \frac{2ax}{a} + \frac{aby}{a} + \frac{a}{a} = \frac{2\cancel{a}^1 x}{\cancel{a}_1} + \frac{{}^1\cancel{a}by}{{}_1\cancel{a}} + \frac{{}^1\cancel{a}}{{}^1\cancel{a}} = 2x + by + 1$$

EXAMPLE 2

Divide: $\dfrac{18ab^2 - 12bc}{6b}$

$$\frac{18ab^2 - 12bc}{6b} = \frac{18ab^2}{6b} - \frac{12bc}{6b} = 3ab - 2c$$

Binomial Divisor

When the divisor has more than one term, the process of long division can be used with dividing polynomials.

EXAMPLE

Divide $(x^2 - 4x - 12)$ by $(x + 2)$.

First see how many x's there are in x^2. That is, what is $\dfrac{x^2}{x}$? $\dfrac{x^2}{x} = x$. Put x in the quotient. Write the product of the divisor and the part of the quotient you found under the dividend. Since $x(x + 2) = x^2 + 2x$, write this underneath, and then subtract.

$$
\begin{array}{r}
x \\
x+2\overline{)x^2 - 4x - 12} \\
-(x^2 + 2x)
\end{array}
$$

Rewrite $-(x^2 + 2x)$ as its opposite $-x^2 - 2x$ so that you can add the opposite. (Adding the opposite is the same as subtracting.)

$$
\begin{array}{r}
x \\
x+2\overline{)x^2 - 4x - 12} \\
-x^2 - 2x
\end{array}
$$

Add $-x^2$ to x^2, and $-2x$ to $-4x$, and bring down -12.

$$
\begin{array}{r}
x \\
x+2\overline{)x^2 - 4x - 12} \\
-x^2 - 2x \\
\hline
-6x - 12
\end{array}
$$

Repeating the process, you get 0 as the remainder and $x - 6$ as the quotient.

$$\begin{array}{r} x - 6 \\ x+2\overline{)x^2 - 4x - 12} \\ \underline{-x^2 - 2x} \\ -6x - 12 \\ \underline{-(-6x - 12)} \\ \end{array}$$

$$\begin{array}{r} x - 6 \\ x+2\overline{)x^2 - 4x - 12} \\ \underline{-x^2 - 2x} \\ -6x - 12 \\ \underline{6x + 12} \\ 0 \end{array}$$

So, $(x^2 - 4x - 12) \div (x + 2) = x - 6$.

Synthetic Division

Before looking at synthetic division, you need to review regular division in arithmetic.

EXAMPLE

Divide 47 by 9.

$$\begin{array}{r} 9 \\ 5\overline{)47} \\ \underline{45} \\ 2 \end{array}$$

So, $47 = 9\dfrac{2}{5}$ or $9 + \dfrac{2}{5}$. Equivalently, $47 = (9 \times 5) + 2$. Here, 5 is called the divisor, 47 is the dividend, 9 is the quotient, and 2 is the remainder. So, $\dfrac{\text{dividend}}{\text{divisor}} = \text{quotient} + \dfrac{\text{remainder}}{\text{divisor}}$ or dividend = quotient $\times$ divisor + remainder.

In algebra, if you divide a polynomial $P(x)$ by a polynomial $D(x)$ where the degree of D is less than the degree of P, you find $P(x) = Q(x) \times D(x) + R(x)$ where $P(x)$ is the dividend, $Q(x)$ is the quotient, $D(x)$ is the divisor, and $R(x)$ is the remainder.

Synthetic division is a shortcut method of polynomial division in the special case of dividing by a linear factor or a factor of the form $(x - c)$. Synthetic division is generally used not for dividing out factors but for finding zeroes (or roots) of polynomials.

Before proceeding with the actual steps of synthetic division, make sure (1) the dividend is in standard form, which means the powers are in decreasing order, and (2) the divisor must be in the form $x - c$.

EXAMPLE 1

Divide $(x^3 - 5x^2 + 3x - 7)$ by $(x - 2)$.

First, the dividend is in standard form, that is, the exponents are in decreasing order.

Step 1: The divisor is also in the required form, that is, $x - c$.

Write the coefficients of the dividend: $1 - 5 + 3 - 7$.

Then, put 2 of the divisor to the left as shown here.

$$2\underline{|1 - 5 + 3 - 7}$$

Step 2: Bring down the leading coefficient (1), multiply it with (2), and write the product ($1 \times 2 = 2$) in the second column.

$$
\begin{array}{r}
2\underline{|1 - 5 + 3 - 7} \\
\underline{+2} \\
1
\end{array}
$$

Then, add the numbers in the second column.

$$
\begin{array}{r}
2\underline{|1 - 5 + 3 - 7} \\
\underline{+2} \\
1 - 3
\end{array}
$$

Step 3: Repeat the process: $-3 \times 2 = -6$ until you finish with the last column.

$$
\begin{array}{r}
2\underline{|1 - 5 + 3 - 7} \\
\underline{+2 - 6 - 6} \\
1 - 3 - 3 - 13
\end{array}
$$

The first three numbers, $1, -3, -3$, in the last row are the coefficients of the quotient, and the last number, -13, is the remainder. Note that the numbers below the horizontal line except the last (remainder) are the coefficients of the quotient. More so, the exponents of the variables of the quotient are all reduced by 1, so start the quotient with an x^2-term.

Step 4: The answer is presented in the following way:

Dividend = (Quotient × Divisor) + Remainder

$$x^3 - 5x^2 + 3x - 7 = (x^2 - 3x - 3)(x - 2) - 13$$

EXAMPLE 2

Divide $(x^4 - 3x^3 - 11x^2 + 5x + 17)$ by $(x + 2)$.

Step 1: The dividend is in standard form since the exponents are in decreasing order. The divisor needs to be rewritten to get the required form: $x - c$. Write $x + 2 = x - (-2)$, so $c = -2$.

Step 2: Using the synthetic division method, you get

$$-2\overline{\left)\begin{array}{l} 1-3-11+5+17 \\ -2+10+2-14 \\ \hline 1-5-1+7+3 \end{array}\right.}$$

The first four numbers, $1 - 5 - 1 + 7$, are the coefficients of the quotient, and the last number, 3, is the remainder. The quotient will start with an x^3-term.

Step 3: The final answer is $(x^4 - 3x^3 - 11x^2 + 5x + 17) = (x^3 - 5x^2 - x + 7)$ $(x + 2) + 3$.

EXERCISE 15

Dividing Polynomials

Directions: Divide.

1. $(2a + 6) \div 2$

2. $(18xy + 45y) \div 9y$

3. $(16z^2 - 24z - 28) \div 4$

4. $(52y^5 + 26y^4 - 65y^3) \div (13y^2)$

5. $(2x^4 - 9x^3 + 21x^2 - 26x + 12) \div (2x - 3)$

Directions: Divide using the synthetic division method.

6. $(x^2 + 7x - 5) \div (x - 12)$

7. $(4x^4 + 9) \div (x^2 - 1)$

8. $(x^2 + 5x + 6) \div (x - 1)$

9. $(x^3 - 5x - 6) \div (x - 2)$

10. $(3x^2 + 7x - 3) \div (x + 2)$

Answers are on page 571.

Factoring

When factoring numbers or factoring polynomials, you are finding numbers or polynomials that divide out evenly from the original numbers or polynomials. But in the case of polynomials, you are dividing expressions by expressions.

Factoring in polynomial expressions uses the distributive property: $a(b + c) = ab + ac$. For example, when you factor $2x + 6$ with this property, you get $2x + 6 = 2(x) + 2(3) = 2(x + 3)$.

The process is to see what can be factored out of every term in the expression. This is called finding the greatest common factor (GCF) from the terms of the expression.

EXAMPLE

Factor $3x - 12$.

Step 1: The only factor common between the two terms (i.e., the only thing that can be divided out of each term and then moved up front) is 3. This is the greatest common factor. So, write 3 in front of parentheses: $3x - 12 = 3(\_)$.

Step 2: When 3 is divided into $3x$, the x-term is left. Write x as the first term inside the parentheses: $3x - 12 = 3(x\_)$.

Step 3: When 3 is divided into -12, -4 is left. Write "-4" in the parentheses: $3x - 12 = 3(x - 4)$.

Step 4: $3x - 12 = 3(x - 4)$.

Factoring Out a GCF

Factoring out the GCF of a polynomial is an important part of simplifying an expression. Finding a GCF is the process of identifying what numbers and variables a group of terms have in common. In the previous example, 3 is the GCF as it is the largest common factor in both $3x$ and -12.

EXAMPLE

Factor $5x^3 + 125x$ completely.

$$5x^3 + 125x = 5 \cdot x \cdot x \cdot x + 5 \cdot 5 \cdot 5 \cdot x$$

The GCF is $5x$ as 5 and x are common in both "$5x^3$" and "$+125x$." Take $5x$ out, and then divide each term by $5x$.

$$5x^3 + 125x = 5x\left(\frac{5 \cdot x \cdot x \cdot x}{5x} + \frac{5 \cdot 5 \cdot 5 \cdot x}{5x}\right) = 5x(x \cdot x + 5 \cdot 5) = 5x(x^2 + 25)$$

The answer is $5x(x^2 + 25)$.

EXERCISE 16

Factoring

Directions: Factor each polynomial completely.

1. $4x^3 + 6x + 2x^2$

2. $6x^2y + 9xy^2$

3. $3x^3 + 6x^2 - 15x$

4. $x^8 + x^7 + x^6 + x^5$

5. $5x^5 - 4x^4 + 3x^3$

6. $x^3 + x^2$

7. $6x^5 + 2x^3$

8. $2x^3 - 4x^2 + x$

9. $3x^6 - 2x^5 + 4x^4 - 6x^2$

10. $36y^{15} - 27y^{10} - 18y^5$

Answers are on page 571.

Factoring a Common Polynomial Factor

When factoring a four-term polynomial, you group the polynomial into two sets of two terms, and factor those sets using the GCF method.

EXAMPLE 1

Factor $x(x-5) + 3(x-5)$ completely.

Here, the common polynomial is $x - 5$. Use the GCF method to factor it out, and you are left with $x + 3$.

So, $x(x-5) + 3(x-5)$ factors as $(x-5)(x+3)$.

EXAMPLE 2

Factor $5x^2(x-2) + 3(x-2)$ completely.

Here, the common polynomial is $x - 2$. Use the GCF method to factor it out, and you are left with $5x^2 + 3$.

So, the factored form is $(x-2)(5x^2 + 3)$.

EXAMPLE 3

Factor $x(x-2) + 3(2-x)$ completely.

Since there is a common factor here, rewrite the expression to get a common factor. Use the commutative property and then factor out -1 to get:

$3(2-x) = 3(-x+2) = -3(x-2)$

A common factor $(x-2)$ is created. Thus, $x(x-2) + 3(2-x) = x(x-2) - 3(x-2)$. Then use the GCF method to get $x(x-2) - 3(x-2) = (x-3)(x-2)$.

So the factored form of $x(x-2) + 3(2-x)$ is $(x-3)(x-2)$.

EXERCISE 17

Factoring a Common Polynomial Factor

Directions: Factor each polynomial completely.

1. $2(x-y) - b(x-y)$ **4.** $x(x+5) + 3(x+5)$ **7.** $x(x+1) - (x+1)$

2. $11x(x-8) + 3(8-x)$ **5.** $x(x+1) + 2(x+1)$ **8.** $x^2(x-5) + 3(x-5)$

3. $x^2(x-5) + 4(x-5)$ **6.** $x(x-2) - 3(x-2)$ **9.** $x^2(x+1) + 9(x+1)$

Answers are on page 571.

Factoring by Grouping

You can use this technique to factor a four-term polynomial. Factor a common factor from the first two terms and then factor another common factor from the second two terms. Then factor the common polynomial from both groups. Sometimes you may have to rewrite in order to use this method of factoring.

EXAMPLE 1

Factor $x^3 + 6x^2 + 5x + 30$ completely.

Step 1: Use parentheses to make two groups: the first group comprising the first two terms and the second group comprising the second two terms.

$$x^3 + 6x^2 + 5x + 30 = (x^3 + 6x^2) + (5x + 30)$$

Step 2: Factor the GCF from each group:

$$(x^3 + 6x^2) + (5x + 30) = x^2(x + 6) + 5(x + 6)$$

Step 3: Now, factor the GCF from the newly written expression:

$$x^2(x + 6) + 5(x + 6) = (x + 6)(x^2 + 5)$$

EXAMPLE 2

Factor $3x^3 - 15x^2 - 2x + 10$ completely.

Step 1: Use parentheses to make two groups: the first group comprising the first two terms and the second group comprising the second two terms.

$$3x^3 - 15x^2 - 2x + 10 = (3x^3 - 15x^2) - (2x - 10)$$

Step 2: Factor the GCF from each group:

$$(3x^3 - 15x^2) - (2x - 10) = 3x^2(x - 5) - 2(x - 5)$$

Step 3: Now, factor the GCF from the newly written expression:

$$3x^2(x - 5) - 2(x - 5) = (3x^2 - 2)(x - 5)$$

EXERCISE 18

Factoring by Grouping

Directions: Factor each polynomial completely.

1. $m^3 + 7m^2 - 2m - 14$ 5. $3x^3 - 15x^2 - 2x + 10$ 9. $x^3 + 2x^2 + 8x + 16$

2. $12x^3 + 2x^2 - 18x - 3$ 6. $x^3 + 2x^2 - x - 2$ 10. $xy - 4y + 3x - 12$

3. $x^3 + x^2 + 3x + 3$ 7. $12x^3 - 6x^2 - 2x + 1$ 11. $xy - 4y - 3x + 12$

4. $2x^3 - 6x^2 + 5x - 15$ 8. $x^3 - 5x^2 + 3x - 15$ 12. $4x^2 + 20x - x - 5$

Answers are on page 571.

Factoring Trinomials

A trinomial is a polynomial with three terms. The process of factoring a trinomial is the opposite of the FOIL method, which is the process used to multiply two binomials. Most trinomials can be factored completely as two binomials.

Factoring by Guessing

This method is used when a is 1 (a is the coefficient of x^2). In other words, you can use this method whenever the leading coefficient of the trinomial is 1.

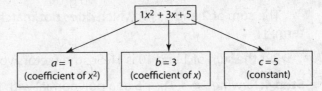

$$1x^2 + 3x + 5$$

| $a = 1$ (coefficient of x^2) | $b = 3$ (coefficient of x) | $c = 5$ (constant) |

EXAMPLE 1

Factor $x^2 + 8x + 15$.

Find numbers that multiply to give 15 and add to give 8.

$5 \times 3 = 15$ and $5 + 3 = 8$

So, $x^2 + 8x + 15$ factors to $(x + 5)(x + 3)$.

Since guessing is used, you need to check that you are correct. The easiest way to check is to multiply the binomials together (FOIL method) and see whether you get the original problem.

EXAMPLE 2

Factor $x^2 + 6x - 27$.

Find numbers that multiply to give –27 and add to give 6.

$(9) \times (-3) = -27$ and $(9) + (-3) = 6$

So, $x^2 + 6x - 27$ factors to $(x + 9)(x - 3)$.

Some trinomials cannot be factored. Take the trinomial $2x^2 + 35x + 7$, for example. You cannot find two integers whose sum is 35 and whose product is $2 \times 7 = 14$. This type of trinomial, which cannot be factored, is called a **prime trinomial**.

Factoring by the *ac* Method

This method is used to factor a trinomial when $a > 1$.

EXAMPLE 1

Factor $2x^2 + 5 + 11x$.

Step 1: Write the trinomial in descending order so that the term of highest degree ax^2 is first followed by the term bx and c last.

$2x^2 + 5 + 11x$ becomes $2x^2 + 11x + 5$.

Step 2: Next, multiply $a \times c = 2 \times 5 = 10$. To factor $2x^2 + 5 + 11x$, you need factors of 10 that add up to the coefficient of the middle term, 11. The factors of 10 are 2, 5 and 1, 10.

Step 3: Now find the pair of factors that allow you to factor the trinomial. Check the sum of each pair of factors:

Pair of Factors	Product	Sum
2, 5	10	7
1, 10	10	11

The sum of 2 and 5 is 7, which does not match the coefficient of the middle term, 11.

But the sum of 1 and 10 is 11. So, the factors you want to use are 1 and 10.

Step 4: Rewrite $2x^2 + 11x + 5$ as a polynomial with four terms: $2x^2 + 10x + 1x + 5$.

Step 5: Follow the grouping method to factor the polynomial.

$$2x^2 + 10x + 1x + 5 = 2x(x + 5) + 1(x + 5)$$

$$= (x + 5)(2x + 1)$$

Step 6: Check the final answer by multiplying the binomials together (FOIL method) and see if you get the original polynomial:

$$(x + 5)(2x + 1) = 2x^2 + x + 10x + 5 = 2x^2 + 11x + 5$$

In some cases you have to factor a GCF out first and then factor the trinomial.

EXAMPLE 2

Factor $-3x^4 + 30x^3 - 75x^2$ completely.

This trinomial has common factors. Factor out the GCF first:

$$-3x^4 + 30x^3 - 75x^2 = -3x^2 (x^2 - 10x + 25)$$

Factor the perfect-square trinomial:

$$-3x^4 + 30x^3 - 75x^2 = -3x^2 (x^2 - 10x + 25) = -3x^2 (x - 5)(x - 5)$$

Express as a perfect square:

$$-3x^4 + 30x^3 - 75x^2 = -3x^2 (x^2 - 10x + 25) = -3x^2 (x - 5)(x - 5) = -3x^2 (x - 5)^2$$

EXERCISE 19

Factoring Trinomials

Directions: Factor each trinomial completely.

1. $2x^2 + 11x + 12$

2. $3x^2 + 5x + 2$

3. $2x^2 + 13x + 20$

4. $2x^2 - 5xy + 3y^2$

5. $2x^2 - 18x - 72$

6. $10x^2 - 7x - 12$

7. $8y^2 - 2y - 3$

8. $-8x^3 - 18x^2 - 4x$

9. $-2x^3 - 6x^2 + 56x$

10. $24x^2 - 6xy - 9y^2$

Answers are on page 571.

Special Forms
Perfect Square

When you square a binomial, the resulting trinomial is called a perfect square. For example, $(x + 1)(x + 1) = (x + 1)^2 = x^2 + x + x + 1 = x^2 + 2x + 1$. Here, $x^2 + 2x + 1$ is a perfect-square trinomial.

When factoring perfect-square trinomials, use the following:

$$a^2 + 2ab + b^2 = (a + b)^2 \text{ and } a^2 - 2ab + b^2 = (a - b)^2.$$

The bases in the binomials are the square roots of the first term and last term of the trinomial. The sign of the binomial comes from the sign of the middle term of the trinomial.

EXAMPLE 1

Factor $x^2 + 24x + 144$.

The trinomial $x^2 + 24x + 144$ can be written as $x^2 + 24x + 12^2$. The first term is x^2 and the base is x. The last term is 12^2 and the base is 12. The second term is twice that of $12x$, that is, $24x = 2(12x)$. Thus, $x^2 + 24x + 12^2$ is a perfect-square trinomial.

Factor the trinomial in this way. Put the bases inside parentheses with a "+" sign between them $(x + 12)$ and write an exponent of 2 outside the parentheses to get $(x + 12)^2$.

When a trinomial has a negative second term, use this formula: $a^2 - 2ab + b^2 = (a - b)^2$.

EXAMPLE 2

Factor $9x^2 - 24x + 16$.

The trinomial $9x^2 - 24x + 16$ can be written as $(3x)^2 - 24x + (4)^2$.

The first term is $(3x)^2$ and the base is $3x$. The last term is $(4)^2$ and the base is 4. Since the second term is $-24x$ and $-2 \times 3x \times 4 = -24x$, $(3x)^2 + (-24x) + (4)^2$ is a perfect square and you factor like this: put the bases inside parentheses with a minus sign between them $(3x - 4)$ and raise everything to the second power to get $(3x - 4)^2$.

Difference of Squares

A difference of two squares is made up of a perfect square subtracted from another perfect square. For example, for the expression $x^2 - 16$, x^2 is a square because it is equal to $x \times x$ and 16 is a square because it is equal to 4×4. Here are some more examples of difference of two squares: $x^2 - 25$, $4x^2 - 49$, $9x^2 - 36$.

To factor these expressions, do the following:

Step 1: Find the square root of each term.

Step 2: Factor into two binomials—one plus and one minus.

EXAMPLE 1

Factor $x^2 - 16$.

Step 1: Find the square root of each term: $\sqrt{x^2} = x$ and $\sqrt{16} = 4$.

Step 2: Factor into two binomials—one plus and one minus: $(x + 4)(x - 4)$.

$x^2 - 16$ factors to $(x + 4)(x - 4)$.

EXAMPLE 2

Factor $x^2 - 25$.

Step 1: Find the square root of each term: $\sqrt{x^2} = x$ and $\sqrt{25} = 5$.

Step 2: Factor into two binomials—one plus and one minus: $(x + 5)(x - 5)$.

Thus, $x^2 - 25$ factors to $(x + 5)(x - 5)$.

EXAMPLE 3

Factor $4x^2 - 49$.

Step 1: Find the square root of each term: $\sqrt{4x^2} = 2x$ and $\sqrt{49} = 7$.

Step 2: Factor into two binomials—one plus and one minus: $(2x + 7)(2x - 7)$.

Thus, $4x^2 - 49$ factors to $(2x + 7)(2x - 7)$.

Sum or Difference of Cubes

The difference of two cubes can be factored as

$$x^3 - y^3 = (x - y)(x^2 + xy + y^2).$$

EXAMPLE 1

Factor $x^3 - 8$.

$$x^3 - 8 = x^3 - 2^3 = (x - 2)(x^2 + 2x + 2^2) = (x - 2)(x^2 + 2x + 4)$$

The sum of two cubes can be factored as:

$$x^3 + y^3 = (x + y)(x^2 - xy + y^2)$$

EXAMPLE 2

Factor $27x^3 + 1$.

Think of $27x^3 + 1$ as $(3x)^3 + 1^3$. Then,

$$27x^3 + 1 = (3x)^3 + 1^3 = (3x + 1)((3x)^2 - (3x)(1) + 1^2) = (3x + 1)(9x^2 - 3x + 1)$$

In either case of the sum or difference of two cubes, the trinomial in the final factored form cannot be factored further.

EXERCISE 20

Special Forms

Directions: Factor each polynomial completely.

1. $3x^3 - 12x$
2. $x^2 + 6x + 9$
3. $p^2 - 18p + 81$
4. $4y^2 + 48y + 144$

5. $8y^3 + 27$
6. $x^2 - 100$
7. $y^4 - 144$
8. $25m^2 - 9n^2$

9. $x^3 + 125$
10. $8x^3 - 27$
11. $2x^3 + 128y^3$

Answers are on page 571.

General Strategy for Factoring

To factor completely any given polynomial, follow the steps given below:

Step 1: Find the GCF. If there is a GCF, factor it out.

Step 2: Find the number of terms in the polynomial. This determines how you should factor the polynomial.

Check the terms in the polynomial.

1. If it is a sum of perfect squares, $a^2 + b^2$, then the polynomial is prime; if it is a difference of perfect squares, $a^2 - b^2$, then polynomial factors as $(a + b)(a - b)$ or $(a - b)(a + b)$.

2. If it is a perfect-square trinomial, use the appropriate formula given below.

   $a^2 + 2ab + b^2 = (a + b)(a + b) = (a + b)^2$

   $a^2 - 2ab + b^2 = (a - b)(a - b) = (a - b)^2$

3. If it is in the form $x^2 + bx + c$, find two numbers that multiply to c and add to b.

   $x^2 + bx + c = (x\_\_\_\_)(x\_\_\_\_)$

   If no such numbers exist, the polynomial is prime.

4. If it is in the form $ax^2 + bx + c$, use the ac method, trial and error, or factor by grouping.

Step 3: Find each factor and see if it can be factored further. The polynomial is factored completely when none of the factors can be factored further.

Step 4: Check the factorization by multiplying. The product of all the factors should be the original polynomial.

EXERCISE 21

General Strategy for Factoring

Directions: Factor the following expressions.

1. $5x^2 - 32x - 21$
2. $a^3 + a^2b + ab^2 + b^3$
3. $8b^3 - c^3$
4. $12x^3y^2 - 38x^2y^3 + 16xy^4$
5. $x^4 - 81$

6. $x^5 - 4x^3 - 8x^2 + 32$
7. $3x^2 + 21x + 18$
8. $x^2 + 3x - 4$
9. $x^2 + 5x + 12$
10. $2x^2 + 13x + 4$

Answers are on page 572.

Rational Expressions

Rational expressions may look like fractions but have polynomials for numerators and denominators. An example of a rational expression is $\dfrac{x^2+7}{x+5}$.

Rational expressions follow all the rules of rational numbers but are more complex because numbers are replaced by variables. This requires you to use some very basic rules and techniques related to polynomial operations to simplify the expressions.

Multiplying Rational Expressions

To multiply rational expressions, multiply the numerators together, multiply the denominators together, and reduce. When multiplying rational expressions, it is generally simpler to cancel common/like factors first and then do the multiplication, since cancelation will leave smaller numbers to deal with. This is the same as if you were multiplying fractions with just numbers.

EXAMPLE 1

Multiply: $\dfrac{7x^2}{3} \cdot \dfrac{9}{14x}$.

Cancel common/like factors, and then multiply.

$$\frac{7x^2}{3} \cdot \frac{9}{14x} = \frac{{}^{1}\cancel{7}{}^{x}\cancel{x^2}}{{}_{1}\cancel{3}} \cdot \frac{{}^{3}\cancel{9}}{{}_{2}\cancel{14}\cancel{x}_{1}} = \frac{x}{1} \cdot \frac{3}{2} = \frac{3x}{2}$$

The answer is $\dfrac{3x}{2}$.

EXAMPLE 2

Multiply: $\dfrac{3y}{x} \cdot \dfrac{x^2+5x}{3y^2}$.

Step 1: Factor both the numerator and the denominator of both fractions.

$$\frac{3y}{x} \cdot \frac{x^2+5x}{3y^2} = \frac{3y}{x} \cdot \frac{x(x+5)}{3y^2}$$

Step 2: Cancel common/like factors. Multiply.

$$\frac{3y}{x} \cdot \frac{x(x+5)}{3y^2} = \frac{\cancel{3}\cancel{y}}{\cancel{x}} \cdot \frac{\cancel{x}(x+5)}{\cancel{3}y^{\cancel{2}}} = \frac{x+5}{y}$$

The answer is $\dfrac{x+5}{y}$.

EXAMPLE 3

Multiply: $\dfrac{x^2+8x+15}{x+6} \cdot \dfrac{x+4}{x^2+7x+12}$.

Step 1: Factor both the numerator and denominator of both fractions.

$$\frac{x^2+8x+15}{x+6} \cdot \frac{x+4}{x^2+7x+12} = \frac{(x+3)(x+5)}{x+6} \cdot \frac{x+4}{(x+4)(x+3)}$$

Step 2: Multiply the two fractions together.

$$\frac{(x+3)(x+5)}{x+6} \cdot \frac{x+4}{(x+4)(x+3)} = \frac{(x+3)(x+5)(x+4)}{(x+6)(x+4)(x+3)}$$

Step 3: Cancel like terms.

$$\frac{(x+3)(x+5)(x+4)}{(x+6)(x+4)(x+3)} = \frac{\cancel{(x+3)}(x+5)\cancel{(x+4)}}{(x+6)\cancel{(x+4)}\cancel{(x+3)}} = \frac{x+5}{x+6}$$

The answer is $\dfrac{x+5}{x+6}$.

EXERCISE 22

Multiplying Rational Expressions

Directions: Multiply. Reduce your answer to lowest terms.

1. $\dfrac{5x^2}{3xy} \cdot \dfrac{9y^2}{20}$

2. $\dfrac{p^3 - p}{5p^2} \cdot \dfrac{15}{p+1}$

3. $\dfrac{4x+8}{x^2-25} \cdot \dfrac{x-5}{1}$

4. $\dfrac{x^2-4}{(x-3)^2} \cdot \dfrac{x^3-27}{x^3+8}$

5. $\dfrac{x^2+x-6}{x^2+2x-3} \cdot \dfrac{x^2-6x+5}{x^2-7x+10}$

6. $\dfrac{y^2-9}{y^2-3y} \cdot \dfrac{y}{y^2+9y+18}$

7. $\dfrac{x^3-27}{4x} \cdot \dfrac{2x+4}{x^2-x-6}$

8. $\dfrac{a^2-ab-4a+4b}{4a^2-b^2} \cdot \dfrac{2a^2-ab}{a^2-ab-3a+3b}$

9. $\dfrac{(a+b)^3}{a^3+b^3} \cdot \dfrac{a^2-ab+b^2}{a^2+2ab+b^2}$

10. $\dfrac{a^3-3a^2-a+3}{14a^2b^2+14ab^2} \cdot \dfrac{21a^2b}{a^2-4a+3}$

11. $\dfrac{a^2+5a+6}{a^2-1} \cdot \dfrac{3+2a-a^2}{a^2-9}$

Answers are on page 572.

Dividing Rational Expressions

When dividing rational expressions, you will use the same method as you use for dividing numerical fractions: find the reciprocal of the divisor and change the sign to multiplication. Then multiply and simplify.

EXAMPLE 1

Divide: $\dfrac{2}{x-2} \div \dfrac{3}{x+1}$

Flip the divisor, and then multiply.

$$\dfrac{2}{x-2} \div \dfrac{3}{x+1} = \dfrac{2}{x-2} \cdot \dfrac{x+1}{3} = \dfrac{2(x+1)}{3(x-2)}$$

The answer is $\dfrac{2(x+1)}{3(x-2)}$.

EXAMPLE 2

Divide: $\dfrac{9x^2}{x^2+12x+36} \div \dfrac{12x}{x^2+6x}$.

Step 1: Flip the divisor.

$$\dfrac{9x^2}{x^2+12x+36} \div \dfrac{12x}{x^2+6x} = \dfrac{9x^2}{x^2+12x+36} \cdot \dfrac{x^2+6x}{12x}$$

Step 2: Factor the numerator and denominator.

$$\frac{9x^2}{x^2+12x+36} \cdot \frac{x^2+6x}{12x} = \frac{9x^2}{(x+6)(x+6)} \cdot \frac{x(x+6)}{12x}$$

Step 3: Multiply the fractions.

$$\frac{9x^2}{(x+6)(x+6)} \cdot \frac{x(x+6)}{12x} = \frac{9x^2(x)(x+6)}{(x+6)(x+6)(12x)}$$

Step 4: Simplify by dividing out the common factors.

$$\frac{9x^2(x)(x+6)}{(x+6)(x+6)(12x)} = \frac{\overset{3}{9}x^2(\cancel{x})\cancel{(x+6)}}{(x+6)\cancel{(x+6)}(\underset{4}{12}\cancel{x})} = \frac{3x^2}{4(x+6)} = \frac{3x^2}{4x+24}$$

The answer is $\dfrac{3x^2}{4x+24}$.

EXAMPLE 3

Divide: $\dfrac{5y^2+20y}{y^3-2y^2} \div \dfrac{y^2-16}{y^2-y-12}$.

Step 1: Flip the divisor.

$$\frac{5y^2+20y}{y^3-2y^2} \div \frac{y^2-16}{y^2-y-12} = \frac{5y^2+20y}{y^3-2y^2} \times \frac{y^2-y-12}{y^2-16}$$

Step 2: Factor the numerator and denominator.

$$\frac{5y^2+20y}{y^3-2y^2} \times \frac{y^2-y-12}{y^2-16} = \frac{5y(y+4)}{y^2(y-2)} \times \frac{(y+3)(y-4)}{(y+4)(y-4)}$$

Step 3: Multiply the fractions.

$$\frac{5y(y+4)}{y^2(y-2)} \times \frac{(y+3)(y-4)}{(y+4)(y-4)} = \frac{5y(y+4)(y+3)(y-4)}{y^2(y-2)(y+4)(y-4)}$$

Step 4: Simplify by dividing out the common factors.

$$\frac{5y(y+4)(y+3)(y-4)}{y^2(y-2)(y+4)(y-4)} = \frac{5\cancel{y}\cancel{(y+4)}(y+3)\cancel{(y-4)}}{y\cancel{y^2}(y-2)\cancel{(y+4)}\cancel{(y-4)}} = \frac{5(y+3)}{y(y-2)} = \frac{5y+15}{y^2-2y}$$

The answer is $\dfrac{5y+15}{y^2-2y}$.

EXERCISE 23

Dividing Rational Expressions

Directions: Divide. Reduce your answer to lowest terms.

1. $\dfrac{3y^2+12}{3y^2-15y} \div \dfrac{y^4-16}{y^2-3y-10}$

2. $\dfrac{x^2-x}{x+5} \div \dfrac{x^4-x^2}{x^2+5x+4}$

3. $\dfrac{3y}{4x-20} \div \dfrac{2x+10}{x^2-25}$

4. $\dfrac{x^2+3x}{x-2} \div \dfrac{x^2+4x+3}{x^2-x-2}$

5. $\dfrac{2x+4}{x} \div \dfrac{6x+12}{3}$

8. $\dfrac{2x^2+x-6}{x^2-2x-8} \div \dfrac{2x^2-x-3}{x^2-3x-4}$

6. $\dfrac{x^2+6x+9}{x^2-9} \div \dfrac{x^2+2x-3}{3x-9}$

9. $\dfrac{x+4}{2x-6} \div \dfrac{3x+12}{4x-12}$

7. $\dfrac{4+2x}{x^2-4} \div \dfrac{x-2}{x^2-4x+4}$

10. $\dfrac{x^2-3x+2}{2x-4} \div \dfrac{x^2-2x+1}{x-1}$

Answers are on page 572.

Adding Rational Expressions with Common Denominators

When adding rational expressions, you need to see if the rational expressions have common denominators. If the denominators are the same, you can add the rational expressions easily as you did with fractions. Be sure to reduce the answer to lowest terms.

EXAMPLE 1

Add: $\dfrac{4x}{5y} + \dfrac{6x}{5y}$.

Step 1: These fractions already have common denominators. So, add the numerators:

$$\frac{4x}{5y} + \frac{6x}{5y} = \frac{4x+6x}{5y}$$

Step 2: Reduce to lowest terms:

$$\frac{4x+6x}{5y} = \frac{10x}{5y} = \frac{\overset{2}{\cancel{10}}x}{\cancel{5}_1 y} = \frac{2x}{y}$$

The answer is $\dfrac{2x}{y}$.

EXAMPLE 2

Add: $\dfrac{7x}{3x+1} + \dfrac{8x+5}{3x+1}$.

Step 1: Add the numerators together since the two denominators are the same.

$$\frac{7x}{3x+1} + \frac{8x+5}{3x+1} = \frac{7x+8x+5}{3x+1} = \frac{15x+5}{3x+1}$$

Step 2: Reduce to lowest terms by factoring out a GCF of 5 in the numerator.

$$\frac{15x+5}{3x+1} = \frac{5(3x+1)}{(3x+1)}$$

Step 3: Divide out the common factor of $3x + 1$:

$$\frac{5(3x+1)}{(3x+1)} = 5$$

The answer is 5.

EXAMPLE 3

Add: $\dfrac{2x^2+15x-6}{x^3+125} + \dfrac{x^2-x+1}{x^3+125}$.

Step 1: Add the numerators together since the two denominators are the same.

$$\frac{2x^2+15x-6}{x^3+125} + \frac{x^2-x+1}{x^3+125} = \frac{2x^2+15x-6+x^2-x+1}{x^3+125} = \frac{3x^2+14x-5}{x^3+125}$$

Step 2: Reduce to lowest terms by factoring the numerator.

$$\frac{3x^2+14x-5}{x^3+125} = \frac{(3x-1)(x+5)}{(x+5)(x^2-5x+25)}$$

Step 3: Divide out the common factor:

$$\frac{(3x-1)(x+5)}{(x+5)(x^2-5x+25)} = \frac{3x-1}{x^2-5x+25}$$

The answer is $\dfrac{3x-1}{x^2-5x+25}$.

EXERCISE 24

Adding Rational Expressions with Common Denominators

Directions: Add. Reduce your answers to lowest terms.

1. $\dfrac{4}{5x} + \dfrac{1}{5x}$

2. $\dfrac{2x+5}{x-7} + \dfrac{8x-10}{x-7}$

3. $\dfrac{2r+2}{6r^2+r-12} + \dfrac{r-6}{6r^2+r-12}$

4. $\dfrac{b-1}{12b^2+8b} + \dfrac{b+5}{12b^2+8b}$

5. $\dfrac{2n-4}{27n^2-54n} + \dfrac{n-2}{27n^2-54n}$

6. $\dfrac{n+4}{6n^3+24n^2} + \dfrac{n+4}{6n^3+24n^2}$

7. $\dfrac{a-5}{2a^2+a-15} + \dfrac{a}{2a^2+a-15}$

8. $\dfrac{2x^3+3x^2-5}{x^3+x^2} + \dfrac{3x^3+5x^2-8}{x^3+x^2}$

9. $\dfrac{5x^2-2x+5}{x^2+3x+2} + \dfrac{x^3+8x^2}{x^2+3x+2}$

10. $\dfrac{3x+5}{2x^2-3x-2} + \dfrac{8x-5}{2x^2-3x-2}$

Answers are on page 572.

Adding Rational Expressions with Different Denominators

When adding rational expressions with different denominators, first you need to find a common denominator. You find the least common denominator (LCD) by including each distinct factor in a denominator as many times as it occurs in any denominator. For example, if a denominator has a factor of x^2 and another denominator has a factor of x^3, the LCD will have x^3 as one of its factors. As with fractions, you convert the rational expressions to equivalent fractions and add or subtract numerators. Finally, you cancel out any factors to simplify.

EXAMPLE 1

Add: $\dfrac{2}{x} + \dfrac{3}{x^2} + \dfrac{1}{2x}$.

Step 1: To find the common denominator, you need to find the LCD of x, x^2, and $2x$ using the factor method.

x: $\quad x$

x^2: $\quad\quad x \cdot x$

$2x$: $\quad\quad 2 \cdot x$

LCD: $\quad 2 \cdot x \cdot x = 2x^2$

To convert $\dfrac{2}{x}$ to the common denominator, you need to multiply by $\dfrac{2x}{2x}$, since the denominator already has one copy of x but needs a 2 and another x to make $2x^2$:

$$\frac{2}{x} = \frac{2}{x} \cdot 1 = \frac{2}{x} \cdot \frac{2x}{2x}$$

Similarly for $\dfrac{3}{x^2}$, you multiply by $\dfrac{2}{2}$; and for $\dfrac{1}{2x}$, you multiply by $\dfrac{x}{x}$.

Step 2:

$$\frac{2}{x} + \frac{3}{x^2} + \frac{1}{2x} = \frac{2}{x} \cdot \frac{2x}{2x} + \frac{3}{x^2} \cdot \frac{2}{2} + \frac{1}{2x} \cdot \frac{x}{x}$$

$$= \frac{4x}{2x^2} + \frac{6}{2x^2} + \frac{1x}{2x^2}$$

$$= \frac{4x + 6 + x}{2x^2}$$

$$= \frac{5x + 6}{2x^2}$$

The answer is $\dfrac{5x + 6}{2x^2}$.

EXAMPLE 2

Add: $\dfrac{4}{x^2-16} + \dfrac{3}{x^2+8x+16}$.

Step 1: Factor each denominator:

$$\frac{4}{x^2-16} + \frac{3}{x^2+8x+16} = \frac{4}{(x+4)(x-4)} + \frac{3}{(x+4)^2}$$

Step 2: Find the LCD $(x-4)(x+4)^2$ and rewrite each fraction so that the LCD is its denominator.

$$\frac{4}{(x+4)(x-4)} + \frac{3}{(x+4)^2} = \frac{4}{(x+4)(x-4)} \cdot \frac{x+4}{x+4} + \frac{3}{(x+4)^2} \cdot \frac{x-4}{x-4}$$

$$= \frac{4x+16}{(x-4)(x+4)^2} + \frac{3x-12}{(x-4)(x+4)^2}$$

Step 3: Add the numerators and keep the LCD as the denominator.

$$\frac{4x+16}{(x-4)(x+4)^2} + \frac{3x-12}{(x-4)(x+4)^2} = \frac{4x+16+3x-12}{(x-4)(x+4)^2} = \frac{7x+4}{(x-4)(x+4)^2}$$

The answer is $\dfrac{7x+4}{(x-4)(x+4)^2}$.

EXERCISE 25

Adding Rational Expressions with Different Denominators

Directions: Add. Reduce your answers to lowest terms.

1. $\dfrac{5}{x+2} + \dfrac{6}{x-3}$

2. $\dfrac{2}{a} + \dfrac{3}{a-5}$

3. $\dfrac{3x}{2x-6} + \dfrac{9}{6-2x}$

4. $\dfrac{5}{x+2} + \dfrac{2}{x-1}$

5. $\dfrac{2}{c+5} + \dfrac{4}{c-8}$

6. $\dfrac{2}{7x-14} + \dfrac{15}{21x+7}$

7. $\dfrac{4}{x^2-16} + \dfrac{3}{x^2+8x+16}$

8. $\dfrac{8x}{x-3} + \dfrac{5}{9-x^2}$

9. $\dfrac{5x-1}{x^2-3x+2} + \dfrac{3}{2x-4}$

Answers are on page 572.

Subtracting Rational Expressions with Common Denominators

You follow the same process as with adding rational expressions with common denominators.

EXAMPLE 1

Subtract: $\dfrac{5x-1}{x+8} - \dfrac{3x+4}{x+8}$.

These fractions have a common denominator. Use parentheses on the numerators to make sure the "minus" is distributed through the terms of the second parentheses.

$$\frac{5x-1}{x+8} - \frac{3x+4}{x+8} = \frac{(5x-1)-(3x+4)}{x+8}$$

$$= \frac{5x-1-3x-4}{x+8}$$

$$= \frac{2x-5}{x+8}$$

The answer is $\dfrac{2x-5}{x+8}$.

EXAMPLE 2

Subtract: $\dfrac{3x}{x^2+3x-10} - \dfrac{6}{x^2+3x-10}$.

Step 1: Since these expressions have a common denominator, combine both and subtract the numerators.

$$\frac{3x}{x^2+3x-10} - \frac{6}{x^2+3x-10} = \frac{3x-6}{x^2+3x-10}$$

Step 2: Factor the numerator and the denominator.

$$\frac{3x-6}{x^2+3x-10} = \frac{3(x-2)}{(x+5)(x-2)}$$

Step 3: Cancel like terms.

$$\frac{3(x-2)}{(x+5)(x-2)} = \frac{3\cancel{(x-2)}}{(x+5)\cancel{(x-2)}} = \frac{3}{x+5}$$

The answer is $\dfrac{3}{x+5}$.

Subtracting Rational Expressions with Common Denominators

Directions: Subtract. Reduce your answers to lowest terms.

1. $\dfrac{2y}{x} - \dfrac{y-1}{x}$

2. $\dfrac{a+b}{2a-b} - \dfrac{2a-3b}{2a-b}$

3. $\dfrac{4x-1}{x+4} - \dfrac{2x-9}{x+4}$

4. $\dfrac{4x+5y}{15x} - \dfrac{x+5y}{15x}$

5. $\dfrac{x+4y}{18x^2y^2} - \dfrac{x+3y}{18x^2y^2}$

6. $\dfrac{x+1}{9x+36} - \dfrac{x-2}{9x+36}$

7. $\dfrac{3b-5}{2b^2-15b+18} - \dfrac{b-2}{2b^2-15b+18}$

8. $\dfrac{6v}{4v^4-16v^3} - \dfrac{3v+12}{4v^4-16v^3}$

9. $\dfrac{4x+4}{x^2-2x-8} - \dfrac{3x+2}{x^2-2x-8}$

10. $\dfrac{4x+5}{36x^2+24x-12} - \dfrac{40x-7}{36x^2+24x-12}$

Answers are on page 572.

Subtracting Rational Expressions with Different Denominators

When subtracting fractions with different denominators, first you need to find a common denominator following these steps and then subtract.

Step 1: Factor each denominator completely.

Step 2: Find the LCD of the denominators.

Step 3: Rewrite each rational expression with the LCD as the denominator.

Step 4: Subtract the numerators.

It is the same process as with adding fractions with different denominators.

EXAMPLE 1

Subtract: $\dfrac{x+4}{2x} - \dfrac{x-1}{x^2}$.

Step 1: To find the common denominator, find the LCD of $2x$ and x^2 using the factor method.

$2x$: $2 \cdot x$

x^2: $x \cdot x$

Step 2: Find the LCD: $2 \cdot x \cdot x = 2x^2$.

To convert $\dfrac{x+4}{2x}$ to the common denominator, you need to multiply by $\dfrac{x}{x}$, since the denominator already has one copy of x but needs another x to make $2x^2$:

$$\frac{x+4}{2x} = \frac{x+4}{2x} \cdot 1 = \frac{x+4}{2x} \cdot \frac{x}{x}$$

Similarly, multiply $\dfrac{x-1}{x^2}$ by $\dfrac{2}{2}$.

Step 3: Rewrite each rational expression with the LCD as the denominator.

$$\frac{x+4}{2x} - \frac{x-1}{x^2} = \frac{x+4}{2x} \cdot \frac{x}{x} - \frac{x-1}{x^2} \cdot \frac{2}{2}$$

$$= \frac{x^2+4x}{2x^2} - \frac{2x-2}{2x^2}$$

Step 4: Subtract the numerators.

$$\frac{x^2+4x}{2x^2} - \frac{2x-2}{2x^2} = \frac{x^2+4x-(2x-2)}{2x^2} = \frac{x^2+4x-2x+2}{2x^2} = \frac{x^2+2x+2}{2x^2}$$

The answer is $\dfrac{x^2+2x+2}{2x^2}$.

EXAMPLE 2

Subtract: $\dfrac{x}{x^2+x-2} - \dfrac{1}{x+2}$.

Step 1: Factor the first denominator.

$$\frac{x}{x^2+x-2} - \frac{1}{x+2} = \frac{x}{(x+2)(x-1)} - \frac{1}{x+2}$$

Step 2: Find the LCD: $(x+2)(x-1)$.

Step 3: Since the first expression already has the LCD, rewrite the second expression with the LCD.

$$\frac{x}{(x+2)(x-1)} - \frac{1}{x+2} = \frac{x}{(x+2)(x-1)} - \frac{1(x-1)}{(x+2)(x-1)}$$

Step 4: Subtract the numerators.

$$\frac{x}{(x+2)(x-1)} - \frac{1(x-1)}{(x+2)(x-1)} = \frac{x}{(x+2)(x-1)} - \frac{x-1}{(x+2)(x-1)}$$

$$= \frac{x-(x-1)}{(x+2)(x-1)}$$

$$= \frac{x-x+1}{(x+2)(x-1)}$$

$$= \frac{1}{(x+2)(x-1)}$$

The answer is $\dfrac{1}{(x+2)(x-1)}$.

EXAMPLE 3

Subtract: $\dfrac{5x+1}{x^2-2x-3}-\dfrac{5x-3}{x^2-x-6}$.

Step 1: Factor each denominator:

$$\frac{5x+1}{x^2-2x-3}-\frac{5x-3}{x^2-x-6}=\frac{5x+1}{(x-3)(x+1)}-\frac{5x-3}{(x-3)(x+2)}$$

Step 2: Find the LCD: $(x-3)(x+1)(x+2)$.

Step 3: Rewrite each expression with the LCD as the denominator:

$$\frac{5x+1}{(x-3)(x+1)}-\frac{5x-3}{(x-3)(x+2)}=\frac{(5x+1)(x+2)}{(x-3)(x+1)(x+2)}-\frac{(5x-3)(x+1)}{(x-3)(x+2)(x+1)}$$

Step 4: Subtract the numerators:

$$\frac{(5x+1)(x+2)}{(x-3)(x+1)(x+2)}-\frac{(5x-3)(x+1)}{(x-3)(x+2)(x+1)}=\frac{(5x+1)(x+2)-(5x-3)(x+1)}{(x-3)(x+2)(x+1)}$$

$$=\frac{(5x^2+10x+x+2)-(5x^2+5x-3x-3)}{(x-3)(x+1)(x+2)}$$

$$=\frac{5x^2+10x+x+2-5x^2-5x+3x+3}{(x-3)(x+1)(x+2)}$$

$$=\frac{9x+5}{(x-3)(x+1)(x+2)}$$

The answer is $\dfrac{9x+5}{(x-3)(x+1)(x+2)}$.

EXERCISE 27

Subtracting Rational Expressions with Different Denominators

Directions: Subtract. Reduce your answers to lowest terms.

1. $\dfrac{1}{x^2-x}-\dfrac{1}{x}$

2. $\dfrac{2}{a}-\dfrac{3}{a-5}$

3. $\dfrac{2x+3}{x+3}-\dfrac{4x^2}{2x^2+5x-3}$

4. $\dfrac{2}{x^2-36}-\dfrac{1}{x^2+6x}$

5. $\dfrac{5x+1}{x^2-2x-3}-\dfrac{5x-3}{x^2-x-6}$

6. $\dfrac{3y}{2y-1}-\dfrac{4}{y-5}$

7. $\dfrac{5}{x+2}-\dfrac{2}{x-1}$

8. $\dfrac{3}{x^2+6x+9}-\dfrac{2}{x+3}$

9. $\dfrac{1}{x+3}-\dfrac{2}{x-5}$

10. $\dfrac{n-3}{n^2+3n-18}-\dfrac{n-2}{n^2+n-20}$

Answers are on page 573.

Rational Expressions with Rational Expressions in the Numerator and/or Denominator

A rational expression in which the numerator and/or the denominator are rational expressions is called a **complex rational expression**. Here are some examples of these rational expressions:

1.
$$\dfrac{\dfrac{x^2+3x-4}{4x+3}}{\dfrac{7x^2+9}{-4x^2+32x-17}}$$

2.
$$\dfrac{\dfrac{x^7+9}{x^3-1}}{3x+61-\dfrac{1}{x}}$$

A complex rational expression is simplified when there are no fractions in the numerator or in the denominator. To simplify a complex rational expression that consists of a single fraction or polynomial in the numerator, and a single fraction or polynomial in the denominator, follow the same process as you did with numerical fractions and use the division symbol to rewrite the expression.

EXAMPLE

Simplify: $\dfrac{\dfrac{x^2+x}{4x+1}}{\dfrac{x}{3x+2}}$.

Step 1: Rewrite the expression in division form.

$$\dfrac{\dfrac{x^2+x}{4x+1}}{\dfrac{x}{3x+2}}=\dfrac{x^2+x}{4x+1}\div\dfrac{x}{3x+2}$$

Step 2: Multiply the first fraction by the reciprocal of the second.

$$\dfrac{x^2+x}{4x+1}\div\dfrac{x}{3x+2}=\dfrac{x^2+x}{4x+1}\cdot\dfrac{3x+2}{x}$$

Step 3: Simplify by factoring and canceling common factors.

$$\dfrac{x^2+x}{4x+1}\cdot\dfrac{3x+2}{x}=\dfrac{x(x+1)}{4x+1}\cdot\dfrac{3x+2}{x}=\dfrac{\cancel{x}(x+1)}{4x+1}\cdot\dfrac{3x+2}{\cancel{x}}=\dfrac{(x+1)(3x+2)}{4x+1}$$

Simplifying by Distributing LCD

Using this method you will first find the LCD of the small fractions, and multiply each term by the LCD so that you can clear the small fractions and simplify.

EXAMPLE

Simplify: $\dfrac{1-\dfrac{1}{x^2}}{1-\dfrac{1}{x}}$.

Step 1: Identify the LCD of all the denominators: x^2.

Step 2: Multiply each term by the LCD:

$$\frac{1-\dfrac{1}{x^2}}{1-\dfrac{1\cdot x^2}{x}} = \frac{1\cdot x^2 - \dfrac{1\cdot x^2}{x^2}}{1\cdot x^2 - \dfrac{1\cdot x^2}{x}}$$

Step 3: Simplify and reduce the fractions:

$$\frac{1\cdot x^2 - 1}{1\cdot x^2 - x}$$

Step 4: Factor and reduce:

$$\frac{x^2-1}{x^2-x} = \frac{(x+1)(x-1)}{x(x-1)} = \frac{x+1}{x}$$

The answer is $\dfrac{x+1}{x}$.

Simplifying by Obtaining Single Rational Expressions on Top and Bottom and Dividing

To simplify a complex rational expression, you can also collapse the numerator and denominator into single fractions.

EXAMPLE

Simplify: $\dfrac{\dfrac{1}{x}+\dfrac{x}{x^2-1}}{\dfrac{1}{x}-\dfrac{x}{x^2+1}}$.

Step 1: Use addition to first change the numerator into a single fraction.

Put the fractions over the common denominator $(x)(x^2-1)$:

$$\frac{1}{x}+\frac{x}{x^2-1} = \frac{1(x^2-1)}{x(x^2-1)} + \frac{x\cdot x}{x(x^2-1)}$$

Then you add and simplify:

$$\frac{x^2-1+x^2}{x(x^2-1)} = \frac{2x^2-1}{x(x^2-1)}$$

Step 2: Do the same for the denominator.

$$\frac{1}{x}-\frac{x}{x^2+1} = \frac{1(x^2+1)}{x(x^2+1)} - \frac{x\cdot x}{x(x^2+1)}$$

$$= \frac{x^2+1-x^2}{x(x^2+1)}$$

$$= \frac{1}{x(x^2+1)}$$

Step 3: After rewriting the numerator and denominator each as a single fraction, simplify the expression.

$$\frac{\dfrac{1}{x}+\dfrac{x}{x^2-1}}{\dfrac{1}{x}-\dfrac{x}{x^2+1}}=\frac{\dfrac{2x^2-1}{x(x^2-1)}}{\dfrac{1}{x(x^2+1)}}$$

Step 4: Divide the top rational expression by the bottom rational expression.

$$\frac{\dfrac{2x^2-1}{x(x^2-1)}}{\dfrac{1}{x(x^2+1)}}=\frac{2x^2-1}{x(x^2-1)}\div\frac{1}{x(x^2+1)}$$

$$=\frac{2x^2-1}{x(x-1)(x+1)}\div\frac{1}{x(x^2+1)}$$

$$=\frac{2x^2-1}{x(x-1)(x+1)}\cdot\frac{x(x^2+1)}{1}$$

$$=\frac{2x^2-1}{\cancel{x}(x-1)(x+1)}\cdot\frac{\cancel{x}(x^2+1)}{1}$$

$$=\frac{(2x^2-1)(x^2+1)}{(x-1)(x+1)}$$

Step 5: The answer is $\dfrac{(2x^2-1)(x^2+1)}{(x-1)(x+1)}$.

EXERCISE 28

Rational Expressions with Rational Expressions in the Numerator and/or Denominator

Directions: Simplify. Reduce your answer to lowest terms.

1. $\dfrac{1+\dfrac{2}{3x}}{\dfrac{2}{x^2}+\dfrac{3}{x}}$

2. $\dfrac{1-\dfrac{9}{x^2}}{1+\dfrac{5}{x}+\dfrac{6}{x^2}}$

3. $\dfrac{\dfrac{5x^2}{y}}{\dfrac{10x}{y^2}}$

4. $\dfrac{\dfrac{18a^3}{b^2}}{\dfrac{6a^2}{b}}$

5. $\dfrac{4-\dfrac{6}{x}}{2-\dfrac{3}{x}}$

6. $\dfrac{y-\dfrac{1}{y}}{1-\dfrac{1}{y^2}}$

7. $\dfrac{\dfrac{1}{x}-\dfrac{1}{x^2}}{1+\dfrac{2}{x}-\dfrac{3}{x^2}}$

8. $\dfrac{\dfrac{1}{x+3}-\dfrac{1}{x-3}}{1+\dfrac{9}{x^2-9}}$

CHAPTER 10

Equations and Inequalities

Equations are central to mathematics at all levels. Equations are used in algebra to model conditions in the real world; solutions to such equations reveal how real-world conditions may be satisfied. In this chapter, you will learn how to solve equations and inequalities and see how they can be used to model the real world.

Understanding Equations and Inequalities

An **equation** is a mathematical statement that shows two expressions as equal. It may contain one or more variables, or letters. Every equation has an equal sign: =. The equal sign can be read as "is equal to."

EXAMPLES

1. $x + 2 = 5$ This equation has one variable: x plus 2 is equal to 5.

2. $x + x = 3 + 2x$ x plus x is equal to 3 plus $2x$.

3. $12 + 18 = 10(3)$ This equation does not have variables. However, it is true.

An **inequality** is a mathematical statement that compares two expressions. An inequality usually has at least one of the following symbols:

>   is greater than

<   is less than

≥   is greater than or equal to

≤   is less than or equal to

EXAMPLES

1. $x + 2 > 5$ x plus two is greater than 5.

2. $x + y \geq 7$ x plus y is greater than or equal to 7.

3. $5x \leq 9$ 5 times x is less than or equal to 9.

4. $-4 < t < 10$ -4 is less than t and t is less than 10.

What Is a Solution to an Equation or an Inequality?

The value or values that make an equation true are known as the **solution** or **solutions to an equation**. An equation can have one unique solution, one or more solutions, or no solution depending on the equation.

Likewise, the value or values that make an equation true are known as the **solution** or **solutions to an inequality**. An inequality can have one unique solution, one or more solutions, or no solution depending on the inequality.

How to Tell Whether a Given Number Is a Solution to a Given Equation

A number is a solution to a given equation if the equation is true when the number is used in place of the variable, that is, the left side of the equation should be equal to the right side.

For example, check whether $x = 3$ is a solution to the equation: $3x + 11 = 20$. If you put the value of $x = 3$ in the left side, you get $3x + 11 = 3 \times 3 + 11 = 9 + 11 = 20$. The right side has a value of 20, and so the left side is equal to the right side. Thus, you say that $x = 3$ is a solution to $3x + 11 = 20$. In fact, it is the only solution of the equation.

How to Tell Whether a Given Number Is a Solution to a Given Inequality

A number is a solution to a given inequality if the inequality is true when the number is used in place of the variable, i.e., its left side should satisfy the right side.

For example, check whether $x = 5$ is the solution to the inequality: $4x + 5 < 29$. If you put the value of $x = 5$ in the left side, you get $4x + 5 = 4 \times 5 + 5 = 20 + 5 = 25$ and the right side is 29. So, $25 < 29$ is a true inequality. Thus, $x = 5$ is a solution to $4x + 5 < 29$.

Solving Equations and Inequalities

For solving equations, it is important to remember that the equation still holds true when any one of the following is carried out:

1. The same number is added to both sides of the equation.

2. The same number is subtracted from both sides.

3. The same number is multiplied to both sides.

4. Both sides are divided by the same number, other than zero.

In cases of inequalities, remember the following points:

1. The same number can be added to or subtracted from both sides of the inequality without changing the direction of the inequality sign.

2. The same positive number can be multiplied or divided in both sides without changing the direction of the inequality sign.

3. When both sides are multiplied or divided by the same negative number, then the inequality sign changes its direction:

    < changes to >

    > changes to <

    ≤ changes to ≥

    ≥ changes to ≤

4. When the left side and right side are switched, then the inequality sign also changes direction.

If the highest power of the variable in an equation is 1, then the equation is called a **linear equation**. There are no squares, cubes, or higher powers of the variable. Similarly, if the highest power of variable in an inequality is 1, then the inequality is called a **linear inequality**.

EXAMPLES

$x + 7 = 2$ is a linear equation.

$y - 2 < 10$ is a linear inequality.

Solving Linear Equations by Adding or Subtracting

Remember that when the same number is added to or subtracted from both sides of the equation, the equation still holds true.

Solve by Adding or Subtracting Integers

The goal of solving an equation or inequality is to find the values (solutions) that make the equation or inequality true. Equations or inequalities having a variable with a coefficient of 1 can be solved by adding or subtracting the same number from both sides of the equation or inequality. These equations are of the form $x + a = b$ or $x + a < b$.

EXAMPLE 1

Solve: $x + 8 = -3$.

Step 1: To solve means to get the variable alone on one side of the equal sign. The number 8 is added to the variable on the left side of the equation. If you do the **inverse**, or reverse, operation of subtracting 8 from both sides, then you can get the variable x by itself and find the value of x that makes the equation true.

Step 2: Solve the equation by subtracting the number 8 from both sides of the equation.

$$x + 8 = -3$$
$$x + 8 - 8 = -3 - 8$$
$$x = -11$$

Therefore, the value of x for the given equation is -11.

Step 3: When solving, you should always check that the solution is the correct one. Substitute -11 for x in the original equation and simplify both sides.

$$x + 8 = -3$$
$$-11 + 8 = -3$$
$$-3 = -3$$

Notice that −11 gives a true statement after simplifying. If you get an untrue equation after simplifying, then you must check your work when solving the equation to find your mistake. Many of the examples will leave the checking step for you to do.

EXAMPLE 2

Solve: $p − 10 = 4$.

Step 1: Find the number that can be added or subtracted from both sides so that the variable is alone on one side of the equality sign.

Here, the number 10 has to be added to both sides.

Step 2: Solve the equation by adding the number 10 to both sides of the equation.

$$p − 10 = 4$$
$$p − 10 + 10 = 4 + 10$$
$$p = 14$$

Therefore, the value of p for the given equation is 14.

Step 3: Be sure to check the solution.

EXAMPLE 3

Solve: $−15 = y − 4$.

Step 1: Find the number that can be added or subtracted from both sides so that the variable is alone on one side of the equality sign. Here, the number 4 has to be added to both sides.

Step 2: Solve the equation by adding the number 4 to both sides of the equation.

$$−15 = y − 4$$
$$−15 + 4 = y − 4 + 4$$
$$−11 = y$$
$$y = −11$$

Therefore, the value of y for the given equation is −11.

Solve by Adding or Subtracting Fractions and Decimals

Equations having fractions and decimals can be solved by adding or subtracting the same fractions or decimals from both sides of the equation. Again, be sure to check the solution of each example or exercise to be sure the solution is correct.

EXAMPLE 1

Solve: $a + \dfrac{2}{3} = −2$.

Step 1: Find the number that can be added to or subtracted from both sides so that the variable is alone on one side of the equality sign. Here, the fraction $\dfrac{2}{3}$ has to be subtracted from both sides.

Step 2: Solve the equation by subtracting $\frac{2}{3}$ from both sides of the equation.

$$a + \frac{2}{3} = -2$$

$$a + \frac{2}{3} - \frac{2}{3} = -2 - \frac{2}{3}$$

$$a = \frac{-6-2}{3}$$

$$a = -\frac{8}{3}$$

Therefore, the value of a for the given equation is $-\frac{8}{3}$.

EXAMPLE 2

Solve: $b + 19.54 = 28$.

Step 1: Find the number that can be added to or subtracted from both sides so that the variable is alone on one side of the equality sign. Here, the decimal 19.54 has to be subtracted from both sides.

Step 2: Solve the equation by subtracting the decimal 19.54 from both sides of the equation.

$$b + 19.54 = 28$$

$$b + 19.54 - 19.54 = 28 - 19.54$$

$$b = 8.46$$

Therefore, the solution for the given equation is 8.46.

EXAMPLE 3

Solve: $-10 = c - 4.80 + \frac{1}{2}$.

Step 1: Find the number that can be added to or subtracted from both sides so that the variable is alone on one side of the equality sign. Here, the decimal 4.80 has to be added and the fraction $\frac{1}{2}$ has to be subtracted from both sides of the equation.

Step 2: Solve the equation by adding 4.80 and subtracting $\frac{1}{2}$ from both sides of the equation. To make things easier, write $\frac{1}{2}$ as 0.5.

$$-10 = c - 4.80 + \frac{1}{2}$$

$$-10 + 4.80 - 0.5 = c - 4.80 + 4.80 + 0.5 - 0.5$$

$$-10 + 4.80 - 0.5 = c$$

$$-5.7 = c$$

$$c = -5.7$$

Therefore, the solution for c is -5.7.

Solving Linear Equations by Adding or Subtracting

Directions: Solve the equations.

1. Solve: $13 = 3 + a$.
   - **A.** $a = 10$
   - **B.** $a = -10$
   - **C.** $a = 16$
   - **D.** $a = -16$

2. Solve: $b + \dfrac{4}{5} = -28$.
   - **A.** $b = 28.80$
   - **B.** $b = -28.80$
   - **C.** $b = 30$
   - **D.** $b = -30$

3. Solve: $c + 3.4 = 20$.
   - **A.** $c = 16.6$
   - **B.** $c = -16.6$
   - **C.** $c = 23.4$
   - **D.** $c = -23.4$

4. $13 = -4.3 + x$

5. $y - 6.4 = 6.1$

6. $48 + p = 136$

7. $\dfrac{40}{7} + a = -10$

8. $s + \dfrac{3}{4} = 12$

9. $q - 3.8 = 3.7$

Answers are on page 573.

Solving Linear Inequalities by Adding or Subtracting

In linear inequalities, the same number can be added to or subtracted from both sides of the inequality without having to switch the inequality sign.

Solve by Adding or Subtracting Integers

The same integers can be added or subtracted from both sides of the inequality to solve the inequality. The solution of an inequality is a set of numbers, not just one number.

EXAMPLE 1

Solve: $-2 + x \leq -6$.

Step 1: Find the number that can be added or subtracted from both sides so that the variable is alone on one side of the inequality sign. Here, the number 2 can be added to both sides.

Step 2: Solve the inequality by adding 2 to both sides of the equation.

$$-2 + x \leq -6$$
$$-2 + 2 + x \leq -6 + 2$$
$$x \leq -4$$

Therefore, the solution of the given inequality is the set of all values of x such that $x \leq -4$. When you write the inequality $x \leq -4$, you are referring to any number that is less than or equal to -4, which is a set of numbers. So, -6 or $-3{,}777$ can be a solution. If you check any number less than or equal to -4, you will get a true statement.

EXAMPLE 2

Solve: $r + 10 \geq 7$.

Step 1: Find the number that can be added or subtracted from both sides so that the variable is alone on one side of the inequality sign. Here, the number -10 has to be added to both sides.

Step 2: Solve the inequality by adding -10 to both sides of the inequality.

$$r + 10 \geq 7$$
$$r + 10 + (-10) \geq 7 + (-10)$$
$$r + 10 - 10 \geq 7 - 10$$
$$r \geq -3$$

Therefore, the solution of the given inequality is $r \geq -3$.

EXAMPLE 3

Solve: $-12 < y - 4$.

Step 1: Find the number that can be added or subtracted from both sides so that the variable is alone on one side of the inequality sign. Here, the number 4 has to be added to both sides.

Step 2: Solve the inequality by adding the number 4 to both sides of the equation.

$$-12 < y - 4$$
$$-12 + 4 < y - 4 + 4$$
$$-8 < y$$
$$y > -8$$

Note that in the previous step, the inequality sign is switched because the left side and right side of the inequality have been switched. Therefore, the solution is $y > -8$.

Solve by Adding or Subtracting Fractions and Decimals

Inequalities with fractions and decimals can be solved by adding or subtracting the same fraction or decimal from both sides of the inequality.

EXAMPLE 1

Solve: $p + \dfrac{2}{3} < -1$.

Step 1: Find the number that can be added or subtracted from both sides so that the variable is alone on one side of the equality sign. Here, $\dfrac{2}{3}$ has to be subtracted from both sides.

Step 2: Solve the inequality by subtracting $\frac{2}{3}$ from both sides of the inequality.

$$p + \frac{2}{3} < -1$$

$$p + \frac{2}{3} - \frac{2}{3} < -1 - \frac{2}{3}$$

$$p + 0 < \frac{-3 - 2}{3}$$

$$p < -\frac{5}{3}$$

Therefore, the solution of the given inequality is $p < -\frac{5}{3}$.

EXAMPLE 2

Solve: $q + 10.62 > 50$.

Step 1: Find the number that can be added to or subtracted from both sides so that the variable is alone on one side of the inequality sign. Here, 10.62 has to be subtracted from both sides.

Step 2: Solve the inequality by subtracting the decimal 10.62 from both sides of the inequality.

$$q + 10.62 > 50$$

$$q + 10.62 - 10.62 > 50 - 10.62$$

$$q > 39.38$$

Therefore, the solution of the given inequality is $q > 39.38$.

EXAMPLE 3

Solve: $-16 \leq r - 2.2 + \frac{2}{3}$.

Step 1: Find the number that can be added or subtracted from both sides so that the variable is alone on one side of the inequality sign. Here, the decimal 2.2 has to be added and the fraction $\frac{2}{3}$ has to be subtracted from both sides of the inequality.

Step 2: Solve the inequality by adding 2.2 and subtracting $\frac{2}{3}$ from both sides of the equation.

$$-16 \leq r - 2.2 + \frac{2}{3}$$

$$-16 + 2.2 - \frac{2}{3} \leq r - 2.2 + 2.2 + \frac{2}{3} - \frac{2}{3}$$

$$\frac{-48 + 6.6 - 2}{3} \leq r$$

$$\frac{-43.4}{3} \leq r$$

$$-14.47 \leq r$$

$$r \geq -14.47$$

Note that in the previous step, the inequality sign is switched as the left side and right side are switched. Therefore, the solution of the given inequality is $r \geq -14.47$.

EXERCISE 2

Solving Linear Inequalities by Adding or Subtracting

Directions: Solve the equations.

1. Solve: $x + 2 < 4$.
   A. $x < -2$
   B. $x < 2$
   C. $x < 6$
   D. $x < -6$

2. Solve: $y - 1.2 > -6$.
   A. $y > -4.8$
   B. $y > 4.8$
   C. $y > 7.2$
   D. $y > -7.2$

3. Solve: $4 + 1 \geq z + \frac{1}{2}$.
   A. $z \geq -4.5$
   B. $z \geq 4.5$
   C. $z \leq 4.5$
   D. $z \leq -4.5$

4. $15 > 8 + a$

5. $-16 \geq x - 4$

6. $18 \leq 2 + y$

7. $5 > x + 3$

8. $7.2 < 3.4 + b$

9. $\frac{1}{3} + c \geq 2$

Answers are on page 573.

Solving Linear Equations by Multiplying or Dividing

Linear equations can be solved by multiplying or dividing the same number on both sides of the equation. The equations you work with in this section do not have numbers added or subtracted from the variable terms. It is good practice to check the solution of each of these types of equations also.

Solve by Multiplication or Division with Integer Coefficients

Refer to the following examples to solve linear equations with integer coefficients by multiplying or dividing by the same number on both sides of the equations.

EXAMPLE 1

Solve: $5x = 60$.

Step 1: Find the number that can be multiplied or divided on both sides so that the variable is alone on one side of the equality sign. Here, the number 5 has to be divided on both sides because the 5 is multiplied with x.

Step 2: Solve the equation by dividing both sides of the equation by 5.

$$5x = 60$$

$$\frac{5x}{5} = \frac{60}{5}$$

$$x = 12$$

Therefore, the solution for the given equation is 12.

Step 3: Check the solution.

$$5x = 60$$

$$5(12) = 60$$

$$60 = 60$$

The solution checks.

EXAMPLE 2

Solve: $-7a = 91$.

Step 1: Find the number that can be multiplied or divided on both sides so that the variable is alone on one side of the equality sign. Here, the integer -7 has to be divided on both sides.

Step 2: Solve the equation by dividing both sides of the equation by -7.

$$-7a = 91$$

$$\frac{-7a}{-7} = \frac{91}{-7}$$

$$a = -13$$

Therefore, the value of a for the given equation is -13. Don't forget to check the solution.

EXAMPLE 3

Solve: $\frac{y}{2} = 4$.

Step 1: Find the number that can be multiplied or divided on both sides so that the variable is alone on one side of the equality sign. Here, the integer 2 has to be multiplied on both sides because the variable y is divided by 2.

Step 2: Solve the equation by multiplying 2 on both sides of the equation.

$$\frac{y}{2} = 4$$

$$\frac{y}{2} \times 2 = 4 \times 2$$

$$y = 8$$

Therefore, the value of y for the given equation is 8.

EXAMPLE 4

Solve: $\dfrac{z}{-3} = 2$.

Step 1: Find the number that can be multiplied or divided on both sides so that the variable is alone on one side of the equality sign. Here, the integer -3 has to be multiplied on both sides.

Step 2: Solve the equation by multiplying -3 on both sides of the equation.

$$\frac{z}{-3} = 2$$

$$\frac{z}{-3} \times -3 = 2 \times -3$$

$$z = -6$$

Therefore, the value of z for the given equation is -6.

Solve by Multiplication or Division with Fractional and Decimal Coefficients

Refer to the following examples to solve linear equations with fractional or decimal coefficients by multiplying or dividing the same fraction or decimal on both sides of the equations. Be sure to reduce all answers to lowest terms when working with fractions.

EXAMPLE 1

Solve: $\dfrac{4}{5} y = 2$.

Step 1: Find the number that can be multiplied or divided on both sides so that the variable is alone on one side of the equality sign. Here, the fraction $\dfrac{4}{5}$ has to be divided on both sides because it is multiplied with the variable term in the equation.

Step 2: Solve the equation by dividing $\dfrac{4}{5}$ on both sides of the equation.

$$\frac{4}{5} y = 2$$

$$\frac{4}{5} y \div \frac{4}{5} = 2 \div \frac{4}{5}$$

$$\frac{4}{5} y \times \frac{5}{4} = 2 \times \frac{5}{4}$$

$$y = \frac{10}{4} = \frac{5}{2}$$

Therefore, the value of y for the given equation is $\dfrac{5}{2}$.

EXAMPLE 2

Solve: $-\dfrac{4}{3} a = 12$.

Step 1: Find the number that can be multiplied or divided on both sides so that the variable is alone on one side of the equality sign. Here, the fraction $-\frac{4}{3}$ has to be divided on both sides.

Step 2: Solve the equation by dividing $-\frac{4}{3}$ on both sides of the equation.

$$-\frac{4}{3}a = 12$$

$$-\frac{4}{3}a \div -\frac{4}{3} = 12 \div -\frac{4}{3}$$

$$-\frac{4}{3}a \times -\frac{3}{4} = 12 \times -\frac{3}{4}$$

$$a = -9$$

Therefore, the value of a for the given equation is -9.

EXAMPLE 3

Solve: $1.2x = 4.8$.

Step 1: Find the number that can be multiplied or divided on both sides so that the variable is alone on one side of the equality sign. Here, the decimal 1.2 has to be divided on both sides.

Step 2: Solve the equation by dividing by 1.2 on both sides of the equation.

$$1.2x = 4.8$$

$$\frac{1.2x}{1.2} = \frac{4.8}{1.2}$$

$$x = 4$$

Therefore, the solution for the given equation is 4.

EXAMPLE 4

Solve: $-3.2y = 32$.

Step 1: Find the number that can be multiplied or divided on both sides so that the variable is alone on one side of the equality sign. Here, the decimal -3.2 has to be divided on both sides.

Step 2: Solve the equation by dividing by -3.2 on both sides of the equation.

$$-3.2y = 32$$

$$\frac{-3.2y}{-3.2} = \frac{32}{-3.2}$$

$$y = -10$$

Therefore, the value of y for the given equation is -10. Again, be sure to check the solution.

EXERCISE 3

Solving Linear Equations by Multiplying or Dividing

Directions: Solve each equation.

1. Solve: $5x = -10$.
   A. $x = 2$
   B. $x = -2$
   C. $x = 50$
   D. $x = -50$

2. Solve: $2.4y = 4.8$.
   A. $y = 2$
   B. $y = -2$
   C. $y = 3$
   D. $y = -3$

3. Solve: $\frac{z}{7} = -2$.
   A. $z = 14$
   B. $z = -14$
   C. $z = 9$
   D. $z = -9$

4. $48x = 336$

5. $\frac{y}{5} = 3$

6. $81.6 = -6.8p$

7. $\frac{q}{1.6} = 20$

8. $\frac{4a}{5} = 24$

9. $-\frac{2r}{7} = 24$

Answers are on page 573.

Solving Linear Inequalities by Multiplying or Dividing

Linear inequalities with integer, fraction, or decimal coefficients can be solved by multiplying or dividing by the same number on both sides of the inequality. Be sure to switch the direction of the inequality sign when multiplying or dividing by a negative number.

Solve by Multiplication or Division with Integer Coefficients

Refer to the following examples to solve linear inequalities with integer coefficients by multiplying or dividing by the same integer on both sides of the inequality.

EXAMPLE 1

Solve: $2 > \frac{x}{3}$.

Step 1: Find the number that can be multiplied or divided on both sides so that the variable is alone on one side of the inequality sign. Here, the integer 3 has to be multiplied on both sides because x is divided by 3.

Step 2: Solve the inequality by multiplying 3 on both sides of the inequality.

$$2 > \frac{x}{3}$$

$$2 \times 3 > \frac{x}{3} \times 3$$

$$6 > x$$

$$x < 6$$

Note that in the previous step, the direction of the inequality sign is changed because the left side and right side are switched. Therefore, the solution to the given inequality is $x < 6$. As before, the solution set of the inequality is a set—the set of all numbers less than 6.

EXAMPLE 2

Solve: $\frac{y}{-2} \leq 4$.

Step 1: Find the number that can be multiplied or divided on both sides so that the variable is alone on one side of the inequality sign. Here, −2 has to be multiplied to both sides.

Step 2: Solve the inequality by multiplying both sides of the inequality by −2. Remember to switch the direction of the inequality sign when multiplying by a negative number.

$$\frac{y}{-2} \leq 4$$

$$\frac{y}{-2} \times (-2) \geq 4 \times (-2)$$

$$y \geq -8$$

Note that in the previous step, the inequality sign is switched because a negative integer is multiplied to both sides of the inequality. Therefore, the solution to the given inequality is

$$y \geq -8.$$

Step 3: Check the solution. Pick a number greater than or equal to −8, say −6. Substitute −6 into the original inequality and simplify.

$$\frac{y}{-2} \leq 4$$

$$\frac{-6}{-2} \leq 4$$

$$3 \leq 4,$$

which is true. The solution set is correct.

EXAMPLE 3

Solve: $44 > 4n$.

Step 1: Find the number that can be multiplied or divided on both sides so that the variable is alone on one side of the inequality sign. Here, the integer 4 has to be divided on both sides.

Step 2: Solve the inequality by dividing both sides of the inequality by 4.

$$44 > 4n$$
$$\frac{44}{4} > \frac{4n}{4}$$
$$11 > n$$
$$n < 11$$

Therefore, the solution to the given inequality is $n < 11$. Again, this is a set of numbers.

EXAMPLE 4

Solve: $-4a \leq 36$.

Step 1: Find the number that can be multiplied or divided on both sides so that the variable is alone on one side of the inequality sign. Here, the integer -4 has to be divided on both sides.

Step 2: Solve the inequality by dividing both sides of the inequality by -4.

$$-4a \leq 36$$
$$\frac{-4a}{-4} \geq \frac{36}{-4}$$
$$a \geq -9$$

Therefore, the solution to the given inequality is $a \geq -9$. You can check the solution by picking a number greater than or equal to -9.

Solve by Multiplication or Division with Fractional and Decimal Coefficients

Refer to the following examples to solve linear inequalities with fractional or decimal coefficients by multiplying or dividing the same fraction or decimal on both sides of the inequality.

EXAMPLE 1

Solve: $4 < \frac{2x}{3}$.

Step 1: Find the number that can be multiplied or divided on both sides so that the variable is alone on one side of the inequality sign. Here, the fraction $\frac{2}{3}$ has to be divided on both sides because it is multiplied with the variable term.

Step 2: Solve the inequality by dividing both sides of the inequality by $\frac{2}{3}$.

$$4 < \frac{2x}{3}$$
$$4 \div \frac{2}{3} < \frac{2x}{3} \div \frac{2}{3}$$
$$4 \times \frac{3}{2} < \frac{2x}{3} \times \frac{3}{2}$$
$$6 < x$$
$$x > 6$$

Therefore, the solution to the given inequality is $x > 6$. This is a set of numbers.

EXAMPLE 2

Solve: $\dfrac{y}{-3} \le 5$.

Step 1: Find the number that can be multiplied or divided on both sides so that the variable is alone on one side of the inequality sign. Here, the integer −3 has to be multiplied on both sides because the variable is divided by −3.

Step 2: Solve the inequality by multiplying both sides of the inequality by −3.

$$\frac{y}{-3} \le 5$$

$$\frac{y}{-3} \times (-3) \ge 5 \times (-3)$$

$$y \ge -15$$

Notice that the inequality sign is switched because both sides are multiplied by −3. Therefore, the solution to the given inequality is $y \ge -15$.

EXAMPLE 3

Solve: $4.4 < 4.4n$.

Step 1: Find the number that can be multiplied or divided on both sides so that the variable is alone on one side of the inequality sign. Here, the integer 4.4 has to be divided on both sides.

Step 2: Solve the inequality by dividing both sides of the inequality by 4.4.

$$4.4 < 4.4n$$

$$\frac{4.4}{4.4} < \frac{4.4n}{4.4}$$

$$1 < n$$

$$n > 1$$

Therefore, the solution to the given inequality is $n > 1$.

EXAMPLE 4

Solve: $\dfrac{a}{-2.2} \le 6$.

Step 1: Find the number that can be multiplied or divided on both sides so that the variable is alone on one side of the inequality sign. Here, the integer −2.2 has to be multiplied on both sides.

Step 2: Solve the inequality by multiplying both sides of the inequality by −2.2.

$$\frac{a}{-2.2} \le 6$$

$$\frac{a}{-2.2} \times (-2.2) \ge 6 \times (-2.2)$$

$$a \ge -13.2$$

Note that the inequality sign is switched because a negative integer was multiplied on both sides.

Therefore, the solution to the given inequality is $a \ge -13.2$.

EXERCISE 4

Solving Linear Inequalities by Multiplying or Dividing

Directions: Solve each inequality.

1. Solve: $48 \leq -4a$.
   A. $a \leq 4$
   B. $a \leq -4$
   C. $a \leq 12$
   D. $a \leq -12$

2. Solve: $\dfrac{x}{1.2} > 2$.
   A. $x > 2.4$
   B. $x < 2.4$
   C. $x > -2.4$
   D. $x < -2.4$

3. Solve: $-\dfrac{2}{3}p > -4$.
   A. $p < 6$
   B. $p < -6$
   C. $p > 6$
   D. $p > -6$

4. $-8 \geq -\dfrac{x}{6}$

5. $-0.3p > -2.1$

6. $\dfrac{y}{6} \geq -10$

7. $3r < -15$

8. $12 \leq \dfrac{a}{1.2}$

9. $\dfrac{2p}{3} < 12$

Answers are on page 573.

Solving Linear Equations—Combined

Solving some linear equations requires multiple mathematical operations.

Solve Equations with Integer Coefficients

Refer to the following examples to solve equations with integer coefficients.

EXAMPLE 1

Solve: $26x - 22 = -2$.

Step 1: Find the number that has to be added or subtracted from both sides so that only the variable remains on one side. Here, 22 is added to both sides because 22 is subtracted from the variable term in the equation.

Step 2: Add 22 to both sides of the equality sign and simplify.

$$26x - 22 = -2$$
$$26x - 22 + 22 = -2 + 22$$
$$26x = 20$$

Step 3: Now divide both sides by the same number such that the variable has no coefficient.

Here, both sides have to be divided by 26.

$$\frac{26x}{26} = \frac{20}{26}$$

$$x = \frac{20}{26} = \frac{10}{13}$$

The answer is reduced to lowest terms. Thus, the value of x for the given equation is $\frac{10}{13}$. Be sure to check the solution.

EXAMPLE 2

Solve: $-14y + 15 = 43$.

Step 1: Find the number that has to be added or subtracted from both sides so that only the variable remains on one side. Here, 15 has to be subtracted from both sides.

Step 2: Subtract 15 from both sides of the equality sign and simplify.

$$-14y + 15 = 43$$
$$-14y + 15 - 15 = 43 - 15$$
$$-14y = 28$$

Step 3: Now divide both sides by the same number such that the variable has no coefficient.

Here, both sides have to be divided by −14.

$$\frac{-14y}{-14} = \frac{28}{-14}$$

$$y = -2$$

Thus, the value of y for the given equation is −2.

Solve Equations with Fractional and Decimal Coefficients

Refer to the following examples to solve linear equations with fractional or decimal coefficients.

EXAMPLE 1

Solve: $-25 + \frac{4}{9}x = 3$.

Step 1: Find the number that has to be added to or subtracted from both sides so that only the variable remains on one side. Here, 25 has to be added to both sides.

Step 2: Add 25 to both sides of the equality sign and simplify.

$$-25 + \frac{4}{9}x = 3$$

$$-25 + \frac{4}{9}x + 25 = 3 + 25$$

$$\frac{4}{9}x = 28$$

Step 3: Divide both sides by the same fraction such that the variable has no coefficient. Here, both sides have to be divided by $\frac{4}{9}$.

$$\frac{4}{9}x \div \frac{4}{9} = 28 \div \frac{4}{9}$$

$$\frac{4}{9}x \times \frac{9}{4} = 28 \times \frac{9}{4}$$

$$x = 63$$

Thus, the value of x for the given equation is 63.

Step 4: Be sure to check the solution.

EXAMPLE 2

Solve: $-3.4p - 8.6 = -4.1$.

Step 1: Find the number that has to be added or subtracted from both sides so that only the variable remains on one side. Here, 8.6 has to be added to both sides.

Step 2: Add 8.6 to both sides of the equality sign and simplify.

$$-3.4p - 8.6 = -4.1$$

$$-3.4p - 8.6 + 8.6 = -4.1 + 8.6$$

$$-3.4p = 4.5$$

Step 3: Divide both sides by the same decimal such that the variable has a coefficient of one.

Here, both sides have to be divided by -3.4.

$$\frac{-3.4p}{-3.4} = \frac{4.5}{-3.4}$$

$$p = -1.32$$

Thus, the value of p for the given equation is -1.32.

EXAMPLE 3

Solve: $\frac{3x}{4} - 2x + 18 = 12 - x$.

Step 1: Combine like variable terms and number terms on each side.

$$\frac{3x}{4} - 2x + 18 = 12 - x$$

$$\frac{3x}{4} - \frac{8x}{4} + 18 = 12 - x$$

$$-\frac{5x}{4} + 18 = 12 - x$$

Step 2: Bring the variable terms over to one side of the equation by doing the appropriate inverse operation. In this case, adding x to each side will bring the variable term to the left side.

$$-\frac{5x}{4} + 18 + x = 12 - x + x$$

$$-\frac{5x}{4} + \frac{4x}{4} + 18 = 12$$

$$-\frac{1x}{4} + 18 = 12$$

$$-\frac{x}{4} + 18 = 12$$

Then subtract 18 from both sides.

$$-\frac{x}{4} + 18 - 18 = 12 - 18$$

$$-\frac{x}{4} = -6$$

Step 3: Multiply both sides by −4.

$$-\frac{x}{4}(-4) = -6(-4)$$

$$x = 24$$

The solution to the equation is $x = 24$.

Step 4: Be sure to check the answer.

EXERCISE 5

Solving Linear Equations—Combined

Directions: Solve each equation.

1. $-30 = 8a - 3a$

2. $7x + 6 + 8 = 28$

3. $16b - 15 = 22$

4. $\frac{3}{5}x + 1 = 15$

5. $0.08y - 0.9 = 0.02y$

6. $1.7a = 30 + 0.2a$

7. $\frac{x}{4} + 2 = 6$

8. $\frac{x}{3} + \frac{x}{7} = 10$

9. $\frac{c}{3} - \frac{c}{6} = 2$

10. $\frac{19}{20}p + \frac{1}{4} = \frac{44}{5}$

Answers are on page 574.

Solving Linear Inequalities—Combined

Solving some linear inequalities requires multiple mathematical operations.

Solve Inequalities with Integer Coefficients

Refer to the following examples to solve linear inequalities with integer coefficients.

EXAMPLE 1

Solve: $29x - 22 > -2 + 3x$.

Step 1: As with equations, combine variable terms on one side of the equation. Subtract 3x from both sides.

$$29x - 22 > -2 + 3x$$
$$29x - 22 - 3x > -2 + 3x - 3x$$
$$26x - 22 > -2$$

Step 2: Find the number that has to be added or subtracted from both sides so that only the variable remains on one side. Here, 22 has to be added to both sides.

Step 3: Add 22 to both sides of the inequality sign and simplify.

$$26x - 22 < -2$$
$$26x - 22 + 22 < -2 + 22$$
$$26x < 20$$

Step 4: Now divide both sides by the same number such that the variable has a coefficient of 1.

Here, both sides have to be divided by 26.

$$\frac{26x}{26} < \frac{20}{26}$$

$$x < \frac{20}{26}$$

$$x < \frac{10}{13}$$

Thus, the solution set is the set of all values of x such that $x < 0.77$.

EXAMPLE 2

Solve: $-14y + 15 \geq 43$.

Step 1: Find the number that has to be added or subtracted from both sides so that only the variable remains on one side. Here, 15 has to be subtracted from both sides.

Step 2: Subtract 15 from both sides of the inequality sign and simplify.

$$-14y + 15 \geq 43$$

$$-14y + 15 - 15 \geq 43 - 15$$

$$-14y \geq 28$$

Step 3: Now divide both sides by the same number such that the variable has a coefficient of 1.

Here, both sides have to be divided by -14. Be sure to switch the direction of the inequality sign.

$$\frac{-14y}{-14} \leq \frac{28}{-14}$$

$$y \leq -2$$

Thus, the solution for the inequality is $y \leq -2$.

Solve Inequalities with Fractional and Decimal Coefficients

Refer to the following examples to solve linear inequalities with fractional or decimal coefficients.

EXAMPLE 1

Solve: $-25 + \frac{4}{9}x < 3$.

Step 1: Find the number that has to be added or subtracted from both sides so that only the variable remains on one side. Here, 25 has to be added to both sides.

Step 2: Add 25 to both sides of the equality sign and simplify.

$$-25 + \frac{4}{9}x < 3$$

$$-25 + \frac{4}{9}x + 25 < 3 + 25$$

$$\frac{4}{9}x < 28$$

Step 3: Now divide both sides by the same fraction such that the variable has no coefficient.

Here, both sides have to be divided by $\frac{4}{9}$.

$$\frac{4}{9}x \div \frac{4}{9} < 28 \div \frac{4}{9}$$

$$\frac{4}{9}x \times \frac{9}{4} < 28 \times \frac{9}{4}$$

$$x < 63$$

Thus, the solution for the inequality is $x < 63$.

EXAMPLE 2

Solve: $-3.4p - 8.6 \geq -4.1$.

Step 1: Find the number that has to be added or subtracted from both sides so that only the variable remains on one side. Here, 8.6 has to be added to both sides.

Step 2: Add 8.6 to both sides of the equality sign and simplify.

$$-3.4p - 8.6 \geq -4.1$$

$$-3.4p - 8.6 + 8.6 \geq -4.1 + 8.6$$

$$-3.4p \geq 4.5$$

Step 3: Now divide both sides by the same decimal such that the variable has no coefficient.

Here, both sides have to be divided by −3.4. Be sure to switch the inequality sign.

$$\frac{-3.4p}{-3.4} \leq \frac{4.5}{-3.4}$$

$$p \leq -1.32$$

Thus, the solution is $p \leq -1.32$.

EXERCISE 6

Solving Linear Inequalities—Combined

Directions: Solve each inequality.

1. $4a + 5 < 29$

2. $3x - 7 \geq 41$

3. $-6t + 14 < -58$

4. $126 < 3g + 6g$

5. $\frac{x}{3} - \frac{x}{6} > 2$

6. $\frac{1}{3} + \frac{1}{x} > \frac{1}{2}$

7. $2.5y - 1.7y > 4$

8. $2a + 3 \geq 0.2a$

9. $\frac{3}{7}c - \frac{1}{7} > 5$

10. $\frac{3}{2}p + \frac{8}{7} - \frac{4p}{7} \leq 3$

Answers are on page 574.

Solving Linear Equations Involving Parentheses

Linear equations involving parentheses can be solved using the following steps.

Step 1: Combine like terms within the parentheses.

Step 2: Multiply the number outside the parentheses with each term of the parentheses and write the individual products along with the appropriate sign.

Step 3: Solve the equation.

Solve Parenthetical Equations with Integer Coefficients

EXAMPLE 1

Solve: $35 = 9(5a - 7)$.

Step 1: Multiply the number outside the parentheses with each term of the parentheses and write the individual products along with the appropriate sign.

$$35 = 9(5a - 7)$$
$$35 = 9 \times 5a - 9 \times 7$$
$$35 = 45a - 63$$

Step 2: Solve the equation.

$$35 + 63 = 45a - 63 + 63$$
$$98 = 45a$$
$$\frac{45a}{45} = \frac{98}{45}$$
$$a = \frac{98}{45}$$

Thus, the solution to the equation is $\frac{98}{45}$.

EXAMPLE 2

Solve: $8(3 + 3 + 4x) = 25$.

Step 1: Simplify within the parentheses.

$$8(3 + 3 + 4x) = 25$$
$$8(6 + 4x) = 25$$

Step 2: Multiply the number outside the parentheses with each term of the parentheses.

$$(8 \times 6) + (8 \times 4x) = 25$$
$$48 + 32x = 25$$

Step 3: Solve the equation.

$$48 - 48 + 32x = 25 - 48$$
$$32x = -23$$
$$\frac{32x}{32} = \frac{-23}{32}$$
$$x = \frac{-23}{32}$$

Thus, the solution to the equation is $\frac{-23}{32}$.

Solve Parenthetical Equations with Decimal and Fractional Coefficients

EXAMPLE 1

Solve: $2\left(\frac{3}{2}x + 1 + 1\right) = 10$.

Step 1: Simplify within the parentheses.

$$2\left(\frac{3}{2}x + 1 + 1\right) = 10$$
$$2\left(\frac{3}{2}x + 2\right) = 10$$

Step 2: Multiply the number outside the parentheses with each term of the parentheses and write the individual products along with the appropriate sign.

$$2\left(\frac{3}{2}x\right) + 2(2) = 10$$
$$3x + 4 = 10$$

Step 3: Solve the equation.

$$3x + 4 - 4 = 10 - 4$$
$$3x = 6$$
$$\frac{3x}{3} = \frac{6}{3}$$
$$x = 2$$

Thus, the solution to the equation is 2.

EXAMPLE 2

Solve: $-4(1 + 2.5x) = -25.5$.

Step 1: Multiply the number outside the parentheses with each term of the parentheses.

$$-4(1 + 2.5x) = -25.5$$
$$(-4 \times 1) + (-4 \times 2.5x) = -25.5$$
$$-4 + (-10x) = -25.5$$
$$-4 - 10x = -25.5$$

Step 2: Solve the equation.

$$-4 - 10x = -25.5$$

$$-4 + 4 - 10x = -25.5 + 4$$

$$-10x = -21.5$$

$$\frac{-10x}{-10} = \frac{-21.5}{-10}$$

$$x = 2.15$$

Thus, the solution to the equation is 2.15.

EXERCISE 7

Solving Linear Equations Involving Parentheses

Directions: Solve each equation.

1. $4(3y + 9) = -33$

2. $-8(1 - 4a) = 18$

3. $15 = -8 + 7(c + 4)$

4. $-20 - 6z = 8(5z + 4 + 5)$

5. $-8 - 9(1 - 7p) = 31$

6. $-8 + 3(2 - 3x) = -16$

7. $\left(1 + \frac{4}{5}s\right)5 + 2 = 12$

8. $-2\left(7 + \frac{3}{7}b\right) = 10$

9. $6 + 3\left(7 - \frac{5}{9}x\right) = 15$

10. $2(2.5a - 4) = 12$

11. $-6 = -3(0.5q - 4)$

12. $7 - 2.5(1 - 3x) = 19.5$

Answers are on page 574.

Solving Linear Inequalities Involving Parentheses

Linear inequalities involving parentheses can be solved using the following steps.

Step 1: Simplify expressions within parentheses. This means to combine any like terms you may see.

Step 2: Multiply the number outside the parentheses with each term of the parentheses and write the individual products along with the appropriate sign.

Step 3: Solve the inequality.

Solve Parenthetical Inequalities with Integer Coefficients

EXAMPLE

Solve: $4(8 - 3a) \leq 32 - 8(a + 2)$.

Step 1: Multiply the number outside the parentheses with each term of the parentheses and write the individual products along with the appropriate sign.

$$4(8 - 3a) \leq 32 - 8(a + 2)$$
$$(4 \times 8) - (4 \times 3a) \leq 32 + (-8 \times a) + (-8 \times 2)$$
$$32 - 12a \leq 32 - 8a - 16$$
$$32 - 12a \leq 16 - 8a$$

Step 2: Solve the inequality.

$$32 - 12a \leq 16 - 8a$$
$$32 - 32 - 12a \leq 16 - 8a - 32$$
$$-12a \leq -8a - 16$$
$$-12a + 8a \leq -8a + 8a - 16$$
$$-4a \leq -16$$
$$\frac{-4a}{-4} \geq \frac{-16}{-4}$$
$$a \geq 4$$

Thus, the solution to the inequality is $a \geq 4$

Solve Parenthetical Inequalities with Decimal and Fractional Coefficients

EXAMPLE 1

Solve: $3\left(\frac{1}{3}x + 1\right) + \frac{1}{2} > -\frac{9}{2}$.

Step 1: Multiply the number outside the parentheses with each term of the parentheses and write the individual products along with the appropriate sign.

$$3\left(\frac{1}{3}x + 1\right) + \frac{1}{2} > -\frac{9}{2}$$
$$3 \times \frac{1}{3}x + 3 \times 1 + \frac{1}{2} > -\frac{9}{2}$$
$$x + 3 + \frac{1}{2} > -\frac{9}{2}$$
$$x + \frac{6+1}{2} > -\frac{9}{2}$$
$$x + \frac{7}{2} > -\frac{9}{2}$$

Step 2: Solve the inequality.

$$x + \frac{7}{2} - \frac{7}{2} > -\frac{9}{2} - \frac{7}{2}$$

$$x > \frac{-9-7}{2}$$

$$x > \frac{-16}{2}$$

$$x > -8$$

Thus, the solution to the inequality is $x > -8$.

EXAMPLE 2

Solve: $-0.3y + 2(-5 + 2.5y) > -25$.

Step 1: Multiply the number outside the parentheses with each term of the parentheses and write the individual products along with the appropriate sign.

$$-0.3y + 2(-5 + 2.5y) > -25$$
$$-0.3y + 2 \times (-5) + 2 \times 2.5y > -25$$
$$-0.3y - 10 + 5y > -25$$
$$-10 + 4.7y > -25$$

Step 2: Solve the inequality.

$$-10 + 10 + 4.7y > -25 + 10$$
$$4.7y > -15$$
$$\frac{4.7y}{4.7} > -\frac{15}{4.7}$$
$$y > -3.19$$

The solution is rounded to the nearest hundredth. Thus, the solution to the inequality is $y > -3.19$.

EXERCISE 8

Solving Linear Inequalities Involving Parentheses

Directions: Solve each inequality.

1. $-9 \leq -(x - 5)$

2. $5(6 - 3y) \leq 5y - 130$

3. $4(3 - 2a) > 9a - 107$

4. $6b - 169 \geq 3(6 - 2b) - 5b$

5. $9c - 158 \leq 4(3 - 2c)$

6. $6p - 234 > 2(4 - 5p) - 6p$

7. $0.4(x - 0.3) \leq 0.2x + 0.4$

8. $3\left(\frac{2}{3}y + 1\right) < 2\left(\frac{1}{2}y - 1\right)$

9. $3(0.3a + 2) < 4.5$

10. $2\left(\frac{5}{4} + \frac{7}{2}x\right) \leq 2\left(2x - \frac{7}{4}\right)$

Answers are on page 574.

Using Equations to Solve Word Problems

Word problems can be solved by converting the problems into equations or inequalities. You represent one of the unknown quantities with a variable and relate all the other unknown quantities, if any, to this variable. Then form an equation or inequality that will relate the known quantities to the unknown quantities. The next step is to solve the equation or inequality formed in the previous step and answer all the questions asked in the problem.

Writing Equations for Simple Word Problems

For writing equations for simple word problems, follow these steps:

Step 1: Find the unknown quantity in the word problem.

Step 2: Assign a variable to the unknown quantity.

Step 3: Set up an equation based on the facts given in the problem.

Step 4: Solve the equation.

Step 5: Answer all the questions asked in the problem.

Age Problems

EXAMPLE 1

A father's age is 10 times the age of his son. If the father's age is 50 years, what is the age of the son?

Step 1: Find the unknown quantity. Here, the unknown quantity is the son's age.

Step 2: Assign a variable to the unknown quantity. Let the son's age be x years.

Step 3: Set up an equation based on the facts given in the problem.

It is given that the father's age is 10 times the son's age.

Write: $50 = 10 \times x$.

Step 4: Solve the equation.

$$50 = 10 \times x$$
$$10x = 50$$
$$\frac{10x}{10} = \frac{50}{10}$$
$$x = 5$$

Step 5: Thus, the son's age is 5 years.

EXAMPLE 2

The ages of two brothers differ by 5 years. If the younger brother is 7 years old, what is the age of the older brother?

Step 1: Find the unknown quantity. Here, the unknown quantity is the age of the older brother.

Step 2: Assign a variable to the unknown quantity. Let the older brother's age be x years.

Step 3: Set up an equation based on the facts given in the problem.

It is given that the ages of the two brothers differ by 5 years.

$x - 7 = 5$

Step 4: Solve the equation.

$$x - 7 = 5$$
$$x - 7 + 7 = 5 + 7$$
$$x = 12$$

Step 5: Thus, the age of the older brother is 12 years.

EXAMPLE 3

Peter's age is 18 years, and he is 10 years older than Sam. What would be the age of Sam after 5 years?

Step 1: Find the unknown quantity. Here, the unknown quantity is the age of Sam. You also have to find Sam's age after 5 years.

Step 2: Assign a variable to the unknown quantity. Let Sam's age be x years.

Step 3: Set up an equation based on the facts given in the problem.

Peter is 10 years older than Sam.

Write: $x + 10 = 18$.

Step 4: Solve the equation.

$$x + 10 = 18$$
$$x + 10 - 10 = 18 - 10$$
$$x = 8$$

The age of Sam is 8 years. Keep in mind that this does not answer the question posed in the problem. You have to find the age of Sam after 5 years to answer the question.

Step 5: Thus, the age of Sam after 5 years would be $8 + 5 = 13$ years.

EXAMPLE 4

A husband's age is twice the age of his wife. If the age of the husband is 70 years, what was the age of the wife 12 years ago?

Step 1: Find the unknown quantity. Here, the unknown quantity is the age of the wife.

Step 2: Assign a variable to the unknown quantity. Let the wife's age be x years.

Step 3: Set up an equation based on the facts given in the problem.

You are given that the husband's age is twice the age of his wife.

$$70 = 2x$$

Step 4: Solve the equation.

$$70 = 2x$$
$$\frac{70}{2} = \frac{2x}{2}$$
$$35 = x$$
$$x = 35$$

The age of the wife is 35 years.

Step 5: Answer the question. The age of the wife 12 years ago was $35 - 12 = 23$ years.

Problems Involving the Distance Formula: Rate × Time = Distance

EXAMPLE 1

A truck travels from town A to town B. The Super Express train travels from town B to town C. The total distance traveled by the truck and the train is 1,000 miles. The total time they spend traveling is 5 hours. If the speeds of the truck and the train differ by 60 mph, find their speeds.

Step 1: Find the unknown quantities. Here, the unknown quantities are the speeds of the truck and the train.

Step 2: Assign variables to the unknown quantities. Let the speed of the truck be x mph. The speed of the Super Express train will be $(x + 60)$ mph.

Step 3: Set up an equation based on the facts given in the problem. Use the equation distance = rate × time.

Distance traveled by the truck: speed × time = $x \times 5 = 5x$ miles.

Distance traveled by Super Express train: $(x + 60) \times 5 = (5x + 300)$ miles.

The total distance is 1,000 miles.

So, $5x + (5x + 300) = 1,000$.

Step 4: Solve the equation.

$$5x + (5x + 300) = 1,000$$
$$5x + 5x + 300 = 1,000$$
$$10x + 300 = 1,000$$
$$10x + 300 - 300 = 1,000 - 300$$
$$10x = 700$$
$$\frac{10x}{10} = \frac{700}{10}$$
$$x = 70$$

Step 5: Thus, the truck's speed is 70 mph. The train's speed is $x + 60 = 70 + 60 = 130$ mph.

EXAMPLE 2

Sean spends 3 hours training for an upcoming marathon. First he runs at 9 mph, and then he walks the same distance at 3 mph. How long does he spend walking? How long does he spend running?

Step 1: Find the unknown quantity. Here, the unknown quantity is the time spent walking and running.

Step 2: Assign a variable to the unknown quantity. Let the time spent walking be x hours. The time spent running will be $(3 - x)$ hours.

Step 3: Set up an equation based on the facts given in the problem.

Distance traveled walking = speed × time = $3 \times x = 3x$ miles.

Distance traveled running = $9 \times (3 - x) = (27 - 9x)$ miles.

Now the distance traveled walking is equal to the distance traveled running.

$3x = 27 - 9x$

Step 4: Solve the equation.

$$3x = 27 - 9x$$
$$3x + 9x = 27 - 9x + 9x$$
$$12x = 27$$
$$\frac{12x}{12} = \frac{27}{12}$$

Since this is a real-life situation, the decimal form of x is more useful.

$x = 2.25$

Step 5: Thus, the time spent walking is 2.25 hours. The time spent running is $3 - x = 3 - 2.25 = 0.75$ hours.

EXAMPLE 3

Two trains are 500 miles apart and moving toward each other. The speed of one train is 100 mph, and the speed of the other train is 70 mph. If both the trains started moving at the same time, how long will it take for the two trains to meet?

Step 1: Find the unknown quantity. Here, the unknown quantity is the time taken for the trains to meet.

Step 2: Assign a variable to the unknown quantity. Let the time taken for the trains to meet be x hours.

Step 3: Set up an equation based on the facts given in the problem.

Distance traveled by the first train before meeting the second train = speed × time = $100 \times x = 100x$ miles.

Distance traveled by the second train before the trains meet = $70 \times x = 70x$ miles.

The total distance traveled by the trains is 500 miles.

Write: $100x + 70x = 500$.

Step 4: Solve the equation.

$$100x + 70x = 500$$

$$170x = 500$$

$$\frac{170x}{170} = \frac{500}{170}$$

$$x = 2.94$$

Step 5: Thus, the time taken for both trains to meet is 2.94 hours.

Concentration Mixture Problems

EXAMPLE 1

Three gallons of a sugar solution were mixed with 9 gallons of a 44% sugar solution to make a 36% sugar solution. Find the percent concentration of the first solution.

Step 1: Find the unknown quantity. Here, the unknown quantity is the percent concentration of the first solution.

Step 2: Assign a variable to the unknown quantity. Let the percent concentration of the first solution be x.

Step 3: Set up an equation based on the facts given in the problem.

3 gallons of x percentage sugar solution = $3x$.

9 gallons of 44% sugar solution = $9 \times 44\% = 3.96$.

12 gallons of 36% sugar solution = $12 \times 36\% = 4.32$.

The total solution is 12 gallons of 36% sugar solution.

Write: $3x + 3.96 = 4.32$.

Step 4: Solve the equation.

$$3x + 3.96 = 4.32$$

$$3x + 3.96 - 3.96 = 4.32 - 3.96$$

$$3x = 0.36$$

$$\frac{3x}{3} = \frac{0.36}{3}$$

$$x = 0.12$$

Step 5: The first solution contained 12% sugar solution.

EXAMPLE 2

Consider a car that runs on ethanol and gas. The tank of the car is 20 gallons that the driver needs to fill up. The driver buys one fuel that is 30% ethanol and a second fuel that is 80% ethanol. He mixes the two fuels to form a mixture of 40% ethanol to fill the tank. How many gallons of each type of fuel does the driver mix to get the 40% fuel mixture?

Step 1: Find the unknown quantity. Here, the unknown quantity is the quantity of both fuels used to prepare the mixture fuel.

Step 2: Assign a variable to the unknown quantity. Let the quantity of 30% ethanol fuel be x gallons.

The quantity of 80% ethanol fuel would be the remaining number of gallons, or $(20 - x)$ gallons.

Step 3: Set up an equation based on the facts given in the problem.

x gallons of 30% ethanol $= 0.30x$.

$(20 - x)$ gallons of 80% ethanol $= 0.80(20 - x) = (0.80 \times 20) - 0.80x = 16 - 0.8x$.

20 gallons of 40% ethanol $= 0.40 \times 20 = 8$.

The total quantity of fuels required to fill the tank is 20 gallons.

So, $0.30x + 16 - 0.80x = 8$.

Step 4: Solve the equation.

$$0.30x + 16 - 0.80\,x = 8$$
$$-0.5x + 16 - 16 = 8 - 16$$
$$-0.5x = -8$$
$$\frac{-0.5x}{-0.5} = \frac{-8}{-0.5}$$
$$x = 16$$

Step 5: Thus, 16 gallons of 30% ethanol and $20 - 16 = 4$ gallons of 80% ethanol were used to prepare the mixture.

Value Mixture Problems

EXAMPLE 1

Two pounds of Colombian coffee that costs $7 per pound is mixed with a Kenyan coffee that costs $4 per pound. How many pounds of Kenyan coffee should be used to make a new mixture of coffee that costs $5.25 per pound?

Step 1: Find the unknown quantity. Here, the unknown quantity is the amount of Kenyan coffee to be used to make a new mixture.

Step 2: Assign a variable to the unknown quantity. Let the quantity of Kenyan coffee be x pounds. The total quantity of the mixture $= 2 + x$.

Step 3: Set up an equation based on the facts given in the problem.

Cost of Colombian coffee $= 2 \times 7 = \$14$.

Cost of Kenyan coffee $= x \times 4 = 4x$.

Total cost of the mixture $= (2 + x) \times 5.25 = 10.5 + 5.25x$.

The cost of Colombian coffee + cost of Kenyan coffee = total cost of the mixture.

So, $14 + 4x = 10.5 + 5.25x$.

Step 4: Solve the equation.

$$14 + 4x = 10.5 + 5.25x$$

$$14 + 4x - 4x = 10.5 + 5.25x - 4x$$

$$14 = 10.5 + 1.25x$$

$$14 - 10.5 = 10.5 - 10.5 + 1.25x$$

$$3.5 = 1.25x$$

$$\frac{3.5}{1.25} = \frac{1.25x}{1.25}$$

$$x = 2.8$$

Step 5: Thus, 2.8 pounds of Kenyan coffee should be used for the mixture.

EXAMPLE 2

A store owner mixes certain quantities of cashews that cost $2 per pound and almonds that cost $5 per pound to prepare 150 pounds of a mixture. If the mixture costs $3 per pound, what quantities of cashews and almonds did the store owner use in the mixture?

Step 1: Find the unknown quantity. Here, the unknown quantities are the quantities of cashews and almonds used in the mixture.

Step 2: Assign variables to the unknown quantities. Let the quantity of cashews used be x pounds and the quantity of almonds used be $(150 - x)$ pounds.

Step 3: Set up an equation based on the facts given in the problem.

Cost of cashews = $2 \times x = 2x$.

Cost of almonds = $5 \times (150 - x) = 750 - 5x$.

Total cost of mixture = $150 \times 3 = \$450$.

The cost of cashews + cost of almonds = total cost of the mixture.

$$2x + 750 - 5x = 450$$

Step 4: Solve the equation.

$$2x + 750 - 5x = 450$$

$$-3x + 750 = 450$$

$$-3x + 750 - 750 = 450 - 750$$

$$-3x = -300$$

$$\frac{-3x}{-3} = \frac{-300}{-3}$$

$$x = 100$$

Step 5: Thus, the store owner used 100 pounds of cashews and $150 - 100 =$ 50 pounds of almonds to prepare the mixture.

Rate of Work Problems

EXAMPLE 1

Erika can paint her room in 6 hours and Celine can paint the same room in 4 hours. How long will it take them to paint the room if they work together?

Step 1: Find the unknown quantity. Here, the unknown quantity is the time taken to paint the room together.

Step 2: Assign variables to the unknown quantities. Let the time taken to paint the room together be x hours.

Step 3: Set up an equation based on the facts given in the problem.

If the complete job is considered to be 1, then the working rate of Erika is $\frac{1}{6}$.

In x hours, Erika can paint $x \times \frac{1}{6} = \frac{x}{6}$ of the room.

The working rate of Celine is $\frac{1}{4}$.

In x hours, Celine can paint $x \times \frac{1}{4} = \frac{x}{4}$ of the room.

The sum of the portion of work done by each is equal to one complete job.

Write $\frac{x}{6} + \frac{x}{4} = 1$.

Step 4: Solve the equation.

$$\frac{x}{6} + \frac{x}{4} = 1$$

$$\frac{2x + 3x}{12} = 1$$

$$\frac{5x}{12} = 1$$

$$\frac{5x}{12} \times 12 = 1 \times 12$$

$$5x = 12$$

$$x = \frac{12}{5} = 2.4$$

Step 5: Thus, the time taken by both Erika and Celine to paint the room together is 2.4 hours.

EXAMPLE 2

A pipe can fill a pool in 5 hours. A second pipe can fill the pool in 3 hours. If both the pipes are used together to fill the pool, how many hours will it take?

Step 1: Find the unknown quantity. Here, the unknown quantity is the time taken by both pipes to fill the pool together.

Step 2: Assign variables to the unknown quantities. Let the time taken by both pipes to fill the pool together be x hours.

Step 3: Set up an equation based on the facts given in the problem.

If the complete job is considered to be 1, then the working rate of the first pipe is $\frac{1}{5}$.

In x hours, the first pipe can fill $x \times \frac{1}{5} = \frac{x}{5}$ of the pool.

The working rate of the second pipe is $\frac{1}{3}$.

In x hours, the second pipe can fill $x \times \frac{1}{3} = \frac{x}{3}$ of the pool.

The sum of the portion of pool filled by each pipe is equal to one complete job.

Write: $\frac{x}{5} + \frac{x}{3} = 1$.

Step 4: Solve the equation.

$$\frac{x}{5} + \frac{x}{3} = 1$$

$$\frac{3x + 5x}{15} = 1$$

$$\frac{8x}{15} = 1$$

$$\frac{8x}{15} \times 15 = 1 \times 15$$

$$8x = 15$$

$$x = \frac{15}{8} = 1.88$$

Step 5: Thus, both the pipes will take 1.88 hours to fill the pool together.

EXAMPLE 3

A man can clean a school compound in 8 hours. Two men can clean the school compound in 5 hours. How long will it take for the second man to clean the school compound by himself?

Step 1: Find the unknown quantity. Here, the unknown quantity is the time taken by the second man to clean the compound.

Step 2: Assign variables to the unknown quantities. Let the time taken by the second man to clean the school compound be x hours.

Step 3: Set up an equation based on the facts given in the problem.

If the complete job is considered to be 1, then the working rate of the first man is $\frac{1}{8}$.

In 5 hours, the first man can clean $5 \times \frac{1}{8} = \frac{5}{8}$ of the compound.

The working rate of the second man is $\frac{1}{x}$.

In 5 hours, the second man can clean $5 \times \frac{1}{x} = \frac{5}{x}$ of the compound.

The sum of the portion of the school compound cleaned by each man is equal to one complete job.

Write: $\dfrac{5}{8} + \dfrac{5}{x} = 1$.

Step 4: Solve the equation.

$$\dfrac{5}{8} + \dfrac{5}{x} = 1$$

$$\dfrac{5x + 40}{8x} = 1$$

$$\dfrac{5x + 40}{8x} \times 8x = 1 \times 8x$$

$$5x + 40 = 8x$$

$$5x - 5x + 40 = 8x - 5x$$

$$3x = 40$$

$$\dfrac{3x}{3} = \dfrac{40}{3}$$

$$x = 13.33$$

Step 5: Thus, the second man will take 13.33 hours to clean the compound alone.

EXERCISE 9

Using Equations to Solve Problems

Directions: Solve each word problem.

1. Caesar's age is three times the age of his sister. If Caesar is 27, how old is his sister?

2. The sum of the ages of Tom and Harry right now is 50. If Tom is 26 years old right now, how old will Harry be in 6 years?

3. Richard is now half as old as Michael. If Richard's present age is 36, how old was Michael 10 years ago?

4. Two cars are traveling on unpaved country roads at different speeds. In 5 hours, the distance traveled by the first car and the distance traveled by the second car together total 200 miles. If their speeds differ by 10 mph, what is the speed of each car?

5. Two boats that are 300 miles apart start out at the same time and travel toward each other. One boat is traveling at twice the speed of the other boat. After 5 hours, the two boats meet. What is the speed of each boat?

6. A bus travels from location A to location B and back to location A in 3 hours. If it travels at a speed of 60 mph from A to B and returns to A at a speed of 40 mph, how long did it take the bus to travel in each direction?

7. A chemist needs 10 liters of 15% acid solution for a certain test, but the supplier provides only a 10% solution and a 30% solution. The chemist mixes the two solutions to prepare his own 15% solution. How many liters of 10% solution and 30% solution does he need to prepare the mixture?

8. Three liters of a fruit drink were mixed with 1 liter of another fruit drink that contains 56% fruit juice. The new drink contains 65% fruit juice. Find the fruit juice concentration of the first drink.

9. Julianne wants to prepare 7.5 mL of a 22% saline solution by mixing together a 25% saline solution and a 20% saline solution. How much of each solution should she use to prepare the mixture?

10. A special recipe is made by mixing 5 pounds of peanuts that cost $0.80 a pound and caramel popcorn that costs $2.40 a pound. How many pounds of caramel popcorn is needed for a mixture that costs $1.40 a pound?

11. Megan's mother decides to create a 20-pound mixture of gumdrops and jellybeans for Megan's school carnival. She buys the gumdrops at $0.95 per pound and the jellybeans at $1.20 per pound. If she plans to sell the mixture for $1.10 per pound, how many pounds of each candy should she use in the mixture?

12. One liter of paint A that costs $8 per liter is mixed with 5 liters of paint B that cost $2 per liter. Find the cost of one liter of the mixture.

13. It takes Jack 1 hour to mow a lawn. Tom can mow the same lawn in 90 minutes. How long will it take for Jack and Tom to mow the lawn together?

14. One pipe can water an entire garden in 5 hours. This pipe, along with a second pipe, can water the same garden in 3.5 hours. How long will it take for the second pipe to water the garden by itself?

15. Sharon can paint the fence in 4 hours. If her sister helps her, then together they can paint the fence in 3 hours. If her sister paints the fence alone, then how long will it take her to complete it?

Answers are on page 574.

Writing Inequalities for Simple Word Problems

To solve simple word problems using inequalities, remember the following key words or phrases that can help you to translate the word problems to inequalities.

- **at most**—means less than or equal to ($\leq$)
- **no more than**—means less than or equal to ($\leq$)
- **less than**—means less than ($<$)
- **at least**—means greater than or equal to ($\geq$)
- **no less than**—means greater than or equal to ($\geq$)
- **greater than**—means more than ($>$)

These are the steps to follow for solving word problems using inequalities:

Step 1: Find the unknown quantity.

Step 2: Assign variables to the unknown quantities.

Step 3: Set up an inequality based on the facts given in the problem. Find the key words and accordingly use the inequality sign.

Step 4: Solve the inequality.

Step 5: Answer the question.

EXAMPLE 1

The sum of twice a number and 10 is at most 20. What are the possible values for the number?

Step 1: Find the unknown quantity. Here, the number is unknown.

Step 2: Assign variables to the unknown quantities. Let the unknown number be x.

Step 3: Set up an inequality based on the facts given in the problem. Here, the key words used are *at most*, so the inequality sign would be $\leq$.

The sum of twice a number and 10 is at most 20.

So, $2x + 10 \leq 20$.

Step 4: Solve the inequality.

$$2x + 10 \leq 20$$
$$2x + 10 - 10 \leq 20 - 10$$
$$2x \leq 10$$
$$\frac{2x}{2} \leq \frac{10}{2}$$
$$x \leq 5$$

Thus, the solution of the given problem is $x \leq 5$.

Step 5: The possible numbers are all those less than or equal to 5.

EXAMPLE 2

A taxi charges a $2 flat rate in addition to $1 per mile. Sarah has no more than $20 to spend on a ride. How many miles can she travel without exceeding her limit?

Step 1: Find the unknown quantity. Here, the distance that can be traveled is unknown.

Step 2: Assign variables to the unknown quantities. Let the distance that Sarah can travel without exceeding her limit be x miles.

Step 3: Set up an inequality based on the facts given in the problem. Here, the key words used are *no more than*, so the inequality sign would be $\leq$.

It is known that Sarah can spend no more than $20.

Write: $1x + 2 \leq 20$.

Step 4: Solve the inequality.

$$1x + 2 \leq 20$$
$$x + 2 \leq 20$$
$$x + 2 - 2 \leq 20 - 2$$
$$x \leq 18$$

Step 5: Thus, Sarah can travel 18 miles or less without exceeding her limit.

EXAMPLE 3

If 5 times a number is increased by 4, the result is less than 19. Find the number.

Step 1: Find the unknown quantity. Here, the number is unknown.

Step 2: Assign variables to the unknown quantities. Let the unknown number be x.

Step 3: Set up an inequality based on the facts given in the problem. Here, the key words used are *less than*, so the inequality sign would be $<$.

It is known that when 5 times a number is increased by 4, you get a result that is less than 19.

Write: $5x + 4 < 19$.

Step 4: Solve the inequality.

$$5x + 4 < 19$$
$$5x + 4 - 4 < 19 - 4$$
$$5x < 15$$
$$x < \frac{15}{5}$$
$$x < 3$$

Step 5: Thus, the number is less than 3.

EXAMPLE 4

Carolyn had saved $1,000 in her savings account for summer. She wants to have at least $500 left in the account by the end of summer. She withdraws $50 each week for expenses. For how many weeks can she withdraw money?

Step 1: Find the unknown quantity. Here, the number of weeks is unknown.

Step 2: Assign variables to the unknown quantities. Let the unknown number of weeks be x.

Step 3: Set up an inequality based on the facts given in the problem. Here, the key words used are *at least*, so the inequality sign would be $\geq$.

You know that the total amount is $1,000 and the withdrawal amount per week is $50. Carolyn wants to have at least $500 left over.

Write $1,000 - 50x \geq 500$.

Step 4: Solve the inequality.

$$1,000 - 50x \geq 500$$
$$1,000 - 1,000 - 50x \geq 500 - 1,000$$
$$-50x \geq -500$$
$$\frac{-50x}{-50} \leq \frac{-500}{-50}$$
$$x \leq 10$$

Step 5: Carolyn can withdraw money for at most 10 weeks.

EXAMPLE 5

Ben earns $8 per hour working at a café. How many hours does he have to work to earn no less than $150?

Step 1: Find the unknown quantity. Here, the number of hours Ben has to work is unknown.

Step 2: Assign variables to the unknown quantities. Let the number of hours be x hours.

Step 3: Set up an inequality based on the facts given in the problem. Here, the key words used are *no less than*, so the inequality sign would be $\geq$.

The earnings should be no less than $150.

Write $8x \geq 150$.

Step 4: Solve the inequality.

$$8x \geq 150$$
$$\frac{8x}{8} \geq \frac{150}{8}$$
$$x \geq 18.75$$

Step 5: Thus, Ben has to work at least 18.75 hours.

EXAMPLE 6

Michelle earned $400 and $500 in interest in the last 2 years. How much interest must she earn so that her average earning over three years is more than $600?

Step 1: Find the unknown quantity. Here, the interest to be earned in the third year is unknown.

Step 2: Assign variables to the unknown quantities. Let the interest be x.

Step 3: Set up an inequality based on the facts given in the problem. Here, the key words used are *more than*, so the inequality sign would be $>$.

It is known that her average earnings for 3 years need to be more than $600.

So, $\dfrac{400 + 500 + x}{3} > 600$.

Step 4: Solve the inequality.

$$\frac{400 + 500 + x}{3} > 600$$

$$\frac{900 + x}{3} > 600$$

$$\frac{900 + x}{3} \times 3 > 600 \times 3$$

$$900 + x > 1,800$$

$$900 - 900 + x > 1,800 - 900$$

$$x > 900$$

Step 5: Thus, the interest for the third year should be greater than $900.

EXERCISE 10

Writing Inequalities for Simple Word Problems

Directions: Solve.

1. The number of goats on a farm is twice the number of sheep. What is the greatest number of goats on the farm if there are at most a total of 48 animals on the farm?

2. Five more than twice a number is at most 45. What are the possible values of the number?

3. Claire wanted to order some books over the Internet. Each book costs $15, and the shipping charge for the entire order is $10. She has no more than $200 to spend. How many books can she order without exceeding her limit of $200?

4. Smith decides to throw a birthday party for his daughter at a hotel. The hotel charges a $60 flat fee for birthday party rental and $5 for each party guest. He has no more than $150 to spend on the party. How many people can Smith invite to the party without exceeding the limit?

5. A girl decides to buy chocolates for her sister. She goes to a store and finds that the chocolates cost $2 each. If she has less than $20, how many chocolates can she buy?

6. The product of a number and 5 is less than 70. What are the possible values of the number?

7. Lisa makes $9 per hour working at a convenience store. If she gets a bonus of $30 this week, how many hours must she work to make at least $210?

8. The length of a rectangular garden is 12 feet. If the area is at least 96 square feet, what is the smallest possible width of the garden?

9. A school wants to collect no less than 5,000 pounds of food for a food drive. The school has already collected 1,000 pounds of food. If each student can bring 20 pounds of food, how many more students are required to bring food for the drive?

10. A salesperson earns $500 a week plus $50 for every product he sells. How many products does he need to sell in order to earn at least $1,200 for the week?

11. The sum of $4x$ and $2x$ is greater than the difference of $5x$ and 13. Find x.

12. Anna is selling bracelets to make money for her summer vacation. She sells the bracelets at $2 each, and she has already earned $100. How many more does she have to sell so that she makes more than $600?

Answers are on page 574.

Systems of Linear Equations

A system of linear equations is a set of linear equations that have to be solved together. In this section, you will learn to solve a system of two linear equations with two variables. For example, the equations below form a system of two equations having two variables, x and y.

$$4x + 5y = 30$$
$$2x + 3y = 25$$

Solution by Substitution

In the substitution method, one variable is substituted with the other variable so that only one variable is present in one equation This allows you to solve the equation for the variable that is present.

The substitution method can be carried out by the following steps:

Step 1: Solve one of the two given equations for one of the variables.

Step 2: Substitute that expression for the variable in the other equation.

Step 3: Solve the equation to find the value of one variable.

Step 4: Substitute this value in the second equation to get the value of the other variable.

Step 5: State the solution.

EXAMPLE 1

Solve the system of equations by the substitution method.

$$3x + 2y = 3$$

$$-x - y = 1$$

Step 1: Solve one of the two given equations to obtain one of the variables.

Solve the second equation for y because it is the simpler equation of the two.

$$-x - y = 1$$

$$-x + x - y = 1 + x$$

$$-y = 1 + x$$

$$y = -1 - x$$

Step 2: Substitute the expression $y = -1 - x$ into the other equation. Be sure to use parentheses.

$$3x + 2y = 3$$

$$3x + 2(-1 - x) = 3$$

Step 3: Solve the equation for the value of x.

$$3x - 2 - 2x = 3$$

$$x - 2 = 3$$

$$x - 2 + 2 = 3 + 2$$

$$x = 5$$

Step 4: Now substitute $x = 5$ in the other equation to solve for the value of y.

$$-x - y = 1$$

$$-5 - y = 1$$

$$-5 + 5 - y = 1 + 5$$

$$-y = 6$$

$$y = -6$$

Step 5: Thus, x is 5 and y is −6.

EXAMPLE 2

Solve the system of equations by the substitution method.

$$2x + 4y = 4$$
$$-x + 3y = 13$$

Step 1: Solve the first equation for y.

$$2x + 4y = 4$$
$$2x - 2x + 4y = 4 - 2x$$
$$4y = 4 - 2x$$
$$\frac{4y}{4} = \frac{4 - 2x}{4} = \frac{2(2 - x)}{4}$$
$$y = \frac{2 - x}{2}$$

Step 2: Substitute the value of $y = \frac{2 - x}{2}$ in the other equation.

$$-x + 3y = 13$$
$$-x + 3\left(\frac{2 - x}{2}\right) = 13$$

Step 3: Solve the equation to get the value of a variable.

$$-x + \frac{3(2 - x)}{2} = 13$$
$$-x + \frac{6 - 3x}{2} = 13$$
$$\frac{-2x + 6 - 3x}{2} = 13$$
$$-2x + 6 - 3x = 13 \times 2$$
$$-5x + 6 = 26$$
$$-5x + 6 - 6 = 26 - 6$$
$$-5x = 20$$
$$\frac{-5x}{-5} = \frac{20}{-5}$$
$$x = -4$$

Step 4: Now substitute $x = -4$ in the other equation to solve for the value of y.

$$-x + 3y = 13$$
$$-(-4) + 3y = 13$$
$$4 + 3y = 13$$
$$4 - 4 + 3y = 13 - 4$$
$$3y = 9$$
$$\frac{3y}{3} = \frac{9}{3}$$
$$y = 3$$

Thus, the solutions are $x = -4$ and $y = 3$.

Solution by Elimination

In the elimination method, two equations in the system are added or subtracted to eliminate one variable and form a new equation with only one variable.

The elimination method contains the following steps:

Step 1: Multiply the two equations with certain numbers such that one variable has the same coefficients in both the newly formed equations.

Step 2: Add or subtract the two new equations so that one variable is eliminated.

Step 3: Solve for the other variable.

Step 4: Substitute the value obtained in the previous step in one of the equations to solve for the other variable.

EXAMPLE

Solve the system of equations by the elimination method.

$$3x - y = 1$$
$$4x + 5y = 14$$

Step 1: Multiply the first equation by 5 such that both equations have one variable with the same coefficients.

$$(3x - y) \times 5 = 1 \times 5$$
$$15x - 5y = 5$$

Step 2: Add the two equations to eliminate y.

$$15x - 5y = 5$$
$$\underline{4x + 5y = 14}$$
$$19x + 0 = 19$$

Step 3: Solve for x.

$$19x = 19$$
$$\frac{19x}{19} = \frac{19}{19}$$
$$x = 1$$

Step 4: Substitute the value of $x = 1$ in the first equation to solve for y.

$$3x - y = 1$$
$$3 \times 1 - y = 1$$
$$3 - y = 1$$
$$3 - 3 - y = 1 - 3$$
$$-y = -2$$
$$y = 2$$

Step 5: The solution is given by $x = 1$ and $y = 2$.

EXERCISE 11

Systems of Linear Equations

Directions: Solve each system of equations by the substitution method.

1. $3x + 2y = 3$
$-2x - y = -1$

2. $3x + 2y = -1$
$4x - 5y = 14$

3. $-x + 5y = -16$
$-3x + 7y = -8$

4. $x - 5y = 21$
$-6x = 24$

5. $7x - 4y = -7$
$5x + y = 22$

6. $x + 3y = 18$
$-x - 4y = -25$

7. $-4x - 3y = 9$
$5x = 15$

8. $2x + 3y = -1$
$3x + 4y = -4$

9. $6x + y = 15$
$-7x - 2y = -10$

10. $-2x + y = 10$
$4x - y = -14$

11. $6x + 7y = -9$
$-4x - 5y = 5$

12. $3x + y = -14$
$-2x - y = 9$

Answers are on page 575.

Using Systems to Solve Word Problems

For writing a system of equations for simple word problems, follow these steps:

Step 1: Find the unknown quantities in the word problem.

Step 2: Assign variables to the unknown quantities.

Step 3: Set up two equations based on the facts given in the problem.

Step 4: Solve the system of equations.

Step 5: Answer all the questions asked in the problem.

Age Problems

EXAMPLE 1

The sum of the ages of a father and his son is 53 years. The father's age is 5 years more than three times the son's age. Find the ages of both the father and son.

Step 1: Find the unknown quantities in the word problem. Here, both the father's and son's ages are unknown.

Step 2: Assign variables to the unknown quantities. Let the father's age be x years and the son's age be y years.

Step 3: Set up two equations based on the facts given in the problem.

The sum of the ages of a father and his son is 53 years. The father is 5 years older than three times the son's age.

Write:

$$x + y = 53$$
$$x = 5 + 3y$$

Step 4: Solve the system of equations.

$$x + y = 53$$
$$x = 5 + 3y$$

Substitute the value of x in the second equation into the first equation.

$$x + y = 53$$
$$(5 + 3y) + y = 53$$
$$5 + 3y + y = 53$$
$$5 + 4y = 53$$
$$5 - 5 + 4y = 53 - 5$$
$$4y = 48$$
$$\frac{4y}{4} = \frac{48}{4}$$
$$y = 12$$

Now, substitute the value of y in the first equation.

$$x + 12 = 53$$
$$x + 12 - 12 = 53 - 12$$
$$x = 41$$

Step 5: The son is 12 years old and the father is 41 years old.

EXAMPLE 2

Six years ago, Bess was 4 times as old as her son. Eight years from now she will be only twice as old as her son. How old are Bess and her son now?

Step 1: Find the unknown quantities in the word problem. Here, the ages of Bess and her son are unknown.

Step 2: Assign variables to the unknown quantities. Let Bess's present age be x years and her son's present age be y years.

Step 3: Set up two equations based on the facts given in the problem.

Given, six years ago, Bess was 4 times as old as her son. Also, 8 years from now, she will be only twice as old.

Write the system of equations:

$$(x - 6) = 4 \times (y - 6)$$
$$(x + 8) = 2 \times (y + 8)$$

Simplifying, the system becomes:

$$x = 4y - 18$$
$$x = 2y + 8$$

Step 4: Solve the equations.

Substitute the value of x in the second equation into the first equation.

$$x = 4y - 18$$
$$(2y + 8) = 4y - 18$$
$$2y - 4y + 8 = 4y - 4y - 18$$
$$-2y + 8 = -18$$
$$-2y + 8 - 8 = -18 - 8$$
$$-2y = -26$$
$$\frac{-2y}{-2} = \frac{-26}{-2}$$
$$y = 13$$

Now, substitute the value of y in the second equation.

$$x = 2y + 8$$
$$x = 2 \times 13 + 8$$
$$x = 26 + 8$$
$$x = 34$$

Step 5: Thus, Bess's age is 34 years and the age of her son is 13 years.

Mixture Problems

EXAMPLE 1

An alloy containing 14% aluminum is mixed with an alloy containing 24% aluminum to make 100 pounds of an alloy containing 18% aluminum. How many pounds of each kind of alloy are used for the new mixture?

Step 1: Find the unknown quantities in the word problem. Here, the quantities of the alloys used in the mixture are unknown.

Step 2: Assign variables to the unknown quantities. Let the quantity of 14% aluminum alloy be x pounds and the quantity of 24% aluminum alloy be y pounds.

Step 3: Set up two equations based on the facts given in the problem.

You are given that the total quantity of the alloy mixture is 100 pounds and that the 14% aluminum alloy is mixed with a 24% aluminum alloy to make an alloy containing 18% aluminum.

Write:

$$x + y = 100$$
$$0.14x + 0.24y = 0.18 \times 100 = 18$$

which becomes

$$x + y = 100$$
$$0.14x + 0.24y = 18$$

Step 4: Solve the equations.

Multiply the second equation by 100 to clear the decimals: $14x + 24y = 1,800$.

Multiply the first equation by 14: $14x + 14y = 1,400$.

Subtract the first equation from the second equation.

$$14x + 24y = 1800$$
$$\underline{14x + 14y = 1400}$$
$$10y = 400$$
$$10y = 400$$
$$\frac{10y}{10} = \frac{400}{10}$$
$$y = 40$$

Now, substitute the value of y in the first equation.

$$x + y = 100$$
$$x + 40 = 100$$
$$x + 40 - 40 = 100 - 40$$
$$x = 60$$

Step 5: Thus, 60 pounds of 14% aluminum alloy and 40 pounds of 24% aluminum alloy are used for the mixture.

EXAMPLE 2

Beth mixed peanuts that sell for $2 per pound with raisins that sell for $1.50 per pound to make a 10-pound mixture that she will sell for $1.75 per pound. How many pounds of peanuts and raisins were used?

Step 1: Find the unknown quantities in the word problem. Here, the quantities of peanuts and raisins used are unknown.

Step 2: Assign variables to the unknown quantities. Let the quantity of peanuts used be x pounds and the quantity of raisins used be y pounds.

Step 3: Set up two equations based on the facts given in the problem.

The peanuts sell for $2 per pound, the raisins sell for $1.50 per pound, and Beth makes a 10-pound mixture that she will sell for $1.75 per pound.

Write:

$$x + y = 10$$

$$2x + 1.5y = 1.75 \times 10 = 17.5$$

Simplify the system.

$$x + y = 10$$

$$2x + 1.5y = 17.5$$

Step 4: Solve the equations using substitution method.

Solve for x in the first equation.

$$x + y = 10$$

$$x + y - y = 10 - y$$

$$x = 10 - y$$

Substitute the value of x in the second equation.

$$2x + 1.5y = 17.5$$

$$2(10 - y) + 1.5y = 17.5$$

$$20 - 2y + 1.5y = 17.5$$

$$20 - 0.5y = 17.5$$

$$20 - 20 - 0.5y = 17.5 - 20$$

$$-0.5y = -2.5$$

$$\frac{-0.5y}{-0.5} = \frac{-2.5}{-0.5}$$

$$y = 5$$

Substitute the value of y in the first equation.

$$x + y = 10$$

$$x + 5 = 10$$

$$x + 5 - 5 = 10 - 5$$

$$x = 5$$

Step 5: Thus, 5 pounds of peanuts and 5 pounds of raisins were used.

Distance Problems

EXAMPLE 1

An airplane travels 600 miles from city A to city B in 2 hours. In this direction, it is flying with the wind, which is blowing in the same direction as the plane is flying. On the return journey, the airplane must fly against the wind. If the return journey takes 2.5 hours, what are the speed of the plane and the speed of the wind?

Step 1: Find the unknown quantities in the word problem. Here, the speeds of the plane and wind are unknown.

Step 2: Assign variables to the unknown quantities. Let the speed of the plane be x mph and the speed of the wind be y mph.

Step 3: Set up two equations based on the facts given in the problem.

You know that an airplane travels 600 miles from city A to city B in 2 hours. The plane covers the same distance in 2.5 hours while returning.

Remember, when the plane is with the wind, it will go faster $(x + y)$, and when the plane is going against the wind, it will go slower $(x - y)$.

Write:

$$2(x + y) = 600$$
$$2.5(x - y) = 600$$

Simplify.

$$2x + 2y = 600$$
$$2.5x - 2.5y = 600$$

The first equation can be simplified as follows: $x + y = 300$.

The second equation can be simplified as follows: $x - y = 240$.

Thus, the system becomes

$$x + y = 300$$
$$x - y = 240$$

Step 4: Solve the equations using substitution method.

Add the equations:

$$x + y = 300$$
$$\underline{x - y = 240}$$
$$2x = 540$$
$$\frac{2x}{2} = \frac{540}{2}$$
$$x = 270$$

Substitute the value of x in the first equation.

$$x + y = 300$$
$$270 + y = 300$$
$$270 - 270 + y = 300 - 270$$
$$y = 30$$

Step 5: Thus, the speed of the plane is 270 mph and the speed of the wind is 30 mph.

EXAMPLE 2

A boat takes 2 hours to go 120 miles downstream. It takes the same time to go 100 miles upstream. Find the speed of the boat and the speed of the stream.

Step 1: Find the unknown quantities in the word problem. Here, the speeds of the boat and stream are unknown.

Step 2: Assign variables to the unknown quantities. Let the speed of the boat be x mph and the speed of the stream be y mph.

Step 3: Set up two equations based on the facts given in the problem.

A boat takes 2 hours to go 120 miles downstream. It takes the same time to go 100 miles upstream. Remember, when the boat moves downstream, it will go faster $(x + y)$, and when the boat is going upstream, it will go slower $(x - y)$.

Write:

$$2(x + y) = 120$$
$$2(x - y) = 100$$

Simplify the equations:

$$x + y = 60$$
$$x - y = 50$$

Step 4: Solve the equations using substitution method.

Add the equations:

$$x + y = 60$$
$$\underline{x - y = 50}$$
$$2x = 110$$
$$\frac{2x}{2} = \frac{110}{2}$$
$$x = 55$$

Substitute the value of x in the first equation.

$$x + y = 60$$
$$55 + y = 60$$
$$55 - 55 + y = 60 - 55$$
$$y = 5$$

Step 5: Thus, the speed of the boat is 55 mph and the speed of the stream is 5 mph.

Miscellaneous Problems

EXAMPLE 1

The digits of a two-digit number are interchanged to make a second number. The sum of the two-digit number and the second number is 121. If the digits of the number differ by 5, find both numbers.

Step 1: Find the unknown quantities in the word problem. Here, the digits of the numbers are unknown.

Step 2: Assign variables to the unknown quantities. Let the digit in the ones place be x and the digit in the tens place be y.

Step 3: Set up two equations based on the facts given in the problem.

The sum of a two-digit number and the number obtained by interchanging the digits of the number is 121.

A number with tens digit x and ones digit y can be written as $10x + y$.

Similarly, a number with tens digit y and ones digit x will be $10y + x$.

Write $(10x + y) + (10y + x) = 121$.

Also, the digits of the number differ by 5.

So, $x - y = 5$.

The system of equations is:

$$11x + 11y = 121$$
$$x - y = 5$$

Step 4: Solve the equations using the elimination method.

Multiply the second equation by 11: $11x - 11y = 55$.

Add the equations.

$$11x + 11y = 121$$
$$\underline{11x - 11y = 55}$$
$$22x \qquad = 176$$
$$\frac{22x}{22} = \frac{176}{22}$$
$$x = 8$$

Substitute the value of x in the second equation.

$$x - y = 5$$
$$8 - y = 5$$
$$8 - 8 - y = 5 - 8$$
$$-y = -3$$
$$y = 3$$

Step 5: Thus, the numbers are 83 and 38.

EXAMPLE 2

If the length of a rectangle is reduced by 2 units and its width is increased by 1 unit, the area is reduced by 6 square units. However, if the length is increased by 3 units and the width is reduced by 1 unit, the area is increased by 9 square units. Find the length and width of the rectangle.

Step 1: Find the unknown quantities in the word problem. Here, the length and width of the rectangle are unknown.

Step 2: Assign variables to the unknown quantities. Let the length be x units and the width be y units.

Step 3: Set up two equations based on the facts given in the problem.

Given, if the length of a rectangle is reduced by 2 units and its width is increased by 1 unit, the area is reduced by 6 square units. However, if the length is increased by 3 units and the width is reduced by 1 unit, the area is increased by 9 square units.

The area of the rectangle is given by the formula, length × width = xy.

Write:

$$(x - 2)(y + 1) = xy - 6$$

$$(x + 3)(y - 1) = xy + 9$$

The first equation can be simplified as follows:

$$(x - 2)(y + 1) = xy - 6$$

$$xy + x - 2y - 2 = xy - 6$$

$$xy - xy + x - 2y - 2 = xy - xy - 6$$

$$x - 2y - 2 = -6$$

$$x - 2y - 2 + 2 = -6 + 2$$

$$x - 2y = -4$$

The second equation can be simplified as follows:

$$(x + 3)(y - 1) = xy + 9$$

$$xy - x + 3y - 3 = xy + 9$$

$$xy - xy - x + 3y - 3 = xy - xy + 9$$

$$-x + 3y - 3 = 9$$

$$-x + 3y - 3 + 3 = 9 + 3$$

$$-x + 3y = 12$$

Step 4: Solve the equations using elimination method.

Add the equations.

$$x - 2y = -4$$

$$\underline{-x + 3y = 12}$$

$$y = 8$$

Substitute the value of y in the first equation.

$$x - 2y = -4$$
$$x - 2 \times 8 = -4$$
$$x - 16 = -4$$
$$x - 16 + 16 = -4 + 16$$
$$x = 12$$

Step 5: Thus, the length of the rectangle is 12 units and the width is 8 units.

EXERCISE 12

Word Problems Solvable by Systems

Directions: Solve the following questions.

1. The sum of a father's age and twice his son's age is 70 years. If twice the father's age is added to the son's age, the sum is 95. Find the ages of the father and son.

2. Nancy is 18 years older than her son. One year ago, she was three times as old as her son. How old are Nancy and her son now?

3. Fran mixed gallons of 40% alcohol solution and gallons of 60% alcohol solution to produce 24 gallons of a 50% alcohol solution. How many gallons of 40% alcohol solution and 60% alcohol solution did she use for the mixture?

4. A store sells lemon tea for $4 per pound and green tea for $7 per pound. A 120-pound blend is prepared from the lemon and green teas and is sold for $5 per pound. How many pounds of each type of tea were used?

5. A swimmer can swim 20 miles downstream in a nearby river in 2 hours. However, it takes him 5 hours to swim the same distance upstream. Find the speed of the swimmer and the speed of the river.

6. An airplane takes 15 hours to travel 1,500 miles, traveling against the wind. The return trip on the same plane using the same route takes 10 hours, traveling with the wind. Find the speed of the plane and the speed of the wind.

7. Nine times a two-digit number is the same as twice the number obtained by interchanging the digits of the number. If the one's digit exceeds the ten's digit by 7, find both numbers.

8. If the length of a rectangle is reduced by 2 units and the width is increased by 1 unit, the area increases by 1 square unit. However, if the length is increased by 2 units and the width by 1 unit, the area increases by 29 square units. Find the width of the rectangle.

9. Four years ago, a mother was four times the age of her daughter. Six years from today, the mother will be 2.5 times as old as her daughter. Find the present ages of the mother and daughter.

10. How many pounds of walnuts selling for $1 per pound and cashews selling for $1.50 per pound should be mixed to make 100 pounds of a mixture that sells for $1.25 per pound?

Answers are on page 575.

Quadratic Equations

A **quadratic equation** is a second-order polynomial equation in a single variable. The standard form of a quadratic equation is $ax^2 + bx + c = 0$.

Here, a, b, and c are known values or coefficients, $a \neq 0$, and x is the variable. Remember that since a quadratic equation is of second order, it has two solutions. For example,

$$3x^2 + 4x + 2 = 0 \qquad \text{Here, } a = 3, b = 4, \text{ and } c = 2.$$

$$x^2 - 5x = 0 \qquad \text{Here, } a = 1, b = -5, \text{ and } c = 0.$$

Solving Quadratic Equations by Factoring

The solutions of a quadratic equation can be obtained by expressing the equation in terms of its factors.

Step 1: Find the factors of the polynomial expression and write them in the form $(x + m)$ $(x + n)$, where m and n are two integers.

Step 2: Set the factors equal to zero.

Step 3: Solve each factor to get two values of x.

EXAMPLE 1

Solve: $x^2 + 5x + 6 = 0$.

Step 1: $x^2 + 5x + 6$ factors as $(x + 2)(x + 3)$.

Step 2: Set the factors equal to zero: $(x + 2)(x + 3) = 0$.

Step 3: Solve each factor to get two values of x.

The first factor can be solved as:

$$(x + 2) = 0$$
$$x + 2 - 2 = 0 - 2$$
$$x = -2$$

The second factor can be solved as:

$$(x + 3) = 0$$
$$x + 3 - 3 = 0 - 3$$
$$x = -3$$

Thus, $x = -2$ or $x = -3$.

EXAMPLE 2

Solve: $x^2 - 15 = -2x$.

The equation can also be written as:

$$x^2 - 15 = -2x$$
$$x^2 - 15 + 2x = -2x + 2x$$
$$x^2 + 2x - 15 = 0$$

Step 1: $x^2 + 2x - 15 = (x - 3)(x + 5)$

Step 2: Set the factors equal to zero: $(x - 3)(x + 5) = 0$.

Step 3: Solve each factor to get two values of x.

The first factor can be solved as:

$$(x - 3) = 0$$
$$x - 3 + 3 = 0 + 3$$
$$x = 3$$

The second factor can be solved as:

$$(x + 5) = 0$$
$$x + 5 - 5 = 0 - 5$$
$$x = -5$$

Thus, $x = 3$ or $x = -5$.

EXAMPLE 3

Solve: $3x^2 + 2x - 8 = 0$.

Step 1: $3x^2 + 2x - 8 = (3x - 4)(x + 2)$

Step 2: Set the factors equal to zero: $(3x - 4)(x + 2) = 0$.

Step 3: Solve each factor to get two values of x.

The first factor can be solved as:

$$(3x - 4) = 0$$
$$3x - 4 + 4 = 0 + 4$$
$$3x = 4$$
$$\frac{3x}{3} = \frac{4}{3}$$
$$x = \frac{4}{3}$$

The second factor can be solved as:

$$(x + 2) = 0$$
$$x + 2 - 2 = 0 - 2$$
$$x = -2$$

Thus, $x = \frac{4}{3}$ or $x = -2$.

EXAMPLE 4

Solve: $2x^2 - 6x = 0$.

Step 1: $2x^2 - 6x = (2x)(x - 3)$

Step 2: Set the factors equal to zero: $(2x)(x - 3) = 0$.

Step 3: Solve each factor to get two values of x.

The first factor can be solved as:

$$2x = 0$$
$$\frac{2x}{2} = \frac{0}{2}$$
$$x = 0$$

The second factor can be solved as:

$$(x - 3) = 0$$
$$x - 3 + 3 = 0 + 3$$
$$x = 3$$

Thus, $x = 0$ or $x = 3$.

Solving Quadratic Equations by the Square Root Property

When $b = 0$, then the solutions of a quadratic equation can be obtained by finding the square root of both sides of the given equation.

Step 1: Write the equation such that the x^2 term is on one side of the equal sign and the constant is on the other side.

Step 2: Find the square root of both sides. Remember, the square root of the constant has two roots: positive or negative. Indicate this with a plus or minus sign ($\pm$).

EXAMPLE 1

Solve: $x^2 - 25 = 0$.

Step 1: Write the equation such that the x^2 term is on one side of the equal sign and the constant is on the other side.

$$x^2 - 25 + 25 = 0 + 25$$
$$x^2 = 25$$

Step 2: Find the square root of both sides.

$$x^2 = 25$$
$$\sqrt{x^2} = \pm\sqrt{25}$$
$$x = \pm 5$$

Thus, the solutions of the equation are $x = 5$ and $x = -5$.

EXAMPLE 2

Solve: $x^2 - 24 = 0$.

Step 1: Write the equation such that the x^2 term is on one side of the equal sign and the constant is on the other side.

$$x^2 - 24 = 0$$
$$x^2 - 24 + 24 = 0 + 24$$
$$x^2 = 24$$

Step 2: Find the square root of both sides.

$$x^2 = 24$$

$$\sqrt{x^2} = \pm\sqrt{24} = \pm 2\sqrt{6}$$

$$x = \pm 2\sqrt{6}$$

Thus, the values of x in the equation are $x = 2\sqrt{6}$ and $x = -2\sqrt{6}$.

EXAMPLE 3

Solve: $3x^2 - 4 = 3$.

Step 1: Write the equation such that the x^2 term is on one side of the equal sign and the constant is on the other side.

$$3x^2 - 4 = 3$$

$$3x^2 - 4 + 4 = 3 + 4$$

$$3x^2 = 7$$

$$\frac{3x^2}{3} = \frac{7}{3}$$

$$x^2 = \frac{7}{3}$$

Step 2: Find the square root of both sides.

$$x^2 = \frac{7}{3}$$

$$\sqrt{x^2} = \pm\sqrt{\frac{7}{3}}$$

$$x = \pm\frac{\sqrt{7} \times \sqrt{3}}{\sqrt{3} \times \sqrt{3}} = \pm\frac{\sqrt{21}}{3}$$

Thus, the values of x in the equation are $x = \frac{\sqrt{21}}{3}$ and $x = -\frac{\sqrt{21}}{3}$.

EXAMPLE 4

Solve: $(x + 4)^2 - 36 = 0$.

Step 1: Write the equation such that the x^2 term is on one side of the equal sign and the constant is on the other side.

$$(x + 4)^2 - 36 = 0$$

$$(x + 4)^2 - 36 + 36 = 0 + 36$$

$$(x + 4)^2 = 36$$

Step 2: Find the square root of both sides.

$$(x+4)^2 = 36$$
$$\sqrt{(x+4)^2} = \pm\sqrt{36}$$
$$x + 4 = \pm 6$$
$$x + 4 - 4 = -4 \pm 6$$
$$x = -4 - 6 \text{ or } x = -4 + 6$$
$$x = -10 \text{ or } x = 2$$

Thus, the solutions of the equation are $x = 2$ and $x = -10$.

Solving Quadratic Equations by Completing the Square

A quadratic equation can also be solved by completing the square. This method is applicable when the coefficient of x^2 is 1.

Step 1: Check if the coefficient of x^2 is 1. If not, then divide the entire equation by the coefficient of x^2.

Step 2: Set the equation such that all x terms are on the left side and the constant is on the right side.

Step 3: Complete the square on the left side by adding $\left(\dfrac{b}{2}\right)^2$ on both sides, where b is the coefficient of x.

Step 4: Solve the equation to get the solutions for x.

EXAMPLE 1

Solve: $x^2 - 2x - 2 = 0$.

Step 1: Check if the coefficient of x^2 is 1. The coefficient of x^2 is 1.

Step 2: Set the equation such that all x terms are on the left side and the constant is on the right side.

$$x^2 - 2x - 2 = 0$$
$$x^2 - 2x - 2 + 2 = 0 + 2$$
$$x^2 - 2x = 2$$

Step 3: Complete the square on the left side by adding $\left(\dfrac{b}{2}\right)^2$ on both sides, where b is the coefficient of x.

Here, $b = -2$. So, $\left(\dfrac{b}{2}\right)^2 = \left(\dfrac{-2}{2}\right)^2 = (-1)^2 = 1$.

$$x^2 - 2x + 1 = 2 + 1$$
$$x^2 - 2x + 1 = 3$$
$$(x - 1)^2 = 3$$

Step 4: Solve the equation to get the values of x.

$$(x - 1)^2 = 3$$
$$x - 1 = \pm\sqrt{3}$$
$$x - 1 + 1 = \pm\sqrt{3} + 1$$
$$x = 1 \pm\sqrt{3}$$

Thus, the solutions of the equation are $x = 1 \pm\sqrt{3}$.

EXAMPLE 2

Solve: $x^2 + 2x = 7$.

Step 1: Check if the coefficient of x^2 is 1. The coefficient of x^2 is 1.

Step 2: Set the equation such that all x terms are on the left side and the constant is on the right side. Here, the constant is on the right side.

Step 3: Complete the square on the left side by adding $\left(\dfrac{b}{2}\right)^2$ on both sides, where b is the coefficient of x.

Here, $b = 2$. So, $\left(\dfrac{b}{2}\right)^2 = \left(\dfrac{2}{2}\right)^2 = (1)^2 = 1$.

$$x^2 + 2x + 1 = 7 + 1$$
$$x^2 + 2x + 1 = 8$$
$$(x + 1)^2 = 8$$

Step 4: Solve the equation to get the values of x.

$$(x + 1)^2 = 8$$
$$x + 1 = \pm2\sqrt{2}$$
$$x + 1 - 1 = \pm2\sqrt{2} - 1$$
$$x = -1 \pm2\sqrt{2}$$

Thus, the solutions of the equation are $x = -1 \pm2\sqrt{2}$.

EXAMPLE 3

Solve: $2x^2 + 6x - 7 = 0$.

Step 1: Check if the coefficient of x^2 is 1. Here, the coefficient of x^2 is 2. So, divide the equation by 2.

$$2x^2 + 6x - 7 = 0$$
$$\frac{2x^2 + 6x - 7}{2} = \frac{0}{2}$$
$$\frac{2x^2}{2} + \frac{6x}{2} - \frac{7}{2} = 0$$
$$x^2 + 3x - \frac{7}{2} = 0$$

Step 2: Set the equation such that all x terms are on the left side and the constant is on the right side.

$$x^2 + 3x - \frac{7}{2} = 0$$

$$x^2 + 3x - \frac{7}{2} + \frac{7}{2} = 0 + \frac{7}{2}$$

$$x^2 + 3x = \frac{7}{2}$$

Step 3: Complete the square on the left side by adding $\left(\frac{b}{2}\right)^2$ on both sides, where b is the coefficient of x.

Here, $b = 3$. So, $\left(\frac{b}{2}\right)^2 = \left(\frac{3}{2}\right)^2 = \frac{9}{4}$.

$$x^2 + 3x + \frac{9}{4} = \frac{7}{2} + \frac{9}{4}$$

$$\left(x + \frac{3}{2}\right)^2 = \frac{14 + 9}{4} = \frac{23}{4}$$

Step 4: Solve the equation to get the values of x.

$$\left(x + \frac{3}{2}\right)^2 = \frac{23}{4}$$

$$x + \frac{3}{2} = \pm \frac{\sqrt{23}}{2}$$

$$x + \frac{3}{2} - \frac{3}{2} = \pm \frac{\sqrt{23}}{2} - \frac{3}{2}$$

$$x = -\frac{3}{2} \pm \frac{\sqrt{23}}{2}$$

Thus, the solutions of the equation are $x = -\frac{3}{2} \pm \frac{\sqrt{23}}{2}$.

EXAMPLE 4

Solve: $3x^2 - 11 = 5x$.

Step 1: Check if the coefficient of x^2 is 1. Here, the coefficient of x^2 is 3. So, divide the equation by 3.

$$3x^2 - 11 = 5x$$

$$\frac{3x^2 - 11}{3} = \frac{5x}{3}$$

$$\frac{3x^2}{3} - \frac{11}{3} = \frac{5x}{3}$$

$$x^2 - \frac{11}{3} = \frac{5x}{3}$$

Step 2: Set the equation such that all x terms are on the left side and the constant is on the right side.

$$x^2 - \frac{11}{3} = \frac{5x}{3}$$

$$x^2 - \frac{11}{3} - \frac{5x}{3} = \frac{5x}{3} - \frac{5x}{3}$$

$$x^2 - \frac{11}{3} - \frac{5x}{3} = 0$$

$$x^2 + \frac{11}{3} - \frac{11}{3} - \frac{5x}{3} = 0 + \frac{11}{3}$$

$$x^2 - \frac{5x}{3} = \frac{11}{3}$$

Step 3: Complete the square on the left side by adding $\left(\frac{b}{2}\right)^2$ on both sides, where b is the coefficient of x.

Here, $b = \frac{-5}{3}$. So, $\left(\frac{b}{2}\right)^2 = \left(\frac{-5}{3 \times 2}\right)^2 = \frac{25}{36}$.

$$x^2 - \frac{5x}{3} + \frac{25}{36} = \frac{11}{3} + \frac{25}{36}$$

$$x^2 - \frac{5x}{3} + \frac{25}{36} = \frac{132 + 25}{36}$$

$$x^2 - \frac{5x}{3} + \frac{25}{36} = \frac{157}{36}$$

$$\left(x - \frac{5}{6}\right)^2 = \frac{157}{36}$$

Step 4: Solve the equation to get the values of x.

$$\left(x - \frac{5}{6}\right)^2 = \frac{157}{36}$$

$$x - \frac{5}{6} = \pm \frac{\sqrt{157}}{6}$$

$$x - \frac{5}{6} + \frac{5}{6} = \pm \frac{\sqrt{157}}{6} + \frac{5}{6}$$

$$x = \frac{5}{6} \pm \frac{\sqrt{23}}{2}$$

Thus, the solutions of the equation are $x = \frac{5}{6} \pm \frac{\sqrt{23}}{2}$.

Solving Quadratic Equations Using the Quadratic Formula

You can solve the general quadratic equation $ax^2 + bx + c = 0$ ($a \neq 0$) by using the meth of completing the squares.

First, the coefficient of x^2 has to be divided throughout the equation.

$$ax^2 + bx + c = 0$$

$$\frac{ax^2}{a} + \frac{bx}{a} + \frac{c}{a} = 0$$

$$x^2 + \frac{b}{a}x + \frac{c}{a} = 0$$

Set the equation such that the x terms are on the left side and the constants are on the right side.

$$x^2 + \frac{b}{a}x + \frac{c}{a} - \frac{c}{a} = 0 - \frac{c}{a}$$

$$x^2 + \frac{b}{a}x = -\frac{c}{a}$$

Add $\left(\frac{b}{2a}\right)^2$ to both sides.

$$x^2 + \frac{b}{a}x + \left(\frac{b}{2a}\right)^2 = -\frac{c}{a} + \left(\frac{b}{2a}\right)^2$$

$$\left(x + \frac{b}{2a}\right)^2 = \frac{b^2}{4a^2} - \frac{c}{a} = \frac{b^2 - 4ac}{4a^2}$$

$$\sqrt{\left(x + \frac{b}{2a}\right)^2} = \sqrt{\frac{b^2 - 4ac}{4a^2}}$$

$$x + \frac{b}{2a} = \pm\frac{\sqrt{b^2 - 4ac}}{2a}$$

$$x + \frac{b}{2a} - \frac{b}{2a} = -\frac{b}{2a} \pm \frac{\sqrt{b^2 - 4ac}}{2a}$$

$$x = \frac{-b \pm \sqrt{b^2 - 4ac}}{2a}$$

The solutions obtained are known as the **quadratic formula**. The value of $b^2 - 4ac$ is known as the **discriminant** of the quadratic equation and is denoted by D.

Thus, the quadratic formula can also be written as:

$$x = \frac{-b \pm \sqrt{D}}{2a}, \text{ where } D = b^2 - 4ac.$$

EXAMPLE 1

Solve: $x^2 - 4x - 8 = 0$.

Here, $a = 1$, $b = -4$, and $c = -8$.

$$x = \frac{-b \pm \sqrt{b^2 - 4ac}}{2a}$$

$$= \frac{-(-4) \pm \sqrt{(-4)^2 - 4 \times 1 \times (-8)}}{2 \times 1}.$$

$$= \frac{4 \pm \sqrt{16 + 32}}{2} = \frac{4 \pm \sqrt{48}}{2}$$

$$= \frac{4 \pm 4\sqrt{3}}{2}$$

$$= \frac{2(2 \pm 2\sqrt{3})}{2}$$

$$x = 2 \pm 2\sqrt{3}$$

Thus, the solutions to the quadratic equation are $2 \pm 2\sqrt{3}$.

EXAMPLE 2

Solve: $6x^2 + 11x - 35 = 0$.

Here, $a = 6$, $b = 11$, and $c = -35$.

$$x = \frac{-b \pm \sqrt{b^2 - 4ac}}{2a}$$

$$= \frac{-11 \pm \sqrt{(11)^2 - 4 \times 6 \times (-35)}}{2 \times 6}$$

$$= \frac{-11 \pm \sqrt{121 + 840}}{12}$$

$$= \frac{-11 \pm \sqrt{961}}{12}$$

$$= \frac{-11 \pm 31}{12}$$

$$x = \frac{-11 + 31}{12} \text{ or } x = \frac{-11 - 31}{12}$$

$$x =. \frac{20}{12} \text{ or } x = \frac{-42}{12}$$

$$x = \frac{5}{3} \text{ or } x = \frac{-7}{2}$$

Thus, the solutions to the quadratic equation are $x = \frac{5}{3}$ and $x = \frac{-7}{2}$.

EXERCISE 13

Quadratic Equations

Directions: Solve by factoring.

1. $x^2 - 5x + 6 = 0$

2. $3x^2 + 8x = 0$

3. $6y - 5y^2 = 0$

4. $6x^2 - 13x - 5 = 0$

5. $9x^2 - 3x - 20 = 0$

6. $2x^2 - 5x = 3$

Directions: Solve by using the square root property.

7. $x^2 + 7 = 36$

8. $x^2 - 48 = 0$

9. $x^2 - 4 = 0$

10. $x^2 - 50 = 0$

11. $(x - 2)^2 - 12 = 0$

12. $(x - 5)^2 - 100 = 0$

Directions: Solve the quadratic equations by completing the square.

13. $x^2 - 4x - 8 = 0$

14. $x^2 - 2x - 1 = 0$

15. $5x^2 - 6x = 8$

16. $2x^2 + 6x - 3 = 0$

17. $3x^2 + 5x - 8 = 0$

18. $7x^2 = 6 - 19x$

Directions: Solve by using the quadratic formula.

19. $x^2 + x - 4 = 0$

20. $x^2 - 3x - 4 = 0$

21. $x^2 - 10x + 20 = 0$

22. $3x^2 - 10x + 5 = 0$

23. $x^2 + 2x - 8 = 0$

24. $x^2 - 5x - 5 = 0$

Answers are on page 575.

Word Problems Leading to Quadratic Equations

Word problems using quadratic equations can be solved by following these steps:

Step 1: Find the unknown quantities and assign the variable x to one of them.

Step 2: Set the equation in the form of a quadratic equation.

Step 3: Solve the quadratic equation using any of the methods discussed in the previous sections.

Step 4: Answer the questions.

Find Two Numbers Given Product and Sum or Difference

EXAMPLE

The sum of the squares of two consecutive positive odd numbers is 394. Find the numbers.

Step 1: Find the unknown quantities and assign variable x to one of them. Let one of the unknown odd numbers be x. The other consecutive odd number would be $x + 2$.

Step 2: Set the equation in the form of a quadratic equation.

$$x^2 + (x + 2)^2 = 394$$
$$x^2 + x^2 + 4x + 4 = 394$$
$$2x^2 + 4x + 4 = 394$$
$$2x^2 + 4x + 4 - 394 = 394 - 394$$
$$2x^2 + 4x - 390 = 0$$

Step 3: Solve the equation using any of the methods discussed in the previous sections.

The equation can be solved by using the quadratic formula.

Here, $a = 2$, $b = 4$, and $c = -390$.

$$x = \frac{-b \pm \sqrt{b^2 - 4ac}}{2a}$$

$$= \frac{-4 \pm \sqrt{4^2 - 4 \times 2 \times (-390)}}{2 \times 2}$$

$$= \frac{-4 \pm \sqrt{16 + 3,120}}{4}$$

$$= \frac{-4 \pm \sqrt{3,136}}{4}$$

$$= \frac{-4 \pm 56}{4}$$

$$= \frac{4(-1 \pm 14)}{4}$$

$$= -1 \pm 14$$

$$x = -1 + 14, \text{ or } x = -1 - 14$$

$$x = 13 \text{ or } x = -15$$

The value -15 is not positive and is not a solution. Thus, $x = 13$ is one of the numbers.

Step 4: The two consecutive odd natural numbers are 13 and $13 + 2 = 15$.

Area of a Square or a Rectangle

EXAMPLE 1

Find the length of the side of a square whose area is 625 square units.

Step 1: Find the unknown quantities and assign variable x to one of them. The side of the square is unknown; let it be x units.

Step 2: Set the equation in the form of a quadratic equation.

$x^2 = 625$

Step 3: Solve the equation using any of the methods discussed in the previous sections.

This can be solved by using the square root method.

$$x^2 = 625$$
$$\sqrt{x^2} = \sqrt{625}$$
$$x = \pm\, 25$$

The negative root, -25, cannot be a solution because the solution represents a length. So, $x = 25$.

Step 4: Thus, the side of the square is 25 units.

EXAMPLE 2

The length of a rectangle is 5 units more than its width. If the area of the rectangle is 84 square units, what are the length and width of the rectangle?

Step 1: Find the unknown quantities and assign variable x to one of them. The length and width are the unknown quantities. Let the width of the rectangle be x units. So, the length will be $x + 5$.

Step 2: Set up the equation in the form of a quadratic equation.

$$(x + 5)\,(x) = 84$$
$$x^2 + 5x = 84$$
$$x^2 + 5x - 84 = 84 - 84$$
$$x^2 + 5x - 84 = 0$$

Step 3: Solve the equation using any of the methods discussed in the previous sections.

$$x^2 + 5x - 84 = 0$$

Here, $a = 1$, $b = 5$, and $c = -84$.

You can use the quadratic formula, $x = \dfrac{-b \pm \sqrt{b^2 - 4ac}}{2a}$.

$$x = \frac{-5 \pm \sqrt{5^2 - 4 \times 1 \times (-84)}}{2 \times 1}$$

$$= \frac{-5 \pm \sqrt{25 + 336}}{2}$$

$$= \frac{-5 \pm \sqrt{361}}{2}$$

$$= \frac{-5 \pm 19}{2}$$

$$x = \frac{-5 + 19}{2} \text{ or } x = \frac{-5 - 19}{2}$$

$$x = 7 \text{ or } x = -12$$

The negative value does not make sense for the width. So, $x = 7$.

Step 4: Thus, the width is 7 units and length is $7 + 5 = 12$ units.

EXERCISE 14

Word Problems Leading to Quadratic Equations

Directions: Solve the following word problems using quadratic equations.

1. The sum of the squares of two consecutive even positive numbers is 580. Find the numbers.

2. The sum of the squares of two consecutive positive numbers is 925. Find the two numbers.

3. The sum of the squares of two positive consecutive numbers is 365. Find the two numbers.

4. The length of a rectangular park is three times its width and the area is equal to 2,700 square units. Find the length and width of the park.

5. A rectangular room has an area of 3,200 square units. If its length is twice its width, find the length and width of the room.

Answers are on page 575.

CHAPTER 11

Graphing

Graphs are mathematicians' response to the saying "A picture is worth a thousand words." A graph supplies a means of visualizing equations, from which details may be apparent that are otherwise hidden. In this chapter you will learn about graphs and how they are made and used.

Cartesian Coordinate System

The **Cartesian coordinate system** consists of two axes, which intersect each other at a point called the **origin**, and is used to define the position of any point by using ordered pairs. The plane on which the points and the axes are drawn is called the **Cartesian coordinate plane**. This plane is a tool for graphing algebraic relationships, functions, figures, and scatter plots.

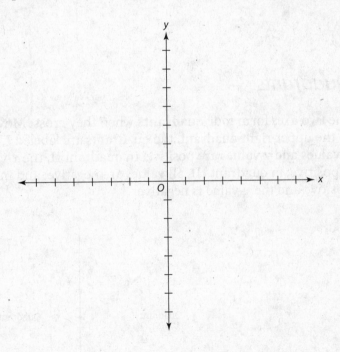

x- and y-Axes

The axes are the horizontal and the vertical number lines of the graph. The horizontal axis is the **x-axis,** and the vertical one is the **y-axis**. The position of any point on the Cartesian plane is described by using two numbers (x, y). The first number, x, is the horizontal position of the point measured from the origin. It is called the **x-coordinate**. The second number, y, is the vertical position of the point measured from the origin. It is called the **y-coordinate**.

Origin

The point of intersection of the x-axis and the y-axis is called the **origin** and is denoted by the letter O.

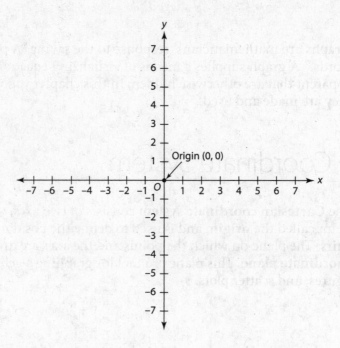

Quadrants

The two axes form four **quadrants** when they cross. Moving counterclockwise, starting in the upper-right quadrant, the quadrants are labeled **I**, **II**, **III**, and **IV**. In quadrant I, all x-values and y-values are positive; in quadrant II, the x-value is negative and the y-value is positive; in quadrant III, all values are negative; and in quadrant IV the x-value is positive and the y-value is negative.

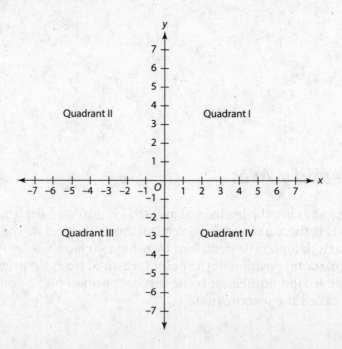

Ordered Pairs = Points

A specific order is used to represent the coordinates, which is very important. The *x*-coordinate is always given first and the *y*-coordinate is always second. The coordinates in such order are called **ordered pairs**. (*x, y*) specifies the location of a point *P* on the plane as shown in the figure.

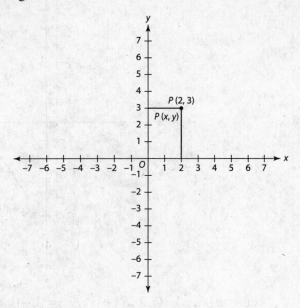

Distance Between Points

To calculate the distance between two points, first join the points with a straight line. The length of this line can be thought of as the distance between the points (x_1, y_1) and (x_2, y_2).

Compute the distance, *d*, by using this formula:

$$d = \sqrt{(x_2 - x_1)^2 + (y_2 - y_1)^2}\,.$$

In this formula, x_1 is the *x*-coordinate of the first graphed point and x_2 is the *x*-coordinate of the second point. Similarly, y_1 is the *y*-coordinate of the first point on the graph and y_2 is the *y*-coordinate of the second point.

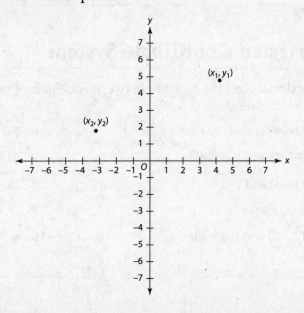

EXAMPLE

What is the distance between the points *A* and *B* given in the coordinate plane?

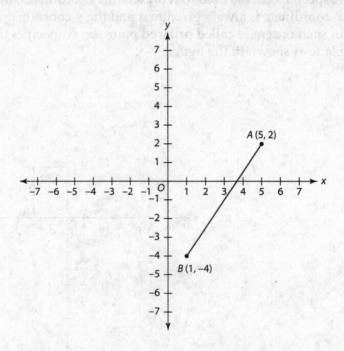

Let *A* be $(x_1, y_1) = (5, 2)$; *B* be $(x_2, y_2) = (1, -4)$. You could alternatively choose to let *A* be (x_2, y_2) and *B* be (x_1, y_1). The distance formula will work with either order. Use $x_1 = 5$, $x_2 = 1$, $y_1 = 2$, and $y_2 = -4$.

$$d = \sqrt{(x_2 - x_1)^2 + (y_2 - y_1)^2}$$

$$= \sqrt{(1-5)^2 + (-4-2)^2}$$

$$= \sqrt{(-4)^2 + (-6)^2}$$

$$= \sqrt{16 + 36} = \sqrt{52} = 7.21$$

EXERCISE 1

Cartesian Coordinate System

Directions: Find the distance between each pair of coordinates. Round to the nearest tenth.

1. (3, −4) and (5, 7)

2. (−1, 3) and (−8, −4)

3. (3, −1) and (−2, 5)

4. (−5, 5) and (0, 5)

5. (2, −9) and (−3, −6)

6. (−2, 1) and (3, −4)

7. (0, 0) and (5, 1)

8. (8, −3) and (5, 3)

9. (9, 4) and (4, 0)

10. (2, 1) and (6, 7)

Answers are on page 575.

Midpoint of a Line Segment

The middle point between two given points is called the **midpoint**. This is the point that divides the line segment between the two points exactly in half.

The formula for finding the midpoint is $\left(\dfrac{x_1+x_2}{2}, \dfrac{y_1+y_2}{2}\right)$.

EXAMPLE

What is the midpoint between the two given points given in the coordinate plane?

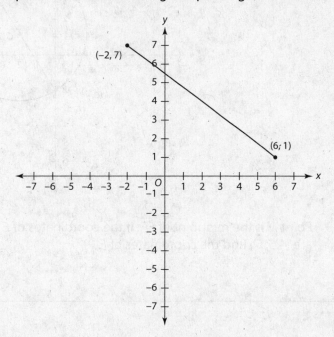

Let $(x_1, y_1) = (-2, 7)$ and $(x_2, y_2) = (6, 1)$. The midpoint of the two points is:

$$\left(\frac{x_1+x_2}{2}, \frac{y_1+y_2}{2}\right) = \left(\frac{-2+6}{2}, \frac{7+1}{2}\right) = \left(\frac{4}{2}, \frac{6}{2}\right) = (2, 3)$$

EXERCISE 2

Midpoint of a Line Segment

Directions: Find the midpoint between each pair of points.

1. $(6, 4)$ and $(3, -4)$

2. $(0, 1)$ and $(2, 4)$

3. $(-2, -5)$ and $(3, 2)$

4. $(-6, -3)$ and $(-2, -9)$

5. Suppose M is the midpoint of $\overline{CD}$ and the coordinates of C are $(-2, 3)$ and M are $(1, 0)$. Find the coordinates of D.

6. Suppose $\overline{AB}$ is a diameter of a circle with its center at (2, 1.3). If the coordinates of A are (0, −2), find the coordinates of B.

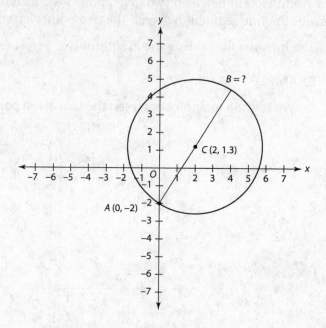

7. Point M is the midpoint of $\overline{EF}$. If the coordinates of E are (2, 3) and the coordinates of M are (4.5, 6), find the coordinates of F.

Answers are on page 575.

Point Symmetry

Points Symmetric About the x-Axis

A graph is said to be **symmetric about the x-axis** when its graph is reflected about the x-axis. If (x, y) is on the graph, then (x, −y) is also on the graph. Here is a graph that is symmetric about the x-axis.

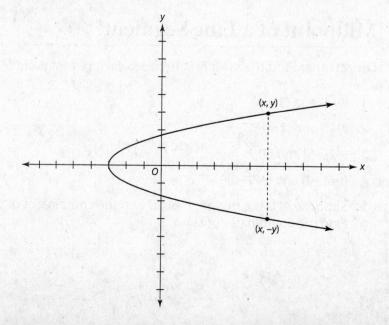

Points Symmetric About the *y*-Axis

A graph is said to be **symmetric about the *y*-axis** when its graph is reflected about the *y*-axis. If (x, y) is on the graph, then $(-x, y)$ is also on the graph. Here is a sketch of a graph that is symmetric about the *y*-axis.

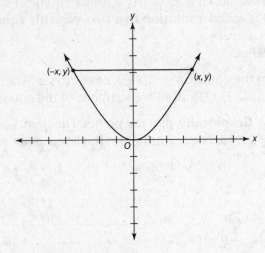

Points Symmetric About the Origin

A graph is said to be **symmetric about the origin** when if whenever (x, y) is on the graph, then $(-x, -y)$ is also on the graph. Here is a sketch of a graph that is symmetric about the origin.

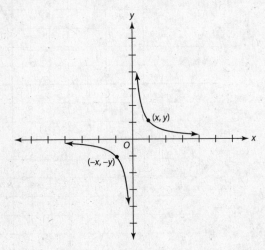

EXERCISE 3

Point Symmetry

Directions: Find the symmetric point for each point with respect to the given axis or with respect to the origin.

1. $(7, 9)$; origin

2. $(8, -1)$; *x*-axis

3. $(12, -15)$; *y*-axis

4. $(-2, -1)$; origin

5. $(-4, 6)$; *y*-axis

6. $(5, -7)$; *x*-axis

Answers are on page 576.

Graphing

Ordered Pairs as Solutions to Two-Variable Equations

When the values of (x,y) satisfy a linear equation with two variables, then the ordered pair (x,y) is called a **solution to a two-variable equation**.

EXAMPLE

For the equation $y = 2x + 3$, check to see whether the coordinate points {(0,3), (1,5), (4,1), (2,7), (3,9), (5,4)} are solutions to the equation or not.

Graphically, plot the points. The points on the straight line are solutions of $y = 2x + 3$. The points not on the line are not solutions.

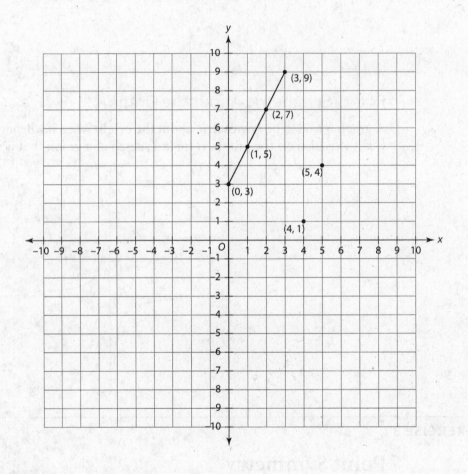

Algebraically, you can also find whether these points are solutions to the equation.

Rewrite $y = 2x + 3$ as $y - 2x = 3$ and then substitute each pair of coordinates into the equation. Then check to see if the left side gives a value of 3.

$(x, y) = (0, 3) : 3 - 2(0) = 3 - 0 = 3.$ Solution.

$(x, y) = (1, 5) : 5 - 2(1) = 5 - 2 = 3.$ Solution.

$(x, y) = (4, 1) : 1 - 2(4) = 1 - 8 = -7 \neq 3.$ Not a solution.

$(x, y) = (2, 7) : 7 - 2(2) = 7 - 4 = 3.$ Solution.

$(x, y) = (3, 9) : 9 - 2(3) = 9 - 6 = 3.$ Solution.

$(x, y) = (5, 4) : 4 - 2(5) = 4 - 10 = -6 \neq 3.$ Not a solution.

Thus, the points (0, 3), (1, 5), (2, 7), and (3, 9) are solutions of the given two-variable equation.

EXERCISE 4

Ordered Pairs as Solutions to Two-Variable Equations

Directions: Determine if the ordered pair is a solution to the given equation.

1. $(x, y) = (2, 3);\ 4y - 2x = 6$

2. $(x, y) = (4, -5);\ 7x - 11y = 6$

3. $(x, y) = (1, -3);\ 6x - 5y = 21$

4. $(x, y) = (1, -1);\ 3x + 2y = 1$

5. $(x, y) = (6, 6);\ x - y + 4 = 0$

6. $(x, y) = (2, -1);\ 2x + 5y = 1$

7. $(x, y) = (-4, 6);\ 3y - 2x = 20$

8. $(x, y) = (0, 4);\ y = -11x + 4$

9. $(x, y) = (1, 12);\ y = x + 12$

10. $(x, y) = (-1, 1);\ 9x + 4y + 5 = 0$

Answers are on page 576.

Graphing y as an Expression of x

Graphing $y = x$

The ordered pairs that are on the graph of $y = x$ are in the table below.

x	y
1	1
−1	−1
2	2
0	0
3	3

This is a graph of the points that are solutions to the equation $y = x$.

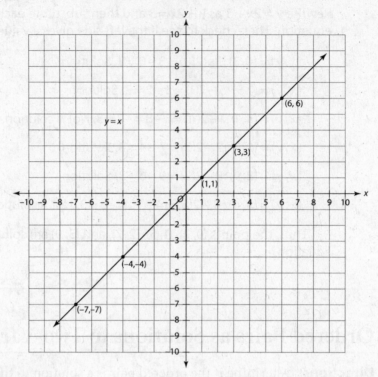

Graphing $y = |x|$

The absolute value of a number or quantity is a mathematical function that tells the distance that the number is from zero on the number line. Example values are $|3| = 3$, $|-6| = 6$, and $|-25| = 25$.

Graphically, $y = |x|$ is in the shape of a V.

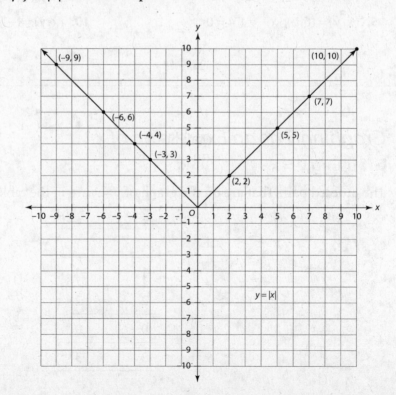

Graphing $y = x^2$

Make a table of values for this expression.

x	$y = x^2$
–3	$(-3)^2 = 9$
–2	$(-2)^2 = 4$
–1	1
0	0
1	1
2	4
3	9

Then graph the points.

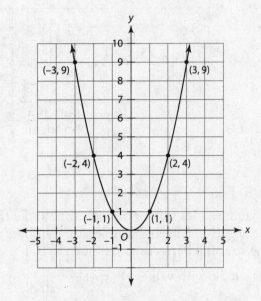

Here, the graph is not a straight line, but curved. It is called a parabola. The bottom point is the vertex at the origin.

EXAMPLE

Graph $y = x^2 + 2$.

Make a table of values.

x	–2	–1	0	1	2
y	6	3	2	3	6

Then graph $(-2, 6)$, $(-1, 3)$, $(0, 2)$, $(1, 3)$, and $(2, 6)$.

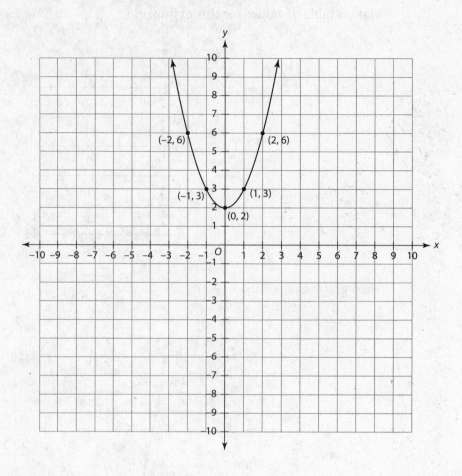

Graphing $y = \sqrt{x}$

This is the square root function. You cannot take the square root of a negative number, so do not use negative values of x. Also, use numbers whose square root is easily calculated. This brings to mind perfect squares such as 0, 1, 4, 9, and so on.

Here is a table with values of (x, y).

x	y
0	0
1	1
4	2
9	3

The graph of the square root starts at the point (0, 0) and then goes off to the right.

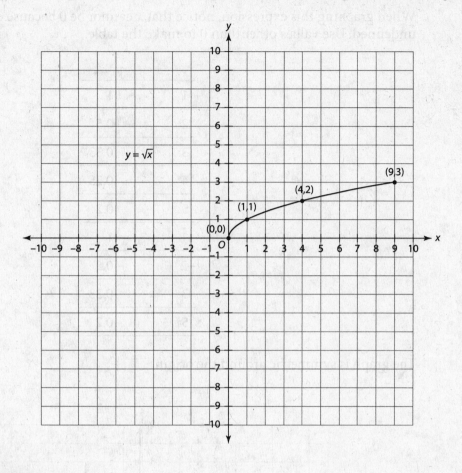

$y = \sqrt{x}$

(0,0) (1,1) (4,2) (9,3)

EXAMPLE

Graph $y = \sqrt{x-3}$.

Make a data table. Use values that will give a perfect square root.

x	3	4	12
y	0	1	$\sqrt{12-3} = 3$

Plot the points from the table: (3, 0), (4, 1), (12, 3).

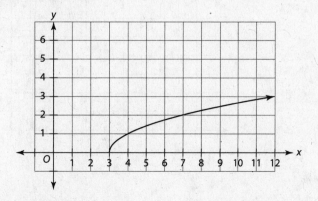

Graphing $y = \dfrac{1}{x}$

When graphing this expression, notice that x cannot be 0 because division by 0 is undefined. Use values other than 0 to make the table.

x	y
1	1
2	0.5
3	0.33
4	0.25
5	0.2
−1	−1
−2	−0.5
3	−0.33
5	−0.2

The graph is symmetric around the origin.

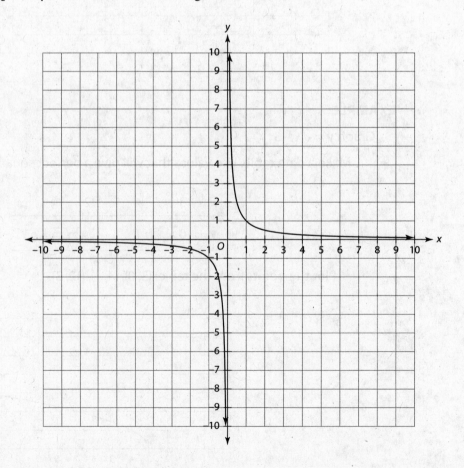

EXAMPLE

Graph $y = \dfrac{1}{x+2}$.

Make a table of the values. Don't forget negative values. Notice that the value of −2 makes the denominator 0, so the value −2 cannot be used in the table.

x	0	1	2	3	4	5	−5	−6	−7
y	0.5	0.33	0.25	0.2	0.16	0.14	−0.33	−0.25	−0.2

Graph the points.

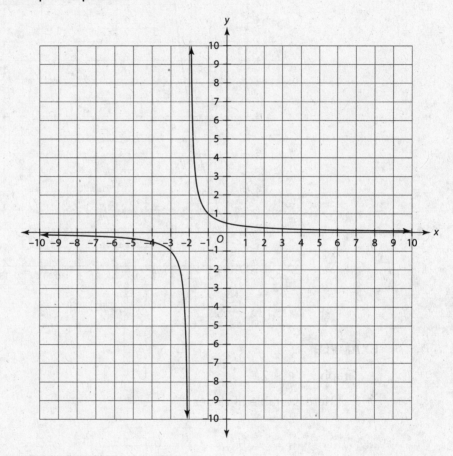

Graphing $y = b^x \ (b > 1)$

Graph $y = 2^x$.

Here is a table of values.

x	y
0	1
1	2
2	4
3	8
4	16

Now graph the points to get an idea of the curve.

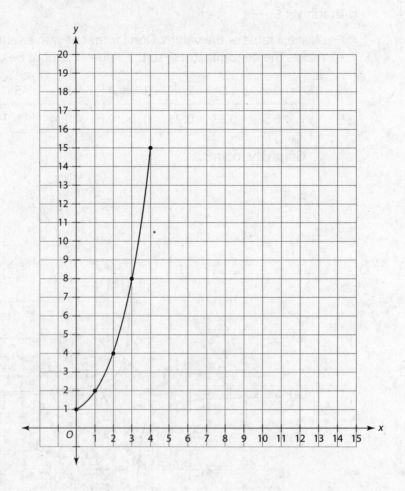

EXAMPLE

Graph $y = 4^x + 2$.

Here is a table of values.

x	0	1	2
y	3	6	18

Graph the ordered pairs.

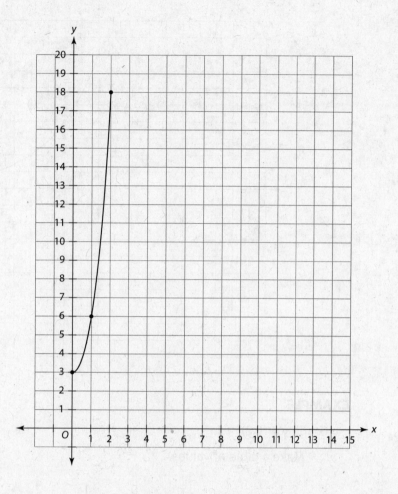

Graphing $y = b^x$ $(0 < b < 1)$

Graph $y = (0.5)^x$.

x	y
0	1
1	0.5
2	0.25
3	0.125
4	0.06

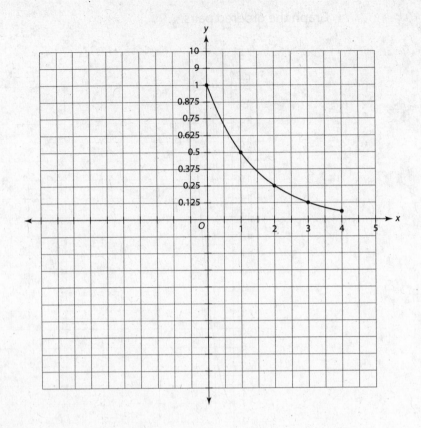

EXAMPLE

Graph $y = (0.2)^x + 1$.

Make a table of values.

x	0	1	2	3
y	2	1.2	1.04	1.008

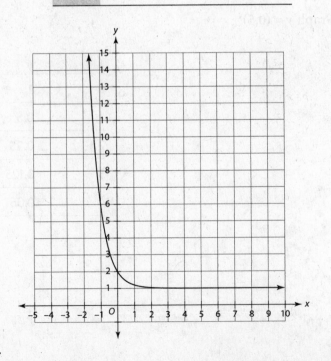

EXERCISE 5

Graphing *y* as an Expression of *x*

Directions: Graph each equation.

1. $y = |x - 3|$

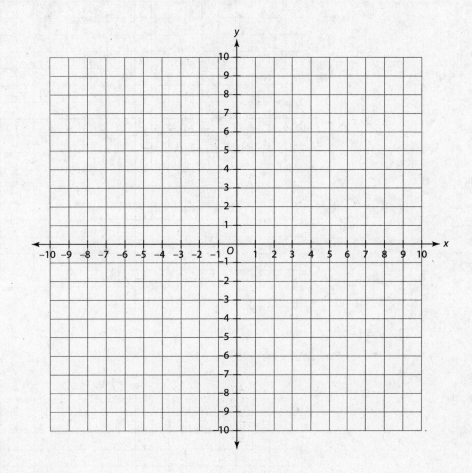

2. $y = \sqrt{x-1}$

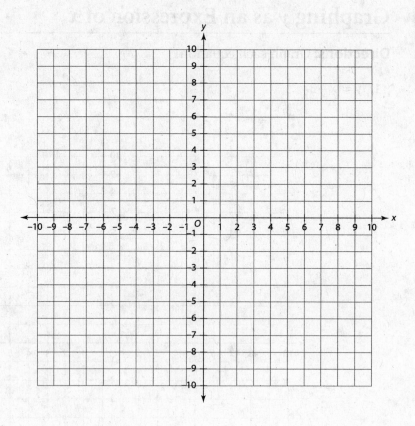

3. $y = 1 - x^2$

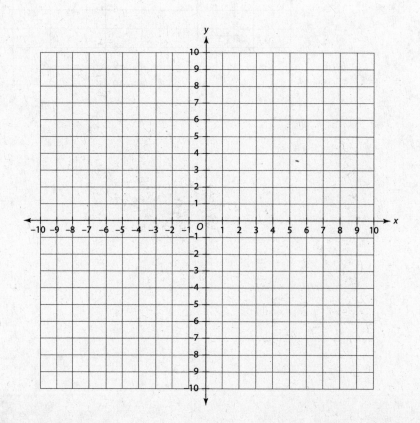

4. $y = -\lvert x - 3\rvert + 2$

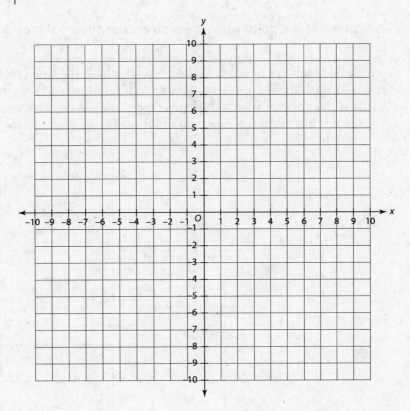

5. $y = 3^x$

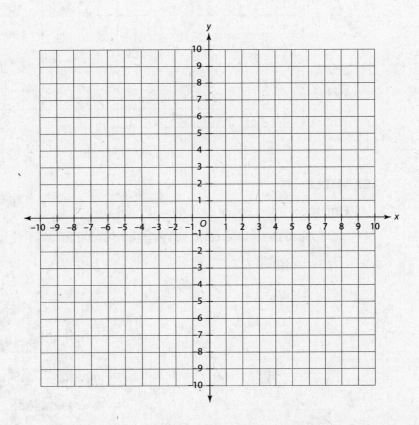

x- and y-Intercepts of a Graph

An **intercept** is a point where a graph crosses the x- or the y-axis. Let's take a look at lines.

The **x-intercept** of a line is the point at which the line crosses the x-axis. The y-value is equal to zero (0). The x-intercept has an ordered pair of the form (x, 0). The **y-intercept** of a line is the point at which the line crosses the y-axis. The x-value is equal to zero (0). The y-intercept has an ordered pair of the form (0, y).

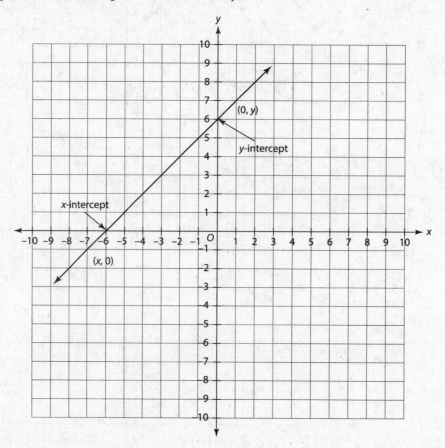

EXAMPLE

Find the x-intercept of $3x + 4y = 12$.

To find the x-intercept, set $y = 0$ and solve for x.

$$3x + 4(0) = 12$$

$$3x + 0 = 12$$

$$3x = 12$$

$$x = \frac{12}{3}$$

$$x = 4$$

Thus, the x-intercept is (4, 0).

To find the *y*-intercept, set $x = 0$ and solve the equation.

$$3(0) + 4y = 12$$

$$0 + 4y = 12$$

$$4y = 12$$

$$y = \frac{12}{4}$$

$$y = 3$$

Thus, the *y*-intercept is (0, 3).

Graphically, you can use the *x*-intercept and *y*-intercept to graph a line. Once these have been found, you can plot them, draw a straight line connecting them, and extend the line at either end. Here is a graph of the equation $3x + 4y = 12$, drawn using intercepts:

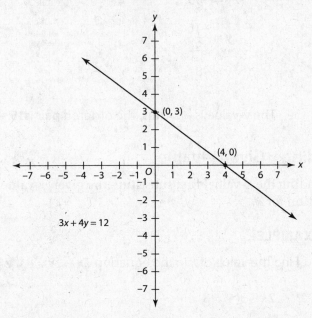

EXERCISE 6

x- and *y*-Intercepts of a Graph

Directions: Find the *x*- and *y*-intercepts of each linear equation.

1. $2x - 3y = -6$

2. $-\dfrac{3}{4}x + 12y = 9$

3. $-2x + \dfrac{1}{2}y = -3$

4. $4x + y = 4$

5. $4x - 6y = 12$

6. $10y + 8x = -40$

7. $-6x + 5y = -30$

8. $y = -3x + 6$

9. $x - y = 4$

10. $20x + 5y = 20$

Answers are on page 579.

Reading Coordinates from Graphs

Finding *y* Given *x*-Value

In finding the *y*-value, first substitute the given *x*-value in the equation and then solve the equation for *y*.

EXAMPLE

Find the value of *y* in the equation $5x + 2y = 9$ if $x = 5$.

$$5(5) + 2y = 9$$
$$25 + 2y = 9$$
$$2y = 9 - 25$$
$$2y = -16$$
$$y = \frac{-16}{2}$$
$$y = -8$$

The *y*-value is −8. Thus, the ordered pair is (5, −8).

Finding *x* Given *y*-Value

In finding the *x*-value, first substitute the given *y*-value in the equation and then solve the equation for *x*.

EXAMPLE

Find the value of *x* in the equation $2x - 3y = 8$ if $y = 4$.

$$2x - 3(4) = 8$$
$$2x - 12 = 8$$
$$2x = 8 + 12$$
$$2x = 20$$
$$x = \frac{20}{2}$$
$$x = 10$$

So, the *x*-value is 10. Thus, the ordered pair is (10, 4).

EXERCISE 7

Reading Coordinates from Graphs

Directions: Solve for the missing value. Write the *x*- and *y*-values as an ordered pair.

1. $2x - 5y = -23;\ y = 5$

2. $-7x + 6y = 15;\ x = 3$

3. $2x + 3y = 3;\ y = 1$

4. $7x + 2y = -1;\ y = 17$

5. $5x - 3y = -14;\ x = -1$

6. $x + y = 5;\ y = 2$

7. $2x + 3y = 26;\ y = 2$

8. $2x + y = 9;\ x = 4$

9. $3x - y = 5;\ x = 1$

10. $x - 3y = 6;\ y = 1$

Answers are on page 579.

Equations of Lines

Graphing $y = mx + b$

The slope-intercept form of a linear equation is $y = mx + b$, where *m* is the slope and *b* is the *y*-intercept. This form of the equation will help you graph the line more easily.

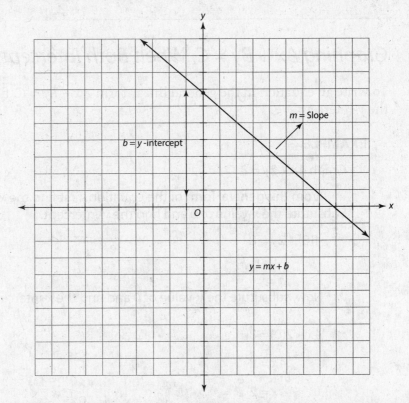

To find the slope and *y*-intercept of the equation of a line, solve the equation for *y*.

EXAMPLE

Find the slope and *y*-intercept of $3x - 7y = 21$.

Solve for *y*.

$$3x - 7y = 21$$

$$-7y = -3x + 21$$

$$y = \frac{-3x + 21}{-7}$$

$$y = \frac{-3x}{-7} + \frac{21}{-7}$$

$$y = \frac{3}{7}x - 3$$

The slope is $\frac{3}{7}$ and the *y*-intercept is $b = -3$.

EXERCISE 8

Equations of Lines

Directions: Find the slope and the *y*-intercept of each line.

1. $x - 3y = 12$ **2.** $2x - y = 4$ **3.** $5x - 2y = 8$ **4.** $4x - y = -4$ **5.** $3x - 2y = -6$

Answers are on page 579.

Graphing Ax + By = C, When Both Intercepts Are Integers

To write an equation in the general linear form $Ax + By = C$, first find the *x*-intercept and the *y*-intercept.

EXAMPLE

Graph $4x + 2y = 8$.

From this general form of the equation, first find the *x*- and *y*-intercepts. Substitute the *x*-value of 0 and find the *y*-intercept.

$$4(0) + 2y = 8$$

$$y = 4$$

Now, substitute the *y*-value of 0 and find the *x*-intercept.

$$4x + 2(0) = 8$$

$$4x = 8$$

$$x = 2$$

So, the intercepts are (0, 4) and (2, 0). Now graph the line.

x	y
0	4
2	0

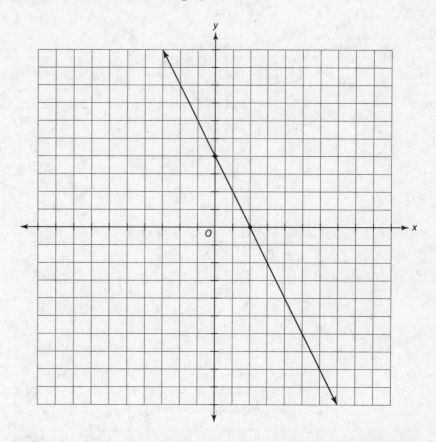

EXERCISE 9

Graphing $Ax + By = C$, When Both Intercepts Are Integers

Directions: Find the intercepts of each line. Graph each line using its intercepts.

1. $-3x + y = 6$

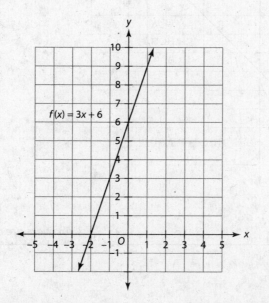

2. $y = 5x - 5$

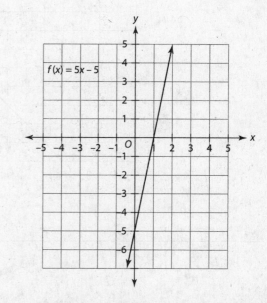

3. $y = 2x + 4$

4. $y = \dfrac{1}{4}x - 6$

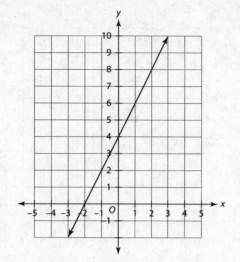

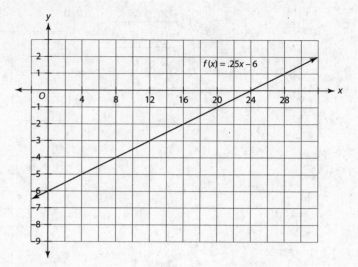

5. $y = x - 1$

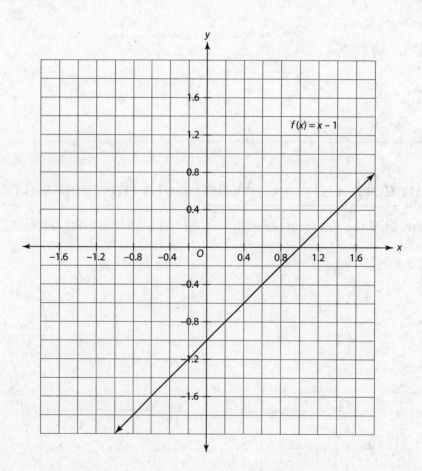

Answers are on pages 579–580.

Graphing Ax + By = C, When One or Both Intercepts Are Not Integers

This section works with finding intercepts that may not be integers.

EXAMPLE

Find the intercepts and graph of $2x + 3y = 1$.

First, substitute 0 for x to find the y-intercept.

$$2(0) + 3y = 1$$

$$3y = 1$$

$$y = \frac{1}{3} = 0.33$$

Substitute 0 for y to find the x-intercept.

$$2x + 3(0) = 1$$

$$2x = 1$$

$$x = \frac{1}{2} = 0.5$$

x	y
0	0.33
0.5	0

The intercepts of the line are (0, 0.33) and (0.5, 0). Graph the line using the intercepts.

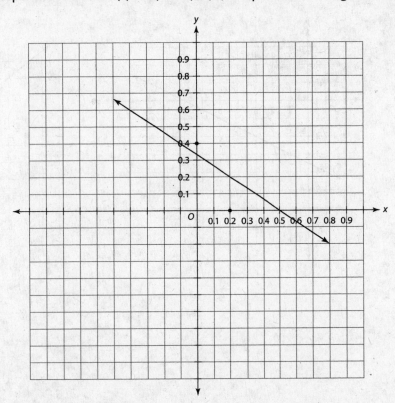

EXERCISE 10

Graphing $Ax + By = C$, When One or Both Intercepts Are Not Integers

Directions: Find the intercepts of each line. Graph each line using its intercepts.

1. $5x + 2y = 8$

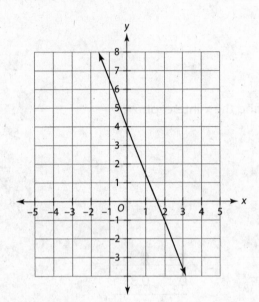

2. $2x - y = 5$

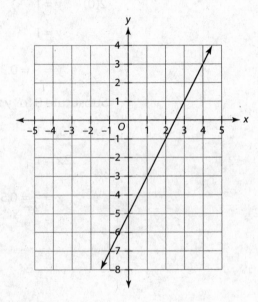

3. $x - 2y = 7$

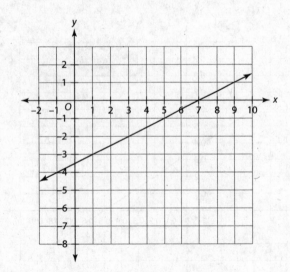

4. $4x + 5y = 12$

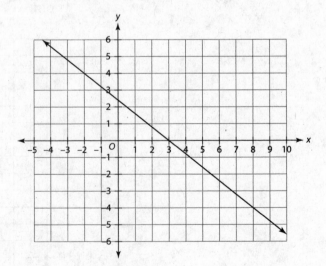

5. $5x + 4y = 38$

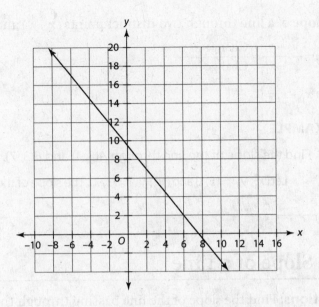

The Slope of a Line
Definition—"Rise Over Run"

The slope compares the vertical change (the **rise**) to the horizontal change (the **run**) when moving from one fixed point to another along the line. A ratio comparing the change in y (the rise) with the change in x (the run) is used to calculate the slope of a line. So, the slope of the line $m = \dfrac{\text{rise}}{\text{run}}$.

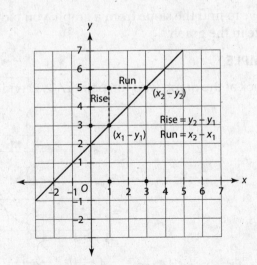

Finding Slope from Two Points with $m = \dfrac{y_2 - y_1}{x_2 - x_1}$

The **slope** of a line through two distinct points (x_1, y_1) and (x_2, y_2) is given by the formula:

$$m = \frac{y_2 - y_1}{x_2 - x_1} = \frac{\text{Change in } y}{\text{Change in } x},$$

where $x_1 - x_2 \neq 0$.

EXAMPLE

Find the slope of the line through $A(5, 1)$ and $B(3, 7)$.

Let $(x_1, y_1) = (5, 1)$ and $(x_2, y_2) = (3, 7)$. The slope of the line is $m = \dfrac{y_2 - y_1}{x_2 - x_1} = \dfrac{7 - 1}{3 - 5} = \dfrac{6}{-2} = -3$.

EXERCISE 11

The Slope of a Line

Directions: Find the slope of the line passing through the coordinates given below.

1. (10,3), (7,9)

2. (7,3), (8,5)

3. (4,2), (4,5)

4. (7,3), (5,9)

5. (13,6), (3,1)

6. (3,2), (12,2)

7. (2,4), (4,9)

8. (2,10), (8,7)

9. (12,11), (9,5)

10. (8,10), (−7,14)

Answers are on page 582.

Finding Slope from a Graph

If you have to find the slope from a graph, you plot the points and then calculate the slope of the line in the graph.

EXAMPLE

Look at the graph with the points $A(2, 2)$ and $B(4, 4)$.

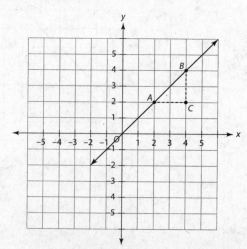

Calculate the rise and run and find the slope.

Rise = $y_2 - y_1 = 4 - 2 = 2$, run = $x_2 - x_1 = 4 - 2 = 2$, and $m = \dfrac{\text{rise}}{\text{run}} = \dfrac{2}{2} = 1$.

So, the slope of the line in the given graph is 1.

EXERCISE 12

Finding Slope from a Graph

Directions: Find the slope of the line in the graph.

1.

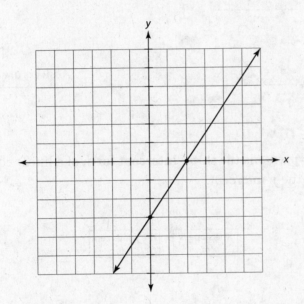

2.

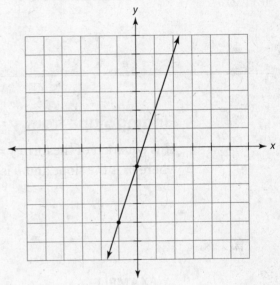

2.

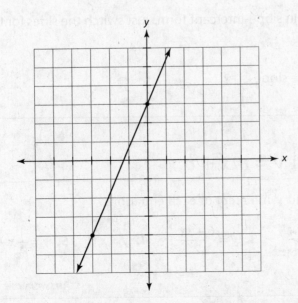

3.

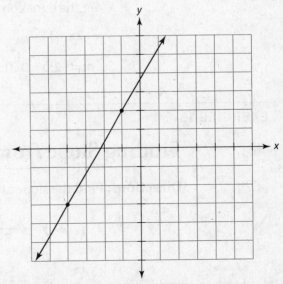

5.

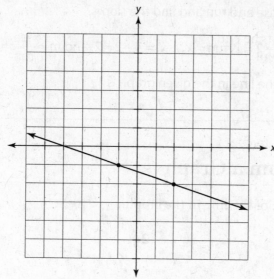

Answers are on page 582.

Finding Slope from $y = mx + b$

This equation of the form $y = mx + b$ is the **slope-intercept form** of a linear equation, where m is the slope and b is the y-intercept.

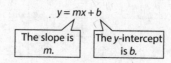

EXAMPLE

Find the slope of the line with equation $3 - 2x = y$.

Write the equation in slope-intercept form. Just switch the sides for this equation.

$y = -2x + 3$

So, $m = -2$; $b = 3$. The slope is -2.

EXERCISE 13

Finding Slope from $y = mx + b$

Directions: Find the slope and y-intercept of each equation.

1. $y = -x + 2$ **2.** $y = \dfrac{9 - 2x}{3}$ **3.** $y = \dfrac{6 - 5x}{2}$ **4.** $y = x$ **5.** $y = \dfrac{1}{4}x + 1$

Answers are on page 582.

Finding Slope from $Ax + By = C$

From this standard form of the equation, convert the equation to slope-intercept form to find the slope and *y*-intercept.

EXAMPLE 1

Find the slope and *y*-intercept of the equation $3x - 5y = -1$.

Find the slope-intercept form of the equation by solving for *y*.

$$3x - 5y = -1$$
$$-5y = -1 - 3x$$
$$-5y = -(1 + 3x)$$
$$5y = 1 + 3x$$
$$y = \frac{1 + 3x}{5}$$
$$y = \frac{3}{5}x + \frac{1}{5}$$

The slope-intercept form of the equation gives $m = \frac{3}{5}$ and $b = \frac{1}{5}$.

EXAMPLE 2

Find the slope of the line $10x - 6y = 72$.

Solve the equation for *y* to put it in the slope-intercept form:

$$-6y = -10x + 72$$
$$\frac{-6y}{-6} = \frac{-10x + 72}{-6}$$
$$y = \frac{-10}{-6}x + \frac{72}{-6}$$
$$y = \frac{5}{3}x - 12$$

The slope of the line is $\frac{5}{3}$.

EXERCISE 14

Finding Slope from $Ax + By = C$

Directions: Find the slope of each equation.

1. $2x + 4y = 10$ **2.** $2x - 4y = -6$ **3.** $4x + 4y = 8$ **4.** $x - y = 2$ **5.** $2x - 3y = -6$

Answers are on page 582.

Interpreting the Slope, Especially in Proportional Relationships ($b = 0$)

If a line passes through the origin, then its y-intercept is 0, that is, $b = 0$.

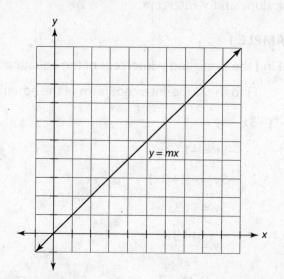

So, the equation of the line is:

$$y = mx + b$$

$$y = mx + 0$$

$$y = mx$$

EXAMPLE

Find the slope of $2y - x = 0$.

$$2y - x = 0$$

$$y = \frac{x - 0}{2}$$

$$y = \frac{x}{2} - 0$$

$$y = \frac{1}{2}x$$

So, the slope is $\frac{1}{2}$ and the line passes through the origin. This represents a proportional relationship between x and y.

Slopes of Parallel Lines

Suppose line 1 with slope m_1 is parallel to line 2 with slope m_2. Then $m_1 = m_2$. The slopes of parallel lines are equal.

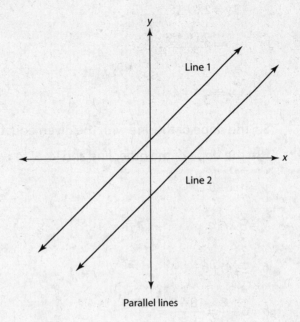

Parallel lines

EXAMPLE 1

Find the slope of the line parallel to a line with equation $-5x + 3y = 15$.

Convert the equation of the line to slope-intercept form $y = mx + b$.

$$-5x + 3y = 15$$

$$3y = 15 - 5x$$

$$y = \frac{15 - 5x}{3}$$

$$y = 5 - \frac{5}{3}x$$

$$y = \left(-\frac{5}{3}\right)x + 5$$

So, $m_1 = -\frac{5}{3}$. You know the slopes of parallel lines are equal, that is, $m_1 = m_2 = -\frac{5}{3}$.

Thus, the slope of a line parallel to the line with the given equation is $-\frac{5}{3}$.

EXAMPLE 2

Find the equation of the line that goes through (4, 6) and is parallel to the line given by the equation $3y - 2x = 15$.

Convert the given equation to the slope-intercept form $y = mx + b$.

$$3y - 2x = 15$$

$$3y = 2x + 15$$

$$y = \frac{2x + 15}{3}$$

$$y = \frac{2}{3}x + 5$$

So, the slope of the line with the given equation is $\frac{2}{3}$.

Use the slope of the other line and (4, 6) to write the equation of the parallel line.

$$y = mx + b$$

$$y = \frac{2}{3}x + b$$

$$6 = \frac{2}{3}(4) + b$$

$$b = 6 - \frac{8}{3} = \frac{18 - 8}{3} = \frac{10}{3}$$

Therefore, the equation of the line through (4, 6) is:

$$y = mx + b$$

$$y = \frac{2}{3}x + \frac{10}{3}$$

$$y = \frac{2x + 10}{3}$$

$$3y = 2x + 10$$

$$3y - 2x = 10$$

$$-2x + 3y = 10$$

$$2x - 3y = -10$$

EXERCISE 15

Slopes of Parallel Lines

Directions: Find the slope of the line parallel to each line whose equation is given.

1. $2y - 4x = 12$ **2.** $y = 5x + 8$ **3.** $8x - 7y = 9$ **4.** $3y + 2x = 3$ **5.** $4x + 5y = 12$

6. $(-2,2); -2x+3y=21$

9. $(3,-3); -2x+5y=10$

7. $(-2,3); y=3x-3$

10. $(-4,1); y=4x-10$

8. $(-4,4); x+y=8$

Answers are on page 582.

Slopes of Perpendicular Lines

Two perpendicular lines intersect at a right angle. Their slopes are negative reciprocals of each other, that is, $m_1 = -\dfrac{1}{m_2}$.

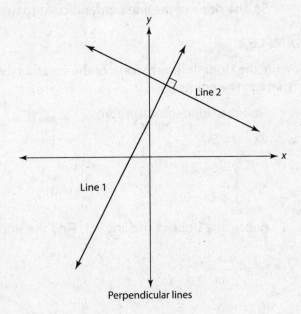

Perpendicular lines

EXAMPLE 1

Find the slope of a line perpendicular to the line whose equation is $x+4y=8$.

Convert the given equation to slope-intercept form.

$$x+4y=8$$

$$4y=8-x$$

$$y=\frac{8-x}{4}$$

$$y=2-\frac{1}{4}x$$

$$y=-\frac{1}{4}x+2$$

So, the slope of the line for the given equation is $-\frac{1}{4}$. Now, find the slope of the line perpendicular to the first line.

$$m_1 = -\frac{1}{m_2}$$

$$m_2 = -\frac{1}{m_1}$$

$$m_2 = -\frac{1}{\left(-\frac{1}{4}\right)} = (-)\frac{1}{1} \times (-)\frac{4}{1} = 4$$

So, the slope of the line perpendicular to the given equation is 4.

EXAMPLE 2

Write the slope-intercept form of the equation of the line perpendicular to $2x - y = 5$ through the points $(2, -5)$.

Find the slope-intercept form.

$$2x - y = 5$$

$$-y = 5 - 2x$$

$$y = 2x - 5$$

Hence, the slope of the line is 2. Find the slope of the perpendicular line.

$$m_1 = -\frac{1}{m_2}$$

$$m_2 = -\frac{1}{m_1} = -\frac{1}{2}$$

Substitute $(x, y) = (2, -5)$ and $m = -\frac{1}{2}$ into the slope-intercept form of the equation to find the y-intercept.

$$y = mx + b$$

$$-5 = -\frac{1}{2}(2) + b$$

$$-5 = -1 + b$$

$$-4 = b$$

Thus, the desired equation is $y = -\frac{1}{2}x - 4$.

EXERCISE 16

Slopes of Perpendicular Lines

Directions: Find the slope of the line perpendicular to each equation.

1. $4x - 3y = -1$
2. $2x + y = 3$
3. $x - 5y = -43$

4. $x - 2y = 4$
5. $2x + y = 81$

Directions: Find the equation of a line passing through the given points and perpendicular to the given equation.

6. $3x + 4y = -2; (-4, 6)$
7. $5x + 2y = -8; (-1, 2)$
8. $4x + 3y = 3; (4, 4)$

9. $7x + 4y = 16; (-5, 0)$
10. $y = -3x - 3; (4, -1)$

Answers are on page 582.

The y-Intercept of a Line

The changes in the y-intercept will change the starting value of the line on the graph.

Interpretation as Starting Value

As studied earlier, the y-intercept is the point of the line that crosses the y-axis. So, the coordinate is $(0, y)$. When graphing, you can plot the y-intercept first and start the line at this point.

Graphing $y = mx + b$ Using b as a Starting Value and m as a Direction

The slope-intercept form of the equation gives m as the slope and b as the y-intercept. You can graph the line by plotting the y-intercept and then using the slope to find another point on the line. Then you can draw the line.

Finding the Equation of a Line

Using the Point-Slope Form $y - y_1 = m(x - x_1)$

The **point-slope form** of the equation of a line with slope m that passes through the point (x_1, y_1) is $y - y_1 = m(x - x_1)$.

When Slope and Another Point Are Known

EXAMPLE

Find the equation of the line passing through (–1, 3) with a slope of 4.

Use $m = 4; (x_1, y_1) = (-1, 3)$.

Use the point-slope form of the equation of the line and then simplify to find the equation.

$$y - y_1 = m(x - x_1)$$
$$y - 3 = 4[x - (-1)]$$
$$y - 3 = 4(x + 1)$$
$$y - 3 = 4x + 4$$
$$y - 4x = 4 + 3$$
$$y - 4x = 7$$
$$y = 4x + 7$$

EXERCISE 17

Finding the Equation of a Line

Directions: Find the equation of the line passing through the given points and with the given slope.

1. $(4, 3); m = -1$

2. $(3, 5); m = -2$

3. $(7, 0); m = 4$

4. $(0, 9); m = -2$

5. $(-5, -6); m = 2$

Answers are on page 582.

When Both Points Are Known

EXAMPLE

Find the equation of the line in point-slope form through the points (–2, 4) and (1, 2).

Use $(x_1, y_1) = (-2, 4)$ and $(x_2, y_2) = (1, 2)$. Find the slope.

$$m = \frac{y_2 - y_1}{x_2 - x_1} = \frac{2 - 4}{1 - (-2)} = \frac{-2}{3} = -\frac{2}{3}$$

Substitute (x_1, y_1) and m into the point-slope form.

$$y - y_1 = m(x - x_1)$$

$$y - 4 = -\frac{2}{3}[x - (-2)]$$

$$y - 4 = -\frac{2}{3}(x + 2)$$

$$y - 4 = -\frac{2}{3}x + \left(-\frac{4}{3}\right)$$

$$y = -\frac{2}{3}x + \left(-\frac{4}{3}\right) + 4$$

$$y = -\frac{2}{3}x + \left(-\frac{4}{3}\right) + \frac{12}{3}$$

$$y = -\frac{2}{3}x + \frac{8}{3}$$

So, the desired equation of the line is $y = -\frac{2}{3}x + \frac{8}{3}$.

EXERCISE 18

Finding the Equation of a Line with Two Given Points

Directions: Find the equation of the line with the two given points.

1. (0,8) and (−1,10)

2. (0,−9) and (2,0)

3. (4,11) and (0,16)

4. (5,2) and (−1,−10)

5. (4,6) and (8,3)

Answers are on page 582.

Using the Slope-Intercept Form $y = mx + b$ When b Is One of the Known Points

EXAMPLE

Find the equation of the line passing through (2, 9) with y-intercept 4.

Here, the y-intercept b, where $x = 0$, is known. Therefore, the points to use to find the equation are $(x_1, y_1) = (0, 4)$ and $(x_2, y_2) = (2, 9)$. Compute the slope:

$$m = \frac{y_2 - y_1}{x_2 - x_1} = \frac{9 - 4}{2 - 0} = \frac{5}{2}$$

Substitute all the values into the slope-intercept form of the equation.

$$y = mx + b$$

$$y = \frac{5}{2}x + 4$$

Using the Slope-Intercept Form to Find *b* When It Is Not Known

EXAMPLE

Find the equation of the line passing through (−1, −2) and (2, 2).

You have $(x_1, y_1) = (-1, -2)$ and $(x_2, y_2) = (2, 2)$. Compute the slope:

$$m = \frac{y_2 - y_1}{x_2 - x_1} = \frac{2 - (-2)}{2 - (-1)} = \frac{4}{3}$$

Substitute the values into the slope-intercept form.

$$y = mx + b$$

$$-2 = \frac{4}{3}(-1) + b$$

$$-2 = -\frac{4}{3} + b$$

$$-2 + \frac{4}{3} = b$$

$$-\frac{2}{3} = b$$

The equation is:

$$y = mx + b$$

$$y = \frac{4}{3}x + \left(\frac{-2}{3}\right)$$

$$y = \frac{4}{3}x - \frac{2}{3}$$

Writing *Ax* + *By* = *C*

The standard form of the equation of a line is:

$$Ax + By = C,$$

where $A > 0, B \neq 0$, and $A, B,$ and C are relatively prime integers.

EXAMPLE

Write $y = 3x + 2$ in standard form.

$$y = 3x + 2$$

$$-3x + y = 2$$

$$3x - y = -2$$

Finding the Equation Given a Table of Values

EXAMPLE

Find the equation of the line that contains the points in the table.

x	y
0	3
1	7
2	11
3	15

Calculate the slope by using any two points. Use the first two points.

$$m = \frac{y_2 - y_1}{x_2 - x_1} = \frac{3 - 7}{0 - 1} = \frac{-4}{-1} = 4$$

Use the slope-intercept form to find the equation.

$$y = mx + b$$

$$y = 4x + b$$

The y-intercept is $b = 3$.

$$y = 4x + 3$$

$$y - 4x = 3$$

$$4x - y = -3$$

Thus, the standard form is $4x - y = -3$.

Finding the Equation Given a Graph

One way to find an equation of a line from its graph is to use the intercepts.

EXAMPLE

Find the equation of the line shown in the graph.

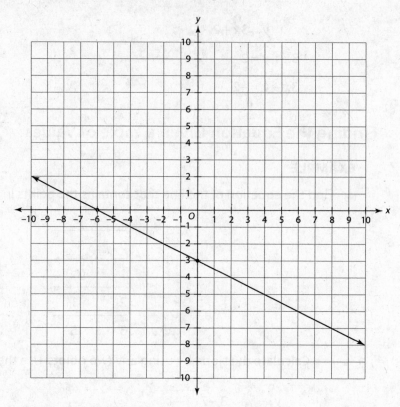

From the graph, x-intercept $= -6$ and y-intercept $= -3$. Find the slope using these points: $(x_1, y_2) = (-6, 0)$ and $(x_2, y_2) = (0, -3)$.

$$m = \frac{y_2 - y_1}{x_2 - x_1} = \frac{-3 - 0}{0 - (-6)} = \frac{-3}{6} = -\frac{1}{2}$$

Now, the equation of the line in slope-intercept form is:

$$y = mx + b$$

$$y = -\frac{1}{2}x + b$$

After substituting the y-intercept in the above equation, the equation is:

$$y = -\frac{1}{2}x + (-3)$$

$$y = -\frac{1}{2}x - 3$$

$$y + \frac{1}{2}x = -3$$

$$2\left(y + \frac{1}{2}x\right) = -3(2)$$

$$2y + x = -6$$

$$x + 2y = -6$$

Notice that to write the equation in standard form, you multiply both sides of the equation by the least common denominator of the fractions, which in this example is 2. Thus, the desired equation is $2y + x = -6$.

Special Cases

Horizontal Lines $y = b$ and Their Slopes

A straight line on the coordinate plane where all points on the line have the same y-coordinate is a horizontal line.

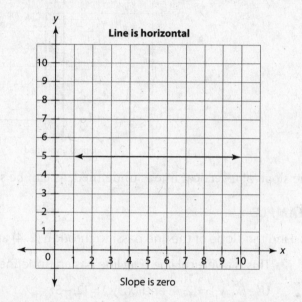

A horizontal line is given by an equation in the form $y = b$, where b is the y-intercept and the slope $m = 0$. Thus, no matter whichever two points you choose on the line, they will always have the same y-coordinate.

EXAMPLE

Find the slope of the line passing through (3,2) and (−8,2).

This is horizontal line. The slope is 0, as shown below. Use $(x_1, y_1) = (3,2)$ and $(x_2, y_2) = (-8, 2)$.

$$m = \frac{y_2 - y_1}{x_2 - x_1} = \frac{2 - 2}{-8 - 3} = \frac{0}{-11} = 0$$

So, the slope of the given line is 0, as is the slope of every horizontal line.

Vertical Lines x = a and Their Slopes

A **vertical line** is given by an equation in the form of $x = a$, where a is the x-intercept of the line.

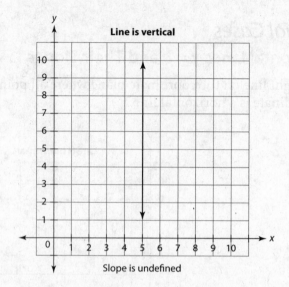

The slope of a vertical line is undefined, as can be seen in the example.

EXAMPLE

Find the slope of the line passing through (2, 4) and (2, –5).

This is a vertical line. The line has an undefined slope as shown below.

Use $(x_1, y_1) = (2, 4)$ and $(x_2, y_2) = (2, -5)$.

Using the formula for slope gives $m = \dfrac{y_2 - y_1}{x_2 - x_1} = \dfrac{4 - (-5)}{2 - 2} = \dfrac{9}{0}$. Division by 0 is undefined, so the slope of a vertical line is said to be undefined.

EXERCISE 19

Special Cases

Directions: Answer these questions about horizontal and vertical lines.

1. Find the slope of the line $y = 3$.

2. What is the equation of a line that passes through the point (5, –5) and is perpendicular to the x-axis?

3. What is the slope of the line whose equation is $y = -5$?

4. What is the slope of the line $x = -8$?

5. What is the equation of the line that passes through (4, 2) and (4, 3)?

Answers are on page 582.

CHAPTER 12

Functions

In day-to-day life, you come across different patterns of relations such as teacher-student, employer-employee, and doctor-patient. In mathematics you study **relations** such as a number m is less than number n, line l is parallel to line m, and set A is a subset of set B. A **relation** is a set of ordered pairs. In this chapter, you will learn about a special type of relation called a **function**.

Understanding Functions

A **function** is a relation in which, for each value of the first component in an ordered pair, there is *exactly one value* of the second component. It is an assignment of values from one set, called the **domain** of the function, to those of another set, called the **range** of the function. The domain values are considered **inputs**, and the range values are **outputs**.

EXAMPLE 1

Suppose each student in a class is assigned a letter grade from the set (A, B, C, D, F): A for Alan, B for Bon, C for Clive, D for Ronnie, and F for Steve (as shown in the following figure). The ordered pairs (student, letter grade), assigning to each student a grade, would be a function.

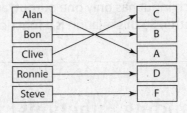

EXAMPLE 2

Tell whether the relation defines a function.

$G = \{(1, 2), (-2, 4), (3, -1)\}$

$H = \{(-4, 1), (-2, 1), (-2, 5)\}$

G is a function because for each different x-value, there is exactly one y-value. H is *not* a function. The last two ordered pairs have the same x-value paired with two different y-values (-2 is paired with 1 and 5), so H is a relation but not a function. In a function, no two ordered pairs can have the same first component and different second components.

EXAMPLE 3

Let set A = {1, 2, 3, 4, 5, 6} and set B = {2, 3, 4, 5, 6, 7}, and the relation R from A to B = {(1,2), (2,3), (3,4), (4,5), (5,6), (6,7)}. Show this relation using a diagram. Then find the domain and range of R, and examine if the relation is a function.

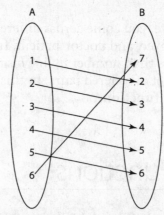

You can see that the domain = {1, 2, 3, 4, 5, 6}, and the range = {2, 3, 4, 5, 6, 7}. The relation R = {(1,2), (2,3), (3,4), (4,5), (5,6), (6, 7)} is a function.

EXAMPLE 4

Is the relation given by {(−3, −6), (−2, −1), (1, 0), (1, 5), (2, 0)} a function?

By definition, the inputs in a function have only one output. The input 1 has two outputs: 0 and 5, so the relation is *not* a function.

EXAMPLE 5

Is the relation given by {(−3, 4), (−2, 4), (−1, 4), (2, 4), (3, 4)} a function?

Each input has only one output, and the fact that it is the same output "4" does not matter. So this relation is a function.

EXERCISE 1

Understanding Functions

Directions: Determine if the relation is a function.

1. R = {(2,1), (3,1), (4,2)}

2. R = {(2,2), (2,4), (3,3), (4,4)}

3. R = {(1, f), (2, g), (3, d), (4, q), (5, t), (6, m)}

4. {(0, 0), (1, 1), (1, −1), (2, 2), (2, −2)}

5. {(−2, 2), (−1, 1), (0, 0), (1, 1), (2, 2)}

6. {(0, 2), (3, 4), (−3, −2), (2, 2)}

Representation of Functions

A function can be represented in several ways, such as verbal descriptions, tables, algebraic expressions, graphs, and lists of ordered pairs. Using functions in mathematics and in real-world applications often involves changing the representation of a function from one form to another.

Mappings

Relations can be represented graphically using **mapping**.

EXAMPLE

Show a mapping of the relation {(*a*, 1), (*b*, 2), (*c*, 3)}.

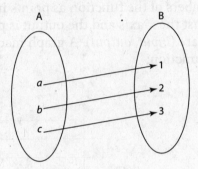

Tables

Another way to show a function is to make a table of input values versus output values.

EXAMPLE 1

Determine whether the relation in the table satisfies the definition of a function.

input	2	3	4	5	6	7	8	9	−1
output	5	4	3	9	1	2	8	6	7

Look at the first value, 2, in the input row. It is paired with 5 and never with a different value in the output row. The same is true for every input. Thus, the entries in the table satisfy the definition of a function.

EXAMPLE 2

Determine whether the table below represents a function.

input	4	0	−5	−6	7	8	−5	3	2
output	−6	2	−3	1	1	1	9	5	8

The third input value, −5, is paired with −3; the same input occurs four columns to the right, paired with a different output value, 9. Having an input value paired with more than a single output value violates the definition of a function. Therefore, this table does not represent a function.

EXAMPLE 3

The following table is a partial representation of the function whose outputs are three more than the square of the inputs. This table could have additional entries, including fractions and decimals, since it is possible to square any number and then add three.

input	-2	-1	0	1	2
output	7	4	3	4	7

Graphs

A function can be represented by a **coordinate graph**. The entries made in tables are **ordered pairs** (x, y). The graph of a function results from plotting the input-output pairs that are members of the function as points in the xy-coordinate system. The input is plotted against the x-axis and the output is plotted against the y-axis. In other words, the points (x, y) are (*input, output*). A graph made up of a collection of separated points can represent a function:

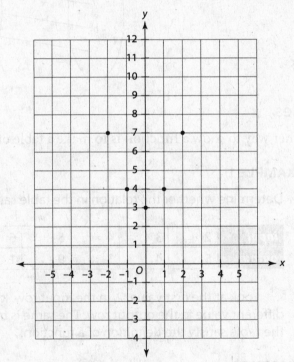

This graph is a function because every input value x is associated with only one output value y.

For instance, for the input value $x = 1$, the output value is $y = 4$, and there is no other output value associated with the input $x = 1$. Compare with the following graph:

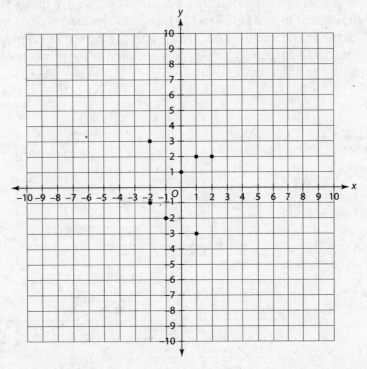

This graph is not the graph of a function because there is at least one input value associated with more than one output value. Specifically, the input value $x = -2$ is associated with two input values, $y = 3$ and $y = -1$. Whether there are other such associations is irrelevant: a single input associated with more than one output is all it takes to keep a graph or any representation from being a function.

A graph may also be a smooth curve:

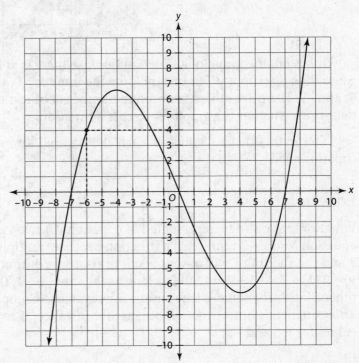

This graph consists of so many points plotted so close together that it appears as a single curve drawn with a single stroke of the pen. In fact there are an infinite number of points plotted, not only where the inputs *x* are integers but also an infinite number of fractional inputs between the integers. The arrowheads indicate that the graph continues in the manner indicated. This graph can be seen to represent a function because every input value (such as *x* = −6) is associated with only one output value (*y* = 4). Compare with the following graph:

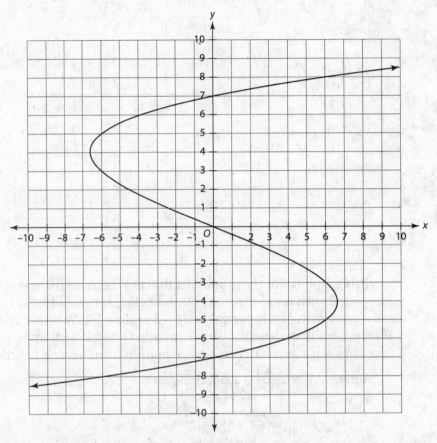

This is not the graph of a function because there is at least one input *x* associated with more than one input *y*. For instance, for the input *x* = 0, the associated outputs are *y* = 7, 0, and −7. There are others, an infinite number of others, in fact, but it only takes one to determine whether the graph represents a function.

Later in this chapter, you will learn about a well-known test of graphs for functionhood.

Equations

Functions may also be represented as equations in two variables, usually *x* and *y*. The equation *y* = 3*x* + 7 represents a function because multiplying a specific input value *x* by 3 and then adding 7 will always result in the same output *y*. For instance, if *x* = −1, then *y* = 3(−1) + 7 = −3 + 7 = 4, and as long as the input is −1, the output will be no number other than 4. The same is true for any input value *x*. Compare the equation $x^2 + y^2 = 25$. This equation is not a function because for instance, if *x* = 0, then there are two possible values for *y*, 5 and −5.

You need to be clear about which variable represents the input and which the output. Does the equation $p = q^2$ represent a function? In this case, it depends which variable is the input and which is the output. If q is the input, then the equation does represent a function because squaring a number isn't going to give different answers for different starting values. On the other hand, if p is the input, then the equation does not represent a function. If $p = 4$, then q could be 2 or –2. With a function, equal outputs can come from different inputs, but no input can lead to more than a single output. When the variables used are x and y, it is safe to take x as the input variable and y as the output variable.

EXERCISE 2

Representation of Functions

Directions: Determine if the tables below represent a function.

1.

Input	Output
–1	3
–2	5
–3	3
–5	–3

2.

Input	Output
3	–1
5	–2
3	–3
–3	–5

3.

Input	Output
1	–2
2	–2
3	–2
4	–2

Directions: Determine if the graph represents a function.

4.

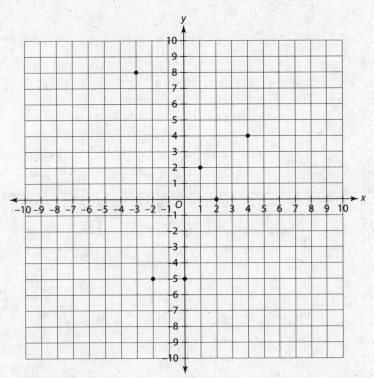

5.

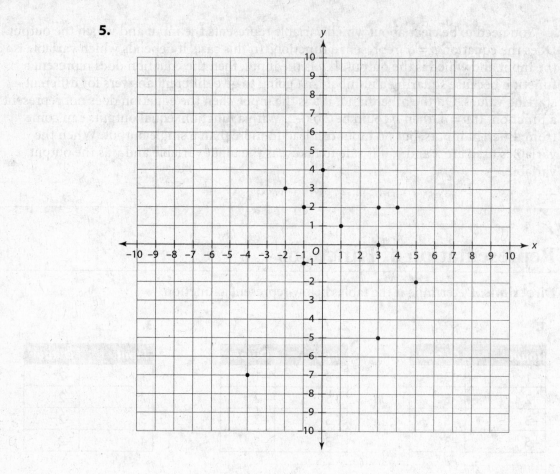

6.

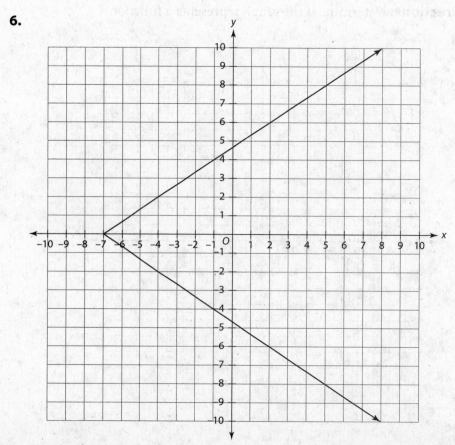

7.

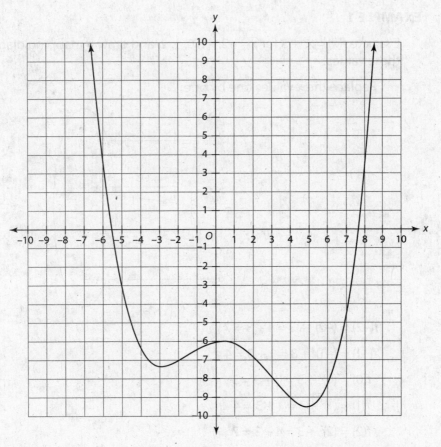

Directions: Determine if the equation represents a function.

8. $y = 2x - 5$

9. $y = x^2 + 2x - 4$

10. $x^2 = y^2$

11. $x^2 + y^2 = 4$

Answers are on page 583.

Evaluation of Functions

Function Notation f(x)

The letter f is generally used for a function. When more than one function is being considered, it is common to use the next few letters of the alphabet, g and h. When the function represents some real-world quantity, a letter suggesting that quantity may be used, perhaps w for the weight of a load of sand. In any case, given an input x, the associated **output is $f(x)$**. Although the expression looks like multiplication, it does not mean "multiply f and x" but is read "f of x" and refers to the unique output value associated with the input value x. You can **evaluate a function** by replacing its variable with a given number or expression.

EXAMPLE 1

Evaluate $f(x) = x^2 + 3$ for $x = -2, -1, 0, 1, 2$, and draw a mapping diagram showing these values.

Replace the x values one by one:

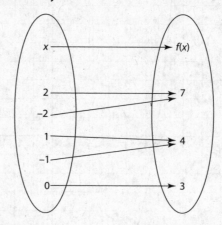

$$f(-2) = (-2)^2 + 3 = 4 + 3 = 7$$

$$f(-1) = (-1)^2 + 3 = 1 + 3 = 4$$

$$f(0) = (0)^2 + 3 = 0 + 3 = 3$$

$$f(1) = (1)^2 + 3 = 1 + 3 = 4$$

$$f(2) = (2)^2 + 3 = 4 + 3 = 7$$

The mapping diagram of the function $f(x) = x^2 + 3$ shows a general input value x being mapped to the corresponding output value $f(x)$ as well as how this mapping works for the chosen inputs.

EXAMPLE 2

If $f(x) = x^2 - 2x + 7$, evaluate $f(-2)$.

To find $f(-2)$, replace all occurrences of x in the algebraic expression with -2 and evaluate the resulting expression.

$$f(-2) = (-2)^2 - 2(-2) + 7$$

$$= 4 + 4 + 7$$

$$= 15$$

EXAMPLE 3

If $f(x) = x^2 + 2x - 1$, evaluate $f(2)$.

To find $f(2)$, replace all occurrences of x in the algebraic expression with 2 and evaluate the resulting expression.

$$f(2) = 2^2 + 2(2) - 1$$

$$= 4 + 4 - 1$$

$$= 7$$

EXAMPLE 4

Evaluate $g(x) = x^2 + 3$ for $x = -3$.

Replace x with -3:

$g(-3) = (-3)^2 + 3$

$\qquad = 9 + 3$

$\qquad = 12$

EXAMPLE 5

What is the value of $h(-3)$ if the function h is defined as $h(x) = 2 + x - x^2$?

Replace x with -3:

$h(-3) = 2 + (-3) - (-3)^2$

$\qquad = 2 - 3 - 9$

$\qquad = -10$

Evaluating a function can also mean replacing the variable with another algebraic expression such as $3m + 1$ or v^2.

EXAMPLE 1

Evaluate the function $f(x) = 1 - x + x^2$ for $x = \dfrac{1}{r}$.

To find the output value, replace all occurrences of x in the algebraic expression with $\dfrac{1}{r}$ and simplify the resulting expression.

$$f\left(\frac{1}{r}\right) = 1 - \frac{1}{r} + \left(\frac{1}{r}\right)^2$$

$$\qquad\qquad = 1 - \frac{1}{r} + \frac{1}{r^2}$$

EXAMPLE 2

Evaluate the function $f(x) = 1 - x + x^2$ for $x = a - 4$.

To find the output value, replace all occurrences of x in the algebraic expression with $a - 4$ and simplify the resulting expression.

$f(a - 4) = 1 - (a - 4) + (a - 4)^2$

$\qquad\quad = 1 - a + 4 + a^2 - 8a + 16$

$\qquad\quad = 21 - 9a + a^2$

You can evaluate functions to answer other questions.

EXAMPLE

If $f(x) = 3x^2 + ax - 1$, and $f(3) = 8$, what is the value of a?

Evaluate $f(3)$: $\qquad f(3) = 3 \cdot (3)^2 + a \cdot 3 - 1$

Then simplify:

$$f(3) = 3 \cdot 9 + 3a - 1$$
$$= 27 + 3a - 1$$
$$= 26 + 3a$$

You know $f(3) = 8$, so you can replace $f(3)$ by $26 + 3a$ and solve the equation that results for a:

$$26 + 3a = 8$$
$$3a = 8 - 26$$
$$3a = -18$$
$$a = \frac{-18}{3} = -6$$

This means that $f(x) = 3x^2 - 6x - 1$.

EXERCISE 3

Evaluation of Functions

Directions: Evaluate each function.

If $f(x) = x^2 + 2x - 1$, evaluate

1. $f(-1)$

2. $f(-2)$

3. $f(-3)$

4. $f(0)$

5. $f(2)$

6. $f(-4)$

7. $f(4)$

8. $f(-5)$

9. $f(6)$

10. $f(8)$

11. Evaluate the function $g(x) = x^2 - 3x + 2$ for $x = a - 2$.

12. If $f(x) = -2x^3 + ax^2 + 2$, and $f(2) = 14$, what is the value of a?

Answers are on page 583.

Changing from One Representation to Another

Table to Graph

The x and y values presented in a table can be plotted as ordered pairs (x, y) in a coordinate system. After plotting the ordered pairs, the dots can be connected by a line or a curve if there is some justification for doing so. One justification can be that the inputs and outputs are related by an equation.

EXAMPLE 1

Draw a graph using the values in the following table.

x	0	1	2	3
$y = f(x) = 3x$	0	3	6	9

Plot the four points and draw a line connecting the points.

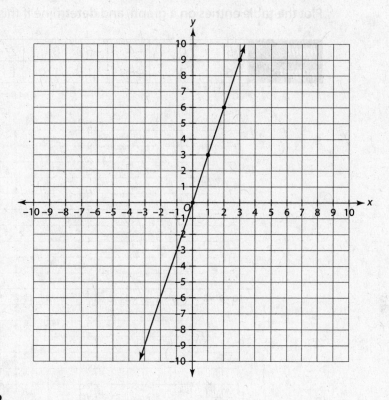

EXAMPLE 2

Plot the table entries on a graph.

x	2	3	1	4	−1	−2	−3
y	−3	4	−2	1	−2	−4	4

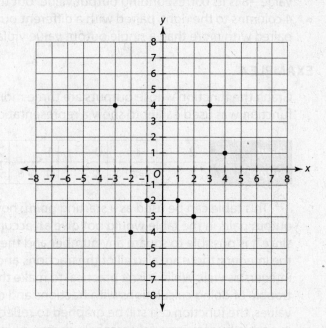

This graph represents a function. Here, there is no justification for connecting the dots.

EXAMPLE 3

Plot the table entries on a graph, and determine if this table represents a function.

input	5	0	−4	−6	8	2	−4	3	7
output	−6	3	−8	1	1	1	9	2	0

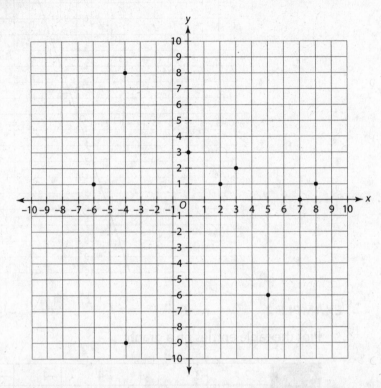

This graph does not represent a function. Look at the third input value, −4. The value −8 is its corresponding output value, but the same input value occurs 4 columns to the right, paired with a different output value, 9. Having an input value paired with more than a single output value violates the definition of a function.

EXAMPLE 4

Graph the function whose outputs are three more than the square of the inputs. This function was used earlier to show a representation of a function as a table:

input	−2	−1	0	1	2
output	7	4	3	4	7

This table can be used as a starting point; however, plotting only the input-output pairs in the table would not give an accurate representation of the function since it is possible to square any number and then add three. But consider not only the integers; there are also all of the fractions and decimals in between consecutive integers as well. While it isn't practical to make the table too large, or to go to the trouble of doing calculations with fractions and decimals and then trying to plot such values, the function can still be graphed to reflect the existence of all the points not in a table by plotting a few carefully chosen points and then drawing a smooth curve through them.

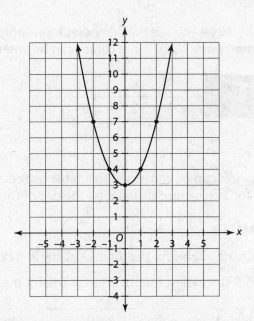

This is not to say that a smooth curve should always be drawn through the points that are actually plotted. A verbal description of the function was not given for the tables presented before this one, and for them, it cannot be assumed that there are additional input values other than the ones given.

Graph to Table

The graph of a function results from plotting the ordered pairs that are members of the function as points in the *xy*-coordinate system. Picking ordered pairs from the *xy*-coordinate system that specifies points on a graph, you can present these in a table.

EXAMPLE

Change the following graphical presentation to a table.

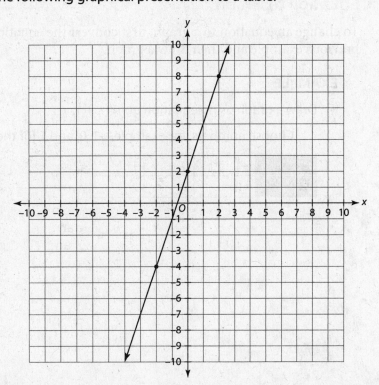

Here, you see the first point represents (−2, −4), the second point (0, 2), and the third point (2, 8). These values can be entered into a table.

x	−2	0	2
y	−4	2	8

Equation to Table

An equation can be converted to a table by replacing x with different values. The values chosen for x either are dictated by the use of the function or can be chosen randomly.

EXAMPLE

Create a table for the function $f(x) = 2 - 2x$.

The easiest numbers to choose for the x values are −1, 0, and 1.

$x = -1$	$x = 0$	$x = 1$
$f(-1) = 2 - 2(-1)$	$f(0) = 2 - 2(0)$	$f(1) = 2 - 2(1)$
$= 2 + 2 = 4$	$= 2 + 0 = 2$	$= 2 - 2 = 0$
$f(-1) = 4$	$f(0) = 2$	$f(1) = 0$

The first ordered pair is (−1, 4). Using the same process, replace x with 0 and 1 and get (0, 2) and (1, 0), respectively. Present the values in the following table.

x	−1	0	1
y	4	2	0

Equation to Graph

To change an equation to a graph, first convert the equation to a table as given in the previous example and then draw a graph.

EXAMPLE

Draw a graph using equation $q(x) = x + 1$.

Choose numbers, for example, −1, 0, and 1 for the x-value and find the y-value.

x	−1	0	1
y	0	1	2

Plot the values on a graph and connect all the points.

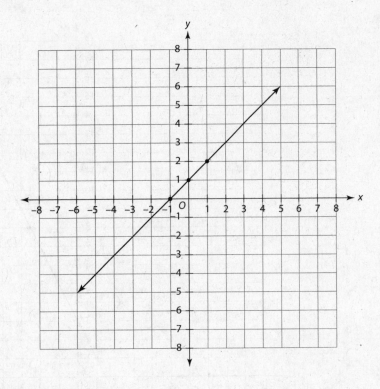

Table or Graph to Equation

In certain cases, you can convert a table of values to an equation. You often need to determine or establish additional information about the table or graph to determine what form of equation is appropriate. If you can verify that the entries in a table exhibit a constant rate of change, you can try to find a slope-intercept form of the equation, $f(x) = mx + b$.

EXAMPLE 1

Write a function for the following table of values.

x	y
−3	−3
−1	1
3	9
6	15
7	17

Using the table of data, you can draw a graph.

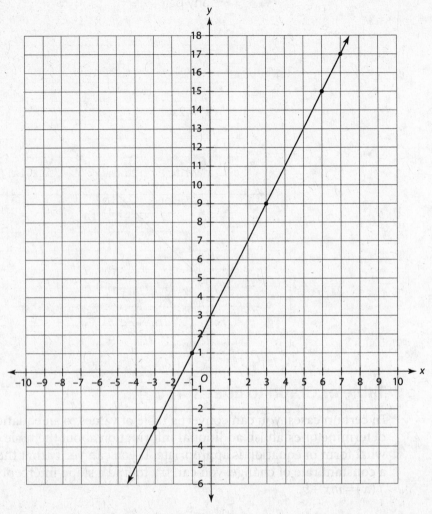

The points appear to lie on a straight line, and actually drawing the line helps to confirm this. To verify this mathematically, you need to check the slope between adjacent pairs of entries in the table. Find the differences between adjacent input values, and also between adjacent output values, as shown below. Then calculate the ratios of the output differences to the corresponding input differences. If this ratio is constant, the entries in the table are linear.

Input differences			Output differences	Ratios

	x	y		
	−3	−3		$\frac{4}{2}=2$
2	−1	1	4	
4	3	9	8	$\frac{8}{4}=2$
3	6	15	6	$\frac{6}{3}=2$
1	7	17	2	$\frac{2}{1}=2$

The constant rate of change is the slope of the line. The equation of the line is $y = 2x + b$. Substitute any pair from the table to find b. Choosing the pair $(-1, 1)$,

$$1 = 2(-1) + b$$
$$1 = -2 + b$$
$$3 = b$$

The function is $f(x) = 2x + 3$.

EXAMPLE 2

Analyze the graph and write a function.

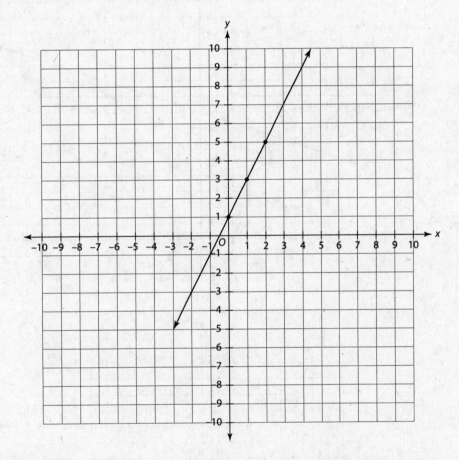

The graph is a straight line, so choosing any two ordered pairs (x, y) and finding the slope-intercept form of the equation will give the function in the form $f(x) = mx + b$. Choosing the points $(1, 3)$ and $(2, 5)$, find the slope: $m = \dfrac{y_2 - y_1}{x_2 - x_1} = \dfrac{5 - 3}{2 - 1} = \dfrac{2}{1} = 2$. To find b, it is clear from the graph that the line passes through the point $(0, 1)$, so $b = 1$. The function is $f(x) = 2x + 1$.

EXERCISE 4

Changing from One Representation to Another

Directions: Make a table of *x*- and *y*-values, and write a function.

1.

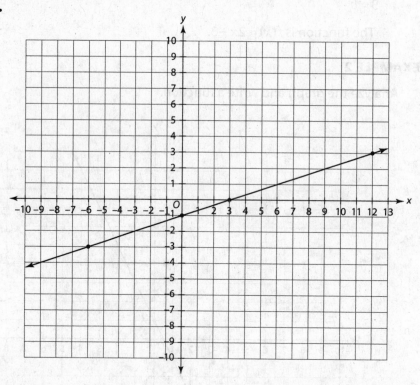

2.

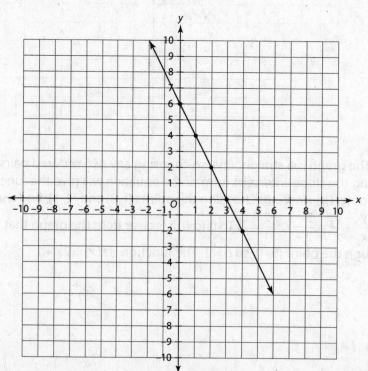

3.

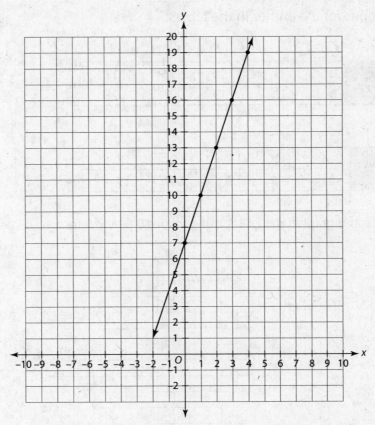

4.

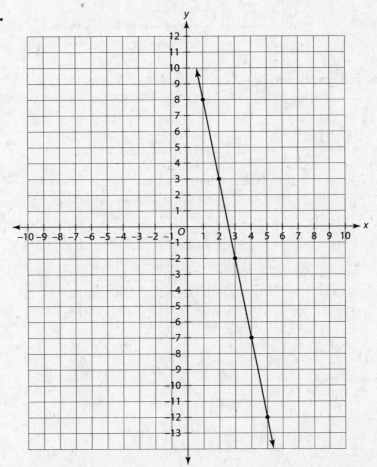

Write functions for the entries in the tables.

5.

x	0	3	6	9	12
y	1	7	13	19	25

6.

x	−4	−1	2	5	8
y	−21	−6	9	24	39

7. Evaluate and graph $f(x) = 2x + 1$ using values 0, 1, and 2 for x.

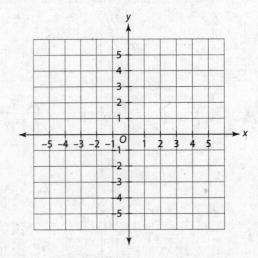

8. Evaluate and graph $g(x) = x − 1$ using values 1, 2, 3, and 4 for x.

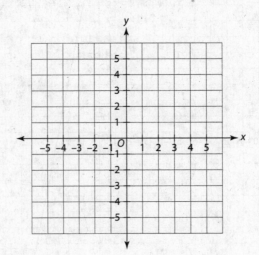

9. Evaluate and graph $f(x) = 2x^2 - 1$ using values 0, 1, −1, 2, and −2 for x.

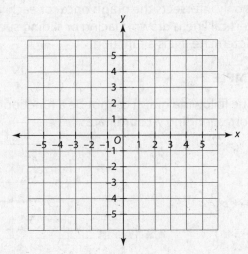

Answers are on pages 583–586.

Identifying Functions

Graphically with the Vertical Line Test

The **vertical line test** is used to determine whether a graph is the graph of a function. If a vertical line can be drawn intersecting the graph in two or more places, then the graph is not the graph of a function. If it is not possible to draw a vertical line intersecting the graph in two or more places, then the graph is the graph of a function. In other words, if every vertical line crosses a graph no more than once, the graph is that of a function.

EXAMPLE 1

The following graph of the function looks like a semicircle. Here, y is a function of x because for each x-coordinate there is exactly one y-coordinate.

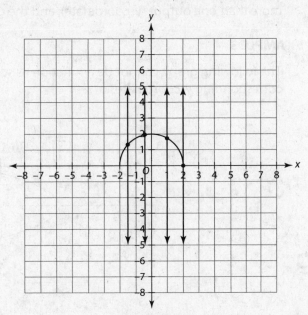

This graph passes the vertical line test. If you draw a vertical line across the graph, it only intersects the graph once for each value of *x*. This is true no matter where the vertical line is drawn. Placing or sliding such a line across a graph is a good way to determine if it is a function.

EXAMPLE 2

The following graph cannot be a function as some of the *x*-coordinates have two corresponding *y*-coordinates.

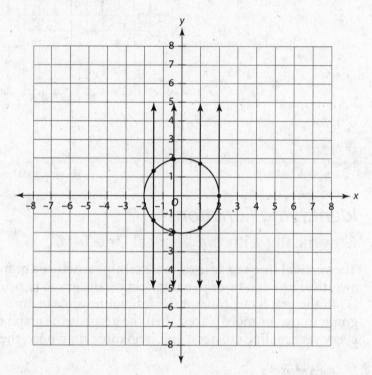

This graph fails the vertical line test. When a vertical line is drawn across the graph, it intersects the graph more than once for some values of *x*. If a graph shows two or more intersections with a vertical line, then an input (*x*-coordinate) can have more than one output (*y*-coordinate), and the graph is not the graph of a function.

EXAMPLE 3

The following graph cannot be a function as some of the *x*-coordinates have two corresponding *y*-coordinates.

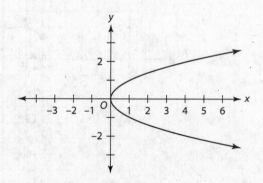

EXAMPLE 4

Draw a graph for $f(x) = 2x$ using values 2, 3, 4, and 5 for x and see if the graph passes the vertical line test.

Find y values by replacing x with values 2, 3, 4, and 5 in $f(x) = 2x$.

$f(x) = 2x$

$f(2) = 2(2) = 4$

$f(3) = 2(3) = 6$

$f(4) = 2(4) = 8$

$f(5) = 2(5) = 10$

So the ordered pairs you get are {(2, 4), (3, 6), (4, 8), (5, 10)}. Now plot the points on the graph and see if it passes the vertical line test.

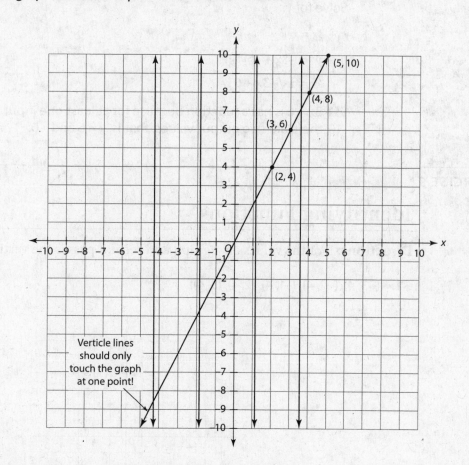

This graph passes the vertical line test. If you draw a vertical line across the graph, it only intersects the graph once for each value of x.

Mathematically from $y = f(x)$

Another way of identifying functions is to try to solve the equation for y. Then try to determine how many outputs can be associated with an input.

EXAMPLE 1

Does the equation $3x - y = 7$ represent y as a function of x?

Solve the equation for y:

$$3x - y = 7$$
$$-y = -3x + 7$$
$$y = 3x - 7$$

Since multiplying a number by three and then subtracting seven will produce equal outputs for equal inputs, the equation does represent a function.

EXAMPLE 2

Does the equation $y^2 + 3x = 6$ represent a function?

Solve for y:

$$y^2 + 3x = 6$$
$$y^2 = -3x + 6$$
$$y = \pm\sqrt{-3x + 6}$$

$y^2 + 3x = 6$ is not a function because for at least one input value, for example, $x = -10$, there are two output values, that is, $y = 6$ and -6.

EXERCISE 5

Identifying Functions

Directions: Plot the values on a graph and see if it passes the vertical line test.

1. {(−3, 4), (−2, 4), (−1, 4), (2, 4), (3, 4)}

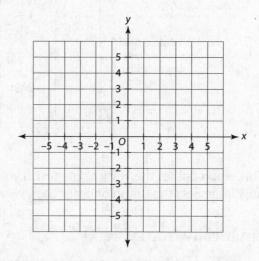

2. {(0, 0), (1, 1), (1, −1), (2, 2), (2, −2)}

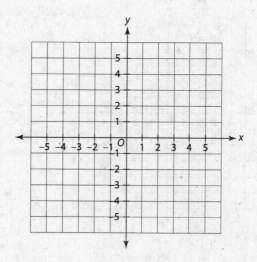

3. {(−2, 2), (−1, 1), (0, 0), (1, 1), (2, 2)}

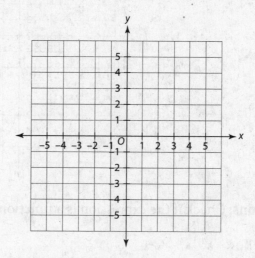

Directions: Plot entries of each table on a graph and determine if it represents a function.

4.

x	y
2	−1
2	−2
2	−3
2	−4

5.

x	y
1	4
4	2
3	−1
4	3

6.

x	y
1	2
2	3
3	4
4	5

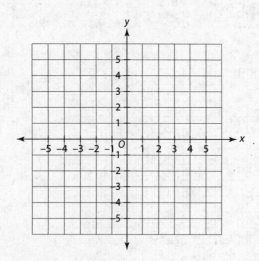

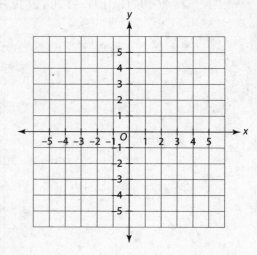

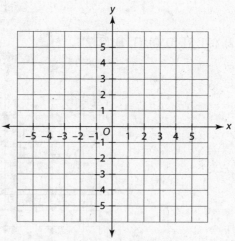

Directions: Check if the expression is a function.

7. $y = 1 - x + x^2$

8. $y = 2y^2 + 6x$

Directions: Does the graph pass the vertical line test?

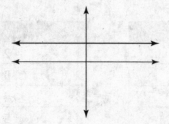

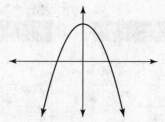

9.

10.

Answers are on pages 587–589.

Operations with Functions

You can do arithmetic operations—**adding**, **subtracting**, **multiplying**, and **dividing**—as well as composite functions with functions.

Arithmetic Operations

Addition

Look at the definition of the sum of two functions.

$$(f + g)(x) = f(x) + g(x)$$

This looks like the distributive law, but it is not. It tells you how to find the output of the sum of two functions: you find the sum of the outputs.

> **EXAMPLE**
>
> Let $f(x) = 9x - 5$ and $g(x) = 4x + 1$. Find $(f + \boldsymbol{g})(\boldsymbol{x})$.
>
> Replace $f(x)$ and $g(x)$ with their respective expressions and simplify.
>
> $$(f + g)(x) = f(x) + g(x)$$
> $$= (9x - 5) + (4x + 1)$$
> $$= 9x + 4x - 5 + 1$$
> $$= 13x - 4$$
>
> The sum of the two functions is the sum of the two polynomials.

Subtraction

You can also subtract two functions using the following definition:

$$(g - f)(x) = g(x) - f(x)$$

Again, this is not the distributive law. You find the output of a difference function by finding the difference of the outputs.

> **EXAMPLE**
>
> If $f(x) = 5x + 6$ and $g(x) = 3x^2 - 4x + 8$, find $(g - f)(x)$.
>
> Replace $g(x)$ and $f(x)$ with their respective expressions and simplify.
>
> $$(g - f)(x) = g(x) - f(x)$$
> $$= (3x^2 - 4x + 8) - (5x + 6)$$
> $$= 3x^2 - 4x + 8 - 5x - 6$$
> $$= 3x^2 - 9x + 2$$

Multiplication

Functions can be multiplied using the definition of multiplication of functions:

$$(f \times g)(x) = f(x) \times g(x)$$

EXAMPLE

Find the product of $f(x) = 2x + 1$ and $g(x) = 5x - 3$.

Replace $f(x)$ and $g(x)$ with their respective expressions and simplify.

$$(f \times g)(x) = f(x) \times g(x)$$
$$= (2x + 1)(5x - 3)$$
$$= 10x^2 - 6x + 5x - 3$$
$$= 10x^2 - x - 3$$

Division

Functions can be divided using the definition of the quotient of two functions:

$$\left(\frac{f}{g}\right)(x) = \frac{f(x)}{g(x)}$$

EXAMPLE

Divide $f(x) = 12x^3 + 15x^2 - 6x$ by $g(x) = 3x$.

Replace $f(x)$ and $g(x)$ with their respective expressions and simplify.

$$\left(\frac{f}{g}\right)(x) = \frac{f(x)}{g(x)}$$
$$= \frac{12x^3 + 15x^2 - 6x}{3x}$$
$$= \frac{3x(4x^2 + 5x - 2)}{3x}$$
$$= \frac{\cancel{3x}(4x^2 + 5x - 2)}{\cancel{3x}}$$
$$= 4x^2 + 5x - 2$$

EXERCISE 6

Operations with Functions

Directions: Perform the indicated function arithmetic.

1. Evaluate $(f + g)(3)$ if $f(x) = 4x + 7$ and $g(x) = 2x^2$.

2. If $f(x) = x - 5$ and $g(x) = -x + 8$, find $(f - g)(5)$.

3. If $f(x) = x^2 - 3x + 4$ and $g(x) = x^2 - 2$, find $(g + f)(x)$.

4. If $g(x) = 5x^2 - 9$, find $(g - g)(x)$.

5. Evaluate $(f \times g)(2)$ if $f(x) = 4x + 7$ and $g(x) = 2x^2$.

6. If $f(x) = (x - 3)^2$ and $g(x) = (5 - x)^2$, what is $(f - g)(x)$?

7. If $f(x) = (x - 3)^2$ and $g(x) = (5 - x)^2$, what is $(f + g)(x)$?

8. If $f(x) = 2x + 3$ and $g(x) = x^2$, what is $\left(\dfrac{f}{g}\right)(x)$?

Answers are on page 589.

Forming Composite Functions

Forming composite functions means using the output of one function as the input of another function. In other words, you can **insert $g(x)$ into $f(x)$**. This is written as $(f \circ g)(x)$ and read as "*f* **of** *g* **of** *x*.*"* The definition of the composition of two functions is:

$$(f \circ g)(x) = f(g(x))$$

That is, insert a value for x into g, simplify, and then insert the result into f.

EXAMPLE 1

If $f(x) = 2x + 3$ and $g(x) = -x^2 + 5$, find $f(g(1))$.

Working from the inside out, substitute the value of $x = 1$ into $g(x)$, evaluate $g(1)$, and then substitute the result into $f(x)$.

First evaluate $g(1)$: $g(1) = -1^2 + 5 = -1 + 5 = 4$.

Next, evaluate $f(4)$: $f(4) = 2(4) + 3 = 8 + 3 = 11$.

So $f(g(1)) = f(4) = 11$.

EXAMPLE 2

If $f(x) = 2x + 3$ and $g(x) = -x^2 + 5$, find $g(f(1))$.

Working from the inside out, substitute the value of $x = 1$ into $f(x)$, evaluate $f(1)$, and then substitute the result into $g(x)$.

First evaluate $f(1)$: $f(1) = 2(1) + 3 = 2 + 3 = 5$.

Then evaluate $g(5) = -5^2 + 5 = -25 + 5 = -20$.

So $g(f(1)) = -20$.

You can see from these two examples that in general, $f \circ g \neq g \circ f$.

You can also form the composition of two functions as an expression.

EXAMPLE

For $f(x) = 2x + 3$ and $g(x) = -x^2 + 5$, find (a) $(f \circ g)(x)$ and (b) $(g \circ f)(x)$.

(a) $(f \circ g)(x) = f(g(x))$

$= f(-x^2 + 5)$

$= 2(-x^2 + 5) + 3$

$= -2x^2 + 10 + 3$

$= -2x^2 + 13$

(b) $(g \circ f)(x) = g(f(x))$

$= g(2x + 3)$

$= -(2x + 3)^2 + 5$

$= -(4x^2 + 12x + 9) + 5$

$= -4x^2 - 12x - 4$

EXERCISE 7

Forming Composite Functions $f(g(x))$

Directions: Evaluate the composite functions.

1. Evaluate $f(g(15))$ when $f(x) = 2x^2$ and $g(x) = 2 - 3x$.

2. If $f(x) = 2x + 3$ and $g(x) = x^2$, evaluate $f(g(x))$.

3. If $f(x) = 3x - 1$ and $g(x) = x^2$, then evaluate $f(g(x))$.

4. If $f(x) = 3x - 1$ and $g(x) = x^2$, then evaluate $g(f(x))$.

Answers are on page 590.

A Few Important Functions

Constant Function

When all of the output values are the same for all input values, the function is a constant function, written as $f(x) = k$. The graph of a constant function is a horizontal line. In the following example, $k = 5$.

x	f(x)
−4	5
−1	5
0	5
3	5

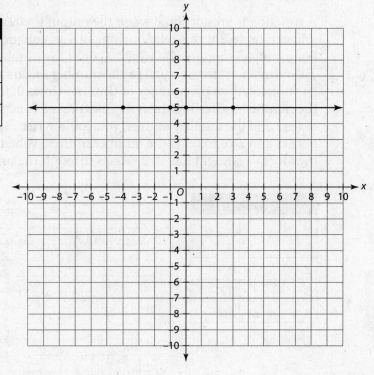

Identity Function

The **identity function** is expressed as $f(x) = x$. The identity function **does not change the input values** at all. The points plotted are $(x, f(x))$ which are the points (x, x). Joining all these points you get a straight line passing through the origin inclined at an angle 45° with the x-axis. The points $(1, 1)$, $(2, 2)$, $(3, 3)$, … are on the line.

x	f(x)
1	1
2	2
3	3

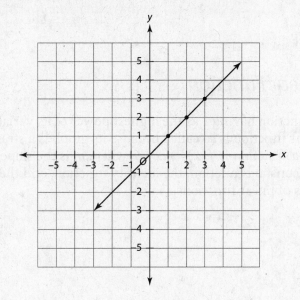

Proportionality Function

A function is proportional when the output is equal to the input multiplied by a constant. You can represent this relationship with an equation: $f(x) = mx$, where m is a constant. For example, suppose you want to count the number of tires on cars in a parking lot. The number of tires is equal to the number of cars times 4. If there are no cars in the parking lot, then the number of tires is 4 times 0, that is, 0. If there are 4 cars in the lot, the number of tires is 4 times 4. To express a functional relationship between the number of cars and the number of tires, you could write $T(c) = 4c$, where c represents the number of cars and T represents the number of tires. When proportional functions are graphed, they form a straight line that passes through the origin.

c	T(c)
0	0
1	4
2	8
3	12
4	16

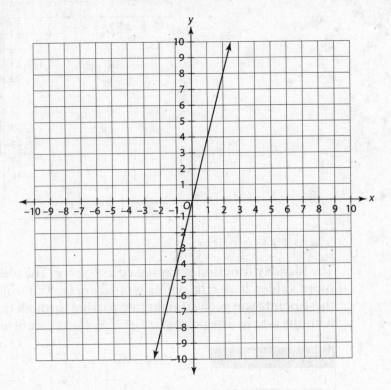

Linear Function

A function having 1 as the highest power of its variable is called a **linear function**. A linear function is so called because its graph is a straight line. The general form of a linear function is $f(x) = mx + b$, where m is the slope of the line and b is the y-intercept. The constant function, the identity function, and the proportional function are all special cases of linear functions.

EXAMPLE

Graph $f(x) = 3x + 2$.

Create a table of values for the function.

x	f(x)
−2	−4
−1	−1
0	2
2	5

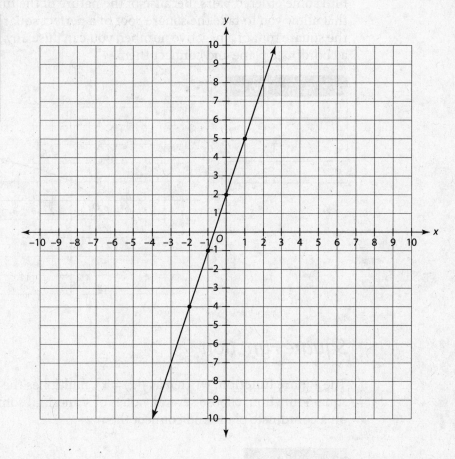

Absolute Value

The absolute value function is written as $f(x) = |x|$. To graph an absolute value function, choose several values of x and find some ordered pairs. Plot the points on a coordinate plane and connect them.

x	f(x)
−2	2
−1	1
0	0
1	1
2	2

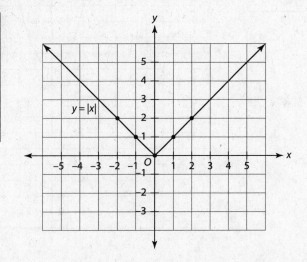

Square Root

The **square root** function is written as $f(x) = \sqrt{x}$. The square root function takes the square root of an input. To graph the square root function, choose some values of x and find some ordered pairs. Because of the nature of the function, it is best to choose values that allow you to take the square root of a perfect square. Notice that since you can't take the square root of a negative number, you can't use any negative inputs. Plot the points on a coordinate plane and connect them.

x	f(x)
0	0
1	1
4	2
9	3

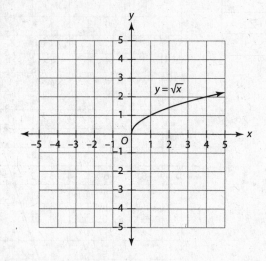

Square Function

The **square function**, written as $f(x) = x^2$, multiplies the input value by itself. To graph the square function, choose several values of x and find some ordered pairs. Plot the points on a coordinate plane and connect them.

x	f(x)
−2	4
−1	2
0	0
1	1
2	4

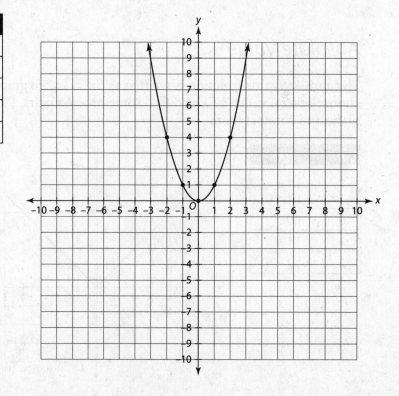

Quadratic Functions

A polynomial function having 2 as the highest power of its variable is called a **quadratic function**. The squaring function is a special case of a quadratic function. The standard form of a quadratic function is $f(x) = ax^2 + bx + c$, where a, b, and c are real numbers with $a \neq 0$. Every quadratic function has a U-shaped graph called a _parabola_.

EXAMPLE 1

Graph $f(x) = x^2 - 3$.

The following table shows several values of x and the function f evaluated at those numbers. Plot the five points on the graph of f from the table, and based on these points, draw the graph of f connecting all the points.

x	f(x)
−2	1
−1	−2
0	−3
1	−2
2	1

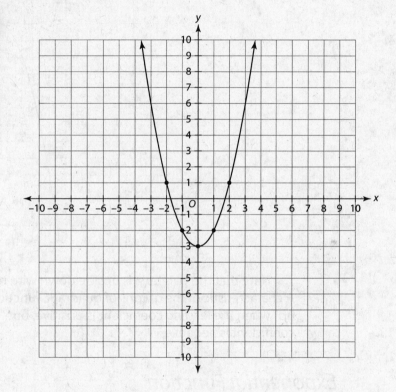

EXAMPLE 2

Graph $g(x) = 3 - x^2$.

Make a table, plot the points, and draw the graph.

x	f(x)
−2	−1
−1	2
0	3
1	2
2	−1

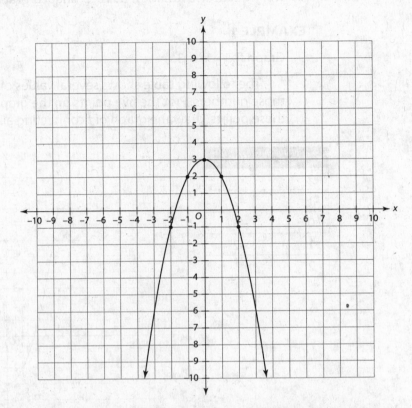

Note that the parabola is upside down with respect to the previous example. A characteristic of the graphs of quadratic functions is that they are "right side up" when the leading coefficient is positive, but "upside down" when the leading coefficient is negative.

Exponential Function

The **exponential function** is expressed as $f(x) = a^x$, where a, the base, is some positive constant other than 1. There are two cases of exponential functions to be considered, $a > 1$ and $0 < a < 1$.

EXAMPLE 1

Graph $f(x) = 3^x$.

To graph the exponential function, choose some values of x and find some ordered pairs. Plot the points on a coordinate plane and connect them.

x	f(x)
−2	1/9
−1	1/3
0	1
1	3
2	9

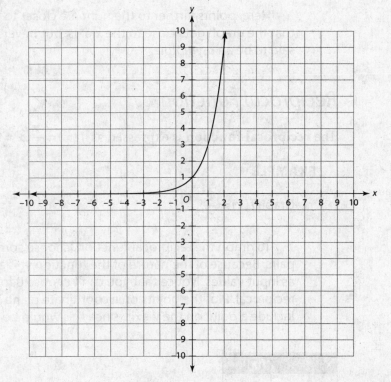

While it is difficult to accurately plot a point such as $\left(-2, \dfrac{1}{9}\right)$ on the coordinate system, the idea isn't to be perfect, but to get the general idea. For instance, the point $\left(-2, \dfrac{1}{9}\right)$ should be closer to the x-axis than the point $\left(-1, \dfrac{1}{3}\right)$, and likewise, points farther to the left should get increasingly closer to the x-axis.

EXAMPLE 2

Graph $g(x) = \left(\dfrac{1}{2}\right)^x$.

x	f(x)
−2	4
−1	2
0	1
1	1/2
2	1/4

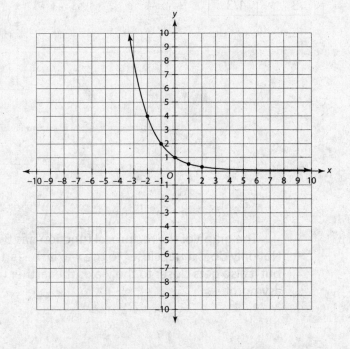

Here, points farther to the right are closer to the x-axis. In both examples, note that the graph gets close to the x-axis, but never crosses or touches it. The x-axis is said to be an *asymptote*.

Reciprocal Function

The **reciprocal function** is expressed as $f(x) = \dfrac{1}{x}, x \neq 0$.

EXAMPLE

Graph $f(x) = \dfrac{1}{x}$.

To graph the reciprocal function, choose some values of x and find some ordered pairs. Because of the nature of the function, it is a good idea to choose some fractions as input values. Notice that you can't choose 0 for an input value because 0 has no reciprocal. Plot the points on a coordinate plane and connect them. Be sure you don't include a point on the y-axis, since this would be a point with input = 0.

x	f(x)
−3	−1/3
−2	−1/2
−1	−1
−1/2	−2
−1/3	−3
1/3	3
1/2	2
1	1
2	1/2
3	1/3

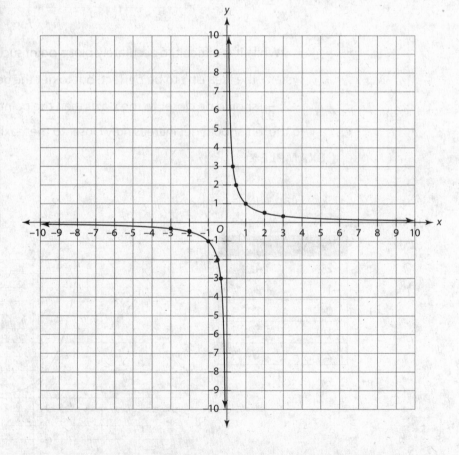

The graph of the reciprocal function has two separate, unconnected branches. Not only does it get closer to the x-axis the farther to the left or right you go, but it also gets closer to the y-axis the farther up or down you go. Both axes are asymptotes.

A Few Important Functions

Directions: Graph the following functions.

1. $f(x) = \sqrt{x+4}$ (*Hint:* Use $x = -4, -3$, and a few others.)

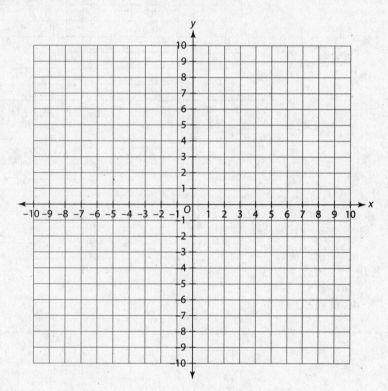

2. $g(x) = |x - 2|$

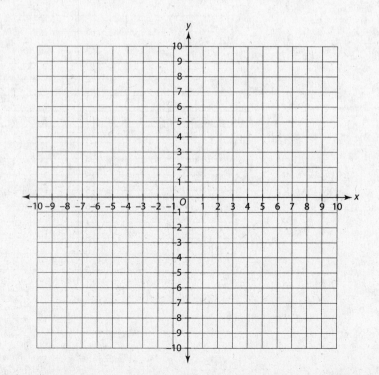

3. $h(x) = x - 5$

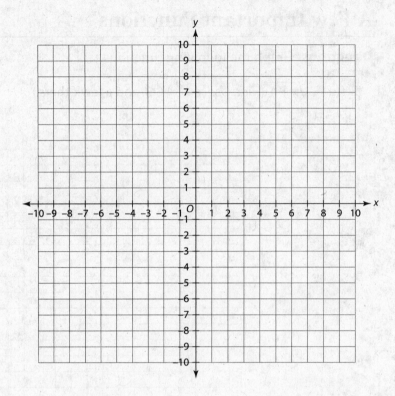

4. $p(x) = 2x$

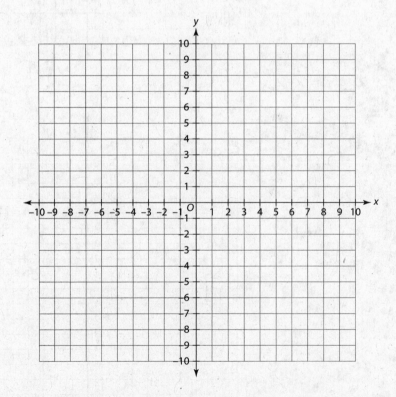

5. $q(x) = (x - 2)^2$

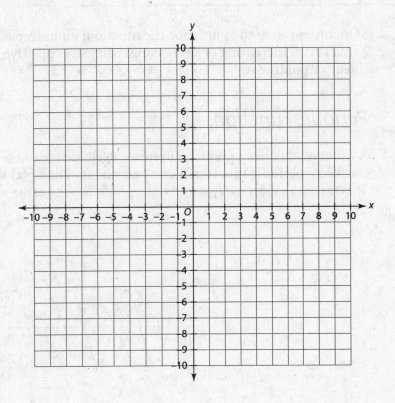

6. $r(x) = |x| - 2$

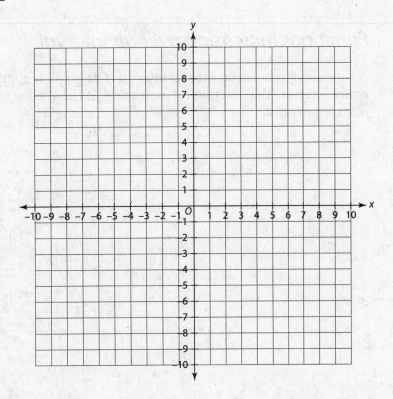

Descriptions of Functions

Sometimes you need to describe the function: for example, you may be asked whether a function is **increasing** or **decreasing**, where it is **positive** or **negative**, or whether it is **linear** or **nonlinear**.

Periodic Functions

A function that has a graph that repeats itself identically over and over a fixed interval is called a **periodic function**. For a periodic function $g(x)$ with period a, $g(x + a) = g(x)$. This means that for every a units, the graph has the same y-values as a units before.

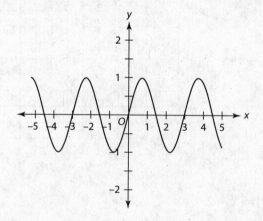

Functions Increasing over an Interval

A function is increasing over an interval if its graph is going up from left to right on the entire interval. The function is "increasing" if the y-value increases as the x-value moves from left to right.

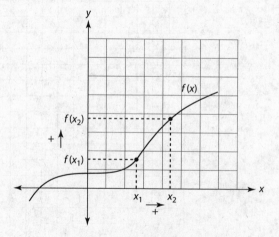

The graph of $y = f(x)$ tends to go up as it goes along from left to right.

Usually, you see intervals where a function is increasing like the one shown here:

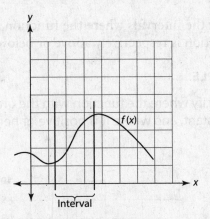

This function is increasing for the interval shown.

Functions Decreasing over an Interval

A function is decreasing over an interval if its graph is going down from left to right on the entire interval. The y-value decreases as the x-value moves from left to right.

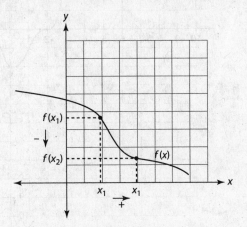

Functions Constant over an Interval

A function is constant over an interval if its graph is horizontal on the entire interval.

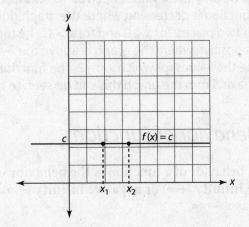

A function is constant on an interval if for any x_1 and x_2 on the interval, $f(x_1) = f(x_2)$.

Functions Positive or Negative over an Interval

To find out the intervals where the function is positive and negative, find where the graph of the function is respectively above or below the *x*-axis.

EXAMPLE

Specify where the function with the given graph is increasing, decreasing, or constant, and where it is positive or negative.

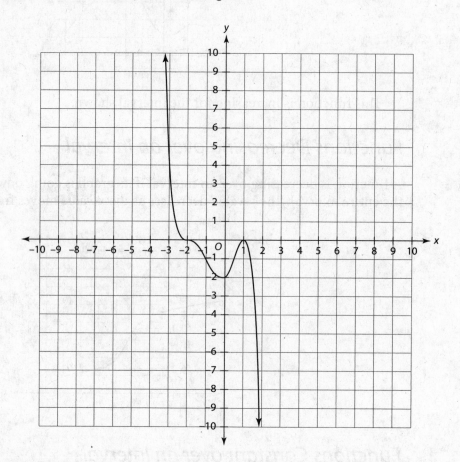

The function is increasing where the graph goes up from left to right. This looks to be only the *x*-values between 0 and 1, so the function is increasing for $0 < x < 1$. The function is decreasing where the graph goes down from left to right. This is occurring in two places: for $x < 0$ and for $x > 1$. The function is constant nowhere. The function is positive where the graph is above the *x*-axis. From the graph this can be seen to be the values for which $x < -2$. The function is negative where the graph is below the *x*-axis. From the graph this can be seen to be the values for which $-2 < x < 1$ or $x > 1$.

End Behavior of Functions

The end behavior of a function is the **behavior of the graph of $f(x)$ as x approaches positive infinity** ($+\infty$) or **negative infinity** ($-\infty$). The statement "x approaches infinity" is written as $x \to \infty$.

The leading coefficient of a polynomial function determines its end behavior. This is because for any polynomial, the leading term overwhelms all of the other terms for large enough values of x. For polynomials, there are only four possibilities:

I. When the leading coefficient is positive and the degree is even:

$$f(x) \to +\infty, \text{ as } x \to -\infty; f(x) \to +\infty, \text{ as } x \to +\infty$$

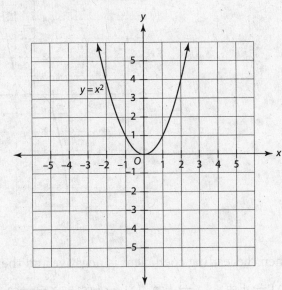

II. When the leading coefficient is negative and the degree is even:

$$f(x) \to -\infty, \text{ as } x \to -\infty; f(x) \to +\infty, \text{ as } x \to +\infty$$

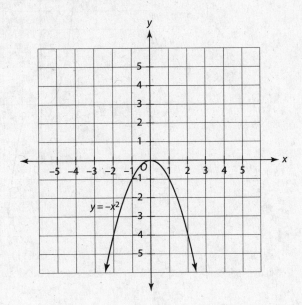

III. When the leading coefficient is positive and the degree is odd:

$f(x) \rightarrow -\infty$, as $x \rightarrow -\infty$; $f(x) \rightarrow +\infty$, as $x \rightarrow +\infty$

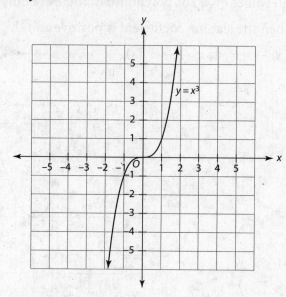

IV. When the leading coefficient is negative and the degree is odd:

$f(x) \rightarrow +\infty$, as $x \rightarrow -\infty$; $f(x) \rightarrow -\infty$, as $x \rightarrow +\infty$

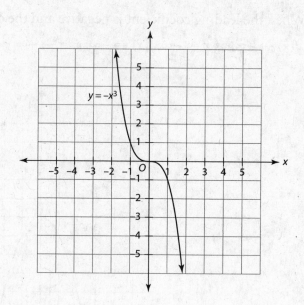

The **reciprocal function** takes the reciprocal (i.e., multiplicative inverse) of an input. The reciprocal of a very large number is a very small number, so the end behavior of a reciprocal function, for example, $f(x) = \dfrac{1}{x}$, is expressed as:

$$f(x) \to 0, \text{ as } x \to +\infty; f(x) \to 0, \text{ as } x \to -\infty$$

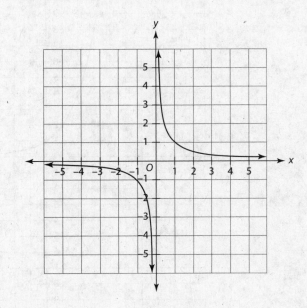

The end behavior of an **exponential function** with base $a > 1$, for example, $f(x) = a^x$, is expressed as:

$$f(x) \to +\infty, \text{ as } x \to +\infty; f(x) \to 0, \text{ as } x \to -\infty$$

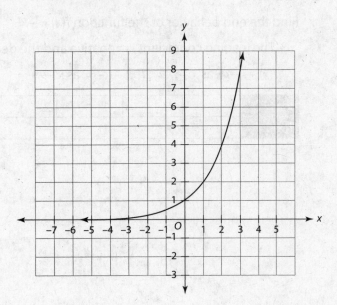

When $0 < a < 1$, the end behavior is:

$$f(x) \rightarrow +\infty, \text{ as } x \rightarrow -\infty; \ f(x) \rightarrow 0, \text{ as } x \rightarrow +\infty$$

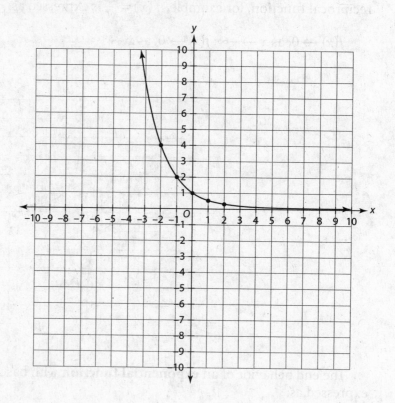

EXAMPLE 1

Find the end behavior of the function $f(x) = -x^2$.

The leading coefficient is negative and the degree is even, so the end behavior is:

$$f(x) \rightarrow -\infty, \text{ as } x \rightarrow -\infty; \ f(x) \rightarrow -\infty, \text{ as } x \rightarrow +\infty$$

x	0	1	−1	2	−2
f(x)	0	−1	−1	−4	−4

The graph of the function looks as follows:

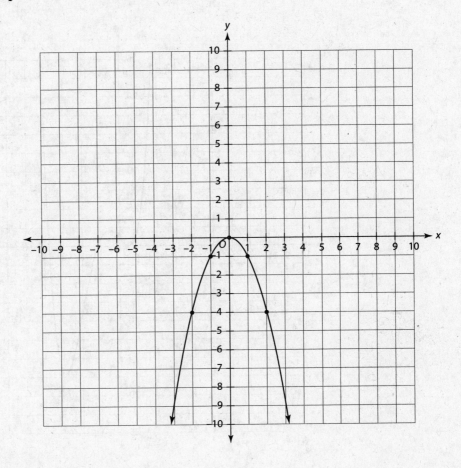

EXAMPLE 2

Find the end behavior of the function $x^4 - 4x^3 + 3x + 1$.

The leading coefficient is positive and the degree is even, so the end behavior is:

$f(x) \to +\infty$, as $x \to -\infty$; $f(x) \to +\infty$, as $x \to +\infty$

x	0	1	−1	2	−2
f(x)	1	1	3	−9	43

The graph of the function looks as follows:

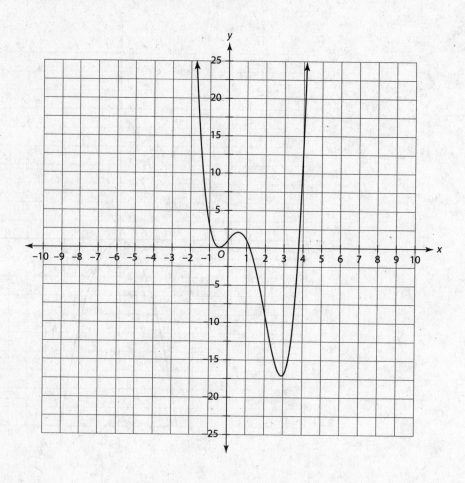

EXAMPLE 3

Find the end behavior of the function $f(x) = \dfrac{1}{x}$.

The end behavior of the function is $f(x) \to 0$, as $x \to -\infty$; $f(x) \to 0$, as $x \to +\infty$.

x	1	−1	2	−2	3	−3
f(x)	1	−1	0.5	−0.5	$0.\overline{3}$	$−0.\overline{3}$

The graph of the function looks as follows:

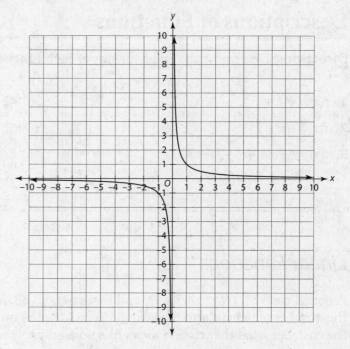

The curve consists of two separate pieces, but they should be regarded as one graph.

EXAMPLE 4

Find the end behavior of the function $f(x) = 2x$.

The end behavior of the function is $f(x) \to +\infty$, as $x \to +\infty$; $f(x) \to 0$, as $x \to -\infty$.

x	0	1	−1	2	−2
f(x)	1	2	0.5	4	0.25

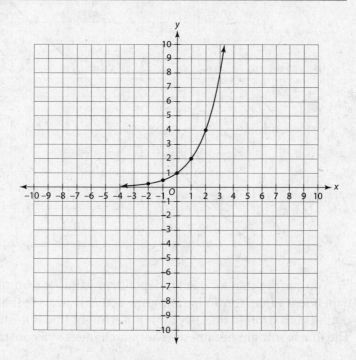

Descriptions of Functions

Directions: Determine the end behavior of each function.

1. $f(x) = x^3$

2. $f(x) = -x^2 + 2$

3. $f(x) = -2x^3 + 4x^2 + 2x - 3$

4. $f(x) = 2x^2$

5. $f(x) = 4^x$

6. $f(x) = \dfrac{2}{x}$

Answers are on page 593.

Linear Functions

A pencil costs $1, two pencils $2, and three pencils $3. So there is a relationship between the number of pencils and the cost in dollars. As the number of pencils increases, so does the cost. See what the relation looks like on a graph.

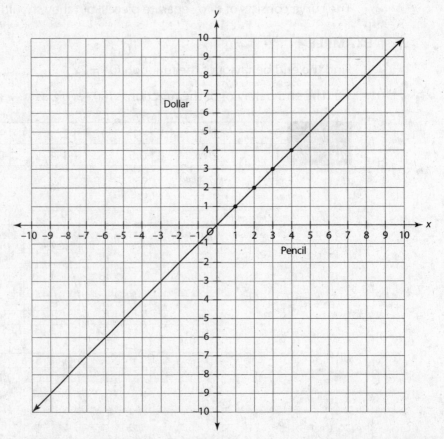

You can see that for each independent value, the number of pencils, there is a single dependent value, the dollar amount. You can also see that the graph of paired inputs and outputs is a straight line. A graph is a straight line if it is the graph of a linear function. The line is straight because the output changes at a constant rate with respect to the input.

Graph Is a Line

A **straight line is produced by a linear function**. So a straight line can be described by an equation that takes the form $y = mx + b$. In the formula, y is a dependent variable, x is an independent variable, m is a constant rate of change, and b is the y-intercept. In a more general straight line equation, x and y are coordinates, m is the slope, and b is the y-intercept. Because the equation $y = mx + b$ describes a line in terms of its slope and its y-intercept, it is called the slope-intercept form.

y-Intercept = Initial Value

The y-intercept of a straight line is where the line crosses the y-axis. Often, linear graphs represent changes over the course of time: how much something changes as time passes. For example, a survey might deal with how the population grows in a certain city, with the population increasing by a certain fixed amount every year. When $x = 0$, the corresponding y-value is the y-intercept. The y-intercept (i.e., the point when $x = 0$) also refers to the starting value; that is, the value when you start counting the time. In the population survey, the y-intercept would be the population when the sociologists started keeping track of the population. If they started taking their measurements or doing their calculations from a year, for example, 1990, then $x = 0$ would correspond to the year 1990, and the y-intercept would correspond to the population in 1990.

Slope = Rate of Change

The slope of a line measures how much the value of y changes for every unit that the value of x changes. For instance, in the line $y = \frac{3}{5}x - 2$, the slope is $m = \frac{3}{5}$. This means that starting at any point on this line you can get to another point on the line by going up 3 units and then going to the right 5 units. But you could also view this slope as a fraction over 1. You can get to a point on the line from another point by going up $\frac{3}{5}$ unit and to the right 1 unit.

As m gets larger, the line gets steeper. When m gets smaller, the slope flattens. For any two distinct points on a line, (x_1, y_1) and (x_2, y_2), the slope is $m = \frac{y_2 - y_1}{x_2 - x_1}$, $x_1 \neq x_2$.

EXAMPLE

A heavy truck travels 10 miles/hour. In 1 hour the truck covers 10 miles, in 2 hours 20 miles, and in 3 hours 30 miles. Find the slope.

The values could be paired as (1, 10), (2, 20), and (3, 30).

$$m = \frac{y_2 - y_1}{x_2 - x_1}, x_1 \neq x_2$$

$$m = \frac{20 - 10}{2 - 1} = \frac{10}{1} = 10$$

$$m = \frac{30 - 20}{3 - 2} = \frac{10}{1} = 10$$

So $m = 10$.

Zero Slope—Constant Function

The **slope of a line can be positive, negative, zero, or undefined**. A horizontal line has slope zero since it does not rise vertically (i.e., $y_1 - y_2 = 0$), while a vertical line has undefined slope since it does not run horizontally (i.e., $x_1 - x_2 = 0$). Just because horizontal lines have a slope equal to zero does not mean that they have no slope. Since $m = 0$ in the case of horizontal lines, they are symbolically represented by the equation $y = b$. Functions represented by horizontal lines are often called constant functions.

Vertical lines have an undefined slope. This is because any two points on a vertical line have the same x-coordinate, making the denominator in the slope formula, $m = \dfrac{y_2 - y_1}{x_2 - x_1}$, zero. Division by zero is an undefined operation, so the slope of a vertical line is undefined. Vertical lines are symbolically represented by the equation $x = a$, where a is the x-intercept. Vertical lines are not functions; they do not pass the vertical line test at the point $x = a$.

Positive Slope—Always Increasing

Lines in slope-intercept form with $m > 0$ have positive slope. Lines with positive slope are always-increasing functions as shown below.

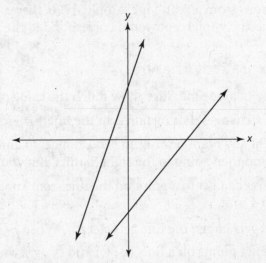

Lines with greater slopes rise more steeply. For a one unit increment in x, a line with slope $m_1 = 1$ rises one unit while a line with slope $m_2 = 2$ rises two units as shown.

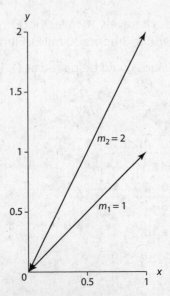

Negative Slope—Always Decreasing

Lines in slope-intercept form with $m < 0$ have negative slope. Lines with a negative slope are always-decreasing functions as shown.

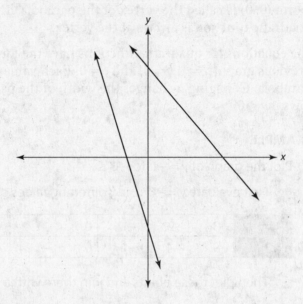

Quadratic Functions

A **quadratic function** is a **second-degree polynomial function** of the form $f(x) = ax^2 + bx + c$, where a, b, and c are real numbers and $a \neq 0$. Every quadratic function has a "U-shaped" graph called a **parabola**. Recall the graph of the squaring function $f(x) = x^2$.

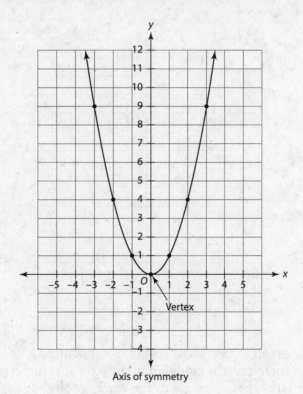

The left side and the right side of the curve are mirror images of each other. This property is called **symmetry**. The graph is said to be **symmetrical** about the y-axis, and the y-axis is called the **axis of symmetry**. The axis of symmetry has equation $x = 0$ in this example. The parabola opens upward. The minimum value of y is zero, and it occurs when $x = 0$. The point $(0, 0)$ is called the **vertex** of the parabola. The maximum or minimum value of the quadratic function is always at the vertex.

The equations for quadratic functions have the form $f(x) = ax^2 + bx + c$ where $a \neq 0$. In the previous graph, $a = 1$, $b = 0$, and $c = 0$. Each value changes the shape and location of the parabola. Changing a changes the width of the parabola, which opens up if $a > 0$ and narrows if $a < 0$.

EXAMPLE

Plot the graph of $y = -x^2$ for $-3 \leq x \leq 3$.

First evaluate $y = -x^2$ using different values of x.

x	−3	−2	−1	0	1	2	3
y	−9	−4	−1	0	−1	−4	−9

Then plot these points and join them with a smooth curve as shown.

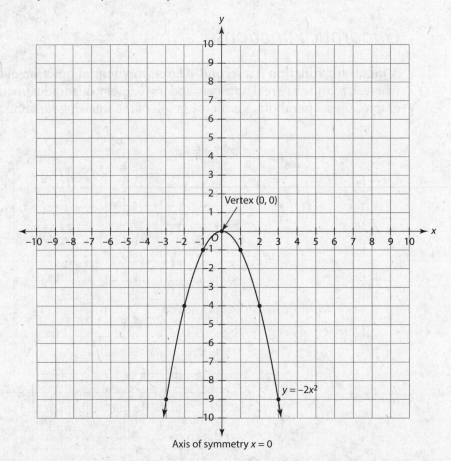

The graph is a parabola that opens downward. The graph is symmetric about the y-axis. Therefore, the equation of the axis of symmetry is $x = 0$. The maximum value of y is 0 and it occurs when $x = 0$. The vertex of the parabola is the point $(0, 0)$.

Note that if $y = ax^2$, where $a < 0$, then the graph is a parabola opening downward with the axis of symmetry $x = 0$ and vertex $(0, 0)$. In this example, $a = -1$.

Finding *x*-Intercept(s) and *y*-Intercept(s)

The *x*-intercept is where the graph crosses the *x*-axis, and the *y*-intercept is where the graph crosses the *y*-axis. The *y*-axis is also the line $x = 0$. In the same way, the *x*-axis is also the line $y = 0$.

Algebraically, an *x*-intercept is a point on the graph where *y* is zero, and a *y*-intercept is a point on the graph where *x* is zero.

EXAMPLE

Find the *x*-intercepts and *y*-intercepts of $25x^2 + 4y^2 = 9$.

Using the definitions of the intercepts, find *x*-intercepts first.

$$y = 0 \text{ for the } x\text{-intercept(s), so } 25x^2 + 4y^2 = 9$$

$$25x^2 + 4(0)^2 = 9$$

$$25x^2 + 0 = 9$$

$$x^2 = \frac{9}{25}$$

$$x = \pm\frac{3}{5}$$

Thus, the *x*-intercepts are the points $\left(\frac{3}{5}, 0\right)$ and $\left(-\frac{3}{5}, 0\right)$.

Next, find *y*-intercepts.

$$x = 0 \text{ for the } y\text{-intercept(s), so } 25x^2 + 4y^2 = 9$$

$$25(0)^2 + 4y^2 = 9$$

$$0 + 4y^2 = 9$$

$$y^2 = \frac{9}{4}$$

$$y = \pm\frac{3}{2}$$

Thus, the *y*-intercepts are the points $\left(0, \frac{3}{2}\right)$ and $\left(0, -\frac{3}{2}\right)$.

Finding Maximum or Minimum Value and Its Location

When describing the graph of a quadratic function, you may need to find a minimum or maximum value, and where the function is increasing or decreasing. The graph of $y = ax^2 + bx + c$ has its maximum or minimum value at its vertex. The vertex is a minimum if *a* is positive, and a maximum if *a* is negative. The vertex can be found by a formula: its location is (x_v, y_v), where $x_v = -\frac{b}{2a}$, $y_v = f(x_v)$.

EXAMPLE

Describe the two functions $f(x)$ and $g(x)$, using the terms *increasing*, *decreasing*, *maximum*, and *minimum*.

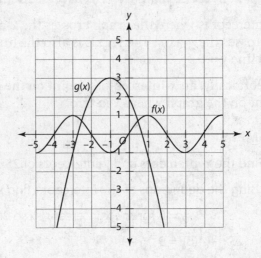

The graph of $f(x)$ is periodic. It decreases on $-3 < x < -1$, then increases on $-1 < x < 1$, then decreases again on $1 < x < 3$, and so on. It has a maximum value of 1 and a minimum value of -1, and it attains these maxima and minima many times.

The graph of $g(x)$ is increasing for $-\infty < x < -1$ and decreasing for $-1 < x < \infty$. The graph takes a maximum value of 3 at $x = -1$. It has no minimum.

Functions in Real Life

Functions can also be used in real life to solve many problems. The following are some examples where functions can be used to calculate real-life problems.

Temperature Conversion Function

Let $f(x)$ be the function to convert a temperature in degrees Fahrenheit to its equivalent temperature in degrees Celsius.

$$f(x) = \frac{5}{9}(x - 32)$$

Let $g(x)$ be the function to convert a temperature in degrees Celsius to its equivalent temperature in degrees Fahrenheit.

$$g(x) = \frac{9}{5}x + 32$$

EXAMPLE 1

Convert 98.6°F into its equivalent °C.

To convert degrees Fahrenheit into degrees Celsius, you can use the function $f(x) = \frac{5}{9}(x - 32)$.

$$f(x) = \frac{5}{9}(x - 32)$$

$$= \frac{5}{9}(98.6 - 32)$$

$$= \frac{5}{9} \cdot 66.6$$

$$= 37$$

Thus, 98.6°F is equivalent to 37°C.

EXAMPLE 2

Convert 63°C into its equivalent °F.

To convert degrees Celsius into degrees Fahrenheit, you can use the function $g(x) = \frac{9}{5}x + 32$.

$$g(x) = \frac{9}{5}x + 32$$

$$= \frac{9}{5} \cdot 63 + 32$$

$$= 113.4 + 32$$

$$= 145.4$$

Thus, 63°C is equivalent to 145.4°F.

EXAMPLE 3

Day and night on the moon can last up to two weeks each. During the daytime, the moon can reach a temperature of 117°C. What is this temperature in degrees Fahrenheit?

To convert degrees Celsius into degrees Fahrenheit, you can use the function $g(x) = \frac{9}{5}x + 32$.

$$g(x) = \frac{9}{5}x + 32$$

$$= \frac{9}{5} \cdot 117 + 32$$

$$= 210.6 + 32$$

$$= 242.6$$

Thus, the moon can reach a temperature of 242.6°F during the daytime.

Ballistic Functions

Ballistic functions are used to model projectile motion. If air resistance is ignored, then the height (h) of the projectile above the ground after t seconds can be given by the function

$$h(t) = -\frac{1}{2}gt^2 + V_0t + H_0$$

where g is the acceleration due to gravity on Earth, which is approximately 32 feet/s², V_0 is the initial velocity (when $t = 0$), and H_0 is the initial height (when $t = 0$).

The maximum height occurs at the vertex of the parabolic graph formed from the quadratic function at time (in seconds) $t = -\dfrac{b}{2a}$.

If an object is dropped, then the distance it falls in t seconds is given by $h(t) = \dfrac{1}{2}gt^2$.

EXAMPLE 1

When an object is thrown straight upward from the top of an 80-foot building, the height (h in feet) of the object above the ground is given by $h(t) = -16t^2 + 32t + 80$ at $t = 0$.

Find:
   a. Time taken by the object to reach the highest point.
   b. The highest point reached by the object.
   c. Time taken to hit the ground.

In the given quadratic function $h(t) = -16t^2 + 32t + 80$, $a = -16$, $b = 32$, and $c = 80$.
   a. First find the time at which the object reaches the maximum height.

The object reaches the maximum height at $t = -\dfrac{b}{2a}$.

$$t = -\frac{32}{2(-16)} = -\frac{32}{(-32)} = 1 \text{ second.}$$

   b. At time $t = 1$ second, the object reaches the maximum height.
So, $h(1) = (-16 \times 1^2) + (32 \times 1) + 80 = -16 + 32 + 80 = 96$ feet.
The maximum height reached by the object is 96 feet.

   c. At the ground, the height of the object is zero. So for $h = 0$, $-16t^2 + 32t + 80 = 0$.
Solve the above quadratic function using the quadratic formula:

$$x = \frac{-b \pm \sqrt{b^2 - 4ac}}{2a}.$$

Here, the variable is t.

So, $t = \dfrac{-b \pm \sqrt{b^2 - 4ac}}{2a}$

$$t = \frac{-32 \pm \sqrt{32^2 - 4 \times (-16) \times 80}}{2(-16)}$$

$$t = \frac{-32 \pm \sqrt{1{,}024 + 5{,}120}}{-32} = \frac{-32 \pm \sqrt{6{,}144}}{-32}$$

$$t = \frac{-32 \pm 78.38}{-32}$$

$$t = \frac{-32 + 78.38}{-32}, \frac{-32 - 78.38}{-32}$$

$$t = -1.45, \; 3.45$$

Time cannot be in negative. So, $t = 3.45$ seconds.

Thus, after 3.45 seconds, the object hits the ground.

EXAMPLE 2

An object is launched from a 70-foot high platform at a velocity of 50 feet/second. What will be the object's maximum height? When will it attain this height?

Initial velocity $= V_0 = 50$ feet/second

Initial height $= H_0 = 70$ feet

The height function can be given as $h(t) = -\left(\dfrac{1}{2}\right)gt^2 + V_0 t + H_0$.

$$\text{So, } h(t) = -\left(\frac{1}{2}\right)gt^2 + V_0 t + H_0$$

$$= -\left(\frac{1}{2}\right) \times 32 \times t^2 + (50 \times t) + 70$$

$$= -16t^2 + 50t + 70$$

Here, $a = -16$, $b = 50$, and $c = 70$.

The object reaches it maximum height at time $t = -\dfrac{b}{2a}$.

$$t = -\frac{50}{2(-16)} = \frac{50}{32} = 1.56$$

Maximum height at $t = 1.56$ seconds is $h(1.56)$.

$$h(1.56) = -16 \times (1.56)^2 + 50 \times 1.56 + 70 = -38.94 + 78 + 70 = 109.06$$

Thus, the object reaches a maximum height of 109.06 feet at 1.56 seconds.

Area of a Circle Function

The area of a circle can be written as a function of the radius or the diameter of the circle, as the area depends on the radius of the circle or the diameter of the circle.

Let $f(x)$ be a function that defines the area of a circle.

So, $f(x) = \pi r^2$, where r is the radius of the circle and the constant $\pi = 3.14$.

Or $f(x) = \dfrac{1}{4}\pi d^2$, where d is the diameter of the circle.

EXAMPLE 1

Find the area of the circle whose radius is 5 units.

The area of the circle can be written in the form of a function:

$$f(5) = 3.14 \times 5^2 = 3.14 \times 25 = 78.5$$

Thus, the area of the circle is 78.5 square units.

EXAMPLE 2

Find the area of the circle whose diameter is 6 units.

The area of the circle can be written in the form of a function:

$$f(6) = \frac{1}{4} \times 3.14 \times 6^2 = \frac{1}{4} \times 3.14 \times 36 = 28.26$$

Thus, the area of the circle is 28.26 square units.

Miscellaneous Problems

EXAMPLE 1

A student's income for the fall semester is given by the function $f(h) = 1,200 + 9h$.

Find $f(300)$.

The given function is $f(h) = 1,200 + 9h$.

For $h = 300$, the value would be:

$$f(300) = 1,200 + 9 \times 300 = 1,200 + 2,700 = 3,900$$

Thus, $f(300) = 3,900$.

EXAMPLE 2

The profit from selling n T-shirts is given by function $p(n) = 8n - 500$. If 70 T-shirts were sold, what is the profit gained?

The given function is $p(n) = 8n - 500$.

For $n = 70$, the profit gained would be:

$$p(70) = 8 \times 70 - 500 = 560 - 500 = 60$$

Thus, the profit gained is $60.

EXERCISE 10

Functions in Real Life

Directions: Convert the following degree temperatures.

1. 73°F
2. 13°F
3. 178°F
4. 214°F
5. 800°F

6. 100°C
7. 20°C
8. 145°C
9. 95°C
10. 56°C

Directions: Answer the following questions.

11. On the moon, the lowest temperature can be as low as −261.4°F. What is this temperature in degrees Celsius?

12. The average temperature of a town that is 100 meters above sea level is 29°C. What is its temperature in degrees Fahrenheit?

13. A typical water heating element can reach a temperature of about 4,200°C. Express this in degree Fahrenheit.

14. In humans, a drop of temperature to 90°F can cause unconsciousness, and a temperature of 78°F can be fatal. Express these temperatures in degrees Celsius.

15. An object is thrown upward at a velocity of 19.6 meters/second from a platform of height 58.8 meters above the ground. The object's height (h) in meters is $h(t) = -4.9t^2 + 19.6t + 58.8$, where t is in seconds. When does the object strike the ground?

16. An object is launched upward from a platform of 80 feet height at a velocity of 64 feet/second. What is the object's maximum height? When will the object reach its maximum height?

17. An object is thrown from the ground at a velocity of 96 feet/second. How long would the object take to reach its maximum height?

Directions: Find the area of the circle from the radius or diameter given.

18. $r = 1.5$ inches

19. $d = 9$ inches

20. $r = 3.5$ inches

21. $r = 15.3$ units

22. $d = 2.8$ units

23. $r = 22$ inches

24. $r = 5$ inches

25. $r = 7$ inches

26. Michael is traveling to France. He needs to exchange his dollars to Euros. The following function describes the exchange rate between dollars and Euros: $E(d) = 0.75d$, where d is dollars and E is Euros. If he has $300, what will be its equivalent in Euros?

Answers are on pages 593–594.

Formulas You Need to Know

You are expected to know a few basic formulas, such as those for the perimeter and area of a square, rectangle, and triangle; the circumference and area of a circle; distance; measures of central tendency (mean, median, and mode); and total cost.

Basic Formulas

distance	$d = rt$	r = rate, t = time
total cost	total cost = unit price $\cdot$ number of units	
measures of	mode = most frequent data value	
central tendency	median = number that has half of the data values above it and half below it	

$$\text{mean} = \frac{x_1 + x_2 + \cdots + x_n}{n}$$

Perimeter and Area

square	$p = 4s$	$A = s^2$
rectangle	$p = 2l + 2w$	$A = lw$
triangle	$p = a + b + c$	$A = \frac{1}{2}bh$
circle	$C = 2\pi r$	$A = \pi r^2$

(C = circumference; $\pi \approx 3.14$)

Surface Area and Volume

cube	$SA = 6s^2$	$V = s^3$
rectangular solid	$SA = 2lh + 2lw + 2hw$	$V = lwh$

(Also, see the formula for a rectangular/right prism on the next page.)

The formulas on the next page will be available when you take the GED. You do not need to memorize them, but you should become familiar with them and know what they mean and how they are used. The letter p stands for the perimeter of the base of an object; s is the length of a side of a square or cube, or the slant height of an object, depending on use; and B stands for the area of the base of a solid. Heights, h, that aren't slant heights must be measured perpendicular to the base. A radius is half of a diameter.

GED Test Mathematics Formula Sheet

Area

parallelogram $A = bh$

trapezoid $A = \frac{1}{2}h(b_1 + b_2)$

Surface Area and Volume

rectangular/right prism $\quad SA = ph + 2B \qquad V = Bh$

cylinder $\qquad SA = 2\pi rh + 2\pi r^2 \quad V = \pi r^2 h$

pyramid $\qquad SA = \frac{1}{2}ps + B \qquad V = \frac{1}{3}Bh$

cone $\qquad SA = \pi rs + \pi r^2 \qquad V = \frac{1}{3}\pi r^2 h$

sphere $\qquad SA = 4\pi r^2 \qquad V = \frac{4}{3}\pi r^3$

(p = perimeter of base B; $\pi \approx 3.14$)

Algebra

slope of a line $\qquad m = \dfrac{y_2 - y_1}{x_2 - x_1}$

slope-intercept form of the equation of a line $\qquad y = mx + b$

point-slope form of the equation of a line $\qquad y - y_1 = m(x - x_1)$

standard form of a quadratic equation $\qquad y = ax^2 + bx + c$

quadratic formula $\qquad x = \dfrac{-b \pm \sqrt{b^2 - 4ac}}{2a}$

Pythagorean theorem $\qquad a^2 + b^2 = c^2$

simple interest $\qquad I = prt$

(I = interest, p = principal, r = rate, t = time)

Mathematical Reasoning Posttest

Now that you have reviewed the topics tested on the mathematics GED® test, take this posttest to get an idea of the skills you learned by going through this review.

This posttest has 46 items, the same number of problems as on the actual GED® test. As on the Pretest, there are multiple-choice and free-response question. On the real GED® test, you will indicate your answers by clicking on the computer screen. For this paper-and-pencil practice test, mark your answers directly on the page.

To get an idea of how you will do on the real exam, take this test under actual exam conditions. Complete the test in one session and limit your total time for both parts of the exam to 115 minutes. Do not use a calculator for Part I of the test, and do not return to Part I after beginning work on Part II. Refer to the second page of formulas as needed, found on page 534, but not the first page. If you do not complete the test in the time allowed, you will know that you need to work on improving your pacing. Try to answer as many questions as you can. There is no penalty for wrong answers, so guess if you have to. In multiple-choice questions, if you can eliminate one or more answer choices, you can increase your chances of guessing correctly.

After you have finished the test, check your answers in the Posttest Mathematical Reasoning Answer Key that begins on page 547. Dividing the number of correct answers by 0.46 will give you the percentage of problems correct.

Mathematical Reasoning

46 questions | **115 minutes**

Part I

Directions: Write your answers in the blanks. Do not use a calculator for this portion of the test. Do not return to this portion of the test after beginning work on Part II.

1. Evaluate: $2^3 + (5 - 1) \div 2 \times 3$ _____

2. Compute: $711.36 - 559.73$ _____

3. Compute: $2{,}798.4 \div 24$ _____

4. Multiply: 57.4×7.92 _____

5. Find 0.4% of 85. _____

PART II

Directions: Use a calculator as needed for this portion of the test. Write your answers in the blanks or circle the correct answer choice. Do not return to Part I.

6. The expanded form of a number is 100,000 + 70,000 + 5,000 + 0 + 90 + 3. What is the number?

   A. 107,593
   B. 175,093
   C. 175,930
   D. 1,075,093

7. Divide: $786 \div (-3)$ _____

8. Multiply: $700 \times 8,000$ _____

9. Evaluate: $2^3 \times 2^2$

   A. 10
   B. 12
   C. 24
   D. 32

10. Simplify: $\sqrt{81b^2}$ _____

11. Simplify: 15^{-2}

    A. -225

    B. $-\dfrac{1}{225}$

    C. $\dfrac{1}{225}$

    D. 225

12. Rewrite $\dfrac{5}{8}$ as a fraction with a denominator of 48. _____

13. Write <, >, or = in the box to make a true statement: $\dfrac{13}{30} \boxed{} \dfrac{9}{20}$

14. Add: $\frac{8}{9}+\frac{3}{7}$. Simplify your answer.

    A. $\frac{11}{16}$

    B. $\frac{11}{8}$

    C. $\frac{83}{63}$

    D. $1\frac{20}{63}$

15. Multiply: $\frac{2}{7}\times\frac{14}{16}\times\frac{5}{10}$ _____

16. Convert 0.525 to a fraction.

    A. $\frac{21}{40}$

    B. $\frac{22}{40}$

    C. $\frac{25}{40}$

    D. $\frac{22}{30}$

17. Determine whether 2:3 and 8:12 are in proportion. _____

18. If $a = 3$, $b = 9$, and $a:b:c = 1:3:7$, find c.

    A. 7
    B. 14
    C. 21
    D. 28

19. If the scale on a map is 1 inch = 200 miles, what is the actual distance between two locations 5 inches apart on the map? _____

20. A concrete mix has 1 part cement and 2 parts sand. If 10 kg of cement are used, how much sand is needed? _____

21. Convert $\frac{1}{5}$ to a percent.

    A. 5%
    B. 15%
    C. 20%
    D. 25%

22. 9.57 is 22% of what number? _____

23. Students of a class held an election for class president. Alex and Megan were the candidates running for class president. Megan received 21 votes and Alex received 29 votes. What percent of the votes did Megan receive?

    A. 41%
    B. 42%
    C. 43%
    D. 44%

24. Jeanne rolls two dice. What is the probability that she will roll a prime number on each of the dice? _____

25. Find the mean, the median, and the mode of the data: 24, 31, 21, 24, 28, 28, 33, 35, 24, 22

    _____

26. A test has two parts, A and B, each containing 10 questions. A student needs to choose 8 questions from part A and 4 questions from part B. In how many ways can he do that?

    _____

27. How many 5-digit numbers can be formed from the digits 2, 0, 4, 3, 8 without repeating a digit?

    A. 14
    B. 96
    C. 120
    D. 144

28. If $\angle a = 120°$, find the other angles. _____

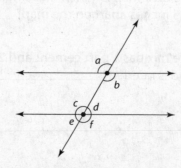

29. What is the measure of $\angle x$ in the following figure?

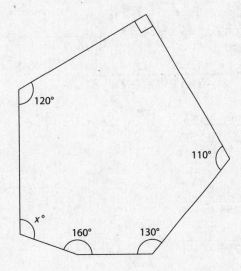

A. 20°
B. 90°
C. 100°
D. 110°

30. The volume of a cylinder is 80 meters³. If a scale factor of 2 is applied, find the new volume of the cylinder. _____

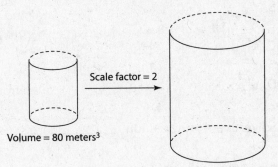

Scale factor = 2

Volume = 80 meters³

31. What is the area of a rectangle having a length of 7 inches and a width of 2 inches?

A. 5 inches²
B. 9 inches²
C. 14 inches²
D. 21 inches²

32. Expand: $(7c + 8)(2c + 9)$ _____

33. Factor: $6x^2 + 7x - 24$ _____

34. Add: $\dfrac{1}{x^2 - 3x + 2} + \dfrac{4}{x^2 + 2x - 3}$

    A. $\dfrac{5}{x^2 + x - 6}$

    B. $\dfrac{5}{x^2 - x - 1}$

    C. $\dfrac{5}{2x^2 + x - 6}$

    D. $\dfrac{5}{2x^2 - x - 1}$

35. Simplify: $\dfrac{1 + \dfrac{2}{3x}}{\dfrac{2}{x^2} + \dfrac{3}{x}}$

    A. $\dfrac{x}{4}$

    B. $\dfrac{x}{3}$

    C. $\dfrac{2x}{5}$

    D. $\dfrac{2x}{3}$

36. Solve: $8x - 4 = 2(2x + 10)$ _____

37. Solve: $7(a + 5) < 4(9 + 2a) + 4$

    A. $a < -5$
    B. $a > -5$
    C. $a < 5$
    D. $a > 5$

38. A father is three times as old as his son. Five years ago, the father was four times as old as his son. Find the present age of both father and son. _____

39. A rectangular room has an area of 1,250 square units. If its length is twice the width, find the length and width of the room. _____

40. What is the midpoint of the line that connects the points (−2, 5) and (8, −3)?

     _____

41. Find the distance between the points (−2, 1) and (1, 5) in a Cartesian plane.

     _____

42. What is the equation of the line with points (11, 100) and (12, 110)?

    A. $10x + 10 = y$
    B. $10 − y = 10x$
    C. $y = 10x − 10$
    D. $y = 10\,x$

43. Which of the points P (−1, 1), Q (3, −4), R (1, −1), S (−2, −3), and T (−4, 4) lie in Quadrant IV?

    A. Q and R
    B. P and T
    C. Only S
    D. Only R

44. Compute the function table and draw a graph of the function $f(x) = x^2 - 5$.

x	f(x)
−3	
−2	
−1	
0	
1	
2	
3	

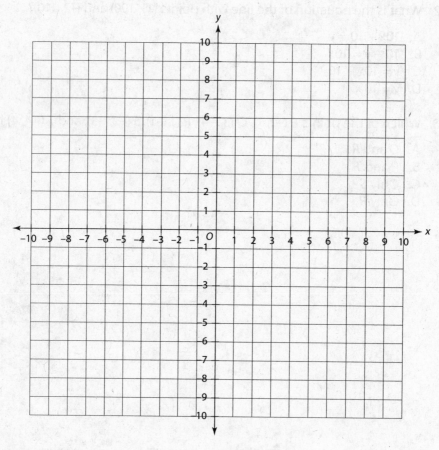

45. $f(x) = x^2 + 4x + 5$ and $g(x) = 3x - 7$. Find $f(g(2))$.

A. 2
B. 10
C. 12
D. 44

46. Over what intervals is the function in the graph increasing?

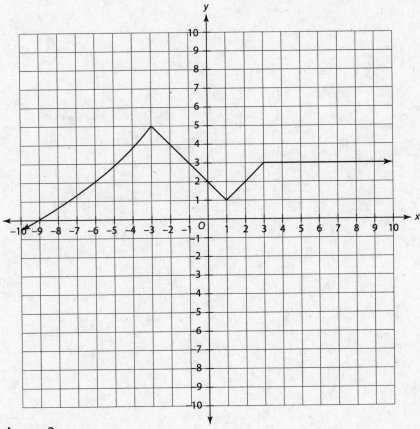

A. $x > 3$
B. $-3 < x < 1$
C. $-3 < x < 1, 1 < x < 3$
D. $x < -3, 1 < x < 3$

THIS IS THE END OF THE MATHEMATICAL REASONING POSTTEST.

Mathematical Reasoning Answer Key

1. 14
2. 151.63
3. 116.6
4. 454.608
5. 0.34
6. B
7. −262
8. 5,600,000
9. D
10. $9b$
11. C
12. $\dfrac{30}{48}$
13. <
14. D
15. $\dfrac{1}{8}$
16. A
17. Yes, they are in proportion.
18. C
19. 1,000 miles
20. 20 kg
21. C
22. 43.5

23. B
24. $\dfrac{1}{4}$
25. mean = 27, median = 26, mode = 24
26. 9,450
27. B
28. $\angle b = \angle c = \angle f = 120°, \angle d = \angle e = 60°$
29. D
30. 640 meters^3
31. C
32. $14c^2 + 79c + 72$
33. $(3x + 8)(2x − 3)$
34. A
35. B
36. $x = 6$
37. B
38. The father is 45 years old; his son is 15 years old.
39. length = 50 units, width = 25 units
40. (3, 1)
41. 5
42. C
43. A

44.

x	f(x)
−3	4
−2	−1
−1	−4
0	−5
1	−4
2	−1
3	4

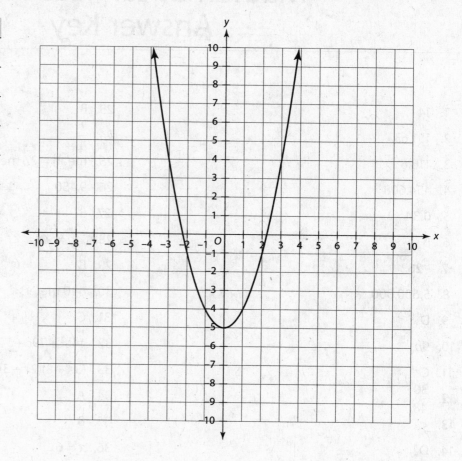

45. A

46. D

Chapter 1 Integers

Exercise 1: Understanding Place Value

1. ten thousands
2. millions
3. 2
4. 4<u>8</u>
5. 2<u>1</u>8
6. 75,3<u>2</u>5
7. 5,5<u>6</u>4
8. 3<u>0</u>8
9. 5<u>3</u>,512
10. 17<u>8</u>,320
11. 1,25<u>4</u>,740
12. 2<u>8</u>,580
13. ten thousands
14. millions
15. 20
16. 800,000
17. 4,000,000
18. hundred billions

Exercise 2: Expanded Form of Whole Numbers

1. 32,127
2. 281,321
3. 51,078
4. 643,260
5. 1,000,000 + 30,000 + 9,000 + 600 + 70
6. 40,000 + 5,000 + 10
7. 300,000 + 20,000 + 6,000 + 700 + 50 + 6
8. 100,000,000 + 20,000,000 + 3,000,000 + 500,000 + 70,000 + 7,000 + 800 + 90 + 9
9. 300,000,000,000 + 10,000,000,000 + 1,000,000,000 + 200,000,000 + 30,000,000 + 4,000,000 + 70,000+7,000 + 90
10. 40,000,000 + 2,000,000 + 100,000 + 90,000 + 8,000 + 500 + 20 + 1
11. forty-six thousand, one hundred forty-two
12. six hundred seventy-eight thousand, four hundred fifty-one

13. four million, six hundred seventy-five thousand, two hundred twelve
14. forty-four million, four hundred eleven thousand, seven hundred sixty-three
15. ninety-one billion, five hundred thirty-two million, two hundred seventy-seven thousand, five hundred sixty-three
16. thirty-four thousand, nine hundred eighty-two

Exercise 3: The Number Line

1. 3
2. 9
3. 16

4–11. (Number lines may vary from what is shown in 4–11.)

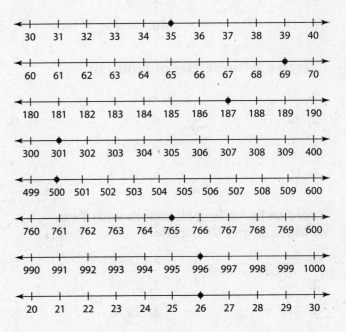

Exercise 4: Absolute Value

1. 12		**8.** 7	
2. 20		**9.** 881	
3. 1		**10.** 1,058	
4. 8		**11.** 144	
5. 8		**12.** 235	
6. 22		**13.** 405	
7. 14			

Exercise 5: Ordering of Integers

1. 0, 9, 65	**4.** <
2. −11, 34, 42	**5.** <
3. −120, −87, −18	**6.** >

Exercise 6: Adding Numbers with One Digit

1. 7	**6.** 11
2. 7	**7.** 17
3. 7	**8.** 7
4. 18	**9.** 14
5. 11	**10.** 12

Exercise 7: Properties of Addition

1. 11	**5.** 0
2. 6	**6.** 7
3. 2	**7.** 0
4. 0	**8.** 14

Exercise 8: Adding Numbers with Two or More Digits Vertically

1. 98	**6.** 1,077
2. 160	**7.** 8,737
3. 170	**8.** 9,776
4. 1,693	**9.** 17,528
5. 421	**10.** 3,579

Exercise 9: Adding Two Integers

1. 130	**5.** −106
2. 13	**6.** 0
3. −43	**7.** 148
4. −166	**8.** −102

Exercise 10: Adding Several Integers

1. 30	**5.** −119
2. −71	**6.** 14
3. −212	**7.** 68
4. −94	

Exercise 11: Subtracting on the Number Line

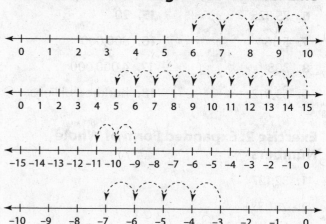

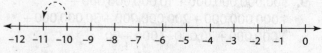

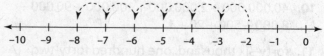

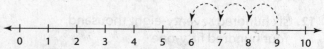

Exercise 12: Subtracting Multi-Digit Numbers Vertically

1. 80
2. 38
3. 15
4. 640
5. 568
6. 1,079
7. 307
8. 318
9. 232
10. 532

Exercise 13: Zero Digits in the Minuend

1. 15
2. 32
3. 139
4. 436
5. 560
6. 5,966
7. 513
8. 5,916
9. 6,621
10. 8,334

Exercise 14: Subtracting Two Integers

1. 103
2. −13
3. 56
4. −667
5. −844
6. −138
7. 175
8. −344

Exercise 15: Multiplying Single Digits

1. 18
2. 9
3. 32
4. 18
5. 63
6. 21
7. 30
8. 8
9. 64
10. 54

Exercise 16: Properties of Multiplication

1. 7
2. 0
3. 0
4. 9
5. 12
6. 63
7. 15
8. 39
9. 21

Exercise 17: Multiplying Multi-Digit Numbers by One-Digit Numbers

1. 345
2. 7,035
3. 4,212
4. 5,184
5. 1,818
6. 10,560
7. 3,369
8. 5,376

Exercise 18: Multiplying Multi-Digit Numbers

1. 336
2. 480
3. 1,120
4. 5,148
5. 64,750
6. 512
7. 5,432
8. 7,475

Exercise 19: Multiplying Two Integers

1. −189
2. 5,550
3. 1,152
4. −5,175
5. 975
6. −2,499
7. −1,488
8. 700

Exercise 20: Multiplying Several Integers

1. 60
2. −40
3. −126
4. −2,268
5. −140
6. 84
7. 945
8. −90

Exercise 21: Dividing on the Number Line

1. 10
2. 8
3. 7
4. 9
5. 4
6. 9
7. 6
8. 8
9. 9
10. 8

Exercise 22: Long Division Algorithm

1. 100
2. 195
3. 450
4. 307
5. 393
6. 380
7. 7,051
8. 114
9. 784

Exercise 23: Answers with Remainders

1. Quotient = 262, Remainder = 2
2. Quotient = 245, Remainder = 2
3. Quotient = 514, Remainder = 6
4. Quotient = 1,591, Remainder = 6
5. Quotient = 949, Remainder = 8
6. Quotient = 654, Remainder = 1
7. Quotient = 616, Remainder = 10
8. Quotient = 473, Remainder = 5

Exercise 24: Fractions Representing Division

1. 4
2. 21
3. 9
4. 12
5. 27
6. 12
7. 9
8. 6
9. 125
10. 49
11. 133
12. 274

Exercise 25: Dividing Two Integers

1. −7
2. −43
3. 180
4. −51
5. −111
6. 47
7. −187
8. 103

Exercise 26: Rules for Rounding Whole Numbers

1. 10
2. 260
3. 150
4. 990
5. 1,280
6. 800
7. 1,000
8. 2,300
9. 1,100
10. 13,200
11. 2,000
12. 10,000
13. 2,000
14. 78,000
15. 13,000

Exercise 27: Rounding to Estimate

1. 590
2. 1,100
3. 9,000
4. 2,400
5. 650
6. 500
7. 400
8. 6,000
9. 2,400
10. 70,000
11. 30,600
12. 1,470,000
13. 12
14. 45
15. 77
16. 29

Exercise 28: Powers of Ten

1. 1,000
2. 10,000,000
3. 1,000,000
4. 1,000,000,000
5. 10,000

Exercise 29: Multiplying by Powers of Ten

1. 5,340,000
2. 123,400,000
3. 6,726,000
4. 65,200,000,000
5. 871,300,000
6. 9,851,000,000
7. 6,540,000,000
8. 431,100

Exercise 30: Multiplying Numbers Ending in Strings of Zeros

1. 15,600,000
2. 1,080,000
3. 91,200,000
4. 70,000
5. 348,000,000
6. 256,000
7. 5,112,000,000
8. 525,000,000

Exercise 31: Integers to Powers—Even and Odd Powers

1. −32
2. 243
3. 4,096
4. 1,024
5. −512
6. 1,296
7. 1,331
8. 16
9. 1,024
10. −1,681

Exercise 32: Order of Operations

1. −327
2. 8
3. 69
4. −34
5. 188
6. −322
7. 167
8. 36
9. 35

Exercise 33: Grouping Symbols

1. 16
2. 29
3. 97
4. 12
5. 14
6. 27
7. 40
8. 61
9. 96
10. 26

Exercise 34: Memory Device for Order of Operations (Pemdas)

1. 7
2. 12
3. 21
4. 96
5. 28
6. 85
7. 520
8. 42
9. 88
10. 608

Chapter 2 Exponents, Roots, and Radicals and Properties of Numbers

Exercise 1: Prime Numbers

1. prime
2. non-prime
3. non-prime
4. non-prime
5. prime
6. non-prime
7. prime
8. prime
9. 31, 37, 41, 43, 47

Exercise 1: Prime Factorization of a Whole Number

1. $2 \times 2 \times 3 \times 3 \times 3 \times 5$
2. $2 \times 3 \times 3 \times 5 \times 7$
3. $2 \times 3 \times 5 \times 5 \times 11$
4. $2 \times 3 \times 5 \times 7$
5. $2 \times 2 \times 5 \times 7$
6. $2 \times 2 \times 5 \times 11$
7. 5×31
8. $2 \times 2 \times 2 \times 2 \times 2 \times 2 \times 3$
9. 5×113
10. $3 \times 7 \times 37$

Exercise 3: Finding All the Factors/Divisors of a Number

1. 1, 2, 4, 17, 34, 68
2. 1, 2, 3, 4, 5, 6, 9, 10, 15, 18, 20, 30, 32, 36, 45, 60, 90, 180
3. 1, 2, 4, 5, 8, 10, 17, 20, 34, 40, 68, 85, 136, 170, 340, 680
4. 1, 5, 29, 145
5. 1, 2, 4, 6, 8, 12, 13, 24, 26, 39, 52, 78, 156, 312
6. 1, 5, 13, 25, 65, 325
7. 1, 3, 5, 13, 15, 39, 65, 195
8. 1, 2, 137, 274
9. 1, 2, 4, 8, 11, 16, 22, 32, 44, 88, 176, 352
10. 1, 2, 4, 5, 8, 10, 20, 25, 40, 50, 100, 200

Exercise 4: Finding All the Common Factors of Two Numbers

1. 1, 3, 9
2. 1, 2
3. 1, 5, 25
4. 1, 11
5. 1, 5

6. 1, 2, 3, 4, 6, 9, 12, 18, 36
7. 1, 2, 4
8. 1, 5
9. 1, 5, 25
10. 1, 2

Exercise 5: Finding All the Common Factors of More Than Two Numbers

1. 1, 3, 5
2. 1, 2, 3, 4, 6, 12
3. 1, 2, 5, 10
4. 1, 2, 5, 10
5. 1, 2

6. 1, 2, 4, 8
7. 1, 5, 25
8. 1, 2
9. 1, 2, 4, 5, 10, 20
10. 1, 2, 4, 8

Exercise 6: Finding the Greatest Common Factor of Two or More Numbers

1. 7
2. 12
3. 30
4. 10
5. 9

6. 10
7. 12
8. 5
9. 4
10. 20

Exercise 7: Finding All the Multiples of a Number

1. 18, 36, 54, 72, 90, 108
2. 25, 50, 75, 100, 125, 150
3. 50, 100, 150, 200, 250, 300
4. 61, 122, 183, 244, 305, 366
5. 76, 152, 228, 304, 380, 456
6. 21, 42, 63, 84, 105, 126
7. 45, 90, 135, 180, 225, 270
8. 55, 110, 165, 220, 275, 330
9. 34, 68, 102, 136, 170, 204
10. 15, 30, 45, 60, 75, 90

11. 62, 124, 186, 248, 310, 372
12. 100, 200, 300, 400, 500, 600

Exercise 8: Finding All the Common Multiples of Two Numbers

1. 180
2. 196
3. 414
4. 90
5. 24

6. 108
7. 380
8. 150
9. 120
10. 360

Exercise 9: Finding All the Common Multiples of More Than Two Numbers

1. 360, 720, 1080
2. 360, 540, 720
3. 90, 180, 270
4. 120, 240, 360
5. 756, 1,512, 2,268

6. 360, 720, 1,080
7. 24, 48, 72
8. 72, 144, 216
9. 672, 1,344, 2,016

Exercise 10: Finding the Least Common Multiple of Two or More Numbers

1. 360
2. 8,400
3. 35,190
4. 168
5. 360
6. 4,200

7. 15,840
8. 2,160
9. 336
10. 480
11. 1,440
12. 360

Exercise 11: Perfect Squares

1. 9
2. 25
3. 49
4. 100
5. 169

6. 225
7. 625
8. 900
9. 3,600
10. 10,000

Exercise 12: Perfect Cubes

1. 8
2. 27
3. 125
4. 343
5. 512
6. 729
7. 1,000
8. 1,331
9. 1,728
10. 2,197

Exercise 13: Square Roots

1. 3
2. 5
3. 9
4. 10
5. 11
6. 14
7. 25
8. 30
9. $2\sqrt{11}$
10. $3\sqrt{11}$

Exercise 14: Cube Roots of Perfect Cubes

1. 2
2. 3
3. 4
4. 7
5. 8
6. 12
7. 13
8. 14
9. 15
10. 20

Exercise 15: Simplifying Cube Roots of Non-Perfect Cubes

1. $2\sqrt[3]{3}$
2. $2\sqrt[3]{4}$
3. $2\sqrt[3]{5}$
4. $2\sqrt[3]{6}$
5. $3\sqrt[3]{2}$
6. $2\sqrt[3]{7}$
7. $2\sqrt[3]{9}$
8. $2\sqrt[3]{10}$
9. $3\sqrt[3]{5}$
10. $2\sqrt[3]{49}$

Exercise 16: *n*th Roots

1. 3
2. 5
3. 7
4. 11
5. 10
6. $4\sqrt[3]{4}$
7. $5\sqrt[3]{5}$
8. $6\sqrt[3]{6}$
9. $9\sqrt[3]{9}$
10. $10\sqrt[3]{10}$

Exercise 17: Properties of Relations

1. Transitive property of inequality
2. Symmetric property of equality
3. Transitive property of equality
4. Transitive property of inequality
5. Transitive property of inequality
6. Transitive property of inequality

Exercise 18: Exponents

1. 1,000
2. 729
3. 10,000
4. 161,051
5. 4,096
6. 1,024
7. 243
8. 5
9. $\dfrac{9}{64}$
10. 1,296
11. Product rule
12. Extended product rule
13. Quotient rule
14. Quotient rule
15. Factor rule
16. Extended factor rule
17. Fraction rule
18. Power rule

Exercise 19: Special Cases of b^n

1. 1
2. 0
3. 32
4. 1
5. 1
6. undefined
7. 1
8. 75
9. 0
10. 81

Exercise 20: Negative Bases

1. −1
2. 1
3. −8
4. −27
5. 625
6. −100
7. 100
8. −1,331

Exercise 21: Negative Powers

1. $\dfrac{1}{8}$

2. $\dfrac{1}{125}$

3. $\dfrac{1}{216}$

4. $\dfrac{1}{729}$

5. $\dfrac{1}{1,000}$

6. $\dfrac{1}{10,000}$

7. $\dfrac{1}{1,331}$

8. $\dfrac{1}{225}$

9. $\dfrac{1}{8,000}$

10. $\dfrac{1}{625}$

Exercise 22: Fractional Exponents

1. 3

2. $\sqrt[3]{4}$

3. $\sqrt[4]{4}$

4. 3

5. 81

6. 5

7. 9

8. 3

9. 2

10. 10

Exercise 23: Simplifying Expressions with More Than One Factor

1. 11,664

2. 4,096

3. $\dfrac{1}{45}$

4. $\dfrac{1}{3,969}$

Exercise 24: Simplifying Radicals

1. 3

2. 6

3. 9

4. 10

5. 10

6. $4\sqrt{3}$

7. $2\sqrt{23}$

8. $3\sqrt{10}$

Chapter 3 Fractions

Exercise 1: Converting Mixed Numbers to Improper Fractions

1. $\dfrac{3}{8}$, $\dfrac{1}{4}$

2. $\dfrac{7}{3}$, $\dfrac{9}{9}$, $\dfrac{5}{1}$

3. $2\dfrac{1}{3}$

4. $\dfrac{19}{10}$

5. $1\dfrac{2}{4}$

6. $1\dfrac{4}{15}$

7. $1\dfrac{4}{5}$

8. $2\dfrac{2}{3}$

9. $\dfrac{17}{3}$

10. $\dfrac{39}{5}$

11. $\dfrac{17}{6}$

12. $\dfrac{209}{15}$

Exercise 2: Reducing Fractions to Lowest Terms

1. 12

2. $\dfrac{1}{2}$

3. $\dfrac{15}{39}$ is in lowest terms because the GCF of 15 and 39 is 1. No other factor greater than 1 divides into 15 and 39.

4. 10

5. $\dfrac{5}{7}$

6. $\dfrac{1}{4}$

7. $\dfrac{3}{17}$

8. 1

9. $\dfrac{1}{2}$

10. $\dfrac{10}{11}$

11. $\dfrac{3}{7}$

12. $\dfrac{11}{30}$

13. $\dfrac{1}{4}$

Exercise 3: Building Up Single Fractions

1. $\dfrac{6}{8}$

2. $\dfrac{12}{28}$

3. $\dfrac{6}{12}$

4. $\dfrac{8}{20}$

5. $\dfrac{16}{10}$

6. $\dfrac{28}{12}$

7. $\dfrac{14}{16}$

8. $\dfrac{102}{36}$

9. $\dfrac{132}{36}$

10. $\dfrac{57}{36}$

11. $\dfrac{486}{36}$

12. $\dfrac{96}{36}$

Exercise 4: Building Up Two or More Than Two Fractions

1. 15

2. 24

3. $\dfrac{9}{12}$

4. $\dfrac{5}{10}, \dfrac{6}{10}$

5. $\dfrac{8}{24}, \dfrac{21}{24}$

6. $\dfrac{35}{70}, \dfrac{42}{70}, \dfrac{50}{70}$

7. $\dfrac{20}{30}, \dfrac{18}{30}, \dfrac{10}{30}$

8. $\dfrac{175}{70}, \dfrac{28}{70}, \dfrac{50}{70}$

9. $\dfrac{12}{36}, \dfrac{20}{36}, \dfrac{21}{36}$

10. $\dfrac{45}{315}, \dfrac{189}{315}, \dfrac{175}{315}$

11. $\dfrac{32}{24}, \dfrac{15}{24}, \dfrac{20}{24}$

Exercise 5: Comparing and Ordering Fractions

1. C

2. D

3. A

4. $\dfrac{7}{12} > \dfrac{5}{21}$

5. $\dfrac{19}{18} < \dfrac{15}{9}$

6. $\dfrac{15}{7} > \dfrac{20}{56}$

7. $\dfrac{7}{20} > \dfrac{5}{21}$

8. $\dfrac{10}{5} = \dfrac{12}{6}$

9. $\dfrac{7}{9} < \dfrac{11}{13}$

10. $\dfrac{3}{8}, \dfrac{9}{16}, \dfrac{11}{12}, \dfrac{7}{4}$

11. $\dfrac{1}{2}, \dfrac{3}{5}, \dfrac{2}{3}, \dfrac{5}{7}$

12. $\dfrac{7}{20}, \dfrac{5}{12}, \dfrac{10}{12}, \dfrac{13}{8}$

13. $\dfrac{17}{14}, \dfrac{6}{7}, \dfrac{3}{21}, \dfrac{2}{35}$

14. $\dfrac{6}{5}, \dfrac{7}{11}, \dfrac{5}{9}, \dfrac{3}{7}$

15. $\dfrac{7}{9}, \dfrac{10}{18}, \dfrac{3}{6}, \dfrac{5}{12}, \dfrac{5}{18}$

Exercise 6: Adding or Subtracting Proper Fractions with the Same Denominator

1. $\dfrac{4}{3}$

2. $\dfrac{5}{9}$

3. $\dfrac{34}{25} = 1\dfrac{9}{25}$

4. $\dfrac{41}{6} = 6\dfrac{5}{6}$

5. $\dfrac{44}{5} = 8\dfrac{4}{5}$

6. $\dfrac{62}{67}$

7. $\dfrac{100}{100} = 1$

8. $\dfrac{9}{20}$

9. $\dfrac{3}{18}$

10. $\dfrac{2}{5}$

11. $\dfrac{33}{8} = 4\dfrac{1}{8}$

12. $\dfrac{35}{54}$

13. $\dfrac{28}{45}$

14. $\dfrac{1}{3}$

Exercise 7: Adding or Subtracting Proper Fractions with Different Denominators

1. $\frac{29}{35}$

2. $\frac{8}{9}$

3. $\frac{839}{550} = 1\frac{289}{550}$

4. $\frac{38}{5} = 7\frac{3}{5}$

5. $\frac{356}{63} = 5\frac{41}{63}$

6. $\frac{4,054}{4,355}$

7. $\frac{149}{15} = 9\frac{14}{15}$

8. $\frac{141}{140} = 1\frac{1}{140}$

9. $\frac{13}{36}$

10. $\frac{3}{28}$

11. $\frac{67}{46} = 1\frac{21}{46}$

12. $\frac{25}{4} = 6\frac{1}{4}$

13. $\frac{2}{3}$

14. $\frac{7}{20}$

Exercise 8: Adding Mixed Numbers

1. $3\frac{2}{3}$

2. 3

3. $12\frac{1}{2}$

4. $16\frac{1}{6}$

5. $11\frac{11}{17}$

6. $8\frac{3}{23}$

7. $32\frac{14}{19}$

8. 7

9. 16

10. $15\frac{2}{3}$

Exercise 9: Adding Mixed Numbers and Simplifying

1. $13\frac{13}{20}$

2. $4\frac{5}{12}$

3. $13\frac{5}{12}$

4. $21\frac{1}{7}$

5. $11\frac{4}{5}$

6. $12\frac{1}{2}$

7. $8\frac{1}{10}$

8. $5\frac{7}{6}$

9. $7\frac{31}{72}$

10. $13\frac{5}{7}$

11. $8\frac{1}{8}$

Exercise 10: Subtracting Mixed Numbers

1. $5\frac{4}{7}$

2. $5\frac{1}{2}$

3. $7\frac{9}{17}$

4. $2\frac{1}{23}$

5. $6\frac{4}{19}$

6. $5\frac{3}{5}$

7. $21\frac{3}{10}$

8. $7\frac{2}{15}$

9. $9\frac{1}{21}$

10. $4\frac{1}{8}$

11. $4\frac{2}{9}$

12. $7\frac{5}{24}$

Exercise 11: Subtracting Mixed Numbers with Borrowing

1. $3\frac{1}{2}$

2. $4\frac{14}{15}$

3. $2\frac{3}{4}$

4. $4\frac{3}{5}$

5. $2\frac{7}{8}$

6. $6\frac{7}{10}$

7. $9\frac{7}{9}$

8. $10\frac{9}{14}$

9. $7\frac{17}{20}$

10. $4\frac{11}{12}$

11. $4\frac{13}{18}$

12. $2\frac{11}{12}$

Exercise 12: Multiplying Fractions

1. $\frac{14}{25}$

2. $\frac{9}{25}$

3. $\frac{25}{27}$

4. $\frac{4}{63}$

5. $\frac{10}{81}$

6. $\frac{160}{693}$

7. $\frac{25}{108}$

8. $\frac{14}{165}$

9. $\frac{2}{5}$

10. 1

11. $\frac{2}{5}$

12. $\frac{1}{2}$

13. $\dfrac{21}{32}$ **15.** $\dfrac{8}{5}$

14. $\dfrac{1}{12}$ **16.** $\dfrac{4}{15}$

Exercise 13: Multiplying Mixed Numbers

1. $19\dfrac{1}{4}$ **6.** 20

2. $38\dfrac{8}{9}$ **7.** $20\dfrac{5}{8}$

3. $7\dfrac{5}{7}$ **8.** $18\dfrac{3}{7}$

4. $70\dfrac{13}{18}$ **9.** $12\dfrac{5}{18}$

5. $84\dfrac{33}{40}$ **10.** $292\dfrac{3}{5}$

Exercise 14: Dividing Fractions

1. $\dfrac{2}{5}$ **6.** $\dfrac{1}{3}$

2. 2   **7.** 1

3. $\dfrac{4}{5}$ **8.** $\dfrac{3}{4}$

4. $\dfrac{2}{3}$ **9.** $\dfrac{1}{6}$

5. 1   **10.** $\dfrac{1}{25}$

Exercise 15: Dividing Mixed Numbers

1. $\dfrac{21}{32}$ **6.** $2\dfrac{2}{21}$

2. $1\dfrac{1}{7}$ **7.** $1\dfrac{5}{46}$

3. $\dfrac{7}{24}$ **8.** $1\dfrac{5}{14}$

4. $1\dfrac{37}{134}$ **9.** 5/9

5. $\dfrac{65}{116}$ **10.** 2-1/52

Exercise 16: Raising Fractions to Powers

1. D   **6.** $\dfrac{25}{36}, \dfrac{125}{216}$

2. A   **7.** $\dfrac{49}{9}, \dfrac{343}{27}$

3. $\dfrac{1}{64}, \dfrac{1}{512}$ **8.** $\dfrac{4}{81}, \dfrac{8}{729}$

4. $\dfrac{9}{16}, \dfrac{27}{64}$ **9.** $\dfrac{9}{64}, \dfrac{27}{512}$

5. $\dfrac{36}{144}, \dfrac{216}{1,728}$ **10.** $\dfrac{4}{49}, \dfrac{8}{343}$

Exercise 17: Square Roots and Cube Roots of Fractions

1. $\dfrac{7}{12}$ **6.** $\dfrac{5}{7}$

2. $\dfrac{13}{11}$ **7.** $\dfrac{6\sqrt[3]{3}}{5}$

3. $\dfrac{4\sqrt{2}}{10}$ **8.** $\dfrac{5}{8}$

4. $\dfrac{4\sqrt{2}}{9}$ **9.** $\dfrac{4}{7}$

5. $\dfrac{15}{25}$ **10.** Should be "3 on the cube root of 4 over 10" [in numbers]

Exercise 18: Fractions and the Order of Operations

1. 75   **6.** 18

2. 33-1/2   **7.** $29\dfrac{1}{2}$

3. $13\dfrac{3}{4}$ **8.** $14\dfrac{1}{4}$

4. 15   **9.** $1\dfrac{3}{5}$

5. $20\dfrac{7}{9}$ **10.** $2\sqrt{5}+4$

Chapter 4 Decimals

Exercise 1: Understanding Decimals

1. 0.1

2. 0.02

3. 0.1

4. 0.008

5. 0.0011

6. 50   60   63   70

7. 70   75.5   80   90

8. 90   100 101.2   110

9. Tenths

10. Thousandths

11. Hundredths

12. Ten-thousandths

Exercise 2: Reading and Writing Decimals

1. 0.6

2. 0.15

3. 0.4008

4. 0.609

5. 0.00001

6. 16.5

7. 1.008

8. 8.004004

9. 30.32

10. 42.05

Exercise 3: Comparing Decimals

1. B

2. D

3. A

4. D

5. 0.0012

6. 0.3113

7. 72.0456

8. 9.01565

9. 105.1

10. 0.6515

11. 0.8901

12. 90.1005

Exercise 4: Rounding Decimals

1. 157.83

2. 0.103

3. 5.7893

4. $125.46

5. 1.4

6. 0.8

7. 1.0

8. 0.8

9. 0.6

10. 10.3

Exercise 5: Addition of Decimals

1. 98.29

2. 238.31

3. 26.63

4. 44.919

5. 16.412

6. 4.87

7. 27.133

8. 114.122

9. 1,021.507

10. 1,003.5242

Exercise 6: Subtraction of Decimals

1. 1.83

2. 81.8109

3. 20.696

4. 0.00072

5. 0.768

6. 71.185

7. 891.0901

8. 14.13

Exercise 7: Multiplication of Decimals

1. 0.004

2. 2133

3. 36.91

4. 0.00292

5. 464.1648

6. 439.4928

7. 781.4118

8. 855.7384

Exercise 8: Division of Decimals

1. 4.73

2. 4.761

3. 32.15

4. 27.87

5. 144.81

6. 87

7. 250.8

8. 2.5

9. 1.1

10. 8.43

Exercise 9: Multiplication and Division by Powers of Ten

1. 207.7
2. 2,159
3. 95,220
4. 252,627
5. 50
6. 6.34
7. 4.5689
8. 0.0684
9. 0.00145
10. 0.000005

Exercise 10: Conversion of Decimals to Fractions

1. $\frac{5}{8}$
2. $\frac{333}{1,000}$
3. $\frac{17}{20}$
4. $\frac{16}{25}$
5. $\frac{3}{8}$
6. $\frac{33}{40}$
7. $\frac{17}{40}$
8. $\frac{3}{20}$
9. $\frac{19}{40}$
10. $\frac{79}{80}$

Exercise 11: Converting Fractions to Non-Repeating Decimals

1. 0.8
2. 0.4
3. 0.75
4. 0.625
5. 0.32
6. 0.85
7. 0.875
8. 0.25
9. 0.152
10. 0.6875

Exercise 12: Converting Fractions to Repeating Decimals with a Single Repeating Digit

1. 0.555…
2. 0.444…
3. 0.333…
4. 0.777…
5. 1.222…
6. 0.666…
7. 0.111…
8. 0.888…

Exercise 13: Converting Fractions to Repeating Decimals with Several Repeating Digits or to Decimals with a Single Repeating Digit Following Non-Repeating Digits

1. $0.8\overline{1}$
2. $0.583\overline{3}$
3. $3.\overline{142857}$
4. $0.0\overline{675}$
5. $0.\overline{142857}$
6. $0.\overline{428571}$
7. $0.\overline{285714}$
8. $0.\overline{571428}$
9. $0.\overline{076923}$
10. $0.\overline{714285}$

Exercise 14: Converting Non-Repeating Decimals or Decimals with a Single Repeating Digit to Fractions

1. $\frac{9}{100}$
2. $\frac{1}{8}$
3. $\frac{7}{9}$
4. $\frac{1}{3}$
5. $\frac{2}{3}$
6. $\frac{5}{9}$
7. $\frac{1}{9}$
8. $\frac{11}{9}$
9. $\frac{4}{9}$
10. $\frac{8}{9}$

Exercise 15: Converting Decimals with Multiple Repeating Digits to Fractions

1. $\frac{9}{11}$
2. $\frac{7}{11}$
3. $\frac{1}{11}$
4. $\frac{21}{37}$
5. $\frac{2}{7}$

Exercise 16: Converting Decimals with Non-Repeating Digits Followed by Repeating Digits to Fractions

1. $\dfrac{1}{12}$

2. $\dfrac{53}{74}$

3. $\dfrac{19}{35}$

4. $\dfrac{77}{600}$

5. $\dfrac{21}{55}$

Exercise 17: Estimating Roots

1. 0.13

2. 0.65

3. 0.0145

4. 1.8

5. 2.861684

6. 27.6

7. 4.2

8. 4.1

9. 4.405434

10. 4.586634

Chapter 5 Ratios and Proportions

Exercise 1: Concept of Ratio

1. $\dfrac{7}{10}$

2. $\dfrac{15}{35}$

3. $\dfrac{50}{40}$

4. $\dfrac{45}{60}$

5. $\dfrac{7}{15}$

6. $\dfrac{1.2}{3.6}$

7. $\dfrac{8}{12}$

8. $\dfrac{19}{76}$

9. $\dfrac{6}{48}$

Exercise 2: Using Ratio Language to Describe Ratio Relationships

1. $\dfrac{5}{1}$

2. $\dfrac{7}{7} = 1$

3. $\dfrac{3}{6}$

4. $\dfrac{4}{8}$

5. $\dfrac{15}{20}$

6. $\dfrac{1}{2}$

Exercise 3: Ratios in Simplest Form

1. $\dfrac{2}{5}$

2. $\dfrac{7}{9}$

3. $\dfrac{2}{3}$

4. $\dfrac{11}{20}$

5. $5 : 6$

6. $\dfrac{1}{2}$

7. $\dfrac{1}{10}$

8. $\dfrac{1}{6}$

9. $\dfrac{2}{1}$

10. $\dfrac{14}{27}$

Exercise 4: Equivalent Ratios and Comparing Ratios

Answers may vary for questions 1–5.

1. $\dfrac{1}{2}, \dfrac{10}{20}$

2. $\dfrac{1}{4}, \dfrac{14}{56}$

3. $\dfrac{4}{6}, \dfrac{6}{9}$

4. $\dfrac{3}{5}, \dfrac{12}{20}$

5. $\dfrac{22}{24}, \dfrac{33}{36}$

6. Bess's Club

7. Bagel Barn

8. jet M

9. car B

10. Sarah's

Exercise 5: Ratios Comparing More Than Two Quantities

1. $\dfrac{2}{5} < \dfrac{3}{5} < \dfrac{16}{20}$

2. $\dfrac{4}{5} > \dfrac{21}{35} > \dfrac{8}{21}$

3. $\dfrac{5}{6} > \dfrac{18}{36} > \dfrac{2}{7}$

4. $\dfrac{20}{24} > \dfrac{12}{16} > \dfrac{12}{20}$

5. $2:2\dfrac{1}{2} = \dfrac{32}{40} > 1:1\dfrac{1}{3}$

6. $\dfrac{1.2}{0.4} > \dfrac{0.4}{0.2} > \dfrac{0.6}{0.8}$

7. $\dfrac{1}{2} > \dfrac{7}{54} > \dfrac{6}{48}$

8. $\dfrac{7.2}{1.2} > \dfrac{0.7}{4.2} > \dfrac{8}{16}$

9. $\dfrac{1}{2}:\dfrac{1}{3} > \dfrac{5}{7}:\dfrac{9}{2} > \dfrac{1}{2}:\dfrac{7}{2}$

Exercise 6: Concept of Rates

1. $\dfrac{450 \text{ cashews}}{32 \text{ people}} = 450$ cashews:32 people

2. $\dfrac{\$145}{20 \text{ minutes}} = \$145$:20 minutes

3. $\dfrac{54 \text{ miles}}{2 \text{ hours}} = 54$ miles:2 hours

4. $\dfrac{\$150}{4 \text{ people}} = \$150$:4 people

5. $\dfrac{45 \text{ flowers}}{2 \text{ children}} = 45$ flowers:2 children

6. $\dfrac{\$790}{4 \text{ books}} = \$790$:4 books

Exercise 7: Use of Rate Language in the Context of Rate Relationships

1. 5 fish per aquarium

2. 1 bench: 5 children

3. 5 trees:14 flowers

4. 10 cashews per student

5. 3 teachers per classroom

6. 1 elephant:2 tigers

Exercise 8: Rates in Simplest Form

1. 225 cashews:16 people

2. $29:4 minutes

3. 27 miles per hour

4. $75:2 people

5. 15 flowers: 1 child

6. $395:2 books

Exercise 9: Computation of Unit Rates

1. 41 houses per block

2. 106 miles per hour

3. $26\dfrac{1}{4}$ flowers per child

4. 4 mice per cage

5. 35.83 rooms per floor

6. $58.5 per book

Exercise 10: Using the Equation Unit Rate × Quantity = Total

1. 800 students

2. $19.95

3. 66 tons

4. 280 miles

5. 960 nails

6. $250

7. 750 square feet

8. 84 hours

Exercise 11: Means and Extremes

1. Mean: 2, 4 and Extremes: 1, 8

2. Mean: 2, 14 and Extremes: 7, 4

3. Mean: 7, 36 and Extremes: 9, 28

4. Mean: 6, 40 and Extremes: 5, 48

5. Mean: 10, 2 and Extremes: 5, 4

6. Mean: 3, 18 and Extremes: 9, 6

Exercise 12: Deciding Whether Two Quantities Are in Proportional Relationships

1. in proportion

2. not in proportion

3. in proportion

4. not in proportion

5. not in proportion

6. not in proportion

7. in proportion

8. in proportion

Exercise 13: Solving Proportions with a Single Missing Value

1. 17.5
2. 9
3. 9
4. 6
5. 4
6. 4
7. 3,750
8. 10,500
9. 15
10. 9

Exercise 14: Solving Proportions with More Than One Missing Value

1. B = 90 and C = 135
2. $x = 15$ and $y = 18$
3. 48 first type of books and 72 third type of books
4. 30 apples and 45 oranges
5. second subject scores = 30 and third subject scores = 42

Exercise 15: Analyzing and Solving Real-World Problems

1. 12 kilograms of sand and 24 kilograms of gravel
2. $5\frac{5}{6}$ or 5.83 feet
3. 28 days
4. $1\frac{2}{3}$ or 1.67 cups of sugar
5. $\frac{1}{3}$ cup of lime juice
6. 10 kilograms sand
7. 600 miles
8. 6 feet
9. 8 meters
10. 25 inches

Chapter 6 Percents

Exercise 1: Converting Percents

1. $\frac{4}{5}$
2. $1\frac{1}{4}$
3. $\frac{1}{8}$
4. $\frac{1}{6}$
5. 0.392
6. 0.0138
7. 1.5
8. 0.00002
9. 40%
10. 6,525%
11. 32%
12. $37\frac{1}{2}$%
13. $83\frac{1}{3}$%
14. $641\frac{2}{3}$%
15. 40,000%
16. 0.75%

Exercise 2: Solving Percent Problems Using a Proportion

1. 1.75
2. 75
3. 400
4. 35%
5. 120
6. 35%

Exercise 3: Solving Percent Problems Using Percent Whole = Part

1. 24
2. 75
3. 50%
4. 5 kilograms
5. 80%
6. 125
7. 5
8. 15%

Exercise 4: Percent Increase or Decrease

1. 1,680

2. $15,200

3. $10,000

4. $16\frac{2}{3}\%$

5. 75%

6. 62%

7. 30%

8. 83%

Exercise 5: Serial Increase or Decrease

1. 450

2. $2,000

3. $2,925

4. $580.92

5. $15,138

6. $12.83

Chapter 7 Probability and Statistics

Exercise 1: Basics of Statistics

1. 12; 87

2.

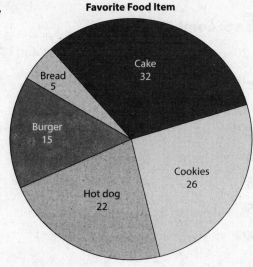

a) English, Math   b) Debate, Social Science

3.

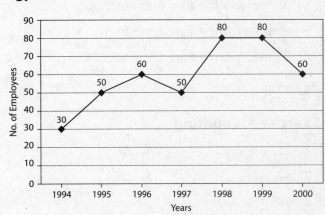

4.

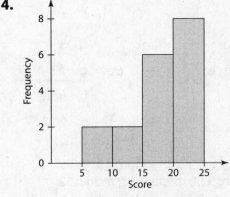

a) 24   b) two (12, 13)

5.

a) 1998–1999   b) 1997–1998

6. a) 13

b) 5

c) No baseballs were sold by the seller on that day.

Exercise 2: Measures of Central Tendency For Data Sets

1. a) 10   f) 4
   b) 10   g) 6
   c) 10   h) 5
   d) 5   i) 16
   e) 5   j) 6

2. a) 14   f) 16
   b) 9   g) 1
   c) 25   h) 21
   d) 7   i) 10
   e) 14   j) 7

3. a) 4, 28   f) 3
   b) none   g) 22
   c) 20   h) none
   d) 11   i) 20,7
   e) none   j) 25

4. a) mean: 52.1; median: 52; mode: 52
   b) mean: 3; median: 2; mode: 2
   c) mean: 5; median: 5; mode: 2
   d) mean: 6; median: 6; mode: 5, 7
   e) mean: 4; median: 3; mode: 3
   f) mean: 5; median: 4.5; mode: 3

5. 77.45

Exercise 3: Counting

1. 15   **4.** 20
2. 42   **5.** 120
3. 12

Exercise 4: Factorials

1. a) 336   d) 30,240
   b) 5,985   e) 56
   c) 3,652,110 f) 20

   g) 420   i) 35
   h) 60   j) 4

2. $7! = 5,040$
3. $15! = 1.31 \times 10^{12}$
4. $4! = 24$
5. $8! = 40,320$

Exercise 5: Permutations

1. a) 60   e) 11,880
   b) 720   f) 3,024
   c) 840   g) 40,320
   d) 90   h) 60

2. 120
3. 840
4. 5,040
5. 336
6. 1,680
7. 5,040
8. 210
9. 552
10. 19,656

Exercise 6: Combinations

1. a) 20   e) 11,440
   b) 126   f) 1
   c) 36   g) 3,003
   d) 55   h) 1,140

2. 210
3. 126
4. 165
5. 2,002
6. 35
7. 3,060
8. 220

Exercise 12: Multiplying Binomials

1. $12n^2 + 14n + 2$

2. $6x^2 + 7x + 2$

3. $6x^2 - x - 2$

4. $3x^2 + 5x - 8$

5. $20x^2 - 23x + 6$

6. $8n^2 + 26n + 6$

7. $6x^2 - 20x + 6$

8. $48p^2 + 4p - 4$

9. $30p^2 - 8p - 64$

Exercise 13: Square of a Binomial

1. $x^2 + 8x + 16$

2. $x^2 + 12x + 36$

3. $4x^2 + 4x + 1$

4. $x^2 - 2xy + y^2$

5. $9x^2 - 12x + 4$

6. $16p^2 - 8p + 1$

7. $4y^2 - 12y + 9$

8. $x^2 + 14x + 49$

Exercise 14: Product of the Sum and Difference of Two Terms

1. $16x^2 - 4$

2. $49y^2 - 25$

3. $4x^2 - 9$

4. $9y^2 - 49$

5. $a^2 - 9b^2$

6. $4x^2 - 25y^2$

7. $144x^2y^2 - 121$

8. $64 - 25t^2$

9. $9x^2 - 4$

10. $25c^2 - 9d^2$

Exercise 15: Dividing Polynomials

1. $a + 3$

2. $2x + 5$

3. $4z^2 - 6z - 7$

4. $4y^3 + 2y^2 - 5y$

5. $x^3 - 3x^2 + 6x - 4$

6. $(x + 19)(x - 12) + 223$

7. $(4x^2 + 4)(x^2 - 1) + 13$

8. $(x + 6)(x - 1) + 12$

9. $(x^2 + 2x - 1)(x - 2) - 8$

10. $(3x + 1)(x + 2) - 5$

Exercise 16: Factoring

1. $2x(2x^2 + 3 + x)$

2. $3xy(2x + 3y)$

3. $3x(x^2 + 2x - 5)$

4. $x^5(x^3 + x^2 + x + 1)$

5. $x^3(5x^2 - 4x + 3)$

6. $x^2(x + 1)$

7. $2x^3(3x^2 + 1)$

8. $x(2x^2 - 4x + 1)$

9. $x^2(3x^4 - 2x^3 + 4x^2 - 6)$

10. $9y^5(4y^{10} - 3y^5 - 2)$

Exercise 17: Factoring a Common Polynomial Factor

1. $(x - y)(2 - b)$

2. $(x - 8)(11x - 3)$

3. $(x^2 + 4)(x - 5)$

4. $(x + 3)(x + 5)$

5. $(x + 2)(x + 1)$

6. $(x - 3)(x - 2)$

7. $(x - 1)(x + 1)$

8. $(x^2 + 3)(x - 5)$

9. $(x^2 + 9)(x + 1)$

Exercise 18: Factoring by Grouping

1. $(m + 7)(m^2 - 2)$

2. $(2x^2 - 3)(6x + 1)$

3. $(x^2 + 3)(x + 1)$

4. $(2x^2 + 5)(x - 3)$

5. $(3x^2 - 2)(x - 5)$

6. $(x^2 - 1)(x + 2)$

7. $(6x^2 - 1)(2x - 1)$

8. $(x^2 + 3)(x - 5)$

9. $(x^2 + 8)(x + 2)$

10. $(y + 3)(x - 4)$

11. $(y - 3)(x - 4)$

12. $(4x - 10)(x + 5)$

Exercise 19: Factoring Trinomials

1. $(x + 4)(2x + 3)$

2. $(3x + 2)(x + 1)$

3. $(2x + 5)(x + 4)$

4. $(2x - 3y)(x - y)$

5. $2(x + 3)(x - 12)$

6. $(2x - 3)(5x + 4)$

7. $(4y - 3)(2y + 1)$

8. $-2x(4x + 1)(x + 2)$

9. $-2x(x - 4)(x + 7)$

10. $3(2x + y)(4x - 3y)$

Exercise 20: Special Forms

1. $3x(x - 2)(x + 2)$

2. $(x + 3)^2$

3. $(p - 9)^2$

4. $(2y + 12)^2$

5. $(2y + 3)(4y^2 - 6y + 9)$

6. $(x + 10)(x - 10)$

7. $(y^2 + 12)(y^2 - 12)$

8. $(5m + 3n)(5m - 3n)$

9. $(x + 5)(x^2 - 5x + 25)$

10. $(2x - 3)(4x^2 + 6x + 9)$

11. $2(x + 4y)(x^2 - 4xy + 16y^2)$

Exercise 21: General Strategy for Factoring

1. $(5x + 3)(x - 7)$
2. $(a + b)(a^2 + b^2)$
3. $(2b - c)(4b^2 + 2bc + c^2)$
4. $2xy^2(3x - 8y)(2x - y)$
5. $(x - 3)(x + 3)(x^2 + 9)$
6. $(x - 2)^2(x + 2)(x^2 + 2x + 4)$
7. $3(x + 1)(x + 6)$
8. $(x - 1)(x + 4)$
9. Prime
10. Prime

Exercise 22: Multiplying Rational Expressions

1. $\dfrac{3xy}{4}$
2. $\dfrac{3(p-1)}{p}$
3. $\dfrac{4x+8}{x+5}$
4. $\dfrac{(x-2)(x^2+3x+9)}{(x-3)(x^2-2x+4)}$
5. 1
6. $\dfrac{1}{y+6}$
7. $\dfrac{x^2+3x+9}{2x}$
8. $\dfrac{a(a-4)}{(a-3)(2a+b)}$
9. 1
10. $\dfrac{3a}{2b}$
11. $\dfrac{2+a}{1-a}$

Exercise 23: Dividing Rational Expressions

1. $\dfrac{1}{y^2-2y}$
2. $\dfrac{x+4}{x^2+5x}$
3. $\dfrac{3y}{8}$
4. x
5. $\dfrac{1}{x}$
6. $\dfrac{3}{x-1}$
7. 2
8. 1
9. $\dfrac{2}{3}$
10. $\dfrac{1}{2}$

Exercise 24: Adding Rational Expressions with Common Denominators

1. $\dfrac{1}{x}$
2. $\dfrac{10x-5}{x-7}$
3. $\dfrac{1}{2r+3}$
4. $\dfrac{b+2}{6b^2+4b}$
5. $\dfrac{1}{9n}$
6. $\dfrac{1}{3n^2}$
7. $\dfrac{1}{a+3}$
8. $\dfrac{5x^3+8x^2-13}{x^2(x+1)}$
9. $\dfrac{x^3+13x^2-2x+5}{(x+1)(x+2)}$
10. $\dfrac{11x}{(2x+1)(x-2)}$

Exercise 25: Adding Rational Expressions with Different Denominators

1. $\dfrac{11x-3}{(x+2)(x-3)}$
2. $\dfrac{5(a-2)}{a(a-5)}$
3. $\dfrac{3}{2}$
4. $\dfrac{7x-1}{(x+2)(x-1)}$
5. $\dfrac{6c+4}{(c+5)(c-8)}$
6. $\dfrac{3x-4}{(x-2)(3x+1)}$
7. $\dfrac{7x+4}{(x-4)(x+4)^2}$
8. $\dfrac{8x^2+24x-5}{(x-3)(x+3)}$
9. $\dfrac{13x-5}{2(x-1)(x-2)}$

Exercise 26: Subtracting Rational Expressions with Common Denominators

1. $\dfrac{y+1}{x}$
2. $\dfrac{-a+4b}{2a-b}$
3. 2
4. $\dfrac{1}{5}$
5. $\dfrac{1}{18x^2y}$
6. $\dfrac{1}{3x+12}$
7. $\dfrac{1}{b-6}$
8. $\dfrac{3}{4v^3}$
9. $\dfrac{1}{x-4}$
10. $-\dfrac{1}{x+1}$

Exercise 27: Subtracting Rational Expressions with Different Denominators

1. $\dfrac{2-x}{x(x-1)}$

2. $\dfrac{-a-10}{a(a-5)}$

3. $\dfrac{4x-3}{2x^2+5x-3}$

4. $\dfrac{1}{x(x-6)}$

5. $\dfrac{9x+5}{(x-3)(x+1)(x+2)}$

6. $\dfrac{3y^2-23y+4}{2y^2-11y+5}$

7. $\dfrac{3x-9}{(x+2)(x-1)}$

8. $\dfrac{-2x-3}{(x+3)^2}$

9. $\dfrac{-x-11}{(x+3)(x-5)}$

10. $\dfrac{-3n-8}{(n+6)(n+5)(n-4)}$

Exercise 28: Rational Expressions with Rational Expressions in the Numerator and/or Denominator

1. $\dfrac{x}{3}$

2. $\dfrac{x-3}{x+2}$

3. $\dfrac{xy}{2}$

4. $\dfrac{3a}{b}$

5. 2

6. y

7. $\dfrac{1}{x+3}$

8. $-\dfrac{6}{x^2}$

Chapter 10 Equations and Inequalities

Exercise 1: Solving Linear Equations by Adding or Subtracting

1. A
2. B
3. A
4. $x=17.3$
5. $y=12.5$
6. $p=88$
7. $a=-15.71$
8. $s=11.25$
9. $q=7.5$

Exercise 2: Solving Linear Inequalities by Adding or Subtracting

1. B
2. A
3. C
4. $a<7$
5. $x\le-12$
6. $y\ge16$
7. $x<2$
8. $b>3.8$
9. $c\ge\dfrac{5}{3}$

Exercise 3: Solving Linear Equations by Multiplying or Dividing

1. B
2. A
3. B
4. $x=7$
5. $y=15$
6. $p=-12$
7. $q=32$
8. $a=30$
9. $r=-84$

Exercise 4: Solving Linear Inequalities by Multiplying or Dividing

1. D
2. A
3. A
4. $x\ge48$
5. $p<7$
6. $y\ge-60$
7. $r<-5$
8. $a\ge14.4$
9. $p<18$

Exercise 5: Solving Linear Equations— Combined

1. −6
2. 2
3. $\frac{37}{16}$
4. $\frac{70}{3}$
5. 15
6. 20
7. 16
8. 21
9. 12
10. 9

Exercise 6: Solving Linear Inequalities— Combined

1. $a < 6$
2. $x \geq 16$
3. $t > 12$
4. $g > 14$
5. $x > 12$
6. $x < 6$
7. $y > 5$
8. $a \geq -1.67$
9. $c > 12$
10. $p \leq 2$

Exercise 7: Solving Linear Equations Involving Parentheses

1. $-\frac{23}{4}$
2. $\frac{13}{16}$
3. $-\frac{5}{7}$
4. −2
5. $\frac{48}{63}$
6. $\frac{14}{9}$
7. $\frac{5}{4}$
8. −28
9. $\frac{36}{5}$
10. 4
11. −4
12. 2

Exercise 8: Solving Linear Inequalities Involving Parentheses

1. $x \leq 14$
2. $y \geq 8$
3. $a < 7$
4. $b \geq 11$
5. $c \leq 10$
6. $p > 11$
7. $x \leq 2.6$
8. $y < -5$
9. $a < -1.67$
10. $x \leq -2$

Exercise 9: Using Equations to Solve Problems

1. 9 years old
2. 30 years old
3. 62 years old
4. 25 mph; 15 mph
5. 20 mph; 40 mph
6. 1.2 hours; 1.8 hours
7. 7.5 liters of 10% solution; 2.5 liters of 30% solution
8. 68%
9. 3 mL of 25% saline solution; 4.5 mL of 20% saline solution
10. 3 pounds
11. 8 pounds of gumdrops; 12 pounds of jellybeans
12. $3/liter
13. 36 minutes
14. 11.67 hours
15. 12 hours

Exercise 10: Writing Inequalities for Simple Word Problems

1. 32 goats
2. The number is less than or equal to 20.
3. No more than 12 books
4. No more than 18 people
5. Less than 10 chocolates
6. The number is less than 14.
7. At least 20 hours
8. 8 feet
9. At least 200 students
10. At least 14 products
11. $x > -13$
12. More than 250 bracelets

Exercise 11: Systems of Linear Equations

1. $x = -1, y = 3$
2. $x = 1, y = -2$
3. $x = -9, y = -5$
4. $x = -4, y = -5$
5. $x = 3, y = 7$
6. $x = -3, y = 7$
7. $x = 3, y = -7$
8. $x = -8, y = 5$
9. $x = 4, y = -9$
10. $x = -2, y = 6$
11. $x = -5, y = 3$
12. $x = -5, y = 1$

Exercise 12: Word Problems Solvable by Systems

1. 40 years old, 15 years old
2. 28 years old, 10 years old
3. 12 gallons, 12 gallons
4. 80 pounds lemon tea, 40 pounds green tea
5. swimmer's speed: 7 mph, river's speed: 3 mph
6. plane's speed: 125 mph, wind's speed: 25 mph
7. 18, 81
8. 6 units
9. 44 years, 14 years
10. 50 pounds, 50 pounds

Exercise 13: Quadratic Equations

1. $2, 3$
2. $0, -\dfrac{8}{3}$
3. $0, \dfrac{6}{5}$
4. $-\dfrac{1}{3}, \dfrac{5}{2}$

5. $\dfrac{5}{3}, -\dfrac{4}{3}$
6. $3, -\dfrac{1}{2}$
7. $\pm\sqrt{29}$
8. $\pm 4\sqrt{3}$
9. ± 2
10. $\pm 5\sqrt{2}$
11. $2 \pm 2\sqrt{3}$
12. $-5, 15$
13. $2 \pm 2\sqrt{3}$
14. $1 \pm \sqrt{2}$
15. $2, \dfrac{-4}{5}$
16. $-\dfrac{3}{2} \pm \dfrac{\sqrt{15}}{2}$
17. $1, -\dfrac{8}{3}$
18. $\dfrac{2}{7}, -3$
19. $\dfrac{-1 \pm \sqrt{17}}{2}$
20. $-1, 4$
21. $5 \pm \sqrt{5}$
22. $\dfrac{5 \pm \sqrt{10}}{3}$
23. $-4, 2$
24. $\dfrac{5 \pm 3\sqrt{5}}{2}$

Exercise 14: Word Problems Leading to Quadratic Equations

1. 16, 18
2. 21, 22
3. 13, 14
4. length = 90 units, width = 30 units
5. length = 80 units, width = 40 units

Chapter 11 Graphing

Exercise 1: Cartesian Coordinate System

1. 11.2
2. 9.9
3. 7.8
4. 5
5. 5.8
6. 7.1
7. 5.1
8. 6.7
9. 6.4
10. 7.2

Exercise 2: Midpoint of a Line Segment

1. $(4.5, 0)$
2. $(1, 2.5)$
3. $(0.5, -1.5)$
4. $(-4, -6)$
5. $(4, -3)$
6. $(4, 4.6)$
7. $(7, 9)$

Exercise 3: Point Symmetry

1. (−7, −9)

2. (8, 1)

3. (−12, −15)

4. (2, 1)

5. (4, 6)

6. (5, 7)

Exercise 4: Ordered Pairs as Solutions to Two-Variable Equations

1. not a solution

2. not a solution

3. solution

4. solution

5. not a solution

6. not a solution

7. not a solution

8. solution

9. not a solution

10. solution

Exercise 5: Graphing y as an Expression of x

1.

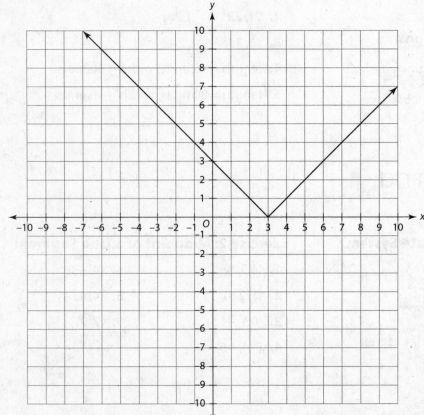

2.

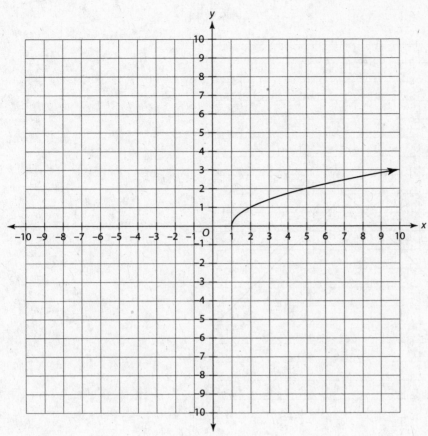

3.

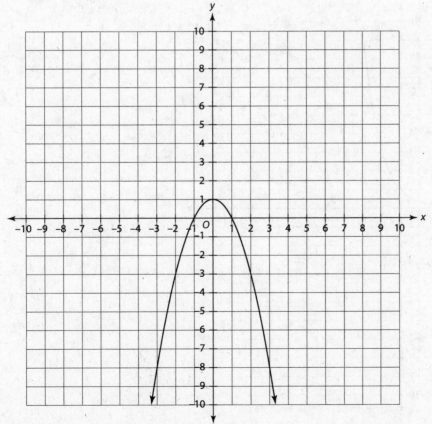

4.

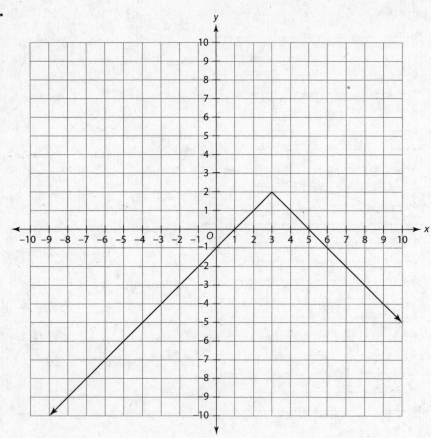

5.

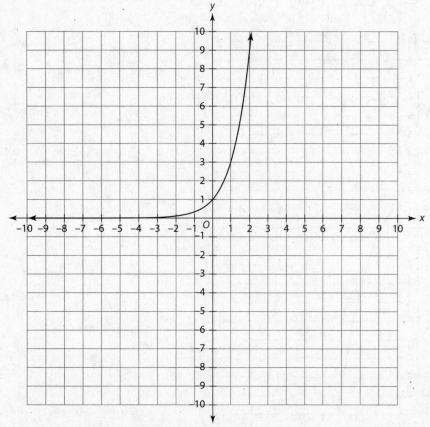

Exercise 6: *x*- and *y*-Intercepts of a Graph

1. (−3, 0), (0, 2)

2. (−12, 0), $\left(0, \dfrac{3}{4}\right)$

3. $\left(\dfrac{3}{2}, 0\right)$, (0, −6)

4. (1, 0), (0, 4)

5. (3, 0), (0, −2)

6. (−5, 0), (0, −4)

7. (5, 0), (0, −6)

8. (2, 0), (0, 6)

9. (4, 0), (0, −4)

10. (1, 0), (0, 4)

Exercise 7: Reading Coordinates from Graphs

1. (1, 5)

2. (3, 6)

3. (0, 1)

4. (−5, 17)

5. (−1, 3)

6. (3, 2)

7. (10, 2)

8. (4, 1)

9. (1, −2)

10. (9, 1)

Exercise 8: Equations of Lines

1. $m = \dfrac{1}{3}; b = -4$

2. $m = 2; b = -4$

3. $m = \dfrac{5}{2}; b = -4$

4. $m = 4; b = 4$

5. $m = \dfrac{3}{2}; b = 3$

Exercise 9: Graphing *Ax* + *By* = *C*, When Both Intercepts Are Integers

1. (−2, 0), (0, 6)

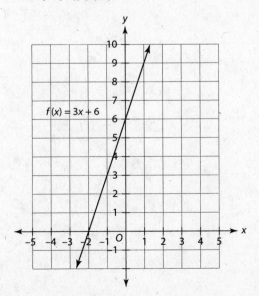

2. (1, 0), (0, −5)

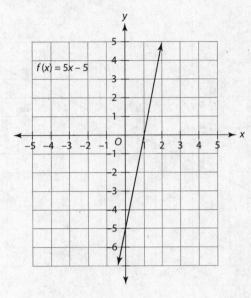

3. (−2, 0), (0, 4)

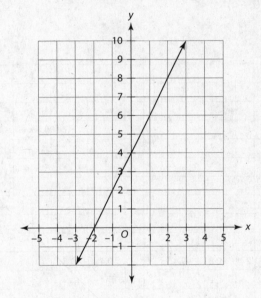

4. (24, 0), (0, −6)

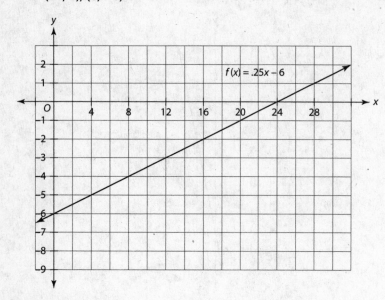

$f(x) = .25x - 6$

5. (1, 0), (0, −1)

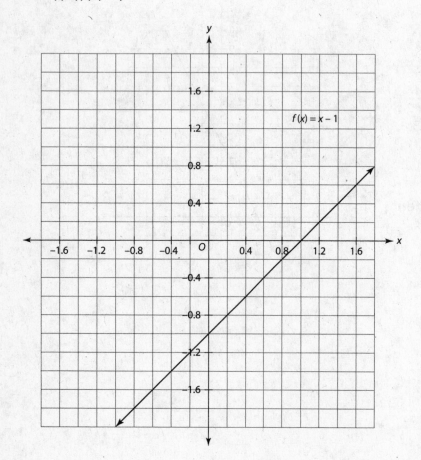

$f(x) = x - 1$

Exercise 10: Graphing $Ax + By = C$, When One or Both Intercepts Are Not Integers

1. (0, 4), (1.6, 0)

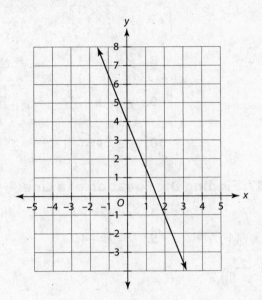

2. (0, −5), (2.5, 0)

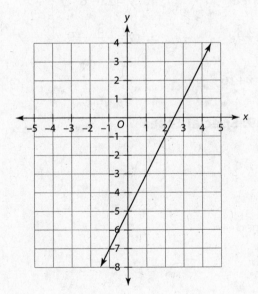

3. (0, −3.5), (7, 0)

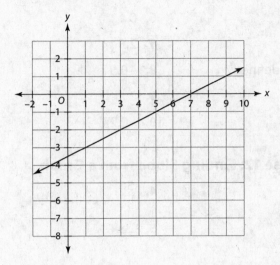

4. (0, 2.4), (3, 0)

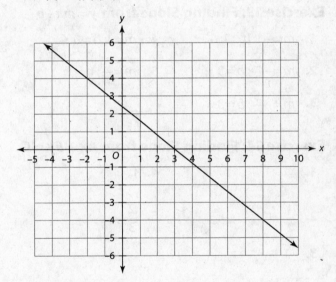

5. (0, 9.5), (7.6, 0)

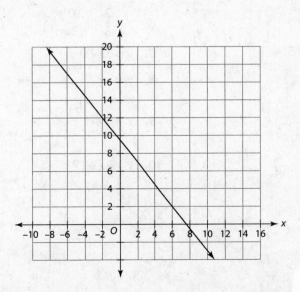

Exercise 11: The Slope of a Line

1. -2
2. 2
3. undefined
4. -3
5. 0.5
6. 0
7. 2.5
8. -0.5
9. 2
10. -0.27

Exercise 12: Finding Slope from a Graph

1. $\dfrac{3}{2}$
2. 3
3. $\dfrac{7}{3}$
4. $\dfrac{5}{3}$
5. $-\dfrac{1}{3}$

Exercise 13: Finding Slope from $y = mx + b$

1. $m = -1; b = 2$
2. $m = -\dfrac{2}{3}; b = 3$
3. $m = -\dfrac{5}{2}; b = 3$
4. $m = 1; b = 0$
5. $m = \dfrac{1}{4}; b = 1$

Exercise 14: Finding Slope from $Ax + By = C$

1. $-\dfrac{1}{2}$
2. $\dfrac{1}{2}$
3. -1
4. 1
5. $\dfrac{2}{3}$

Exercise 15: Slopes of Parallel Lines

1. 2
2. 5
3. $\dfrac{8}{7}$
4. $-\dfrac{2}{3}$
5. $-\dfrac{4}{5}$
6. $y = \dfrac{2}{3}x + \dfrac{10}{3}$
7. $y = 3x + 9$
8. $y = -x$
9. $y = \dfrac{2}{5}x - \dfrac{21}{5}$
10. $y = 4x + 17$

Exercise 16: Slopes of Perpendicular Lines

1. $-\dfrac{3}{4}$
2. $\dfrac{1}{2}$
3. -5
4. -2
5. $\dfrac{1}{2}$
6. $y = \dfrac{4}{3}x + \dfrac{34}{3}$
7. $y = \dfrac{2}{5}x + \dfrac{12}{5}$
8. $y = \dfrac{3}{4}x + 1$
9. $y = \dfrac{4}{7}x + \dfrac{20}{7}$
10. $y = \dfrac{1}{3}x - \dfrac{7}{3}$

Exercise 17: Finding the Equation of a Line

1. $y = -x + 7$
2. $y = -2x + 11$
3. $y = 4x - 28$
4. $y = -2x + 9$
5. $y = 2x + 4$

Exercise 18: Finding the Equation of a Line with Two Given Points

1. $y = -2x + 8$
2. $y = \dfrac{9}{2}x - 9$
3. $y = -\dfrac{5}{4}x + 16$
4. $y = 2x - 8$
5. $y = -\dfrac{3}{4}x + 9$

Exercise 19: Special Cases

1. 0
2. $x = 5$
3. 0
4. undefined
5. $x = 4$

Chapter 12 Functions

Exercise 1: Understanding Functions

1. function

2. not a function

3. function

4. not a function

5. function

6. function

Exercise 2: Representation of Functions

1. function

2. not a function

3. function

4. function

5. not a function

6. not a function

7. function

8. function

9. function

10. not a function

11. not a function

Exercise 3: Evaluation of Functions

1. −2

2. −1

3. 2

4. −1

5. 7

6. 7

7. 23

8. 14

9. 47

10. 79

11. $a^2 - 7a + 12$

12. 7

Exercise 4: Changing from One Representation to Another

1.

x	−6	0	3	12
y	−3	−1	0	3

$f(x) = \dfrac{1}{3}x - 1$

2.

x	0	1	2	3	4
y	6	4	2	0	−2

$f(x) = -2x + 6$

3.

x	0	1	2	3	4
y	7	10	13	16	19

$f(x) = 3x + 7$

4.

x	1	2	3	4	5
y	8	3	−2	−7	−12

$f(x) = -5x + 13$

5. $f(x) = 2x + 1$

6. $f(x) = 5x - 1$

7.

x	0	1	2
y	1	3	5

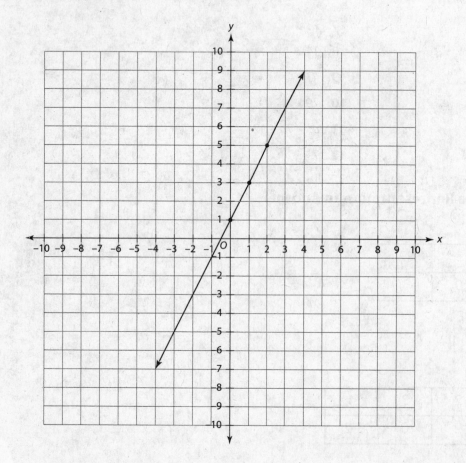

8.

x	1	2	3	4
y	0	1	2	3

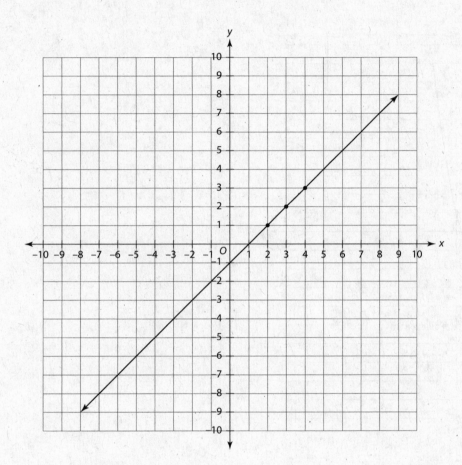

9.

x	0	1	−1	2	−2
y	−1	1	1	7	7

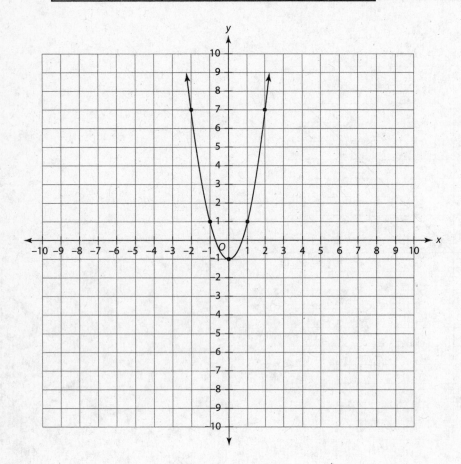

Exercise 5: Identifying Functions

1.

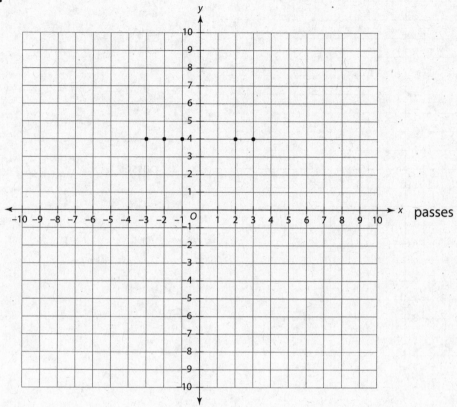

passes

2.

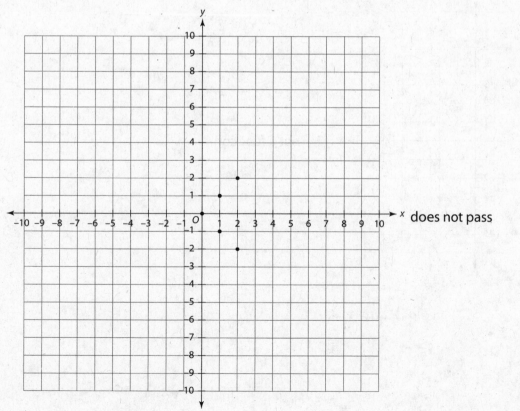

does not pass

3.

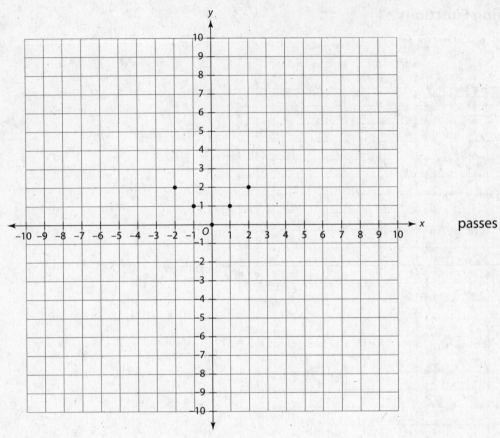

passes

4.

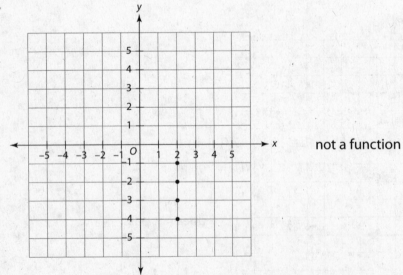

not a function

5.

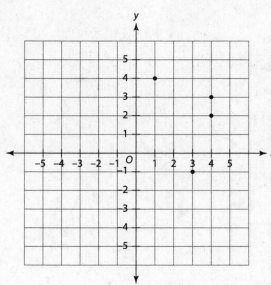

not a function

6.

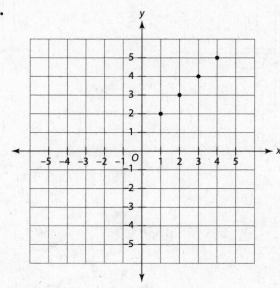

function

7. function

8. not a function

9. yes

10. yes

Exercise 6: Operations with Functions

1. 37

2. −3

3. $2x^2 - 3x + 2$

4. 0

5. 120

6. $4x - 16$

7. $2x^2 - 16x + 34$

8. $\dfrac{2x+3}{x^2}$

Exercise 7: Forming Composite Functions $f(g(x))$

1. 3,698

2. $2x^2 + 3$

3. $3x^2 - 1$

4. $9x^2 - 6x + 1$

Exercise 8: A Few Important Functions

1.

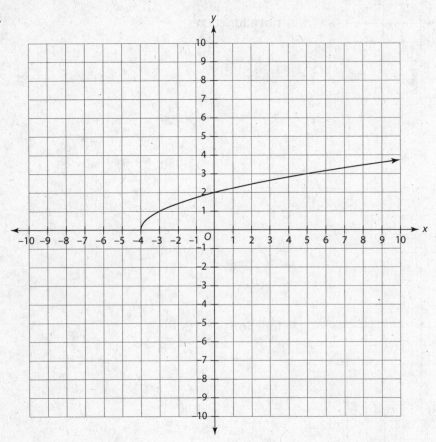

2.

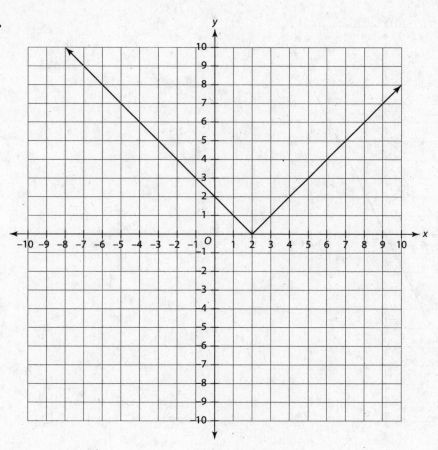

3.

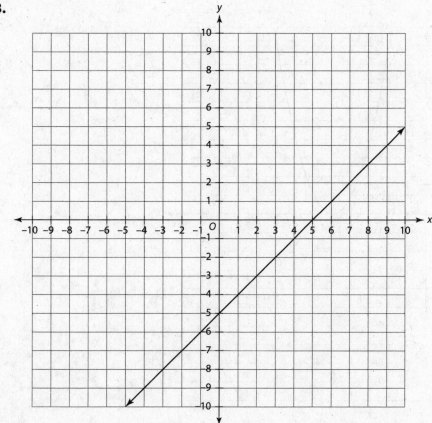

4.

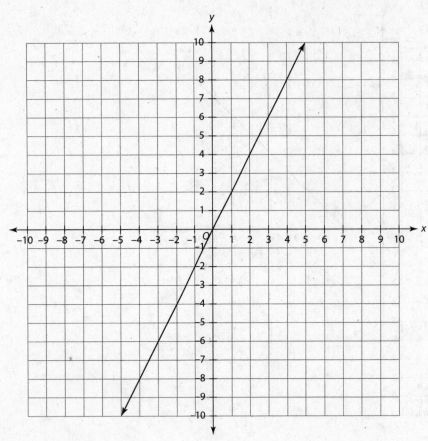

5.

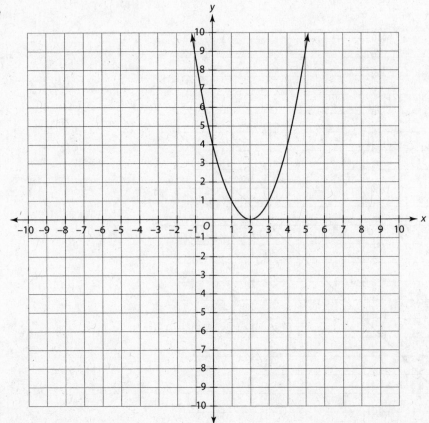

6.

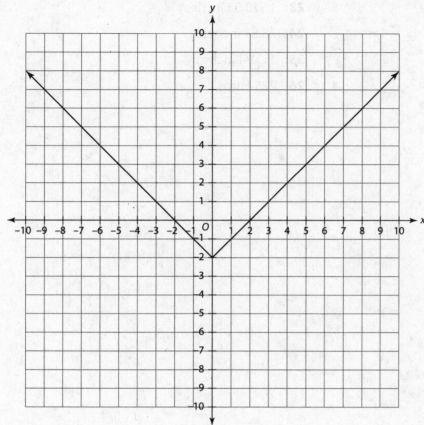

Exercise 9: Descriptions of Functions

1. $f(x) \to -\infty$, as $x \to -\infty$; $f(x) \to +\infty$, as $x \to +\infty$

2. $f(x) \to -\infty$, as $x \to -\infty$; $f(x) \to -\infty$, as $x \to +\infty$

3. $f(x) \to +\infty$, as $x \to -\infty$; $f(x) \to -\infty$, as $x \to +\infty$

4. $f(x) \to +\infty$, as $x \to -\infty$; $f(x) \to +\infty$, as $x \to +\infty$

5. $f(x) \to +\infty$, as $x \to +\infty$; $f(x) \to 0$, as $x \to -\infty$

6. $f(x) \to 0$, as $x \to -\infty$; $f(x) \to 0$, as $x \to +\infty$

Exercise 10: Functions in Real Life

1. 22.8°C

2. −10.6°C

3. 81.1°C

4. 101.1°C

5. 426.7°C

6. 212°F

7. 68°F

8. 293°F

9. 203°F

10. 132.8°F

11. −163.0°C

12. 84.2°F

13. 7,592°F

14. 32.22°C, 25.56°C

15. 6 seconds

16. 144 feet, 2 seconds

17. 3 seconds

18. 7.07 inches²

19. 63.62 inches^2

20. 38.48 inches^2

21. 735.42 square units

22. 6.16 square units

23. 1,520.53 inches^2

24. 78.54 inches^2

25. 153.94 inches^2

26. 225 Euros